The Expanding Boundaries of Black Politics

THE NATIONAL POLITICAL SCIENCE REVIEW

EDITOR
Georgia A. Persons
Georgia Institute of Technology

ASSOCIATE EDITORS
Robert C. Smith
San Francisco State University
Cheryl M. Miller
University of Maryland-Baltimore County

EDITORIAL BOARD

The National Political Science Review   Volume 11

The Expanding Boundaries of Black Politics

Georgia A. Persons
Editor

Transaction Publishers
New Brunswick (U.S.A.) and London (U.K.)

Library of Congress Catalog Number: 2006103024
ISBN: 978-0-7658-03757
Printed in the United States of America

Library of Congress Cataloging-in-Publication Data

The expanding boundaries of Black politics / Georgia A. Persons, editor.
        p. cm.—(The national political science review ; v. 11)
    Includes bibliographical references and index.
    ISBN-13: 978-0-7658-0375-7
        1. African Americans—Politics and government—20th century—Con-
    gresses. 2. African Americans—Politics and government—21st cen-
    tury—Congresses. 3. Political participation—United States—Congresses.
    4. Elections—United States— Congresses. 5. African Americans—Social
    conditions—1975—Congresses. 6. United States—Race relations—Po-
    litical aspects—Congresses. 7. United States—Race relations—Political
    aspects—History—20th century—Congresses. I. Persons, Georgia Anne.
    II. National political science review.

E185.615.E93 2007
324.089'96073—dc22   2006103024

Contents

Part II. Maximizing the Black Vote: Recognizing the Limits of Electoral Politics

BOOK FORUM

Book Reviews

Acknowledgements

The Editor offers special thanks to all of the contributors featured in this volume of the *National Political Science Review*. Special thanks to Todd Shaw, Symposium Editor, for his outstanding efforts in organizing the collection of papers around which this volume is anchored. Thanks also to Associate Editors Robert C. Smith and Cheryl M. Miller, and colleagues in the discipline who served as reviewers and made completion of this volume possible.

Thanks to Melissa Nobles, President of NCOBPS and Kathy Stromile-Golden, Executive Director of NCOBPS for their support and assistance with the business and financial aspects of managing the journal. I would also like to extend deep appreciation to Matthew Holden, former Editor of the *National Political Science Review* for his ongoing support and assistance in raising the profile of the journal.

Thanks to the copy editors at Transaction Publishers for providing outstanding technical assistance and for ensuring that the journal meets the highest standards of quality and accuracy. Carmen Williams and Katara Jones of the School of Public Policy, Georgia Institute of Technology, have provided administrative assistance, kindness, mirth and good humor in support of the ongoing logistical needs of the journal.

The National Political Science Review is currently indexed in the following publications: American History & Life, Historical Abstracts, International Index to Black Periodicals, International Political Science Abstracts, Social Planning-Policy & Development Abstracts, Sage Race Relations Abstracts, Social Science Abstracts, and Sociological Abstracts.

Thanks to all of the contributors and reviewers over the years, editorial board members past and present, and members of NCOBPS. Because of your support, The National Political Science Review has been established and sustained as a nationally and internationally respected peer-reviewed journal and a leader in the field of African American Politics.

Editor's Note

One of the challenges to political science research and scholarship as pursued outside of highly resourced and privileged environments of think-tanks is the inability of scholars to rapidly shift foci to produce substantive analyses of newly breaking debates on societal problems. The result is that there is usually a considerable lag time between "breaking news" issues which dominate public debate and discourse and political science analyses of these issues. There are several reasons for this state of affairs. One is the resource constraint. Most of us do not have the benefit of an extensive team of well trained research assistants. Nor are we exempt from the multifaceted demands of teaching. Thirdly, scholarship is ultimately about knowing and understanding, ends which require a level of deeply engaged and sustained inquiry. Indeed, much of what scholars do is to attend to the maintenance needs of their disciplines. We busy ourselves with filling in the conceptual, theoretical and analytical gaps in the knowledge base. It is our critical duty as scholars to do so. Moreover, the customs, traditions, and rewards of the academy strongly dictate that individuals become experts in some specific area, a goal which requires much concentration, dedication and time.

The end result of the convergence of these factors is that sometimes it very much appears that the world of politically significant and compelling societal developments evolves at a rapid-fire pace in comparison to the production of political science analyses of those issues which scholars decide are interesting. Such is the nature of the present moment in history. One readily observes that the oral discourse among political scientists, especially that community of scholars which is loosely organized around concerns about race, gender, social inequality and social justice—a significant portion of whom are served by this journal—is rife with concerns such as the dire social conditions exposed by Hurricane Katrina; the mass-scale failure of public organizations which accompanied Hurricane Katrina; the injustices associated with the war in Iraq; the alarming marginalization of African American males and the attendant risks to all of Black America; the persistent failure of America's public schools which disproportionately serves African Americans; the heated debate and policy stalemate over immigration reform; the absence of a mobilizing ethos within the black community with the potential for generating and sustaining a meaningful policy agenda. These are the kind of compelling issues which comprise the oral discourse among black political scientists. However, our scholarly productivity woefully lags behind and only partially addresses our political concerns and interests.

The encouraging news is that there are moments when the scholarly foci of our community of political scientists comes together to address a broad portion of political and social developments and policy issues which are both timely and compelling vis-à-vis the interests of the black community. *The National Political Science Review* has sought to strategically position itself at this critical nexus over the years. We have sought to do so in this volume, and have done so with some success.

The anchoring symposium, the Expanding Boundaries of Black Politics, presents the scholarship of a cadre of young black political scientists. All of the contributors to this symposium are junior, untenured faculty. All yet in the critical maturation stages of finding their voice as scholars. They are also all actively engaged in the critical tasks of moving forward the study of black politics and black political concerns. By their works included in this volume, we see that they are strongly positioned for the challenges of these tasks. Most importantly, we see that they are expanding the boundaries of black politics along lines of epistemology and methodological approaches, and in regard to issue-areas incorporated within the field as well. The introductory essay by symposium editor, Todd Shaw, situates the works of the young scholars featured here within the context of temporal shifts in scholarly emphases; overlapping issues and concerns across time; as well as the derivations of the featured body of work from the black politics scholarship which has defined the field from its founding. Indeed, the symposium makes for an interesting reflection on legacy and progeny.

Part II of this volume has been titled "Maximizing the Black Vote; Recognizing the Limits of Electoral Politics." To a significant extent the distinction between the foci of the anchoring symposium and Part II is more apparent than real. The bounty of this volume lies in the focus and coverage of the whole. We see the tending to matters of scholarly understanding of lingering questions such as the policy significance of black mayors and the concomitant impact of the black vote. We see the pushing of boundaries in consideration of the conjunction of black theology and sexual identity. We see the discussion of a gendered analysis of familial policies echoed in a critical essay on the newly crystallizing debate about the deepening social and economic plight of young black males, and echoed as well in the article on felon disfranchisement. The continuing search for understanding the relationship between religion, the black church and black political behavior is captured in this volume. The article on cross-racial group coalitions provides a very timely backdrop against which to reflect on matters of immigration, growing multiculturalism, and the impact on black politics. Continuing concerns about maximizing the impact of the black vote are variably addressed in the articles on voting rights enforcement; the black vote in presidential elections; and the voice of the Congressional Black Caucus in American foreign policy. And issues of persistent social inequalities are the focus of two articles which address dimensions of ideology, federalism, and social welfare policy. Finally the review of Ira Katznelson's book was solicited to provide the readership with exposure to a timely and useful analysis which entails the possibility for rebuilding the contours of the intellectual debate on affirmative action. This volume joins the archives of preceding volumes in attempting to capture the expanding boundaries of black politics and the persistent interests of the black community at large.

Georgia A. Persons

Part I

The Expanding Boundaries of Black Politics:
A Symposium

The Expanding Boundaries
of Black Politics

Todd C. Shaw
Symposium Editor

Introduction

Contemporary black politics must still grapple with George Santayana's admonition that our failure to learn history only dooms us to repeat it. Mindful of how history can repeat itself in both the practice and praxis of black politics, this symposium takes seriously the claim by Persons (1999) that black political science confronts a "malaise" and thus needs fresh intellectual blood. In a 1999 *National Political Science Review* editorial essay, Persons asserts: "the study and the practice of black politics in America has reached a state of seeming inertia. There is very little which is new in terms of theory building or engaging analyses on the part of scholars" (1993:3). Nine years earlier Mack Jones sanguinely echoes Persons concern when he concludes black political science, "has yet to get beyond it most rudimentary stage" (Jones 1990). Furthermore, Persons feels that absent a critical re-examination of this malaise, "analysts of black politics, especially black analysts, endlessly lament what they see as the lack of purpose in black politics as an actual practice" (1993:3). Robert Smith's *We Have No Leaders*, now ten years old, is among the best exemplars of this intellectual cynicism (Persons 1999a; Smith 1996). Persons attributes the above analytical and actual stupor to two failures. First, scholars and practitioners fail to grasp changing political conditions and to adapt by creating appropriately new analytical lens as well as *realpolitik* strategies and tactics. Second, the lack of innovative approaches to American racial politics and black politics inhibits our ability to derive useful comparative lens for understanding dominant-subordinate politics outside as well as inside the United States. Interestingly, Persons wrote these words in 1999 when Cathy Cohen published her book *The Boundaries of Black Blackness: Aids and the Breakdown of Black Politics*.

Cohen's Marginalization Theory

This symposium is entitled "The Expanding Boundaries of Black Politics" because we use Cohen's work as a point of thematic departure to demonstrate how the newest generation of black politics scholarship—the third— answers Persons call for theoretical and practical innovation. Like Persons, Cohen was concerned about the rigidity of American and black politics, so she advances a "new" political power theory called "marginalization theory" whereas an: "observable characteristic or distinguishing behavior shared by a group of individuals," such as race, class, gender, or sexual orientation, "is systematically used within the larger society to signal the inferior and subordinate status of the group" (Cohen 199: 24-25). This theory asserts that political power is not a one-dimensional dichotomy of the powerful vs. the powerless as political scientists had traditionally conceived. Instead it is a multi-dimensional continuum whereas the oppressed have varying levels of political power and agency as defined by cross-cutting systems of privilege and disadvantage—that is, black house slaves vs. field slaves; affluent white gay males vs. working-class Chicana lesbians, etc. Generalizability and dynamics are inherent features of marginalization theory, for it applicable to several dominant group-subordinate group contexts and recognizes varying levels of oppression overtime. Cohen imaginatively employs this theory to explain both the external and internal dimensions of African American politics.

With the *external dimension*, she explains that overtime the black freedom struggle has pressured American society to modify its ideologies and practices of racism and white supremacy. First, there is the absolute or "categorical marginalization" imposed by slavery, when all or nearly all blacks faced racial subjugation and exclusion. Next, there is the "integrative marginalization" imposed by the late- and immediate post-Jim Crow period, when a few blacks broke color barriers. Lastly, there is the "advanced marginalization" of the current post-Civil Rights Movement era, when *de jure* racial segregation is outlawed and a burgeoning black elite and middle class enjoy significant opportunities in employment and elective office. Progress notwithstanding, race has and still predominates African American life and constrains black opportunities and individual perceptions of "linked fate" as many students of black political attitudes and ideology have observed (Dawson 1994a; Dawson 2001; Gurin, Hatchett, and Jackson 1989; Tate 1993).

With the *internal dimension*, Cohen delineates the difference between the above primary marginalization process that constrains most black life chances and a secondary form of marginalization that affects important sub-sections. Secondary marginalization occurs when indigenous black leaders are so preoccupied with the anti-racist policing of the boundaries of black identity, interests, and politics that they disregard or subsume other oppressions—class, gender, sexual orientation, etc.—because attention to the latter supposedly fractures black unity. Elites instead choose to invest the community's ideological and institutional resources in race-based "consensus issues" like affirmative action or voting rights at the expense of "cross-cutting issues" like rape and domestic violence that can equally mean life or death for those affected. Cohen decides to focus on one of the most contentious, cross-cutting, policy issues to confront the black community—the HIV/AIDS epidemic among African Americans. Black moral consternation with homosexuality and intravenous drug-use prevents many black elected officials, ministers, and civil rights leaders from directing sufficient attention to this crisis. Despite black gays, lesbians, and intravenous drug users racially identifying as fellow African Americans, they face secondary marginalization because key black leaders consider their cross-cutting needs and interests as outside the main purview of black politics. In this instance, black linked fate is "qualified" by a "politics of respectability." Even while some black leaders and groups support and provide limited social services to those at-risk, Cohen labels the inability of black leaders to move beyond traditional moral prohibitions in waging a full assault on the HIV/AIDS epidemic as a "willingness to serve, but not to lead."

Moreover, we believe Cohen's dynamic framework provides a starting point from which to further expand the theoretical, epistemological, and methodological boundaries of the black politics literature. While it is true we answer Persons' call for innovation, I label this chapter *The Expanding Boundaries of Black Politics* precisely because I do not believe that this symposium's contributions are without precedent. In fact, the next section argues that the black politics literature as a corpus is an inherently self-critical enterprise. I establish the groundwork for arguing in the fourth section how third generationists assume the mantle of helping to push the literature beyond any intellectual malaise.

Black Politics, Boundaries, and the Black Political Science Tradition

At the 37th Annual Meeting of NCOBPS held in March of 2006, the audience members who attended the roundtable session that prospectively introduced this *NPSR* symposium raised a number of provocative questions in response to the presentations.[1] Two of the most important *a priori* questions were: *What is this symposium's definition of black politics? How do you define the (intellectual) boundaries you seek to expand?*

With regard to defining black politics, black political scientists by the mid-1970s formed an uneasy consensus that the practice of *black politics* entails those individual and collective black struggles that seek political power, whether internal and external to the American polity, so to define and achieve black group liberation amidst the realities of racism and/or white supremacy (Barnett and Hefner 1976; Henderson 1972; Holden 1973; Milton 1975; Walton 1972). Accompanying this agreement was a call for a "black political science" as a response to the perceived racial myopia as well as the atheoretical lacuna of mainstream political science, which had ignored the fundamental insights racialized persons and the Third World brought to studies of political power. Jones explains, "Just as conventional American political science takes 'maintaining a stable commonwealth' as a point of beginning, black political scientists must begin with the need to subvert that order ... [therefore] we must first of all develop a political science which grows out of a black perspective; a black political science if you will"(Jones 1977). Similar to their sisters and brothers in sociology, history, psychology, and other disciplines, black political scientists debated the need for the fruits of their intellectual labors to have explicit normative assumptions—e.g., black freedom—and to be applicable to the real word political and policy needs of African American/African peoples (Morris 1990; Pinderhughes 1990; Shaw 1991).

Where are the boundary lines? Notwithstanding this tentative agreement, students of black politics vigorously and contentiously debate whether placing race and racism at the center of their analysis is necessary but not sufficient in properly defining the scope and boundaries of black politics and black political science. Black nationalist scholars with varying intensity argue that race or "the nation" must be primary to black political analysis (Howard and Smith 1978; Karenga 1977; Nelson 1990; Obadele 1990; Smith 1996). Scholars of black women studies disagree and argue that black politics must at least include the parallel consideration of gender, patriarchy, and sexism (Gay and Tate 1998; Githens and Prestage 1977; King 1990; King 1977; Locke 2000; Robinson 1987; Simien 2006; Smith and Prestage 1977). Neo-Marxist or other class analysts argue black politics must also consider class, capitalism, and/or economic exploitation (Dawson 1994b; Jones 1972; Marable 1983; Reed 1985; Reed 1999b). A number of black politics scholars intersect lines of normative or ideological demarcation and identify race/nation, gender, and class as co-determinants of the black political condition, though often race still has primacy (Alex-Assensoh and Stanford 1997; Cohen and Dawson 1993; Harris Lacewell 2004; Marable 1990; Preston and et al. 1987; Reed 1988; Smith and Prestage 1977).

Thus debates about whether the boundary lines of black politics end at the edges of race are not new, but are in fact a recurring discourse within black political science. What is new, however, is Cohen's interjection of sexual orientation and health status as a heretofore underexamined cleavage within black politics (until the late 1990s) as well as the way her work has uniquely though not singularly encouraged the growth of what I call the third generation of black politics scholarship and its use of several "new" paradigms—specifically *marginality, intersectionality, multiraciality, and deep democracy.* Below I explain how these paradigms distinguish this third generation from its predecessors before summarizing the contributions of each symposium author.

The Third Generation of Black Politics Scholarship

As should be evident from the foregoing discussion, there are several standpoints from which we can categorize the evolution of the black politics corpus—e.g., the epistemological, theoretical, ideological, or methodological. Within the epistemological approach, I choose a genealogical typology and conclude there have been at least three waves of so-called *grand research questions* that have animated the inquiries of African American politics scholars since the early 1970s. I use the term "generations of black politics scholarship" and not "scholars" to stipulate that I am characterizing cohorts of research questions and not age-cohorts of research- ers. In fact, several senior scholars extend beyond the field's immediate post-1970s research questions in fascinating ways so to examine the current complexities confronting black com- munities (Dawson 1999; McClain and Karnig 1990; Nelson 2000; Pinderhughes 2003; Walton 1997) and several junior scholars provocatively revisit questions previously thought answered (Brown 1996; Calhoun-Brown 1996; Harris, Sinclair-Chapman, and McKenzie 2006; Owens 2003). Albeit, I qualify my categorization in two important ways. First of all, certain complex works quite naturally fall into more than one generation—(e.g., Jennings 1992; Reed 1999a; Tate 2003; Thompson 2005). Second, there is a plethora of excellent work that examines the historical development of black politics (Gaines 1996; Hahn 2003; Lawson 1976; Lawson 1997; Payne 1995), but I am confining my discussions to the literature on the post-Civil Rights Movement era of the late 1960s up to the present day.

Broadly speaking, the first generation of this post-Civil Rights Movement scholarship is the *initial empowerment & incorporation generation.* It includes a series of texts that examine the various pre-conditions for black political incorporation and/or autonomy between the mid-1960s and 1970s. Questions about political inclusion and group autonomy were extremely relevant in the immediate aftermath of the Civil Rights Movement, the civil rights reforms, and the Black Power Movement because all of them newly empowered black voters, black community leaders, and black candidates and/or public officials (Browning, Marshall, and Tabb 1984; Carmichael and Hamilton 1967; Hamilton 1973; Henderson 1972; Holden 1973; Jones 1972; Kleppner 1985; Nelson and Meranto 1977; Pinderhughes 1987; Preston 1987; Walton 1972; Williams 1989). Since race still polarizes the vote and renders black political empowerment precarious, there are scholars who either continue to investigate the conditions under which black mayors and other elected officials first came to power in the 1960s and 1970s or they explain the reasons for or against contemporary black electoral/policy breakthroughs (Jeffries 2000; Moore 2002; Pohlmann and Kirby 1996; Reeves 1997). Historians (Colburn 2001; Moore 2002; Thomp- son 2001) and students of deracialization theory (McCormick and Jones 1993; Persons 1993; Wright 2000) remain quite interested in this line of inquiry. Likewise, the substantial body of behavioral and institutional literature regarding black presidential politics, blacks in Congress, and the politics of black representation is a very important outgrowth of this genre (Gay 2001; Morris 1988; Reed 1985; Tate 2003; Walters 1988; Whitby 1998).

The second generation includes a wide range of works that evaluate the performance of African Americans elected to federal, state, and local office ten or more years after the emer- gence of the post-1960s black voter. This *racial and economic impact generation* of literature chiefly wonders if and how black political empowerment has led to black policy efficacy and substantive black economic opportunity (Bobo and Gilliam 1990; Brown 1996; Eisinger 1983; Howard and Smith 1978; Jennings 1992; Karnig and Welch 1980; Keller 1978; Nelson 1990), especially for the black working class and/or poor (Akalimat 1988; Banks 2000; Jones 1978; Orr and Stoker 1994; Reed 1999b). Most notably are the volumes by Preston and his colleagues that declare the arrival of a "New Black Politics" due to increased numbers of black elected officials (Preston 1987; Preston et al. 1982; Preston et al. 1987; Williams 1987). Given that the black middle-class is the chief beneficiary of the educational and employment doors opened by civil rights reforms while the black poor experienced a deepening poverty in cities like Detroit, Atlanta, and Chicago, these widening inter-group disparities indicate the relevance of line of questioning. While this generation of scholarship implicitly disagrees with Wilson's thesis in *The Declining Significance of Race*, it clearly believes that in the post-Civil Rights era economic inequalities among blacks and between blacks and whites are increasing in salience, despite greatly increased numbers of black elected officeholders (Akalimat 1988; Dawson 1994a; Hill 1983; Marable 1985; Reed 1985; Tate 1993).

Lastly, third generation questions are logical outgrowths of the previous two generations for this newest cohort focuses upon the cross-cutting cleavages, divides, and conflicts within black politics due to widening stratification, perceived leadership failures, and/or the inequities of lop-sided policy outcomes. The central question of this *cross-cutting class and social cleavages generation* of the literature is whether the increasing heterogeneity among African American communities in the post-Civil Rights Movement era has and will lead to new as well as significant political fissures. Black scholars have long debated whether race vs. class (or other social constructs) shape and determine black political life (Allen 1990; Drake and Cayton 1993; DuBois 1935; Frazier 1957). As aforementioned, there are several theoretical innovations this third generation has made in explicating the contemporary dimensions of internecine black politics—including *marginality, intersectionality, multiraciality, and deep democracy*.

First of all, a *marginality* approach as Cohen (1999) tell us begins its analysis with those social groups and identities that are farthest from the centers of power; while *intersectionality* contemplates how various integrations of race, class, gender, age, sexual orientation, and/or other social identities as well as positions complicate unitary definitions of group political interests. To be sure, third generation scholarship flows from many previous trajectories of social science theory but most directly borrows from interdisciplinary fields like feminist and gender studies, cultural studies, critical race theory, and of course African American studies (Crenshaw 1995; Fuery and Mansfield 2000; Hill Collins 1990; Marable 2000). Explanations for the ways in which contemporary black politics is shaped by ideology, the media, public discourse, political and popular culture, context, and activist traditions are among the mass political processes that intrigue this generation (Dawson 1999; Dawson 2001; Gay 2004; Hanchard 2006; Harris 2001; Harris Lacewell 2004; Iton 2000; Orr 1999; Shelby 2005; Williams 2004). Due to the overwhelming social and political influence of Hip Hop upon contemporary popular culture, third generationists also return to 1970s queries about the political socialization, attitudes, and behavior of African American youth (Brown 2005; Simpson 1998; Spiller 2004).

Second, more so than it predecessors, this generation is aware of the subtly shifting minority status of self-identified African Americans due to the emergence of increasingly solidified Latino and Asian American communities. Thus, black politics is not simply confined to the so-called "black-white paradigm." Toward these ends, these scholars overall argue this phenomenon represents both opportunities and challenges for new black-and-brown coalitions.[2] Third generationists join previous schools in criticizing the patronizing, white-referential, "race relations" literature (Harris Lacewell 2000; Walton, Miller, and Joseph P. McCormick 1995) but they go further and plumb the current depths of *multiraciality* or rather multiracial forms of as well as tensions within black politics (Alex-Assensoh and Hanks 2000; McClain and Karnig 1990; Pinderhughes 2003; Thompson 2005). In effect, the whole question of what constitutes "blackness" is more complicated because post-1965 immigration dynamics increased the numbers of persons in the U.S. who are black and are from Africa, the Caribbean, and Latin America, but still distinguish themselves from native-born African Americans (Assensoh 2000; Rogers 2000).[3]

Lastly, as part of a renewed academic and grassroots consideration of new leftist politics and activism in an era of neoliberalism or conservatism, third generationists join calls to manifest a new *"deep democracy"* within *black politics* and American politics (West 2006). As inspired by Civil Rights and Black Power Movement scholarship, third generationists use a deep democracy lens to re-examine contemporary black grassroots activism and to understand if black insurgent politics can be and have been combined with black institutional politics to reinvigorate black freedom struggles (Franklin 2002; Jennings 1992; Reed 1985; Reed 1999b; Shaw 2003; Simpson 2005; Thompson 2005; Williams 2004). While they share no consensus as to whether black grassroots activism is alive and well, they vigorously debate this question between themselves and with those of previous generations (Dawson 1995; Jennings 1992; Reed 1999c; Smith 1996). Below I discuss how each of the above theoretical innovations—marginality, intersectionality, multiraciality, and/or deep democracy—are evident throughout the works of this symposium's contributors.

Expanding Beyond Margins and Boundaries

As aforementioned, this symposium features some of the cutting-edge third generation black politics scholarship, but it also provides a venue for a handful of the newest scholars within the field of black political science.[4] In fact, all of the contributors to this symposium are either untenured faculty members, junior scholar fellows, and/or newly minted Ph.D.s, who in a Kuhnian (1970) sense, borrow from and revise political science theories and paradigms. Although these authors ponder the implications of recent events such as Hurricane Katrina or the 2004 election, the works in this volume go beyond immediate issues to consider perennial aspects of the black political experience: black urban representation and policy responsiveness; new labor activism; changing multiracial demographics; health risks and behaviors; gender and the status of black women and girls; black youth participation and generational differences; voting rights; criminal justice and social welfare policy; as well as the black church and the politics of morality.

In addition, this symposium's contributors practice not only *methodological* but *epistemological pluralism*. They are not captive to the simplistic quantitative-qualitative divide that for years intellectually constrained the political science discipline and caused unnecessary rifts among students of black political science, especially presenters at the National Conference of Black Political Scientists (NCOBPS) (Dawson and Wilson 1991; Morris 1990; Pinderhughes 1990). They go beyond this dichotomy and artfully blend theoretical, historical, and empirical insights to support their arguments. These authors use a wide array of qualitative and quantitative techniques—from case-study, ethnographic interviews to large-sample, multivariate regression—and in some cases pose both their questions and their answers in imaginative and unorthodox ways.

Robert Brown's article "Race & Politics Matter" begins this symposium. Among all the articles, his represents the clearest bridge between the second and third generations of scholarship for he assesses the urban fiscal expenditure patterns of cities with black versus white mayors and city councilors. Although Brown concedes that he does not use Cohen's work as his theoretical lens, he examines a time period—the early 1970s to the mid-1990s—that undeniably is part of what Cohen labels the advanced marginalization phase of black politics. While Brown's work directly counters the skepticism of thinkers like Watts (2005) because cities led by black mayors and city councilors, for all of their political and fiscal constraints, do make larger investments in housing and community development than their white counterparts. Brown readily admits, as most evident from New Orleans, that black-led efforts still fall far short of the need.

Next, Dorian Warren's piece "A New Labor Movement?" adeptly analyzes the historical record as well as original survey data to argue what he believes are the "missing intersections between Black and Labor Politics". In contrast to Brown, Warren's article is more squarely third generationists because, inspired by Cohen, he uses marginality, intersectionality, and deep democracy to explain why the current labor movement suffers from fragmentation and demobilization. Blame for this situation is laid both at the feet of myopic mainline white unionists and their unimaginative black unionist comrades. Is this sense the missing link is a problem internal and external to black politics. Khalilah Brown-Dean and her third generationist piece "Permanent Outsiders" argues the necessity of black policy agendas more strongly embracing felon disenfranchisement as an issue. Like Warren, she too employs the marginality and intersectionality features of Cohen's marginalization theory to explain those external and internal dynamics of a black politics that acquiesce to "consensus issues" at the expense of "cross-cutting issues." Given Tavis Smiley's popular *The Covenant with Black America* mentions ex-felon enfranchisement as part of its laundry list of demands, this suggests that there is a nominal (if not yet a sufficient) awareness that this form of deep democracy is painfully absent (Henderson 2006).

From a different third generationist angle, Lorrie Frasure's piece "Beyond the Myth of the White Middle Class" also helps to expand the boundaries of black politics. She expertly analyzes census data to investigate how the increasing multiracial diversity of suburbia is driven by differing group settlement choices and can conceivably lead to differing inequalities. In this respect, her focus upon the implications of suburban multiraciality serves as a vibrant scholarly juncture between urban politics, racial and ethnic politics (to which African American politics belongs), and urban political economy. Her piece is also timely given recent debates about American immigration policy. To a degree, Frasure work also follows in the footsteps of Dawson (1994a), for she demonstrates the insights and foibles of the rationalist or rationale choice paradigm.

The works of Lester K. Spence and Rena Boss-Victoria in their piece "AIDS, Context, and Black Politics" as well as Ruth Nicole Brown in her piece "Remembering Maleessa" both nicely provide ethnographic evidence that illuminates the difficult circumstances and choices African American youth confront as they make political sense of their world. In one respect, their pieces harken back to the early political ethnography of Lane (1962), for both works observe the political in the everyday narratives of these young people's struggles. Their respective articles also prove my point about third generationist literature for they consider marginality, intersectionality, and deep democracy as part of their theories. On the one hand, Spence and Boss-Victoria contemplate the political geographies of race, poverty, and public health risks as each frames political learning. So they adhere to Cohen's thinking by remapping her specific public health concerns of HIV/AIDS and drug use. On the other hand, Ruth Nicole Brown provocatively argues for a new theory of black girl political socialization as inflected by Hip Hop and feminist theories. Thus she echoes Cohen's theoretical concern with understanding the core of political power by beginning at its extreme margins. No work in this symposium wrestles more with the theoretical and methodological conventions of political science than does the piece by Ruth Nicole Brown—and thus it is literally the newest of the new.

To further demonstrate this symposium's commitment to expanding boundaries, Marwin Spiller contributes an additional piece on African American youth and young adult politics. From a longitudinal analysis of National Election Study data (1960-1998), he concludes that the "Protest" and "Hip Hop" generations vary as to how race and class attitudes motivate their reported political participation. As our lone sociologist, he nicely retests Wilson's *Declining Significance of Race* thesis (1980) and not only creates a bridge between elements of the second and third genres of inquiry but retests the intersection between race and class, while of course adding the variable of age.

Last but not least, Julia Jordan-Zachery in her "Let Men Be Men" as well as Todd Shaw's and Eric McDaniel's piece "Whosoever Will," both push the boundaries of black politics by similarly asking how African American leadership and institutions grapple with (or fail to grapple with) difficult moral and social policy issues. Both works tackle third generationist assumptions of gender and sexuality as these constructs provide conflicting impulses for black community and black policy leaders. Shaw and McDaniel conclude from their analyses of various survey datasets that the black political church, whether gay-led or gay-affirming, is more inclined to be accepting of homosexuality than its more apolitical counterparts. Again, Cohen's discussions of marginality and intersectionality are directly applicable because they two focus upon homophobia and the reactions of black indigenous leaders and individual group members. Jordan-Zachery argues that Black Nationalist and Integrationist thought must better meld conceptions of racist patriarchy into their worldviews if they are to better equip the black community to critique conservative policy prescriptions like attacking poverty through marriage initiatives, in a Moynihan-sense, which in turn attacks the fictive "Black Matriarch." Her conception of "racist patriarchy" is directly borrowed from a presumption of black feminist theory that race and gender equally matter.

Conclusion: Whither the Fourth Generation?

In this editorial essay, I argue that the newest or third generation of the U.S. black politics literature, like its predecessors, understands the inherent limitations that racial and economic oppression impose upon African Americans, but frames its questions of external and internal dynamics using theories of marginality, intersectionality, multiraciality and/or deep democracy. This generation did not originate with the work of Cohen (1999), but her theory of marginalization has been a seminal contribution to the approach. Furthermore, not only is there a third generation of U.S. black politics literature, but conceivably this generation of inquiry extends across black political science to comparative students of race and the politics of blackness in Latin America, the Caribbean, Africa, and the larger African Diaspora (Hanchard 1999; Nobles 2000; Persons 1999b; Sawyer 2006). At the onset, I fully concede that this review of literature has had a limited purpose of making a case for what is newest in African American politics. However, I believe this essay, if critically engaged, will spark or reignite a self-conscious awareness of and debate about the important distinctions between the various generations of black political science.

To look ahead is to naturally ask whether there is a fourth generation of black politics scholarship on the horizon? Quite conceivably, its seeds may be evident in at least two ways. On the theoretical front, scholars will further pursue the logical ends of current grand research questions by vigorously debating the increasing difficulties of defining blackness and African American politics. On the epistemological and methodological front, I predict debate will increase regarding the merits of the positivist-empirical paradigm, in which most political scientists are still trained, versus the more interpretative-subjective paradigm of literature and humanities.[5] Moreover, we believe from an normative standpoint this symposium is an important contribution to black political science because at the beginning of this new century it demonstrates that this field is still pursuing the goal of "being relevant" to the black experience. Nearly forty years ago, the National Conference of Black Political Scientists was founded and assumed as its motto: "a growing organization in the struggle for African liberation." (Jones 1990; Morris

1990; Pinderhughes 1990) Mindful of the necessary growing pains that stem, in part, from the tough intellectual criticism of various colleagues, we hope both the scholarly study and actual practice of black politics will at least modestly benefit from our efforts.

Notes

1. My thanks to Robert Brown, Eric McDaniel, Lorrie Frasure, Khalilah Brown-Dean, and Julia Jordan-Zachery for their ability to participate. I also thank the other volume contributors who wanted to participate but were unable to attend the conference.
2. Recently, there have been vigorous on-line debates among members of the National Conference of Black Political Scientists as to whether policy and political coalitions between African Americans and Latinos are feasible and desirable. The deep intellectual and ideological divisions emanating from these debates essentially represent not only clashes between nationalist versus radical pluralist conceptions, but conceivably clashes between first versus third generation approaches.
3. In fact, one current convention among some Black Studies scholars is to reserve use of the term "Black" to only denote all persons of African descent and the term "African American" to mean persons who self-identify as native black Americans.
4. Just a few examples of outstanding third generationist books by students of black politics include Harris, Fredrick C., Valeria Sinclair-Chapman, and Brian D McKenzie. 2006. *Countervailing Forces in African-American Civic Activism, 1973–1994*. Cambridge: Cambridge University Press, Harris Lacewell, Melissa. 2004. *Babershops, Bibles, and BET: Everyday Talk and Black Political Thought*. Princeton, NJ: Princeton University Press, Iton, Richard. 2000. *Solidarity Blues: Race, Culture, and the American Left*. Chapel Hill and London: University of North Carolina Press, Marie Hancock, Ange. 2005. *The Politics of Disgust: The Public Identity of the Welfare Queen*. New York: New York University Press, Thompson, J. Phillip. 2005. *Double Trouble: Black Mayors, Black Politics, and the Call for Deep Democracy*. Oxford: Oxford University Press.
5. Long before the 1990s "Perestroika" counter-movement within the American Political Science Association that called for a recognition of a greater breadth of methods and a deeper associational democracy—see 2000. An Open Letter to the American Political Science Association and Members. *PS: Political Science & Politics* 33:735-37—there have routinely been discussions and tensions at the National Conference around qualitative versus quantitative approaches. See Pinderhughes, Dianne. 1990. NCOBPS: Observations on The State of the Organization. *National Political Science Review* 2:13-21.

References

2000. An Open Letter to the American Political Science Association and Members. *PS: Political Science & Politics* 33:735-37.

Akalimat, Abdul. 1988. Chicago: Black Power Politics and the Crisis of the Black Middle Class. *Black Scholar* 19 (3):45-54.

Alex-Assensoh, Yvette M, and Lawrence J Hanks, (eds.) 2000. *Black and Multiracial Politics in America*. New York and London: New York University Press.

Alex-Assensoh, Yvette, and Karin Stanford. 1997. Gender, Participation, and the Black Urban Underclass. In *Women Transforming Politics: An Alternative Reader*, (ed.) C. Cohen, K. Jones and J. C. Toronto. New York: New York University Press.

Allen, Robert L. 1990. *Black Awakening in Capitalist America: An Analytic History*. New edition (ed.) Trenton, NJ: African World Press.

Assensoh, Akwasi B. 2000. Conflict or Cooperation? Africans and African Americans in Multiracial America. In *Black and Multiracial Politics in America*, (ed.) Y. M. Alex-Assensoh and L. J. Hanks. New York and London: New York University Press.

Banks, Manley. 2000. A Changing Electorate in a Majority Black City: The Emergence of a Neo-conservative Black Urban Regime in Contemporary Atlanta. *Journal of Urban Affairs* 22 (3):265-278.

Barnett, Marguerite Ross, and James Hefner, (eds.) 1976. *Public Policy for the Black Community*. New York, NY: Alfred.

Barry, John. 1997. *Rising Tide: The Great Mississippi Flood and How It Changed America*. New York: Simon & Schuster.

Bobo, Lawrence, and Franklin Gilliam. 1990. Race, Sociopolitical Participation, and Black Empowerment. *American Political Science Review* 84:377-93.

Brown, Robert A. 1996. A Tale of the Cities: Urban Fiscal Policy, the Transformation of American Cities, and the Influence of African American Urban Representation, University of Michigan, Ann Arbor, MI.

Brown, Ruth Nicole. 2005. Between Empowerment and Marginalization: A Study of Political Socialization in an After-School Mentoring Program for Sixth Grade Girls. Ph.D., Political Science and Women Studies, University of Michigan, Ann Arbor, MI.

Browning, Rufus P, Dale Rogers Marshall, and David H Tabb. 1984. *Protest Is Not Enough: The Struggle of Black and Hispanics for Equality in Urban Politics.* Berkeley and Los Angeles, CA: University of California Press.

Calhoun-Brown, Allison. 1996. African American Churches and Political Mobilization: The Psychological Impact of Organizational Resources. *Journal of Politics* 58:935-53.

Carmichael, Stokley, and Charles Hamilton. 1967. *Black Power: The Politics of Liberation in America.* New York: Vintage Press.

Cohen, Cathy, and Michael Dawson. 1993. Neighborhood Poverty and African American Politics. *American Political Science Review* 87 (2):286-301.

Colburn, David R. 2001. Running for Office: African-American Mayors from 1967 to 1996. In *African-American Mayors: Race, Politics, and the American City*, (ed.) D. R. Colburn and J. S. Adler. Urbana and Chicago, IL: University of Illinois Press.

Crenshaw, Kimberle, et al, (ed.) 1995. *Critical Race Theory: The Key Writings that Formed the Movement.* New York: New Press.

Dawson, Michael. 1994a. *Behind the Mule: Race and Class in African American Politics.* Princeton, NJ: Princeton University Press.

Dawson, Michael. 1994b. *Behind the Mule: Race and Class in African-American Politics.* Princeton, NJ: Princeton University Press.

Dawson, Michael. 1995. A Black Counterpublic?: Economic Earthquakes, Radical Agenda(s), and Black Politics. In *The Black Public Sphere: A Public Culture Book.* Chicago, IL: University of Chicago.

Dawson, Michael. 1999. Dis Beat Disrupts: Rap, Ideology, and Black Political Opinion. In *The Cultural Territories of Race: White and Black Boundaries*, (ed.) M. Lamount. Chicago, IL: University of Chicago Press.

Dawson, Michael. 2001. *Black Visions: The Roots of Contemporary African-American Political Ideologies.* Chicago and London: University of Chicago Press.

Dawson, Michael, and Ernest J III Wilson. 1991. Paradigms and Paradoxes: Political Science and African American Politics. In *Theory and Practice of Political Science*, (ed.) W. Crotty. Evanston, IL: Northwestern University Press.

Drake, St. Clair, and Horace Cayton. 1993. Black Metropolis: A Study of Negro Life in a Northern City. Chicago, IL: University of Chicago Press.

DuBois, W.E.B. 1935. *Black Reconstruction in America, 1860-1880.* New York: Antheneum.

Eisinger, Peter K. 1983. *Black Employment in City Government, 1973-1980.* Washington, DC: Joint Center for Political Studies.

Fine, Sidney. 1989. *Violence in the Model City: The Cavanagh Administration, Race Relations, and the Detroit Riot of 1967.* Ann Arbor, MI: University of Michigan Press.

Franklin, Sekou. 2002. Community Organizing and Strategy in Post-Black Power Grass-Roots Activism.

Frazier, E. Franklin. 1957. *Black Bourgeoisie.* New York: Free Press.

Fuery, Patrick, and Nick Mansfield. 2000. *Cultural Studies and Critical Theory.* Melbourne, New York: Oxford University Press.

Gaines, Kevin K. 1996. *Uplifting the Race: Black Leadership, Politics, and Culture in the Twentieth Century.* Chapel Hill and London: University of North Carolina Press.

Gay, Claudine. 2001. The Effect of Black Congressional Representation on Political Participation. *American Political Science Review* 95 (3):589-602.

Gay, Claudine. 2004. Putting Race in Context: Identifying the Environmental Determinants of Black Racial Attitudes. *American Political Science Review* 98 (4):547-562.

Gay, Claudine, and Katherine Tate. 1998. Doubly Bound: The Impact of Gender and Race on the Politics of Black Women. *Political Psychology* 1:169-184.

Githens, Marianne, and Jewel Prestage. 1977. *A Portrait of Marginality: The Political Behavior of the American Woman.* New York: McKay Co.

Gurin, Patrica, Shirley Hatchett, and James Jackson. 1989. *Hope and Independence: Blacks' Response to Electoral and Party Politics*. New York, NY: Sage Foundation.

Hahn, Steven. 2003. *A Nation Under Our Feet: Black Political Struggles in the Rural South from Slavery to the Great Migration*. Cambridge, MA: Harvard University Press.

Hamilton, Charles. 1973. *The Black Experience in American Politics*. New York: JP Putnam & Sons.

Hamilton, Donna Cooper, and Charles V. Hamilton. 1997. *The Dual Agenda: Race and Social Welfare Policies of the Civil Rights Organizations*. New York: Columbia University Press.

Hanchard, Michael, (ed.) 1999. *Racial Politics in Contemporary Brazil*. Durham, NC: Duke University Press.

Hanchard, Michael. 2006. *Party/Politics: Horizons in Black Political Thought*. Oxford: Oxford University Press.

Harris, Fredrick C. 2001. 'It Takes a Tragedy to Arouse Them': Collective Memory and Collective Action During the Civil Rights Movement. In *Presented at the Theorizing Black Communities Conference: New Frontiers in the Study of African-American Politics*. Rochester, NY: University of Rochester.

Harris, Fredrick C., Valeria Sinclair-Chapman, and Brian D McKenzie. 2006. *Countervailing Forces in African-American Civic Activism, 1973–1994*. Cambridge: Cambridge University Press.

Harris Lacewell, Melissa. 2000. The Heart of the Politics of Race: Centering Black Ideology in the Study of White Political Attitudes.

Harris Lacewell, Melissa. 2004. *Barbershops, Bibles, and BET: Everyday Talk and Black Political Thought*. Princeton, NJ: Princeton University Press.

Henderson, Lenneal, (ed.) 1972. *Black Political Life in the United States: A Fist As a Pendulum*. San Francisco, CA: Chandler.

Henderson, Wade. 2006. Claiming our Democracy. In *The Covenant with Black America*, (ed.) T. Smiley. Chicago, IL: Third World Press.

Hill Collins, Patricia. 1990. *Black Feminist Thought: Knowledge, Consciousness, and the Politics of Empowerment*. New York: Routledge.

Hill, Richard C. 1983. Crisis in the Motor City: The Politics of Economic Development in Detroit. In *Restructuring the City: The Political Economy of Urban Redevelopment*, (ed.) S. Fainstein and et al. New York: Longman.

Holden, Matthew. 1973. *The Politics of the Black 'Nation'*. New York: Chandler Publishing.

Howard, John R, and Robert C Smith. 1978. Urban Black Politics. *Annals of the American Academy of Political and Social Science* 438.

Iton, Richard. 2000. *Solidarity Blues: Race, Culture, and the American Left*. Chapel Hill and London: University of North Carolina Press.

Jeffries, Judson L. 2000. *Virginia's Native Son: The Election and Administration of Governor L. Douglas Wilder*. Lafayette: Purdue University Press.

Jennings, James. 1992. *The Politics of Black Empowerment: The Transformation of Black Activism in Urban America*. Detroit, MI: Wayne State University Press.

Jones, Mack. 1972. A Frame of Reference for Black Politics. In *Black Political Life in the US*, (ed.) L. Henderson. San Francisco, CA: Chandler.

Jones, Mack. 1977. Responsibility of Black Political Scientists to the Black Community. In *Black Political Scientists and Black Survival: Essays in Honor of a Black Scholar*, (ed.) S. L. Smith and J. L. Prestage. Detroit, MI: Belamp Publishers.

Jones, Mack. 1978. Black Political Empowerment in Atlanta. *Annals of the American Academy of Political and Social Science* 438:90-117.

Jones, Mack. 1990. NCOBPS Twenty Years Later. *National Political Science Review* 2:2-13.

Karenga, Maulana. 1977. Kawaida and Its Critics: A Sociohistorical Analysis. *Journal of Black Studies* 18 (4):395-414.

Karnig, Albert, and Susan Welch. 1980. *Black Representation and Urban Policy*. Chicago, IL: University of Chicago Press.

Keller, Edmond. 1978. The Impact of Black Mayors on Urban Policy. *Annals of the American Academy of Political and Social Science* 439:40-52.

King, Deborah. 1990. Multiple Jeopardy, Multiple Consciousness: The Context of Black Feminist Ideology. In *Black Women in America: Social Science Perspectives*, (ed.) M. Malson. Chicago, IL: University of Chicago Press.

King, Mae C. 1977. The Political Role of the Stereotype Image of the Black Woman in America. In *Black Political Scientists and Black Survival: Essays in Honor of a Black Scholar*, (ed.) S. L. Smith and J. L. Prestage. Detroit, MI: Belamp Publishers.

Kleppner, Paul. 1985. *Chicago Divided: The Making of a Black Mayor*. Dekalb, IL: Northern Illinois University Press.

Kuhn, Thomas S. 1970. *The Structure of Scientific Revolutions*. 2nd ed. Chicago, IL: University of Chicago Press.

Lane, Robert Edwards. 1962. *Political Ideology: Why the American Common Man Believes What He Does*. New York: Free Press of Glencoe.

Lawson, Steven F. 1976. *Black Ballots: Voting Rights in the South, 1944-1969*. New York: Columbia University Press.

Lawson, Steven F. 1997. *Running for Freedom: Civil Rights and Black Politics in America since 1941*. 2nd ed. New York: McGraw-Hill.

Locke, Mamie. 2000. Deconstruct to Reconstruct: African American Women in the Post-Civil Rights Era. In *Black and Multiracial Politics in America*, (ed.) Y. M. Alex-Assensoh and L. J. Hanks. New York and London: New York University Press.

Marable, Maning. 1983. *How Capitalism Underdeveloped Black America*. Boston, MA: South End Press.

Marable, Maning, (ed.) 2000. *Dispatches from the Ebony Tower: Intellectuals Confront the African American Experience*. New York: Columbia University Press.

Marable, Manning. 1985. *Black American Politics: From Washington Marches to Jesse Jackson*. London: Verso.

Marable, Manning. 1990. Race, Reform, and Rebellion: The Second Reconstruction of Black America, 1945-1990. Jackson, MS: University of Mississippi Press.

Marie Hancock, Ange. 2005. *The Politics of Disgust: The Public Identity of the Welfare Queen*. New York: New York University Press.

McClain, Paula, and Albert Karnig. 1990. Black and Hispanic Socioeconomic and Political Competition. *American Politiacl Science Review* 84 (2):535-545.

McCormick, Joseph 2nd, and Charles E Jones. 1993. The Conceptualization of Deracialization: Thinking Through the Dilemma. In *Dilemmas of Black Politics: Issues of Leadership and Strategy*, (ed.) G. Persons. New York: Harper Collins.

Milton, Morris. 1975. *The Politics of Black America*. New York: Harper & Row.

Moore, Leonard M. 2002. *Carl B. Stokes and the Rise of Black Political Power*. Urbana and Chicago, IL: University of Illinois Press.

Morris, Lorenzo. 1988. *The Social and Political Implications of the 1984 Jesse Jackson Presidential Campaign*. New York: Praeger Press.

Morris, Lorenzo. 1990. Preparing the Harvest: The Future of African Americans in Political Science. Paper read at Annual Meeting of the National Conference of Black Political Scientists, 1990, at Atlanta, GA.

Nelson, William. 2000. *Black Atlantic Politics: Dilemmas of Political Empowerment in Boston and Liverpool*. Albany, NY: State University of New York Press.

Nelson, William E. 1990. Black Mayoral Leadership: A Twenty-Year Perspective. *National Political Science Review* 2:188-195.

Nelson, William, and Phillip Meranto. 1977. *Electing Black Mayors: Political Action in the Black Community*. Columbus, OH: Ohio State University Press.

Nobles, Melissa. 2000. *Shades of Citizenship: Race and the Census in Modern Politics*. Stanford, CT: Stanford University Press.

Obadele, Imari. 1990. The Macro-Level Theory of Human Organization. In *A Brief History of Black Stuggle in America*, (ed.) K. Afoh, C. Lumumba, I. Obadele and A. Obafemi. Atlanta & Cypress, TX: The Malcolm X Generation.

Orr, Marion. 1999. *Black Social Capital: The Politics of School Reform in Baltimore*. University of Kansas Press: Lawrence, KN.

Orr, Marion, and Gerry Stoker. 1994. Urban Regimes and Leadership in Detroit. In *Urban Affairs Quarterly*.

Owens, Michael Leo. 2003. Doing Something in Jesus' Name: Black Churches and Community Development Corporations. In *New Day Begun: African American Churches and Civic Culture in Post-Civil Rights America*, (ed.) by R. D. Smith. Durham, NC: Duke University Press.

Payne, Charles. 1995. *I've Got the Light of Freedom: The Organizing Tradition and the Mississippi Freedom Struggle*. Berkeley and Los Angeles, CA: University of California Press.

Persons, Georgia, (ed.) 1993. *Dilemmas of Black Politics: Issues of Leadership and Strategy*. New York: Harper Collins.

Persons, Georgia. 1999a. Politics and Social Change: The Demise of the African-American Ethnic Movement? *National Black Political Science Review* 7:3-19.

Persons, Georgia. 1999b. *Race and Ethnicity in Comparative Perspective*. Vol. 7, *National Political Science Review*. News Brunswick and London: Transactions.

Pinderhughes, Dianne. 1987. *Race and Ethnicity in Chicago Politics: A Reexamination of Pluralist Theory*. Urbana & Illinois, IL: University of Illinois Press.

Pinderhughes, Dianne. 1990. NCOBPS: Observations on the State of the Organization. *National Political Science Review* 2:13-21.

Pinderhughes, Dianne. 2003. Chicago Politics: Political Incorporation. In *Racial Politics in American Cities*, (ed.) R. Browning, D. R. Marshall and D. Tabb: Longman.

Pohlmann, Marcus D, and Michael P Kirby. 1996. *Racial Politics at the Crossroads: Memphis Elections Dr. W.W. Herenton*. Knoxville, TN: The University of Tennessee Press.

Preston, Michael. 1987. The Election of Harold Washington: An Examination of the SES in the 1983 Mayoral Election. In *The New Black Politics: the Search for Political Power*, (ed.) M. Preston et al. New York: Longman.

Preston, Michael, and et al., (eds.) 1982. *The New Black Politics*. New York: Longman.

Preston, Michael, and et al., (eds.) 1987. *The New Black Politics: The Search for Political Power*. 2nd ed. New York: Longman.

Reed, Adolph, Jr. 1999a. *Stirrings in the Jug: Blacks Politics in the Post-Segregation Era*. Minneapolis, MN: University of Minnesota Press.

Reed, Adolph Jr. 1985. *The Jesse Jackson Phenomenon*. New Haven, CT: Yale University Press.

Reed, Adolph Jr. 1988. The Black Urban Regime: Structural Origins and Constraints. In *Power, Community, and the City: Comparative Urban and Community Research*, (ed.) P. Smith. New Brunswick, NJ: Transaction.

Reed, Adolph Jr. 1999b. Sources of Demobilization in the New Black Political Regime: Incorporation, Ideological Capitulation, and Radical Failure in the Post-Segregation Era. In *Stirrings in the Jug: Black Politics in the Post-Segregation Era*, (ed.) A. J. Reed. Minneapolis and London: University of Minnesota Press.

Reed, Adolph, Jr. 1999c. Sources of Demobilization in the New Black Political Regime: Incorporation, Ideological Capitulation, and Radical Failure in the Post-Segregation Era. In *Stirrings in the Jug: Black Politics in the Post-Segregation Era*, (ed.) A. Reed, Jr. Minneapolis, MN: University of Minnesota Press.

Reeves, Keith. 1997. *Voting Hopes or Fears?* New York Oxford: Oxford University Press.

Robinson, Deborah. 1987. The Effect of Group Identity among Black Women on Race Consciousness, University of Michigan, Ann Arbor, MI.

Rogers, Reuel. 2000. Afro-Caribbean Immigrants, African Americans, and the Politics of Group Identity. In *Black and Multiracial Politics in America*, (ed.) Y. M. Alex-Assensoh and L. J. Hanks. New York and London: New York University Press.

Sawyer, Mark Q. 2006. *Racial Politics in Post-Revolutionary Cuba*. Cambridge: Cambridge University Press.

Shaw, Todd. 2003. "We Refused to Lay Down Our Spears": The Persistence of Welfare Rights Activism, 1966-1996. In *Black Political Organizations in the Post Civil Rights Movement Era*, (ed.) O. Johnson and K. Stanford. New Brunswick, NJ: Rutgers University Press.

Shaw, Todd C. 1991. A Relevant Politics: The Internal Logic and Importance of African American Politics, Practice and Praxis. Ann Arbor, MI.

Shelby, Tommie. 2005. *We Who Are Dark: The Philosophical Foundations of Black Solidarity*. Cambridge, MA: Belknap Press of Harvard University Press.

Simien, Evelyn. 2006. *Black Feminists Voices in Politics*. Albany, NY: SUNY University Press.

Simpson, Andrea Y. 1998. *The Tie That Binds: Identity and Political Attitudes in the Post-Civil Rights Generation*. New York: New York University Press.

Simpson, Andrea Y. 2005. Halting, Heroic, Hopeful: Today and Tomorrow in the Environmental Justice Movement.

Smith, Robert C. 1996. *We Have No Leaders: African Americans in the Post-Civil Rights Era*. Albany, NY: State of New York University Press.

Smith, Shelby Lewis, and Jewel Limar Prestage, (eds.) 1977. *Black Political Scientists and Black Survival: Essays in Honor of a Black Scholar*. Detroit, MI: Belamp Publishers.

Spiller, Marwin. 2004. The Effects of Race and Class Patterns of Political Participation on African-American Young Adults. Ph.D., Sociology, University of Illinois, Urbana and Champaign, IL.

Tate, Katherine. 1993. *From Protest to Politics: The New Black Voters in American Elections*. Cambridge and London: Russell Sage and Harvard University Press.

Tate, Katherine. 2003. *Black Faces in the Mirror: African Americans and Their Representatives in the US Congress*. Princeton and Oxford: Princeton University Press.

Thompson, Heather Ann. 2001. Rethinking the Collapse of Postwar Liberalism: The Rise of Mayor Coleman Young and the Politics of Race in Detroit. In *African-American Mayors: Race, Politics, and the American City*, (ed.) D. R. Colburn and J. Adler. Urbana and Chicago, IL: University of Illinois Press.

Thompson, J. Phillip. 2005. *Double Trouble: Black Mayors, Black Politics, and the Call for Deep Democracy*. Oxford: Oxford University Press.

Walters, Ronald W. 1988. *Black Presidential Politics: A Strategic Approach*. Albany, NY: State University of New York.

Walton, Hanes Jr. 1972. *Black Politics: A Theoretical and Structural Analysis*. Philadelphia, PA: J.P. Lippincott.

Walton, Hanes Jr. 1997. *African American Power and Politics: The Political Context Variable*. New York, NY: Columbia University Press.

Walton, Hanes Jr., Cheryl Miller, and II Joseph P. McCormick. 1995. Race and Political Science: The Dual Traditions of Race Relations Politics and African-American Politics. In *Political Science in History: Research Programs and Political Traditions*, (ed.) J. Dryzek, J. Farr and S. Leonard. New York: Cambridge University Press.

Watts, Jerry. 2005. *What Use Are Black Mayors?* [on-line article]. Black Commentator.Com, 2005 [cited 28 November 2005]. Available from www.blackcommentator.com/159/159_cover_black_mayors.html.

West, Cornel. 2006. A Call to Action. In *The Covenant with Black America*, (ed.) T. Smiley. Chicago, IL: Third World Press.

Whitby, Kenny. 1998. *The Color of Representation: Congressional Behavior and Black Constituents*. Ann Arbor, MI: University of Michigan Press.

Williams, Linda. 1987. Black Electoral Progress in the 1980s: The Electoral Arena. In *The New Black Politics: the Search for Political Power*, (ed.) M. B. Preston et al. New York: Longman.

Williams, Linda. 1989. White/Black Perceptions of the Electability of Black Political Candidates. *National Political Science Review* 2:45-64.

Williams, Rhonda Y. 2004. *The Politics of Public Housing: Black Women's Struggles Against Urban Inequality*. Oxford and New York: Oxford University Press.

Wilson, William Julius. 1980. *The Declining Significance of Race*. Chicago, IL: University of Chicago Press.

Wright, Sharon D. 2000. *Race, Power, and Political Emergence in Memphis*. New York, NY: Garland Press.

Race and Politics Matter: Black Urban Representation and Social Spending during the Urban Crisis

Robert A. Brown
Emory University

Introduction

One of the major developments of American politics over the past thirty years has been the dramatic increase in the numbers of African Americans elected to serve in the nation's federal, state, and local governments. While blacks have made strong inroads at the national level, with thirty-nine black Representatives in the 107th Congress, they have had far greater success at the local level, especially in the nation's central cities. For instance, from 1965 to 1993, the number of blacks elected to Congress increased from four to thirty-eight, while the numbers among city council members increased from seventy-four to well over 3,000 and among city mayors from three to 356 (Jayes and Williams 1989: 239; Joint Center for Political and Economic Studies 1993: xv). Nonetheless, in a somewhat unfortunate irony, African Americans achieved a higher level of urban political representation during the 1970s and 1980s when many cities experienced hard times—economically, socially, and politically—enduring a struggle for continued viability, as they lost staggering numbers of residents, businesses, and jobs to the suburbs.[1] Hence, it is often said that black mayors assumed control of "hollow cities" during this time, as they presided over cities experiencing severe economic decline (Friesema 1967). Yet, how did black mayors and city council members govern their cities during these two decades of significant economic and demographic change?

A central question in the literature examining the influence of black urban officials concerns their alteration of city government decision-making to benefit black citizens. Have they responded to the policy interests of black constituents? Have black mayors governed cities in ways different from white mayors? And specifically, for this article, did black officials alter urban fiscal budgets to devote more money to social policies? This article examines city government expenditures to answer the question whether black mayors and city council members altered these governments' fiscal priorities by increasing the expenditures devoted to social policy: Did African American urban elected officials have a significant effect upon increases in city governments' social spending for housing and community development, public welfare, and health?

A chief assumption of my argument is that these black leaders consciously sought to implement measures that helped to alleviate the economically distressing conditions experienced by many of their black constituents. Whereas my work does not directly draw upon the marginalization theory of Cohen (1999), the problem and post-Civil Rights Movement period I study is clearly within the purview of what she considers the advanced marginalization phase of black politics. This article demonstrates that despite considerable barriers black mayors and city council members were not completely powerless when it came to increasing fiscal expenditures of potential benefit to African American communities, most especially low and moderate citizens. In my conclusion, I extend upon these thoughts. After a brief review of the literatures relevant to this article, I analyze the attitudes of black and white mayors using the U.S. Fiscal Austerity and Urban Innovation (FAUI) dataset, demonstrating that black mayors are more likely than white ones to favor spending increases for social policies. I next compare black mayoral cities to white mayoral ones, developing several hypotheses that will be tested in the empirical analysis. Using a dataset of the universe of the nation's largest cities from 1972 to 1990, I conduct panel regression analyses of several models of urban expenditures for the two social policy areas and for the infrastructural policy area for highways. I conclude with a discussion of the major results and their implications for research in race and American representation.

African American Urban Representation and Urban Governance

The dramatic rise in black urban elected officials has been a topic of considerable research attention in the study of American urban politics, with much of it focused towards understanding the material benefits that have accrued to black urban communities as a result of greater black political representation (Browning, Marshall, and Tabb 1984; Eisinger 1980, 1982; Jones 1978; Karnig and Welch 1980; Keller 1978; LaVeist 1992; Meier and England 1984; Mladenka 1989; Nelson 1978; Pinderhughes 1987; Preston 1976; Saltzstein 1989; Welch and Karnig 1979). Most studies assessing the impact of black mayors and city council members upon city governments have focused upon the following policy areas: the use of minority contractors for city services and projects, municipal hiring and employment, bureaucratic and commission appointments, the adoption of police review boards, and urban fiscal expenditures. Much of the other research has primarily examined black officials' influence upon municipal hiring practices and employment. Many of these works have established that black citizens received concrete benefits as a result of black representation. A major assumption of the research on black urban representation centers on the policy preferences of black citizens and black urban elected officials. Black citizens are assumed to desire the following: increases in the hiring and employment of blacks in government jobs (civil service, police, and fire); greater representation of blacks on city commissions and boards; a larger share of city contracting for minority businesses; and spending increases for social welfare programs. However, only a few (Karnig and Welch 1980; Keller 1978) have attempted to determine black officials' effect upon municipal expenditure patterns, specifically their effect upon spending on social policies of importance to many black urban residents.

Albert Karnig and Susan Welch's *Black Representation and Urban Policy* is the primary work examining the effect of black representation upon urban spending. Using city expenditure data from the U.S. Census' *Government Finance* series records, they analyzed a sample of 139 cities for the periods 1968-1969 and 1974-1975. In descriptive analysis of their data, they found that, on average, cities with black mayors and higher levels of black city council representation increased their cities' total spending and social welfare spending (spending on health, housing, welfare, and education) more than did other cities (Karnig and Welch 1980: 118, 122). Their regression results supported these findings: cities with black mayors devoted more money towards social policies than did those with white mayors. However, though the effect was statistically significant, it was not a large effect, and in the case of black city council representation, the evidence of effect was both inconsistent and insignificant.

Although Karnig and Welch's study establishes evidence for the influence of black mayors upon spending increases in social programs, African Americans' assumption of elective office, over the course of the 1970s and 1980s, coincided with an era in which cities experienced significant population and employment losses. Moreover, during the 1980s, the Reagan administration cut federal aid to the cities by nearly 50 percent, with the sharpest reductions in public service jobs and job training, social services, and community development block grants (Caraley 1992: 7-12). Hence, a comprehensive analysis of black urban political power must take into account the constraints upon that power, if we seek to assess accurately the capacity of black elected officials to effect policy changes within such a formidable context. I argue that such an analysis is necessary in order to determine the effects of black representation upon city governments' social spending. Data across a number of years are necessary because of the obvious lag time between black candidates' electoral victories, assumption of their positions, and the implementation of actual policy changes. These data are also critical because of the growth in the number of black elected officials that took place after 1975. Of the 6,016 black elected officials in 1985, 2,513 or 42 percent of them were elected after 1975 (Jayes and Williams 1989: 238). And of the 286 black mayors in 1985, 151 or 53 percent of them were elected after 1975—the latest year that Karnig and Welch examined in their study (Jayes and Williams 1989: 240).

Urban Fiscal Policy and Social Welfare Expenditures

Although urban politics scholars have devoted some attention to urban fiscal policy (Schneider 1989), Paul Peterson's *City Limits* is the major work in urban politics that examines the fiscal economies of city governments. Peterson assumes that a city's economic viability and the enhancement of that viability are the primary concerns of urban officials and citizens (Peterson 1981: 21). Urban residents, he argues, naturally want to reside in a city that is in an attractive and prosperous environment and that offers them ample opportunity in which to live and work. Thus, a city's principal interest is the maintenance and development of its economic prosperity. Public policy that enhances the desirability or attractiveness of the territory is in the city's interest, because it benefits all residents—in their role as residents of the community (Peterson 1981: 21). Moreover, cities within the United States are engaged in an economic competition with one another; they all seek to improve their economic standing in comparison with other cities in order to attract businesses and the jobs and economic activity that they provide.

While this article seeks to extend our understanding of the influence of black city officials upon concrete policy outcomes, it also tests one of the major theories of American urban politics. Paul Peterson's *City Limits* (1981) has been one of the most influential theoretical works in urban politics over the eighteen years. He devotes much of his attention to the question whether city governments devote money towards social (or within his framework, redistributive) policy. He essentially argues that it is not in a city's interests to allot significant amounts of money for social policies because of the negative effects they have upon keeping and attracting middle and upper income, tax-paying citizens and businesses providing economic investment and employment opportunities. Furthermore, a city's internal politics—specifically, Peterson maintains, the demands of black and low income citizens for greater social spending—will play a minor role in determining the city's fiscal commitment to social policy. Using econometric analyses of city governments' social spending, this article examines the aforementioned claims by including measures of formal political representation—that is, the presence of black mayors and city council members—as well as group demands for economic and political social programs—the percentage of a city's population comprised of black and poor citizens.

Working from these basic assumptions, Peterson outlines a theory of urban governments, their policies, and the nature of the politics affecting those policies. He divides urban public policy into three broad areas: developmental policy, allocational policy, and redistributive policy. For this article, I concentrate upon his discussion of redistributive policy. Redistributive policies are those programs that assist lower income citizens and that have a negative effect upon urban economies by redistributing income from higher income, tax-paying residents to lower income, low-tax-paying residents (Peterson 1981: 41-4, 132). Concern with enhancing a city's economic prosperity—a concern supposedly held by all residing within the city—determines the essential character of policy and politics within cities. And because of the primacy of urban economic competition, urban politics is, in Peterson's words, "limited politics." Dominant economic concerns determine the nature of urban policymaking: "It is these city interests, not the internal struggles for power within cities, that limit city policies and condition what local governments do," he writes (Peterson 1981: 4).

Since cities' internal politics play a less important role in determining their fiscal commitment to various policies, Peterson concludes that black and lower income citizens have little political influence upon urban governments' social spending. Black and low-income populations, Peterson maintains, are indicators of political influence, yet their presence will not cause cities to increase the money devoted to social programs. Peterson concludes from his analyses that they indicate "the impotence of the needs of blacks and low-income groups as determinants of redistributive policy" (Peterson, 1981: 57). Hence, economic factors, not political ones, wield the primary influence upon urban social spending. Clearly, he is arguing that the political power of black urban communities was not very meaningful in affecting urban social policy.

Though his theory is a parsimonious explanation of urban politics, I believe Peterson's argument has a number of shortcomings that limit its utility in explaining and understanding the contemporary social, economic, and political context of American cities. Such factors as the dramatic losses in urban employment and population and the sizable increases in the numbers of lower income residents have altered the social and economic environment of many cities. Since these changes have occurred over the past several decades, they necessarily have been dynamic in nature. Yet Peterson's argument lacks a consideration of these shifts and their consequences. Perhaps most importantly, although he argues that political factors have little substantive effect upon cities' fiscal policymaking, Peterson includes economic and demographic variables in his econometric analysis of cities' expenditures and includes no political variables to test his claims. This article is a test of Peterson's contention that the politics *within* cities have a lower level of relevance to the fiscal agenda of urban governments. It focuses specifically upon the effect of black elected officials upon cities' social spending, though it will include measures of cities' black and poor populations to test the argument he makes regarding these groups.

The other major research of relevance to this article is the extensive state politics literature on state governments' welfare spending. Much of this literature developed in response to a well-known proposition advanced by V.O. Key, Jr. in his book *Southern Politics in State and Nation* (1949). He hypothesized that states with more competitive two-party systems would provide higher levels of social welfare provision than those with less competitive systems, arguing that the competition between the parties for the votes of considerably less mobilized poorer citizens would compel them to offer and ultimately enact policies of greater social welfare provision. Accordingly, much of the research in this area concentrated on the potential effects of the parties and the competition between upon state governments' welfare policies. Later efforts discovered that the levels of income, education, and urbanization of states—rather than the degree of their party competition—were more pivotal in determining state governments' welfare policies (Dye 1984: 1099). The research in this literature is similar in approach to the analysis offered in this article as it tends to utilize regression analyses of welfare spending with a complement of political and economic variables (Dye 1984; Gray 1976; Jennings 1979). However, because of its general focus upon the effects of the political parties, the literature is less helpful in contributing to our understanding of the relationship between racial politics and social policy provision.

A Theoretical Argument for African American Urban Representation

Although there has been little research that attempts to link urban black citizens' policy preferences with those of black municipal officials, this assumption is neither an invalid nor an unreasonable one. Clark and Ferguson reported that blacks generally exhibited greater support for increased government spending for cities, education, health, and welfare than whites did (Clark and Ferguson, 1983: 128). These results were from the 1973 and 1980 NORC-General Social Surveys in which questions were asked whether too little was spent on the following: conditions of blacks, cities, education, health, welfare, crime, the environment, and drug addiction. Depending on the question, there was a difference of about ten to thirty percentage points between the responses of blacks and whites across total family income levels. These policy differences between blacks and whites appear to be rather consistent and enduring ones: for example, in the case of welfare, there has been a consistent difference of approximately thirty percentage points from 1972 to 1987 separating black and white support of increased funding for the program (Sigelman and Welch 1991: 139-140).

As for black elected officials themselves, in one of the few studies examining the policy preferences of black and white local chief executives (mayors and city managers), Gilliam and Wallin (1990) found that black officials clearly favor an expansion of existing city services in the areas of health and housing more than white leaders. Interestingly, they found some regional effects: New Jersey black executives supported increased spending in social policy areas while California black leaders were more supportive of increased expenditures for public safety areas.

While I do expect the presence of a black mayor in a city will result in increased social spending, it is reasonable to expect that the cities in which black mayors were elected were quite diverse and that black mayoral presence operated differently in different contexts. Table 1 displays a breakdown of the cities by black mayoral presence according to city government structure, city population, city poverty rate, city black population percentage, and presidential era. Well over 50 percent of black mayors were elected in cities with mayor-council systems, with well over half of these mayors in cities with black city council representation that exceeded 50 percent. In contrast, about 45 percent of black mayors were in cities with council-manager systems, but the majority of these mayors were in cities having black city council representation under 50 percent. Over a third of black mayors presided over cities having populations below 100,000. However, just over 40 percent of black mayors were in cities of over 200,000 in population. As expected, cities with higher poverty rates were more likely to elect black mayors: over 90 percent of black mayors were in cities with poverty rates over 10 percent. Additionally, the vast majority of black mayors were elected in cities having black population percentages greater than 20 percent. Finally, nearly two-thirds of the years of black mayoral presence in cities occurred during the 1980s during the Reagan administration.

Given the results of this table, how might the effects of a black mayor upon city governments' social spending vary by different contexts? There are several ways that I believe varying context might affect the nature of the effect a black mayor has upon social spending. First of all, black mayors in cities with larger black populations might be more likely to increase social spending than those black mayors in cities with smaller black populations. Presumably, black mayors governing cities with larger black populations can draw upon electoral and governing

Table 1

Analysis of Number of Years Black Mayors and White Mayors by City Government Structure, City Population, City Poverty Rate, City Black Population Percentage, and Presidential Era {Number of Black Mayoral Years in bold} (Number of White Mayoral Years in parentheses)

Cities by Different Category (Number of total cities in each category in parentheses)	(1) Number of Black Mayoral Years	(2) Number of Black Mayoral Years in Cities with Black City Council Representation *under* 50%	(3) Number of Black Mayoral Years in Cities with Black City Council Representation *over* 50%	(4) Missing Cases[4]
Mayor / Council System (2754)	**205** (2549)	**88** (2474)	**117** (43)	32
Council / Manager System (3468)	**163** (3305)	**136** (3257)	**26** (24)	25
Cities by Population:				
Below 100,000 (3630):	**138** (3492)	**76** (3431)	**61** (30)	32
Between 100,000 to 200,000 (1674):	**80** (1594)	**62** (1544)	**18** (37)	13
Between 200,000 to 400,000 (626):	**63** (563)	**39** (555)	**24** (1)	7
Over 400,000 (547):	**87** (460)	**47** (449)	**40** (2)	9
Cities by Poverty Rate:[1]				
Below 10% (2076):	**7** (2069)	**6** (2048)	**1** (16)	5
Between 10% to 20% (3592):	**199** (3393)	**148** (3326)	**50** (17)	51
Over 20% (788):	**162** (626)	**70** (584)	**92** (37)	5
Cities by Black Population Percentage:[2]				
Below 10% (3343):	**12** (3331)	**12** (3310)	——[3]	21
Between 10% to 20% (1160):	**41** (1119)	**40** (1089)	**0** (16)	15
Over 20% (1814):	**315** (1499)	**172** (1420)	**143** (54)	25
Cities by Presidential Era:				
Nixon / Ford (1972-1976) (1905):	**74** (1831)	**52** (1811)	**21** (12)	9
Carter (1977-1980) (1524):	**78** (1446)	**46** (1437)	**32** (9)	0
Reagan (1981-1988) (3048):	**216** (2832)	**126** (2731)	**90** (49)	52

Total Number of City-Years=6477 (381 cities x 17 years).
Total City-Years with Black Mayoral Presence=368. Total City-Years with White Mayoral Presence=6109.
[1] The total number of city-years equals 6456 because there are 21 cases with missing data for poverty rate.
[2] The total number of city-years equals 6317 because there are 160 cases with missing data for black population percentage.
[3] —— indicates that there were no cases that satisfied the attributes of the cell.
[4] The sum of city-years in columns 2 and 3 do not equal the total number of city-years for many of the categories because of missing data in the numbers of black city council members in a total of 61 cities. Column 4 indicates the number of missing cases in each category row.

coalitions that readily expect responsiveness to black policy interests. Moreover, such a constituency might hold that mayor accountable and make sure that the official is responsive to its needs and concerns. In essence, being in a city with a larger black population might operate as both a support and a constraint for a black mayor's policymaking. Hence, I expect that black mayors in cities with larger black populations will devote more money to social programs than those in cities with smaller ones. Another significant factor affecting how context might influence the nature of a black mayor's capacity to represent black citizens is a city's poverty rate. Here I believe that context operates in a different manner in that a black mayor would be forced to respond to the economically depressed environment of a city and thus would be more likely to increase social spending than a black mayor in a more prosperous city.

Of course, there are other attributes of context that might prove pivotal in shaping a black mayor's capability to effectively represent black constituents. Time is another factor shaping context. Here I am specifically referring to the politics of a time period—in other words, the national political environment and how it might shape what a black mayor can do and achieve at the city level. Given African Americans' contemporary allegiance to the Democratic Party, the fact that virtually all of the black mayors who have been elected have been Democrats, and the general political ideologies of the Democratic and Republican parties, I believe that black mayors were more likely to increase social spending during the administrations of Democratic Presidents and to decrease such spending during Republican ones. Finally, I argue that the local political context of the city government a black mayor confronts also matters a great deal. The numbers of politically like-minded city council members on a city council—and for this article, black council members—will undoubtedly influence what a black mayor, or any mayor, can do and hope to accomplish. Having more political allies clearly gives a mayor greater opportunity and capability to enact his or her policy agenda, and higher levels of black council representation would ostensibly bolster the power of a city's black mayor. Browning, Marshall, and Tabb's (1984) concept of *incorporation*, or the degree to which blacks are in the dominant policymaking coalition, is especially relevant here. Thus, consistent with their measure of incorporation, the interaction of a black mayor with greater levels of black city council representation will be more likely to increase social spending than that of a black mayor with lower levels.

Dataset and Method for Analyses of City Governments' Social Spending

This analysis of urban fiscal policy uses revenue and expenditure data of the city governments. These data are compiled by the Census Bureau of the U.S. Department of Commerce and are available in its *Censuses and Annual Surveys of Governments*. The data I developed have annual fiscal data for American cities from 1972 to 1988 and include all of the nation's cities having population sizes of at least 50,000 residents, with the total number being approximately 380 cities. I use urban government expenditure data because they enable me to examine measures of the programmatic spending and priorities of urban governments, given their varying social, economic, and political contexts. I examine per capita total expenditures on housing and community development, public welfare, and health as measures of social policy. The level of analysis is the city government in a year (city by year); urban governments' expenditures are the dependent variable.

I supplement these fiscal data with data from a number of other sources. The *U.S. County and City Data Books* provide the data for the economic and demographic factors I examine in the descriptive analyses. I use the Joint Center for Political and Economic Studies' annual publication *Black Elected Officials: A National Roster* as my reference in indicating the presence of black mayors and city council members. This source is the most comprehensive list of all of the black elected officials at the federal, state, and local government levels and provides annual data for the presence of black urban officials for all of the cities in the dataset. I used International City Managers Association's annual publication *Municipal Year Book* as a reference in determining the total number of city council members for each city's city council.

I used pooled regression analysis of the cities across time to estimate each of the models of per capita spending for housing and community development policy and public welfare policy. Pooled analysis is essentially the regression analysis of cross sections of units across time. However, pooled analysis entails considerably more trouble in managing potential violations of the basic ordinary least squares error assumptions. Violations of the assumptions can appear either in the simpler forms of heteroscedasticity or autocorrelation or in the considerably more complex form of the simultaneous presence of both. Nonetheless, pooled analysis can be quite powerful in its capability of modeling and estimating the causal dynamics of a process over a sample of units.[2] In the analyses, I included only those cities that exhibited consistent spending in the policy area. My procedure here is patterned after the work of Liebert (1976); cities were included for analysis if they had expenditures in the policy area for at least half (nine or more years) of the seventeen-year time period.

Analysis of the Effect of Black Representation Upon Urban Social Expenditures

The Empirical Model

The goal of the analysis is to estimate the effect of the presence of black elected officials on city governments' social spending on housing and community development, public welfare, and health. The dependent variables are a city government's total per capita spending in each of these areas. In this section, I discuss each of the independent variables of the models I use for analysis and my expectations of their effect upon cities' social spending.

Black mayoral presence is measured by a dummy variable indicating whether the city was governed by a black mayor in a particular year. *Black city council representation* is a proportional measure dividing the total number of black city council members by the total number of city council members. For the analyses of spending for the three policy areas, I use five models based on my discussion of the varying contexts of black mayors: a basic model with black mayoral presence, a model of the interaction of black mayoral presence with poverty rate, a model of the interaction of black mayoral presence with black population percentage, a model of the interaction of black mayoral presence with black city council representation, and a model of black mayoral presence categorized by presidential era. I expect all of these variables to have a positive effect on social expenditures, given my earlier argument. Because of the endogeneity of black mayoral presence, it is necessary to create instrumental variables for black mayoral presence and all of the interaction variables with it.

White mayoral presence is measured by a dummy variable indicating whether the city was governed by a white mayor in a particular year. I include this variable because it is well known that black-led cities tend to have more black and lower-income citizens; hence, white-led cities with similar populations of black and poor residents as black mayoral ones might also increase social spending. In order to test this possibility, I included the following variables related to white mayoral presence: two dummy variables for white mayoral cities by poverty rate in the basic model and in the poverty rate model, two dummy variables for white mayoral cities by black population percentage in the black population percentage model, and two dummy variables for white mayoral cities during the Carter and Reagan administrations in the presidential era model.

The next set of variables in the analyses control for the influence that the federal and state governments have upon expenditures at the city government level. *Federal Intergovernmental Grant for Cities' Housing and Community and Development Spending, for their Public Welfare Spending, and for their Health Spending* measure the total intergovernmental assistance granted by the federal government to a city government for its programs in these policy areas. *State Intergovernmental Grant for Cities' Housing and Community and Development Spending, for their Public Welfare Spending, and for their Health Spending* measure the total intergovernmental assistance granted by the state government to a city government for its programs in these policy areas. The history of urban social policy, the development of federalism in addressing cities' inadequate fiscal resources for providing necessary public services, and the subsequent reliance of urban governments upon intergovernmental fiscal assistance all point to the need to examine the interaction between the federal and city governments as well as the social and economic environment of urban centers. I expect federal and state aid will have a strong positive effect upon cities' social spending.

Mayor-Council System and *Council-Manager System* are measures for city government structure (the excluded category is for commission systems). I expect these two systems to have opposite effects upon social spending. Because of their developmental emphasis, council-manager systems will tend to devote lower amounts to social spending and have a negative influence upon social policy expenditures. On the other hand, mayor-council systems will devote greater amounts to social policies because of the potentially incendiary nature of politics in the area. Mayors will not want to be regarded by a city's residents as being insensitive to the needs of lower income citizens, especially in those cities that have had to address the needs of increasing poor populations.

The next set of variables controls for the potential affects that region might have upon cities' social spending. *Northeast, Midwest,* and *South* are region dummy variables and indicate whether the city is either in the northeast, the midwest, or the south. The west is the excluded category. I expect that northeastern cities probably devoted more money towards social spending in that they tend to be older cities, to have more fiscal responsibilities, and to be politically more liberal, while southern cities can be expected to spend less money on social policy due to the region's general political conservatism. I expect that midwestern cities will behave in a manner between northern and southern cities, devoting money at levels lower than northern cities and higher than southern areas. My expectation here is due to the political environment of the midwest, one that is seemingly less liberal than the northeast and less conservative than the south.

The final set of variables includes all of the demographic and economic controls that are necessary for effective estimation of city government expenditure models. *Total Median Family Income* and *Median Value of Owner-Occupied Single-Family Units* provide a measure of the economic health of a city. Higher levels of median income and housing value indicate the economic base that a city can potentially tap for collecting tax revenues to pay for the public goods and services it provides. I believe that both of these variables will have strong positive effects upon city governments' social expenditures.

American cities have become considerably more diverse racially and economically over the past twenty-five years. The numbers of blacks living in cities have increased, as have the numbers of urban residents living below the poverty line. *Percent of a City's Total Population that is Black* and *Percent of a City's Total Population that is Poor* provide a test of how these demographic and socioeconomic changes affected urban social spending. I expect them to have positive effects upon social spending. I believe that urban governments were forced to respond to the needs of lower income citizens over the 1970s and 1980s, especially as these populations were growing and their presence was being felt by other urban residents. I expect a positive effect associated with black urban populations because of the needs of many black urban citizens and the historical memories of many urban officials. The urban uprisings of the latter half of the 1960s continue to serve as grim markers of black political and economic discontent. I argue that urban officials overall increased social spending as black urban communities grew in order to respond to the political demands of black urban communities as well as to keep those demands from becoming a great deal more than demands. My expectations here stand in contrast to Peterson's argument regarding the political influence of black and poor citizens and the results he found in his analysis.

Per Capita Civilian Employment provides some measure of the economic and employment context of a city, controlling for the effects of that context upon social expenditures. I expect this variable will have a negative relationship upon social expenditures. An increase in jobs ostensibly provides greater employment opportunities for urban residents overall and subsequently less poverty and less need for social provision by city governments.

Finally, I included two variables to measure the potential effects of cities' population changes upon their social spending. As I noted earlier, many American cities lost substantial numbers of their residents during the 1970s and 1980s. *Population Change from 1970 to 1980* and *Population Change from 1980 to 1990* are dummy variables coded '1' if the city increased in population and '0' if it decreased. I expect these variables will have a negative effect upon social spending in that demographically more prosperous cities will be less likely to increase their social spending.

Empirical Results

Table 2 reports the results for city governments' housing and community development expenditures. It is evident that context matters a great deal for black urban representation. The presence of a black mayor alone (Basic Model) had a substantive impact upon increased spending for housing and community development but came short of having a statistically significant effect. While the interaction of black mayoral presence with a city's poverty rate did not have a significant effect upon spending in this analysis, the interaction with a city's black population percentage was quite significant (p-value < .005) and indicated that black mayors in cities with larger black populations substantially increased spending for housing and community development. Model 4 indicates that who occupies the mayor's office makes quite a difference in expenditures for this policy area: the combination of a black mayor with black city council representation led to sizable and highly significant spending increases while such an interaction with a white mayor resulted in dramatic reductions. Finally, the time during which a black mayor presided was pivotal. Black mayors were more likely to decrease housing and community development expenditures during the early 1970s and to increase them during the 1980s under the Reagan administration. The late 1970s of the Carter administration were not more favorable for black mayors as they had no distinguishing effect upon expenditures during this time. This was not the case for white mayors who increased housing spending during the Carter administration. However, this was the only white mayoral variable that was significant in this table's analyses.

The other variables generally performed according to my expectations, though several had no significant effect upon housing spending. As expected, federal and state government assistance for cities' housing and community development spending were both highly correlated with cities' expenditures. The political structure of a city government had virtually no effect upon spending indicating that expenditures for this policy area differ very little whether a city has a mayor-council or council-manager system. Results were somewhat different for regional context as it made quite a difference in a city's housing and community development spending: in all of the models, northeastern cities devoted more money to housing and community development spending than western cities, while southern and midwestern cities failed to exhibit any real difference from western ones in their housing spending.

Table 2
Analysis of Housing and Community Development Spending

Independent Variables	(1) Basic Model	(2) Poverty Rate Model	(3) Black Population Percentage Model	(4) Black City Council Representation Model	(5) Presidential Era Model
Black Representation Variables					
Black Mayoral Presence	18.408 (9.573)	---	---	---	---
Black Mayoral Presence x City's Poverty Rate	---	4.758 (97.056)	---	---	---
Black Mayoral Presence x City's Black Population Percentage	---	---	112.923*** (33.819)	---	---
Black Mayoral Presence x City's Black City Council Representation	---	---	---	278.581**** (63.325)	---
White Mayoral Presence x City's Black City Council Representation	---	---	---	-125.521**** (34.696)	---
Black Mayoral Presence x Nixon / Ford	---	---	---	---	-82.072* (41.950)
Black Mayoral Presence x Carter	---	---	---	---	11.836 (39.502)
Black Mayoral Presence x Reagan	---	---	---	---	28.661* (12.797)

Table 2 (continued)

White Mayoral Comparison Variables

	(1)	(2)	(3)	(4)	(5)
White Mayoral Presence in Cities with Poverty Rates between 9% to 14%	5.078 (2.744)	3.125 (2.564)	----	----	----
White Mayoral Presence in Cities with Poverty Rates over 14%	5.279 (3.525)	1.731 (3.035)	----	----	----
White Mayoral Presence in Cities with Black Population Percentages between 2% to 13%	----	----	4.046 (2.418)	----[c]	----
White Mayoral Presence in Cities with Black Population Percentages over 13%	----	----	1.382 (2.624)	----	----
White Mayoral Presence x Carter	----	----	----	----	5.558* (2.479)
White Mayoral Presence x Reagan	----	----	----	----	-0.127 (2.545)

Federal and State Governmental Assistance Variables

	(1)	(2)	(3)	(4)	(5)
Total Federal Intergovernmental Grant for Cities' Housing and Community Development Spending	2.26×10^{-7}**** (2.77×10^{-8})	2.31×10^{-7}**** (2.77×10^{-8})	2.21×10^{-7}**** (2.78×10^{-8})	1.94×10^{-7}**** (2.90×10^{-8})	2.20×10^{-7}**** (2.80×10^{-8})
Total State Intergovernmental Grant for Cities' Housing and Community Development Spending	3.09×10^{-7}* (1.48×10^{-8})	2.91×10^{-7} (1.51×10^{-7})	3.87×10^{-7}* (1.50×10^{-7})	5.25×10^{-7}*** (1.57×10^{-7})	3.13×10^{-7}* (1.49×10^{-7})

City Governmental Structure Variables

	(1)	(2)	(3)	(4)	(5)
Mayor - Council System	-7.715 (5.140)	-7.294 (5.231)	-8.759 (5.182)	-3.610 (5.321)	-7.879 (5.134)
Council - Manager System	-4.994 (5.132)	-4.055 (5.321)	-6.322 (5.191)	-3.334 (5.134)	-4.269 (5.124)

Region Variables

	(1)	(2)	(3)	(4)	(5)
Northeast	12.042*** (3.577)	10.707*** (3.632)	12.020*** (3.528)	14.760**** (3.609)	10.940*** (3.524)
Midwest	-5.759 (3.613)	-6.712 (3.607)	-5.405 (3.662)	-0.959 (3.826)	-5.269 (3.672)
South	-2.471 (3.365)	-4.691 (4.403)	4.254 (4.219)	20.253*** (6.647)	-4.955 (3.266)

Table 2 (continued)

Demographic and Economic Variables					
Median Value of Owner-Occupied Single-Family Units ($)	5.93×10^{-5}	6.14×10^{-5}	4.53×10^{-5}	4.49×10^{-5}	5.66×10^{-5}
	(3.83×10^{-5})	(3.87×10^{-5})	(3.79×10^{-5})	(3.78×10^{-5})	(4.09×10^{-5})
Total Median Family Income ($)	-6.12×10^{-4}	-6.73×10^{-4}	-6.98×10^{-4}	-7.35×10^{-4}*	-6.76×10^{-4}
	(3.72×10^{-4})	(3.79×10^{-4})	(3.65×10^{-4})	(3.64×10^{-4})	(4.27×10^{-4})
Percent of a City's Total Population that is Black	9.780	21.127	-39.198	-82.724***	16.260
	(10.524)	(17.888)	(21.077)	(23.842)	(9.938)
Percent of a City's Total Population that is Poor	-67.360	-47.686	-51.864	-36.202	-55.366
	(42.042)	(49.389)	(37.677)	(37.825)	(38.618)
Per Capita Civilian Employment	-14.106	-9.947	-13.676	-10.430	-29.957
	(20.238)	(20.159)	(20.154)	(20.134)	(24.222)
Population Change from 1970 to 1980 (1=Population Growth; 0=Population Loss)	-14.143****	-14.307****	-15.678****	-19.171****	-13.230****
	(2.393)	(2.393)	(2.414)	(2.643)	(2.448)
Population Change from 1980 to 1990 (1=Population Growth; 0=Population Loss)	-4.443*	-4.958*	-4.003	0.819	-4.954*
	(2.160)	(2.171)	(2.167)	(2.556)	(2.174)
Lag of Housing and Community Development Spending	0.391****	0.392****	0.391****	0.392****	0.391****
	(0.013)	(0.013)	(0.013)	(0.013)	(0.013)
Constant	61.210***	60.073***	69.515****	71.484****	72.039****
	(17.738)	(19.406)	(17.539)	(17.281)	(17.686)
Number of cases	4682	4682	4682	4682	4682
Adjusted R^2	0.270	0.270	0.272	0.273	0.272
Standard Error of the Estimate	59.936	59.960	59.878	59.827	59.873

OLS Analyses with Panel Corrected Standard Errors. Unstandardized Coefficient Estimates with Standard Errors in Parentheses. ---- indicates that variable was not included in the model. *indicates $p < .05$. **indicates $p < .01$. ***indicates $p < .005$. ****indicates $p < .001$. Values are rounded to 0.001, with some exceptions. STATA 5.0 was used for the analysis.

The economic and demographic context of a city generally did not have a great effect upon cities' housing and community development spending. First of all, the economic measures of median housing value and median family income failed to display consistent, significant effects. Although per civilian employment had a negative relationship with housing and community development spending, it also was not a factor of statistical consequence in these analyses. With the exception of the population change variables, the demographic environment of a city did not prove to be much of a factor influencing cities' expenditures for this policy. Nonetheless, as expected, cities that experienced population growth during these two decades were more likely to decrease spending for housing and community development. Finally, the lag variables of housing and community development spending displayed strong positive effects across all of the analyses—a result that is not particularly surprising in that a previous year's spending greatly influences the amount spent in a later year.

Table 3 displays the results from analyses of cities' public welfare spending. It is quite apparent here that black mayoral presence and the interactions associated with it did not exhibit the effects shown in Table 2. Black mayoral presence did not have a significant effect in Models 1, 2, and 3. In Model 5, during the 1970s, black mayors were no more likely to increase or decrease public welfare spending in comparison to white mayors during the Nixon/Ford administrations, yet during the Reagan administration black mayors significantly decreased their cities' public welfare spending. However, Model 4 was a notable exception: the combination of a black mayor with black city council representation led to considerable spending increases for public welfare, and as in Table 2, such a combination with a white mayor resulted in sizable decreases in this area. However, unlike the results in Table 2, several of the white mayoral variables displayed significant effects. In Models 1 and 2, white mayors in cities with poverty rates between 9 percent to 14 percent increased public welfare spending in their cities. This result stands in contrast with the insignificance of black mayors for these models. However, in Model 4, white mayors performed in a similar fashion to black mayors during the 1980s, decreasing public welfare expenditures during the Carter and Reagan administrations.

As expected, federal and state governmental assistance in this policy area greatly influenced increases in a city's welfare spending. City governmental structure had much more of an effect upon public welfare expenditures than in Table 2's results. While mayor-council systems were only significant in Model 4 and associated with spending increases in this analysis, council-manager systems interestingly performed contrary to my expectations and were more likely to devote more money for public welfare in three of the five models. Region displayed consistent, negative effects in all of the models: in comparison to western cities, northeastern, midwestern, and southern cities all tended to decrease public welfare expenditures during the 1970s and 1980s. These decreases appear to have had the greatest effect upon midwestern cities as they experienced decreases of over $20 per capita.

With the exceptions of a city's poverty rate and its population change from 1970s to 1980, many of the demographic and economic variables were statistically insignificant. Although they were exceptions in some of the models, median housing value, per capita civilian employment, and 1980-1990 population change displayed little consistent effect in the analyses. Median family income had a negative effect upon cities' public welfare spending in Models 3, 4, and 5. While it failed to exhibit a significant effect in Models 2, 3, and 4, a city's black population percentage was significantly related to spending increases in Models 1 and 5. On the other hand, a city's poverty rate did not have a similar effect upon public welfare spending: it consistently and significantly was associated with sizable decreases in all of the models. Finally, 1970-1980 population change was consequential in all of the models, as population growth resulted in decreases in a city's public welfare spending.

Table 3
Analysis of Public Welfare Spending

Independent Variables	(1) Basic Model	(2) Poverty Rate Model	(3) Black Population Percentage Model	(4) Black City Council Representation Model	(5) Presidential Era Model
Black Representation Variables					
Black Mayoral Presence	-12.518 (7.793)	---	---	---	---
Black Mayoral Presence x City's Poverty Rate	---	54.002 (79.289)	---	---	---
Black Mayoral Presence x City's Black Population Percentage	---	---	21.487 (29.597)	---	---
Black Mayoral Presence x City's Black City Council Representation	---	---	---	205.786** (76.110)	---
White Mayoral Presence x City's Black City Council Representation	---	---	---	-105.232** (37.674)	---
Black Mayoral Presence x Nixon / Ford	---	---	---	---	-19.372 (39.913)
Black Mayoral Presence x Carter	---	---	---	---	-5.758 (35.534)
Black Mayoral Presence x Reagan	---	---	---	---	-21.218* (9.976)

Table 3 (continued)

White Mayoral Comparison Variables

White Mayoral Presence in Cities with Poverty Rates between 9% to 14%	5.438* (2.369)	7.023*** (2.193)	----	----	----
White Mayoral Presence in Cities with Poverty Rates over 14%	1.560 (2.713)	4.177 (2.258)	----	----	----
White Mayoral Presence in Cities with Black Population Percentages between 2% to 13%	----	----	1.224 (2.027)	----	----
White Mayoral Presence in Cities with Black Population Percentages over 13%	----	----	0.973 (2.039)	----	----
White Mayoral Presence x Carter	----	----	----	----	-8.108**** (2.025)
White Mayoral Presence x Reagan	----	----	----	----	-10.809**** (2.171)

Federal and State Governmental Assistance Variables

Total Federal Intergovernmental Grant for Cities' Public Welfare Spending	9.10×10^{-7}**** (4.70×10^{-8})	8.81×10^{-7}**** (4.71×10^{-8})	8.57×10^{-7}**** (5.65×10^{-8})	4.16×10^{-7}* (1.74×10^{-8})	9.01×10^{-7}**** (4.58×10^{-8})
Total State Intergovernmental Grant for Cities' Public Welfare Spending	5.14×10^{-8}**** (2.43×10^{-9})	5.21×10^{-8}**** (2.60×10^{-9})	5.19×10^{-8}**** (2.54×10^{-9})	5.44×10^{-8}**** (2.70×10^{-9})	5.19×10^{-8}**** (2.41×10^{-9})

City Governmental Structure Variables

Mayor - Council System	4.895 (3.861)	3.788 (3.879)	3.950 (3.833)	9.480* (4.246)	5.807 (3.818)
Council - Manager System	9.002* (3.948)	7.545 (4.053)	7.334 (3.947)	9.960* (3.955)	9.255* (3.900)

Region Variables

Northeast	-15.049**** (3.447)	-13.634**** (3.538)	-16.779**** (3.330)	-14.707**** (3.403)	-17.761**** (3.303)
Midwest	-23.817**** (3.717)	-23.495**** (3.744)	-24.672**** (3.757)	-21.125**** (3.954)	-23.614**** (3.797)
South	-10.368*** (3.405)	-6.939 (4.369)	-8.790* (4.235)	9.394 (7.997)	-12.082**** (3.345)

Table 3 (continued)

Demographic and Economic Variables

Median Value of Owner-Occupied Single-Family Units ($)	7.06×10^{-5}	6.77×10^{-5}	5.05×10^{-5}	5.78×10^{-5}	1.15×10^{-4}**
	(3.88×10^{-5})	(3.96×10^{-5})	(3.93×10^{-5})	(3.87×10^{-5})	(4.31×10^{-5})
Total Median Family Income ($)	-5.75×10^{-4}	-5.93×10^{-4}	-6.79×10^{-4}*	-7.34×10^{-4}*	-1.17×10^{-3}***
	(2.98×10^{-4})	(3.03×10^{-4})	(2.96×10^{-4})	(2.94×10^{-4})	(3.49×10^{-4})
Percent of a City's Total Population that is Black	38.638****	22.418	15.067	-32.898	36.383****
	(8.227)	(14.380)	(17.463)	(23.670)	(7.751)
Percent of a City's Total Population that is Poor	-81.146*	-111.350***	-100.296****	-116.397****	-89.645***
	(31.718)	(37.406)	(28.715)	(29.187)	(29.080)
Per Capita Civilian Employment	-3.668	-6.507	-5.397	3.470	40.350*
	(16.688)	(16.583)	(16.579)	(16.869)	(19.772)
Population Change from 1970 to 1980 (1=Population Growth; 0=Population Loss)	-16.414****	-16.764****	-17.021****	-21.152****	-15.496****
	(2.155)	(2.160)	(2.235)	(2.737)	(2.284)
Population Change from 1980 to 1990 (1=Population Growth; 0=Population Loss)	-0.583	0.281	0.748	4.717*	-0.381
	(1.796)	(1.784)	(1.776)	(2.274)	(1.766)
Lag of Public Welfare Spending	0.711****	0.710****	0.713****	0.712****	0.706****
	(0.012)	(0.012)	(0.012)	(0.012)	(0.012)
Constant	39.513**	44.619***	52.406****	53.319****	44.008***
	(14.100)	(14.915)	(13.808)	(13.646)	(13.941)
Number of cases	2125	2125	2125	2125	2125
Adjusted R^2	0.911	0.910	0.910	0.910	0.911
Standard Error of the Estimate	32.682	32.699	32.772	32.711	32.537

OLS Analyses with Panel Corrected Standard Errors. Unstandardized Coefficient Estimates with Standard Errors in Parentheses. --- indicates that variable was not included in the model. *indicates $p < .05$. **indicates $p < .01$. ***indicates $p < .005$. ****indicates $p < .001$. Values are rounded to 0.001, with some exceptions. STATA 5.0 was used for the analysis.

Table 4 displays the results from analyses of cities' health spending. Black mayoral presence clearly had a dramatic positive effect upon increasing cities' health spending. Black mayors alone, those in cities with higher poverty rates, and those in cities with larger black populations were all the more likely to increase city expenditures for health policy (p-value < .001). Once again, the interaction of a black mayor with the black representation on a city council proved to be pivotal, leading to considerable increases in cities' health spending. As in the previous two tables, this particular result contrasted with the negative effect associated with the combination of a white mayor and black city council representation. Presidential era also made quite a difference: black mayors were more likely to increase health expenditures during the Carter administration, while decreasing health spending during the Nixon administration. The white mayoral variables did not exhibit any consistent significant effects across the five models, although they were associated with statistically significant increases in Model One.

The other groups of variables generally displayed effects similar to those reported in the previous tables. Federal and state intergovernmental grants for cities' health spending were highly significant and led to spending increases. City government structure was not much of a factor in these analyses as the variables for both mayor-council systems and council-manager systems were insignificant. As for regional effects, northeastern cities were more likely to decrease health expenditures over the time period. Finally, the demographic and economic variables exhibited greater influence upon cities' health spending than they did upon expenditures for housing and community development and for public welfare. A city's black population percentage was the only variable that failed to show consistent significance across the models. Cities with higher median housing value were more likely to increase their health spending in all of the models. Per capita civilian employment also had a consistent positive effect upon expenditures. However, this was not the case for either median family income or a city's poverty rate. Both of these variables were significantly associated with decreases in health spending. Population change from 1970 to 1980 led to decreases in spending, while interestingly, population change from 1980 to 1990 resulted in modest increases in three of the five models.

Conclusion: The Context of Representation

In a provocative essay entitled, "What Uses are Black Mayors? An Open Letter to the National Conference of Black Political Scientists," Watts (2005) admonishes students of black politics, and black political scientists in particular, for their "scholarly failures" of merely celebrating and not fully critiquing the election of black chief executives—most notably in the wake of Hurricane Katrina's devastation of New Orleans and the missteps of Mayor Ray Nagin. He asks, "why do we scholars of black politics spend so much time explaining how a black became mayor if becoming mayor has so little substantive political importance? Such analyses are utterly technocratic and ultimately establishmentarian" (2005: 1, 3.) His aim is to challenge the notion that black mayors are insurgent figures and instead demand they recast themselves as actual protest spokespersons willing to lead the charge against the fiscal austerity of state and federal governments.

Albeit Watts admirably calls for accountability from black mayors and others, my analysis empirically challenges his claim that black mayors have made no difference. Watts' failure is that he does not heed Walton's (1997) insight that context matters in determining the range of black political opportunities for victory and defeat. For black mayors to have the capacity to effect meaningful change in cities' fiscal priorities, as Watts suggests, certainly is a daunting prospect. There are a number of formidable constraints restricting the political power of all urban mayors. Furthermore, the electoral ascendance of many black mayors occurred during the culmination of the pivotal economic and demographic forces I discussed earlier. As a result,

Table 4
Analysis of Health Spending

Independent Variables	(1) Basic Model	(2) Poverty Rate Model	(3) Black Population Percentage Model	(4) Black City Council Representation Model	(5) Presidential Era Model
Black Representation Variables					
Black Mayoral Presence	11.673**** (2.108)	----	----	----	----
Black Mayoral Presence x City's Poverty Rate	----	79.682**** (19.877)	----	----	----
Black Mayoral Presence x City's Black Population Percentage	----	----	27.575**** (7.328)	----	----
Black Mayoral Presence x City's Black City Council Representation	----	----	----	50.926*** (14.662)	----
White Mayoral Presence x City's Black City Council Representation	----	----	----	-22.124** (8.021)	----
Black Mayoral Presence x Nixon / Ford	----	----	----	----	-31.527*** (9.488)
Black Mayoral Presence x Carter	----	----	----	----	46.473**** (9.019)
Black Mayoral Presence x Reagan	----	----	----	----	-0.085 (2.813)

Table 4 (continued)

Demographic and Economic Variables

Median Value of Owner-Occupied Single-Family Units ($)	3.38×10^{-5}****	2.84×10^{-5}***	2.97×10^{-5}****	3.03×10^{-5}****	4.68×10^{-5}****
	(1.00×10^{-5})	(1.02×10^{-5})	(1.00×10^{-5})	(1.00×10^{-5})	(1.10×10^{-5})
Total Median Family Income ($)	-2.40×10^{-4}***	-3.24×10^{-4}****	-2.54×10^{-4}****	-2.76×10^{-4}****	-4.14×10^{-4}****
	(8.42×10^{-5})	(8.58×10^{-5})	(8.32×10^{-5})	(8.30×10^{-5})	(9.89×10^{-5})
Percent of a City's Total Population that is Black	2.454	-4.036	-5.714	-9.865	6.000**
	(2.250)	(3.775)	(4.565)	(5.310)	(2.210)
Percent of a City's Total Population that is Poor	-39.141****	-45.868****	-21.490*	-19.978*	-28.071***
	(9.490)	(10.644)	(8.288)	(8.294)	(8.454)
Per Capita Civilian Employment	12.123**	14.551***	13.929***	15.746****	13.745**
	(4.329)	(4.312)	(4.316)	(4.357)	(5.242)
Population Change from 1970 to 1980 (1=Population Growth; 0=Population Loss)	-1.937****	-1.963****	-2.295****	-2.895****	-1.437**
	(0.522)	(0.523)	(0.526)	(0.585)	(0.531)
Population Change from 1980 to 1990 (1=Population Growth; 0=Population Loss)	0.918*	0.798	0.704	1.508**	0.935*
	(0.463)	(0.464)	(0.463)	(0.558)	(0.469)
Lag of Health Spending	0.716****	0.719****	0.718****	0.718****	0.709****
	(0.012)	(0.012)	(0.012)	(0.012)	(0.012)
Constant	6.402	10.773**	6.239	6.348	9.835**
	(3.788)	(4.068)	(3.709)	(3.674)	(3.761)
Number of cases	3822	3822	3822	3822	3822
Adjusted R^2	0.687	0.686	0.686	0.686	0.688
Standard Error of the Estimate	11.594	11.616	11.616	11.618	11.585

OLS Analyses with Panel Corrected Standard Errors. Unstandardized Coefficient Estimates with Standard Errors in Parentheses. ---- indicates that variable was not included in the model. *indicates $p < .05$. **indicates $p < .01$. ***indicates $p < .005$. ****indicates $p < .001$. Values are rounded to 0.001, with some exceptions. STATA 5.0 was used for the analysis.

Table 4 (continued)

Demographic and Economic Variables

Median Value of Owner-Occupied Single-Family Units ($)	3.38 x 10^{-5}**** (1.00 x 10^{-5})	2.84 x 10^{-5}*** (1.02 x 10^{-5})	2.97 x 10^{-5}**** (1.00 x 10^{-5})	3.03 x 10^{-5}**** (1.00 x 10^{-5})	4.68 x 10^{-5}**** (1.10 x 10^{-5})
Total Median Family Income ($)	-2.40 x 10^{-4}**** (8.42 x 10^{-5})	-3.24 x 10^{-4}***** (8.58 x 10^{-5})	-2.54 x 10^{-4}**** (8.32 x 10^{-5})	-2.76 x 10^{-4}**** (8.30 x 10^{-5})	-4.14 x 10^{-4}**** (9.89 x 10^{-5})
Percent of a City's Total Population that is Black	2.454 (2.250)	-4.036 (3.775)	-5.714 (4.565)	-9.865 (5.310)	6.000** (2.210)
Percent of a City's Total Population that is Poor	-39.141**** (9.490)	-45.868**** (10.644)	-21.490* (8.288)	-19.978* (8.294)	-28.071*** (8.454)
Per Capita Civilian Employment	12.123** (4.329)	14.551*** (4.312)	13.929*** (4.316)	15.746**** (4.357)	13.745** (5.242)
Population Change from 1970 to 1980 (1=Population Growth; 0=Population Loss)	-1.937**** (0.522)	-1.963**** (0.523)	-2.295**** (0.526)	-2.895**** (0.585)	-1.437** (0.531)
Population Change from 1980 to 1990 (1=Population Growth; 0=Population Loss)	0.918* (0.463)	0.798 (0.464)	0.704 (0.463)	1.508** (0.558)	0.935* (0.469)
Lag of Health Spending	0.716**** (0.012)	0.719**** (0.012)	0.718**** (0.012)	0.718**** (0.012)	0.709**** (0.012)
Constant	6.402 (3.788)	10.773** (4.068)	6.239 (3.709)	6.348 (3.674)	9.835** (3.761)
Number of cases	3822	3822	3822	3822	3822
Adjusted R^2	0.687	0.686	0.686	0.686	0.688
Standard Error of the Estimate	11.594	11.616	11.616	11.618	11.585

OLS Analyses with Panel Corrected Standard Errors. Unstandardized Coefficient Estimates with Standard Errors in Parentheses. ----- indicates that variable was not included in the model. *indicates $p < .05$. **indicates $p < .01$. ***indicates $p < .005$. ****indicates $p < .001$. Values are rounded to 0.001, with some exceptions. STATA 5.0 was used for the analysis.

many of the cities that black mayors presided over were among those with decreasing economic viability and growing populations of lower income citizens with increasing economic needs.

Nonetheless, this article establishes that black mayors had a significant influence upon increasing city governments' spending for social programs. Furthermore, it shows how the demographic, temporal, political and policy context shaping urban representation matters, thus influencing the ability of black mayors to alter cities' fiscal agenda. Cities' social spending are not only influenced by economic factors, as Peterson argued. Black urban communities and the politics associated with them are much more salient and apparently have much greater influence than his analysis and argument suggest. Black mayors clearly had an effect upon increasing cities' social spending in the three policy areas I examined, even controlling for the intergovernmental aid to city governments provided by the federal and state governments. And if their political influence has an effect upon urban fiscal priorities, then the internal politics of cities do matter with regard to social policy.

There is clearly variation in the seeming ability of mayors to affect the spending devoted to their cities' social policies: for example, black mayors alone, and those in cities with higher poverty rates and larger black populations, failed to exhibit a consistent significant influence upon public welfare spending. Yet, these mayors and their interactions with these critical variables were quite salient in increasing expenditures for housing and community development and for health programs. These results indicate that certain policy areas are perhaps more malleable than others with regard to the potential effect a mayor can have upon the spending devoted to that area. Another explanation might also lie in the general level of regard (or criticism) that citizens have for certain policies. Health programs and those for housing and community development are presumably less controversial than those for public welfare; thus, a mayor might be more likely to try to alter the fiscal agenda to increase funding for these policies rather than risking a possible political backlash in increasing public welfare spending. However, there was one notable exception in the public welfare analysis: the combination of a black mayor and black city council representation resulted in significant funding increases for this policy area. It is apparent that context in the form of political allies coupled with control of the mayor's office was quite pivotal in this case.

A city's context for a black mayor proved to be consequential throughout the results. In the basic model's results, the sole presence of a black mayor was significant only in the case of health spending. The context of a city's poverty rate and its interaction with black mayoral presence was also significant only in the case of funding for health. The size of a city's black population made a difference: black mayors in cities with larger black populations were more likely to increase spending for housing and community development and for health than those in cities with smaller black communities. It was also significant whenever a black mayor was in power. Although there were several exceptions, the results generally indicated that the periods during Republican presidential administrations caused black mayors to decrease spending in all three policy areas, while they increased health expenditures during the Carter administration. The one contextual attribute that consistently stood out from the rest was the racial balance on city councils. The combination of a black mayor with black city council representation consistently led to spending increases for all three policy categories. Moreover, the race of who occupied the mayor's office was very important as the interaction of a white mayor with black city council representation consistently led to decreases in spending for the three policies. Additionally, despite a few exceptions in the results, the economic and demographic context of a city did not consistently cause white mayors, even those in cities with higher poverty rates and larger black populations, to increase their cities' social spending.

Consequently, this article reiterates the assertion that black mayors and city council members have a continuum of political influence over urban spending and thus it dovetails with Cohen's

(1999) thinking about advanced marginalization in the post-Civil Right Movement Era. Within the margins imposed by race, economic disparity, and federalism, local black elected officials have the ability to help shape vital policy priorities and return necessary if often not sufficient benefits to black communities. To be sure, these leaders are still very limited in their ability to make all of the needed reforms in areas like public health, affordable housing, and jobs that would significantly close black-white racial disparities. However, the degree to which these black elected officials neglect the redistributive policy needs of black poor and other marginalized communities is the degree to which both Cohen and Watts are rightly critical about their motives and their larger conceptions of black group interests.

Moreover, what do these results tell us about the nature of American representation within the nation's cities? How is urban representation in a multilevel democracy—especially in cities' attempts to respond to the economic distress within them—affected when that very latitude is constrained by a formidable environment affecting urban governments? Representation in a democracy is an opportunity to have some influence upon policymaking and to effect actual changes in policy. Of course, representation and citizens' support of a representative do not promise that they will ultimately result in concrete policy changes that those citizens might desire. However, if the context in which urban representation occurs greatly shapes the nature of that representation and its capacity to bring about substantive policy change, then urban representation appears to be highly contingent on a context that no one can control. For black mayors, certain contexts—larger black populations and greater black representation on city councils—enhanced their ability to substantively alter city governments' fiscal agenda in ways responsive to the needs of black constituents. A provocative question to consider, given this article's focus and how race apparently plays such a critical role in the governing of American cities, is whether the changes enacted by black mayors led to demographic and economic responses that only abetted these cities becoming "hollow cities?"

Notes

1. Throughout this article, I will be referring to black urban representation. In using this term, I am referring specifically to political representation in the form of black elected officials of central cities, notably black mayors and city council members. Additionally, my use of 'urban' throughout this article refers primarily to central cities.
2. I draw upon the following sources in my use of pooled regression in this article: Beck and Katz 1996; Hsiao 1986; Kmenta 1986; Sayrs 1989; and Stimson 1987. I follow the approach suggested by Beck and Katz (1996). They suggest including a lag of the model's dependent variable in regression analyses of time-series-cross-sectional (TSCS) continuous data. The standard errors are adjusted by a procedure calculating panel-corrected standard errors to correct for the many problems possible with TSCS data. STATA 5.0 was used for the econometric analyses. All results were generated using the xtgls command with the pcse option.

References

Beck, Nathaniel and Jonathan N. Katz. 1996. "Nuisance vs. Substance: Specifying and Estimating Time-Series-Cross-Section Models." Political Analysis 6:1-36.
Browning, Rufus P., Dale Rogers Marshall, and David H. Tabb. 1984. Protest Is Not Enough. Berkeley, CA: University of California Press.
Caraley, Demetrios. 1992. "Washington Abandons the Cities." Political Science Quarterly 107:1-30.
Clark, Terry Nichols and Lorna C. Ferguson. 1983. City Money. New York: Columbia University Press.
Cohen, Cathy. 1999. The Boundaries of Blackness: AIDS in the Black Community. Chicago, IL: University of Chicago Press.
Dye, Thomas R. 1984. "Party and Policy in the States." The Journal of Politics 46:1097-1116.
Eisinger, Peter K. 1980. Politics of Displacement: Racial and Ethnic Transition in Three American Cities. New York: Academic Press.

Eisinger, Peter K. 1982. "Black Employment in Municipal Jobs: The Impact of Black Political Power." American Political Science Review 76:380-392.

Friesema, H. Paul. 1967. "Black Control of Central Cities: The Hollow Prize." Journal of American Institute of Planners. pp. 75-79.

Gilliam, Franklin D., Jr. and Bruce Wallin. 1990. "Municipal Black Political Empowerment and Active Representation." Presented at the annual meeting of the National Conference of Black Political Scientists, Atlanta, GA.

Gray, Virginia. 1976. "Models of Comparative State Politics: A Comparison of Cross-Sectional and Time Series Analysis." American Journal of Political Science 20:235-256.

Hsiao, Cheng. 1986. Analysis of Panel Data. Cambridge: Cambridge University Press.

International City Managers Association. 1972. The Municipal Year Book. Chicago: International City Managers Association.

International City Managers Association. 1976. The Municipal Year Book. Chicago: International City Managers Association.

International City Managers Association. 1982. The Municipal Year Book. Chicago: International City Managers Association.

International City Managers Association. 1987. The Municipal Year Book. Chicago: International City Managers Association.

Jaynes, Gerald D. and Robin M. Williams, Jr., (eds.) 1989. A Common Destiny: Blacks and American Society. Washington, DC: National Academy Press.

Jennings, Edward T., Jr. 1979. "Competition, Constituencies, and Welfare Policies in American States." American Political Science Review 73:414-429.

Joint Center for Political and Economic Studies Press. 1993. Black Elected Officials: A National Roster. Washington, DC: Joint Center for Political and Economic Studies Press.

Jones, Mack H. 1978. "Black Political Empowerment in Atlanta: Myth and Reality." Annals of the American Academy of Political and Social Science. 439:90-117.

Karnig, Albert K. and Susan Welch. 1980. Black Representation and Urban Policy. Chicago, IL: University of Chicago Press.

Keller, Edmond. 1978. "The Impact of Black Mayors on Urban Policy." The Annals of the American Academy of Political and Social Science 439: 40-52.

Key, V.O., Jr. 1949. Southern Politics in State and Nation. New York: Random House.

Kmenta, Jan. 1986. Elements of Economics. New York: Macmillan.

LaVeist, Thomas A. 1992. "The Political Empowerment and Health Status of African-Americans: Mapping a New Territory." American Journal of Sociology 97:1080-1095.

Liebert, Roland J. 1976. Disintegration and Political Action: The Changing Functions of City Governments in America. New York: Academic Press.

Meier, Kenneth J. and Robert E. England. 1984. "Black Representation and Educational Policy: Are They Related?" American Political Science Review 78:392-403.

Mladenka, Kenneth R. 1989. "Blacks and Hispanics in Urban Politics." American Political Science Review 83:165-191.

Nelson, William E., Jr. 1978. "Black Mayors as Urban Managers." Annals of the American Academy of Political and Social Science. 439: 53-67.

Peterson, Paul E. 1981. City Limits. Chicago, IL: University of Chicago Press.

Pinderhughes, Dianne M. 1987. Race and Ethnicity in Chicago Politics. Urbana, IL: University of Illinois Press.

Preston, Michael. 1976. "Limitations of Black Urban Power: The Case of Black Mayors." In New Urban Politics, (ed.) Louis H. Masotti and Robert L. Lineberry. Cambridge: Ballinger Publishing Company.

Saltzstein, Grace Hall. 1989. "Black Mayors and Police Policies." Journal of Politics 51:525-544.

Schneider, Mark. 1989. The Competitive City Pittsburgh, PA: University of Pittsburgh Press.

Sigelman, Lee and Susan Welch. 1991. Black Americans' Views of Racial Inequality. New York: Cambridge University Press.

Stimson, James A. 1987. "Regression in Space and Time: A Statistical Essay." American Journal of Political Science 29:914-947.

U.S. Department of Commerce. 1984. U.S. County and City Data Book: 1983 Files on Tape Technical Documentation. Washington, DC: Bureau of the Census.

U.S. Department of Commerce. 1991. Annual Survey of Governments, 1988: Finance Statistics—Technical Documentation. Washington, DC: Bureau of the Census.

U.S. Department of Commerce. 1992. Government Finance and Employment Classification Manual. Washington, DC: Bureau of the Census.

Walton, Hanes Jr. 1997. African American Power and Politics: The Political Context Variable. New York, NY: Columbia University Press.

Watts, Jerry. 2005. What Use Are Black Mayors? [on-line article]. Black Commentator.Com, 2005 [cited 28 November 2005]. Available from www.blackcommentator.com/159/159_cover_ black_mayors. html.

Welch, Susan and Albert K. Karnig. 1979. "The Impact of Black Elected Officials on Urban Social Expenditures." Policy Studies Journal 7:707-714.

A New Labor Movement?:
Race, Class, and the Missing Intersections between Black and Labor Politics

Dorian T. Warren
Columbia University

Introduction

Unfortunately the "color line" that W.E.B. DuBois decried as detrimental to African American well-being at the beginning of the twentieth century remains a problem at the beginning of the twenty-first century. However, in post-industrial twenty-first century America, scholars have noted how this color line has been joined by the lines of class, gender, and sexuality, and thus they profoundly shape and structure the life chances and opportunities of black Americans (Cohen 1999; Wilson 1978, 1996). Overall levels of poverty and inequality in the United States are the highest among Western industrial nations, and maldistributions in income and wealth are at their highest levels since the Gilded Age and the Great Depression (Krugman 2002; Iceland 2003; Phillips 2002). Even North Carolina Sen. John Edwards referenced these increasing inequalities when during his 2004 Democratic bid for vice-president he spoke of "Two Americas" where a growing economic polarization and inequality disadvantages working-class Americans and especially black Americans (Edwards 2004).

Organized labor has been one of the key political actors in efforts to combat various inequalities. Labor unions help to decrease economic, racial and gender inequalities directly through labor market intervention and indirectly through the political system as they support redistributive social policies (Bradley, et al.; Wallerstein 1989). In the United States, the labor movement has been in serious decline for more than the last quarter century, coinciding with the increase in economic inequality. The overall union density rate in 2005 was 12.5 percent, down from a post-war high of 35 percent in 1955 (Bureau of Labor Statistics 2006). In 1995, this "crisis" of the decline of American trade unions prompted the first contested election for President of the American Federation of Labor and the Congress of Industrial Organizations (AFL-CIO). The insurgent candidate, John Sweeney, emerged victorious and promised to institute labor movement reforms that would organize new members and thus halt the membership decline (Mantsios 1998). Much has changed since 1995: labor has increased its public profile with campaigns like "Justice for Janitors" (which was even made into a motion picture); union political mobilization has increased in national elections; and especially significant for communities of color, labor-community coalitions have been active and pronounced in many urban areas. However, ten years after the promise of "a new labor movement for a new century," organized labor's decline continues. Its economic and political influence is questionable, and a new and invigorated debate about the future direction of the labor movement is taking place.

As Adolph Reed (2002) notes, race and class politics have long commanded a dual and central importance in American politics. Thus, both African American politics and the labor movement have principally attempted to organize against racial and class inequalities. By African American politics, I mean the political struggles black workers and their allies have waged within the labor movement and broader public arenas. In this article, I examine the longstanding contradictory relationship between race and class politics, and more specifically between the black freedom movement and the labor movement. I argue that the major unresolved political problem of both the labor movement and black politics over the last forty years since the passage of the 1964 Civil Rights Act and the heyday of industrial unionism has been the failure of both to address race and class simultaneously (though not without notable exceptions). Indeed, in the case of the American labor movement, its continuing inability to fuse a class politics with an "identity politics" of race, gender, and sexuality, despite the claims of "universalists" who advocate for focusing on issues of class alone, is the major reason why unions continue to suffer from serious decline. I will argue that these "missing intersections" particularly around race and class need to be resolved in order for both movements to tackle the complex inequalities facing marginalized communities in the twenty-first century. Instead, unions should engage in a form of "intersectional" or "complex solidarity" through taking on the complex and multiple inequalities marginalized workers face.

Using data from an original survey of labor unions, interviews with union leaders and primary and secondary sources, I combine historical analysis with conventional social science tools to assess the evolving relationship between organized labor and African American politics. By focusing on the political organizing of black Americans and workers in this country, I revisit what has always been the grand and all too elusive political promise of what used to be called the "black/labor alliance." The next section introduces my theoretical framework drawing on Cathy Cohen's (1999) theory of marginalization, followed by a brief analysis of the current political-economic context of black communities. I then proceed with the historical analysis, evidence from the contemporary period, and conclude by suggesting that unions can draw upon their own historical legacy of fighting against the multiple inequalities affecting black workers.

The Politics of Universal, Consensus, and Cross-Cutting Issues

The dominant political ideology and strategy for addressing issues of inequality in American politics is the politics of "universalism." The specific form of inequality based on class is universalized to include almost everyone. "Identity politics" or the politics of recognition is seen here as divisive or undermining of a broader politics of redistribution or "class politics." This political strategy is to unify around the one system or set of issues that allegedly exploits everyone. Often advancing a "backlash thesis" positing that white working-class voters reacted to the excesses of the civil rights and women's movements of the 1960s by exiting the Democratic Party (the traditional party of redistribution), analysts focused on mainstream American politics have argued for strategies creating a "progressive coalition"—usually on pragmatic grounds—to promote universal social policies that the broader American public can support (Carmines and Stimson 1989; Edsall and Edsall 1991; Gitlin 1995; Greenberg and Skocpol 1997; Skocpol 1995; 2001; Teixeira and Rogers 2000; Wilson 1987, 1996, 1999). Indeed, many interest group leaders who represent the disadvantaged in American politics argue that political organizations should ignore issues pertaining to race or gender precisely because they divide the electorate and undermine broader solidarity around universal policies. Instead, groups and voters should unite around "lowest-common-denominator" issues, the issues everyone has in "common" (Strolovitch 2002). This concern about the impact of "identity" (and specifically racial) issues plays itself out in labor union politics in the use of the strategy of universalism. Even though advocates of universalism might agree that racial or gender inequality is significant and important, either as practical political strategy or due to the lack of a readily available political language through which to discuss complex inequalities, political actors and scholars rely on universal redistributive appeals.

Contrary to this debate, the major theoretical lens I use in this article is marginalization theory as advanced by Cathy Cohen (1999), which explains the disjuncture between African American politics and community responses to the HIV/AIDS crisis. This framework is useful because it gives us a sense of how well marginalized workers and their political interests are represented by their unions. Specifically, I draw on her distinction between "consensus" and "cross-cutting" issues. A consensus issue is an issue that is "*framed* as somehow important to every member of 'the black community', either directly or symbolically ... "(11) (emphasis added). In addition, "they are often the most visible segments of any black political agenda, and they often receive the bulk of resources and attention from black political leaders and organizations" (11). Alternatively, a cross-cutting issue:

> refers to those concerns which *disproportionately and directly* affect only certain segments of a marginal group. These issues stand in contrast to consensus issues, which are understood to constrain or oppress with equal probability (although through different manifestations) all identifiable marginal group members. Cross-cutting issues, in addition to disproportionately impacting one segment of a group, are also often situated among those subpopulations of marginal communities that are the most vulnerable economically, socially, and politically, and whose vulnerable status is linked to narratives that emphasize the "questionable" moral standing of the subpopulation (13-14).

In the union context, I identify consensus, cross-cutting, and *universal* issues. Universal issues are issues that affect not just union members, the working-class or marginalized workers, but potentially have a direct impact on everyone in the society. Civil liberties, such as the right to free speech protected by the First Amendment, is an example of a universal issue, and one the labor movement has historically fought to secure. Notwithstanding the etymological similarities, in my framework, universal issues are just that: universal. Consensus issues refer to those issues that proponents of an ideology or politics of "universalism" advocate; they are often "framed" as somehow important to every member of a labor union or society, though in reality they often target a specific group. For example, New Deal social welfare policies aimed at reducing poverty are often considered "universal" by scholars and advocates and counter posed to "cross-cutting" racially-targeted social policy (Skocpol 1995, 2001; Wilson 1996, 1999). Yet in reality, they are really class-targeted policies framed as "consensus issues" that do not affect the entire population (McCall 2001). Finally, cross-cutting issues in the union context are those issues which "disproportionately and directly" affect marginalized workers. I define "marginalized workers" as those workers who experience multiple forms of inequality both at work and at home, and those workers who have been historically excluded or discriminated against by unions because of their racial, ethnic, national, gender, or sexual identities.

Following the scholarship of those who have examined and advanced such concepts of "ascriptive inequalities and hierarchies," "multiple oppressions," "complex inequalities," and "intersectionality," I start from the premise that race, class, gender, and sexuality are all structural and historically specific determinants of inequality (Crenshaw 1989; Cohen 1999; Guy-Sheftall 1995; Hennessey and Ingraham 1997; McCall 2001; Reed 2002; Reskin 2003; Smith 2000; Young 1990). While multiple systems of inequalities in the U.S. case might be endogenous and constitutive of one another, I maintain that there is value in identifying their distinctive processes and logics of reproduction. Instead of race, gender, or sexuality fragmenting an already unified "working class," at this particular juncture and throughout most of twentieth century American history, race, gender, and sexuality have been hidden yet fundamentally constitutive of the processes of capitalist development and (working) class formation (Katznelson and Zolberg 1986). As I show, unions have historically struggled with these intersecting systems of inequality, and they continue to do so in the current context of "complex inequality" (McCall 2001), especially around the cross-cutting issues affecting African American workers and communities.

The Economic and Political Intersections of Urban Black Communities

The present political and economic context of black communities under globalization, increasing inequality and "advanced marginalization" (Cohen 1999), and the role of unions in African American politics is important to know in order to understand the current era of missing and broken intersections between labor and African American communities. This contemporary context of complex inequality makes advancing a politics of "complex" or "intersectional" solidarity even more challenging for labor unions and the black workers they seek to organize and represent.

Several economic, social and political developments have shaped the politics of race and class in the present era including globalization, deindustrialization, and conservative government retrenchment. In turn they have led to a black condition of intersecting oppressions. The first development of "globalization," is a constellation of economic, political and demographic processes that affect the American and global economy—e.g., NAFTA, employer assaults on labor, increased mobility of capital, a shift to a service and information-based economy, racial and gender changes in the workforce, and a substantial 1990s increase in economic inequality (Clawson and Clawson 1999; Sassen 1998; Wilson 1996). Over the last thirty-five years, the racialized impacts of globalization and structural changes in the political economy have engendered adverse outcomes for urban communities. Chicago, for example, used to be one of the many "rustbelt" manufacturing cities primarily of the industrial Northeast and Middle West—that is, Detroit, Philadelphia, Toledo, and, further west, Los Angeles (Sides 2003)—that served as a base for World War II and post-war industrial American capitalism. The unionization of manufacturing industries, through the relatively race-inclusive Congress of Industrial Organizations (CIO), led to stable employment, decent working conditions, and a path to the middle-class for many African Americans. Another path to middle-class life for many black Americans was through expanded public sector employment in the mid-1960s. The benefits from public sector unions enabled blacks to create ethnic niches in local, state, and federal employment (Johnston 1994).

In contrast to this political-economic regime of Fordist industrialism, the current post-industrial era of globalization has resulted in deindustrialization, the restructuring of the economy, and a shift to a service, information and technologically based economy (Wilson 1996; Holt 2001; Madigan 2004). As a result, many of the old rustbelt cities have experienced devastating economic decline due to the loss of hundreds of thousands of manufacturing jobs and have led directly to the de-unionization of the workforce and increased unemployment. The effects of these changes on the urban political economy of Chicago have been most pronounced in African American communities where work has literally "disappeared" (Wilson 1996). Overall Chicago manufacturing jobs declined from a post-war high of 688,000 factory jobs to 187,000 in 1992 and 100,000 by 2004 (Abu-Lughod 2000; IDES 2004), and the city has not created the requisite amount or quality of employment that highly unionized manufacturing jobs once provided (Abu-Lughod 2000; Sassen 2004).

The third development over the past fifty or so years has been the emergence and institutionalization of several movements known as the "minority rights revolution": civil rights, women, gay and lesbian liberation, among others (Skrentny 2002). These movements have had a broad impact on American politics and civil society, and a more direct impact on the marginalized communities from which they sprang. For instance, the most significant legislative achievements of the civil rights movement—the 1964 Civil Rights Act, the 1965 Voting Rights Act, the 1968 Fair Housing Act , the War on Poverty Program—all dramatically changed the conditions of and political landscape for racial equality and economic justice (MacLean 2005; Skrentny 2002). These social movement outcomes also shaped the labor movement in the form of union desegregation, the institutionalization of racial, gender and sexuality "identity caucuses" within unions, and were a source of new union leadership after the decline of these movements (Frymer 2003; Needleman 2003; Stein 1998; Voss and Sherman 2000). The subsequent racial integration of unions along with the emergence and consolidation of the various identity caucuses within unions began to place more cross-cutting issues affecting marginalized workers on unions' agendas, but not without controversy and not always successfully (Needleman 2003).

In addition, there has been an ideological and political shift to the right in all three branches of government. This has a direct impact upon union strategies over the past few decades (Levi 2003). One of the effects of this shift has been the triumph of neo-liberal market ideology, which creates a political environment that discourages and delegitimizes collective action especially through the vehicle of union organizing (Frank 2001; Milkman and Voss 2004). Another major aspect of this conservative shift and the breaking down of the "New Deal consensus" is retrenchment of the public sector and the welfare state (Pierson 1995; Fraser and Gerstle 1989). Beginning with Reagan era retrenchment, aggressive deregulation, and privatization, the dominant ideology of neo-liberalism and the reemergence of laissez-faire market-driven economics fomented a decline in public sector employment that continues (Clawson and Clawson 1999). Mary Pattillo (1999) demonstrates that this means marginalized workers, especially the black middle-class dependent on this sector of the economy, have seen their already precarious positions become more uncertain.

As a result of these developments, the political context *within* racialized communities has changed in the post-civil rights era. Under Cohen's (1999) aforementioned "advanced marginalization," social cleavages and divisions of gender, sexuality and class have taken on increased importance together with race in determining the lived experience and political behavior of African Americans and other racially marginalized groups such as Latinos and many immigrants from Latin America, Africa, Asia and the Caribbean. The resulting crisis in "linked-fate" politics (Dawson 1994) calls into question the utility of single-identity political organizations—only race, class, or gender—in fighting against the multiple hierarchies of inequality many black Americans and marginal groups face. Indeed, effective political responses have been limited in this economic and political context of increasing economic inequality and advanced marginalization in black and racialized communities (Cohen 1999; Reed 1999). It is with the class, racial, and gender dimensions of the problem of inequality that labor unions, particularly those in the service sector, might play a role. Unionization helps to reduce levels of economic inequality for both union and non-union workers directly through the labor market and indirectly through the state (Wallerstein 1989; Bradley, et al. 2003). Unionization also disproportionately impacts marginalized groups by reducing race- and gender-specific inequalities (Zeitlin and Weyher 2001; Reskin 2003).

In addition to their economic effects, labor unions have political muscle as well. When the labor movement does not succumb to the status quo, it has also been a valuable and useful political institution in African American communities, particularly when it comes to reducing inequalities, advocating for public and social policies, and political mobilization. Several unions that were racially egalitarian—what Robert Korstad (2003) calls "civil rights unionism"—had a significant impact on the economic, social and political conditions of black Americans—before and during the Civil Rights Movement. While there have been many studies about the role other political institutions—political parties (Frymer 1999), the black church (Morris 1984; Harris 1999; Harris-Lacewell 2004)—have had upon African American politics and the civil rights movement, scant attention has been paid to the role of organized labor, especially in the contemporary era. As mentioned earlier, the major unresolved problem for both labor and black politics has been the failure to address issues of race and class simultaneously. These missing intersections of race, class and gender need to be reconciled in order to deal with the complex inequalities facing marginalized communities in the new economy of the twenty-first century. Under the old industrial economy of the twentieth century, unions were sometimes able to create intersectional solidarities among black and white workers fighting for economic and racial justice. It is to this history that I now turn.

"Negro and White, Unite and Fight!": The CIO Legacy of Race and Class Intersections

To examine this historic political impact of unions in black communities, I briefly review the era of the CIO in the 1930s and 1940s. The long history of neglect, exclusion, discrimination, and violence against black workers by white craft unionists make the emergence of an alternative model of unionism in the 1930s extremely significant (Foner 1982; Gould 1977). The Committee of Industrial Organizations, later changed to the Congress of Industrial Organizations, was formed in 1935. It was constituted by several industrial unions that were kicked out of the craft-dominated American Federation of Labor (AF of L), and by other industrial unions that wanted to use an alternative organizing model to that of the exclusionary AFL model. This is especially significant in the case of black workers, as several CIO unions took on both consensus and cross-cutting issues; they often used the slogan of "Negro and White, Unite and Fight" in their early organizing drives and organized black workers in an unprecedented way. Of course, recent labor historiography documents the wide variation, limitations, and flaws of the CIO's racially egalitarian legacy, but it is worth pointing to a few of the contributions of the early CIO unions (Goldfield 1997).

The CIO's surging unionism promoted the popular notion in American political culture of "industrial democracy" (Lichtenstein 2002). In response to rapid industrialization and the harsh and exploitative conditions that came with it, Progressive middle-class reformers along with radicals and grassroots CIO labor organizers wanted to extend notions of citizenship and political democracy to the workplace. This extension of what historian Nelson Lichtenstein calls the "responsibilities and expectations of American citizenship—due process, free speech, the right of assembly and petition—would now find their place in factory, mill, and office" (Lichtenstein 2002: 32). But more than that, industrial democracy also meant a bevy of shared material benefits including: the end of exploitative and unsafe working conditions, a democratic voice and decision-making power in the work one does, more democratic and shared governance at the workplace, seniority rights and job security, a fair grievance procedure, and the equivalent of a social wage—social security, pensions, and health care. At a moment when African Americans could not exercise their political rights in the voting booth, CIO unions provided an opportunity for black workers to exercise privileges of political and economic citizenship in the workplace.

Another important contribution of CIO unions came in their mixed but much better record on the cross-cutting issue of race and racial inequality, and their intersectional model of inter-racial unionism or "civil rights unionism" (Korstad 2003). At the time, several scholars and commentators were enthusiastic about the CIO's explicit progressivism on the "Negro question" in comparison to AFL craft unions. By the end of World War II, over 500,000 black workers had joined CIO unions. In October 1941 an NAACP *Crisis* reporter wrote that the CIO is a "lamp of democracy" throughout the old Confederate South. "The South has not known such a force since the historic Union Leagues in the great days of the Reconstruction era" (Quoted in Lichtenstein, 2002: 79). The great scholar-activist W.E.B. DuBois wrote in 1948: "Probably the greatest and most effective effort toward interracial understanding among the working masses has come about through the trade unions. The organization of the CIO in 1935. … Probably no movement in the last thirty years has been so successful in softening race prejudice among the masses" (as quoted in Goldfield 1995: 79). But what made this model of unionism possible, particularly under the harsh conditions of corporate monopolies, anti-union sentiment and white supremacy? The two most important factors that made interracial unionism possible were the role of left organizations and leaders, and the role of black workers. For a brief moment, the labor movement took an intersectional approach to organizing and politics by considering both racial and class inequalities simultaneously.

Left Organizations and Intersecting Interests

The first major condition that made interracial unionism possible was the role of "Left" organizations and leaders, who supplied an alternative and much more progressive leadership group within certain unions. The main organization and most controversial was the Communist Party, but other leftists affiliated with the progressive coalition of activists known as the "Popular Front" included a broad collective of "laborites, independent radicals, progressive New Dealers, and [Communist] Party activists" who infused their labor organizing and politics with a racial egalitarianism (Goldfield 1995; Korstad 2003: 8; Rosswurm 1992). John L. Lewis, then president of the Mineworkers and the CIO explicitly enlisted the support of the Communist Party for organizers. Black left organizations also played a vital role in supplying leadership to organizing struggles. For instance, in the campaign to organize the steel industry in the 1930s, the Steel Workers Organizing Committee developed an alliance with the black left-wing organization the National Negro Congress, which played a significant role in organizing black workers (Foner 1982; Needleman 2003). In 1937, after being shunned by the AFL's Tobacco Workers International Union who refused to organize the interracial workforce at a Richmond, VA tobacco plant, four hundred Black women stemmers walked out, eventually getting most, if not all of their support from the Southern Negro Youth Congress, a Communist Party led student organization of the National Negro Congress (Goldfield 1995; Korstad 2003). These tobacco workers eventually affiliated with the Food, Tobacco, Agricultural, and Allied Workers (FTA)-CIO, a radical left-led union of mostly black and Chicana women. In the case of the Mine, Mill and Smelter Workers Union, the early communist leaders made a conscious choice to appeal to black workers by emphasizing cross-cutting and intersectional demands for racial equality.

One of the main reasons why left-wing led organizations were better on race came down to their unique political principles. Self-identified leftists tended to be much more committed to radical social change and racial equality although for many different reasons. Communists, for example, saw the "Negro Question" as a central component of their U.S.-based strategy: "African Americans were more potentially revolutionary than other segments of the population, the struggle for civil rights had a revolutionary galvanizing potential for the whole population, and the support of white workers for this struggle was *the* key to *their* development of class consciousness" (Goldfield 1995: 103; Kelley 1990). While this intersectional analysis of race and class was not limited to Communist labor organizers, it did infuse many CIO unions during this period.

Black Workers and Intersecting Issues

A second condition that made an intersectional and interracial unionism possible were black workers themselves, who through their aggressive internal organizing and external pressure pushed their unions to fight for both racial and class equality both within and outside of the workplace. Black union leaders such as A. Philip Randolph did this throughout their careers, but most importantly, Randolph and other black union leaders organized black workers through various independent organizations which incubated an intersectional analysis of American (and global) race and class inequalities. Among them were the National Negro Labor Council from 1950-1955, the Negro American Labor Council, and both the Coalition of Black Trade Unionists and the A. Philip Randolph Institute, two of the six current constituency or identity groups of the AFL-CIO (Foner 1982). Arguably, the organization of black workers into CIO unions would not have been possible without the preexisting self-organization of African Americans around their racial identity. Indeed, as Ruth Needleman (2003) aptly puts it in her work examining the organization of black steelworkers, the role of independent race-based organization and movements was crucial in black steelworkers' struggles for economic and racial justice. For instance, had it not been for the working class activism of Marcus Garvey's Universal Negro Improvement Association (UNIA), a black nationalist mass organization, and the Communist Party's (CP) unemployment councils, it is doubtful the Steelworkers Organizing Committee (SWOC) would have had much success organizing black workers, and eventually the entire industry. Garvey's movement, black churches, and black civil rights organizations fomented what social movement scholars call an "oppositional consciousness" against racism and economic exploitation among black working-class residents of northwest Indiana and nationwide (Mansbridge and Morris 2001). They also helped create social, political and survival networks among the recent African American migrants to the North. So when SWOC organizers came to town in 1936, they were not union staff members there to do a workplace-based blitz campaign among black workers. The steelworkers' organizing campaign was not a workplace campaign; instead, from the start, it was a community-wide campaign which drew on the indigenous resources and networks of the African American community prior to the CIO. Thus, CIO unions often drew upon black workers' already existing intersectional analysis of racial and class inequalities and their political networks in their organizing and political activities.

The Impact of the CIO's Race, Class, and Gender Intersections

The inclusionary wing of the labor movement in the form of the CIO had a significant impact on the economic, social and political conditions of black Americans and black politics *before* the emergence of the civil rights movement, while also contributing to the emergence of the movement. Thus there are at least three contributions the CIO made in addressing cross-cutting issues by intersecting race, class, and often times gender, though its activism also dealt with consensus issues. First, *CIO unionism created a form of industrial democracy and provided a semblance of "citizenship rights on the shop floor" for black workers*. These consisted of a number of new rights: legal structures; bureaucratic procedures; signed contracts; seniority rights; clearly defined wage scales; shop stewards; and grievance procedures. In the midst of the poll tax, the white primary, segregation and condoned violence, black workers found that the slogan of "one man, one vote" or "one woman, one vote" actually applied in one sphere of their lives: the workplace. Through participation in National Labor Relations Board union elections, black industrial workers who had never before voted or had any political rights in the larger public sphere were enfranchised in the workplace. Here, their votes counted. Second, *most egalitarian CIO unions mobilized their members to fight for the civil, political and economic rights of African Americans*. Essentially, these unions fought for the rights of full citizenship in the broadest sense. For many of the activists and leaders of these unions at the time, there were clear and indistinguishable links between workplace democracy, civil rights, and economic justice. They fought for universal, consensus and cross-cutting issues: the abolition of the poll tax, the right to vote, anti-lynching and broad social welfare legislation (Goldfield 1995).

Third, *organized black workers influenced campaigns for racial and economic justice through other black organizations.* In Winston-Salem, NC, hundreds of Food, Tobacco and Agricultural Workers Union (FTA) Local 22 members joined the local NAACP, transforming it from a membership of eleven in 1941 into a large and militant branch with 2,000 members by 1946 (Korstad 2003). Robert Black, one of the union's leaders explained it this way, "We saw the need of strengthening the NAACP, not to dominate it with our members, but to build it. Because that was the political arm of the blacks, short of our union. By building and getting our members to support these organizations, it gave us extra strength in our community" (Korstad 2003: 260). As the NAACP and its national structure of local organizations became an essential organizational resource during the civil rights movement, there is no doubt that the labor movement, through CIO unions and the intersectional or complex solidarities they enabled among black (and white) workers, played a pivotal role.

But while the progressive wing of the labor movement had an impact on black communities before the emergence of the civil rights movement, it was also involved with the movement when it did emerge. Dr. Martin Luther King, Jr. described this objective intersectional relationship best at an address to the 1961 AFL-CIO national convention when he said, "Negroes are almost entirely a working people. There are pitifully few Negro millionaires, and few Negro employers. .... That is why Negroes support labor's demands and fight laws which curb labor. That is why the labor-hater and labor-baiter is virtually always a twin-headed creature spewing anti-Negro epithets from one mouth and anti-labor propaganda from the other mouth. The duality of interests of labor and Negroes makes any crisis which lacerates you a crisis from which we bleed" (King 1961: 203).

In 1941, A. Philip Randolph, backed up by his powerful Brotherhood of Sleeping Car Porters, planned the March on Washington for Jobs and Equal Participation in National Defense, with the goal of pressuring the Roosevelt Administration to end racial discrimination in the war and defense industries. The result of this effort was Roosevelt's 1941 executive order establishing the Fair Employment Practices Commission or FEPC. Ultimately, the Negro/Labor, Black/Labor alliance and its successful lobbying effort pushed Congress to create a permanent FEPC, in the form of Title VII of the 1964 Civil Rights Act. Even though the AFL-CIO did not endorse the 1963 March on Washington, whose original goal was to focus on the economic dimensions of racial justice, the idea for the march its and main organizers came from Randolph's chief lieutenant Bayard Rustin, who contributions as a civil rights and gay rights activist have been long overlooked. The model for the 1963 March was based upon Randolph's threatened 1941 march. At the 1962 convention of the Negro American Labor Council (NALC), the delegates voted to endorse Randolph's and Rustin's idea and plan a march on Washington for the late summer or fall of 1963 to deal with black unemployment, demand jobs for African Americans, and call for an end to industry and union racism. In the late spring of 1963, Dr. King called on Randolph to expand the aims of the march to pass the pending civil rights legislation (what eventually became the 1964 Civil Rights Act). The NALC officially hired Rustin to plan and organize the march in early June, and he was paid out of District 65 of the Distributive, Processing, and Office Workers Union in New York. Cleveland Robinson, Vice-President of District 65 and a leader in the NALC, was treasurer of the March. Thus, Philip Foner (1982) is correct when he concludes, "the climax of the civil rights movement—the March on Washington for Jobs and Freedom—was initiated and planned largely by black trade unionists" (346).

The impact of the March on Washington created the necessary pressure to pass the 1964 Civil Rights Act and for the first time ever in American history, visually highlighted a broad movement for major change in racial equality. However, just two months after having organized the march, Bayard Rustin wrote an essay in October of 1963 that was overly optimistic about the historic impact of the March. While often interpreted as being a pragmatist and realist, his optimism clearly articulates what would be the ultimate failure of the civil rights and labor movements over the last forty years in the wake of the political and economic developments discussed earlier. Rustin discusses the impact of the March and writes, "It began the process of focusing attention where it belongs: on the problem of what kind of economic and political changes are required to make it possible for everyone to have jobs. The civil rights movement alone cannot provide jobs for all." (Rustin 1963: 382). A few pages later in that essay, Rustin incorrectly predicts how history would interpret the March—"the significance of the March will be seen to have less to do with civil rights than with economic rights: the demand for jobs. The problem of how to get jobs for Negroes is really the problem of how to get jobs for people." However, he was accurate in his reading of its significance with regards to the American political economy, "We must put the total structure of the country under scrutiny, including the war economy. Not only does the war industry fail to provide butter and schools, houses and hospitals, but it provides the least jobs per dollar spent of any sector of industry" (Rustin 1963: 384). Like DuBois, King, and Randolph, Rustin and his disciples, such as Norman Hill, were farsighted and even foresaw the coming difficulties of deindustrialization and globalization, well before scholars noticed the impact these political and economic changes inflicted upon black communities (Foner 1974/1982: 439). But despite this foresight, these intersecting connections between labor and black politics would be fleeting outside of Washington, DC.

Labor's Hope for the South: Race, Class, and Broken Intersections

As W.E.B. DuBois argued (1935), the South has always held the key for achieving racial justice in this country as it holds the key for the growth of the labor movement. Historically, many leaders within the labor movement, including some Southerners, have been sympathetic to the civil rights movement and, in some cases, provided political resources and assistance. But they did so not out of moral or political conviction, but because according to historian Alan Draper, "they expected the civil rights movement to resolve the southern political problem for labor. Blacks would do the political work that southern white workers [that] the unions had failed to organize in the 1930s and 1940s should have done. Black enfranchisement, then, would initiate the realignment of southern politics the labor leaders desired" (Draper 1994: 14). Civil rights leaders also assumed that black enfranchisement would help defeat southern Dixiecrats and cement the black-liberal-labor alliance (Rustin 1963). However, rank-and-file white southern union members saw these possible benefits of the civil rights movement as a path toward "undercutting" white skin privilege and the racial caste system. (Draper 1994: 15).

Thus, due to differences around race, white union members differed sharply from their unions' political leaders in the South, and had a different vision of how the civil rights movement affected their interests. Ultimately, according to Draper, there was a tension created by the civil rights movement and racial justice organizing for southern organized labor. On the one hand, the civil rights movement created new and transformative political possibilities for labor in the form of a fundamental political electoral realignment. This represented the converse of what we now know was Nixon's "southern strategy" where white working-class voters were convinced to switch to the Republican Party. On the other hand, by precipitating conflict or rather racial fault lines, between the rank-and-file and the leadership of southern unions, it posed a threat to labor's organizational maintenance objectives. This led to the ultimate failure of organized labor to organize the South in the 1930s, 1940s, and 1950s through its "Operation Dixie" campaign. This challenge remains. According to political scientist Michael Goldfield (1997), the defeat of Operation Dixie is the most important factor in explaining all of American politics from WWII to the present. He argues three internal factors led to its ultimate defeat. First, it was at bottom a corporate strategy, not a mass mobilization and effort to build a militant social movement.

Second, it deemphasized race and an intersectional approach to organizing; the consensus issue of class took center-stage from the 1950s onward. Third, most leftists—those who did have an intersectional analysis of race and class—were purged from the staff. These three factors also account for labor's present day struggles in making intersections between class and other dimensions of inequality such as race or gender. The ultimate failure of organized labor to organize the South in the post-war era is remarkable not only for cross-cutting interests of black workers whom the labor movement conceded. It is also because of: the consolidation of an anti-labor South especially with the new industrialization of the Black and Sun Belts; the elimination of what could have possibly been a broad progressive movement for massive social change; and the total transformation of Southern politics whose national political impact is still ever present.

Contemporary Black Politics and the New Labor Movement's Missing Intersections

Having very briefly examined the historical legacy of CIO unionism, I ask in this final section—what is the present relationship of African Americans and the "new" labor movement over the past ten years and what evidence is there for a failure to (re)create intersecting appeals? Using data from an original survey of national and local labor unions and interviews with African American labor leaders, I argue that organized labor has yet to recover from the failure of Operation Dixie, the last major attempt to organize black workers and to create intersections. In addition, the role of black unionists in African American politics remains uncertain. First I explain my data and methodology, and then discuss basic results.

Data and Methodology

Along with a series of twenty-five personal interviews I conducted with predominantly African American labor leaders between the dates of April 2002 and December 2004, I use data from the 2003 Survey of National and Chicago Unions. The latter examines the conditions under which marginalized and historically excluded groups of workers are represented in unions' structures and activities. This telephone survey of union elected officials and staff was conducted by the Northern Illinois University Public Opinion Lab in the summer and fall of 2003. The 2003 Survey of National and Chicago Unions has a national population of 112 and a response rate of 36.6 percent with a total of forty-one national unions in the sample. The unions in the national sample represent about 68.5 percent of all unionized workers in the U.S. (11 million out of 16 million). The Chicago survey has a population of 222 and a response rate of 31.9 percent with a total of seventy-one local unions in the sample. The unions in the Chicago sample represent about 53.4 percent of all unionized workers in the Chicago Metropolitan Area (361,644 out of 676,890). While the response rates are low, (the general range of response rates for organizational surveys tends to be somewhere between 25 percent to 50 percent), both samples are representative of the labor movement in terms of industry and sector of the economy, and variation in size and type of political behavior.

Basic Results and Discussion

The AFL and CIO merged into one organization in 1955, and today constitute a national federation of fifty-two labor unions consisting of 9 million of the 16 million total union members in the U.S. As I mentioned earlier, John Sweeney's election as president of the national labor federation in 1995—the AFL-CIO's first contested election in the federation's history—brought promises of a new and more inclusive labor movement. The newly elected insurgent leadership committed itself not only to organizing marginalized workers into its ranks, but also to addressing the multiple issues of inequality that shape these workers' lived and work experiences (Clawson 2003; Hunt and Rayside 2000; Mantsios 1998; Krupat and McCreery 2001). Yet just ten years later in 2005, on the 50th anniversary of the merger of the AFL-CIO, another group of insurgents provoked a serious internal debate and subsequently started a new and rival labor federation with the goal of "changing to win," and recruiting marginalized workers into labor's ranks on a massive scale.[1] Led by the Service Employees International Union (SEIU)—the very union out of which AFL-CIO President John Sweeney campaigned as a reformer in 1995—several unions boycotted the convention and went even further by disaffiliating from the AFL-CIO. The charge leading the break away from the national federation by these "dissident" unions was that the AFL-CIO under Sweeney's leadership had not "changed enough" to stem the continuing decline in organized labor's numbers over the previous ten years. The Change To Win Federation now consists of seven unions representing about six million workers, especially black and Latino workers in the service sector of the economy.

Issues such as immigrant rights, police brutality, public education, affordable housing, welfare reform, HIV/AIDS, and hate crimes— cross-cutting issues not directly related nor relegated to the workplace—have received, in some cases, prominent attention and advocacy from organized labor, both on the national and local levels. On the local level especially, unions have engaged with black and Latino communities through labor-community alliances around economic justice campaigns such as living wage campaigns, campaigns against Wal-Mart and through local electoral politics. However, on several measures including basic membership inclusion in old AFL building and construction trade unions, the labor movement is failing to secure justice and equality for black workers. However, black unionists share part of the blame. I examine my data by considering if new labor has made diverse appeals along the lines of organizational inclusion and political action.

Levels of Organizational Inclusion

I define *organizational inclusion* as the extent to which previously excluded workers are selected or recruited as leaders and members of unions. This issue of basic inclusion is important not only for normative reasons of social justice, but also for the future vitality of the movement. While there is a self-interested and strategic imperative to recruit more members, some unions have been very slow to admit workers of color into their ranks. Often notorious for discrimination, building and construction trade unions actually made more progress between the late 1960s and early 1980s than they did during the 1990s, counter to the expectations of activists and scholars (Frymer 2003; Warren 2005). In fact, in many cases, we see a retreat and downturn in racial and ethnic minority levels of membership

To place unions' membership numbers in a broader context, I compare them to national aggregate data on the demographic composition of private industry. The key category in the industry-wide EEOC data to examine is the racial and ethnic composition of "Craft Workers." With the exception of a couple of manufacturing and/or service sector unions, all of the unions which must report data to the EEOC are classified as craft workers. As is clear from the industry-wide data, whites are overrepresented among craft workers (76.5 percent), compared to their participation in the workforce as a whole (70 percent), whereas blacks are underrepresented (9.7 percent compared to 13.9 percent overall) while Latinos are about even with their overall workforce numbers (10.6 percent compared to 10.9 percent overall). Similar patterns of black worker underrepresentation of African Americans emerge when we compare demographic breakdowns among union craft workers in the 1990s. In twenty-one out of twenty-six total unions, African Americans are underrepresented compared to their overall workforce numbers, and in seventeen out of twenty building and construction trade unions, they are underrepresented compared to their industry numbers. See Table 1.

Table 1

Blacks In Building and Construction Trade Unions, 1990-1998

International	Black 1990	Black 1992	Black 1996	Black 1998
Asbestos Workers	6.1	5.8	4.5	4.5
Boilermakers	7.1	3.5	4	4.6
Bricklayers	10.4	7.7	9	8.4
Carpenters	4.5	4.4	4.8	4.2
Electrical Workers, IBEW	4.2	4	4.7	4.9
Elevator Constructors	3.8	4	5.3	5.3
Operating Engineers	4.3	6.4	5.1	5.6
Iron Workers	5.1	5.3	4.5	5.2
Laborers	18.9	16.6	15.5	15
Marble Polishers	4.3	4.7	4.2	0.7
Painters	5.2	7.5	7.1	8.2
Plasterers	13.5	12.8	10.8	14.6
Plumbers	3.6	3.6	3.7	4
Roofers	9.1	10.6	9.8	10.6
Sheet Metal Workers	3.3	3.3	3.6	3.6
Graphic Arts	6.8	6.8	8	10.2
HERE	14.7	15	15.9	13.1
Longshoremen	78.8	66	79.6	75.4
Longshoremen and Warehousemen	8	7	17.1	16.6
Machinists	15.1	7.8	7.5	6.3
Pattern Makers	10.6	0.8	0.8	0.8
Printing Pressmen		10.4	11.1	7.7
Service Workers	29.3	16.2	19.9	23.9
Stage and Motion Picture Operators	3.4	3.8	3.9	4.5
Teamsters	16.3	15.4	18.4	17.5
Typographical	2.8	3.3	3.3	4.3

The same patterns of continual exclusion are present on the local level. Building and Construction trade unions in Chicago still have trouble integrating blacks into their memberships, and have lost ground over the last several years. For instance, the percentages of African Americans in apprenticeship programs, the mandatory gateways to gaining entrance into trade unions and skilled crafts, fall far behind whites. In a city in which African Americans constitute more than a third of the population, their percentage of new apprenticeship program registrations was just 10.1 percent from 2000-2003, down from a paltry 12.8 percent from 1996-1999 (Warren 2005). Out of sixteen local building and construction trade unions, only in one do African Americans come close to their overall city-wide demographic numbers (laborers at 32 percent). Thus, on both the national and local levels, African Americans in the building and construction industry are still excluded from basic membership in craft unions.

Despite black politicians' and activists' active efforts over the last four decades to integrate the most exclusionary unions within the labor movement, resistance still remains strong. For example, the most recent past president of the Chicago collective of building and construction trade unions, the Chicago and Cook County Building and Construction Trades Council, denied that racial discrimination is still a valid explanation. Those who believe that racism is still an obstacle are "about 10 percent right" according to Mike O'Neill (Taylor 2004). Other explanations that fault blacks for not having the adequate skills or work ethic necessary for entry into these unions are common among many white union officials (Taylor 2004). However, not all agree. One high-ranking white union official in Chicago told me frankly that the "only instrument that has moved many of the building trades is legal action. If you sue the crap [sic] out of them, if you hit their pocketbooks, then they start to change" (Anonymous Interview, April 2002).

Black unionists' views are also much less sanguine about the issue. One black labor leader explained, "This issue of the exclusion of African Americans from craft unions, what we might call the exclusionary wing of the labor movement, has been one of the primary defining characteristics of the American labor movement throughout history. It is no surprise to me that there has been so little progress (Anonymous Interview, December 2004). Another black unionist agreed, "... there is just so much at play. Nepotism, closed social and work networks ... of course racist attitudes and behavior. Then there is the denial and the lack of strong leadership, especially among white union leaders that they won't tolerate such racism" (Anonymous Interview, June 2002). Thus, according to EEOC and BLS data, throughout the 1990s and well into the new century, many building and construction trade unions still practice and confirm the long pattern of the basic exclusion of black workers from their workforces, crafts, and unions. Because these referral unions have control over the hiring process in their trades, especially through apprenticeship programs, they remain a key agent and institution responsible for the exclusion of African American workers from these particular jobs. This is despite the impact of the civil rights movement, legal suits, consent decrees, other court decisions, and affirmative action over the last thirty years. This situation is particularly egregious given the disappearance of viable manufacturing employment for African American residents in Chicago. Unlike their CIO counterparts, many of today's unions continue to miss the intersections between race and class on the most basic of levels: recruitment and inclusion in their organizations.

Levels of Political Issue Activity

Subsequently, I define *political action* as those activities in which unions engage to pursue their interests in the public arena. The political influence of labor reaches from local grassroots involvement in urban politics to election activity, policymaking and lobbying on the national level (Dark 1999). This section examines the extent to which today's new labor movement ad-

Table 2
National Political Issue Activity

Issue	% Active	% Very Active	Mean
Health Care Reform	76.4	58.8	3.21
Occupational Health and Safety	73.6	41.2	3.00
Social Security	64.8	32.4	2.82
Corporate Accountability	60.6	30.3	2.70
Raising the Minimum Wage	60.6	24.2	2.67
Living Wage Campaigns	61.7	23.5	2.65
Protecting and Expanding Civil Liberties and Human Rights	58.9	26.5	2.56
Protecting and Expanding Affirmative Action	48.5	18.2	2.36
Immigration Rights/Reform	42.5	15.2	2.21
Reforming the Electoral System	39.4	12.1	2.15
Eliminating Gender Wage Gap	33.3	9.1	2.06
Protecting Welfare	30.3	12.1	2.06
Protecting GLBT Workers from Discrimination	30.3	9.1	2.00
Restoring Federal Safety-net for Immigrants	30.3	9.1	1.97
Contraceptive Equity	24.3	9.1	1.85
Banning Racial Profiling	24.2	3.0	1.85
Protecting and Expanding Hate Crime Laws	20.6	5.9	1.85

dresses the intersections of race, class, gender and sexuality in their political activities. Again, the original survey of national and Chicago unions uses several indicators to measure the range of union political activity. Respondents were asked to rate on a scale of 1 to 4, where 1 is "not active at all" and 4 is "very active," how active they were on a list of seventeen issues that I determined were national and local political issues. In addition, an open-ended question asked unions to list their three most important policy issues. The two lists, in rank order of activity and importance, are below [See Tables 2 and 3].

Clearly, the issues receiving the most attention from organized labor tend to be "bread and butter" consensus economic and workplace related issues that affect the broadest range of workers. Unions are particularly concerned about the crisis in health care in this country for both self-interested and broader normative reasons. In addition, the number of uninsured Americans continues to rise, partly as a result of declining union density. However, in terms of the least powerful and most marginalized workers in society who experience discrimination based on their race (or other identities such as immigrant status, sexual orientation, and gender) in addition to their class position and status as workers, the cross-cutting issues that most directly impact these groups of workers receive the least amount of attention from their unions.

According to Table 2, the top five political issues receiving the most attention from national unions are: (1) health care reform, (2) occupational health and safety regulations, (3) social security, (4) corporate accountability, and (5) raising the minimum wage. According to Table 3, the top five political issues receiving the most attention from local unions in Chicago are the same with the exception of social security, which ranks seventh. The top five there include: (1) occupational health and safety, (2) health care reform, (3) living wage campaigns, (4) corporate accountability, and (5) raising the minimum wage. While it is the case that all of these issues have a disproportionate impact on black workers and communities, compared to several other issues that might have a more direct impact on African Americans such as banning racial profiling they receive much more attention and fewer resources from unions.

Table 3
Local Political Issue Activity

Issue	% Active	% Very Active	Mean
Occupational Health and Safety	76.9	44.6	3.03
Health Care Reform	70.8	37.5	2.88
Living Wage Campaigns	61.5	27.7	2.65
Corporate Accountability	60.6	31.1	2.62
Raising the Minimum Wage	59.4	29.7	2.61
Protecting and Expanding Civil Liberties and Human Rights	53.2	27.4	2.55
Protecting and Expanding Affirmative Action	58.7	19.0	2.51
Social Security	56.9	21.5	2.51
Eliminating Gender Wage Gap	45.3	20.3	2.31
Protecting Welfare	44.7	18.5	2.26
Immigration Rights/Reform	42.8	19.0	2.21
Protecting GLBT Workers From Discrimination	42.8	9.5	2.11
Restoring Federal Safety-net for Immigrants	36.9	12.3	2.03
Banning Racial Profiling	34.4	18.8	2.03
Reforming the Electoral System	34.4	14.1	1.98
Contraceptive Equity	32.2	16.1	1.97
Protecting and Expanding Hate Crime Laws	31.3	9.4	1.95

In the union context, I identify *consensus*, *cross-cutting*, and *universal* issues. To reiterate, universal issues are issues that have impact not just on union members, the working-class or marginalized workers, but potentially have a direct impact on everyone in the society. So, for instance, I code electoral reform and civil liberties and human rights as universal issues. Consensus issues are those that are framed as important to every member of a union or working-class people. I code social security, corporate accountability, health care reform, minimum and living wage, and health and safety. Of course, one could make the argument that consensus and cross-cutting issues both have effects on and benefit everyone in a society. Notwithstanding that argument, I code as cross-cutting those issues that disproportionately and directly effect marginalized subpopulations of workers. Thus, cross-cutting issues directly affecting workers of color, women workers, or gay and lesbian workers are coded into the race, gender, and sexuality categories. The "mixed" category includes those cross-cutting issues that include some combination of race, gender, class, and sexuality, such as hate crimes. Refer to Table 4.

Based on previous research showing that cross-cutting issues receive the least amount of political activity from political organizations while consensus issues garner the most (Cohen 1999; Strolovitch 2002), I hypothesize that in the case of unions' political activities, class issues (my consensus issues) will also receive the highest amount of activity, while race, gender, sexuality and mixed issues (my cross-cutting issues) will get the least. As we might expect based on the previous discussion of the policy issues at the top of unions' agendas, in terms of mean levels of activity, consensus class issues receive the most amount of political activity from both national and local unions (2.85 national, 2.71 local), followed by universal issues (2.37 national, 2.24 local). The differences between the means of consensus class issues compared with the five other types of issues are all statistically significant at the 0.001 level. Mixed issues have the next highest level of mean political activity from both sets of samples, although there is a much greater level of drop-off in activity among national unions from class and universal issues to mixed issues. Nonetheless, mixed issues receive more attention than

Table 4
Mean Level of Political Activity by Issue Type

Issue	Rank	National Mean	Rank	Local Mean
Class	1	2.85	1	2.71
Universal	2	2.37	2	2.24
Mixed	3	2.07	3	2.23
Race	4	2.01	6	2.08
Gender	5	2.00	4	2.15
Sexuality	5	2.00	5	2.11

race issues (2.01 national, 2.08 local), sexuality issues (2.00 national, 2.11 local) and gender issues (2.00 national, 2.15 local).[2] This finding suggests unions are beginning to address some cross-cutting issues that fall at the intersections of multiple systems of inequality. However, the challenge will be how unions balance universal and consensus issues on the one hand, with cross-cutting issues on the other.

One common explanation I heard from black labor leaders of the low priority assigned to cross-cutting racial issues effecting African American workers was fear. White labor leaders tend to worry that any political issue that is not considered a universal class issue will somehow divide a heterogeneous membership. As one African American labor activist explained, "There is a great deal of fear around race in the AFL-CIO. Unions rarely want to discuss basic civil rights issues or affirmative action...and don't dare bring up the issue of 'institutional racism.' They will run scared ... " (Anonymous Interview, November 2002). Other leaders I interviewed offered a different interpretation for unions that have a reputation as being "progressive." The politics of "tokenism" or "race-blindness" is prevalent in many unions with a significant number or even majority of workers of color and black workers but with mostly white leadership. A prominent black labor official explained that among progressive unions, what we see today is "the illusion of inclusion. Sure, you might see some black faces at the top, but it makes no difference for the empowerment of rank-and-file black workers. And it makes no difference in terms of the union's political agenda" (Anonymous Interview, December 2004). Another African American labor leader, in speaking about the popular president of SEIU (Service Employees International Union), a union known for its progressive politics, explained that "Andy Stern is one of the few who tries to cut a different path. But there is kind of a prevailing sentiment that they [SEIU] have moved beyond race" (Anonymous Interview, November 2004). He continued, "The staff of unions are much more conscious and progressive on these issues than the backwards 'handkerchief heads' of these organizations. Their attitudes are calcified with homophobia, racism and sexism." This sentiment was all too common among the many African American labor activists I interviewed.

As mentioned earlier, there is a real fear that focusing on cross-cutting issues among a heterogeneous political organization threatens the group's political solidarity. It could be the case that diverse organizations can only focus on universal or consensus issues that affect the broadest group of constituents, as James Q. Wilson (1974) cogently suggests, "diversity is the enemy of solidarity" within political organizations (127). However, historical evidence of CIO unions that had consensus, universal and cross-cutting issues at the core of their agendas should give us pause from generalizing to all labor unions. Indeed, even in the contemporary period, there are many unions which are now active on cross-cutting issues. As I detail in other work, the hotel workers union (UNITE-HERE) has been active on issues affecting both immigrant workers and African American workers (Warren 2005). And the two rival labor federations, the AFL-CIO and Change to Win, are also advancing competing positions on the cross-cutting issue of immigration reform.[3] Many unions also advocate for gender-specific issues affecting women such as contraceptive equity, while many others include cross-cutting issues that impact gay and lesbian workers as central elements of their political agendas (Warren 2005). A question for future research will be to ascertain under what conditions unions are active on cross-cutting issues, and under what conditions they are not. In the meantime, there are enough historical and contemporary unions that show that at the very least, it is not outside of the realm of possibility.

Conclusion

As we have seen throughout history and in the contemporary period, the role of race in the labor movement and its relationship with black communities and the African American freedom movement have always posed fundamental questions about the character of both movements and the democratic and transformative possibilities within American politics. Does unionism only amount to higher wages and better working conditions or does the agenda of the labor movement include broader social and political goals of social and economic justice for all? Historically, it was the CIO's activism around both consensus and cross-cutting issues at the intersections between race, class and gender that attracted black workers and led to racial and economic justice in black communities. If unions hope to organize marginalized workers in the future, they might consider increasing their level of political activity on cross-cutting issues, but not as a zero-sum trade-off with their activity on universal and consensus issues.

As of this writing, it does not seem like there will be a radical shift in the priorities or strategies of the Change to Win Federation unions that broke away from the AFL-CIO in 2005. What will happen in the next ten years with the AFL-CIO and the Change to Win Federation will surely be the topic of many more articles. But more importantly is what will become of the "dissident" unions who broke away from the AFL-CIO. Will they be the catalyst for a labor revival much like the CIO was in the 1930s, labor's "golden age?" Most significantly, what are the implications of these most recent changes for the plight of African American workers? Will the competition between the two rival labor federations be good or bad for workers of color? It is too early to say at this point, but we might expect that with the heightening concentration of black workers in the service sector where unions in both labor federations are targeting future campaigns, there is hope that they will learn from their predecessors and focus on rebuilding a movement that takes seriously how the complex inequalities of race, class, and gender structure the lives of workers of color.

I have argued in this article that there was a moment when the labor movement did address racial and class inequalities simultaneously. That is not the case today, though there are some promising possibilities for unions to rebuild intersectional and complex solidarities among all workers in order to tackle the multiple inequalities facing marginalized communities in the post-industrial twenty-first century. One of the black union leaders who organized the Reynolds tobacco plants in Winston-Salem, North Carolina in the 1940s once explained, "It wasn't just wages we wanted, but freedom" (Korstad 2003: 294). Much like the best of the CIO aimed to do—and did achieve for millions of workers of all races and genders—organized labor needs to wage a broad campaign for democracy and justice for the twenty-first century by fusing the intersections of race, class, gender and sexuality into an agenda for "freedom."

Notes

1. The name of the rival federation is the "Change to Win Coalition."
2. However, the differences between the means of each of the cross-cutting issues (race, gender, sexuality, mixed) are not statistically significant.

3.   In a remarkable shift from labor's historically anti-immigrant politics, both national labor federations are in favor of immigration reform that benefits immigrants, though they disagree on the substance and details of such reform. What is notable is that both federations are actively involved in a "cross-cutting" issue that affects a less powerful subgroup of their membership.

References

Abu-Lughod, J.L. 2000. *New York, Chicago, Los Angeles: America's Global Cities.* Minneapolis, MN: University of Minnesota Press.

Bradley, D., Huber, E., Moller, S., Nielsen, F., and Stephens, J.D. 2003. "Distribution and Redistribution in Postindustrial Democracies." *World Politics*, 55, 193-228.

Bureau of Labor Statistics. 2006. "Union Members in 2005." http://www.bls.gov/news.release/union2.nr0.htm

Carmines, E. G. and J. A. Stimson. 1989. *Issue Evolution: Race and the Transformation of American Politics.* Princeton, NJ: Princeton University Press.

Clawson, D. 2003. *The Next Upsurge: Labor and the New Social Movements.* Ithaca, NY: Cornell University Press.

Clawson, D., and Clawson, M.A. 1999. "What Has Happened to the U.S. Labor Movement? Union Decline and Renewal." *Annual Review of Sociology*, 25, 95-119.

Cohen, C. J. 1999. *The Boundaries of Blackness: Aids and the Breakdown of Black Politics.* Chicago, IL: University of Chicago Press.

Crenshaw, K. 1989. "Demarginalizing the Intersection of Race and Gender." *The University of Chicago Legal Forum* 139.

Dark, T. E. 1999. *The Unions and the Democrats: An Enduring Alliance.* Ithaca, NY: Cornell University Press.

Dawson, M. C. 1994. *Behind the Mule: Race and Class in African-American Politics.* Princeton, NJ: Princeton University Press.

Draper, A. 1994. *Conflict of Interests: Organized Labor and the Civil Rights Movement in the South, 1954-1968.* Ithaca, NY: Cornell University Press.

DuBois, W. E. B. 1935. *Black Reconstruction in America 1860-1880.* New York: Free Press.

Edsall, T. B. and M. D. Edsall. 1991. *Chain Reaction: The Impact of Race, Rights, and Taxes on American Politics.* New York: W.W. Norton.

Edwards, J. 2004. "Speech to the 2004 Democratic National Convention." http://www.johnkerry.com/pressroom/speeches/spc_2004_0728.html.

Foner, P. S. 1974/1982. *Organized Labor and the Black Worker: 1619-1973, 1982.* New York: International Publishers.

Frank, T. 2001. *One Market Under God: Extreme Capitalism, Market Populism, and the End of Economic Democracy.* New York: Anchor Books.

Fraser, S. and Gerstle G. 1989. *The Rise and Fall of the New Deal Order 1930-1980.* Princeton, NJ: Princeton University Press.

Frymer, P. 1999. *Uneasy Alliances: Race and Party Competition in America.* Princeton, NJ: Princeton University Press.

Frymer, P. 2003. "Acting When Elected Officials Won't: Federal Courts and Civil Rights Enforcement in U.S. Labor Unions, 1935-85." *American Political Science Review*, 483-499.

Gitlin, T. 1995. *The Twilight of Common Dreams: Why America Is Wracked by Culture Wars.* New York: Metropolitan Books.

Goldfield, M. 1995. "Was There a Golden Age of the CIO? Race, Solidarity, and Union Growth during the 1930s and 1940s." in Glenn Perusek and Kent Worcester, (eds.), *Trade Union Politics: American Unions and Economic Change 1960s-1990s.* Atlantic Highlands, NJ: Humanities Press International.

Goldfield, M. 1997. *The Color of Politics: Race and the Mainspring of American Politics.* New York: The New Press.

Gould, W. B. 1977. *Black Workers in White Unions: Job Discrimination in the United States.* Ithaca, NY: Cornell University Press.

Greenberg, S.B. and T. Skocpol. 1997. *The New Majority: Toward a Popular Progressive Politics.* New Haven, CT: Yale University Press.

Guy-Sheftall, B. (ed.) 1995. *Words of Fire: An Anthology of African-American Feminist Thought.* New York: New Press.

Harris, F. 1999. *Something Within: Religion in African-American Political Activism.* New York: Oxford University Press.

Harris-Lacewell, M. V. 2004. *Barbershops, Bibles and B.E.T.: Everyday Talk and Black Political Thought.* Princeton, NJ: Princeton University Press.

Hennessy, R. and C. Ingraham. 1997. *Materialist Feminism: A Reader in Class, Difference, and Women's Lives.* New York: Routledge.

Holt, T. C. 2001. *The Problem of Race in the Twenty-first Century.* Cambridge, MA: Harvard University Press.

Hunt, G. and Rayside, D. 2000. "Labor Union Response to Diversity in Canada and the United States." *Industrial Relations, 39, 3.*

Iceland, J. 2003. *Poverty In America: A Handbook.* Berkeley, CA: University of California Press.

Illinois Department of Employment Security. 2004. Labor Market Information Unit. http://www.ides.state.il.us/

Johnston, P. 1994. *Success While Others Fail: Social Movement Unionism and the Public Workplace.* Ithaca, NY: Cornell University Press.

Katznelson, I. and A. R. Zolberg. 1986. *Working-Class Formation: Nineteenth-Century Patterns in Western Europe and the United States.* Princeton, NJ: Princeton University Press.

Kelley, R.D.G. 1990. *Hammer and Hoe: Alabama Communists During the Great Depression.* Chapel Hill, NC: University of North Carolina Press.

King, M.L.K., Jr. 1961. "Address at the Fourth Annual Convention of the American Federation of Labor and Congress of Industrial Organizations (AFL-CIO) on 12/11/61." *Proceedings of the Fourth Constitutional Convention, Volume I,* pp. 282-289. Washington, DC: AFL-CIO.

Korstad, R. 2003. *Civil Rights Unionism: Tobacco Workers and the Struggle for Democracy in the Mid-Twentieth Century South.* Chapel Hill, NC: University of North Carolina Press.

Krugman, P. 2002. "For Richer," *New York Times Magazine,* 20 October. http://www.pkarchive.org/economy/ForRicher.html

Krupat, K. and McCreery, P., (eds.) 2001. *Out at Work: Building a Gay-Labor Alliance.* Minneapolis, MN: University of Minnesota Press.

Levi, M. 2003. "Organizing Power: The Prospects for an American Labor Movement." *Perspectives on Politics.* 1: 45-68.

Lichtenstein, N. 2002. *State of the Union: A Century of American Labor.* Princeton, NJ: Princeton University Press.

MacLean, N. 2005. *Freedom Is Not Enough: How the Fight for Jobs and Justice Changed Race and Gender in America, 1950-2000.* Harvard University Press.

Madigan, C. (ed.) 2004. Global Chicago. Champaign, IL: University of Illinois Press.

Mansbridge, J.J. and Morris, A. (eds.) 2001. *Oppositional Consciousness: The Subjective Roots of Social Protest.* Chicago, IL: University of Chicago Press.

Mantsios, G. (ed.) 1998. A New Labor Movement for the New Century. New York: Monthly Review Press.

McCall, L. 2001. *Complex Inequality: Gender, Race and Class in the New Economy.* New York: Routledge.

Milkman, R. and Voss, K. 2004. *Rebuilding Labor: Organizing and Organizers in the New Union Movement.* Ithaca, NY: Cornell University Press.

Morris, A. D. 1984. The Origins of the Civil Rights Movement. New York: Free Press.

Needleman, R. 2003. *Black Freedom Fighters In Steel: The Struggle for Democratic Unionism.* Ithaca, NY: Cornell University Press.

Pattillo-McCoy, M. 1999. *Black Picket Fences: Privilege and Peril Among the Black Middle Class.* Chicago, IL: University of Chicago Press.

Phillips, K. 2002. *Wealth and Democracy.* New York: Broadway Books.

Pierson, P. 1995. *Dismantling the Welfare State?: Reagan, Thatcher and the Politics of Retrenchment.* New York: Cambridge University Press.

Reed, A., Jr. 1999. *Stirrings in the Jug: Black Politics in the Post-Segregation Era.* Minneapolis, MN: University of Minnesota Press.

Reed, A., Jr. 2002. "Unraveling the Relation of Race and Class In American Politics." *Political Power and Social Theory.* V. 15, pp. 265-313.

Reskin, B. F. 2003. "Including Mechanisms in our Models of Ascriptive Inequality." *American Sociological Review,* 68, 1-21.

Rosswurm, S. 1992. *The CIO's Left-Led Unions.* Newark, NJ: Rutgers University Press.

Rustin, B. 1963/1971. "The Meaning of Birmingham." In *Beyond the Line: The Collected Writings of Bayard Rustin.* New York: Quadrangle Books.

Sassen, S. 1998. *Globalization and Its Discontents.* New York: The New Press.

Sassen, S. 2004. "A Global City." in Madigan, Charles. (ed.) 2004. *Global Chicago*. Champaign, IL: University of Illinois Press.

Sides, J. 2003. *L.A. City Limits: African-American Los Angeles From the Great Depression to the Present*. Berkeley, CA: University of California Press.

Skocpol, T. 1995. *Social Policy in the United States: Future Possibilities in Historical Perspective*. Princeton, NJ: Princeton University Press.

Skocpol, T. 2001. *The Missing Middle: Working Families and the Future of American Social Policy*. New York: W.W. Norton and Co.

Skrentny, J. D. 2002. *The Minority Rights Revolution*. Cambridge, MA: Harvard University Press.

Smith, B. (ed.) 2000. *Home Girls: A Black Feminist Anthology*. New Brunswick, NJ: Rutgers University Press.

Stein, J. 1998. *Running Steel, Running America: Race, Economic Policy and the Decline of Liberalism*. Chapel Hill, NC: University of North Carolina Press.

Strolovitch, D. Z. 2002. "Closer to a Pluralist Heaven?: Women's, Racial Minority, and Economic Justice Advocacy Groups and the Politics of Representation." *Dissertation, Yale University*.

Taylor, T. S. 2004. "Blacks Find Progress Slow in Joining Trade Unions." *Chicago Tribune*. August 1.

Teixeira, R. and J. Rogers. 2000. *America's Forgotten Majority: Why the White Working Class Still Matters*. New York: Basic Books.

Voss, K. and Sherman, R. 2000. "Breaking the Iron Law of Oligarchy: Union Revitalization in the American Labor Movement." *American Journal of Sociology*,106, 303-349.

Wallerstein, M. 1989. "Union Organization in Advanced Industrial Democracies." *American Political Science Review*, 83, 481-501.

Warren, D. T. 2005. "A New Labor Movement for a New Century?: The Incorporation of Marginalized Workers Into U.S. Unions." *Dissertation, Yale University*.

Wilson, J. Q. 1974. *Political Organizations*. Princeton, NJ: Princeton University Press.

Wilson, W. J. 1978. *The Declining Significance of Race: Blacks and Changing American Institutions*. Chicago, IL: University of Chicago Press.

Wilson, W.J. 1987. *The Truly Disadvantaged: The Inner City, the Underclass and Public Policy*. Chicago, IL: University of Chicago Press.

Wilson, W.J. 1996. *When Work Disappears: The World of the New Urban Poor*. New York: Vintage.

Wilson, W. J. 1999. *The Bridge Over the Racial Divide: Rising Inequality and Coalition Politics*. Berkeley, CA: University of California Press; New York: Russell/Sage Foundation.

Young, I. M. 1990. *Justice and the Politics of Difference*. Princeton, NJ: Princeton University Press.

Zietlin, M. and Weyher, F. 2001. "Black and White, Unite and Fight: Interracial Working-Class Solidarity and Racial Employment Equality." *American Journal of Sociology*. 107, 430-67.

Beyond the Myth of the White Middle-Class: Immigrant and Ethnic Minority Settlement in Suburban America

Lorrie A. Frasure[1]
Cornell University

Introduction

The suburbs of metropolitan areas are where most Americans live. Yet the social, economic, and political implications of immigrant and ethnic minority suburbanization remain severely marginalized in the political science discipline. Recent immigrant and ethnic minority suburbanization trends must be understood within the historical and social context of the racial exclusion and subsequent economic and place inequalities. Historically, government action and private sector power have been important influences in accelerating suburbanization (Danielson 1976; Drier, Mollenkopf, and Swanstrom 2001; Fishman 1987; Jackson 1985; Kleinberg 1995; Ross and Levine 200l; Williams 2003). The Federal Housing Administration (FHA), established by Congress in 1934, provided federal assistance to provide middle- and working-class families a means to buy suburban homes by providing loan insurance for up to 80 percent of the value of an approved property. By reducing the risk of making a home loan, banks were more willing to finance homes for millions of Americans—lowering down payment requirements and interest rates (Jackson 1985; Drier, Mollenkopf, and Swanstrom 2001; Williams 2003). The federal government also provided such assistance to millions of veterans returning home following World War II. Under the GI bill of 1944, the Veterans Administration was authorized to insure home mortgages to veterans.

The "helping hand" of these government interventionist policies helped to secure young, white, middle- and working-class families an opportunity to obtain suburban homes in flight from America's central cities, while retarding the growth of African American and largely non-European immigrant suburbanization. Such programs also gave little attention to the purchase of apartments or renovations of older housing in central cities (Jackson 1985; Drier, Mollenkopf, and Swanstrom 2001; Ross and Levine 2001). With the exodus of business- and the middle-class, many urban communities were deemed blighted and unfit for habitation and investment. These federal housing finance programs exacerbated the racial and economic imbalance between central cities and suburbs (Drier, Mollenkopf, and Swanstrom 2001).

However, following the 1960s race riots, and passage of landmark Civil Rights Act (1964) and Voting Rights Act (1965) legislation, the federal government faced new pressures to amend their pro-suburban bias, particularly in FHA and VA loan guarantees. The passage of the Fair Housing Act of 1968 and other programs such as the Community Reinvestment Act of 1977 have helped to relieve, but not eliminate, some of these constraints. These measures coupled with the Immigration and Nationality Act Amendments of 1965, helped to crack the closed-system of suburban life for existing immigrant and ethnic minority groups as well as newcomers.

As numerous scholars and commentators have pointed out, suburbs are also geographically where the tide of recent patterns of unprecedented immigration has settled. By 2000, 94 percent of immigrants lived in metropolitan areas. Of those residing in American metros, 48 percent lived in central cities and 52 percent lived in suburbs (Singer 2001). Like those immigrants and ethnic minorities who journeyed to urban enclaves for greater social and economic opportunities in the early Twentieth century, newer immigrant groups are often lead to suburbia seeking greater opportunities and privileges, historically and disproportionately enjoyed by white suburbanites.

Given the historical legacy of structural and institutional constraints on *minority* suburbanization, such groups have made spatial location decisions from a severely constrained set of choices. Unlike their predecessors, however, immigrant newcomers are *not* faced with the same institutional and structural barriers to suburban entry at the hand of government and private lenders. Suburbanization is an attainable dream for some newcomers to America because there is greater opportunity in the housing market for recent immigrants, than their predecessors. Such opportunities are even greater for minority groups with higher incomes and levels of educational attainment, such as Asians who are the most suburbanized minority group in the United States (Logan 2003).

In fact, newcomers to the U.S. are headed for the suburbs of metropolitan areas in unprecedented numbers.[2] Despite the conventional wisdom that suburbs are white and affluent, many suburban jurisdictions are facing extraordinary racial/ethnic heterogeneity and economic inequality. As Frey (2003) notes, "among the nation's 102 largest metropolitan areas, with populations exceeding half a million, minorities constituted more than a quarter (27.3) of the suburban populations in 2000, up from 19.3 percent in 1990" (155). According to the 2000 Census, 58 percent of Asians lived in suburbs, up from 53 percent in 1990. Latino suburbanization grew 3 percent from 46 percent in 1990 to 49 percent in 2000. However, while African American suburbanization increased by 5 percent, from 34 percent in 1990 to 39 percent in 2000, it remains significantly lower than both Asian and Latino suburbanization, and trails white suburbanization at 71 percent by thirty-two percentage points (Logan 2003).

Paradoxically, some suburbanization researchers have observed, "minority segregation and isolation has increased in suburbs during the 1990s as suburbs have become more diverse" (Logan 2003a, 238; also see Massey and Denton 1987, 1988, 1989, 1993; Massey and Eggers 1990 for evidence of continued suburban racial segregation).[3] Many recent immigrant and ethnic minority settlements have occurred in suburban "melting pot metro" areas. Demographer William Frey (2003) defines "melting pot metros" as metropolitan statistical areas where the non-Hispanic white percentage of population is less than their percentage of the total U.S. population (69.1 percent in 2000), and where at least two of the minority groups comprise a percentage larger than their total U.S. percentage of the population (18 percent in 2000).[4] Nationwide, thirty-five of the 102 metropolitan areas with populations exceeding 500,000 fit this geographic classification. Frey (2003) observes, "melting pot metro areas and the Hispanics locating within them are the major drivers of national minority suburbanization trends. The new suburban diversity patterns, particularly the fact that minorities are dominating suburban growth in more than half of the nations largest metropolitan areas, raises questions about 'race and space' in America's metropolitan areas" (174). Melting pot metros are found primarily in high immigration zones of the U.S. such as New York, Los Angeles, San Francisco, Miami, and Chicago. Concurrently, such areas also experienced the greatest share of non-Hispanic white out-migration (Frey 2003:160).

To date there is little empirical research concerning why some suburban areas—specifically "melting pot" metros—have become more diverse while other suburban metro areas remain homogenously white or dichotomously black/white in their demographic composition.[5] The demographic transformations of some suburban areas, particularly since 1980, provide fertile ground for the empirical examination of key sociological and political economy spatial location theories. While fewer scholars have examined suburbanization patterns between recent immigrant and ethnic minority groups, (but see Alba et al. 1999; Alba and Logan 1991; Frey 2003; Logan 2003) an interdisciplinary group of scholars have long examined the determinants of micro-level spatial location decision-making. Some of these sociological and political economy explanations are examined below.

Sociological and Political Economy Explanations of Spatial Location Choice

Sociological explanations for minority location decisions tend to underscore models of spatial assimilation and place-stratification. Spatial assimilation theory suggests that a rise in income and educational attainment for immigrant and ethnic minority groups increases their propensity to exit urban ethnic enclaves for (ideally) more heterogeneous suburban neighborhoods. Thus, after having achieved some socioeconomic success, the model predicts that immigrant and ethnic minorities move to suburbia seeking greater resources, goods and services long enjoyed (disproportionately) by white suburbanites (Alba et al. 1999; Alba and Logan 1991; Frey and Speare 1988; Jackson 1985; Massey 1985; Massey and Denton 1988). According to this model, immigrant groups typically spend a generation or more in central city enclaves, with the expectation that second or third generation descendants would subsequently spread outwards to suburban jurisdictions.

However, the emergence of suburban "melting pot metro" areas may undermine the applicability of these sociological expectations regarding immigrant theories of spatial assimilation. As Alba and colleagues (1999) contend, "recent immigrants seem much more inclined to settle outside of urban enclaves than were immigrants in previous eras, whose experience is recorded in the spatial assimilation model" (458). They further note, "the pattern of rapid or immediate suburban entry, combined with the large concentration of recent immigrants in a few metropolitan areas, raises the question of whether suburbanization holds the same meaning for recent immigrants that it held for previous groups" (446). Thus, unlike the distinct cues of the "American dream"—individualism, upward mobility, and prosperity, inherent in post-WWII suburban mobility patterns, migration to those loosely defined non-rural areas outside the central city—"suburbia"—may reveal little about "upward mobility," or "greater opportunity" for recent immigrant and ethnic minority migrants. In fact, the recent phenomenon of immigrant groups forgoing the traditional ethnic succession course, facilitated by passage through the urban core undermines the individual-level processes inherent in spatial assimilation theory. These processes include achieving socioeconomic mobility and capital for "purchase of entry" into suburbia (Alba et al. 1999).

Moreover, the experiences of some racial/ethnic groups have long challenged the spatial assimilation model. For African Americans, place-stratification models work better toward explaining their spatial location patterns (Massey 1985; Massey and Denton 1993). Advocates of the place-stratification model find that structural and institutional discriminatory practices restrain opportunities for mobility for groups with distinct African ancestry phenotype such as blacks,

Dominicans, and Puerto Ricans (Logan and Alba 1993; Logan and Molotch 1987) and these restrictions impact their residential choices in spite of increases in income and educational attainment. In *American Apartheid* (1993), Massey and Denton contend that middle-class blacks are still more likely to live near poor blacks than middle-class whites are to live near poor whites. The vast majority of African Americans continue to live in highly segregated communities, even in suburbia. Yet, other communities of color, in particular Asian Americans and to some extent Latinos, are somewhat more likely to live in ethnically and racially diverse neighborhoods.

While sociologists often look to spatial assimilation and place-stratification theories to explain spatial location decisions, some political economist examine macroeconomic determinants such as local tax and service packages to deduce microeconomic motivations for location choices. Residential mobility is especially important to political economist interested in the efficiency of local municipal government, particularly the provision of local public goods and services. Though often examined to a lesser extent regarding explanations of *minority* spatial location decisions, at least a brief theoretical discussion of economic sorting models also referred to as "exit option" models of spatial location is warranted in any discussion of immigrant and ethnic minority settlement in suburban jurisdictions. This is particularly important since such theoretical models are commonly celebrated on efficiency grounds in lieu of racial, economic, and distributive justice concerns.

Economic sorting models predict that individuals will move to the communities that hold tax and expenditure policies that match their preferences (Hirschman 1970; Peterson 1981; Schneider 1989; Tiebout 1956) with little, if any, attention to racial tastes or constraints. For example, variants of the Tiebout (1956) hypothesis remains particularly interesting to an interdisciplinary group of scholars concerned with how spatial sorting models explain mobility patterns. As the original Tiebout hypothesis contends:

> The consumer-voter may be viewed as picking that community which best satisfies his preference pattern for public goods. At the central level the preferences of the consumer-voter are given and, the government tries to adjust to the pattern of those preferences, whereas at the local level various governments have their revenue and expenditure more or less fixed. Given these revenue and expenditure patterns, the consumer-voter moves to that community whose local government best satisfies his set of preferences (418).

Accordingly, individuals' location decisions convey some information about their preferences and this helps to overcome the "free-rider" problem, ideally resulting in a more efficient provision of goods and services at the local level (Conley and Wooders 1997: 421).

Closer examination of the *original* Tiebout hypothesis finds these limited notions problematic for the study of minority suburbanization. Gary Miller (1981) observes that while Tiebout model allows for individual revelation of demand (i.e. preferences), the model fails to introduce an analogous pricing mechanism that will, in practice, *ration* public goods (such as local public education) efficiently. Bruce Hamilton (1975) finds that the Tiebout model does not guarantee efficiency by itself but the extra element of *income stratification* drives such efficiency. To be clear, unlike the expectations of the Tiebout hypothesis, in practice efficiency gains accrue through a pricing mechanism based on property taxation, government-backed exclusionary zoning practices, and separation of income classes.

Economic sorting models can result in creating and maintaining economically homogenous suburban neighborhoods resulting in the negative by-products of sorting—residential, income, and, subsequently, racial segregation. In his pivotal contribution to the debate, Miller (1981) contents, "Because, the distribution of consumers is linked with the distribution of resources, low-income cities have also been low resources cities; the sorting out of metropolitan population by income class has been detrimental to low-income individuals" (182). In short, the poorest can only live in an area with the weakest property tax requirement. Consequently as Miller (1981) further explains, "while fragmentation may promote multiple, responsive, small-scale demand-revealing mechanisms for homogenous neighborhoods, it may also result in increases in income and economic segregation. And if income and racial segregation are empirically associated with either the concentration of resource-draining problems like crime, then fragmentation may actually work against the welfare of individuals in the low-income and minority jurisdictions, contrary to the original Tiebout expectation" (182).

Thus, the *practice* of sorting models proved to overcome "preference revelation" concerns only with great partiality and bias toward the upper income. Since income dynamics are inextricably linked to racial/ethnic dynamics, the "exit option" may be less viable for lower-income groups who are also disproportionately among immigrant and ethnic minority populations. When the "exit option" *is* undertaken, some have the means to relocate to better suburban areas, while for others suburban migration may leave them worst off, given sharp distinctions in terms of tax bases and the quality of public services. Moreover as Charles (2003) points out, "minority suburbs, although better off than poor minority neighborhoods tend to be less affluent, have poorer quality public services and schools, and experience more crime and social disorganization compared to the suburbs that comparable whites reside in" (also see Alba et al. 1994; Logan et al. 2002).

Suburbia is an area in which the less affluent are often separated from the more affluent. While historically the "burbs" were fashioned to accept only a select group of individuals into the "club," the emergence of suburban "melting pot metros" raise important questions concerning how political economy sorting models will fair in light of recent immigrant and ethnic minority suburbanization trends.

To begin to fill these gaps in the literature, and to help bring the concerns of immigrant and ethnic minority suburbanites from marginalization to the fore, we must first examine why some immigrant and ethnic minority groups sort themselves into certain types of suburban areas. Although this research does not directly borrow from the groundbreaking work of Cathy Cohen's (1999) framework on marginalization, in which this volume was inspired, it does speak to her broad concern for racial marginalization. This is particularly true for groups who, by choice, chance, or constraint, reside in multi-ethnic suburban areas and the implications of these spatial location decisions.

Until recently, researchers were left to make indirect inferences regarding individual groups' spatial location decisions. However, in 1998, the Current Population Survey Annual March Supplement added a "main reason for moving" question to the survey's section on migration, thus reducing the need to make indirect inferences about micro-level migration decisions. In the multivariate analysis to follow, I use logit regression analysis to examine the impact of these migration related measures along with some features of the spatial assimilation/social mobility theory, and family/household composition factors. I also control for some metropolitan contextual variables on the propensity of suburban melting pot metro settlement (SMPM). I test this model among recent non-Hispanic white, non-Hispanic black non-Hispanic Asian, and Latino (including Mexicans, Central/South Americans, and Puerto Ricans) migrants residing in thirty-three U.S. suburban melting pot metro areas. The next section describes the data and methods used to test the model of suburban melting pot metro (SMPM) settlement, followed by the results and a discussion of the findings.

Data and Methods

The empirical analysis of immigrant and ethnic minority populations raises important challenges for researchers. Several questions must be ascertained when attempting to develop empirical models related to immigrant and ethnic minority groups based on the secondary analysis of survey data. For immigrant groups, migration-related variables such as place of birth, year of entry into the U.S., parents' place of birth and citizenship status are imperative. It is also important to employ a dataset with significant numbers of immigrant sub-populations to allow for disaggregated immigrant and racial/ethnic group comparisons.

This study relies on pooled data from the U.S. Census Bureau's Current Population Survey (CPS Annual March Supplement) from 2000-2004.[6] The data consists of a representative probability sample of the U.S. non-institutionalized population. The March CPS public use micro-data file provides a treasure trove of information on socio-economic and demographic characteristics such as income, poverty, education, age, sex, race, Latino origin, household composition, and migration.[7] The full national sample consists of coverage in about 790 sample areas comprising over 2,000 counties and independent cities with coverage in every state and the District of Columbia. This allows for the individual-level statistical estimation for the entire country, at the state level, or at the Metropolitan Statistical Areas level. Moreover, the CPS March supplement is ideal for conducting a cross-sectional analysis of spatial location patterns among recent immigrants and racial/ethnic migrants to U.S. suburban melting pot metro areas, as recent as one year ago. This empirical analysis provides an informative "snapshot" into the life of recent international and domestic migrants who relocated one year ago. This analysis will focus on the estimation of separate models of non-Hispanic whites, non-Hispanic blacks, non-Hispanic Asians as well as Latinos including three subgroups (Mexicans, Central/South Americans, and Puerto Ricans).

The CPS March supplement pooled dataset (2000-2004) used in this study consisted of several hundred thousand cases. However, given the immense specificity necessary to develop a model of suburban settlement in "melting pot metro" areas (based on William Frey's geographic typology) between various immigrant and ethnic minority groups, the CPS pooled dataset was truncated in several ways to allow for a cross-sectional comparison of spatial location patterns across several suburban melting pot metros. I created a dummy variable for SMPM Settlement (SMPM=1, 0=other).[8] The truncated final sample includes thirty-three SMPM areas. There are fifty-seven "other=0" suburban metropolitan statistical areas included in the sample.[9] I also dropped all non-movers as well as central city and rural cases from the sample. The percentages and metropolitan statistical area FIPS codes for the thirty-three Suburban "Melting Pot Metros" included in this study are listed in Table 1.

The individual level unit of analysis in this study is adult householders (assuming they facilitate migration decisions) of prime mobility and full-time employment age (twenty-five to sixty-four). Movers are defined as respondents who were living in a different house or apartment one year prior to the year surveyed (Schachter 2001). To differentiate among various racial and ethnic groups, I created filters or qualifiers for each model using dummy variables for non-Hispanic whites, non-Hispanic blacks, non-Hispanic Asians, and Latinos. I also created dummy variables for Mexican, Central/South American, and Puerto Rican national origin groups.[10] Following the previous work of Frey (2001, 2003), this analysis does not include multiracial-categories and all whites, blacks, and Asians are of non-Hispanic descent.

I focus on several plausible determinants of migration to examine the impact of both economic and non-economic factors on suburban melting pot metro (SMPM) settlement, among various immigrant and ethnic minority groups. The independent measures include those relevant to residential location including housing-, family-, and employment- migration-related reasons, some features of spatial assimilation, family/household composition, period of immigration, and some metropolitan contextual variables. Historically, the availability of national data on individual level reasons for moving has been limited. As previously noted, in 1998 the Current Population Survey added a question on main reason for moving. In this study, to operational-

Table 1
List of 33 Suburban "Melting Pot Metros," * Metro Areas with Populations Over 500,000**
(in Percentages, by MSA/PSMA FIPS Code)

	Percentages	MSA/PMSA FIPS Code
Los Angeles-Long Beach, CA	10.74	4480
Chicago, IL	11.11	1600
Washington, DC, MD, VA	7.58	8840
Las Vegas, NV-AZ	9.32	4120
Newark, NJ	3.92	5640
Miami, FL	3.03	5000
Honolulu, HI	3.47	3320
Riverside-San Bernardino	4.11	6780
Dallas, TX	4.90	1920
Houston, TX	4.55	3360
Orlando, FL	4.53	5960
Fort Lauderdale, FL	4.63	2680
Bergen-Passaic, NJ	1.63	0875
New York, NY	1.93	5600
Orange County, CA	2.68	5945
Phoenix-Mesa, AZ	2.87	6200
Middlesex-Somerset-Hunterdon, NJ	1.95	5015
Oakland, CA	2.37	5775
San Diego, CA	2.18	7320
Sacramento, CA	2.11	6920
Albuquerque, NM	0.95	0200
San Francisco, CA	1.45	7360
Fort Worth-Arlington, TX	1.29	2800
Austin-San Marcos, TX	0.89	0640
Bakersfield, CA	0.61	0680
Tuscan, AZ	1.50	8520
San Antonio, TX	0.63	7240
San Jose, CA	0.92	7400
Fresno, CA	0.82	2840
Jersey City, NJ	0.34	3640
McAllen-Edinburg-Mission, TX	0.37	4880
Stockton, Lodi, CA	0.34	8120
Vallejo-Fairfield-Napa, CA	0.29	8720
Total Suburb MPM		3,799
Total Suburb Non-MPM		5,923
Total Suburb Sample (MPM and Non-MPM)		9,722

Source: Current Population Survey (CPS) Annual March Supplement 2000-2004

"Melting pot metros" are areas where non-Hispanic whites comprise no more than 69 percent of the 2000 population (the percentage of non-Hispanic whites nation-wide) and where the combined populations of all other racial/ethnic groups exceed 18 percent of the population (the sum of these groups nationwide is 18 percent of the population) (Frey 2001, 2003).

*El Paso, TX (MSA) and Ventura, CA (PMSA) were listed in the March CPS as "non-identifiable" regarding the number central city versus non-central city cases, and thus were not included in this analysis. **All areas except McAllen, TX, Stockton, Lodi, CA and Vallejo, CA hold populations greater than 500,000. These three contain populations between 250,000 and 500,000 and are included in the model to remain consistent with Frey's (2001, 2003) typology.

ize the "reasons for migrating" variables, I used the responses to the CPS question "What was your main reason for moving in the previous year?" I used the pre-established groupings, which include "housing-related," "employment-related," "family-related," and "other" reasons to create separate migration-related dummy variables (ex. housing related=1, 0=otherwise). In this study "other" reasons will serve as the reference group (see footnote 10 for full list of categories per grouping).[11] Only one reason is reported per mover.

Recent Census Bureau reports of the findings from the addition of these migration related groups of measures do not examine disaggregated models by immigrant group (Schachter 2001a, 2001b). Yet, the rapidly changing demographics in the U.S. lend support to the need to examine disaggregated racial and ethnic models of suburban settlement. I expect to find the significance of these migration related variables on settlement in SMPMs would vary by immigrant and ethnic minority group.

The features of spatial assimilation remain important in examining spatial location patterns for immigrant and ethnic minority groups. Immigrant groups enter the U.S. with different levels of socio-economic status. Thus, income (and educational attainment) factors will shape opportunities and constraints facing suburban settlement. Alba and Logan (1991) find that socioeconomic variables like income and education are more likely determinants of suburbanization for some minority groups than for the majority groups (434). Recent findings using 2000 Census data reports both native and immigrant Asians have substantially higher incomes and lower poverty levels than both blacks and Latinos. Latino immigrants have lower levels of education than natives while the differences in income and poverty rates are less substantial (see Logan 2003a). To test the variability of these measures in this multivariate model, I include standard measures to account for income (in 10,000s) and educational levels (from one to twenty-two years) of recent household migrants. Education is often viewed as a spatial assimilation measure of "cultural adaptation." It is generally believed that rises in education deter the likelihood of ethnic or multi-ethnic neighborhood settlement (Logan, Zhang and Alba, 307: 2002). Therefore, it is predicted that as educational attainment rises, minority groups may be less inclined to settle in a "melting pot metro" area.

I am also particularly interested in how low-income status impact individuals' propensity to move to a SMPM. Thus, I also create a dummy variable for individuals below the poverty level. Notably, a 2001 CPS report examining these migration related variables finds that lower income groups are more likely to move for family reasons and less likely to move for work-related reasons than higher income groups. Moreover, this report concludes that "work-related reasons were not as important for movement of the poor as economic theory suggests, with house-related reasons taking precedence for this group, and family reasons being more important for the poor than the non-poor" (Schachter 2001: 9). To further examine *how* the relationship between the aforementioned migration-related variables and SMPM settlement is modified by low-income status for immigrant and racial/ethnic group, I included an interaction term for "below the poverty level" and each of dichotomous migration related variable. I expect the interaction between low income and the migration related measures would modify the effects of these measures on SMPM settlement. The effect of low-income status will increase the propensity of these migration related variables on SMPM settlement for some groups, controlling for all other factors.

In order to examine the relationship between some family and household variables on suburban settlement between immigrant and ethnic minority groups, I created dummy variables to examine the marital status of the householder, whether the householder has school age children, and whether the householder is a homeowner. Moreover, I also controlled for the age of the householder.

I also examine the impact of immigration period on the propensity to settle in suburban melting pot metro areas. Numerous studies have noted that immigrants grow increasingly similar to the native-born population with length of residence in the U.S. (Capps et al. 2003). In order to examine whether maturated (pre-1980s) immigrants, who having achieved some economic prosperity are more likely to move to suburban melting pot metros, I control for the pre-1980s wave of immigrants (pre-1980=1, 0=otherwise). Given the influx if immigrants since the 1980s and their reported boom in SMPMs, I also include separate dummy variables for immigrants who entered the U.S. from 1980-1989 and for those who entered the country from 1990-present. I seek to take account of possible changes in the effects between these two heavy immigration decades, between the groups studied. U.S.-born serves as the reference category for the immigration period measures (Alba et al. 1999).

Additionally, I included regional controls including a set of dummy variables for the four main regions (with "south" as the reference category). In this analysis, these geographic contextual variables will not play a role in the interpretation and are therefore not include in the tables, but they are included in the logit regression models to account for varying distributions of the groups across metro areas (see Alba et al. 1999 for a similar method).[12] Finally, I also included controls for survey year (2000-2004).

A Closer View of SMPM Settlers: Some Key Characteristics

Prior to exploring the logit regression results, I provide a closer look at recent racial and ethnic suburbanization in melting pot metros. Table 2 reports some relevant summary statistics of SMPM settlement, by non-Hispanic whites, blacks, Asians, and Latinos using data from the Current Population Survey (Annual March Supplement) micro-data file 2000-2004. These findings reveal some interesting variations regarding immigrant and ethnic minority groups' settlement in SMPMs.

According to Table 2, on average, Latinos who moved to SMPM areas in the previous survey year are more likely to have self-reported migrating for housing-related reasons while Asians are the least likely. On the other hand Asians and non-Hispanic whites are slightly more likely, on average, to have reported a move to a SMPM for employment-related reasons, while Latinos are the least likely. While there is not much variation among recent migrants concerning the influence of family-related reasons on their migration decisions, on average, whites were the least likely to report family-related reasons than any other group.

Not surprisingly, the greatest variation among recent migrants to SMPMs can be found in their spatial assimilation summary statistics. Asians residing in suburban MPMs have the highest mean income, and are more likely to have attended at least one year of college. They are also more likely to be employed in upper white-collar jobs (where upper white collar refers to professional, technical, managerial, and executive occupations), and are the least likely to be unemployed. On average, Latinos in the sample hold the lowest levels of mean income and are the least likely to be affluent (defined as holding annual family income greater than $50,000). Latinos on average are the least likely to have attended at least one year of college and are the most likely to maintain households with an income below the poverty level.

Regarding some family and household characteristics, Asians and whites in SMPMs are more likely, on average, to be homeowners than blacks and Latinos. Asians are also more likely on average to be married, while blacks are the least likely. Black households, on average, are more likely to be headed by a female than the other racial/ethnic groups. While the average ages of SMPM householders do not vary much, Latinos householders on average are slightly younger than the other racial and ethnic groups.

These average scores also emphasize the reported boom in the Asian and Latino population in the post-1980s. On average, the Asian and Latino settlement in SMPMs rose significantly in the 1980s and increased dramatically in the 1990s. Notably, there were also significant increases

Table 2
Suburban Melting Pot Metro Summary Statistics, by Race/Ethnicity of Householder*

	White	Black	Latino	Asian
All Suburbs	7893	1080	1359	603
(SMPM Only)	2855	516	905	365
Housing-Related	.54	.56	.58	.47
	(.49)	.49)	(.49)	(.49)
Family-Related	.19	.21	.23	.22
	(.39)	(.41)	(.42)	(.42)
Work-Related	.21	.17	.14	.25
	(.41)	(.38)	(.35)	(.43)
College	.66	.61	.42	.81
	(.47)	(.48)	(.49)	(.38)
Age	39.64	38.45	36.90	37.58
	(10.13)	(9.11)	(8.99)	(9.39)
White-collar	.54	.48	.36	.61
	(.49)	(.50)	(.48)	(.48)
Unemployed	.21	.24	.22	.19
	(.41)	(.42)	(.41)	(.39)
Income	6.15	5.13	4.72	6.43
	(3.34)	(3.11)	(2.94)	(3.43)
Affluent	.45	.32	.23	.49
	(.49)	(.47)	(.42)	(.50)
Below poverty	.10	.16	.18	.12
	(.30)	(.36)	(.39)	(.33)
Owner	.46	.31	.34	.42
	(.49)	(.46)	(.47)	(.49)
School age	.36	.42	.50	.35
	(.48)	(.49)	(.50)	(.47)
Married	.59	.39	.65	.72
	(.49)	(.48)	(.47)	(.44)
Female	.46	.58	.45	.38
	(.49)	(.49)	(.49)	(.48)
Pre-1980	.06	.06	.15	.17
	(.23)	(.24)	(.36)	(.38)
Post-1980	.17	.15	.47	.65
	(.38)	(.36)	(.49)	(.47)
Northeast	.07	.12	.06	.10
	(.26)	(.33)	(.24)	(.30)
Midwest	.10	.09	.05	.07
	(.30)	(.29)	(.23)	(.25)
West	.46	.25	.49	.58
	(.49)	(.43)	(.50)	(.49)
South	.35	.51	.37	.23
	(.47)	(.50)	(.48)	(.42)

Source: Current Population Survey March Supplement 2000-2004

Notes: Table entries represent the means with standard deviations in parentheses

a. Sample Population reflects adult head of household in MPM. All data is weighted to reflect 2000 Census. The March supplement (marsupwt) weight was normalized to avoid the potential problem of weights changing in magnitude between years.

in the white and black immigrant populations in SMPM areas in the post-1990s. Finally, the summary statistics also underscore some longstanding racial/ethnic regional variations. On average, southern and northeastern blacks were more likely to reside in suburban MPMs, while Asians in the West were more like to reside in SMPMs, followed by Latinos.

Logit Regression Results for Latinos and Non-Hispanic Whites, Blacks, Asians

In this study, I used the Current Population Survey Annual March Supplement (2000-2004) to carry out a multivariate logit regression analysis to access the impact of housing-, family-, and employment-related measures; socioeconomic status; family and household characteristics; immigration period; and metropolitan contextual variables have on recent suburban melting pot metro settlement. In Table 3, I evaluate the determinants of SMPM settlement among recent white, black, Asian, and Latino migrants. In Table 4, to better evaluate the differences between Latino national origin groups, I compare the impact of these measures across some select groups.

In logit regression analysis, the clear-cut interpretation of the coefficients, are more difficult to navigate than OLS regression estimates. Therefore, for each logit model, I calculate the conditional effects on suburban melting pot metro settlement for each independent measure having statistically significant results. In the tables below, Column I represents estimates for the logit regression coefficients with standard errors in parentheses. Column II represents the conditional effects of each statistically significant variable.[13]

Table 3 details the multivariate regression model for non-Hispanic white, non-Hispanic black, non-Hispanic Asian, and Latino groups. When each group is examined independently we see that some variables become more salient than others in predicting the likelihood of the dependent variable, SMPM settlement. First, we examine the "reason for moving" measures. Each migration related measure is positively associated with SMPM settlement for each group in the model. However, the housing-related variable is only significant for whites and Latinos in the sample. On the other hand, the family-related measure is only significantly related to SMPM settlement for Latinos and Asians. The conditional effects reveal that non-Hispanic whites were 6.3 percent more likely and Latinos were 16.5 percent more likely to report a housing related reason for their recent move. Notably, while the work-related measure failed to reach statistical significance for any of the groups, the interaction effect of "work-related" reasons and "low-income" status on SMPM settlement were significant and positive for Asians. For Asians we must proceed with caution in examining the impact of work-related reasons on SMPM settlement prior to accounting the effects of poverty for this group. The introduction of the interaction term modifies the relationship between work and SMPM settlement, whereas low-income Asians are 12 percent more likely to settle in SMPMs for a work-related reasons, than an Asian whose income is above the poverty level.

The family-related measure was positive and significantly correlated to SMPM settlement for Latinos and Asians, whereas Latinos were 18 percent and Asians were 25 percent more likely to report a family-related reason for their recent move to a SMPM. Yet, the model failed to reach statistical significance for both whites and blacks, and there were no statistically significant interaction effects between family reasons and low-income status for any of the subgroups.

Income was included in the model as a measure of spatial assimilation. It was positively associated with SMPM settlement for each group and statistically significant for each group except Latinos. Among recent white, black, and Asian migrants to SMPMs, the model predicts as black income rises, the propensity of blacks to move to SMPM areas is slightly greater than Asians and much greater than whites in the sample. *Traditional* assimilation theory does not appear to explain the impact of social mobility measures such as income upon the likelihood

Table 3
Logit Analysis of Suburban Settlement in "Melting Pot Metros" for Select Independent Variables[a], Select Racial/Ethnic Groups, with Cond. Effects

Independent Variables	White I Coeff./SE	White II Con. Eff.	Latino I Coeff./SE	Latino II Con. Eff.	Black I Coeff./SE	Black II Con. Eff.	Asian I Coeff./SE	Asian II Con. Eff.
Reason for Migrating								
Housing-Related	0.268* (0.142)	6.3	0.838** (0.365)	16.5	0.504 (0.358)	--	0.488 (0.457)	--
Family-Related	0.131 (0.149)	--	1.142*** (0.390)	18.3	0.558 (0.374)	--	1.520*** (0.533)	25.1
Work-Related	0.072 (0.148)	--	0.288 (0.384)	--	0.479 (0.385)	--	0.058 (0.466)	--
SES								
Education	0.007 (0.010)	--	0.026 (0.019)	--	-0.052* (0.031)	-5.3	-0.007 (0.034)	--
Income	0.095*** (0.011)	15.7	0.041 (0.030)	--	0.171*** (0.034)	21.0	0.119*** (0.041)	19.6
Below poverty	0.544* (0.323)	13.1	0.654 (0.668)	--	0.373 (0.704)	--	0.311 (1.105)	--
Interactions								
Below*house	-0.100 (0.345)	--	-0.466 (0.701)	--	0.169 (0.738)	--	0.055 (1.218)	--
Below*family	-0.228 (0.366)	--	-1.110 (0.744)	--	-0.057 (0.813)	--	-0.112 (1.307)	--
Below*work	-0.355 (0.383)	--	-0.614 (0.744)	--	-0.016 (0.849)	--	2.779* (1.528)	12.0
Fam/Household Status								
Married	-0.215*** (0.064)	-5.1	0.040 (0.155)	--	-0.200 (0.170)	--	-0.127 (0.267)	--
School age	-0.019 (0.056)	--	-0.120 (0.136)	--	-0.094 (0.145)	--	-0.067 (0.237)	--
Female	0.194*** (0.054)	4.5	0.063 (0.137)	--	-0.078 (0.151)	--	-0.060 (0.220)	--
Age	0.008*** (0.003)	0.7	0.009 (0.008)	--	0.012 (0.008)	--	0.002 (0.012)	--
Owner	-0.222*** (0.060)	-5.3	-0.403*** (0.153)	-8.0	-0.104 (0.170)	--	-0.354 (0.254)	--
Immigration Period (U.S-born)								
Pre-1980	0.937*** (0.129)	24.5	0.218 (0.214)	--	1.885*** (0.481)	26.1	0.207 (0.405)	--
During 1980s	1.234*** (0.144)	29.7	0.242 (0.193)	--	0.451 (0.292)	--	0.344 (0.363)	--
1990-present	1.133*** (0.100)	27.5	-0.167 (0.166)	--	1.407*** (0.279)	31.4	-0.077 (0.319)	--

Table 3 (continued)

Constant	-1.617***	-0.264	-1.381**	-1.096
	(0.229)	(0.575)	(0.633)	(0.917)
Observations	7893	1359	1080	603
Log Likelihood	-4478.389	-750.417	-652.915	-304.831
PseudoR2	0.153	0.073	0.126	0.229

Source: Current Population Survey Annual March Supplement Micro-data File 2000-2004.

Notes: a. All models contain contextual measures including region and year of survey controls, whose coefficients are available upon request.

b. Column I represents estimates for logit regression coefficients. Standard errors are in parentheses.

c. Column II represents the conditional effects or the differences between the top 20th percentile and lower 20th percentile for each continuous explanatory variable (unless otherwise specified) and the differences between the minimum and maximum values for each dichotomous explanatory variable, when other variables are held constant at their mean.

Dashes (--) indicate that the variables were not statistically significant. A slash (\) indicates that the variable was not included in model for the national origin group.

* significant at 10 percent; ** significant at 5 percent; *** significant at 1 percent

of black suburbanization (Massey and Denton 1993, Massey 1995); instead place stratification models provide more explanatory power. Recall that the spatial assimilation model emphasizes group differences in SES, while place stratification models account for persistent prejudice and/or discrimination as determinants of spatial location for some groups such as blacks. Yet, this finding is far from an anomaly and actually fairs nicely with the central tenets of both assimilation and place-stratification theories. By definition, SMPMs are stratified multi-ethnic neighborhoods. However, in such areas, blacks are still likely to be racially separated from whites. Given the historical legacy of racism and discriminatory practices excluding blacks from some neighborhoods (coupled with their current preferences based on such exclusion), we would expect that as economic prosperity increases some blacks remain more likely to sort themselves into SMPM areas, controlling for all other factors. Interestingly, while education had no statistically significant effect on SMPM settlement for whites, Latinos, or Asians, it was negative and statistically significant for blacks. For blacks, unlike a rise in income the model predicts that as educational attainment increases blacks are more likely to opt for residence outside of the melting pot.

Next, Table 3 reveals variations in the impact of family/household status measures between each racial/ethnic group. The family/household status findings corroborate much of the findings from Alba et al. (1999) and similarly these finding also yield quite modest results. A white married couple was 5 percent less likely to move to a suburban melting pot metro area than a white non-married couple, while marital status had no statistically significant effect on SMPM settlement for the other groups. Homeownership was negatively related to settlement in SMPM areas for each group. However, it was only statistically significant for whites and Latinos. Latino homeowners were 8 percent less likely to settle in suburban melting pot metros than Latino non-homeowners, while white homeowners were 5 percent less likely than white non-homeowners.

Finally, unlike expected, the period of immigration factors had no significant effect on the propensity of Latinos or Asians to settle in SMPMs. However, immigration period was a positive predictor of SMPM settlement for black immigrants in each period. Yet, this measure only proved statistically significant for pre-1980 and post-1990 immigrants. Blacks who immigrated before 1980 were 26 percent more likely to reside in SMPMs, relative to their native counterparts during the same immigration period. The conditional effects of immigration period on SMPM settlement for black immigrants arose to 31 percent in the 1990s. Prior to a discussion of these findings, the next section presents the results logit regression analysis for some disaggregated Hispanic national origin groups.

Logit Regression Results for Some Hispanic National Origin Groups

By the year 2000, Mexicans comprised nearly two-thirds (65 percent) of Latinos in the United States while Puerto Ricans, the second largest Latino group in the United States, made up 10 percent of the Latino population. Yet, as Logan (2001) notes, there was a substantial increase in the presence of Central and South Americans to the U.S. in during the 1990s (from 3.0 in 1990 to 6.1 million in 2000), referring to the most recent arrivals as the "New Latinos" (Logan 2001: 1). Numerous studies have examined Latino assimilation and incorporation (particularly related to their civic/political incorporation, or lack of, in the American political process) for groups residing in urban areas (de la Garza et al. 1992; de la Garza and DeSipio 1999; DeSipio 1996; Jones-Correa 1998, 2001; Mollenkopf and Gertsle 2001; Sonenshein 1989; Waldinger 1999, 2001). However, fewer studies have examined factors related to Latino suburbanization (but for some exceptions see Alba et al. 1999; Logan 2001, 2003; Iceland 2004; Frey 2001, 2003; and for local studies Jones-Correa 2003, 2004; Frasure and Jones-Correa 2005).

Table 4 examines three Latino subgroups: Mexican, Central/South American, and Puerto Rican. With one exception, the model predicts that each migration related factor is positively associated with SMPM settlement. For Mexicans the work related measure is negatively related to SMPM settlement and none of the migration related measures reached statistical significance for this national origin group.

The model predicts that Central/South Americans are 26 percent more likely to cite family-related reasons for their move to a SMPM. On the other hand, while there is no statistically significant effect of housing-related reasons, there is an interaction effect present between both the family and housing predictors and low-income status. Without the inclusion of the interaction term, we would have missed the impact of housing-related factors on the location decisions of low-income Central/South Americans. Low-income Central/South American suburbanites are about 2 percent more likely to have moved to a MPM area for housing-related reasons than their counterparts above the poverty line. They are 19 percent more likely to sort themselves into SMPMs for family related reasons than those above the poverty line.

Puerto Ricans were 41 percent more likely to have located to a SMPM for housing-related reasons and 33 percent more likely to have located to a SMPM for family-related reasons. However, the location decisions of Puerto Ricans were not affected by low-income status. Traditionally, along with blacks, place-stratification theories have been more useful in explaining the settlement patterns of Puerto Ricans. Massey and Denton (1993) argue that groups of distinct African phenotype are often similarly disadvantaged with regard to their spatial location choices. As Sacks (2003) points out "of all long-term Latino groups in the U.S., Puerto Ricans have been more economically disadvantaged that any other major Latino group" (Sacks, 2003: 11). In *Between Two Nations,* Jones-Correa (1998) examines the assimilation of Latino immigrants noting, "for many immigrants the value of the company of their ethnic compatriots more than outweighs the prejudice they may suffer for choosing to live in mixed-race neighborhood (122)." These factors may help to account for the robustness of the Puerto Rican model.

Recall that in the Latino full sample the family/household status measures offered little

Table 4
Logit Analysis of Suburban Settlement in "Melting Pot Metros" for Select Independent Variables[a], Select Latino National Origin Groups, with Cond. Effects

Independent Variables	Latino (All)		Mexican		Central/ South		Puerto Rican	
	I	II	I	II	I	II	I	II
	Coeff./ SE	Con. Eff.	Coeff./ SE	Con. Eff.	Coeff./ SE	Con. Eff.	Coeff./ SE	Con. Eff.
Reason for Migrating (other)								
Housing-Related	0.838**	16.5	0.166	--	0.941	--	2.018*	41.2
	(0.365)		(0.776)		(0.637)		(1.136)	
Family-Related	1.142***	18.3	0.288	--	1.572**	26.3	2.165*	32.5
	(0.390)		(0.800)		(0.753)		(1.158)	
Work-Related	0.288	--	-0.356	--	0.277	--	0.739	--
	(0.384)		(0.795)		(0.705)		(1.135)	
SES								
Education	0.026	--	0.074**	3.0	0.001	--	0.032	--
	(0.019)		(0.029)		(0.042)		(0.103)	
Income	0.041	--	0.028	--	0.069	--	0.143	--
	(0.030)		(0.048)		(0.070)		(0.120)	
Below poverty	0.654	--	-0.203	--	-17.530***	-45.2	-0.537	--
	(0.668)		(1.362)		(1.282)		(1.811)	
Interactions								
Below*house	-0.466	--	0.615	--	17.218***	1.5	0.878	--
	(0.701)		(1.381)		(1.426)		(2.148)	
Below*family	-1.110	--	0.893	--	15.383***	11.8	0.626	--
	(0.744)		(1.463)		(1.452)		(2.248)	
Below*work	-0.614	--	0.252	--	\	\	2.960	--
	(0.744)		(1.415)				(2.564)	
Fam/Household Status								
Married	0.040	--	0.004	--	-1.160***	-22.0	1.332**	29.1
	(0.155)		(0.226)		(0.414)		(0.579)	
School age	-0.120	--	-0.271	--	0.217	--	0.616	--
	(0.136)		(0.204)		(0.316)		(0.515)	
Female	0.063	--	-0.034	--	0.107	--	-0.518	--
	(0.137)		(0.199)		(0.322)		(0.519)	
Age	0.009	--	0.011	--	0.015	--	0.006	--
	(0.008)		(0.012)		(0.020)		(0.032)	
Owner	-0.403***	-8.0	-0.050	--	-0.810**	-17.5	-0.533	--
	(0.153)		(0.225)		(0.338)		(0.560)	

Table 4 (continued)

Immigration Period (U.S.-born)							
Pre-1980	0.218	--	0.184	--	1.399**	29.4	\
	(0.214)		(0.340)		(0.651)		\
During 1980s	0.242	--	-0.100	--	1.029*	18.8	\
	(0.193)		(0.282)		(0.547)		\
1990-present	-0.167	--	-0.566**	-10.4	0.991**	20.4	\
	(0.166)		(0.253)		(0.483)		\
Constant	-0.264		0.377		-0.476		-2.646
	(0.575)		(1.072)		(1.251)		(2.156)
Observations	1359		748		281		147
Log Likelihood	-750.417		-367.488		-146.602		-72.958
PseudoR2	0.073		0.105		0.176		0.259

Source: Current Population Survey Annual March Supplement Micro-data File 2000-2004.

Notes: a. All models contain contextual measures including region and year of survey controls, whose coefficients are available upon request.

b. Column I represents estimates for logit regression coefficients. Standard errors are in parentheses.

c. Column II represents the conditional effects or the differences between the top 20th percentile and lower 20th percentile for each continuous explanatory variable (unless otherwise specified) and the differences between the minimum and maximum values for each dichotomous explanatory variable, when other variables are held constant at their mean.

Dashes (--) indicate that the variables were not statistically significant. A slash (\) indicates that the variable was not included in model for the national origin group.

* significant at 10 percent; ** significant at 5 percent; *** significant at 1 percent

insight into Latino SMPM settlement. Yet, once the full model is disaggregated we see some greater variation in the effect of these measures. Married Central/South American householders are 22 percent less likely than their unmarried counterparts to reside in SMPMs. Conversely, Puerto Rican married couples are 29 percent more likely to reside in a SMPM, than unwed Puerto Ricans. Like the full Latino model, homeownership remains negatively correlated with SMPM settlement, but with the exception of Central/South Americans, homeownership fails to account for location attainment among any other national origin group.

Finally, the disaggregated Latino national origin controls for immigration period reveal more variability in the impact of post-1980 immigration on SMPM settlement. Pre-1980 Central/South American immigrants were nearly 30 percent more likely to move to a SMPM relative to their native counterparts. These results decreased but remained positive and significant for newcomers in the 1980s at 19 percent, and rose to 20 percent in the 1990s. On the contrary, immigration period posed no statistically significant results for Mexicans who immigrated prior to 1980 and posed a negative effect on SMPM for post 1980 Mexicans. The most recent (post 1990) immigrants from Mexican are 10 percent less likely to have moved to a SMPM.

Discussion

These finding indicate that some direct migration related measures including housing- and/or family-related concerns are significant predictors of SMPM settlement for whites, Asians, and Latinos in the model, but posed no significant effect for blacks. It is likely that housing- and family-related factors draw some immigrant groups to pre-established melting pot suburbs since, as Logan (2001) points out, the "costs" of integration, particularly for more recent immigrants, is much higher. To be sure, while the income and educational attainment of Asians, for example, tends to be higher than for suburban whites, blacks, and Latinos, Asians are still more likely to settle in SMPM areas for family-related reasons. Family ties may lower the financial cost associated with moving to the suburbs. For immigrant newcomers, family ties are also likely to reduce linguistic and cultural barriers associated with suburbanization. Moreover, some groups may be drawn to suburban MPMs because of a combination of affordable housing and a relatively better neighborhood.

These results also reveal that income has a stronger impact on the propensity of blacks to settle in SMPM than it does for whites and Asians, while posing no effect for Latino settlement. Notably, these findings differ in some ways from the traditional predictions of spatial assimilation theories regarding blacks, yet fare well when noting the place stratification element inherent in suburban melting pot metro areas that are—by definition—distinct and separated from locals dominated by the majority population.

Finally as expected, the examination of the Latino subgroup populations reveal some notable variations in comparison to the non-disaggregated Latino model, underscoring the increasing need to evaluate separate national origin group models of suburbanization. Notably, unlike the full Latino sample, when Latino national origin groups are disaggregated, the interaction effect of low-income status and some migration-related measures becomes pronounced, particularly for Central/South Americans.

Conclusion

Some observers of American suburbanization have applauded the recent trends in "suburban diversity," as heterogeneous groups of ethnic minorities more readily make their way out of central cities, while some recent immigrant newcomers choose to by-pass the urban core altogether. Rest assured, however, all parties do not view suburban diversity as an asset. To be sure, diversity complicates matters. If history is our guide, racial/ethnic, economic, cultural, civic, or political heterogeneity have not historically been treated as a positive in the American society. This is particularly true for prearranged, politically fragmented suburban areas. The study of recent suburbanization patterns between immigrant and ethnic minority groups intersect with concerns raised about racial/ethnic relations, immigration, quality of life issues, as well as the appropriate role of government in addressing these concerns. The increasing reality of mixed-race, mixed-income, and mixed-land use suburban places marks a reason to dream for some and a dream deferred for others.

Recent findings from Iceland and Wilkes (forthcoming) suggest that at all levels of socioeconomic status blacks continue to be more segregated from whites than Asians or Latinos. Other communities of color, such as Asian Americans and to some extent Latinos, are also more likely to live in ethnically and racially diverse neighborhoods. All minority groups have not experienced rapid suburbanization. For some groups, such residential mobility does not necessarily garner an upward mobility move. African Americans continue to live in highly segregated communities relative to other racial/ethnic groups, many of which are situated on the periphery of deteriorating urban areas.

This is particularly important given how black immigrants versus their native-born counterparts are faring in the United States. According to the Census 2000 (Supplemental Survey Data) black immigrants have an advantage over native-born blacks regarding education and income. On the other hand, native blacks are more likely than black immigrants to be unemployed at 10 percent and 6.5 percent respectively, and to fall *below* the poverty level at 25 percent and 16 percent respectively (Logan 2003b).[14] Using 2000 Census data specifically for groups residing in suburban melting pot metro areas, Frasure (2005) found similar intra-group comparison results regarding black foreign-born and native-born populations. On average, black immigrants held higher levels of educational attainment than native-born blacks, were less likely to be unemployed than native-born blacks, yet were equally as likely to hold incomes below the poverty level, as native-born blacks. These factors raise concerns about the so-called "exodus" of the black middle-class toward suburbia as well as the political implications of these demographic transformations. Where sufficient data is available, future research should examine disaggregated groups of blacks from the U.S., Caribbean, and Africa to examine the factors propels or deters increases in black suburbanization.

As more astute scholars remind us, despite increasing diversity, suburban areas are paradoxically faced with increasing minority segregation and isolation (Logan 2003a, 238). This is, in part, because recent immigrant and ethnic minority settlements have often occurred in multi-ethnic areas such as suburban "melting pot metros." This research set out to examine some of these complexities in light of unprecedented suburban growth in the last decades. This multivariate model of suburban melting pot metro (SMPM) settlement help us to better capture the idiosyncratic nature of immigrant and ethnic minority settlement in suburbia. This research moves beyond the outdated, insular characterization of suburban spatial location research as a black/white dichotomy. Likewise, this analysis extends the lens of social science research beyond the study of central cities *versus* suburban localities toward the examination of the differences contained *within* suburbia.

This project is one step in a host of necessary research concerning suburban jurisdictions and their changing demographics. Several unanswered questions remain regarding racial/ethnic suburbanization. Scholars must contend with the civic and political implications of politically fragmented suburban governments particularly in light of emerging multi-ethnic suburban areas such as "melting pot metros," which paradoxically are also increasingly bifurcated in their social, economic, and political composition.

Despite a suburban street address, the clustering of immigrant and ethnic minority groups into suburban "melting pots" may have a negative effect on the advancement of civic and political participation. Some scholars suggest that metropolitan fragmented government structures like those exacerbated by post-World War II suburbanization may be "undermining the health of American democracy" (Oliver 1999:206; also see Oliver 2001; Drier, Mollenkopf, and Swanstrom 2001; Putman 2000). As Oliver (1999) observes, "By creating politically separated pockets of affluence, suburbanization reduces the social needs faced by citizens with the most resources to address them, by creating communities of homogeneous political interests, suburbanization reduces the local conflicts that engage and draw the citizenry into the public realm" (205). Such critiques argue, "municipal competition may empower some people to shop as consumers, but it immobilizing and isolating them as citizens in the democratic process" (Oliver 1999: 206). The densely populated and increasingly ethnically segregated areas in suburban jurisdictions can make it difficult to form coalitions with those with usable social and political capital to expend. Thus, one cannot assume that newcomers enjoy the same level of opportunity for civic and political engagement—across suburban communities—to voice their concerns or can as readily exit when their needs are not met.

The opportunities for choice *and* participation (exit and voice) provided by local municipalities are important components of a well-functioning democracy. However, will immigrant and ethnic minority suburbanization place the foundation for modes of civic or political incorporation in suburban areas, providing the resources and networks necessary for groups to gain social and economic ground in a democratic society, and in turn take a more active role in ensuring its maintenance?

Notes

1. The author thanks Linda Faye Williams, Joe Oppenheimer, Bart Landry, Irwin Morris, Michael Jones-Correa, and Tony Affigne for their helpful comments and suggestions. She also thanks Todd Shaw for his endless commitment to this volume, the 2006 NCOBPS roundtable participants and the anonymous reviewers of this volume for their comments and suggestions.

2. This study uses the Office of Budget and Management (OMB) definitions of Metropolitan Statistical Areas (MSAs) and Primary Metropolitan Statistical Areas (PMSAs). A Central County must be first established. A Central County is a County that contains a Central City of at least 50,000 people. A metropolitan statistical area exists if it contains a Census defined Urbanized Area of 50,000 or more people and has a total metro area population (including surrounding Counties) or at least 100,000 people. A city with the largest population in each metropolitan area is a central city. Moreover, other cities may also qualify as a central city bases on factors such as population size, commuting patterns and employment/residence ratios (Frey 2003:258). The U.S. Census defines a suburb as a metropolitan area outside of the metro's central cities.

3. Logan's 2003 study was based on dissimilarity indices used to examine residential segregation in the suburbs between 1990-2000. Empirically, to examine spatial location patterns among racial and ethnic groups, scholars have employed some statistical measures of racial or ethnic segregation. Two commonly use measures are the "dissimilarity index"—the percentage of individuals holding a given characteristic who would have to migrate for the group to be equally represented in each neighborhood and the "exposure index"—the probability that members of one group live in the same area as members of other groups.

4. In other words, melting pot metros are found in metropolitan places where non-Hispanic whites comprised less than 69 percent of the population and where two or more racial/ethnic groups made up more than 18 percent of the population. For example, blacks > 12.6 percent, or Hispanics > 12.5 percent, and at least 5 percent for Asians) (Frey 14: 2001, 2003).

5. Multi-ethnic and melting pot areas are used interchangeably because both are classified as metro areas in which "two or more of the three minority groups (Latinos, Asians, and blacks) make up a greater share of the metro area's population than the national population" (Frey and Farley 1996: footnote page 41, compare to Frey 2001, 2003). In contrast, "mostly white-black, mostly white-Latino, and mostly white-Asian areas house only one group whose share exceeds the national share. In the remaining "mostly white" areas none of the three minorities exceeds the national share" (Frey and Farley 1996: footnote page 41).

6. Conducted for more than fifty years, the Current Population Survey (CPS) is a monthly survey of about 60,000 households, with an additional 3,500 Latino households. The CPS Annual March Supplement surveys approximately 100,000 households (before 2001 roughly 65,000 households were sampled). The March CPS Annual March Supplement was referred to as the Annual Demographic File until its name change in 2003 to the Annual Social and Economic Supplement (ASEC) micro data file.

7. The CPS March Supplement micro-data files were made available through the Center for Economic and Social Research at Cornell (CISER). Each year of the CPS employed in this study include 2000 census weights to ensure consistency across survey year. Since neither the 2000 nor 2001 CPS March supplement files included the 2000 Census weights, prior to appending these documents to years 2002-2004 to create a pooled data set, I merged the 2000 weighs to the original CPS document files. I obtained the weights in raw data format for the years 2000 and 2001 from the U.S. Census Bureau. Together with Kerry Papps, a statistical consultant at CISER, I developed a do-file (STATA), which successfully merges the 2000 Census weights to the CPS March Supplement for 2000 and 2001. This do-file is available upon request or the merged data files for the 2000 and 2001 CPS with 2000 Census weights are also available upon request.

8. Notably, two MPM areas, El Paso, TX (MSA) and Ventura, CA (PMSA) were listed in the March CPS as "non-identifiable." This means that the observations for these areas could not be identified as central city, suburban, or rural. Thus, in order to avoid distorting the data, these two areas were excluded from this analysis. Moreover, according to the CPS, the metro areas sampled in McAllen, TX, Stockton, Lodi, CA, and Vallejo CA fell below the population threshold of 500,000 for this analysis, yet to remain as consistency as possible with Frey's (2001, 2003) typology these three areas remain include in this analysis. Thirty areas have populations over 500,000 while three areas have populations between 250,000 and 500,000.

9. Each of these non-melting pot metro areas includes populations over 500,000.

10. Upon truncation of the dataset excluding those under twenty-five and over sixty-four, non-movers, central city and rural cases and the filtering of household migrants to suburbia, by various migrant

types, the cases were too sparse to include disaggregated groups of blacks, Asians, or Native Americans.

11. Housing related options: wanted to own home, not rent; wanted new or better house/apartment; wanted better neighborhood cheaper housing; other housing reason. Family-related options: change in marital status; to establish own household; other family reason. Employment related options: new job or job transfer; to look for work or lost job; to be closer to work/easier commute; retired; other job-related reason. Other related options: to attend college; change in climate; health reason, other reason (specify). Each group of options (i.e. family-related) were coded 1=family-related, 0=otherwise). In order to detect potential problems of multicollinearity among all the variables in the model, correlation matrices were generated. None of these variables indicated the possibility of multicollinearity. However, the correlations between the migration variables are reasonably high given that they were disaggregated from the same survey question, whereas respondents were asked to specify the main reason for their move. Running the models with some of the more highly correlated variables omitted had no effect on the explanatory power of the variables. Therefore, we can safely conclude that the results are stable in terms of the varying specifications of the model.

12. Tables including geographic contextual measures are available upon request.

13. The statistical program CLARIFY (King et al.. 1998), used in the statistical software package STATA, employs stochastic simulation techniques to help researchers overcome limitations in interpreting and presenting logic results. To be clear, after estimating each logit regression, I use the CLARIFY program to calculate the conditional effects, or the impact on suburban melting pot metro settlement. In doing so, I simulate the changes in the probability of SMPM settlement for various "scenarios" of interest concerning SMPM settlement between non-Hispanic whites, blacks, Asians, and Latinos householders. For example, I evaluate how the probability of SMPM settlement would change at varying levels of income, educational attainment, or factors thought relevant in explaining SMPM settlement. The conditional effects for each dichotomous explanatory variable, is the difference in the predicted probabilities for the two values of that variable, when other variables are held constant at their mean. The conditional effects for each continuous variable represent the differences between the upper twentieth and lower twentieth percentiles (unless otherwise specified), when other variables are held constant at their mean.

14. Hispanic immigrants also have lower levels of education than their native counterparts, while the differences in income and poverty rates are less substantial. Both native and immigrant Asians have substantially higher incomes and lower poverty levels than both blacks and Hispanics.

References

Alba, Richard., Victor Nee. 2003. *Remaking the American Mainstream: Assimilation and Contemporary Immigration.* Cambridge, MA: Harvard University Press.
Alba, Richard, Logan John. 1991. "Variations on Two Themes: Racial and Ethnic Patterns in the Attainment of Suburban Residence." *Demography* 28:431-453.
Alba, Richard D. and Logan, John R. 1993. Minority Proximity to Whites in Suburbs: An Individual-level Analysis of Segregation. American Journal of Sociology 98 (6) May. 1388-1427.
Alba Richard, Logan JR, Stults BJ, Marzan G, Zhang W. 1999. "Immigrant Groups in the Suburbs: A Reexamination of Suburbanization and Spatial Assimilation." *American Sociological Review* 64:446-460.
Capps, Randy, Jeffrey S. Passel, Daniel Perez-Lopez Michael Fix. 2003. "The New Neighbors: A Users' Guide to Data on Immigrants in U.S. Communities" The Urban Institute Washington, DC.
Charles, Camille Z. 2003. "Dynamics of Racial Residential Segregation." *Annual Review of Sociology* 29(1):167-207.
Cohen, Cathy. 1999. *The Boundaries of Blackness: Aids and the Breakdown of the Black Community.* The University of Chicago Press. Chicago, IL.
Conley, John., Wooders, Myrna. 1997. "Equivalence of the Core and Competitive Equilibrium in a Tiebout Economy with Crowding Types." *Journal of Urban Economics*, Vol. 41: 421-440.
Danielson, Michael N. 1976. *The Politics of Exclusion.* New York: Columbia University.
de la Garza, Rodolfo., Louis DeSipio, F. Chris Garcia, John Garcia and Ángelo Falcón. 1992. *Latino Voices: Mexican, Puerto Rican, and Cuban Perspective on American Politics.* Westview Press, Inc
de la Garza, Rodolfo., and Louis DeSipio. 1996. *Awash in the Mainstream: Latino Politics in the 1996 Elections.* Boulder, CO: Westview Press.
DeSipio, L. 1996. *Counting on the Latino Vote: Latinos as a New Electorate.* University of Virginia Press. Charlottesville, VA.

Dreier, Peter. John Mollenkopf and Todd Swanstrom. 2001. *Place Matters: Metropolitics for the Twenty-First Century.* Lawrence, KN: University Press of Kansas.

Fishman, Robert. 1987. *Bourgeois Utopias: The Rise and Fall of Suburbia. Basic Books,* Inc. NY.

Frasure, Lorrie., co-authored with Michael Jones-Correa. 2005. "NIMBY's Newest Neighbors: Bureaucratic Constraints, Community-Based Organizing and the Day Laborer Movement in Suburbia." Paper presented at the Annual Meeting of the Midwest Political Science Association, Chicago, IL. April 7-10.

Frasure, Lorrie., 2005. "We Won't Turn Back: The Political Economy Paradoxes of Immigrant and Ethnic Minority Settlement in Suburban America." Unpublished dissertation manuscript. University of Maryland, College Park, MD.

Frey, William H. 2001. "Melting Pot Suburbs: A Census 2000 Study of Suburban Diversity." Census 2000 Series, Center on Urban and Metropolitan Studies, Washington, DC. The Brookings Institution.

Frey, William H. 2003. "Melting Pot Suburbs: A Study of Suburban Diversity." in Bruce Katz and Robert E. Lane (eds.) *Redefining Urban and Suburban: Evidence for Census 2000.* The Brookings Institution Press.

Frey, William H., and Alden Speare, Jr. 1988. Regional and Metropolitan Growth and Decline in the United States. New York: Russell Sage Foundation.

Hamilton, Bruce W. 1975. "Zoning and Property Taxation in a System of Local Governments." *Urban Studies* 12 (June): 205-211.

Hirschman, Albert O. 1970. *Exit, Voice, and Loyalty: Responses to Decline in Firms, Organizations, and States.* Cambridge, MA: Harvard University Press.

Iceland, John. (forthcoming) Wilkes, Rima. forthcoming. "Does Socioeconomic Status Matter? Race, Class and Residential Segregation." *Social Problems.*

Jackson, Kenneth. 1985. *Crabgrass Frontier: The Suburbanization of the United States.* Oxford University Press.

Jones-Correa, Michael. 1998. *Between Two Nations: The Political Predicament of Latinos in New York City.* Ithaca, NY: Cornell University Press.

Jones-Correa, Michael. 2002. "Reshaping the American Dream: Immigrants and the Politics of the New Suburbs." American Political Science Association Meeting, Boston, MA; August 30-September 1, 2002.

Kleinberg, Benjamin. 1995. *Urban American in Transformation: Perspectives on Urban Policy and Development.* Sage Publications, Thousand Oaks, CA.

Logan, John R. 2003a. "America's Newcomers." Albany, NY: Lewis Mumford Center for Comparative Urban and Regional Research, University at Albany, NY.

Logan, John. 2003b. "Ethnic Diversity Grows, Neighborhood Integration Lags." in Bruce Katz and Robert E. Lane (eds.) *Redefining Urban and Suburban: Evidence for Census 2000.* The Brookings Institution Press.

Logan, John R. 2001. "The New Latinos: Who They are, Where They Are." Report from the Lewis Mumford Center For Comparative Urban and Regional Research, University at Albany, NY.

Logan, John R., Richard D. Alba, and Shu-Yin Leung. 1996. "Minority Access to White Suburbs: A Multiregional Comparison." *Social Forces* 74 (3): 851-881.

John R. Logan, Richard D. Alba, and Wenquan Zhang. 2002. "Immigrant Enclaves and Ethnic Communities in New York and Los Angeles" *American Sociological Review* 67 (April):299-322.

Logan, J. and Molotch H. 1987. *Urban Fortunes: The Political Economy of Place.* Berkley, CA: University of California Press.

Massey, Douglas. 1985 "Ethnic Residential Segregation: A Theoretical Synthesis and Empirical Review." *Sociology and Social Research* 69: 315-50.

Massey, Douglas S. and Nancy A. Denton. 1988 "The Dimensions of Residential Segregation." *Social Forces* 67(2):281-315.

Massey, Douglas. and Mitchell Eggers. 1990. "The Ecology of Inequality: Minorities and the Concentration of Poverty." *American Journal of Sociology* 95:1153-88.

Massey, Douglas S. and Nancy A. Denton. 1993. *American Apartheid: Segregation and the Making of the Underclass.* Cambridge, MA: Harvard University Press.

Miller, Gary J. 1981. *Cities by Contract: The Politics of Municipal Incorporation.* MIT: Cambridge, MA.

Mollenkopf John and Gary Gerstle (eds.), 2001. *E Pluribus Unum? Contemporary and Historical Perspectives on Immigrant Political Incorporation.* New York: Russell Sage Foundation.

Oliver, Eric. 2001. *Democracy in Suburbia.* Princeton, NJ: Princeton University Press.

Oliver, Eric. 1999. "The Effects of Metropolitan Economic Segregation on Local Civic Participation." *American Journal of Political Science.* Vol. 43, No 1.

Peterson, Paul. 1981. *City Limits*. Chicago, IL: University of Chicago Press.

Putnam, Robert. 2000. *Bowling Alone: The Collapse and Revival of American Community*. New York: Simon & Schuster

Ross, Bernard., and Levine, Myron, 2000. *Urban Politics: Power in Metropolitan America* 6th ed. Itsaca, IL: F.E. Peacock.

Sacks Michael P. 2003. "Suburbanization and the Racial/Ethnic Divide in the Hartford Metropolitan Area." Unpublished Manuscript

Schneider, Mark. 1989. *The Competitive City: The Political Economy of Suburbia*. Pittsburgh, PA: University of Pittsburgh Press

Singer, Audrey., Samantha Friedman, Ivan Cheung, and Marie Price 2001. "The World in a Zip Code: Greater Washington, DC as a New Region of Immigration." The Brooking Institutions, Center on Urban and Metropolitan Policy, Survey Series.

Sonenshein, Raphael 1989. *Politics in Black and White*. Princeton, NJ: Princeton University Press.

Tiebout, Charles. 1956. "A Pure Theory of Local Expenditures." *Journal of Political Economy* 64(5): 416-24.

Tomz, Michael Jason Wittenberg, and Gary King (2003). *Software for Interpreting and Presenting Statistical Results*. Version 2.1. Stanford University, University of Wisconsin, and Harvard University. Available at http://gking.harvard.edu/

U.S. Dept. of Commerce, Bureau of the Census. Current Population Survey: Annual March Supplement 2000-2004 [Computer file]. NBER version. Washington, DC: U.S. Dept. of Commerce, Bureau of the Census [producer].

Waldinger, Roger 1999. *Still the Promised City: African-Americans and New Immigrants in Postindustrial New York*. Cambridge, MA: Harvard University Press.

Waldinger, Roger (ed.) 2001. *Strangers at the Gates: New Immigrants in Urban America*. Berkeley, CA: University of California Press

Williams, Linda. 2003. *The Constraint of Race: Legacies of White Skin Privilege in America*. Pittsburg, PA: Penn State Press.

AIDS, Context, and Black Politics

Lester Spence
Johns Hopkins University and Morgan State University

Rena Boss-Victoria
Morgan State University

Introduction

At least since V.O. Key penned the seminal *Southern Politics*, scholars have recognized the role that neighborhood context plays in political behavior (Key 1949). Similarly, public health scholars have recognized the growing role that neighborhood context plays in morbidity—whether talking about asthma, sexually transmitted diseases, or even stress (Brown, Mayer, and Zavestoski 2003; Diaz, Ayala, and Bein 2001; Fullilove 2003; Harrell 2000). Scholars have also begun to revisit some of the central findings of the political socialization literature (Gimpel, Lay, and Schuknecht 2003; Gimpel, Lay, and Schuknecht 2002). But very rarely have scholars attempted to look at links between youth political socialization, context, *and* health. We argue that one of the key variables that wed the politics of hyper-segregated urban space to the public health of those spaces is risk perception. Perceptions of risk (youth perceptions in particular) make citizens less likely to believe they have the capacity to change the world around them, less likely to trust authority figures, and as a result, more likely to become vulnerable to health issues. Baltimore is a city characterized by its large black population and its high crime rate. Indeed, two of the most riveting crime dramas of the last ten years (*The Wire* and *Homicide*) were set (and filmed) in Baltimore. It is also known as having one of the highest HIV/AIDS rates in the country. In many ways it represents the perfect site to study the intersection between health, context, and political attitudes. In this paper we use qualitative data collected for the purpose of grappling with the high incidence of HIV/AIDS among youth, in order to examine the theoretical relationship between context, risk perception, youth political socialization, and public health.

Context, Health, and Politics

We know that a variety of individual level factors play a significant role in health outcomes. A person's degree of education, socio-economic status, and health history (including the family's health history), all exert an effect on the person's health (LaVeist 2002; Wadsworth 2003). However scholars also recognize that context plays a role in health outcomes. Low birth-weight, asthma rates, and sexually transmitted diseases, have all been linked to neighborhood context (Brown, Mayer, and Zavestoski 2003; Fullilove 2003; Roberts 1997). The research indicates that mental health and well-being are related to context as well (Schulz et al. 2000).

Political scientists have thought carefully about the role of context, but with a totally different set of social phenomena in mind As far back as V.O. Key, political scientists have recognized the role context plays in influencing both behavior and opinion. For Key, the racial composition of southern counties were extremely influential in predicting the degree of party competition—southern counties with large black populations tended to be two-party counties in name only with the Republican party being largely invisible (Key 1949). As scholars began to be interested in the political socialization in youth, particularly in the late 1960s and early 1970s, they focused on the role of racial context in structuring the political attitudes of black and white youth (Abramson 1972; Abramson 1977).

Looking specifically at adult political attitudes and behavior, more recent works continued this thread, finding that some combination of aggregate political, racial, and socio-economic context influenced a variety of attitudes and behaviors (Cohen and Dawson 1993; Dawson 1994; Gay 2004). And studying political socialization, James Gimpel, Celeste Lay, and Jason Schuknecht have shown that political homogeneity influences adolescent political attitudes about a range of phenomena (Gimpel, Lay, and Schuknecht 2003; Gimpel, Lay, and Schuknecht 2002). However, there are some questions as to how context works: is it something about information flows; about social networks; about feelings of threat; or is it some combination of all three?

How Context Works

Public Health

There are a few different ways of thinking theoretically about the relationship between the environment in which one lives and/or works and one's health. One way scholars have thought about it is to argue that living in areas of concentrated poverty make it more likely that one lives near certain types of hazards. In the case of asthma for example, there are strong indicators that poorer communities are older and more prone to be built near highways, environmental waste sites, and more prone to contain allergens (Juhna et al. 2005; Lwebuga-Mukasa, Oyana, and Johnson 2005; Oyana and Lwebuga-Mukasa 2004; Oyana, Rogerson, and Lwebuga-Mukasa 2004). Living in such a neighborhood would make one much more likely to come into direct contact with material elements (asbestos or certain types of mold for example) that cause asthma. Hazardous waste sites are often more likely to be situated near poor neighborhoods, and it is possible that individuals in these neighborhoods imbibe the effluvia from these waste sites thus making them more likely to become sick. Taking a slightly different approach, some focus on the lack of physical amenities that promote healthy lifestyles. Thomas LaVeist and John Wallace find that people living in poor urban neighborhoods are much more likely to live near liquor stores and fast food restaurants than grocery stores (LaVeist and Wallace 2000).

Some focus more generally on social isolation. Hyper-segregation is measured along several dimensions, two of which are isolation and concentration. Chiquita Collins and David Williams found that the mortality rates of blacks in socially isolated environments were higher than among those in environments not so isolated (Collins and Williams 1999). If poorer residents who are less likely to have health care are both concentrated together and isolated from other communities, then whatever contagious illnesses they catch are more likely to breed and spread within those communities. Furthermore, living in neighborhoods where the level of health care is low may exacerbate the degree to which individuals become susceptible to diseases contracted by others in that neighborhood, and hence should make those individuals more likely to become carriers.

Finally, Mindy Thompson Fullilove (2004) has used the term "root shock" to refer to the malaise of disconnectedness and dislocation that happens in formerly vibrant black communities leveled by "urban renewal." She argues that when the sense of connectedness that ties people together in solid neighborhoods dissolves abruptly, people are more likely to feel angst, more likely to feel anxious and fearful. As James House, Karl Landis, and Debra Umberson (1988) show in their work looking at the relationship between health (both physical and mental) and relationship quality these have mental and physical health have consequences.

Political Science

One argument is that the political context shapes access to information as well as the nature of the information that youth and adults alike receive (Huckfeldt and Kohfeld 1989). Living in an environment of concentrated poverty makes an individual much more likely to be surrounded by people who have the least ability to transmit valuable information largely because they do not necessarily *have* the information in the first place. Furthermore, individuals in these spaces are much less likely to be exposed to more information rich networks. Whatever networks an individual is able to create within these spaces will be resource-poor and unable to provide them with the same quality or quantity of knowledge received from other less vulnerable sites.

A similar argument is institution- based. In discussing the role context plays in linked fate, Cathy Cohen and Michael Dawson assert institutions—that is, churches, fraternities, civil rights groups—play critical roles in cultivating a sense of linked fate in black citizens by reducing the cost of attaining information (Cohen and Dawson 1993). While Cohen and Dawson are unable to test this empirically, Claudine Gay (2004) does. Social networks are thought to be important as well, but what is important is the degree to which these networks are information rich. Thus citizens receive the information they need to participate.

Political scientists interested in white racial attitudes and political behavior still emphasize the role of "group threat." V.O. Key argued that the racial composition of counties in the south structured the political party system in those counties because of the group threat that blacks represented for whites (Key 1949). Lynching as a particularly brutal form of political terrorism was arguably a response to two forms of perceived black behavior—the move to become economically independent, and the move to engage in relationships with white women (Dray 2002). More than forty years later, J. Eric Oliver and Tali Mendelberg show that white racial attitudes are not evenly distributed throughout physical space, but rather take on their darkest tones in settings of low education and status, where whites fearful for their own economic safety and security are more likely to blame their insecurity on African Americans (Oliver and Mendelberg 2000).

Context and Youth

Arguably one of the most vulnerable populations in urban communities is youth. Since they cannot vote, they do not have representatives upon which they can make political demands. They are even less mobile than their adult counterparts, because they are not old enough to drive or, in most cases, work. If adults in organizations, cities, and states have the options of exit, voice, and loyalty (even if those options are truncated because of poverty)—youth, comparatively speaking, have no options. How does context influence their political lives?

The early studies of black youth indicate that they are less likely than their white counterparts to exhibit trust in political officials (particularly the police). Studies also reveal that black youth do not feel as efficacious as their white counterparts (Abramson 1977; Clarke 1973; Easton and Dennis 1969; Greenberg 1970a; Greenberg 1970b; Jackson 1973). Two main theories attempted to explain this gap. The social deprivation hypothesis posits that the reason blacks are less trusting and efficacious is because they are deprived relative to their white peers and end up having less trust in the system and a smaller degree of faith in their own ability to work within that system. The political reality hypothesis posits that black youth actually understand the differences between black and white political access. When black youth compare their own reality to that of whites and realize the difference, they are less trusting and efficacious (Abramson 1977). While black youth, particularly those in poor neighborhoods, may engage in the above comparison/contrast where they perceive somehow that they "get less" than their white counterparts, which negatively affects black youth political efficacy and trust, this explanation that does not quite fit. From an informational standpoint, there is much more information to be gained from interactions in poor urban environments than suggested by either the political reality or the social deprivation theses. Information about threat and risk looms large here.

Threat as a concept has most recently been applied to white and black racial attitudes. In delineating the possible ways that the environment may influence white racial attitudes, J. Eric Oliver and Tali Mendelberg (p. 576) note that being exposed to the effluvia of urban spaces wracked by concentrated poverty can lead to feelings of anxiety, fear, alienation, and mistrust. But again they only apply this to the study of white racial attitudes. If we go beyond the study of black and white inter- and intra-racial attitudes there are enormous possibilities for understanding how risk and anxiety influence attitudes and behavior. Areas of concentrated poverty are not just dead information spaces, nor are they simply resource poor spaces in comparison to middle class urban neighborhoods and suburbs. They are also spaces of immediate *danger*. They expose citizens to crime, to environmental hazards, and to disease on a regular basis. While we can overestimate the degree to which these spaces are disorganized and disheveled, we should not underestimate the degree to which citizens in these spaces have to live with threat and risk. And as youth are often the least likely to have the agency to exert either exit (poor youth in particular have neither the transportation options nor the ability to simply pack up and move) *or* voice (they cannot vote), they may be the most susceptible to the type of threat that incapacitates their potential political capacity. Theorizing about the role threat plays in youth assessments of their environment may pay off in more ways than one.

The Role of Risk and Trauma

In studying the way that black youth in contexts of hyper-segregation define themselves, Elijah Anderson and Mary Patillo McCoy both refer to the significant role that violence plays in their lives (Anderson 1999; Pattillo 1998; Pattillo-McCoy 1999). James Anderson, Terry Grandison, and Laronistine Dyson argue that violence is so inextricably linked to disability that it should be considered a public health problem (Anderson, Grandison, and Dyson 1996). In fact, there is a growing literature that deals with the relationship between urban space, violence, and trauma (Bell, Baptiste, and Madison 2003; Okundaye 2004; St. Lawrence 1993; Zimmerman, Ramirez-Valles, and Maton 1999). People living in contexts beset by urban poverty live in environments characterized by trauma. They encounter violence as a routine part of their lives.

Often the rates of interpersonal violence among low-income residents far outstrip those of the society at large. In Denise Hien and Claudia Bukszpan's study of a group of low-income women they found that these women were much more likely to have experienced a variety of traumatic experiences from childhood sexual abuse and physical abuse to partner violence (Hien and Bukszpan 1999). Joshua Nosa Okundaye posited that youth living in contexts in which drug trafficking and violence was endemic are much more likely to exhibit symptoms of Post-Traumatic Stress Disorder (PTSD). He found that not only did youth perceive drugs and violence to be widespread in these communities but also they found themselves to be at-risk (Okundaye 2004). This fact alone made them susceptible to PTSD. In fact, trauma is now recognized to be the leading cause of death and disability among children and adolescents.

Perceived risk in the health literature refers to "… people's perceptions about their susceptibility to various ailments and diseases" (Rimal, 2001, p. 633). As scholars have begun to think about violent crime as a public health crisis in many communities, the concept of perceived risk begins to take on a new meaning. Looking at the relationship between perceptions of risk and preventative health behavior, some of the literature clearly suggests a negative relationship—with those who perceive themselves in greatest danger of being inflicted with an ailment as the least likely to gather information and/or act on information given to them. Overall, this relationship mediated is by self-efficacy (Rimal 2001; Rimal and Real 2003). Again, information is a critical catalyst. As perceptions of danger increase, the likelihood of gathering information from other people in the social space may indeed decrease. But here information from peers, or family members, or neighbors is not the only source of information individuals have access to. What about information gleaned directly from the environment—information that in turn alters one's ability to process and act on other information? Okundaye was specifically interested in examining perceptions of threat among urban youth connected to the drug trade. However there is no a priori reason to confine Okundaye's findings about threat and risk to that of the drug trade.

Researchers have noted that HIV/AIDS rates are growing significantly in urban spaces and among non-white youth (National Center for HIV 2004). The city of Baltimore, while beset with many of the crises that characterize rustbelt cities—that is, white and increasingly black flight, urban disinvestment, high unemployment, high crime rate, etc.—has a particularly high rate of HIV/AIDS among its adolescent population (Department of Health and Mental Hygiene 2004). The Baltimore RARE Project was designed to both analyze and stem the tide of HIV/AIDS among youth in select Baltimore neighborhoods. While ostensibly created in order to address a significant public health issue, the interviews conducted through the project can grant insight into the role that threat and risk play in the political socialization of urban youth.

The Baltimore R.A.R.E. Project

R.A.R.E. stands for Rapid Assessment Response Evaluation. It represents an attempt to quickly evaluate the processes involved in disease transmission and prevention within a given environment. The assessment methods used in RARE are drawn from epidemiology, ethnography, survey research, and evaluation strategies. It uses a combination of observation, interviews, focus groups, and street intercept surveys to determine HIV risk behaviors, attitudes and beliefs, environmental and broader social influence, barriers to HIV prevention, and HIV program strategy effectiveness.

The Baltimore Project was conducted in order to address the growing HIV/AIDS epidemic among a specific black youth and young adult population (ages eighteen to twenty-four who resided within east and westside neighborhoods. A significant component of the RARE Project is physical and cultural mapping. Individuals from the research team create a physical map of the communities under study as well as a map of the social and psychic environments. Among the physical aspects that the researchers noted were a significant number of abandoned houses (some of them used as large scale crack houses, some only used periodically by scattershot groups for drugs and sex), intermittent street light maintenance, illicit activity (drug sales, sex workers soliciting clients, drug use), vacant lots and storefronts. In many ways the sites in which researchers conducted this study resembled the stereotypical view of the crime-ridden "inner city" that is broadcasted far and wide by television news and detailed in the works of Martin

Table 1
Demographics of Focus Group Participants

Age	N	percent	Male	Female	GED	Some HS	HS Grad	Some College	College Grad	Yes	NO
14-17	7	6.7	4	3	4	1	1			2	5
18-24	75	72.1	37	37	31	13	16	9	6	28	44
25-34	7	6.7	5	2					6	1	6
35-70	15	14.4	7	8	4		1	5	5	1	14
	104	100.0	51.5	48.5	39	14	18	14	17	32	69
Avg.					38.2	13.7	17.7	13.7	16.7	31.7	68.3

Gilens (1999), Frank Gilliam and Shanto Iyengar (2000) . Massey and Denton (1993) coined the term "hypersegregation" to refer to urban areas wracked by segregation not only by race but also by class. Areas like these are in many ways Massey and Denton's poster children, and in Baltimore (and many other cities) these neighborhoods are the epicenter for HIV/AIDS.

Researchers were particularly interested in the various ways that youth negotiated these spaces with an eye towards garnering knowledge about their level of awareness about HIV/AIDS and neighborhood programs designed to combat HIV/AIDS. Over 100 respondents selected from neighborhoods within three zip codes (21215, 21218, and 21213) participated.

Looking at the demographics of the participants, what stands out is the high number of respondents with a GED. Looking specifically at the two youngest groups (fourteen to seventeen and eighteen to twenty-four) a full 43 percent of them have GEDs as opposed to formal high school diplomas. Furthermore out of that same population approximately 60 percent are without insurance. All of them are African American. But these demographics only tell a small part of the story. Individuals were recruited for participation in the focus groups through street recruiting, and the recruiters were themselves part of the community.

In a speech given to commemorate the fiftieth anniversary of Brown vs. Board, Bill Cosby (2004) excoriated the black residents of urban neighborhoods like those in east and west Baltimore, arguing that they were responsible for their own condition. Talking for example about a stereotypical case of police brutality in which a child was murdered by police for stealing a piece of pound cake, Cosby asks plaintively "what was the child doing stealing the pound cake in the first place?" To Cosby, like many black and white conservatives (be they nationalist or integrationist) the problem of black children in poor neighborhoods is that their cultural baggage prevents them from learning the fundamental skills needed to thrive in American life. According to this view, the problem may have been structural some time ago, that time has passed. Looking at the demographic data, particularly the data about education, it appears as if the focus group participants are part of the group that Cosby excoriates. And perhaps in some vulgar way they are—in as much as they live in neighborhoods that black and white conservatives damn. After all, a significant number of them only have GEDs.

On the other hand if we take the point of view of structuralists such as Massey and Denton, it is not that hard to view these individuals as victims of forces beyond their control. The forces of poverty and racism have significantly hamstrung the ability of these individuals to survive much less thrive. Most of them do not have health insurance and have low levels of education thus their challenges are predisposed to a structural explanation.

Although the structural argument is much more persuasive given the data, neither view accurately fully captures the lives of these individuals). While on the one hand these individuals are not the type of ignorant carjacking welfare mothers that the conservatives would have citizens believe they are, they are also not the blind automatons dictated to by forces outside of their control. They are individuals who are trying to make a way for themselves in the communities they live in without letting that community kill their spirit. These are youth (and young adults) who have in some cases lost family members to drugs and to HIV. While some of them are to some extent connected to the illicit economy, most are not. To be sure, the use of alcohol is not illegal, though underage alcohol purchases *are*. To the degree they are working, they work in the various low-wage, no-benefits service, positions that dot the area (i.e. McDonalds, Walgreen's, Mobil's gas stations, etc).. Although none of them are married, some of them have children. One poignantly details having to literally beat up a man in an alley behind her house because he exposed himself to her daughter. At least one of them is currently on parole.

In the focus groups and interviews, these individuals were asked a variety of questions about four broad interest areas: behavior risk and harm-producing behaviors, prevention services and resource access, physical and environmental barriers, as well as gaps in knowledge, and HIV program effectiveness. While the purpose of the Baltimore RARE Project was not to assess the political socialization of metropole youth, the responses youth give in the focus groups and individual interviews can be used to theorize about the political socialization process in as much as the responses reflect perceptions about the lived environment.

How AIDS affects the Baltimore Community

In Baltimore, Maryland, as in the United States as a whole, epidemiologic data indicates that HIV and AIDS are disproportionately affect African Americans. Baltimore ranks fifth in the United States in terms of the number of AIDS cases, with 39.3 cases per 100,000 populations, and has a documented steady increase among minority populations. Baltimore ranks tenth in prevalent (living) AIDS cases. Even more alarming is the documented increase in new HIV+ diagnoses in black Baltimoreans between the ages of thirteen and twenty-four. African American youth and teens represented 63 percent of all new HIV+ diagnoses in this age-specific group between 1994 and 1997 as documented by the Maryland State AIDS Administration (Department of Health and Mental Hygiene 2004). The consequences of the spread of this disease for the general welfare of citizens are potentially enormous. Individuals interviewed may not be as familiar with the statistics here, but they recognize the potential consequences as noted below. (Pseudonyms were used to protect the identities of all respondents).

Interviewer: How is HIV and AIDS affecting young people in this community?

Quentin: Well I think its affecting them because if you not really, you not really, you not really certain who has what. You can't tell by, you know, how they look if they have AIDS or something like that.

Cash: A lot of young people that I know, friends of mine that have HIV, so it's a real, real big affect in this community. The problem is everybody knows it's in the community [but] hardly no one is taking the prevention or doing what they need to do to prevent getting AIDS. It's like they don't care. That's what it is in this community.

John John: It's spreading, and it's killing people.

C Mill: It makes you be more aware of who you interact with and how you interact with them because you're not really sure who has what.

Interviewer: Can I hear from the ladies because the dudes are like carrying it? What's up?

Kesha: They already said everything really. The way I see it affecting people it's like you don't want to get close to nobody because you don't know what's going on with them and how they look.

Note here the recognition of the health consequences of growing numbers of HIV/AIDS cases, as well as the recognition of the impact it has on the social ties of trust that bind people together. While on one level "not knowing who has what" should really only influence decisions regarding physical intimacy, there is a great deal more tied up in that decision with these respondents. The decision on whether to befriend or even simply be seen with others may be influenced by the degree to which people make assumptions about their HIV status. The concept of stigma plays an important role here, as scholars have all found that stigma plays a significant role in black attitudes about HIV/AIDS and at-risk groups (Cohen 1999; Fullilove and Fullilove 1999; Herek and Capitanio 1993; Herek and Capitanio 1995; Herek and Capitanio 1999).

Drug Risk

Looking specifically at respondent perceptions of drug use and drug dealing in their Baltimore neighborhoods, respondents were asked where drugs were sold, as well as the types of drugs available.

Interviewer: Drugs, where are drugs at?

Chuck: Everywhere.

Franchot: When you step out your door you will see drugs, man.

Nadia: Everywhere.

Sandy: Everywhere.

B Willis: Everywhere.

Boyer: I go to Harbor City, you see people there selling drugs. You might even see teachers there buying weed and stuff, like dope and everything. Then they will go in the bathroom and do their little thing and come out of the bathroom and be dumb high. They look like they are stupid.

Interviewer: What kind of drugs?

Group: Dope, coke, rain, E, weed, acid, all of that.

Interviewer: What about the use of needles?

Cash: They be on the corner selling needles too, new ones. You can get a whole box of them for like a dollar.

Sandy: If you shoot dope or any kind of drugs they will give you a box of needles and the next thing you know they will be out there selling them so they can get their high.

Interviewer: Tell me some place where people are not getting high.

Sandy: I can say in the county morgue.

Although the group did not mention methadone—which is largely produced in rural environments for rural consumers—every other drug was bought and sold within the confines of a few Baltimore neighborhoods. According to the respondents the clean needles were available, but the trade was so ubiquitous that the needles themselves became commodities to sell for more drugs.

One of the ways that youth learn about politics and legitimacy is from authority figures that are supposed to model correct behavior and serve as arbiters of right and wrong. While the literature on youth socialization specifically notes that black youth sentiment about the police has no bearing on their degree of trust or political efficacy, these young people's comments about their teachers are telling. Bill Cosby and other conservatives focus clearly on culture and on the importance of role models. William Julius Wilson (1987) would not necessarily consider himself a conservative, but his prescription for urban poverty by exposing black poor citizens to black middle class mores is based on the same theoretical foundation. Along the lines of a strictly cultural narrative, neither of them consider the degree to which state authorities may be complicit in creating the results they decry—that is, increased crime, increased teenage pregnancy, increased single parenthood, etc.

The focus groups noted that they could find drugs "everywhere." What exactly does this mean? How do the youth who were interviewed communicate this when asked to unpack the term? From another focus group they reveal:

Interviewer: Where [are] the young people in the neighborhood buying drugs, sharing

needles, tricking, and having unprotected sex?

Tracy: Where?

Interviewer: Right. What type of places?

Tracy: Um, on the corners, speaking from the neighborhood where I'm from ... I live on Biddle and [inaudible] it's crazy. It's like mainly the drugs and selling drugs is like it really happens, like on, the corner. Around our corner stores like Barnes, stuff like that and sharing needles you usually see that a lot. They do it around vacant houses in ... the backyard. Like we have a playground in the back of our yard and at night a lot, a lot of you know people come over there. I see, it's been to the point; I wouldn't think they would be so rude, like you know ... knowing children play there. I think, what's it called? You know when, a new drug comes out and they giving out like free [samples] like all these people just come like running for it?

Interviewer: Mhmm.

Tracy: And they did that one day in the playground and I'm like "oh my gosh" and

I'm like all these kids are here but it's like this everywhere. Schools,

everywhere. I done seen girls being you know ...

Here schools and playgrounds are implicated as being high-risk areas. Indeed Tracy notes that playgrounds are places in which new products are rolled out for consumers. Sellers do not seem to evince much care for *when* they do it—on one occasion children were actually playing during a product rollout. So not only are teachers buying drugs in front of their students — presumably authority figures who are supposed to help young boys and girls transition into adulthood—but the schools are spaces of risk. They are places where drugs are freely sold and where product rollouts are conducted. Furthermore, as shown below, they are places where boys and girls, as well as men and women, engage in sex.

In asking about areas that were risky or threat-ridden sex-wise, the respondents gave some of the same responses as they did to the questions about drugs. As aforementioned, one of the respondents got into a fight with a man because he exposed himself to her daughter:

> Natasha: I feel as though, just like [others] said, that it's everywhere. Not meaning every single place, but meaning that it's all around you—clubs, schools, it doesn't matter. Nowadays they don't even care if they have privacy. It will be two niggas and two females doing it on a full size bed. They do not care nowadays. They will do it on steps, in kitchens, and they don't care. In their own house, on the floor, on the couch. It doesn't matter. It's like sex is not private like it used to be. It's out there. It's open and it's expected, and that's why they do it. Now, if it was the old days like when my mother and them grew up or even back then, sex was private, sex back then was like a secret. It was valued; it had morals. Nowadays it's 2004 and it has none of them. It's just out there. Everybody is doing it so 'why not me?' and that's why the younger children are doing it. It's sad because my daughter is three years old and a nigga was pissing in the alley and my daughter had to experience seeing a male's thing. So I had to teach my child about body parts and other things at the age of three years old. That killed me to my heart because you could be walking down the street and just see that. No he didn't close it, but the thing is my daughter got to the alley before me because she knows to stop at alleys. So she stopped and she stared and I'm not blaming her because she didn't know what she was looking at. But that male I did fight him and it got into a confrontation on the street.

Natasha's story is agonizing on many different levels. It is clear that she cares deeply about her daughter, and about raising her properly. It is also clear though that she felt she had to take matters into her own hands—it is not as if she could have called the police. In the event that she would have been arrested, she would have become another statistic—single mother arrested for assault. Not only are there a variety of public spaces in which sex is occurring, in many cases sex is occurring between adults *and children*. In the perception of the respondents, neither age group nor space is immune. In fact, one respondent caught a couple having sex in a church. People not only perceive these behaviors as risky behaviors to the individuals engaging in them, they perceive these behaviors as dangerous to others as well as the mores of the community. What the above transcripts reflect is the degree to which perceptions of threat and risk impact the everyday lives of youth in Baltimore. To what degree do these perceptions influence political attitudes?

Modeling the Influence of Threat

Again, previous research indicates that poor urban neighborhoods produce a significant degree of anxiety and illness in their residents (Fullilove 2003; Harrell 2000; House, Landis, and Umberson 1988; Lincoln, Chatters, and Taylor 2003). Presenting a model of this process should help detail some of the direct and indirect ways in which perceptions of threat and risk also influence political attitudes and political knowledge.

Figure 1 contains a somewhat simplified model of the relationship between political knowledge/political attitudes and a variety of factors thought to influence knowledge and attitudes. The mechanisms associated with political knowledge are not exactly the same as that associated with political attitudes—e.g., a school setting influences knowledge but not attitudes—and the schema does not deconstruct all factors—e.g., "school" encompasses both classroom level and campus-wide factors .

What we are particularly interested in is the role of context. Context is thought to influence political attitudes through three different theoretical routes. All of them are indirect. Context influences an individual's social networks, as well as her access to information sources. As both the social deprivation and political reality theories note context also influences an individual's perceptions of her neighborhood in relationship to others and this in turn influences her attitudes.

Figure 1
Model of Political Socialization

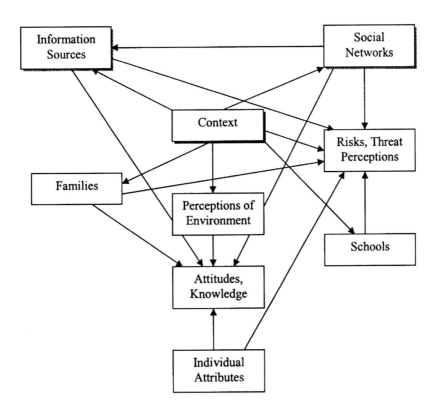

What we are arguing is that context exerts an influence upon perceptions of risk, threat, and danger, and these perceptions in turn influence youth political attitudes and knowledge. However we also posit that other factors influence perceptions of risk, threat, and danger. Schools are supposed to be safe havens, but as noted in the transcripts they are, in too many cases, sites for both illicit sex and drugs and thus can be sites of danger. In this way schools can actually exacerbate perceptions of risk. Families can operate in a similar manner.

We also note a relationship between information sources and perceptions of risk, threat, and danger, as well as a relationship between social networks and those same self-perceptions. Individuals, particularly youth, do not move in social settings by themselves, but often do so through networks of other youth and of authorities. These networks may serve as buffers; protecting youth and making them feel safer. Information sources may work in the same way. However on the other hand both may make individuals feel a heightened sense of risk, and this should lead to them holding more negative political attitudes.

Risk, Threat, and Their Political Implications

The focus groups and interviews above were conducted with the central goal of getting information about the knowledge adolescents and young adults had about HIV/AIDS. It also sought to understand the trouble spots they recognized in their own neighborhoods, the type of risks they felt they were exposed to on a daily basis, and the types of programs that would be most effective in dealing with HIV/AIDS. As such there was no explicit discussion of the state and how state agents do or do not influence the degree to which their neighborhoods serve as danger spots. Nor was there an explicit discussion about the degree of political agency they felt they had or did not have as far as dealing with the problems their communities face.

However, examining the transcripts it is impossible to ignore the way that politics informs the lives of the respondents. The reason that the HIV/AIDS epicenter in Baltimore is in its hardest hit neighborhoods is because of the politics behind hypersegregation (Fullilove 2003; Massey and Denton 1993). One of the most significant reasons why more resources are not poured into HIV/AIDS on the local, state, and federal levels is because of the stigma associated with many of the at-risk groups (Fullilove and Fullilove 1999; Herek 1999; Herek 2003; Herek and Capitanio 1999; Herek, Capitanio, and Widaman 2002). And many of the physical dangers associated with the spaces the respondents inhabit are themselves violations of various city codes that have not been enforced. The decision to enforce (or not enforce) various rules and regulations is a political decision as well. The omnipresent perceptions of risk and threat in as much as they exist in these spaces and not in others are the byproduct of the same political decisions. While health scholars have begun to identify the ways that context influences health outcomes (Adimora and Schoenbach 2005; Bruce 2004; Chen et al. 2003; Diaz, Ayala, and Bein 2001; Fiscella and Williams 2004; Fullilove 2003), very few have begun to outline the impact of politics on this process (Laveist 1993; LaVeist 1997). And very few have examined the way that mental health—and here we focus on perceptions of risk and threat—influence politics and political socialization. What do the comments above reveal about perceptions of risk, threat, and danger?

How does context influence political attitudes according to the literature? Scholars focus on the importance of networks. They discuss how people are enveloped within networks that in turn can expose them to information networks; networks that can inculcate values across generations. Theorizing about linked fate, Michael Dawson argues that black people exposed to black information networks are more likely to evince a sense of group common fate than those not similarly exposed (Dawson 1994). Going back to the theory of social deprivation posited by Abramson, children are supposed to see their environment, make comparisons to other environments and then embrace certain types of attitudes as a result of this process. What the transcripts suggest is that context exposes people to a type of information not accounted for by political scientists. Knowing that a specific area is dangerous or risky, or that the people one encounters on a regular basis are themselves potential menaces, is similar to knowing that a certain type of state agent (police for example) are usually not (in urban environments) friendly. But in as much as perceptions of risk influence stress levels—a dynamic that influences a variety of mental health indicators—assertions that "risk is everywhere" are very different from knowing that a given political party does (or does not) tend to have one's own political interest in mind. When the respondents point to the degree to which abandoned buildings pockmark their neighborhoods they are not simply saying "these abandoned buildings serve as a signal that the political system does not have my best interests at heart." They are saying: "these abandoned buildings and the space around them constitute a clear and present danger to my life and to my health."

These perceptions of risk and threat are associated with stress levels as noted above. They are also associated with depression, with post-traumatic stress disorder, and a variety of mental health indicators (Dempsey 2002; Duckworth, Hale, and Clair 2000; Fang and Myers 2001; Farrell and Bruce 1997; Fitzpatrick and Boldizar 1993; Giaconia, Reinherz, and Silverman 1995). Given that youth are already a particularly vulnerable population, these perceptions should influence the degree to which they evince trust in the political system, the degree of efficacy they exhibit, and the extent to which their political attitudes as a whole are characterized by political apathy.

Conclusion

Cities such as Detroit, Saint Louis, Baltimore, and Washington, DC, have in many ways not only remained segregated but have become hyper-segregated. During much of the twentieth century, a modest proportion of black citizens could find work good enough to buy housing (albeit in segregated environments), and provide for the schooling of their children through college (albeit in segregated schools). However with the decentralization of what Thomas Sugrue has referred to as the "arsenals of democracy," as well as the growing political strength of black populations, whites began to move to suburban enclaves, which excluded blacks (Sugrue 1996; Thompson 2001). Poor blacks that were already segregated by race began to be segregated by class as well or the process known as hyper-segregation. With the beginning of the twenty-first century, this dynamic has not gotten better but in many ways has grown worse.

As a result, citizens living within these spaces find themselves beset with a host of social ills ranging from crime and systemic unemployment to health problems. HIV/AIDS is now one of the top five causes of death among both black men and black women. While some may blame this on the "down low" phenomenon of black men having homosexual sex that they do not disclose to their female partners, it is more likely the result of the growing incarceration of black men and women, which has increased under both Democratic and Republican regimes (National Center for HIV 2004). How does this general dynamic influence the political attitudes of youth—the most vulnerable of populations?

While we have some idea about how these contexts influence the political attitudes and behaviors of adults, we have only begun to explore the degree to which the political attitudes of youth are influenced by these contexts. At the same time scholars in public health have begun to explore the ways that context influences health outcomes, with a specific eye towards understanding how neighborhood context exacerbates health disparities. Research is beginning to uncover the degree to which health is the byproduct of political decisions and political institutions. What our work suggests is that we must begin to think about how health actually structures individual political attitudes and behaviors. Context can structure social networks that provide information. It can also give individuals a comparative lens with which to view other contexts and then make decisions based on those comparisons. However, context also provides information related to threat and risk. As neighborhoods like those on the East side of Detroit or in East Saint Louis shape the perceptions of a growing number of urban youth, it is clear that these perceptions are going to have a seminal role in structuring black youth attitudes from hereon. One can only hope that in the course of studying this relationship we can begin to also study interventions that return an agency to youth which they can use to change the world around them.

References

Abramson, Paul R. 1972. Political Efficacy and Political Trust Among Black Schoolchildren: Two Explanations. *The Journal of Politics 34* (4):1243-1275.

Abramson, Paul R. 1977. *The Political Socialization of Black Americans: A Critical Evaluation of Research on Efficacy and Trust*. New York: Free Press.

Adimora, A. A., and V. J. Schoenbach. 2005. Social Context, Sexual Networks, and Racial Disparities in Rates of Sexually Transmitted Infections. *Journal of Infectious Diseases* 191:S115-S122.

Anderson, Elijah. 1999. *Code of the Street: Decency, Violence, and the Moral Life of the Inner City*. 1st ed. New York ; London: W.W Norton.

Anderson, James F., Terry Grandison, and Laronistine Dyson. 1996. Victims of Random Violence and the Public Health Implication: A Health Care or Criminal Justice Issue? *Journal of Criminal Justice* 24 (5):379-91.

Bell, Carl, Donna Baptiste, and Sybil Madison. 2003. The Role of Personal Contact With HIV-Infected People in Explaining Urban, African American Preadolescents' Attitudes Toward Peers With HIV/AIDS. *American Journal of Orthopsychiatry* 73 (1):101-8.

Brown, Phil, Brian Mayer, and Stephen Zavestoski. 2003. The Health Politics of Asthma: Environmental Justice and Collective Illness Experience in the United States. *Social Science & Medicine* 57 (3):453-64.

Bruce, M. A. 2004. Contextual Complexity and Violent Delinquency Among Black and White Males. *Journal of Black Studies* 35 (1):65-98.

Chen, Y. Y., S. V. Subramanian, D. Acevedo-Garcia, and I. Kawachi. 2003. Qualitative and Quantitative Aspect of Health Behaviors in Context: A Multivariate Multilevel Analysis. *American Journal of Epidemiology* 157 (11):S64-S64.

Clarke, James W. 1973. Family Structure and Political Socialization Among Urban Black Children. *American Journal of Political Science* 17 (2):302-315.

Cohen, Cathy, and Michael Dawson. 1993. Neighborhood Poverty and African American Politics. *American Political Science Review* 87 (June):286-302.

Cohen, Cathy J. 1999. *The Boundaries of Blackness: AIDS and the Breakdown of Black Politics.* Chicago, IL: University of Chicago Press.

Collins, Chaquita A., and David R. Williams. 1999. Segregation and Mortality: The Deadly Effects of Racism? *Sociological Forum* 14 (3):495-523.

Cosby, William. 2004. *Dr. Bill Cosby Speaks* [World Wide Web]. 2004 [cited 10.15.04 2004]. Available from http://www.eightcitiesmap.com/transcript_bc.htm.

Dawson, Michael C. 1994. *Behind the Mule: Race and Class in African American Politics.* Princeton, NJ: Princeton University Press.

Dempsey, Margaret. 2002. Negative Coping as Mediator in the Relation Between Violence and Outcomes: Inner-City African American Youth. *American Journal of Orthopsychiatry* 72 (1):102-9.

Department of Health and Mental Hygiene, Maryland. 2005. *Baltimore City HIV/AIDS Epidemiological Profile* 2004 [cited 3/2/2005 2005]. Available from www.dhmh.state.md.us/AIDS/pdf/Baltimore-Quarterly.pdf.

Diaz, Rafael M., George Ayala, and Edward Bein. 2001. The Impact of Homophobia, Poverty, and Racism on the Mental Health of Gay and Bisexual Latino Men: Findings from Three U.S. cities. *American Journal of Public Health* 91 (6):927-32.

Dray, Philip. 2002. *At the Hands of Persons Unknown: The Lynching of Black America.* 1st ed. New York: Random House.

Duckworth, Melanie P., D. Danielle Hale, and Scott D. Clair. 2000. Influence of Interpersonal and Community Chaos on Stress Reactions in Children. *Journal of Interpersonal Violence* 15 (8):806-26.

Easton, David, and Jack Dennis. 1969. *Children in the Political System: Origins of Political Legitimacy.* New York: McGraw-Hill.

Fang, Carolyn Y., and Hector F. Myers. 2001. The Effects of Racial Stressors and Hostility on Cardiovascular Reactivity in African American and Caucasian Men. *Health Psychology* 20 (1):64-70.

Farrell, Albert D., and Steven E. Bruce. 1997. Impact of Exposure to Community Violence on Violent Behavior and Emotional Distress Among Urban Adolescents. *Journal of Clinical Child Psychology* 26:2-14.

Fiscella, K., and D. R. Williams. 2004. Health Disparities Based on Socioeconomic Inequities: Implications for Urban Health Care. *Academic Medicine* 79 (12):1139-1147.

Fitzpatrick, Kevin M., and Janet P. Boldizar. 1993. The Prevalence and Consequences of Exposure to Violence Among African American Youth. *Journal of the American Academy of Child and Adolescent Psychiatry* 32:424-30.

Fullilove, Mindy Thompson. 2003. Neighborhoods and Infectious Diseases. In *Neighborhoods and Health,* (ed.) I. Kawachi and L. F. Berkman. New York City: Oxford.

Fullilove, Mindy Thompson. 2004. *Root Shock: How Tearing Up City Neighborhoods Hurts America, and What We Can Do About It.* 1st ed. New York: One World/Ballantine Books.

Fullilove, Mindy Thompson, and Robert E. Fullilove. 1999. Stigma as an Obstacle to AIDS Action: The Case of the African American Community. *American Behavioral Scientist* 42 (7 (April)):1117.

Gay, Claudine. 2004. Putting Race in Context: Identifying the Environmental Determinants of Black Racial Attitudes. *American Political Science Review* 98 (4 (November 2004)):547-562.

Giaconia, Rose M., Helen Z. Reinherz, and Amy B. Silverman. 1995. Traumas and Posttraumatic Stress Disorder in a Community Population of Older Adolescents. *Journal of the American Academy of Child and Adolescent Psychiatry* 34:1369-80.

Gilens, Martin. 1999. *Why Americans Hate Welfare: Race, Media, and the Politics of Antipoverty Policy.* Chicago, IL: University of Chicago Press.

Gilliam, Franklin D., and Shanto Iyengar. 2000. Prime Suspects: The Influence of Local Television News on the Viewing Public. *American Journal of Political Science* 44 (3 (Jul. 2000)):560-573.

Gimpel, James G., J. Celeste Lay, and Jason E. Schuknecht. 2003. Cultivating Democracy: Civic Environments and Political Socialization in America. Washington, DC: Brookings Institution Press.

Gimpel, James, J. Celeste Lay, and Jason E. Schuknecht. 2002. Party Identification, Local Partisan Contexts and the Acquisition of Participatory Attitudes.

Greenberg, Edward S. 1970a. Black Children and the Political System. *Public Opinion Quarterly* 34 (3):333-345.

Greenberg, Edward S. 1970b. Children and Government: A Comparison Across Racial Lines. *Midwest Journal of Political Science* 14 (2):249-275.

Harrell, Shelly P. 2000. A Multidimensional Conceptualization of Racism-related Stress: Implications for the Well-being of People of Color. *American Journal of Orthopsychiatry* 70 (1):42-57.

Herek, Gregory M. 1999. AIDS and Stigma. *The American Behavioral Scientist* 42 (7 (April, 1999)):1106-1116.

Herek, Gregory M. 2003. Stigma, Social Risk, and Health Policy; Public Attitudes Toward HIV Surveillance Policies and the Social Construction of Illness. *Health Psychology* 22 (5 (September 2003)):533-540.

Herek, Gregory M., and John P. Capitanio. 1993. Public Reactions to AIDS in the United States: A Second Decade of Stigma. *American Journal of Public Health* 83 (April 1993):574-577.

Herek, Gregory M., and John P. Capitanio. 1995. Black Heterosexuals' Attitudes Toward Lesbians and Gay Men in the United States. *The Journal of Sex Research* 32 (2 (1995)):95-105.

Herek, Gregory M., and John P. Capitanio. 1999. AIDS-related Stigma and Attitudes Toward Injecting Drug Users Among Black and White Americans. *The American Behavioral Scientist* 42 (7 (April 1999)):1148-1161.

Herek, Gregory M., John P. Capitanio, and Keith F. Widaman. 2002. HIV-related Stigma and Knowledge in the United States: Prevalence and Trends, 1991-1999. *American Journal of Public Health* 92 (3 (March 2002)):371-377.

Hien, Denise, and Claudia Bukszpan. 1999. Interpersonal Violence in a "Normal" Low-income Control Group. *Women & Health* 29 (4):1-16.

House, James S., Karl R. Landis, and Debra Umberson. 1988. Social Relationships and Health. *Science* 241 (4865):540-545.

Huckfeldt, R. Robert, and C. W. Kohfeld. 1989. *Race and the Decline of Class in American Politics.* Urbana, IL: University of Illinois Press.

Jackson, John S. 1973. Alienation and Black Political Participation. *The Journal of Politics* 35 (4):849-885.

Juhna, Young J., Jennifer St Sauver, Slavica Katusic, Delfino Vargas, Amy Weaver, and John Yunginger. 2005. The Influence of Neighborhood Environment on the Incidence of Childhood Asthma: A Multilevel Approach. *Social Science & Medicine* 60 (11):2453-2464.

Key, V. O. 1949. *Southern Politics in State and Nation.* 1st ed. New York: A. A. Knopf.

LaVeist, T. A., and J. M. Wallace. 2000. Health Risk and Inequitable Distribution of Liquor Stores in African American Neighborhood. *Social Science & Medicine* 51 (4):613-617.

Laveist, Thomas A. 1993. Segregation, Poverty, and Empowerment: Health Consequences for African Americans. *Milbank Quarterly* 71 (1):41-64.

LaVeist, Thomas A. 1997. The Political Empowerment and Health Status of African Americans: Mapping a New Territory Part of a Symposium On: New Directions in the Sociology of Medicine. *American Journal of Sociology* 97:1080-95.

LaVeist, Thomas Alexis. 2002. *Race, Ethnicity, and Health: A Public Health Reader.* 1st ed. San Francisco, CA: Jossey-Bass.

Lincoln, Karen D., Linda M. Chatters, and Robert Joseph Taylor. 2003. Psychological Distress among Black and White Americans: Differential Effects of Social Support, Negative Interaction and Personal Control. *Journal of Health and Social Behavior* 44 (3):390-407.

Lwebuga-Mukasa, Jamson Jlwebuga buffalo edu, Tonny Oyana, and Caryn Johnson. 2005. Local Ecological Factors, Ultrafine Particulate Concentrations, and Asthma Prevalence Rates in Buffalo, New York, Neighborhoods. *Journal of Asthma* 42 (5):337-348.

Massey, Douglas S., and Nancy A. Denton. 1993. *American Apartheid: Segregation and the Making of the Underclass.* Cambridge, MA; London, Eng.: Harvard University Press.

National Center for HIV, STD, and TB Prevention. 2004. *HIV/AIDS Among Americans* [World Wide Web]. February 6, 2004 2004 [cited October 12, 2004 2004]. Available from http://www.cdc.gov/hiv/pubs/facts/afam.htm.

Okundaye, Joshua Nosa. 2004. Drug Trafficking and Urban African American Youth: Risk Factors for PTSD. *Child & Adolescent Social Work Journal* 21 (3):285-302.

Oliver, J. Eric, and Tali Mendelberg. 2000. Reconsidering the Environmental Determinants of White Racial Attitudes. *American Journal of Political Science* 44 (3):574-89.

Oyana, Tonny J., and Jamson S. Lwebuga-Mukasa. 2004. Spatial Relationships Among Asthma Prevalence, Health Care Utilization, and Pollution Sources in Neighborhoods of Buffalo, New York. *Journal of Environmental Health* 66 (8):25-37.

Oyana, Tonny J., Peter Rogerson, and Jamson S. Lwebuga-Mukasa. 2004. Geographic Clustering of Adult Asthma Hospitalization and Residential Exposure to Pollution at a United States-Canada Border Crossing. *American Journal of Public Health* 94 (7):1250-1257.

Pattillo, Mary E. 1998. Sweet Mothers and Gangbangers: Managing Crime in a Black Middle-Class Neighborhood. *Social Forces* 76 (3):747-774.

Pattillo-McCoy, Mary. 1999. *Black Picket Fences: Privilege and Peril Among the Black Middle Class.* Chicago, IL: University of Chicago Press.

Rimal, Rajiv N. 2001. Perceived Risk and Self-efficacy as Motivators: Understanding Individuals' Long-term Use of Health Information. *Journal of Communication* 51 (4):633-54.

Rimal, Rajiv N., and Kevin Real. 2003. Perceived Risk and Efficacy Beliefs as Motivators of Change: Use of the Risk Perception Attitude (RPA) Framework to Understand Health Behaviors. *Human Communication Research* 29 (3):370-99.

Roberts, E. M. 1997. Neighborhood Social Environments and the Distribution of Low Birthweight in Chicago. *American Journal of Public Health* 87 (4):597-603.

Schulz, A., D. Williams, B. Israel, A. Becker, E. Parker, S. A. James, and J. Jackson. 2000. Unfair Treatment, Neighborhood Effects, and Mental Health in the Detroit Metropolitan Area. *Journal of Health and Social Behavior* 41 (3):314-332.

St. Lawrence, Janet S. 1993. African American Adolescents' Knowledge, Health-related Attitudes, Sexual Behavior, and Contraceptive Decisions: Implications for the Prevention of Adolescent HIV Infection. *Journal of Consulting and Clinical Psychology* 61:104-12.

Sugrue, Thomas J. 1996. *The Origins of the Urban Crisis: Race and Inequality in Postwar Detroit, Princeton Studies in American Politics.* Princeton, NJ: Princeton University Press.

Thompson, Heather Ann. 2001. *Whose Detroit?: Politics, Labor, and Race in a Modern American City.* Ithaca, NY: Cornell University Press.

Wadsworth, Michael. 2003. Early Life. In *Social Determinants of Health*, (ed.) M. Marmot and R. G. Wilkinson. Oxford: Oxford University Press.

Wilson, William Julius. 1987. *The Truly Disadvantaged: The Inner City, the Underclass, and Public Policy.* Chicago, IL: University of Chicago Press.

Zimmerman, Marc A., Jesus Ramirez-Valles, and Kenneth I. Maton. 1999. Resilience Among Urban African American Male Adolescents: A Study of the Protective Effects of Sociopolitical Control on Their Mental Health. *American Journal of Community Psychology* 27 (6):733-51.

Permanent Outsiders: Felon Disenfranchisement and the Breakdown of Black Politics

Khalilah L. Brown-Dean
Yale University

"The Negro is a sort of seventh son, born with a veil, and gifted with second-sight in this American world,—a world which yields him no true self-consciousness, but only lets him see himself through the revelation of the other world. It is a peculiar sensation, this double-consciousness, this sense of always looking at one's self through the eyes of others, of measuring one's soul by the tape of a world that looks on in amused contempt and pity. One ever feels his twoness,—an American, a Negro; two warring souls, two thoughts, two unreconciled strivings; two warring ideals in one dark body, whose dogged strength alone keeps it from being torn asunder. The history of the American Negro is the history of this strife,—this longing to attain self-conscious manhood, to merge his double self into a better and truer self. ...—W. E. B. DuBois (1903).

May the conscience of a great nation rise and rebuke all dishonesty and unrighteous oppression toward the American Negro, and grant him the right of franchise [and] security of person and property."—W. E. B. DuBois (1903).

Introduction

DuBois's *The Souls of Black Folk* represents one of the most impressive accounts of black political life to date. Together, the above passages highlight DuBois's awareness of both the institutional and societal constraints on black advancement. With these profound statements, DuBois highlights African Americans' fractured self-image, while also affirming the importance of active political participation for redefining that image. Since this country's founding, numerous political movements have focused on securing access to the simplest tool of democracy: the franchise. The right to vote separates citizens from outsiders, and provides citizens with the opportunity to influence their government and promote their interests. Access to voting is particularly important for helping minority communities affirm their membership in the polity. Although voting is certainly not the only means of participating, it is one of the most efficient means of translating citizens' preferences into governmental action. In choosing political leaders, citizens can use the vote as a tool for protecting other rights and privileges. As affirmed in the 1964 *Wesberry v. Sanders* decision, "other rights, even the most basic, are illusory if the right to vote is undermined."

Table 1
Voter Registration Rates by Race, 1965-1988

	March 1965			November 1988		
	Black	White	Gap	Black	White	Gap
Alabama	19.3	69.2	49.9	68.4	75.0	6.6
Georgia	27.4	62.6	35.2	56.8	63.9	7.1
Louisiana	31.6	80.5	48.9	77.1	75.1	-2.0
Mississippi	6.7	69.9	63.2	74.2	80.5	6.3
North Carolina	46.8	96.8	50.0	58.2	65.6	7.4
South Carolina	37.3	75.7	38.4	56.7	61.8	5.1
Virginia	38.3	61.1	22.8	63.8	68.5	4.7

Source : Brown-Dean (2006)

   This struggle for inclusion has been a defining feature of Black Politics. Indeed the Civil Rights Movement represents the ultimate culmination of this focus. The movement helped stimulate African Americans' political awareness while also forcing the United States to reduce the gap between the principle and practice of equality. As others have argued, one of the most enduring legacies of the Movement was its emphasis on dismantling the institutional mechanisms of exclusion. Indeed, legislation such as the Civil Rights Act of 1964 and the Voting Rights Act of 1965 provided blacks with the necessary tools to challenge injustice in both the private and public sectors.

   Many argue that as a country, we have made significant strides in the march toward equality (Carmines and Stimson 1993; Thernstrom 1994; Sniderman and Piazza 1995). Certainly one cannot deny that African Americans have successfully raised their visibility both as voters and candidates. For example, when the VRA was passed in 1965, there were only seventy-two African American elected officials. The most recent statistics from the Joint Center for Political and Economic Studies places the number of black elected officials at around 8,000. As Table 1 indicates, less than 20 percent of blacks in Alabama were registered to vote in 1965. By 1988, nearly 70 percent of black Alabamians were registered to vote.

   The importance of active voting for articulating a community's concerns has been well-documented, both in the academic literature and within popular discourse (Walton 1985; Dawson 1994; Conyers 1999; Hutchinson 2000). Much of the post-Civil Rights Movement literature focuses on the movement of the African American community from protest politics to electoral politics (Tate 1993). For many, the fruits of the Civil Rights Movement insured inroads to political incorporation, and ultimately, racial inclusion for African Americans. The marches, boycotts, and non-violent rallies that took place finally resulted in the implementation of measures that outlawed "Jim Crow" in the South, and institutional discrimination in the United States. As former Attorney General William Rogers (1968) once stated, "When minority groups exercise their franchise, it almost invariably follows that they achieve a greater measure of other fundamental freedoms as well" (2). Unfortunately, after years of struggle and only minimal progress, mechanisms still exist that impede the full political incorporation of the African American community. Because expanding and strengthening the electorate is a necessary condition for achieving full political incorporation, felon disenfranchisement laws present a formidable barrier to African Americans' full electoral development.

Felon disenfranchisement laws prohibit current, and in many states, former felony offenders from voting. As a result, there are over 5 million people in this country who are permanently barred from voting. Of particular interest to this research, African Americans comprise some 40 percent of all Americans who have permanently unable to vote. This number stands in sharp contrast to the latest Census statistics that number blacks as being about 13 percent of the total U.S. population. According to Fellner and Mauer (1998), the rate of black voter disenfranchisement is nearly seven times the national average. Together, blacks and Latinos comprise nearly 60 percent of all Americans who have permanently lost the right to vote. As a result, such laws have significantly impaired the ability of black communities to participate in civil society.

Despite the devastating impact of these laws, political elites have failed to properly address this issue. Constrained by this country's current "zero-tolerance" climate and a desire to promote a more positive public image, black elites' silence on this issue has stifled the community's ability to mobilize against these statutes. Guided by Cohen's Theory of Marginalization, this article seeks to show that disenfranchisement laws are more than just matters of criminal justice. Rather, they represent significant threats to the sustenance of black political power. Part of that power rests in the ability to vote and enjoy the most fundamental benefits of living in a democratic system. Felon disenfranchisement laws are unique because they explicitly limit political participation, while making implicit claims regarding who is worthy of accessing the political process.

To provide a context for evaluating the current dynamics surrounding felon disenfranchisement laws, I begin with a discussion of how Cohen's Theory of Marginalization helps us better understand the importance of social stigma for suppressing black elites' response to felon disenfranchisement. Using this theoretical framework as a foundation, I discuss the historical roots and contemporary impact of disenfranchisement laws on black political development. Finally, I provide suggestions for future research on how the nexus of race and crime complicate traditional notions of Black Politics.

Theories of Marginalization, Incorporation, and Felon Disenfranchisement Laws

In *Boundaries of blackness: AIDS and the Breakdown of Black Politics*, Cohen (1999) argues that societal perceptions coupled with structural and institutional processes help re-enforce the marginal status of the African American community. Subsequently, the African American community helps to perpetuate existing stereotypes by participating in the marginalization of members of its own community. For Cohen, the marginalization of certain sub-groups within African American communities stifles the group's overall development of political power, because its political agenda does not adequately address the varied needs and interests of community members. This primarily results from both the limited amount of resources available to elite leaders, and the desire to protect and promote a positive African American image. Based on this, this research seeks to apply the central tenets of Cohen's theoretical analysis to the issue of felon disenfranchisement and its impact on African Americans' political participation. Further, understanding Cohen's analysis will be crucial for evaluating the black elite's failure to effectively mobilize on this issue.

Cohen begins her work by providing a theoretical foundation for the emergence of marginalization in society. Within the framework of marginalization, four factors are essential to the subordination of certain sub-groups: 1) identities and norms, 2) ideologies, 3) institutions, and 4) social relationships. In discussing the role of identities and norms, Cohen asserts that a "group's stigmatized identity works to constrain the opportunities and rights afforded community members" (1999:38). Although African American felons and ex-felons are viewed as members of the black community, the stigma of being a convicted felon negatively shapes the views of both the dominant group, as well as the broader racial group to which these felons belong. Thus, black felons are accepted by neither the dominant group, nor their own minority community. As a result, the concerns of this stigmatized group are pushed further to the periphery of the political process.

The second factor that shapes levels of marginalization is the prevalence of ideologies. Cohen (1999) contends that ideologies frame our understanding of what is "normal" and/or "deviant," and also what is "right" and/or "wrong." Ideological constructs essentially help to reinforce and legitimize the marginalization of groups in society. Society constructs an image of (ex) offenders as "deviant" and unworthy of rights and protections. As a result of this belief, the disenfranchisement of convicted felons is viewed as a legitimate form of punishment. Although administrators of the criminal justice system claim to promote and implement strategies of rehabilitation, ideologies of marginalization persist, and prisoners continue to experience secondary citizenship in American society. For many, this sense of secondary citizenship persists even after individuals have served their time.

Institutions like the criminal justice system play an important role in the process of marginalization by excluding and regulating marginal groups. Higginbotham (1996) discusses the historical role that institutions have played in the perpetuation of racism and racial stereotypes by providing ample evidence of periods in time where the judicial system validated racist and exclusionary practices. Such practices have a disproportionate impact on black communities. Policies mandated by the judicial system result in a system of political exclusion that infringes upon the citizenship rights of convicted felons while weakening the overall representation of the broader groups to which they belong (Brown and Paul 2000). Further, the system promotes a form of "American apartheid" that permanently strips individuals of some of the most fundamental benefits of living in a democratic society.

Lastly, Cohen's (1999) theory illuminates the importance of social relationships to the maintenance of marginalization. Informal interactions and prejudices of individuals in society perpetuate marginalization by increasing opportunities for the conveyance and dissemination of such beliefs. At the micro level, if citizens adopt dominant ideologies, identities, and norms associated with marginal groups that are negative, then those images of the stigmatized group are further solidified. Although the dominant structure may choose to ban the formal processes of exclusion, marginalization persists through routine social interactions. Applying this tenet highlights the importance role that individuals play in the stigmatization of convicted felons, as well as limiting opportunities for convicted felons to fully re-integrate back into society.

As previously stated, certain ideologies, identities, and norms help relegate certain groups to a marginalized status. For convicted felons, the road to full political incorporation is blocked by both their stigmatized status and the lack of resources necessary to gain political access. Yet their position can be further explained using Cohen's stages of marginalization: categorical marginalization, integrated marginalization, advanced marginalization, and secondary marginalization. Important to our analysis of felon disenfranchisement are three of the four categories: categorical, advanced, and secondary marginalization. Within each of these categories, power relations as well as the interactions between dominant and subordinate groups are explored. Essential to the different categories of marginalization is the understanding that only certain members of marginalized groups are allowed to completely enter the dominant structure, and that their ability to be incorporated into that group impacts the manner in which they interact with other marginal members.

Many scholars agree that the stigma associated with being a convicted felon is enduring (Kennedy 1997). Furthermore, the stigma of being a "black convicted felon" can be even more damaging. The complete categorical marginalization of African American felons can be seen in the ability of the judicial system to limit the voting potential of this group even after they have paid their proverbial debt to society. This exclusion from the voting process promotes the idea that they are somehow deserving of their marginal and secondary status. Yet it also impairs the ability of African American communities to move beyond their marginalized political status. Thus, African American felons are shut out of the political system because of ideological constructs that validate their position as a marginal group.

In the advanced marginalization stage, select groups members have successfully assimilated into the dominant structure and are placed in positions of power within that structure. Yet their position also warrants a "policing" of the marginal community to which they belong:

> Through the process of public policing, which communicates the judgments, evaluations, and condemnations of recognized leaders and institutions of black communities to their constituencies, the full membership of certain segments of black communities is contested and challenged (1999:74).

Thus, those who conform to the dominant group's norms and values are "legitimized" within the dominant group structure. Furthermore, they act as "authentic" leaders of the marginal group community. Their leadership status results in the secondary marginalization of "deviant" groups within marginal communities.

Although Cohen applies her theoretical framework to the issue of AIDS in the black community, her analysis holds similar implications for the issue of felon disenfranchisement and its impact on black communities. At the mass level, political incorporation is minimal for marginal groups, and is essentially determined by the group's cadre of leaders. As a result of their need to promote a positive image to the broader community, African American community leaders often view the interests of convicted felons as outside of the desired political agenda. Thus, the policing efforts of elite members help push the issue of felon disenfranchisement onto the periphery. Essentially, convicted felons are denied access to both dominant resources and institutions, in addition to indigenous resources and organizations based on this process of secondary marginalization. As Adolph Reed, Jr. (1999) argues, the face of African American politics has changed. A new black regime has emerged, one in which African American leaders have adapted to the dominant structure, both in their approach to politics, and their interactions with the black community. In essence, the focus for many black leaders has been self-empowerment and not community empowerment. As a result, the voices of certain groups within black communities are muted in the political process. Thus, efforts to successfully mobilize black communities necessarily exclude certain individuals and groups. Guided by Cohen's framework, I turn now to an historical overview of disenfranchisement laws.

Historical Perspectives on Black Exclusion

Disenfranchisement laws have existed in many states since the founding of this great nation over 200 years ago. Throughout earlier periods in this country's history, the vote was seen as the privilege of wealthy white men, and therefore not extended to women, ethnic and racial minorities, certain criminals, the poor, and illiterates (Dollard 1949). Since that time, several Constitutional amendments and other key acts of legislation have enabled these groups to successfully gain suffrage, and therefore secure a voice in the political process.

However, one fairly large and resource poor group remains excluded from the electorate: felons and ex-felons. [1] According to Marc Mauer (1996) of The Sentencing Project, disenfranchisement laws in the United States are "a vestige of medieval times when offenders were banished from the community and suffered 'civil death' (23)."[2] Though some form of criminal disenfranchisement has always existed in this country, the end of the nineteenth century marked an important era for the expansion and strict enforcement of these restrictions.

As African Americans gained greater access to the political process, southern white opposition soared. As such, the year 1890 marked the beginning of several southern conventions aimed at stifling blacks' political involvement. Through these conventions, white legislators were able to devise numerous strategies for keeping African Americans out of the voting booth. Though white primaries, poll taxes, grandfather clauses, and outright violence are most often identified as the most prominent of these strategies, most state's criminal disenfranchisement laws were explicitly designed to suppress blacks' electoral participation. As Andrew Shapiro writes, "criminal disenfranchisement—the denial of the vote to citizens convicted of crimes—was the most subtle method of excluding blacks from the franchise."[3]

Recognizing the strength of these plans, from 1895 to 1910, eleven other states including Virginia, Alabama, Tennessee, and Florida expanded the scope of their disenfranchisement provisions. Further, the crimes covered by these provisions were based on those crimes that "blacks supposedly committed more frequently than whites, and to exclude crimes whites were believed to commit more frequently (Lewinson 1932)." For example, archival research reveals that in South Carolina:

> Among the disqualifying crimes were those to which [the Negro] was especially prone: thievery, adultery, arson, wife-beating, housebreaking, and attempted rape. Such crimes as murder and fighting to which the white man was as disposed as the Negro were significantly omitted from the list.[4]

Similarly, in a 1901 speech, Alabama lawmakers boasted of basing disenfranchisement on crimes of "moral turpitude" in an effort to "establish white supremacy (Wang 1997)."[5] In affirming this proposition, the 1896 case of *Ratliff v. Beale* stated the following:

> By reason of its previous condition of servitude and dependence, this [Negro] race had acquired or accentuated certain peculiarities of habit, or temperament, and of character which clearly distinguished it as a race from that of the whites—a patient docile people—but careless, landless, and migratory within narrow limits, without forethought, and its criminal members given rather to furtive offenses than to the robust crimes of the whites. Restrained by the federal constitution from discriminating against the Negro race, the convention discriminated against its characteristics and the offenses to which its weaker members were prone.[6]

From this historical overview, we can see that criminal disenfranchisement laws emerged as a means of depressing black political participation. As Chief Justice William Rehnquist wrote in *Hunter v. Underwood* (1985), "the historical evidence demonstrates conclusively that these laws were deliberately enacted with the intent of disenfranchising blacks."

From Exclusion to Marginalization

Though the laws are the only restriction of that era that remain in effect, they have been sharply challenged over time. Guided by the Civil Rights Movement's expansive efforts to liberalize American politics, reform activists argued that disenfranchisement laws violated the spirit of American democracy. In attempting to merge grassroots organizing with legal challenges, activists hoped to convince the courts that disenfranchisement laws were unconstitutional.

Inspired by the protest tactics of the Civil Rights Movement, the 1970s witnessed a surge in efforts to focus attention on the plight of incarcerated citizens. The most prominent of these strategies were the prison protests and riots in states such as New York, California, and Illinois. Building upon these events, various leaders and advocacy groups came together to initiate a movement aimed at challenging what they viewed as a flawed system of justice. The first phase of the movement focused on resisting the growth of the "Prison Industrial Complex." According to a pamphlet published by the Critical Resistance Organization, the term *Prison Industrial Complex* refers to:

A complicated system situated at the intersection of governmental and private interests that uses prisons as a solution to social, political, and economic problems. The PIC depends upon the oppressive systems of racism, classism, sexism, and homophobia. It includes human rights violations, the death penalty, industry and labor issues, policing, courts, media, community powerlessness, the imprisonment of political prisoners, and the elimination of dissent.

Organizations such as Citizens United for Rehabilitation of Errants (CURE), the Prison Reform Trust, the Sentencing Project, and the ACLU mobilized grassroots campaigns to raise the public's awareness of both the growth of the prison industry and the consequences of massive incarceration. The goal of these campaigns was to encourage citizens to demand more constructive approaches to fighting crime. To this end, these campaigns often focused on eradicating the structural and institutional causes of criminal behavior. Out of these outreach campaigns came later efforts to promote a holistic transformation of America's approach to crime control. Advocates believed that this transformation was necessary to overcome the historical roots of the penal system. In referencing this history former black Panther leader Assata Shakur asserts that:

> Prisons were introduced in Africa, the Americas, and Asia as by-products of slavery and colonialism, and they continue to be instruments of exploitation and oppression. In the heart of the imperialist empires, prisons also meant oppression. The Prison-Industrial Complex is not only a mechanism to convert public tax money into profits for private corporations, it is an essential element of modern neoliberal capitalism. It serves two purposes. One to neutralize and contain huge segments of potentially rebellious sectors of the population, and two, to sustain a system of super-exploitation, where mainly black and Latino captives are imprisoned in white rural, overseer communities.[7]

Ultimately, these efforts led to a broader movement to re-focus the purpose of incarceration on rehabilitation rather than just punishment. Concerned advocates challenged politicians and citizens to consider what should happen *after* offenders were released from prison. Thus, it became necessary to provide individuals with incentives to not commit further crimes, as well as prepare them for life beyond the prison walls. Reflecting on her own experiences as a political prisoner and exile, Assata Shakur used her poem "Affirmation" to remind practitioners that, "And, if I know anything at all, it's that a wall is just a wall and nothing more at all. It can be broken down." These words later became the guiding belief for many organizations demanding a critical assessment of America's criminal justice system.

The prison reform movement addressed felon disenfranchisement on the grounds that the laws were outdated and served no clear purpose. Further, former offenders as well as their advocates believed that the laws impeded the full rehabilitation of ex-offenders. For example, Shapiro (1993) documents the importance of groups such as the American Bar Association and the American Law Institute who "came out against lifetime disenfranchisement ... back when there were still criminologists who bothered to report that the stigma of exclusion might actually deter rehabilitation and increase the likelihood of recidivism" (p. 13). Building upon these views, many believed that the removal of criminals' voting rights violated the protections of the Constitution. This was particularly important given the many legal battles during this time to secure civil liberties protections for both the accused and the convicted. Prison reform advocates also believed that the stigma associated with being ineligible to vote violated the country's commitment to social justice.

In addition to seeing the loss of rights as a threat to justice, others feared that voting restrictions would eventually lead to other, more severe restrictions. However, broader social and economic changes significantly changed the tenor of this support. Economic downturns and conservative judicial decisions led many prisoners' rights advocates to shift their focus to more immediate threats such as the increased use of the death penalty, changes in the sentencing structure, and the privatization of prisons. As a result, felon disenfranchisement became a low priority on the grassroots political agenda. In addition to this change in reformers' agenda, the alarming increases in drug use and drug-related crimes thrust issues surrounding enforcement to the forefront of the nation's political agenda. The prominence of these concerns silenced many elites who had previously supported more rehabilitative approaches to crime control. This was particularly true of black elites who feared that speaking out on the issue would heighten the overlap between race and crime in the public's thinking.

As previously stated, the Civil Rights Movement inspired massive efforts to transform America's political and social landscape. Yet ironically, the contemporary function of the criminal justice system in general and felon disenfranchisement laws in particular, threatens to undermine many of the Movement's gains. According to a recent report released by The Sentencing Project (2004), nearly 98,000 African Americans were incarcerated when the *Brown v. Board* decision was reached in 1954. Fifty years later, the number of African Americans behind bars has risen to more than 880,000. That same report found that over 52 percent of young black men who are high school dropouts also have a prison record. Further, one in three young black men can expect to serve time in prison at some point in their lifetime.

Much of this change can be attributed to shifting views on the purpose and function of incarceration. Beginning with the Anti-Drug Abuse Acts of the Reagan administration and the accompanying War on Drugs Movement, the criminal justice system shifted from an emphasis on rehabilitation to incapacitation. However, one should not limit this issue to the Republican agenda. Schiraldi (2001) details how "tough policies, more prisons, officers, and longer sentences [have] led to more Americans going to prison during Clinton than any other administration."[8] For example, 673,000 individuals were sent to state and federal jails and prisons during Clinton's two terms compared to 448,000 and 343,000 during the Reagan and Bush (Sr.) administrations, respectively.

This movement changed the face of law enforcement policies while also drawing greater public support for harsher punishment. The most prominent of these changes included the adoption of mandatory-minimum sentences, the abolishment of parole in many states, and the adoption of differential sentencing plans for certain crimes. In 1992, U.S. Attorney General William P. Barr issued a report entitled *The Case for More Incarceration*. The report introduced a federal strategy aimed at encouraging state criminal justice systems to reduce crime by increasing incarceration rates. Following the guidelines of the report, most states aggressively pursued incarceration as a deterrent to future crime. By 1990 the national imprisonment rate swelled by 110 percent (282 per 100,000 citizens in the population), with over 713,000 inmates housed in state and federal prisons (Bureau of Justice Statistics, 1992).

These new crime-fighting strategies exponentially increased the size of the criminal population under supervision. Yet, they also gave way to substantial racial disparities. Aside from disparities in arrest and incarceration rates, harsher sentencing policies reinforced racial distinctions by lengthening the period of supervision for certain criminals (Brown-Dean 2005). One of the most notable examples of this disparity is the sentencing guideline for crack versus powder cocaine. When Congress adopted mandatory minimum sentencing laws for all drugs in 1986, it also decided to impose harsher penalties for crack cocaine than for powder cocaine. For example, the mandatory penalty for selling five grams of crack cocaine was five years in prison, while the penalty for selling 500 grams of powder cocaine was also five years. Since the adoption of these guidelines the policy has become known as the "100:1 disparity." Two years later, Congress made crack cocaine the only drug for which there was a mandatory prison term for possession. Given the possibility that many of the individuals convicted of these offenses lacked the resources to successfully fight these charges, the new guidelines meant that a tremendous number of citizens would be serving longer sentences for non-violent offenses. Based on this,

Figure 1
Severity of Felon Voting Restrictions by State

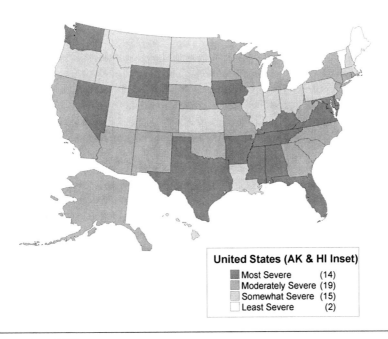

United States (AK & HI Inset)

■ Most Severe   (14)
▨ Moderately Severe (19)
▧ Somewhat Severe   (15)
□ Least Severe   (2)

Source : Brown-Dean (2006)

opponents of the zero-tolerance approach argue that the increasing incarceration rates do not necessarily translate into safer communities (Stimson, 2001). Instead, the approach only serves to perpetuate existing disparities on a variety of dimensions such as race and class.

In referencing the racial consequences of these sentencing strategies, the ACLU (2000) documented that although 93.7 percent of crack cases were brought against African Americans and Latinos, only about 6 percent of the cases were brought against whites. However, Whites represented 64.4 percent of crack users compared to 35 percent for African Americans and Latinos. In contrast, 17.8 percent of powder cocaine cases were brought against Whites compared to 50.8 percent against Latinos.[9]

These consequences laid the foundation for a new set of voices arguing against disenfranchisement because of disparities in arrest, prosecution, and sentencing. Opponents argued against disenfranchisement on the grounds that the penalty emanated from a system marred by racial discrimination. Though earlier activists had used this reasoning to fight against policies such as mandatory-minimums, the second wave of activists focused on the broader, community-wide implications of this systemic bias.

Given the increasing numbers of minorities who were permanently losing the right to vote, there was a growing concern that these policies would eventually create disparities in political access for minority groups struggling to gain political representation. Scholars and activists such as the National Coalition on black Voter Participation (NCBVP), the League of United Latin American Citizens (LULAC), Lani Guinier, the black Leadership Forum, Cornel West, Jesse Jackson, Sr. and the Southern Christian Leadership Center feared that the high numbers of disenfranchised minorities would dismantle the gains secured during the Civil Rights Movement. For example, a report issued by the U.S. Conference on Civil Rights (2001) cautioned that criminal disenfranchisement laws:

Necessarily [deplete] a minority community's voting strength over time by consistently placing a greater proportion of minority than majority voters under a voting disability at any given time. For this reason, the effects of the intentional discrimination that originally motivated felony disenfranchisement still lingers.

The Impact of Marginalization

Although there are certain federal guidelines regarding voting rights, it is important to note that state law establishes electoral qualifications. This discretion has created an inconsistent patchwork of regulations that is often quite confusing. Presently, forty-eight states and the District of Columbia prohibit prisoners serving a felony sentence from voting, while Vermont and Maine allow inmates to vote.[10] Thirty-two states do not allow individuals on parole or probation to vote, while felony convictions can result in permanent disenfranchisement in thirteen states.[11]

States that disenfranchise former felons maintain a process that allows for the restoration of rights, but these requirements are often cumbersome and challenging. For example, of the 200,000 ex-convicts who are residents of the state of Virginia, only 404 have had their rights restored in a recent two-year period (Fellner and Mauer 1998).[12] This failure can be attributed to a number of factors including: (1) a lack of information regarding the process necessary to regain the right to vote, (2) an emphasis on more immediate needs (e.g., finding housing, jobs, etc.) and, (3) a lack of political and financial resources necessary to successfully navigate this arduous restoration process. For example, an ex-offender seeking to regain the right to vote in Mississippi must either secure an executive order from the governor, or convince a state legislator to introduce a bill on his or her behalf, get two-thirds of the legislators in each house to vote for it, and then have the governor sign off on it. In other states like Alabama, ex-felons must first submit a DNA sample to the state's department of forensic science before they can apply to have their voting rights restored. The state of Florida created a so-called fast track program which previously required applicants to fill out a twenty-page questionnaire that asked everything from what your parents died of (if deceased), to the full names and social security numbers of the fathers/mothers of your children.

Figure 2
African Americans in Prisons and Jails, 1954-2002

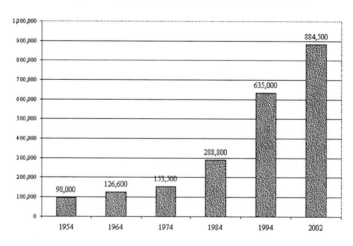

Table 2
Disenfranchisement Rates for Men by Race

State	# Disenfranchised black men	% of Felons who are black	% Disenfranchised black men	# Disenfranchised white men	% of Felons who are white	% Disenfranchised white men
Alabama	42,072	66.4	31.5	73,429	33.3	6.3
Florida	109,063	55.4	31.2	169,931	42.6	3.5
Mississippi	81,700	75.3	28.6	9,088	24.2	1.1
Virginia	40,852	66.5	25.0	25,792	32.6	1.4
Texas	156,610	44.5	20.8	425,382	28.3	7.9
Iowa	10,746	24.2	26.5	15,157	68.9	1.5

Source: Based on data from the U.S. Department of Justice, Voting Section, http://www.usdoj.gov/crt/voting/

Undoubtedly, felon disenfranchisement laws have had a disproportionate impact on communities of color, and that impact is becoming more pronounced each year. Convicted felons constitute the largest single group of American citizens who are prohibited by law from participating in elections. According to the latest report from the Bureau of Justice Statistics, African Americans represent more than one-third of all Americans who are temporarily or permanently unable to vote because of a felony conviction.

Of the states with felony voter restrictions, Alabama and Florida have experienced the most devastating effects with nearly one-third of black men having permanently lost the right to vote. In Alabama, Florida, Mississippi, and Virginia, one in four black men is permanently disenfranchised. [13]

Many have suggested that this disparity in disenfranchisement rates is a direct consequence of harsher sentencing policies, particularly for violent crimes. Likewise, the National War on Drugs has been important for stimulating the high number of African Americans barred from voting. Mauer and Fellner (1997) assert that "the increased rate of black imprisonment is a direct and foreseeable consequence of harsher sentencing policies, particularly for violent crimes, and for the national war on drugs…drug control policies that have led to the arrest, prosecution, and imprisonment of tens of thousands of African Americans represent the most dramatic change in factors contributing to the disproportionate rate of incarceration (3)." For example, in Washington, DC, 42 percent of black men aged eighteen to thirty-five were under some form of criminal justice control in 1992. In that same year, 56 percent of black men aged eighteen to thirty-five in Baltimore were under some form of criminal justice control.

The figures below track both the increase in adult drug arrests and correctional populations over the last twenty years.

The presidential election of 2000 provides us with a practical example of the increasing importance of the criminal justice system. In the state of Florida alone, at least 300,000 ex-felons were unable to vote in that election. Focusing on a community's ability to have a voice

Figure 3
Adult Correctional Population, 1980-2001

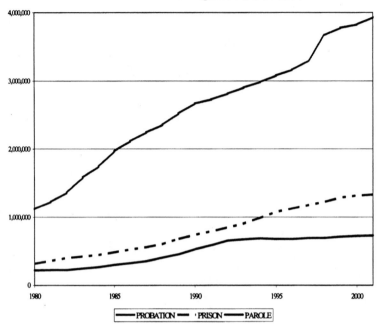

Source : Brown-Dean (2006)

Figure 4
Adult Correctional Population, 1970-2001

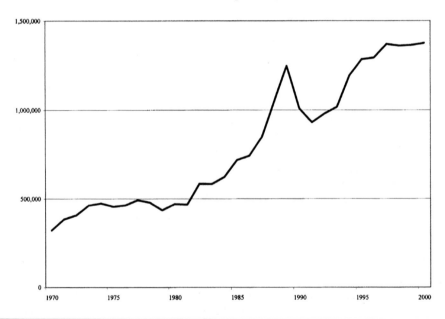

Source : Brown-Dean (2006)

in the political process, 31 percent of black men in that state and 12.4 percent of Latinos were ineligible to vote. Florida is indeed a unique case because of the allegations that many eligible voters were erroneously purged from the voting rolls. However, it does point to the possibility that extending the right to vote to former felons could potentially alter the outcome of political contests. If we accept the conventional knowledge that African Americans and non-Cuban Hispanics tend to overwhelmingly identify with the Democratic Party, it follows that Gore could have secured a more decisive, and uncontested, victory in that state.

It is interesting to note that in the Presidential election of 2004, thirteen of the eighteen battleground states have rather restrictive bans on felon voting. In those eighteen states alone, these restrictions account for a loss of over 1.5 million potential voters (Brown-Dean 2006). These figures affirm the belief that these policies don't just affect the individual offender. Rather, they hold powerful consequences for the broader community to which that (ex) offender belongs. By reducing the size of the eligible electorate, these laws also reduce the potential for a community to support legislation—such as revamping the school funding system—that promotes its best interests.

The Need to Move from Silence to Action

Despite the pervasive impact of these laws, they are relatively understudied in the realm of social science. Illuminating the political consequences of this phenomenon is critical because as Verba, Schlozman, and Brady (1995) suggest, voice and equality are central to democratic participation. In conceptualizing these terms the authors note: "in a meaningful democracy, the people's voice must be clear and loud—clear so that policymakers understand citizen concerns and loud so that they have an incentive to pay attention to what is said. Since democracy implies not only governmental responsiveness to citizen interests but also equal consideration of the interests of each citizen, democratic participation must also be equal (1)."

A great deal of the political science literature, specifically in the fields of race politics and urban politics, argues that when African Americans can effectively mobilize their numbers, they can play an essential role in the electoral process. Yet contrary to traditional voting behavior literature that tends to homogenize African American communities, there are certain persistent patterns that shape the policy interests and pursuits of these communities. For example, the growing gender gap among African American voters results from the fact that African American women tend to vote in larger numbers than African American men (Tate 1993; Verba et al. 1995). This can be partially explained by the fact that more black women are eligible to vote than black men. Such disparities in male and female voting behavior, coupled with felon disenfranchisement create a problem for African American electoral participation. As African American men are disproportionately incarcerated in many states, their electoral power is diluted. In turn, the overall voting power of the African American community is threatened. This phenomenon has implications for the policy agenda of African American communities. Essentially, policy concerns of the African American community are jeopardized as the numbers needed for political mobilization is undercut by a decrease in the number of African American males who are eligible to vote; a possible voting bloc for the African American community. Thus, mobilization against felon disenfranchisement is necessary to the political mobilization and incorporation of the African American community.

Felon disenfranchisement also poses a threat to black political representation. Debates over the Voting Rights Act of 1965 and majority-minority redistricting call into question issues of racial inclusion and representation (Grofman and Davidson 1992). Some argue that redistricting is important because it insures the election of African American representatives and leaders (Grofman and Davidson 1992). Other literature shows that African Americans are important to the election of minority mayors in cities with large black populations (Browning, Marshall, and Tabb 1984). The controversy over African Americans' political representation is further complicated when considering felon disenfranchisement in two ways: (1) at the individual level and, (2) at the mass level. At the individual level, felon disenfranchisement hinders the ability of large numbers of individuals to participate in the political process. Taking away the voting rights of felons and ex-felons fosters a sense of political distrust and anomie resulting in lack of interest in the political process. Ultimately, felon disenfranchisement may stunt individual political growth. Subsequently, if the goal of the prison system is rehabilitation, felony disenfranchisement counters attempts at rehabilitation, especially when considering that felons and former felons have lost the most important citizenship right, the right to vote.

At the mass level, felon disenfranchisement impedes the ability of African Americans to elect black representatives. Browning, Marshall, and Tabb (1984) argue that one necessary resource to minority incorporation is the ability to mobilize sufficient numbers. The disproportionate incarceration of black men blocks mobilization efforts in that the number of potential participants is less. Furthermore, their inability to vote hinders the ability of the African American community to make electoral gains in terms of black representation. Thus racial inclusion becomes more of a myth as black representation becomes difficult to obtain. On the other hand, the failure of African American leaders to recognize felony disenfranchisement as an issue that is detrimental to the African American community results in ignorance about the issue. African American leaders and organizations have the resources necessary to make the issue of felony disenfranchisement a part of their political agenda. Undoubtedly, felon disenfranchisement is an issue that the black community chooses to separate itself from, yet it is an issue that has negative consequences for the African American community. Therefore, African American leaders and organizations need to take the initiative to mobilize the community against felon disenfranchisement laws, and to spread awareness about the implications of such laws for basic democratic inclusion.

Aside from potentially shaping the outcomes of elections, enduring features of the criminal justice system provide yet another reason to assess felon disenfranchisement. The most recent numbers released by the Bureau of Justice Statistics indicate that the number of individuals under criminal supervision has reached an all time high. African Americans continue to be disproportionately represented within the system. Henry Louis Gates found that in 1995, one in four young black men (aged twenty-one to twenty-nine) were under some form of criminal control. Thus, as the number of those convicted of felony offenses continues to increase, and the number of ex-felons leaving prisons continues to climb, we can expect a steady increase in the number of citizens who will be permanently barred from voting in this country. These figures speak to the need for lawmakers and practitioners to address the impact of ostensibly race-neutral criminal control policies.

This topic also allows us to examine the often contradictory nature of public policy in this country. For example, during the 2003 Congressional elections, Jim Traficant was able to run for Congress from prison, but not able to vote for himself. Further, as we continue to witness growth in the number of prisons in this country, we must also assess the fairness of including prison populations in census counts to grant states a greater share of government resources (e.g., congressional districts; federal dollars). Yet, these prisoners have no input into how they are represented, and thus their interests are often neglected.

Lastly, we must also begin to aggressively re-consider the purpose and function of incarceration. And what happens to offenders once they are released. Certainly preventing individuals from voting neither limits criminals' capacity to commit further crimes, nor furthers their rehabilitation. Instead, what this policy does is exacerbate the collateral consequences of incarceration.

One of the dimensions that I am particularly interested in is the generational effects of this policy. We know for example, that the best predictor of whether you vote is whether your parents voted. This form of political socialization is important for conveying to young people the importance of participating in the process. Thus as the number of parents who are barred from voting increases, we will also begin to see that the children of these offenders are at a greater political disadvantage.

The fundamental conclusion to be reached from this study is that felon disenfranchisement is an important research domain for those interested in race, crime, and politics. Furthermore, African American leaders and organizations need to challenge the democratic principles of the dominant structure. As minorities have gained rights as a protected class under American democratic laws, they have simultaneously become victims of those same so-called democratic principles. Essentially, the idea of a democracy is porous especially when discussing the position of minorities within the American political system. Felon disenfranchisement infringes upon the fundamental right of every citizen in the United States, the right to vote. The disenfranchisement of African American felons and ex-felons mirrors the historical exclusion of African Americans before the Civil Rights Movement. It also foreshadows the creation of other initiatives to hinder the political progress of African American communities in the post-civil rights era.

Notes

1. Three Civil War Amendments in particular were critical for gradually extending constitutional protection of the franchise for these groups. The Thirteenth Amendment (1865) forbade slavery and therefore secured a minimal degree of citizenship for blacks. The Fourteenth Amendment (1868) granted citizenship to all persons "born or naturalized in the United States," but failed to explicitly prohibit vote discrimination on racial grounds. The Fifteenth Amendment (1870) stated that "the rights of citizens of the United States to vote shall not be denied or abridged by the U.S. or by any State on account of race, color, or previous condition of servitude" and gave explicit constitutional protection to the voting rights of blacks in the North and South (Grofman and Davidson 1992:10)."
2. Part of this notion of "civil death" involved the "deprivation of all rights, confiscation of property, and exposure to injury and even to death (Mauer 1996)."
3. Source: http://www.herald.com/content/archive/news/elect97.htm.
4. Source: Courthouse Records, State of Alabama.
5. Interestingly, Alabama currently has one of the highest rates of permanent disenfranchisement with nearly one-third of black men in that state having lost the right to vote.
6. Ratliff v. Beale, 74 Miss. 247,266; 20 S. 865,868 (1896).
7. Source: http://www.afrocubaweb.com/assata2.htm#Prison.
8. http://www.freep.com/news/nw/pris19_20010219.htm.
9. http://archive.aclu.org/congress/l052102a.html.
10. Data analysis based on state policies as of 2004. Most states define a felony as an offense punishable by death, or imprisonment in a penitentiary or state prison. However, there is still a great deal of variation across jurisdictions regarding what constitutes such an offense.
11. Another unique feature of this state discretion is that whether a (former) felon can vote generally depends on the state they reside in, not the state they were convicted in. For example, a former felon living in Ohio would be eligible to vote. However, that individual would lose that right if he moved to Virginia. Although this practice would seem to violate the full faith and credit clause, the Court has ruled that states can impose such restrictions.
12. It should be noted that there have been several attempts in the state of Virginia to make the restoration process more accessible. Since taking office in January of 2002, Governor Mark Warner has shortened the length of the application and also encouraged state legislators to pass a bill that would require corrections officials to make ex-felons aware of restoration procedures.
13. To the extent that there have been detailed estimates developed on disenfranchisement, these have primarily been produced for black males (e.g., Fellner and Mauer). Therefore, it was necessary to restrict my analysis to men in order to examine changes in the patterns of disenfranchisement over time. In the future, I hope to incorporate women and people of color (more broadly) into my analysis in order to produce a more comprehensive picture of the impact of felon disenfranchisement.

References

Brown, Khalilah L. and Javonne A. Paul. 2000. "Stolen Democracy: Felony Disenfranchisement Laws and the Future of Black America." Paper presented at the National Conference of Black Political Scientists, Washington, DC.

Brown-Dean, Khalilah L. 2006. "Once Convicted, Forever Doomed: Felon Disenfranchisement Laws and American Political Inequality." Unpublished manuscript.

——. 2006. "The Criminal Justice System and the Challenge of Black and Latino Political Empowerment." In *The Politics of Community Building: African American and Latino Political Actors*, (ed.) William E. Nelson, Jr. and Jessica Lavariega Monforti. Miami, FL: Barnhardt and Ashe.

——. 2005. "Trading *Brown* for Prison Orange: Reflections on Racial Justice Fifty Years after *Brown v. Board of Education*." *Journal of the Institution for Social and Policy Studies.*

Browning, Rufus, Dale Rogers Marshall, and David Tabb.1984.*Protest is Not Enough: The Struggles of Blacks and Hispanics for Equality in Urban Politics.* Berkeley, CA: University of California Press.

Carmines, Edward G. and James A. Stimson. 1989. *Issue Evolution: Race and the Transformation of American Politics.* Princeton, NJ: Princeton University Press.

Cohen, Cathy. 1999. *The Boundaries of blackness: AIDS and the Breakdown of Black Politics.* Chicago, IL: University of Chicago Press.

Conyers, John. 1999. (ed.) "The Commission to Study Reparations Proposals." In *When Sorry Isn't Enough: The Controversy Over Apologies and Reparations For Human Injustice.*

Dawson, Michael. 1994. *Behind the Mule: Race and Class in African American Politics.* Princeton, NJ: Princeton University Press.

Dollard, John.1949. *Caste and Class in a Southern Town.* New York: Doubleday.

DuBois, W.E.B. 1903. *The Souls of Black Folk: Essays and Sketches.* Chicago, IL: A.C. McClurg and Co.

Fellner, Jamie and Marc Mauer. 1998. "Losing the Vote: The Impact of Felony Disenfranchisement Laws in the United States." Washington, DC: The Sentencing Project.

Higginbotham, A. Leon. 1996. *Shades of Freedom: Racial Politics and Presumptions of the American Legal Process.* New York: Oxford University Press.

Huffington, Arianna. 2000. "Jim Crow Nestled in Latest Drug Law." *Boston Sunday Herald.* October.

Hutchinson, Earl Ofari. 2000. Lift the Ban Against Felons Being Able to Vote. *Los Angeles Times*, September 27.

Hunter v. Underwood. 471 U.S. 222 (1985).

Jones, Mack. 1972. "A Frame of Reference for Black Politics." In *Black Political Life in the United States.* (ed.) Lenneal Henderson. San Francisco, CA: Chandler.

Kennedy, Randall. 1997. *Race, Crime, and the Law.* New York: Pantheon Books.

Lewinson, Paul. 1932. *Race, Class, and Party: A History of Negro Suffrage and White Politics in the South.* New York: Oxford University Press.

Mauer, Marc. 1996. *Losing the Vote: The Impact of Felony Disenfranchisement Laws in the United States.* Washington, DC: The Sentencing Project.

Mauer, Marc, and Jamie Fellner. 1998. Losing the Vote: The Impact of Felony Disenfranchisement Laws in the United States. Washington, DC: The Sentencing Project.

Mauer, Marc, and Ryan Scott King. 2004. Schools and Prisons: Fifty Years After Brown v. Board of Education. Washington DC: The Sentencing Project.

Reed, Adolph Jr. 1986. *The Jesse Jackson Phenomenon: The Crisis of Purpose in Afro-American Politics.* New Haven, CT: Yale University Press.

Reed, Adolph Jr. 1999. *Stirrings in the Jug: Black Politics and the Post-Segregationist Era.* Minneapolis, MN: University of Minneapolis Press.

Rights, U.S. Commission on Civil. 2001. Voting Irregularities in Florida During the 2000 Presidential Election. Washington, DC: US Commission on Civil Rights.

Roy L. Brooks. New York: New York University Press.

Schiraldi, Vincent. 2001. A Tale of Two Jurisdictions: Youth Crime and Detention Rates in Maryland and the District of Columbia. Washington, DC: Building Blocks for Youth.

Shapiro, Andrew. 1993. Note: Challenging Criminal Disenfranchisement Under the Voting Rights Act: A New Strategy. *Yale Law Journal* 103:537-66.

Sniderman, Paul and Thomas Piazza. 1995. *The Scar of Race.* Cambridge: Harvard University Press.

Statistics, Bureau of Justice. 1992. National Corrections Reporting Program. Washington, DC: U.S. Department of Justice.

Stimson, Elizabeth. 2001. "Justice Denied: How Felony Disenfranchisement Laws Undermine American Democracy." DC: Americans for Democratic Action Education Fund.

Tate, Katherine. 1993. *From Protest to Politics: The New black Voters in American Elections.* New York: Russell Sage Foundation.

Thernstrom, Abigail. 1987. *Whose Votes Count?: Affirmative Action and Minority Voting Rights.* Cambridge, MA: Harvard University Press.

Thernstrom, Abigail. 1994. *Whose Votes Count?: Affirmative Action and Minority Voting Rights.* Cambridge, MA: Harvard University Press.

Verba, Sidney, Kay Schlozman, and Henry Brady. 1995. *Voice and Equality: Civic Voluntarism in American Politics.* Cambridge: Harvard University Press.

Walton, Hanes. 1985. *Invisible Politics: Black Political Behavior.* Albany, NY: State University of New York Press.

Wang, Xi. 1997. *The Trial of Democracy: Black Suffrage and Northern Republicans, 1860-1910.* Albany, NY: University of Georgia Press.

Wesberry v. Sanders, 376 U.S. 1 (1964).

Remembering Maleesa:
Theorizing Black Girl Politics and the
Politicizing of Socialization

Ruth Nicole Brown
University of Illinois at Urbana-Champaign

Ruth Nicole: What issues do you think are important for girls to talk about?

Maleesa: Sex. Like they be—they nasty, cuz they—sometimes they do what the boys want them to do at that school—they just do whatever. If they say do something really nasty, they will. Like, on Friday, I think somebody was doing something to this boy, and while she was bending down, and the boy was sitting on this chair, and then this teacher's like, "Get up, get up," telling them to move. Like it's weird, you be growing up and stuff, and then they be—you don't know if that's the right boy, and he might beat you and stuff like that.

Introduction

In the living room of a garden level apartment, Maleesa, the twelve-year-old girl who I met in an after school mentoring program,[1] waited patiently to begin the interview while her father signed the necessary consent forms. The brilliance of her eight freshly twisted, shiny, and short ponytails, held tight by bright red balls, muted the red v-neck T-shirt and blue sweatpants she sported and signaled to me that our visit was special. Exuding a kind of humbleness that comes from a mature sense of personal peace, Maleesa's contentment, as I soon learned, was an artifact of her recent move from Detroit to the "quiet" suburbs. Yet, the sixth grade musings she spoke of during our conversations seemed contrary to the serene setting in which they occurred.

She easily expressed how her mother's extended incarceration, a loving but defensive grandmother, the "wild" sister who was responsible for hair-do, and her father who was doing the best he could, were key players in the shaping of her girlhood. Yet, the questions and curiosities that also defined her experiences could not be posed to her caregivers. They were, as I soon learned, reserved for our meeting. Completely surprised by Maleesa's agenda, she reminded me that although I saw myself as a researcher in need of an interview that was not who she knew me to be. To Maleesa, I was her mentor and she felt just as entitled as I did to ask questions and expect answers.

Bearing witness to oral sex acts in school, confessing a lack of knowledge about what it means to be a girl, and expressing concerns of dating violence, Maleesa's version of girlhood reeked of powerlessness and inequality. Hiding her questions with observations and showing her power by initiating connection, Maleesa wanted me to make sense of her experiences. From listening, I learned that the typical agents of adolescent socialization including family, school, and peers greatly influenced who she was and wanted to be. However, what I lacked was a language to explain the politics that structured Maleesa's socialization.

Research on children in the discipline of political science is typically discussed in terms of political socialization and/or political learning. The study of political learning has been central to the discipline since its inception (Fesler et al., 1951) while political socialization became the mode after the twenty-sixth amendment lowered the voting age to eighteen in 1971 (Jennings and Niemi, 1974). Herbert Hyman (1969) coined the term political socialization and was among the first to research and publish a collection of scholarship on the development of political attitudes. Early studies were generally concerned with understanding how individuals change over time as a result of what they learn and know about the nature of citizenship (Easton and Hess, 1962; Easton and Dennis, 1969). In light of the suggestion that political socialization studies originated in the 1950s, developed in the 1960s, piqued in the 1970s, declined in the 1980s, and made obsolete in the 1990's (Peng, 1994) political scientists have recently moved beyond critique to create a field of study that is considerate of the ways in which new variables such as entertainment (Jackson, 2002) and local context (Gimpel et al., 2003) expand the boundaries of political socialization research.

However, as a scholar of political socialization, there was nothing in the literature that gave me the theoretical foundation to make sense of Maleesa's interview. Political socialization studies concerned with "subgroup differences" did not identify African-American girls as an important group for analysis, nor did they adequately address the processes and outcomes of their socialization. It seems that political scientists have forgotten black girls. Maleesa's interview inspires this remembering.

Maleesa's story illustrates the research problem I address in this article, the absence of a theoretical foundation that explains how power shapes the social construction of black girlhood in the United States. Admittedly, this is a first step in a larger research agenda that aims to center the lived experiences of black girls in the study of politics. As a necessary first step, I critique the literature on mainstream political socialization because it is a subfield of study that has been the traditional lens through which political scientists have viewed young people's lives. I then move from critique to construction, outlining a new framework that *politicizes* socialization, by remixing traditional approaches to make central the lived experiences of black girls. The remix is interdisciplinary, drawing from political science, women and girls' Studies, psychology, anthropology, and cultural studies. The remix also departs somewhat from the accepted epistemology of behavioralist political science. As a result, I must warn the "average" political scientist that what you are about to experience is not your mentor's scholarship. It is a political science that is just as informed by literary and cultural studies as the social scientific therefore disrupting the boundaries of the discipline to the point of creating ruptures for new ideas, aesthetics, and stories to sneak in.

In the next section, I detail how my search for articulating an African American Girls' politics of socialization led me back to academic literature on girlhood as well as to Hip Hop via the 2004 National Political Hip Hop Convention (NPHHC). I found that it was black girls and women mobilized by our passion for Hip Hop that provided a platform to discuss, debate, and share the questions young girls must ask of themselves on their way to womanhood. It was at the NPHHC that girls' lives mattered politically and where the kind of questions Maleesa asked gave shape, form, and purpose to my theoretical framework of the politics of African American girls' socialization.

Hip Hop Feminists Call for an African American Girls' Politics

As a participant in the National Hip Hop Political Convention (NHHPC) on June 16-19, 2004 in Newark, New Jersey, my objective was clear: I wanted a political movement that defined itself as representing the Hip Hop generation to create a politics that would offer Maleesa strategies, power, love, and information in her girlhood. Nevertheless, I wondered if my peers, who came from all regions of the U.S. had also forgotten black girls. I wasn't sure if girls' and women's issues would make the agenda since the organizing mission of the conference was primarily dedicated to registering more Democrats to defeat George W. Bush in the 2004 presidential election. Although a worthy goal in its own right, I wondered if young people mobilized by Hip Hop were interested in articulating a political agenda that was broad enough to include formal political incorporation and Maleesa's political situation; a black girl, self-identified decision-maker, who remained subject to what boys tell girls to do, and was denied a girlhood free from boys who beat girls.

As moderator of the "Reading Misogyny: Knowledge of Self for Women" I learned from the four panelists[2] and the audience of more than seventy-five Hip Hop advocates, who were both curious and initially critical of feminism, that we have not forgotten girls. The panelist questioned why we as artists, writers, feminists, womanists, scholars, activists, and first- and second-generation Hip Hop enthusiasts found it necessary to condemn misogyny in our music and culture and to acknowledge the empowerment that comes from recalling all the ways Hip Hop shaped our girlhood memories and inspires our dissident womanhood. The "Reading Misogyny" panel represented a space free of domination "where black women speak freely" (Collins, 2000; p.100)" and as an act of political resistance we recognized that African American girls' struggle to negotiate Hip Hop was intimately tied to our own liberation.

Gwen Pough (2004; p. 221) argues that black feminism has to work within Hip Hop culture or else we will lose the war on young black girls. As Hip Hop feminists, womanists, and label-denouncers, many of us on the panel and in the audience were thinking about how power shapes girls' lives because we realized that our Hip Hop legacy requires girls to ask questions in order to survive. Hip Hop feminists have found it necessary to encourage the curiosity of black girls and mentor them into critical consciousness. Hip Hop feminist Joan Morgan (1999; pg. 26) recalled one particular mentoring situation that inspired a similar reflection,

> I was asking this sixteen-year-old to sift through so many conflicting interpretations of femaleness and blackness and free her voice. In order to do this she was going to have to liberate it from the stranglehold of media-stereotypes—the pathetic SheNayNay impersonations of black male comedians, the talk-to-the hand Superwomen, the video-hos, crackheads, and lazy welfare queens—that obscure so much of who we are. And she was going to have to push her foremothers' voice far enough away to discover her own.

Panelist Toni Blackman, founder of the Artist Development Institute, offered another practical example of how Hip Hop can positively mediate the lives of girls. Besides emceeing, Ms. Blackman life's work includes formally developing girls into professional artists. With the sacredness afforded only by the power of a Hip Hop infused cipher, she coaches girls to understand how and why their IndiaArie[3] inspired poetry represents worthwhile political voices that possess just as much Hip Hop currency as the raunchiest of rap lyrics.

Communications scholar, Angie Beatty used the word "female" in her analysis of gansta rap lyrics instead of "woman" to make the point that many of our favorite emcees were *girls* when they started in the industry. This insight led me to wonder if one reason Hip Hop feminists remember girls is because many of the artists we love and love to hate including LiL' Kim, Roxanne Shante, and Foxy were girls when they started and many of us grew up with them. Although we pick and choose the kind of music we listen to and the kind of images we watch, we noted that even some of the popular artists reflect some aspect of our lives as African American girls. With great deliberation, we consume their music and love them for it.

Hip Hop feminists are not up and coming, we are present and doing, acting as muses to black girls. We understand the experiences of black girls to be political because we know that all too often gender entraps them in less than healthy situations. Youth renders them invisible and powerless. Race marks them as promiscuous and loud. Ask any one of the women at that NHHPC that wore "This is What a Feminist Looks Like" sticker. They organized to make sure that women's and girls issues were voted onto the agenda, and agreed to work to end misogyny in Hip Hop well after the conference was over. Among them, you will find someone rhyming resistance, teaching women's contributions to Hip Hop, creating multidimensional images of women a la Rachel Ramist, raising courageous, wise, girls of strength, and mentoring girls in our communities. Hip Hop feminists remember Maleesa and we are working to bring the politics of African American girls front and center.

In this chapter, I present a theory of black girls' politics in context of the academic literature on political socialization. In political science, we have no other framework for understanding young people's political experience and stories of African American girls' political socialization have yet to be told. I make the case that what is needed is a better understanding of the politicizing of socialization—the negotiations, influences, and structures that shape who girls are and who they want to be. The politicizing of socialization acknowledges the value in asking questions such as: In their political journey of girlhood, how do black girls define who they are and desire to be in the world? Politicizing socialization becomes necessary when we think about the experiences of girls of color. To theorize from this position, it is useful to acknowledge, as did earlier studies that the relationships between young people and politics is important. Yet given that early studies failed to articulate how processes of political socialization were structured by politics, race, class, gender, and sexual orientation among other factors, it is necessary to start afresh with contemporary and updated assumptions about who young people are and how they live in the world as political actors.

As an extension of Patricia Hill Collins' "standpoint theory" I too argue that U.S. black women and girls encounter a distinctive set of social practices that accompany our particular history within a unique matrix of domination characterized by intersecting oppressions (Collins, 2000). My work builds on black feminist theory by reclaiming black women's and girls' ideas, challenging the very terms of intellectual discourse, as well as including the voices and experiences of black girls typically not thought of as intellectuals (ibid.). Likewise, my intent is that the theoretical framework outlined in this article may be applied to future research on black youth as well as in the practical application of black girl empowerment. To this end I discuss the relevance of the remix for programming and policy efforts aimed at girl empowerment at the close of this article.

The next section of this article provides a critique of the literature on political socialization. I make the case that even though political socialization studies have maintained a continuous albeit inconstant position in the discipline of political science, the story of African American girls' political socialization has yet to be told. Following the critique, I outline a new assumptive framework I call *Politicizing Socialization: This is the remix*. *The remix* is a theoretical framework I constructed to address previous inadequacies as well as to illustrate how the centering of black girls' experiences contributes to and expands what we know about political socialization more generally.

Importantly, as with any much of Hip Hop music the verses in the song may be hard to understand and perhaps even a bit unclear. However if catchy enough, the audience can always remember the hook. My refrain is simple: Hip Hop feminists remember Maleesa and we are working to bring the politics of African American girls front and center. Consider this a theoretical commencement.

Why We Should Care About the Politicizing of Socialization

From the beginning, within political socialization studies, "subgroup differences"—race, sex, class, age, and more recently gender—were identified as key variables influencing children's political socialization (Dennis, 1968; Greenberg, 1970; Greenstein, 1970; Orum and Cohen, 1973; Hess and Torney, 1967). However, without considering the structural and contextual variables necessary for providing a theoretical understanding of race, gender, class, and age, previous literature did not produce conclusive and satisfactory explanations regarding the roles identity and difference play in the production of political socialization (Sapiro, 1987). For example, In *Invisible Politics,* Hanes Walton (1985) provided a theory of political socialization relevant to black communities. Walton argued that in the black community, political socialization occurs differently and leads to different results. He explained that African-American political socialization occurs in indigenous institutions and that re-socialization and counter socialization in response to dominant attitudes and behavior are just as important, if not more so, in the black community than traditionally defined socialization processes concerned with measuring system support.

Following up on Walton's insights the theory presented in this article fundamentally challenges assumptions of previous political socialization studies. The politicizing of socialization is meant to press the boundaries of what scholars view as political as well as challenge academic constructions of youth and childhood. When we theorize how young people's formal exclusion from politics inspires non-traditional resources, participation, and socialization only then do African American girls become politically visible.

Politicizing socialization also has an impact on current public policy. President Bush proposed a $150 million initiative to provide "at-risk" boys with "a positive model" through prevention and intervention programs called "Passport to Manhood." The model is one of system support that does not challenge the structural factors that contribute to why a passport to manhood is needed in the first place. With such goals as ensuring a successful future for black boys, the ways program participants will be socialized is inherently political and given the implications of Bush's administration on black and brown communications, it is worthwhile to interrogate the program's model of success.

Politicizing socialization also requires us to understand why Bush's policies and interventions have forgotten black girls. The Bush's administration silence regarding girls of color may actually do many communities more good than harm if it means they will not be subject to socializing efforts for system support. However, Bush's "Passport to Manhood" programming dangerously support the myth of the endangered black male, at the expense of black girls whose lives tell a different story about the kinds of danger facing black communities. The ultimate tragedy for those who forget black girls is that without their inclusion, they remain subject to a role that depends on their powerlessness, lack of integrity, and complete submission.

Overview of Politicizing Socialization: This is the Remix

In Hip Hop and popular music, the remix refers to an updated version of a song that has been changed by adding new elements of verse and music. The remix is usually released after the original and exists as a way to extend the original song's radio life and enhance an artist's marketability. In this vein, I present a new framework of political socialization I call *"Politicizing Socialization: This is the Remix."* This new iteration of research pays tribute to original theories of political socialization and acknowledges the study of children and young people's relationship to politics as a valuable contribution to the discipline of political science. The remix incorporates new epistemological and theoretical claims that facilitate an analysis of the politics of socialization inspired by the lived experiences of African-American girls. Signaling more than just a modification of a dated research paradigm, *"Politicizing Socialization: This is the Remix"* changes the tune, breathes new life into an old song (or, in this case, a subfield of study), and invites readers to consider an innovative approach to a familiar subject of study in political science.

The remixed framework of political socialization I present centers the lived experiences of black girls. To include black girls in a field of study that has historically forgotten them, I have relied on practices of feminist knowledge. Feminist theorizing in particular has supported the goal of enabling a discussion across disciplines, proving an interdisciplinary lens to consider questions of how the meaning of the subject is produced (Stewart and Herrmann, 1995). Drawing on literature from women's studies, anthropology, and sociology was necessary to create a broad understanding of black girls' political experiences.

In the tradition of black feminisms and womanism, the remix also relies heavily on lived experiences as a criterion for bestowing creditability on experience-based knowledge claims (Collins, 2000). The assumptions in the remix grow out of my threefold experience as an ethnographer of Celebrating All Girls[4] the mentoring program where I first met Maleesa, a black woman surviving her own girlhood, as well as an individual that values listening, observing, and working with young people. It is my hope that the premises I present in the framework make sense and speaks to the reader in ways that informs their own thinking about how the process of girls' socialization is full of political meaning, and worthy of renewed interest as political science.

The remix makes the following normative as well as positive claims about: (1) children and young people are political and social actors; (2) politics and the "political" should be broadly and inclusively defined; (3) the ways girls are counter-socialized are just as significant to democratic practice as are the ways they are socialized to acquiesce; (4) the socialization of girls is not only related to their psychological sense of self, but is also determined by the relationships they negotiate within the social structures and institutions that predominate their lives; (5) our starting assumptions about the politics of socialization is directly related to the methodological techniques of data collection and interpretation; and (6) black girls matter; their lived experiences not only suggest the great influences agents of socialization (family, school, media, etc.) have on them but also they way in which girls' agency influences the context in which they were socialized. The next section explains these assumptions in more detail.

Politicizing of Socialization: This is the Remix

Defining the Actors

The remix assumes children and young people are political and social actors. Studies of political socialization have largely justified their importance and worth by the proposition that political orientations socialized in childhood and/or adolescence are the bases of adult orientations, with the latter being important for the operation and maintenance of a stable political system (Dawson and Prewitt, 1969; Easton and Dennis, 1969). This assumption relies on childhood socialization theories are psychological-functionalist, whereby children were regarded as important only as far as they one day will politically develop into adults. However, there has been little empirical research to successfully trace the origins of political socialization. Although some scholars have continued to assume a direct causal relationship between child and adult political orientations, there has been little evidence of this link (Cutler, 1977). This has led many researchers to abandon transmission models of socialization as critiques of these models have disproved the validity, credibility, and prediction power of such analysis (Markus, 1975).

Young people's experiences with politics and learning politics are important to study because they inform the current political and social climate in which we live as citizens. This assumption is consistent with Moor, Lave, and Wagner's (1985; p.16) claim that in the child's political world, it is enough that early childhood has a significant impact on the developing citizen even if it not fully determinative. Young people are not merely becoming citizens they are *already* citizens (McDevitt, M. and S. Chaffee, 2002; Skelton, Boyte, and Sordelet-Leonard, 2002) although they are rarely recognized as such.

Assuming that young people exist as social and political actors and thus citizens, this requires redefining a traditional conception of citizenship. Political scientists tend to privilege adults, beginning at age eighteen, as "real" citizens with "real" political experiences, assuming that voting is the definitive political practice of citizens. As such, studies have been more concerned with childhood as a means to an end; suggesting that what really matters is whether or not children will become good voting partisan patriotic citizens. In contrast, I argue that the worth and value of researching young people's political experiences rests on what they contribute to their communities, how they interpret their life experiences, as well as the actions they take to influence the political systems.

My work with young people has led me to distant places mostly because adults are afraid to speak with young people they know they have failed. From Ann Arbor, Michigan to Florence, South Carolina I have found that young people know what needs to change in their homes, schools, communities, and world to make these spaces more safe and youth inclusive. More than feeling "apathetic," they are actively discontented with policies, procedures, and rules that excluded them from participating in structures that govern their lives. I believe young people embody a distinct political voice worthy of receiving a hearing in the political process (Williams, 1996). However, class, gender, age, ethnicity, and race places them, especially black girls, in socially marginalized positions that do not grant a public hearing of their experience, strength, or knowledge (Gilligan, 1991; p.18).

Defining Politics

The remix assumes that the absence of African-American girls in political socialization literature is not because they do not have political experiences but a result of mainstream definitions of politics. The way researchers define politics is important to consider because definitions represent contested sites of power, which often determine what groups get studied, for what purpose, and under what conditions. Traditional definitions of political socialization typically operationalized some variation of Greenstein's formula of political socialization; who learns what, from whom, under what circumstances, and with what effects (Greenstein, 1971). I find a broadened and revised definition of politics more agreeable with understanding the politics of African-American girls. Because issues as leadership, influence, and conflict are political regardless of whether they occur in government or classrooms, individuals encounter political phenomena at all ages Rosenau (1975; p.163). Such a broad view of politics easily accommodates an exploration of mentoring as site of political socialization.

Many scholars have long since acknowledged that the way politics is traditionally defined excludes marginal group members such as girls of color. Political scientists Cohen, Tronto, Jones (1997; p.1) state,

> By continuing to define politics as what happens exclusively within the institutional arenas of government, or by allowing traditional practices of political interest brokering to limit the scope of our

understanding of political process, political analysts have missed the ways women's actions have transformed politics even though women do not hold the majority of seats in the legislature or have access to most of the economic power. Therefore, so much of what might be regarded as women's political work is regarded as social or personal because it does not take place under the institutional conditions men associate with politics, and because it does not review the obvious political reward of power, or because it is seen as stemming from the "nonpolitical" value of nurturance of social commitment.

If we substitute the word women for girls in the above quote, the meaning does not change. Part of the reason political socialization—the only framework we have for studying people under eighteen in the discipline of political science—fails to have anything significant to say about black girls is not because girls of color are not political, but rather the ways we as political scientists define politics and political socialization have insured their exclusion and marginalization. Girls participate in politics by expressing their political beliefs about political officials. In a Celebrating All Girls activity that asked girls to write down on a piece of poster board what would make a town safe for girls to live in, they frequently commented, "No George Bush!" However, girls also do extra-institutional political work; most familiar perhaps is black girl/woman hair politics.

In Celebrating All Girls, girls were instructed to write down a negative comment someone told them, ball the piece of paper up and give to a volunteer that would help them strategize collectively about ways to turn the negative into a positive. Negative comments about hair, skin color, and body size were the norm. Many girls shared that the thing girls were most "teased" about was hair. That particular CAG semester two girls got in a fight because one girl was teased about her "short," "bad" hair. The girls who got in a fight were in the program, and all of the girls in the program knew the cause of the fight. During this exercise without using names the girls decided that hair was not a good reason to fight someone. In this conversation girls contemplated and articulated issues of fairness (what difference does it make to someone else how I do my hair), identity (what does my hair express about who I am), and decision-making (what influences how I wear my hair) based on their participation in hair politics (Hooks, 1996).

The politics black girls practice is structured by their exclusion from formal politics. Political scientists' definitions of politics are so often narrowly defined that it perpetuates the marginalization of youth in the study of political science. In the remix, politics is broadly defined acknowledging that the negotiations young girls make as girls becoming women has everything to do with power, taking action, and using political skills. In the context of Celebrating All Girls, I politicize socialization by understanding the politics that are inherent in socialization practices like mentoring. I assume mentoring is a political process as girls and young women negotiate leadership, authority, power, connection, conflict, and conflict-resolution while deciding who they are and want to be.

Dissident Citizenship and Ties to Democratic Theory

The remix assumes that the ways girls are counter-socialized are just as significant, if not more so to democracy as are the ways they are socialized into acquiescence. One of the most important goals of early political socialization research was to understand how citizens came to be a part and indeed the basis of a political system, especially a stable democratic system (Sapiro, 1987). Previous studies of political socialization reflected a bias toward system maintenance theories of democracy. That is, they were typically interested in answering questions related to young people that involve positive associations and the effects of governmental policies, persons, and institutions. Yet, critics have suggested that mere system persistence is a strange object to pose as a primary goal of political socialization, particularly in a political culture that otherwise value such objects as representation, responsiveness, and other democratic values (ibid). These "other" democratic values enable a vision of democracy that values the experiences of young people and in particular those of girls of color. Dissent and processes of counter socialization provide a more relevant lens to explore the politics of African-American girls' socialization.

Halloway Sparks (2001) theorizes dissident practices and activism as central to theorizing U.S. democracy. She argues that traditional democratic theory is overly concerned with system maintenance and patriotic system support. Through the exemplar of Rosa Park's activism, Sparks asserts that political courage is vital to understanding particularly how "women marginals" participate and negotiate citizenship. Sparks' conception of dissident citizenship represents the practices of marginalized citizens who publicly contest prevailing arrangements of power by means of oppositional democratic practices that augment or replace institutionalized channels of democratic opposition when those channels are inadequate or unavailable (Sparks, 2001; p. 444). A crucial element in the practice of dissident citizenship is the discourse and practice of courage, the commitment to resolution and persistence in the face of risk, uncertainty, or fear (ibid; p.458). Spark's work supports black politics assumptions that have long realized the significance of counter-socialization as equally important to what individuals learn as citizens (Walton, 1985).

Gilligan and Brown (1990) found that their research, which they originally intended to create a new psychology of women and girl's voices, widened into a political inquiry that found political resistance and courage led girls to take action against social and/or cultural conventions that encouraged them to disconnect from themselves and others in order to preserve emotional and psychological health. Gilligan and Brown argue that political resistance can take two forms. It can be covert when a girl conceals her feelings and knowledge because she is aware of the consequences of speaking out. She outwardly expresses compliance with social conventions but does so as a strategy of self-protection and self-preservation. However, political resistance can also be overt as when a girl speaks out or acts against relationships and conventions that require self-sacrifice or silence. Although not traditionally identified as characteristics associated with politics both political resistance and the role of courage, when interpreted from the experiences of women and girls, they are given political currency in the context of their daily lives.

CAG explicitly operates as a method of counter socialization. In CAG girls often come back to the program to visit and share memories of what they learned in the program. One former participant—Danielle—although hesitant, felt confidant enough to stand in front of the group and state that what she remembered most about the program was that she had a lot fun. She also learned what to do if someone touches her in an inappropriate way. Danielle went on to share with the girls the story of her sister's rape. She encouraged the girls to find strength in each other, and to not be afraid to share similar stories. The most important element of this story is that Danielle and other girls' comeback to participate in this practice of sharing. Apparently, their experiences in CAG produced a certain political obligation to assist the development of future generations.

Danielle's story also sheds light on another concern of political socialization and democratic theory. It was previously assumed that political socialization mattered because what children learn about politics influences the way they will behave politically, especially in terms of voting. As a result, many scholars became concerned with measuring and predicting the impact of political learning on the system. While I do assume there is a link between political education and political structures, I do not think the link should automatically be interpreted in the direction of positive support or as a direct relationship at all. More than some measurable outcome between what the girls learn, what it means for their lives, and what impact their learning has on the world, knowledge created by and with young people was understood in CAG as a process of "planting seeds." The concept of planting seeds acknowledges that the "outcomes" of girls' experiences within mentoring relationships may take on all types of meaning within their life times. However, most important is that the learning process takes place in a safe space supportive and inclusive of all girls. This means that girls' ideas are taken seriously, that girls are listened to, and that they learn in ways that value who they are. The planting seeds concept is antithetical to assumptions of system relevance, primarily because the political implications of what girls are learning matters not only politically but also personally.

The purpose of political socialization is to learn about the ways children are taught conformity in order to insure the status quo. The purpose of remixing political socialization enables an exploration of system maintenance from a different perspective, while also going beyond that to explore the political processes aimed at "raising resisters" to understand how young people engage in social and political transformation (Ward, 2000). In this study mentoring toward the goal of girl empowerment requires a framework that assumes counter socialization processes as valuable routes to the production of a healthier political self and more inclusive democracy.

Focus on Relationships

The remix assumes that who girls are socialized to be and become is not only related to their psychological sense of self, but is also determined by the relationships they negotiate with other people. Since political socialization theory is informed by psychological theories of development, it led to a behavioral revolution in political science in which questions shifted from what "ought" to be to what "is." This resulted in a shift away from institutions to a focus on the individual as the primary unit of analysis (Greenberg, 1970). However, focusing on people leads inevitably and logically to the weakness and imperfections inherent in individuals and away from the imperfections and weakness of the political system (Walton, 1985). Middle school girls in particular have received adequate scholarly attention regarding how they construct their sense of self, primarily because the tumultuous nature of adolescence is typically associated with a decline in self-esteem.

For example, Mary Pipher's *Reviving Ophelia* (1999) claims that white middle-class adolescent girls experience a loss of self-esteem due to the sexist toxicity of U.S. culture and offers psychological remedies to increase girls' self-esteem. The American Association of University Women (2001) finds that the general decline in girls' self-esteem attributed to early adolescence does not characterize the experience of black girls, and argue that the "decline in girls' self-esteem" argument erases the experiences of black girls of all classes.

Practitioners and policy analysts also agree that the developmental needs of black girls are frequently erased in stereotypical discussions about black youths that center on the delinquency of black boys and the pregnancy of black girls (Radford-Hill, 2000). This erasure in confronted head on in Rebecca Carroll's *Sugar in the Raw* (1997), a collection of oral histories of black girls in the U.S. between the ages of eleven and twenty, Carroll uses first person narration as a way to resist the typical silencing and entrapment of black girls. In response to both popular and academic debates about self-esteem, "Jaminica" a fourteen- year-old from San Francisco, California states:

> I read somewhere once that young white girls lose their self-esteem around this age and that black girls don't, which is kind of weird, since black girls have so much more to deal with. Maybe it's because we have so much to deal with that we don't want to risk giving up our self-esteem because then we'd really be in trouble" (Carroll, 1997; p.94).

When girl's voices are heard, how they interpret their experiences often complicates academic inquiries (Inness, 2000; Shandler, 1999). What is the "self" Jaminica suggests she experiences differently because of race? Patricia Hill Collins (2001) state that the "self" is not defined by the increased autonomy gained by defining one's self in opposition to others but is instead found in the context of family and community. Rather, their connectedness among individuals provides black women and girls more meaningful self-definitions (ibid). Gilligan and colleagues (1990) have also asserted that the psyche, or self, is best understood not as a linear evolution of growth or movement along a demarcated timeline, but through the variety of evolving relationships that individuals maintain over the course of their lives. In their attempt to understand political self-hood through the analysis of individuals, political scientists failed to notice dependency of our political selves on the relational and interpersonal structures that define social actions.

Joyce Ladner's *Tomorrow's Tomorrow* (1971) confirms this assumption in her definitive study of African-American girl socialization. Ladner provides a sociological explanation of the transition adolescent black girls make to womanhood in a low income St. Louis community housing project. Rather than affirming social deviance theories treating black girls as patholo-gized and less completely socialized, Ladner (1971; P. 11) writes,

> Becoming a woman in the low-income black community is somewhat different from the routes fol-lowed by the white middle-class girls. The poor black girl reaches her status of womanhood at an earlier age because of different prescriptions and expectations of her culture. There is no single set of criteria for becoming a woman in the black community; each girl is conditioned by a diversity of factors depending primarily upon her opportunities, role models, psychological disposition and the influence of the values, customs and traditions of the black community.

Courageously fascinating and compelling, Ladner's ethnography provides a historically grounded and socially conscious response to her primary question, "what is life like in the urban black community for the 'average' girl" (ibid. p.12). She finds that a host of relation-ships—cultural and familial—influence how girls grow up. More insightful than Pipher's work regarding girls of color, Ladner does not shy away from understanding how racism, sexism, and other systems of oppression and domination shape girls' realities. The community space in which Ladner observers and participates makes clear that girls relationships, whether incidental and or deliberate, matter in terms of how they view themselves.

Whether lost as a result of popular culture (Pipher, 1999), dominated and manipulated by mean girls and their peer groups (Wiseman, 2001), or nurtured through relationships (Collins, 2001; Gilligan et al., 1990), scholars assume that girls have a sense of self that they must con-stantly and continually negotiate. There is also an increasing call for studies to take into account the role of human interactions in the process of political socialization (Verba, Burns, Schlozman, 1997). Many psychologists have already begun to expand their analysis to include contextual and structural factors (Bronfenbrenner, 1992). They expand notions of democracy to include not only cognition—or individual's privately held assumptions inside their brains --- but also the ways in which citizens mingle and interact (Taylor, Gilligan, and Brown, 1995).

Methodological Considerations

   The remix assumes that what we know about the politics of socialization is directly related to the methodological techniques of data collection and interpretation. As political scientists what we do know about children we gather from the definitions we have applied to them. Previous studies of political socialization relied on the questionnaire as the predominant instrument of data gathering. The application of survey methodology to the study of political socialization raised a number of problems concerning the accessibility of research sites, the design and administration of the interview and questionnaires, and validity of findings (Niemi, 1973). In a context where the demographic areas were not mapped out, questionnaire methodologists employed adult behavior as the dominant model, and did not give adequate attention to balancing and including a range of questionnaire choices (Renshon, 1977; p.10). Questionnaires proved to be a barrier and prevented researchers from actually participating in the child's world or at the very least provided a "scientific" way out.

In early political socialization studies there were also methodological problems concerning the investigation of group comparisons. Comparison studies often analyzed subgroups through an oppositional lens of inherent inequality, which used group privilege as an index of normativity. Girls are only known through the comparative lens of research on boys and black children are only known in comparison to white children. Yet, limiting marginal group experiences to comparative studies suggests that there is little value in the contribution of knowledge indigenous to marginalized groups. This is highly problematic both because insight about the variations and dynamics within groups is lost and because non-comparison studies often articulate knowledge and ways of knowing that challenge and resist mainstream ideas about these marginalized groups.

The methodological limitations of survey data and comparison studies suggests the need for future political socialization research to become more involved in naturalistic observations in a variety of contexts (Reshon, 1977). Policy analysts, Skelton, Boyte, and Sordelet-Leonard (2002; p.15) state,

> Ways to assess youth civic engagement lag far behind the emerging consensus on what youth civic engagement means. Today, testing and evaluation remain narrowly focused on quantitative measures of individual knowledge and participation rates in activities such as voting.

There are simply too few qualitative studies of political socialization that take an interest in understanding how young people describe themselves, what they identify as politics, as well as what choices they feel are theirs to make.

In October 2000, an email from an anonymous "Mr. Perestroika," a coalition of faculty and graduate students, prompted much discussion and action within the discipline of political science (Warren, 2003). Mr. Perestroika was concerned with the epistemological and methodological hegemony within political science of whereby research was valued if it adhered to positivism, behavioralism, rational-choice, formal and game theory, or quantitatively driven methods. While it does not really matter whether or not one is sympathetic to strategies employed by Perestroika, the goal of methodological pluralism within the field begs for critical reflection on our practices as scholars of politics. The current Perestroika movement/debate has rightly served as a catalyst for (re)thinking methodology as it relates to larger epistemological and theoretical issues within the discipline (ibid.). Questions such—as who is doing the asking, who can be subjects, what the relationship is between the observer and the observed, and what counts as text (Harding, 1991)—will hopefully transform meanings of what political science is fundamentally about.

Conclusion

As a political scientist, I wanted to be able to talk about the girls and young women I worked with as political actors, actively engaging in shaping politics. I was not concerned if these girls and young women excelled in political trivia as defined by previous political socialization research; what mattered most as a political scientist seeking to create a relevant and responsive political socialization study, were the ways in which girls resisted dominant organizational narratives and constructed a sense of self against a culture and at times a program that did not value their inherent worth. As an ethnographer, I witnessed and learned to appreciate the political nature of the negotiations made by girls as they attempted to "become empowered." I needed a political science that could explain the nuances of power dynamics that influenced individual actions, created and maintained organizational narratives, as well as structured systems of oppression and domination that create a need for girl empowerment.

Remembering Maleesa's heartrending musings about girlhood, I had to construct a theoretical framework that could enable me to make sense of my observations of Celebrating All Girls and the individual interviews I conducted with program participants. As I listened to and worked with young girls, I learned that they were keenly aware of the way power structured their lives and their politics. I considered the girls I worked with political actors because they were often required to negotiate power on a daily basis and strategically sought out mentors and allies that responded to their curiosities with personal, political, and social musings of their own.

Aside from my practical experiences working with girls in the community, Hip Hop was an inspirational resource for the theoretical remix. As a participant of the 2004 National Hip Hop Political Convention, I was relieved that many Hip Hop activists remembered the political struggles of African American girls and understood their relationship to Hip Hop as intimately tied to those that weren't organized and not old enough to vote. Hip Hop artists, activists, and scholars widely acknowledged that the politics of girls' lives included the daily negotiation of misogyny in Hip Hop culture and thus require greater public discussions and grassroots interventions.

Typically, the study of children from a political perspective is subsumed under the rhetoric of political socialization. However, as an old and pervasive field of study, political science has said little about the political socialization of African-American girls. As a result, I introduced *"Politicizing Socialization: this is the remix"* as a theoretical framework to better understand the political experiences of black girls.

A political science that does not understand the role of power in defining politics and in selecting and validating political actors to the exclusion of young people reproduces a kind of inequality and marginalization that is unnecessarily undemocratic and unimaginative. The academic turn presented in this article from political socialization to *politicizing socialization* provides an opportunity to re-center youth as worthy of political science inquiry. The goal is that such a centering will incite debates and discussions that will lead to the articulation and mobilization of greater youth inclusion, fairness, and power, particularly for African American girls. More research is needed on the ways politics and power play a part in the social construction of African American girlhood. We have much to learn about the ways black youth shape and are shaped by Federal, State, and Local political and policy initiatives. Undoubtedly, Cathy Cohen's forthcoming black Youth Project (2005) will set the standard for future research on the politics of black youth. For political scientists, who like me aspire to the arts, our voice is desperately needed on a variety of subjects including and extending beyond that of black youth politics.

Because this article focused on the critique and construction of the literature on political socialization, the contribution of this article is primarily theoretical. While the hardcore empiricists with positivist leanings may ask what's the point, I want to be clear that without a new theory of political socialization that seeks not only to add new variables to the (re) mix but challenges the fundamental epistemological claims of what political scientists call political socialization, we will continue to know very little about young people's lived experiences. Political socialization as we have known it only reifies notions of young people as passive and conflates political trivia with political learning. My work seeks to politicize socialization, drawing attention to the ways young people act with agency and therefore make decisions and participate in the myriad of ways politics structure their lives. Importantly, politicizing socialization questions the role of institutions, programs, and individuals in creating and constructing a kind of young person that serves status quo political ends.

The primary policy issue that arises from my theoretical framework concerns girl empowerment programming. Because black girls are considered "at-risk" they are often the target of many social programming efforts aimed at "empowering" them. The stories and assumptive framework of the remix supports girls' agency and would question programming empowerment initiatives that:

1. Do not involve girls in the decision making structure of the program or organization.
2. Do not take into account the ways black girls lives are structured by intersecting structures of domination.
3. Claim to be for the good of black girls without actively listening to who they are and who they want to be.

During the 2004 National Hip Hop Political Convention, State Senator Nia Gill (D-NJ) passionately proclaimed that young people need power, not programs. The remix supports Gill's insight by assuming girls' political actors. When girls' are acknowledged as political actors then the goal becomes power and the radical revision thereof, not programming black girls to become who well-intention adults need them to be.

Programming that avoids politics does not translate into a kind of sustained empowerment that extends beyond individual girls' lives. Programming that avoids politics attempts to manage girls' lives, instead of inspire their resistance. Programming alone benefits from constructions of girls as weak and powerless, rather than benefit society by creating a public hearing of girls' voices and an empathetic understanding of their silences. Programming lacking a power analysis results in adults making decisions for girls in lieu of organizational processes whereby girls make decisions for themselves. Programming requires someone to serve and someone to receive a service; it does not illuminate the mythology of binary categorizations. Programming too often focuses on the number of girls served versus focusing on the quality of working relationships. Programming reinforces what adults think they know about girls, without creating spaces for girls to define themselves. Programming that does not acknowledge how girls' lives are structured by power socializes girls to become someone they may or may not desire to be; while programs aimed at politicizing socialization illuminate how relations of power shape and influence girls' self-definition, volunteers' intentions, and staff decisions.

Programming for the sake of programming does not radically transform girls and women's realities. Similarly, without discussions about the resources and mobilization it would take to create a kind of girl power that refuses to tolerate status quo gender, race, and class inequality, commodified "Girl Power" and "girl-empowerment programming" only encourages girls to cope with the material realities of second class citizenship. But the kind of power demonstrated, felt, and shared during the NHHPC made possible discussions and actions that account for the politics of black girls' lives.

As a result of the relationships formed during the conference a group of women have continued to organize well after the conference under the name of the Progressive Women's Caucus. The caucus is currently operating out of New Jersey and has begun to practically translate how we experience and explain black girlhood in context of Hip Hop culture in the community by working with girls on issues of media literacy. Articulating the need for power, recognition, and respect, the Progressive Women's Caucus is organizing to gain and share power not to create one more program. We are imagining the kind of power we need as women and girls, the kind of power our families could exercise to insure our equality as mothers, sisters, and aunts, and are transforming our communities so that girls like Maleesa have more power in this world.

Notes

1.   I conducted participant observation for three years of a mentoring program aimed to empower sixth grade girls. In the program, I was program assistant to the Director and Maleesa was a program participant. My observations of the program served as the basis for my research on political socialization of African American girls.
2.   I would like to thank panelists Angie Beatty, Toni blackman, Aisha Durham, and Rachel Ramist for sharing their academic research, personal experiences, poetic verse, and captivating artistry to make the panel a great success.
3.   India.Arie is a contemporary singer that some categorize as neo-soul. In her 2001 debut hit, "Video" she sang, "I'm not the average girl from your video". The song became a popular anthem for girl empowering initiatives dedicated to countering negative media images of girls and women.
4.   Celebrating All Girls (CAG) is a pseudonym for the after-school girl-empowerment program where I met Maleesa. CAG was located in a primarily working class suburb of a large Midwestern city. On average, the program worked with thirty girls and twelve volunteers per academic semester. Typically, the girls that participated were predominately African American and the volunteers were mostly white college age women. The insights and observations gained from my research experiences of CAG are presented throughout the theoretical remix.

References

AAUW Educational Foundation. 2001. *"Beyond the "Gender Wars" A Conversation About Girls, Boys, and Education."* Washington, DC American Association of University Women.

Bronfenbrenner, U. 1992. *Ecological Systems Theory. Six Theories of Child Development: Revised Formulations and Current Issues.* Bristol: Jessica Kingsley Publishers.

Brown, Lyn M. and Carol Gilligan. 1992. *Meeting at the Crossroads: Women's Psychology and Girls' Development.* Cambridge, MA: Harvard University Press, 1992.

Carroll, Rebecca. 1997. *Sugar in the Raw: Voices of Young Black Girls in America.* New York: Three Rivers Press.

Cohen, Cathy, K. Jones, J. Tronto. 1997. *Women Transforming Politics An Alternative Reader.* New York: New York University Press.

Cohen, Cathy. 1999. *The Boundaries of Blackness AIDS and the Breakdown of Black Politics.* Chicago, IL: The University of Chicago Press.

Cohen, Cathy. 2005. Black Youth and Empowerment: Sex, Politics, and Culture. Online. Internet <http://www.blackyouthproject.uchicago.edu/>.

Collins, Patricia Hill. 2000. *Black Feminist Thought*, Second Edition. New York: Routledge.

Collins, Patricia Hill. 2000. *Black Feminist Thought*, Second Edition. New York: Routledge.

Cutler, Neal. 1977. Political Socialization as Generational Analysis: The Cohort Approach Versus the Lineage Approach. *Handbook of Political Socialization.* New York: Free Press.

Dawson, Richard and K. Prewitt. 1997. *Political Socialization.* Boston, MA: Little Brown and Company.

Dennis, Jack. 1968. Major Problems of Political Socialization Research. *Midwest Journal of Political Science.* 12, 1, 85-114.

Easton, David and J. Dennis. 1969. *Children in the Political System.* New York: McGraw Hill.

Easton, David and R. Hess. 1962. The Child's Political World. *Midwest Journal of Political Science.* 6, pp. 229-46.

Fesler, James et al. 1951. Goals for Political Science: A Discussion. *The American Political Science Review*, 45, 4, pp. 996-1024.

Gilligan, Carol, Nona Lyons, and Trudy Hanmer. 1990. *Making Connections: The Relationship Worlds of Adolescent Girls At Emma Willard School.* Cambridge: MA Harvard University Pres.

Gimpel, James, J.Celeste Lay, Jason E. Schuknecht. 2003. *Cultivating Democracy: Civic Environments and Political Socialization in America.* Brookings Institution Press.

Greenberg, Edward (ed.) 1970. *Political Socialization.* New York: Atherton Press.

Greenstein, Fred. "A Note on the Ambiguity of Political Socialization: Definitions, Criticisms, and Strategies of Inquiry." *Journal of Politics* 21 (Nov.) 1970: 969-78.

Greenstein, Fred. 1970. A Note on the Ambiguity of Political Socialization: Definitions, Criticisms, and Strategies of Inquiry. *Journal of Politics.* 21, pgs. 969-78.

Harding, Sandra. 1991. *Whose Science? Whose Knowledge? Thinking From Women's Lives.* Ithaca, New York: Cornell University Press.

Hess, Robert and J. Torney. 1967. *The Development of Political Attitudes in Children.* Chicago, IL: Aldine Publishing Company.

Hooks, Bell. 1996. *Bone Black Memories of Girlhood*. New York: Henry Holt and Company.

Hyman, Herbert. 1969. *Political Socialization*. Glencoe, IL: Free Press.

Inness, Sherrie (ed.) 2000. *Running for Their Lives, Girls, Cultural Identity, and Stories of Survival*. Maryland: Rowman and Littlefield Publishers.

Jackson, David. 2002. *Entertainment and Politics*. New York: Peter Lang.

Jennings, Kent and R. Niemi. 1974. *The Political Character of Adolescence: The Influence of Families and Schools*. Princeton, NJ: Princeton University Press.

Ladner, Joyce. 1971. *Tomorrow's Tomorrow*. Garden City, New York: Doubleday and Company, Inc.

Markus, Gregory. 1975. "Continuity, Change, and the Political Self: A Model of Political Socialization." Doctoral Dissertation. University of Michigan.

McDevitt M. and Chaffee S. 2002. From Top-Down to Tickle-Up Influence: Revisiting Assumptions About the Family in Political Socialization. *Political Communication*, 19, no.3, pp. 281-301(21)

Moore, Stanley, J. Lare, K. A. Wagner. 1985. *The Child's Political World A Longitudinal Perspective*. Praeger.

Morgan, Joan. 1999. When Chickenheads Come Home To Roost: A Hip Hop Feminist Breaks It Down. New York: Simon and Schuster.

Niemi, Richard. 1973. Collecting Information About the Family: A Problem in Survey Methodology. *Socialization to Politics: A Reader*. New York: John Wiley and Sons, Inc.

Orum, Anthony and R. Cohen. 1973. The Development of Political Orientations Among Black and White Children. *American Sociological Review*. 38, pgs. 62-74.

Peng, Yali. "Intellectual Fads in Political Science: The Cases of Political Socialization and Community Power Studies." (The Profession) *PS: Political Science and Politics* March 1994 v27 n1 p100(9)

Pipher, Mary. 1994. *Reviving Ophelia: Saving the Selves of Adolescent Girls*. Random House New York.

Pough, Gwendolyn. 2004. *Check It While I Wreck It: Black Womanhood, Hip Hop Culture, and the Public Sphere*. Boston, MA: Northeastern Press.

Radford-Hill, Sheila. 2000. *Further to Fly: Black Women and the Politics of Empowerment*. Minneapolis: University of Minnesota Press.

Renshon, Stanely A. 1977. *Handbook of Political Socialization Theory and Research*. New York: The Free Press.

Rosenau, Norah. "The Sources of Children's Political Concepts: An Application of Piaget's Theory." *New Directions In Political Socialization*, (eds.) David Schwartz and Sandra Schwartz. New York: New York: The Free Press. 1975

Sapiro, Virginia. 1987. What the Political Socialization of Women Can Tell Us About the Political Socialization of People. *The Impact of Feminist Research in the Academy*. Bloomington, IN: University of Indiana Press.

Shandler, Sara. 1999. *Ophelia Speaks: Adolescent Girls Write About Their Search for Self*. New York: Harper Colllins Publishers.

Skelton, Nan, Harry Boyte, and Lynn Sordelet Leonard. 2002. *Youth Civic Engagement: Reflections on an Emerging Public Idea*. Center for Democracy and Citizenship. Minneapolis: MN.

Sparks, Halloway. 2001. Dissident Citizenship: Democratic Theory, Political Courage, and Activist Women. Boulder, CO: Westview Press.

Steward Abigail and Anne Hermann. 2001. Westview Press. Boulder, CO.

Taylor Jean, C. Gilligan, and A. Sullivan. 1995. *Between Voice and Silence: Women and Girls, Race and Relationship*. Cambridge, MA: Harvard University Press.

Verba, Sidney, Nancy Burns, Kay Lehman Scholzman. 1997. Knowing and Caring about Politics: Gender and Political Engagement. *The Journal of Politics*. 59, 4, pgs. 1051-1072.

Walton, Hanes. 1985. *Invisible Politics*. State University of New York Press.

Ward, Janie V. 2000. Raising Resisters: The Role of Truth Telling in the Psychological Development of African-American Girls. *Construction Sites: Excavating, Race, Class, and Gender Among Urban Youth*. Teachers College, Columbia University: Teachers College Press.

Warren, Dorian. (forthcoming). "Will the Real Perestroikniks Please Stand Up?: Race and Methodological Reform in the Study of Politics (Or, What Does Race Have to do with It?) *Perestroika: Methodological Pluralism, Governance and Diversity in Contemporary American Political Science* (ed.) Kristen Renwick Monroe. New Haven, CT: Yale University Press.

Williams, Melissa S. 2000 "The Uneasy Alliance of Group Representation and Deliberative Democracy." *Citizenship in Diverse Societies*, (eds.) Will Kymlicka and Wayne Norman. 2000; pp.124-153.

Wiseman, Rosalind. 2002. *Queen Bees and Wannabes: Helping Your Daughter Survive Cliques, Gossip, Boyfriends, and Other Realities of Adolescence*. Crown Books.

"Whosoever Will": Black Theology, Homosexuality, and the Black Political Church

Todd C. Shaw
University of South Carolina at Columbia

Eric L. McDaniel
University of Texas at Austin

Introduction

Scholars of American racial politics have routinely observed that blacks are much more likely than whites to favor liberal prescriptions for guaranteeing political equality and improving the economic status of the working class and poor (Dawson, 1994; Kinder and Sanders, 1996; Sigelman and Welch, 1991). However, the 2004 presidential election posed a crosscutting cleavage between black political and social attitudes. It confirmed that on certain moral issues a majority of African Americans are religious or social conservatives (Cohen, 1999; Dawson, 1994; Kinder and Sanders, 1996; R. C. Smith and Seltzer, 1992). With more than eighty percent of African Americans in the states of Arkansas, Georgia, Kentucky, Michigan, Mississippi, Ohio, and Oklahoma voting for Democratic presidential candidate John Kerry, exit polls revealed that as many as eighty percent of blacks in those states also voted to have their state constitutions ban same-sex marriages. At center stage was a fundamental clash between the liberal civil rights proclivities of African Americans, which are in part shaped by the Black Christian church, and the religious opposition or at least discomfort these same churches have toward homosexuality and gay rights. The later stance dovetails with the social agenda of the Christian Right and the Republican Party. Not only did a number of black ministerial alliances and individual African American ministers—e.g., Walter Fauntroy, Jesse Jackson, Sr.—vocally object to same-sex marriage during this election season, a handful of black pastors, impressed by President George W. Bush's Christian moralism, publicly endorsed the Republican candidate's re-election (Abdo, 2004; Deggans, 2004; Kirkpatrick, 2004; Lattin, 2004).

Mindful of the black church's centrality in the African American experience, several quantitative studies and poignant qualitative accounts have concluded that a majority of African Americans strongly oppose homosexuality, principally upon religious grounds (Blaxton, 1998b; Boykin, 1996; Cohen, 1999; Fullilove and Fullilove III, 1999; Griffin, 2000; C. G. Harris, 1986; Herek and Capitanio, 1995; Lemelle and Battle, 2004; Lewis, 2003; McDaniel, 2004; Schulte and Battle, 2004). Researchers have consistently found that church attendance or traditional religiosity is the independent variables most associated with black heterosexual opposition to homosexuality (Smith, 1992 #41)(Smith and Seltzer, 1992). Thus, this religious intolerance is the predominant focus in the growing quantitative literature on black religiosity, the black church, and attitudes toward homosexuality (Fullilove and Fullilove III, 1999; Herek and Capitanio, 1995; Schulte and Battle, 2004). However, an equally important set of considerations—though ones that have received little attention in the quantitative literature—are the attitudes of the minority of religious African Americans who are self-identified lesbians and gays as well as their heterosexual allies who are tolerant or accepting of homosexuals (Battle, Bennett, and Shaw, 2004; Boykin, 1996; Comstock, 1998). We posit that various gay-inclusive ministries, whether heterosexual or homosexual led, are often inspired by a variant of liberation theology, which in the Christian tradition asserts that the Gospel of Jesus rejects all forms of oppression. These Christian ministries take place within black political churches that see political action for social justice as a part of their religious duty.

Moreover, we believe an investigation of these kinds of individual attitudes, and thus by implication their corresponding ministries, is important for two key reasons. First of all, their very existence runs counter to conventional wisdom in the wake of the 2004 same-sex marriage bans, which many black churchgoers endorsed. If neither the African American community nor the church generally serves as political resources to those who are gay-inclusive, how, if at all, do these individuals and groups circumvent this strong ideological opposition? Second of all, this topic merits scholarly investigation because it better maps the slowly but perceptibly shifting political "boundaries of the black church" in the current conservative era—precisely as the work of Cohen (1999) suggests. Ironically, this research problem highlights a paradox—African American politics is simultaneously contracting and expanding as gay-suppressive and gay-inclusive wings of the black religious community debate very different conceptions of morality and group interests in the early twenty-first century.

Thus, we present analyses from three surveys that tap national populations --- the Black Pride Survey 2000; the 1993-1994 National Black Politics Survey; and the 2004 Religion and Politics Study. Three central hypotheses animate our discussion as well as frame our analysis: (1) African American lesbians or gays who belong to gay-accepting churches are more likely to report higher levels of political and civic participation than those who do not; (2) African Americans who identify with liberation theology (broadly defined) are more likely to be accepting of homosexuality than those who do not; and (3) African Americans who belong to a black political church are likely to be more accepting of homosexuality than those who do not. Our analysis follows after our theoretical and historical discussion of homosexuality, the politics of the black church, and the relevance of liberation theology.

Homosexuality and the Mainline Black Church

Qualitative and quantitative accounts have concluded that black heterosexual attitudes toward homosexuality are determined by a multiplicity of concerns—from issues of race, sexuality, and gender roles to the health of black heterosexual marriage, the raising of children, and the black family's well-being (Battle et al., 2004; Beam, 1986; Clarke, 1983; Cohen, 1999; Hemphell and Beam, 1991). black anti-homosexual sentiments or "homophobia" is one result of the black community's historical anxiety over white racist depictions of black sexuality (Douglas, 2003). Yet, in this section, we discuss how religion is clearly the major determinant of black attitudes toward homosexuality.

Since the three mainline Black Protestant denominations—the Baptists, Methodists, and Pentecostals—all originated within the cauldron of American slavery or Jim Crow segregation, these institutions intrinsically have been sympathetic to those who are politically marginalized, especially the poor and racial minorities (Lincoln and Mamiya, 1990). It also true, however, that these mainline churches subscribe to the theological conclusions of orthodox American Protestantism, whose Christian biblical interpretation sees homosexuality as a sin and likely an "abomination" (Boykin, 1996; Gomes, 1996).

Recently the Pew Research Center found that Black Protestants were just as resistant to homosexual rights as their white counterparts—roughly 67 percent of both black and white Protestants objected to same-sex marriage. In fact, a larger percentage of Black Protestants or 60 percent believed that homosexuality was a lifestyle choice as opposed a matter of biology, while a lesser number of white Protestant Evangelicals or 52 percent agreed (Press, 2003). Likewise, the Joint Center for Political and Economic Studies discovered 46 percent of their black respondents felt that gays should neither be able to marry or to have civil unions—in comparison to 37 percent of their white counterparts (Studies, 2004a). Due to contrasting findings, there has been a vigorous debate within the limited quantitative literature as to whether African Americans are more, less, or equally homophobic as compared to their white counters (Herek and Capitanio, 1995; Lewis, 2003; Nyberg and Alston, 1977; R. C. Smith and Seltzer, 1992). As one way to mediate these differences, and as a testament to the prevalence of American religious orthodoxy, work by Schulte and Battle (2004) suggests that religion may be such a strong determinant of predicting black and white American opposition to homosexuality that it renders racial differences statistically insignificant.

Albeit many observers have concluded that religiosity is the strongest predictor of black heterosexual opposition to homosexuality (Battle et al., 2004; Blaxton, 1998a; Boykin, 1996; Constantine-Simms, 2000; Douglas, 2003; Herek and Capitanio, 1995), this opposition also stems from a fundamental anxiety of equating the African American civil rights struggle, and racial oppression, with the gay rights struggle, or homophobia (B. Smith, 1999). In fact, recent black ministerial opposition to the Massachusetts Supreme Court's same-sex marriage verdict as well as the mobilization of black support for anti-gay marriage ballot initiatives clearly demonstrated this anxiety (Deggans, 2004; Institution, 2004; Lattin, 2004; Lawton, 2004). At Harvard University, the Rev. Jesse Jackson, Sr., during a 50th anniversary commemoration of the *Brown v. Board of Education* case, was widely quoted as calling it a "stretch" to compare the two movements for, "gays were never called three-fifths a human in the Constitution"(Abdo, 2004). Bishop Donald Green of the anti-gay marriage Traditional Values Coalition echoed the sentiments of many mainline black pastors when he declared that such comparisons, "are offensive and belittle the cause of freedom and racial justice" (Lattin, 2004).

The dual liberal and conservative dimensions of black religiosity—often characterized as 'love the sinner and hate the sin' when it comes to homosexuality—creates a dilemma within black politics and black church politics. This dilemma confronts both those who oppose and support the advocacy of lesbian and gay issues within the church. Among ministers who object, many felt an ironic sense of frustration in the 2004 election because they were socially aligned with the Christian right on the gay marriage issue (Baird, 2004) but opposed the re-election of Bush and his conservative political and economic agenda. For example, the Joint Center found that in U.S. House races even 56 percent of Black Christian conservatives said they would casts their votes for Democrats—31 percent for Republicans (Studies, 2004b).

For gay-inclusive advocates, whether heterosexual or gay, they acknowledge the criticism that race and sexual orientation are not the exact same struggles (Boykin, 1996; B. Smith, 1999) and race remains the predominant determiner of black group identity. For instance, seventy-seven percent of black lesbians and gays who were surveyed by the Black Pride Survey 2000 said their racial identity was most important of all their identities (Battle, Cohen, Warren, Ferguson, and Audam, 2003). Still supporters claim that the homophobia of mainline black churches colludes with the adversaries of black civil rights (Ehrenstein, 2004; Lisotta, 2004); hinders the black church's ability to be a resource for the black HIV/AIDS crisis (Cohen, 1999; J. Williams, 2000); and imposes a false polarity upon the debate—black or gay (Boykin, 1996; Hemphell and Beam, 1991; B. Smith, 1999). The last outcome renders those who are black and homosexual invisible and forces them to choose sides. In the next section, we discuss how pro-gay advocates and their allies ideologically overcome the mainline black church's doctrine and actions.

Liberation Theology, Homosexuality, and the Black Political Church

Given that the black religious experience has both emphasized individual spiritual salvation and group deliverance whether from chattel slavery, Jim Crow segregation, or contemporary racism and poverty (Lincoln, 1984), we assume that black theology and the African American church have the intrinsic capacity to issue inclusive calls to "whosoever will" (Cole and Guy-Sheftall, 2003b; Douglas, 2003; Gomes, 1996; McDaniel, 2004; West, 1982; D. S. Williams, 1993). Those who send and receive such calls likely believe that at certain moments the church can and should be a forum for black political empowerment (McDaniel, 2004). Among those empowered African Americans, it is significant that at least a handful of political churches include women in general as well as lesbians and gay men.

Liberation Theology: Inclusive calls within the contemporary black church partly have their roots in variants of the liberation theology tradition that sees God and Jesus of Nazareth as liberators of the oppressed. Activist Catholic priests who worked with the Latin American poor and indigenous communities first formally developed this school, which paralleled the earlier social gospel of Walter Rauschenbusch and Paul Tillich (Schall, 1982; Walton, 1971). Prior to these thinkers, there was the slavery-temporized black sacred cosmos and its emphasis upon Old and New Testament narratives of justice, deliverance, and freedom (Levine, 1977). Frederick Douglass's oppositional encounter with his zealous Christian slave master and Sojourner Truth's anti-slavery baptism by fire reminds us of the radical differences between African American readings of Christianity versus those of their white slave masters (Douglass, 1999; Painter, 1997). During the 1950s and 1960s Civil Rights Movement, theologians Benjamin Mays and Howard Thurmond extended upon this tradition and held that racial oppression was fundamentally incompatible with the Gospel of Jesus. Martin Luther King, Jr. followed his mentors by calling for a "Beloved Community" of a universal, anti-racist brotherhood (Carson, 1997; Lincoln and Mamiya, 1990; Mays, 1964; Walton, 1971).

In the late 1960s, black liberation theology further borrowed from black religious nationalism as first exposited by the likes of Bishop Henry Neil Turner, Marcus Garvey, Elijah Muhammad, and Malcolm X (Brown, Torres, and Jackson, 1999; Douglas, 1998). This theology radically asserted that black consciousness ought to be the specific lens and black liberation—free of an "anti-Christ" white supremacy—ought to be the ultimate goal of African American Christianity (Cone, 1970). James Cone's books—*Black Theology and black Power* (1969) as well as *A Black Theology of Liberation* (1970)—first launched this school of thought, and he was joined by a diverse generation of liberation theologians including Gayraud Wilmore, Pauli Murray, Jacqueline Grant, and Albert Cleage; the latter founded Detroit's Shrine of the Black Madonna, a Black Christian Nationalist church (Lincoln and Mamiya, 1990). As a product of the Black Power Movement, black liberation theology embraced three theological tenets, which were to have great utility for later generations of black womanist and black gay theologians.

First of all, these theologians believe that racial and social justice is a part of Old and New Testament narratives about divine justice. As aforementioned, black religion has intrinsically viewed Old and New Testament stories of divine justice as prophecies for how God and "King

Jesus" would deliver African Americans from racial oppression (Cone, 1970; Levine, 1977; Lincoln, 1984; Lincoln and Mamiya, 1990; Painter, 1997; West, 1982). As preached by Nat Turner or Malcolm X through the Muslim lens, the black political Jeremiad or the belief that God's retribution will befall America if it does not free African Americans is an exemplar of this tenet (Howard-Pitney, 1990). Second, there is the belief that the divine could, in the words of Marcus Garvey, be viewed through "African spectacles" or that black people could just as easily view God and Jesus of Nazareth through their own cultural lens as have whites. Black thinkers ranging from Langston Hughes to J. DeOtis Roberts have employed the icon of a "Black Christ" to draw an analogy between black racial suffering and struggles to redeem America and the sacrifice Jesus made to redeem humanity. Evidence of how black consciousness and Afrocentricism have affected the church is seen in such artifacts as Kente cloth priestly vestments, sanctuary images of a Black Christ, or African and African American heritage bible translations (Brown et al., 1999; Lincoln and Mamiya, 1990). Lastly, there is the belief that the Bible must be interpreted through a prism of liberation and social activism—thus it does not condone any form of oppression and actually opposes all oppressors. As Cone declared, "God is active in human history, taking side with the oppressed of the land. If God is not involved in human history, then all theology is useless, and Christianity itself is a mockery, a hollow, meaningless diversion" (Cone, 1970).

Currently, Cone aligns his anti-racist theological views with the empowerment of lesbians and gays, but not all adherents of black liberation theology readily view homophobia as an evil just as they view racism as an evil. In fact, black womanists and gays lamented the open homophobia of some black nationalists and liberation theologians, who like their other straight counterparts "failed to transform" their thinking on homosexuality (Clarke, 1983; Cole and Guy-Sheftall, 2003b). Thus below we explain how black womanists and later black gay liberation theologians broadened the tenets of the theological tradition to fashion faith communities that do no simply embrace those oppressed because of race but also gender and sexual orientation differences.

Black Gay Liberation Theology and Black Gay Ministries: As compared to roughly 70 percent of all black Americans, about 52 percent of the black lesbian and gay respondents to the Black Pride Survey 2000 stated that religion had some influence in their lives (Battle et al., 2003). A common refrain among African Americans lesbians or gays is that they can either choose to be silent about their sexuality in black mainline churches or leave these places of spiritual and cultural refuge. Those who persevere and stay, because spirituality is so important in their lives, risk enduring homophobic Sunday sermons, stigma if they or their loved ones contract the HIV/AIDS virus, or alienation if their homosexuality is ever openly disclosed (Beam, 1986; Boykin, 1996; Clarke, 1983; Cohen, 1999; Fullilove and Fullilove III, 1999; Putre, 2002). Yet the complexities of black church homophobia is explained by Fullilove (1999) when he calls the black church's tacit acceptance of its gay members—if they observe a code of silence and possibly play a valuable worship role (e.g., choir director, church organist)—as the "open closet" phenomenon.

Weary of mainline black church ambivalence and intolerance, a cadre of black womanist and/or lesbian and gay theologians and ministers has, since the late 1970s, embraced non-literal counter-interpretations of Christian scripture. They have preached that Jesus' Gospel, first and foremost, embraced an ethic of love while saying nothing about homosexuality (Boykin, 1996). Some of the openly-gay theologians and ministers who fuse elements of black liberation theology with gay liberation theology include: Carl Bean, Renee L. Hill, Elias Farajaje-Jones, Irene Moore, James Tinney, Tanya Rawls, Wanda Floyd, and Rainey Cheeks (Boykin, 1996; Cole and Guy-Sheftall, 2003b; Gomes, 1996; Jameson, 2003; Kyle, 1993). The now Archbishop Bean is noteworthy because he is the founder and prelate of the Los Angeles-based Unity Fellowship Church, which began in 1982. With an ethic of "God is Love, and Love is for Everyone" this small Christian denomination has fifteen congregations nation-wide and roughly 4,000 members that are predominantly but not exclusively black. As head of the largest, connectional church that is black gay-led and inclusive, Bean explains that the bible, "is a wonderful book of faith. It has all one would need, if one studies it properly, to enlighten us to proceed in a path of life. But it has the history of the time," in which it was written including prejudices against women, the sanctioning of slavery, and other social prohibitions most modern worshipers do not condone (Church, n.d.; Kyle, 1993)—homosexuality notwithstanding. We posit that the work of the Unity Fellowship Church, a handful of other black gay-led churches, as well as the Metropolitan Community Church, which is the largest gay-led denomination in the United States, have helped create an oppositional gay-inclusive theology where individual black homosexuals can find spiritual acceptance and view the Christian church as a political resource open to their interests (Boykin, 1996; Collier, 2004).

Black Political Churches and Gay Inclusive Ministries: Another contributor to gay-inclusive theology and ministries, are liberal white and/or black-led churches that are more often heterosexual led but whose institutional identities include social justice and political engagement. To be sure, the Black Christian Church has played a multitude of civil roles including serving as a political resource for those seeking social change (Billingsley, 1999; Brown and Wolford, 1994; Calhoun-Brown, 1996; Childs-Brown, 1980; F. C. Harris, 1999; Tate, 1993). However, the work of McDaniel (2004) extends upon previous research (Brown and Wolford, 1994; Calhoun-Brown, 1996; F. C. Harris, 1999; McKenzie, 2001; Tate, 1993) to understand what constitutes a black political church. Like the black call and response worship ritual, he concludes that the processes of *conveyance*—a minister sending out a call to be political—and *receptivity*—congregants responding to that call—constitute the key variables of an intricate negotiation process. Ultimately, what matters is whether a black church sees a political identity as one of its many salient identities—spiritual salvation being foremost. We expect gay-inclusive attitudes to be fostered more in the context of these political churches than in apolitical churches, for the former more often attract congregants who are higher educated, liberal, and/or amenable to the church's social engagement in the broader world (McDaniel, 2004). These individual demographic characteristics predispose one to be more tolerant toward homosexuals (Herek and Capitanio, 1995).

There is a handful of white or multiracial Protestant denominations or individual churches that embrace gays and lesbians including the United Church of Christ, the Unitarian Church, and the Episcopalian or Anglican Church (Boykin, 1996), not to mention non-Christian churches. In turn, these denominations have African American ministers as well as congregations who tout a liberation theology that accepts racial, class, gender, and sexual orientation differences. A few examples of such ministers and/or congregations are James Forbes (Riverside Church, New York), Jeremiah Wright, Jr. (Trinity Church, Chicago), Kenneth Samuels (Victory Church, Stone Mountain, GA), Cecil Williams (Glide Memorial Church, San Francisco), and Carl Wallace (Trinity Church, Cleveland) (Cole and Guy-Sheftall, 2003a, 2003b; Putre, 2002). Non-denominational churches and progressive black Baptist churches are also part of the minority of gay-accepting, black or multiracial congregations. Two examples are Edwin Sanders (Metropolitan Interdenominational, Memphis) and Carl Kenny II (Orange Grove Baptist, Durham, NC). Kenny's pastorship over Orange Grove Baptist is illustrative of the dangers inclusive ministries face within in mainline denominations because his explicit involvement in local politics and radical calls for inclusion—women, gays, and young people—eventually clashed with a group of powerful church elders who dismissed him (Comstock, 1998; Harris-Lacewell, 2004; Kenney, 2005). Ostensibly, all of the above types of churches, who have liberal and educated congregants, are political churches because they see the representation of lesbian and gay parishioners as consistent with the social justice of the Christian gospel.

Moreover, the participation of gay-accepting ministers or parishioners in various political causes and issues of social justice strongly attests to the possibility that gay-led or accepting ministries can uniquely legitimize and mobilize the political participation of black lesbians and gay men in the civic life of their communities—e.g., the pro-same-sex marriage campaign, HIV/AIDS awareness efforts, civil rights and educational equity, etc. (Collier, 2004; Jameson, 2003; Kyle, 1993). Thus we predict these pro-gay churches are political resources to their lesbian and gay parishioners just as the traditional black church is for its presumed heterosexual members (F. C. Harris, 1999).

Summary

Having thoroughly explicated the theory under girding our analysis, we now turn to our analysis. We remind the reader that our three hypotheses are: (1) African American lesbians or gays who belong to gay-accepting churches are more likely to report higher levels of political and civic participation than those who do not; (2) African Americans who identify with liberation theology (broadly defined) are more likely to be accepting of homosexuality than those who do not; and (3) African Americans who belong to a black political church are likely to be more accepting of homosexuality than those who do not.

Datasets

To tap the attitudes of self-identified African American homosexuals, we analyze data from the *Black Pride Survey 2000* (BPS2000). It was a short self-administered survey sponsored by the Policy Institute of the National Lesbian and Gay Task Force. It is not a scientific random sample, and thus is not statistically representative of the population. Yet, this dataset is well suited to our purposes because to date it is the most comprehensive survey of black homosexual attitudes asked within one of the community's most significant social/cultural contexts—gay pride celebrations. Among its battery of questions were questions about respondents' religious experiences. The BPS2000 collected a total of 2,645 surveys—944 women, 1,371 men, and thirty-eight transgender persons—from nine black gay pride events including the cities of New York, Philadelphia, Oakland, Los Angeles, Chicago, Detroit, Atlanta, Washington, DC, and Houston. The South was the best-represented region with 43 percent of the total. With a median age of thirty-four, the survey took roughly fifteen to twenty minutes for each consenting respondent to complete, and it asked questions about each person's demographic background, social identities, group memberships, public policy concerns, political attitudes, and perceptions of various forms of discrimination. The vast majority or 75 percent of all respondents sexually identified as a variant of homosexual—lesbian, gay, same-gender-loving; 11 percent as bisexual, 1 percent as transgender, and the remaining percentage as another identity.

To tap a representative sample of African Americans and to examine sentiments towards lesbians and gay men based upon religious questions, we analyze data from the 1993-*1994 National Black Politics Study (NBPS)*. The NBPS is a telephone survey and stratified random sample based upon national population projections of African Americans, eighteen years or older. With a total of 1,206 surveys, each interview ranged from about forty-five minutes to an hour. Conducted between the late fall of 1993 and the early winter of 1994, it is an ideal data source for this study for two key reasons. The survey asks a wealth of questions related to black religion; and it provides numerous questions that examine not only church attendance and religious beliefs, but also asks question pertaining to religious experiences.

Lastly, to tap African American church leaders' attitudes toward homosexuality, we analyze data from the 2004 Religion and Politics Study. It was a self-administered questionnaire distributed during the African Methodist Episcopal Church's 47th General Conference. This study is ideal because the AME church is the oldest and largest black connectional church in the United States; and black Methodists are among the most politically active (and conceivably the most liberal) of all black mainline Protestant churches (Lincoln and Mamiya, 1990). The General Conference was held in Indianapolis, Indiana from June 29 to July 7, 2004 and the survey was conducted between June 30 and July 3, 2004. The survey asked questions relating to religious beliefs and religious experiences. In addition, the survey targeted attitudes about numerous groups and individuals as well as asked opinions about current public policy. Over 300 of the conference attendees were surveyed. Of those persons surveyed, 98 percent were members of the denomination, 19 percent were delegates to the General Conference, and 25 percent were members of the clergy.

Analyses and Findings

We reiterate that our first hypothesis posits that African Americans who belong to gay-accepting churches are more likely to engage in politics and civic life as an outgrowth of the church's social justice mission. Along with the questions of a respondent's religious affiliation, there are four questions from the BPS2000 that comprised the key independent variables of our multivariate analysis: (1) "Rate your experiences with black straights/heterosexuals in the following situations with 1 being very negative and 7 being very positive straight/heterosexual black church/religious institutions"; (2) "Rate how your church/religion views homosexuality with 1 being wrong and sinful and 7 being full acceptance"; (3) "Rate how your church/religion's position on homosexuality influence[s] your daily life with 1 being not at all and 7 being constantly." The one additional independent variable that permits us to understand the degree that a respondent believes the mainstream African American community is anti-homosexual reads as follows: "Homophobia is a problem within the Black/African American community (circle a number [1 strongly disagree to 7 strongly disagree] to indicate your level of agreement/disagreement)".

As a confirmation of the black mainline church's often antagonistic but sometimes ambiguous sentiments toward homosexuality—"love the sinner but hate the sin"—the largest plurality or 43 percent of all BPS2000 respondents reported having negative experiences within black churches and religious institutions; while about a third or 31 percent reported positive as well as negative experiences, and 26 percent reported positive experiences. Overall, fifty-four percent of BPS2000 respondents stated that their churches or religions considered homosexuality "wrong and sinful." A little more than a fifth (21 percent) said their churches or religions assumed neutral stances, and almost a fourth (24 percent) felt their churches were gay-accepting. Ironically, it was those respondents who embraced non-traditional forms of religion or spirituality—that is, they checked "other" as their religious affiliations—that believed their churches or religions were most accepting of homosexuality (42 percent). They were followed by "other Protestants" (27 percent) and Baptists (20 percent), which is the largest Black Christian denomination. As aforementioned, the church's intolerance has likely steered a significant minority of black homosexuals away from religiosity as compared to their heterosexual counterparts. Only a small majority or 52 percent (as opposed to 70 to 80 percent) of BPS2000 respondents reported that their church or their religion exerted a partial to constant influence upon their daily lives. Black homosexuals are acutely aware of the black community's intolerance or discomfort with sexual diversity and thus why two-thirds or 66 percent of BPS2000 respondents reported that homophobia is a major problem in the black community (Battle et al., 2003).

Table 1
OLS Regression of Black Lesbian, Gay, Bisexual and Transgender Persons' Reported
Experiences with Religion and Politics, 2000 Black Pride Survey

Independent Variables	Model 1: Church Accepts Homosexuality	Model 2: Political Participation Index
Church Accepts Homosexuality	---	.069* (.031)
Church's Views Influences Life	.400*** (.036)	.000 (.033)
Negative black Church Experience	-.121** (.043)	.070 (.036)
Black Homophobia Major Problem	-.027 (.040)	.130*** (.034)
Belongs to Liberal Denomination	.216*** (.039)	.029 (.033)
Female	.019 (.024)	-.046* (.020)
Age	.004** (.001)	.003* (.001)
Income	-.030 (.036)	.051 (.032)
Sexual Orientation	.165* (.067)	.074 (.056)
Ideology (Liberal=1)	.002 (.045)	.123** (.037)
South	-.019 (.025)	.041* (.021)
Constant	.068 (.076)	-.081 (.064)
Adjusted R-square	.215	.068
N	720	720

Entries are unstandardized regression estimates with standard errors in parentheses. All variables were recoded on a 0-1 interval, unless indicated otherwise. All tests are two-tailed. * indicates $p < .05$. ** indicates $p < .01$. *** indicates $p < .001$

With Table 1, we present an Ordinary Least Squares (OLS) regression model of the BPS2000 data where we regress the dependent variable of a respondent's reported political participation against the aforementioned independent variables of a respondent's religious and discrimination experiences as well as a series of controls. Except for those variables that have a natural metric (age), we recode all of the variables in this analysis section along a 0 to 1 scale as consistent with Achen's methodological recommendations (Achen, 1982). To measure political participation (Model 2), we created an addictive index using the following eight questions: "In the last five years, have you done any of these things to protest something you encountered? (check all that apply) ... [1] Contacted a public official ... [2] Contacted a white GLBT organization ... [3] Contacted a straight/heterosexual Black/African American organization ... [4] Signed a Petition ... [5] Taken part in a protest meeting ... [6] Taken part in a march or rally ... [7] Voted in a local election ... [8] Joined an organization." The Cronbach's Alpha for this scale is .778, which indicates a strong goodness of fitness between these items. The control variables include: gender or Female = 1.0; Age; Family Income (below \$8k = 1.0 to \$100k and over = 0.0); Sexual Orientation (heterosexual = 0.0; lesbian, gay, homosexual = 0.5; transgender = 1.0); Ideology (Liberal = 1.0); and Region (South = 1.0, Non-South = 0.0). Although a small number of white Latinos and other non-blacks responded to this survey, we only included individuals in this analysis who self-identified as African American/Black.

In Model 1 of Table 1, we analyze the characteristics of those who belong to churches or religions that are accepting of homosexuality. True to the self-esteem reinforcement that religion provides in traditional African American religious settings, Model 1 indicates a very strong, positive, and significant association between BPS2000 respondents who believe that their churches or religion's views on homosexuality greatly affect the conduct of their daily lives and those who said their churches accept homosexuality. For every unit increase in the dependent variable there is a 40 percent increase in the independent variable. This is an indirect or broad test of our liberation theology thesis for it suggests that when openly lesbian and gay African Americans (or at least those who frequent black pride events) embrace religion they are more likely to embrace theologies that empower as opposed to condemn their lifestyles. Inversely and not surprisingly, there is a negative and significant relationship between those BPS2000 respondents who endured negative (as in homophobic) experiences in the traditional black church and those who say their churches or religions are gay-inclusive. Although there is no significant relationship between believing homophobia is a major problem in the black community and belonging to a gay-inclusive church or religion, there is a strong, positive, and significant association between membership in a liberal denomination and affiliation with a gay-inclusive church. In this instance, we coded this dummy variable to include those who belonged to either non-traditional churches or religions they categorized as "other" or those who belonged to the following Christian churches: Anglican/Episcopalian, Disciples of Christ/United Church of Christ, Christian/Religious Scientists, Metropolitan Community Church, Unity Fellowship Church Movement, and Unitarian Universalists. They were coded as 1.0, and all others were coded as 0.0. Lastly, younger respondents (Age) and those who self-identified as transgender (Sexual Orientation) were significantly more likely to be members of gay-accepting religious communities.

In Model 2, the first coefficient indicates that those respondents who reported higher levels of political participation were also more likely to report that their church or religion as accepting of homosexuality. We consider this an indirect measure that taps whether respondent's churches serve as political resources for lesbians and gay men. Given what we know about the traditional African American church as a potential political mobilizer (F. C. Harris, 1999), it is quite plausible that these institutions played a similar role for their prospective lesbian and gay congregants. On the flip side, neither those who say their daily lives were greatly influenced by their church's or religion's views on homosexuality nor those who had negative (as in homophobic) experiences with the black church were significantly related to lower reported levels of political participation. This contradicts our hypothesis that church intolerance will decrease the potential mobilization of lesbians and gays. However, a threat-mobilization relationship may exist with regards to the political participation of persons who self-identify as lesbian or gay. There is a positive and very significant relationship between respondents who were more convinced the black community suffers from homophobia and those who reported higher levels of political participation. An implicit self-selection bias may exist in this finding, because those who are mostly likely to be "out" and civically engaged by virtue of their attendance at a gay pride event are also those most frustrated by black homophobia. Still these results suggest that "push" and "pull" factors are at the heart of the political participation of black homosexuals. It appears that those BPS2000 respondents who were male, older, highly liberal, and from the South were associated with higher levels of political participation.

Turning to Table 2, where we present analysis from the 1993-1994 National Black Politics Study, we include a set similar of control variables in an OLS regression equation—age; gender (Female = 1.0); income; education; region (South = 1.0, Non-South = 0.0); and urbanicity. Relevant to our hypotheses and analysis, we include the variables of political church exposure, the belief that Jesus Christ could have been black, and a measure of church attendance. The political church index is comprised of the six measures found in the 1993-1994 NBPS including hearing discussion of politics in church, talking to someone in church about politics, having a leader come speak at the church, having a clergy member encourage people to become generally more politically active, clergy recruiting members to take part in non-electoral activity, and clergy encouraging people to vote for or against a particular candidate. Slightly more than sixteen percent of the respondents (16.4 percent) had no contact with a political church, while slightly less than a tenth of the respondents (9.8 percent) were exposed to all six functions of a political church. We test the influence of black liberation theology on gay-inclusive attitudes by understanding the effects of one of its key propositions—the importance African Americans attach to Black Christ and by extension other Afrocentric religious imagery in the church (Cone and Wilmore, 1993; Lincoln and Mamiya, 1990). The Black Christ question read, "How important is it that all images and pictures of Christ in black churches show him as being black ...?" It ranged from one representing "very important" to zero representing "not important at all." Roughly 38 percent of all NBPS respondents feel that it is very or fairly important to have Black Christ images in the black church. Church attendance is a four point scale, where zero indicates "never attend" and one indicates attending at least "once a week." Over half (51.4 percent) of the respondents report attending church at least once a week.

The results from this analysis provide mixed support for our hypotheses. Model 1 indicates that those exposed to a political church are more likely to have warmer feelings towards gay men than those who do not. The political church coefficient for Model 2 is not significant and thus the same may not be true about feelings toward lesbians, however, this coefficient is positive. We also find that our black liberation theology measure—belief in a Black Christ—is in the predicted direction or positive, but it is not significant with either feelings toward gay men or lesbians. Only the church attendance measure is significant in both cases as those who attend church more frequently hold cooler feelings towards gay men and lesbians. Along the lines of racial group consciousness, we find that black linked fate or the sentiment that one's individual well-being as an African American is connected to the well-being of the group (Dawson, 1994; Gurin, Hatchett, and Jackson, 1989; Tate, 1993) is positively but not significantly associated with feelings toward gay men and lesbians. Among our control variables, it appears that older respondents, women, and self-identified liberals are warmer toward gay men, while those with higher incomes and self-identified liberals are warmer toward lesbians. Overall, these results

Table 2
OLS Regression of Black Attitudes Toward Gay Men and Lesbians by Religious and Demographic Variables, 1993-1994 National Black Politics Study

Independent Variables	Model 1: Gay Men	Model 2: Lesbians
Political Church Exposure	.077*	.038
	(.034)	(.035)
Black Christ	.04	.035
	(.028)	(.029)
Church Attendance	-.097*	-.093*
	(.046)	(.047)
Age	.133*	.053
	(.059)	(.061)
Female	.097**	.032
	(.023)	(.024)
Income	.051	.089*
	(.037)	(.038)
Education	.065	.074
	(.100)	(.103)
South	-.004	-.006
	(.023)	(.024)
Urban	.042	.033
	(.035)	(.036)
Linked Fate	.059	.062
	(.035)	(.036)
Ideology (Conservative=1)	-.125**	-.100**
	(.031)	(.032)
Constant	.133	.197**
	(.072)	(.075)
Adjusted R-square	.0781	.0432
N	681	676

Entries are unstandardized regression estimates with standard errors in parentheses. All variables were recoded on a 0-1 interval, unless indicated otherwise. All tests are two-tailed. * indicates $p < .05$. ** indicates $p < .01$. *** indicates $p < .001$.

Table 3
Principal Components Factor Analysis of Gay-friendly Measures,
2004 Religion and Politics Study

	Gay-friendly Factor
Allow homosexuals to preach	0.70831
Churches can conduct outreach ministry to Gay Community	0.69159
Clergy can work with Gay Rights Groups	0.74400
Churches should conduct more outreach to Gay community	0.61954
Churches should not oppose gay rights legislation	0.51287
Eigenvalue	2.18039
percent of Variance Explained	43.61
N	238
α	.6283

Varimax Rotation

The analysis was done using STATA 8

show that the context of the black church is important in shaping these sentiments. We see that while going to church promotes cool feelings towards homosexuals, the type of church a person attends may counteract this coolness. At least with this analysis, liberation theology does not appear to be a significant factor in shaping attitudes toward homosexuals.

Lastly, we turn to our analysis of the 2004 Religion and Politics Study (RPS2004.) Our objective is to further understand how African American church leaders, in this case the African Methodist Episcopal church, view homosexuals within the context of religion. From the 312 surveys collected, we discovered that, as expected, this group of African Americans embraced the "love the sinner and hate the sin" axiom. Only 8 percent believed "churches can allow homosexuals to preach" and little more than 6 percent believed that "clergy can work with gay-rights groups." On the other hand, 41 percent agreed that the "clergy should conduct more outreach to the gay community" and almost a third or 31 percent agreed that, "churches should not oppose any legislation that would give homosexuals the same rights as others." Table 3 presents the results from our conducting a principal components factor analysis of measures that are at least nominally gay-friendly—though in this context some RPS2004 respondents may have interpreted the term "outreach" to mean "proselytize" or "convert." With 43 percent of the variance explained by this six-variable factor and with this factor having a Cronbach's alpha of .62, there is a fairly strong statistical relationship between the beliefs that gays should preach, the church should reach out to gays, the clergy should work with gay rights groups, and churches should not oppose gay rights legislation.

Because of the relatively small sample size of the RPS2004 (n=312), we opted to not do a multivariate analysis but instead present a series of bivariate relationships in the form of pair-wise correlations between the gay-friendly scale and several other survey measures.[1] Beginning with demographics, we see that the only significant correlate is education—those with higher levels of education rank higher on the gay-friendly scale. With the ideology and partisanship

Table 4
**Pair-wise correlation between Gay-friendly scale and various measures,
2004 Religion and Politics Study, N=312**

	Gay-friendly Factor
Age	.022
Female	-.007
Education	.162**
Income	.046
Conservative	-.179**
Republican	-.004
Member of the Clergy	.025
Pastor	.007
Delegate to Conference	.085
Orthodoxy	-.047
Receptive to Politically Active Church	.402***
Receptive to Politically Active Pastor	.350***
Pastor should be more politically active	.143*
Churches should be involved in political matters	.176***
Political matters should never be discussed in a church service	-.201***
Religious Right is harmful to Black America	.273***
Jesus is Black	.150**
Discrimination Scale	.122*

Two-tailed test * significant at .1 **.05 ***.01

questions, we find that not surprisingly self-identified conservatives score lower on this scale. As evident from the fairly widespread coolness RPS2004 respondents demonstrated toward homosexuals, it appears that no specific leadership position in the church is significantly correlated with a higher score on the scale. We also do not find a significant correlation between religious orthodoxy and the gay-friendly scale, which is somewhat surprising. Turning to issues of church political activism, however, our hypotheses are confirmed. We see that the more open a respondent is to clergy and church political involvement or the discussion of political matters inside the church the higher her score. In addition, the evaluation of religious conservative groups is significantly and positively correlated with the gay-friendly scale. Those who feel that the Religious Right is harmful to African Americans rank higher on the scale, which stands in contrast to the implicit alliances of anti-same-sex marriage campaigns. While it was not significant in the analysis of the 1993-1994 NBPS, we see that those who view Jesus as black in the RPS2004 rank higher on the scale than those who do not. This is at least a partial confirmation of our thinking about the association between black liberation theology and gay-inclusion. Finally, we measure the connection between perceptions of racial discrimination and attitudes toward homosexuals. This is scale is comprised of three items that asked respondent whether blacks suffered discrimination in employment and housing and whether discrimination explains black-white employment, income, and housing differences. We discover a strong, positive, and statistically significant correlation between those respondents who believe discrimination is a significant problem and those had higher scores on the gay-friendly scale. Below we summarize our findings and discuss their implications.

Discussion and Conclusion

Our examination has lent evidence for the prevailing conclusion that due to traditional religious prohibitions African Americans generally oppose homosexuality (Herek and Capitanio, 1995; Schulte and Battle, 2004) and such gay rights initiatives as same-sex marriage (Lattin, 2004). Yet, it has gone much further than this well-rehearsed refrain. Since America's history of racial discrimination has readily compelled some black churches to embrace anti-oppression theologies, the church as an institution and its belief systems have the intrinsic capacity to be a political resource to those who broadly seek liberation. Sometimes this even includes the small but growing minority of African Americans who depart from the norm of condemning homosexuality. These persons can range from black members of the clergy who are openly lesbian and gay to heterosexual allies who belong to radically inclusive ministries. Our analysis of three datasets provided nuanced but fairly strong confirmation for our three central hypotheses. First, based upon the BPS 2000, prospectively gay and lesbian African Americans who belonged to gay-accepting ministries were more likely to engage in various forms of political and civic participation than those who did not. Second, based upon the 1993-1994 NPBS those African Americans (in general) who were exposed to politics within their churches felt warmer toward gay men than those who did not; but our results were not significant with regards to lesbians. And lastly, according to the RPS2004, those mainline African American church leaders who embraced the liberation theology concept of a Black Christ and believed politics have a place in the church were more likely to be more accepting of homosexuals.

Admittedly the RPS2004 dataset confirmed that the belief in a Black Christ is associated with gay-inclusiveness while the 1993-1994 NBPS did not. As evident from the homophobic rhetoric of the Nation of Islam or the many black ministries who stress racial pride but shun any form of lesbian and gay pride (Cole and Guy-Sheftall, 2003b; Simmons, 1991), sometimes there may be a disjuncture between black nationalist-inspired visions of salvation such as a Black Christ and calls for gay rights. What is apparent from our analysis, however, is that the broad fight against racial discrimination is positively associated with mainline church leaders' greater acceptance of homosexuals. This finding lends support to the interpretation of black liberation theology as a school of thought that stresses overcoming discrimination for all. After all, it has greatly inspired black womanist and gay theologians who seek the inclusion of homosexuals (Cone and Wilmore, 1993; Douglas, 2003). We also found that those black religionists who wanted their churches to be more politically active were also more supportive of the church working with homosexuals. This suggests that there are at least small opportunities to widen the black church's political activism.

We believe that by studying the politics of the black church we understand questions that have a direct bearing upon vital social policy debates and thus African American livelihoods. As only one issue, homosexuality involves questions as vital as community responses to the HIV/AIDS crisis (Fullilove and Fullilove III, 1999), the same-sex marriage debate (Ly and Harris, 2004), or vigorous discussions about whether undisclosed sex between black men or the so-called "down-low" phenomenon is becoming prevalent and effecting public health as well as sexual dynamics (Boykin, 2005; Denizet-Lewis, 2003; King and Hunter, 2004). However, as we examine the boundaries of African American politics and the black church in the coming decades, we must not only characterize the major trends but also unpack the variance. In her conclusions about black homophobia and the HIV/AIDS crisis, Cohen cautions us, "Without increased recognition of the broadening of identities through which people exist in and understand the world, traditional black leaders and scholars may end up so out of touch with the differing experiences of multiple segments of black communities that they fill no real function in their communities and thus are left to talk to themselves" (Cohen, 1999). Towards the ends of greater understanding, we have raised not only the troubling implications but also the prospective changes in the intersection between black religiosity and attitudes toward homosexuality. In this work nothing less than the political meanings of blackness and morality are at stake.

Notes

1. A separate Ordinary Least Squares (OLS) multivariate analysis had only 101 cases, only fifteen degrees of freedom, and with an adjusted R2 value of .238. But for informational purposes we ran a model that included: age, education, income, conservative ideology, member of the clergy, delegate to conference, orthodoxy, receptive to politically active church, receptive to politically active church, receptive to politically active pastor, belief that churches should be involved in political matters, belief that political matters should never be discussed in church service, the belief that the religious right is harmful to black America, the belief that Jesus is black, and a discrimination scale. With this model the church receptivity and the belief that the religious right is harmful to black America were the only to coefficients that had a statistically significant and positive relationship with the gay-friendly scale, given a 95 percent confidence interval—church receptive (= 1.4, p =.006); religious right's harm (=.75, p = .026).

References

Abdo, G. 2004. *Black Ministers Join Drive Against Same-Sex Marriage*, from http://www.anotheran-narbor.org/news_details.php

Achen, C. 1982. *Interpreting and Using Regression*. Beverly Hills, CA: Sage.

Baird, W. 2004. *Black Pentecostals Vote Values, but not Part of 'Religious Right.'* Retrieved 11 November, 2004, from http://www.tcpalm.com/tcp/wptv/article/0,2547,TCP_1213_33820...

Battle, J., Bennett, N., and Shaw, T. C. 2004. From the Closet to a Place at the Table: Past, Present, and Future Assessments of Social Science Research on Black Lesbian, Gay, Bisexual, and Transgender Populations. *African American Research Perspectives, 10*(1), 9-26.

Battle, J., Cohen, C. J., Warren, D., Ferguson, G., and Audam, S. 2003. *Say It Loud, I'm Black and I'm Proud: Black Pride Survey 2000*. New York, NY: Policy Institute of the National Gay and Lesbian Task Force.

Beam, J. 1986. *In the Life: A Black Gay Anthology* 1st ed. Boston, MA: Alyson Publications.

Billingsley, A. 1999. *Mighty Like A River: The Black Church and Social Reform*. New York: Oxford University Press.

Blaxton, R. G. 1998a. 'Jesus Wept': Black Churches and HIV. *Harvard Gay and Lesbian Review, 4*, 13-16.

Blaxton, R. G. 1998b. 'Jesus Wept': Reflections on HIV Disease and the Churches of Black Folk. In E. Brandt (ed.), *Dangerous Liaisons: Blacks, Gays, and the Struggle for Equality* (pp. 102-141). New York, NY: The New Press.

Boykin, K. 1996. Bearing Witness: Faith in the Lives of Black Lesbians and Gays. In *One More River to Cross: Black and Gay in America* (pp. 123-154). New York: Anchor Books.

Boykin, K. 2005. *Beyond the Down Low: Sex, Lies, and Denial in Black America*. New York: Caroll and Graff.

Brown, R. E., Torres, M., and Jackson, J. S. 1999. *The Remembered Past: The Black Christ in an Imagined Pan-African Community*. Unpublished manuscript.

Brown, R. E., and Wolford, M. 1994. Religious Resources and African American Political Action. *National Political Science Review, 56*, 118-134.

Calhoun-Brown, A. 1996. African American Church and Political Mobilization: The Psychological Impact of Organizational Resources. *Journal of Politics, 58*(4), 935-953.

Carson, C. 1997. Martin Luther King, Jr. and the African-American Social Gospel. In T. E. Fulop, and Albert J. Raboteau (ed.), *African-American Religion: Interpretive Essays in History and Culture*. New York: Routledge Press.

Childs-Brown, J. 1980. *The Political Black Minister: A Study in Afro-American Politics and Religion*. Boston, MA: G.K. Hall.

Church, U. F. n.d. *Who We Are: The Unity Fellowship Church Movement*. Retrieved December 18, 2004, from http://www.ufc-usa.org/history.htm

Clarke, C. 1983. The Failure to Transform: Homophobia in the Black Community. In (pp. 197-208). New York: Kitchen Table: Women of Color Press.

Cohen, C. J. 1999. *The Boundaries of Blackness: AIDS and the Breakdown of Black Politics*. Chicago and London: University of Chicago.

Cole, J. B., and Guy-Sheftall, B. 2003a. The Black Church: What's the Word? In *Gender Talk: The Struggle for Women's Equality in African-American Communities* (pp. 102-127). New York: Ballantine.

Cole, J. B., and Guy-Sheftall, B. 2003b. Black, Lesbian, and Gay: Speaking the Unspeakable. In *Gender Talk: The Struggle for Women's Equality in African-American Communities* (pp. 154-181). New York: Ballantine.

Collier, J. G. 2004. Black, Christian and Gay: Couple Fights Religious Bias, Legal Hurdles. *Herald Sun*, pp. 1, 8.

Comstock, G. D. 1998. "Whosoever" Is Welcome Here: An Interview with Reverend Edwin C. Sanders II. In E. Brandt (ed.), *Dangerous Liaisons: Blacks, Gays, and the Struggle for Equality* (pp. 142-157). New York, NY: The New Press.

Cone, J. H. 1969. *Black Theology and Black Power*. New York: Seasbury Press.

Cone, J. H. 1970. *A Black Theology of Liberation*. New York: J.P. Lippincott.

Cone, J. H., and Wilmore, G. S. 1993. *Black Theology: A Documentary History* 2nd ed. Maryknoll, NY: Orbis.

Constantine-Simms, D. (ed.). 2000. *Is Homosexuality the Greatest Taboo?* Los Angeles, CA: Alyson Books.

Dawson, M. 1994. *Behind the Mule: Race and Class in African-American Politics*. Princeton, NJ: Princeton University Press.

Deggans, E. 2004. *Gays Rights and Civil Rights*. Retrieved 7 July, 2004, from http://www.sptimes.com/2004/01/18/news_pf/Perspective/Gay_rights_civil_rig.shtml

Denizet-Lewis, B. 2003, August 3. Double Lives on the Down Low. *New York Times Magazine*, p. 28.

Douglas, K. B. 1998. *Black Christ*. Maryknoll, NY: Orbis.

Douglas, K. B. 2003. Homophobia and Heterosexism in the Black Church and Community. In *Sexuality and the Black Church: A Womanist Perspective* (pp. 87-108). Maryknoll, NY: Orbis Books.

Douglass, F. 1999. Slaveholding Religion and the Christianity of Christ. In M. C. Sernett (ed.), *African American Religious History: A Documentary Witness*. Durham, NC: Duke University Press.

Ehrenstein, D. 2004. The Black Divide: African-Americans Who Refuse to Support Equal Marriage Rights for Gays and Lesbians Are Shoving Their Own History into the Closet. *The Advocate,* 34, 36, 38.

Fullilove, M. T., and Fullilove III, R. E. 1999. Stigma as an Obstacle to AIDS Action. *American Behavorial Scientist, 42*(7), 1113-1125.

Gomes, P. J. 1996. The Bible and Homosexuality: The Last Prejudice. In *The Good Book: Reading the Bible with Mind and Heart.* New York, NY: William Morrow and Co.

Griffin, H. 2000. Their Own Received Them Not: African American Lesbians and Gays in Black Churches. In D. Constantine-Simms (ed.), *The Greatest Taboo: Homosexuality in Black Communities* (pp. 110-111). Los Angeles, CA: Alyson Books.

Gurin, P., Hatchett, S., and Jackson, J. S. 1989. *Hope and Independence: Blacks' Response to Electoral and Party Politics.* New York: Russell Sage Foundation.

Harris, C. G. 1986. Cut Off from Among Their People. In J. Beam (ed.), *In the Life: A Black Gay Anthology* (pp. xxx). Boston, MA: Alyson Publications.

Harris, F. C. 1999. *Something Within: Religion in African-American Political Activism.* New York and Oxford: Oxford University Press.

Harris-Lacewell, M. V. 2004. Ideology in Action: The Promise of Orange Grove. In *Barbershops, Bibles, and BET.* Princeton and Oxford: Princeton University Press.

Hemphell, E., and Beam, J. 1991. *Brother to Brother: New Writings by Black Gay Men.* Boston, MA: Alyson Publications.

Herek, G. M., and Capitanio, J. P. 1995. Black Heterosexuals' Attitudes Toward Lesbians and Gay Men in the United States. *Journal of Sex Research, 32*(2), 95-105.

Howard-Pitney, D. 1990. *The Afro-American Jeremiad: Appeals for Justice in America.* Philadelphia, PA: Temple University Press.

Institution, B. 2004. *Event Summary: Marriage Movement and the Black Church.* Retrieved 28 July, 2004, from http://www.brook.edu/printme.wbs?page=/comm/op-ed/20040602marriage.htm

Jameson, T. 2003, Nov. 1, 2003. Finding Spiritual Acceptance: At Unity Fellowship Church, All Are Welcome—and for Black Gays Especially, It's a Nurturing Haven. *Charlotte Observer.*

Kenney, C. 2005, January 12. Gays and the Black Church: A Conversation that Can't Be Heard. *Independent Weekly,* pp. 21-23.

Kinder, D., and Sanders, L. 1996. *Divided by Color: Racial Politics and Democratic Ideals.* Chicago and London: University of Chicago.

King, J. L., and Hunter, K. 2004. *On the Down Low: A Journey into the Lives of "Straight" Black Men Who Sleep With Men* 1st ed. New York: Broadway Books.

Kirkpatrick, D. K. 2004. *Black Pastors Backing Bush Are Rare, But Not Alone.* Retrieved 7 December, 2004, from http://www.nytimes.com/2004/10/05/politics/campaign/05church.html?ex=110256 8400anden=f1c58113dbc4db01andei=5070andoref=login

Kyle, R. B. 1993. Rev. Carl Bean. In M. B. Hunter (ed.), *Sojourner: Black Gay Voices in the Age of AIDS* (pp. 33-46). New York, NY: Other Countries Press.

Lattin, D. 2004. *Black Clergy Gathering to Fight Gay Matrimony.* Retrieved 7 July, 2004, from http://sfgate.com/cgi-bin/article.cgi?file=/c/a/2004/05/15/MNBUP6MM3ON1.DTLGandtype

Lawton, K. 2004. Black Churches and Gay Marriage [television program], *Religion and Ethics Newsweekly*: PBS.

Lemelle, A. J., and Battle, J. 2004. Black Masculinity Matters in Attitudes Toward Gay Males. *Journal of Homosexuality, 47*(1), 39-51.

Levine, L. W. 1977. *Black Culture and Black Consciousness: Afro-American Folk Thought from Slavery to Freedom.* New York: Oxford University Press.

Lewis, G. B. 2003. Black-White Differences in Attitudes Toward Homosexuality and Gay Rights. *Public Opinion Quarterly, 67,* 59-78.

Lincoln, C. E. 1984. *Race, Religion, and the Continuing American Dilemma.* New York: Hill and Wang.

Lincoln, C. E., and Mamiya, L. H. 1990. *The Black Church in the African American Experience.* Durham and London: Duke University Press.

Lisotta, C. 2004, 17 May 2004. Homophobia of All Hues. *The Nation,* 15-17.

Ly, P., and Harris, H. R. 2004. *Blacks, Gays in Struggle of Values.* Retrieved 7 July, 2004, from http://www.washingtonpost.com/ac2/wp-dyn/A58627-2004Mar14

Mays, B. 1964. *Seeking to be Christian in Race Relations.* New York: Friendship Press.

McDaniel, E. 2004. *Politics in the Pews: The Creation and Maintenance of Black Political Churches.* Unpublished Ph.D., University of Illinois at Urbana-Champaign, Urbana-Champaign, IL.

McKenzie, B. D. 2001. Self-Selection, Church Attendance, and Local Civic Participation. *Journal for the Scientific Study of Religion, 40*(3), 479-488.

Nyberg, K. L., and Alston, J. P. 1977. Analysis of Public Attitudes Toward Homosexual Behavior. *Journal of Homosexuality, 2,* 541-546.

Painter, N. I. 1997. *Sojourner Truth: A Life, A Symbol* (Norton pbk. ed.). New York: W.W. Norton.

Press, P. C. f. P. t. 2003. *Homosexuals and Marriage.* Washington, DC: Pew Center for People and the Press.

Putre, L. 2002, 19 February. Amazing Grace and Resolve: Gay African-American Christians too Often Find Themselves at Odds with the Churches They've Called Home... *The Advocate,* 22-25.

Schall, J. V. 1982. *Liberation Theology in Latin America.* San Francisco, CA: Ignatius Press.

Schulte, L., and Battle, J. 2004. The Relative Importance of Ethnicity and Religion in Predicting Attitudes Toward Gays and Lesbians. *Journal of Homosexuality, 47*(2), 127-142.

Sigelman, L., and Welch, S. 1991. *Black Americans' View of Racial Inequality: The Dream Deferred.* Cambridge: Cambridge University Press.

Simmons, R. 1991. Some Thoughts on the Challenges Facing Black Gay Intellectuals. In E. Hemphell and J. Beam (eds.), *Brother to Brother: New Writings by Black Gay Men* (pp. 211-228). Boston, MA: Alyson Publications.

Smith, B. 1999. Blacks and Gays: Healing the Great Divide. In E. Brandt (ed.), *Dangerous Liaisons: Blacks, Gays, and the Struggle for Equality* (pp. 14-24). New York: The New Press.

Smith, R. C., and Seltzer, R. 1992. *Race, Class, and Culture: A Study in Afro-American Mass Opinion.* Albany, NY: State University Press of New York.

Studies, Joint Center for Political and Economic 2004a. *2004 National Opinion Poll Snapshots: Politics.* Washington, DC: Joint Center for Political and Economic Studies.

Studies, Joint Center for Political and Economic 2004b. *National Opinion Poll Snapshots: Politics.* Washington, DC: Joint Center for Political and Economic Studies.

Tate, K. 1993. *From Protest to Politics: The New Black Voters in American Elections.* New York and Cambridge, MA: Russell Sage and Harvard University Press.

Walton, H., Jr. 1971. *The Political Philosophy of Martin Luther King, Jr.* Westport, CT: Greenwood Press.

West, C. 1982. *Prophesy Deliverance! An Afro-American Revolutionary Christianity.* Philadelphia, PA: Westminister Press.

Williams, D. S. 1993. *Sisters in the Wilderness: The Challenge of Womanist God-talk.* Maryknoll, N.Y.: Orbis Books.

Williams, J. 2000. The Black Church and AIDS [television program], *Religion and Ethics Newsweekly*: WNET New York 13.

Race, Class, and the Political Behavior of African American Young Adults, 1960-1998

Marwin J. Spiller
University of Maine

Introduction

In the 1960s and 1970s the fight to end race-based segregation and discrimination took center stage in the black community. Dissatisfied with their unequal status, black people and their allies set out to change American laws, customs, and practices. Their collective efforts were organized into the modern civil rights movement, which utilized tactics of nonviolence and civil disobedience, as well as the energy and political ambitions of young people. Young people participated in local boycotts, organized mass meetings, engaged in sit-ins, marched in demonstrations, and went to jail by the thousands. In the last few decades, however, African American youth involvement in efforts toward social change has been considerably less visible, leaving many to wonder if this group has become politically dormant. Indeed, with the exception of several highly publicized youth-focused initiatives to increase voter turnout in the 2004 presidential election ("Vote Or Die," "Black Youth Vote," and "Rock-the-Vote"), African American men and women under age thirty have been seemingly absent from activities directed at influencing the structure of government, the selection of government authorities, or public policies.

The question of whether African American young people are less politically active today than were African American young people in the 1960s and 1970s has been the subject of much speculation and debate, but little empirical analysis. In fact, much of what is known about the political behavior of this group stems largely from the activities and organizing of black youth involved in the civil rights movement (Carson, 1981; Chafe, 1981; Morris, 1984; Payne, 1995). To update the discussion of African American youth politics and move it from the realm of conjecture to that of factual information, I plan to provide a more coherent and comprehensive examination of race, class, and civic attitudes as determinants of political participation than was possible in previous research. I maintain that changes in political campaign activity among African American young adults from 1960 to 1998 were driven in large measures by changes in both the levels and effects of socioeconomic status, racial affinity, and psychological political engagement.

157

The Increasing Significance of Social Class

Historical accounts reveal that the 1960s and 1970s were replete with racial tension and civil unrest. Blatant forms of prejudice, discrimination, and segregation placed race and the elimination of its' social, economic, and political consequences at the forefront of black thought and on top of the black political agenda. Issues associated with social class concerned blacks to be sure. However, to the extent that black people of all social classes confronted legal barriers to their civil rights and were considered second class citizens thinking, organizing, and identifying around race proved much more efficient and practical than accenting social and economic status. Then, and to a lesser degree now, the life chances of individual blacks were essentially more a function of race than of class. As such, the quest for racial equality is believed to have given rise to a political culture that encouraged African American young men and women to think of themselves as a racial group and to get involved in politics. Armed with a sense of purpose and group consciousness, young African Americans in the 1960s and 1970s participated in protest rallies, demonstrations, voter registration drives and a host of other activities aimed at challenging society's major social institutions (Carson, 1981; Morris, 1984; Payne, 1995).

By the 1980s and 1990s, however, many of the political, social, and economic barriers to opportunities for blacks were substantially lowered, yet traditional forms of racial segregation and discrimination did not disappear. In many respects problems of race in contemporary America are as pervasive today as they were thirty to forty years ago but much more subtle, covert, and complex. The Voting Rights Act of 1965, for example, makes it illegal to intimidate, coerce or prevent any individual from exercising his or her right to vote, yet large numbers of African American Florida voters experienced frustration and anger on Election Day in 2000 as they endured excessive delays, misinformation, and confusion, which resulted in the denial of their right to vote or to have their vote counted (Scheff, 2001). Compounding such voting irregularities are the large number of African- Americans who are disproportionately denied access to the ballot for having been convicted of a felony because of state laws (Sengupta, 2005). According to DEMOS, a progressive policy advocacy group, felony convictions have barred an estimated 4.7 million Americans from the polls, and of these, approximately two million are black (Chen, 2005). Clearly, whereas the old tactics to keep black people from voting, working, going to school, and residing in certain communities were based explicitly on racial motivations, the new maneuvers have racial significance only in their consequences, not their origins.

On the surface then, race relations in contemporary America appeared to have changed. For even the most casual observer could see that calls for overt bigotry, demands for strict segregation, advocacy of government-mandated discrimination, and adherence to the belief that blacks and other minorities are intellectually inferior to whites had virtually disappeared (Abramson, 1983; Schuman et al., 1997). Upon closer observation, however, we see that very little has changed. The presence of African Americans, for instance, is still firmly resisted in many areas of contemporary America, including residential neighborhoods, prestigious occupations, educational institutions, and private social clubs. In addition to persistent forms of racial segregation and discrimination, black people in the 1980s and 1990s also witnessed depression-level unemployment, declining wages, cuts in social programs, and vicious attacks on affirmative action (Glasgow, 1980; Kluegel and Smith, 1983; Hacker, 1992; Jaynes and Williams, 1989; Simpson, 1998; Williams, 1982). Given the changes in African Americans' social and economic status from 1960 to 1998 on the one hand and the continuities and rigidities in race relations during this time period on the other hand, it is appropriate to consider the effects of these broad trends on the political behaviors of African American young adults. To assess these relationships, I consider the impact of racial affinity, socioeconomic status, and psychological political engagement on the political campaign activity of two independent samples of African Americans who were under the age of thirty-five during the years of 1960–1978 (protest generation) and 1980–1998 (hip-hop generation).

Theories of Political Behavior

Traditionally, the factors thought to encourage African American involvement in politics have included group consciousness (Miller et al., 1981; Verba and Nie, 1972), social class (Verba and Nie, 1972; Verba, Schlozman, and Brady, 1995), and civic attitudes (Abramson, 1983; Carmines, 1978; Lasswell, 1948). Drawing on this body of work, my analysis highlights the influences of these variables on the political campaign activity of African American young adults. Looking first at racial affinity, the assumption is that African American young people who feel a strong sense of connection to or identification with other African Americans, believe that the social position of black people have not changed in the past few years, and are of the opinion that the government in Washington should make every effort to improve the social and economic positions of black people will be more likely to get involved in politics than those who think otherwise. At the base of this argument is the belief that the primary imperative in black politics is to advance the political interests of the group (Dawson, 1994:6). Central here is the assumption that race is still a major determinant of African Americans' life-chances and a dominant theme in American society. Hence, I expect the effect of racial affinity to have a positive effect on African American young people's political campaign activity in the 1960s and 1970s, as well as the 1980s and 1990s. However, I anticipate the effect to be significantly stronger during the former time period than during the latter time period.

The influence of socioeconomic status on political participation is also considered. This perspective asserts that differential access to social and economic resources best explains variations in political participation (Ferree, 1992; McAllister and Makkai, 1992). Pointing to such socioeconomic factors as education, occupation and income, advocates of this theory maintain that individuals located on the lower rungs of the social hierarchy are less likely to participate in the political process because they lack both the cognitive and motivational characteristics found to encourage participation (Park, 1993). Subsequently, it is generally argued that due to less education, more restricted occupation-related learning experiences, greater social isolation and higher levels of alienation, lower status persons, as compared to higher status persons are: less interested in politics; less aware of the need for or possible benefits of participation; less politically efficacious; less likely to possess those social and political skills that facilitate participation and are less likely to have the time, money and energy to expend in the political arena (Axelrod, 1956; Almond and Verba, 1963; Lipset, 1981; Verba and Nie, 1972; Wilson, 1987; and Jaynes and Williams, 1989). To the extent that the black community was more economically polarized in the 1980s and 1990s than in the 1960s and 1970s, I expect the effect of racial affinity on political activity to be weaker during the former time period, as compared to the latter time period. Moreover, I anticipate the effect of socioeconomic status on African American young people's political campaign activity to be positive and stronger in the 1980s and 1990s than in the 1960s and 1970s.

In addition to assessing whether racial affinity or socioeconomic status is more important in shaping African American young adults' political behavior, I also investigate the interaction between the two of them. The idea here is that although both racial and economic oppression have influenced black politics since the first slave revolt, the effects of race and class on political behavior are not constant but change at different time periods and for different socioeconomic groups. Essentially, so long as race-based discrimination and segregation remain major forces in the lives of African Americans against a backdrop of economic progress for some and economic devastation for others, a comprehensive understanding of black youth political activity must inevitably consider the interaction between race and class. The assumption here is that whereas racial affinity was a major and overwhelming determinant of political participation among African American young people in the 1960s and 1970s regardless of social class, in the 1980s and 1990s the most important influences on African American young people's political behavior were inspired by both race- and class-based concerns. In this regard, I expect racial affinity to have a strong and positive effect on the political campaign activity of African American young people in the 1980s and 1990s that are low in social and economic status. By contrast, I anticipate racial affinity to have a strong and positive effect on the political campaign activity of African American young people in the 1960s and 1970s that are high in social and economic status.

A final factor offered to understand political participation among African American young adults highlights the importance of interest in politics. According to this perspective, internal orientations, such as attitudes, beliefs and values are key determinants of varied patterns of political involvement (or the lack thereof) (Abramson, 1983; Abramson and Alrich, 1982; Carmines, 1978; Lasswell, 1948; Seeman, 1966; Sigelman et al., 1985). While acknowledging the joint impact of environmental constraints and personal factors, theorists who associate political behavior with psychological characteristics tend to place increased emphasis on the latter, arguing that personality traits affect basic processes of perception, judgment and learning endemic to all areas of life, including politics. In this regard, I suspect that interest in politics is a major prerequisite of political participation. Hence, it is believed to be an important determinant of involvement in politics among African American young people in the 1960s and 1970s, as well as the 1980s and 1990s. However, to the extent that political leaders and organizations are no longer the most salient factors shaping African American political activity because of changes in American race relations and African Americans' social and economic status, I expect the effect of interest in politics on political campaign activity to be positive and stronger among members of the hip-hop generation than members of the protest generation.

Hypotheses

H_1:

> *Racial Affinity.* Although race relations in America improved dramatically from 1960 to 1998 (Jaynes and Williams, 1989; Schuman et al., 1997; Wilson, 1980), prejudice, segregation, and discrimination are still permanent, but subtle fixtures in the culture. To the extent that African American young adults continue to be haunted by ambiguous and sophisticated forms of race and racism, I expect them to think of themselves as being apart of a group with a common set of political interests and desires to act collectively. In this connection, I hypothesize that racial affinity will have a positive effect on political participation among members of the protest and hip-hop generations. However, I expect the effect to be stronger in the former group than in the latter group.

H_2:

> *Socioeconomic Status.* As a result of social, economic, and political victories won during the civil rights era, many African American young people in the 1980s and 1990s saw doors of opportunity previously shut to them open up. Those who were well-trained, highly educated, and financially stable moved in neighborhoods outside of the black community took jobs serving white clienteles, and established social and professional networks based less on racial interests and more on class interests. By contrast, unskilled, poorly educated African American young people

could neither move out of the black community nor take advantage of employment opportunities in prestigious occupations (Wilson, 1980). The division of the black community into those who were positioned to take advantage of opportunities created by the civil rights legislation and those who could not is believed to have reduced the salience of race as a factor in African American lives on the one hand and raised the importance of social class on the other hand. In this connection, I hypothesize that measures of socioeconomic status will have positive effects on political participation among members of the protest and hip-hop generations. However, I expect the effects to be significantly stronger in the latter group than in the former group.

H_3:

Interest in Politics. The link between internal orientations, such as attitudes, beliefs, and values and involvement in politics has remained constant over the past thirty to forty years (Verba, Schlozman, and Brady, 1995). Among African Americans in the 1960s and 1970s, however, I argue that the push to participate in politics was strong enough to need not warrant a defined or intense set of political attitudes and opinions to achieve a high level of political behavior. To the contrary, the link between the political behavior of African American young people in the 1980s and 1990s and their attitudes and opinions toward politics is argued to be strong. Without the presence of an active and organized social movement mobilizing black interest and political activity, involvement in politics today is believed to require a more meaningful consideration of those internal orientations, such as political attitudes, believes, and values. In this connection, I hypothesize that psychological political engagement will have a positive effect on African American young adults' involvement in politics in both the protest and hip-hop era. However, the effects of interest in politics and external political efficacy on political participation will be positive and stronger among members of the hip-hop generation than members of the protest generation.

H_4:

Interaction Effect. The black experience in America has been shaped as much by race as it has class (Dawson, 1994; DuBois, 1899). On the one hand, racial discrimination and segregation are still dominant themes in black life regardless of individual African American's own or their family's social and economic status. On the other hand, class divisions within the black community have grown so much that the opportunities, life styles, and aspirations of affluent members are radically different from those who are less affluent. In this connection, I hypothesize that racial affinity will have a strong and positive effect on political participation among members of the hip-hop generation who are low in social and economic status, as compared to members of the protest generation who were high in social and economic status.

Data and Study Design

To test these hypotheses, I examine the effects of racial affinity, socioeconomic status, and civic attitudes on African American young adults' involvement in politics from 1960 to 1998. The data are from the American National Elections Studies (NES) Cumulative Data file (Miller, 1999). The NES is a full probability sample of English speaking adults living in households in the continental United States and has been conducted during each election year since 1948. The cumulative surveys covered a total of 35,996 respondents; only African Americans between the ages of eighteen to thirty-five are included in this study. My analyses are based primarily on data for 1,753 respondents—677 were surveyed between the years 1960–1978 and 1,076 were surveyed between the years 1980–1998. Further details on the sample design may be obtained from Miller and the National Election Studies (1999).

I identified three items in the NES cumulative data file that I thought fit into a composite measure of racial affinity and thus might predict African American young people's involvement in politics. One item asked respondents to indicate how close or comfortable (*warm* to *cold*) they felt toward African Americans as a group. Similar to a thermometer, individuals who did not feel either "warm" or "cold" toward African- Americans were placed in the middle, at the 50-degree mark. However, for those who exhibited warm or favorable feelings toward African Americans, they were given a score somewhere between 50 and 100 degrees. Likewise, if one felt cold or did not feel very favorable toward African Americans, then they were given a score somewhere between 0 and 50 degrees. For purposes of analysis, this item was recoded to reflect a 3-point scale, with "3" specifying favorable feelings toward African Americans and "1" specifying unfavorable feelings toward African Americans.

A second item asked African American young people to assess "how much real change they think there has been in the position of black people in the past few years." Possible responses were "a lot," "some," and "not much at all." The third question making up the racial affinity composite measure taps African American young adults' feelings concerning the federal government's responsibility to the black community. More specifically, it asks whether "the government in Washington should make every effort to improve the social and economic position of blacks" or should "the government not make any special efforts to help blacks because they should help themselves." The initial coding for this item was from "1" to "7"; with "7" designating that blacks should help themselves and "1" designating that government should help blacks. For purposes of analysis, this item was recoded to reflect a 3-point scale. The new response category is as follows: "7" through "5" was coded "1"; " 4" was coded "2"; and "3" through "1" was coded "3."

In addition to racial affinity, social class is also thought to influence African American young people's political behavior. Measured using three standard indicators, I considered respondents' level of education, income, and occupational status. Education was coded "1" to "4"; with "4" connoting having completed an advanced graduate and/or professional degree, "3" represent having completed the equivalent of an associate and/or bachelor's degree, "2" represent having attended college, but not graduated and "1" connote having completed at least high school. The scale used to measure income ranged from "1" to "5" and is based on percentiles. In a similar regard, occupation is measured using a 6-point prestige scale. The most prestigious occupation was coded "6" and the least prestigious occupation was coded "1."

A final determinant of participation to be considered here is civic attitudes. Two questions were used to measure this concept. The interest in politics item asked respondents how interested (or not) they were in following political campaigns over the past year. The coding for this question was from "1" to "3"; with "3" designating being "very interested" and "1" representing "not interested." (External Political Efficacy Discussion Here) I also included several socio-demographic variables as controls in my analysis. These consist of gender, urbanism, and region. Each has been found in previous research to affect levels of involvement in politics (Verba and Nie, 1972; Brady, Verba, and Schlozman, 1995). The dependent variable, political activity, is measured by a standard set of NES items: "Did R work for a party or candidate," "Did R attend political meetings," "Did R donate money to a party/candidate," "Did R display a candidate button/sticker," "Did R try to influence to others vote." These items were summed to create a political activity index (alpha reliability = .72).

Results

A basic premise of this analysis is that fundamental changes in racial identity, socioeconomic status, and psychological political engagement has brought in their wake notable shifts in political campaign activity among African American young adults over the past thirty to forty years. Simple comparisons of African American young people's feelings of racial affinity, levels of socioeconomic status, intensity of civic attitudes, and volume of political participation in the 1960s and 1970s versus the 1980s and 1990s provides an assessment of the overall nature of social, economic, and political change. Table 1 gives the mean responses for members of the protest and hip-hop generations for these variables.

In general, shifts in racial affinity, socioeconomic status, and civic attitudes did not accompany substantial changes in involvement in politics. The means for the "political campaign activity" variable indicate that while, on average, fewer African American young people reported having worked for a party or candidate, attended a political meeting, donated money to a party or candidate, displayed a candidate button or sticker, or tried to influence others to vote in the 1980s and 1990s (X = 1.32) than in the 1960s and 1970s (X = 1.65), the percentage who did participate was consistently small.

As can be seen, the means for this item are just under 2 on a 6-point scale. In fact, at no time during the period covered by this analysis did African American young adult's involvement in campaign activity exceed 20 percent.

Despite having lower mean political participation levels in the 1980s and 1990s, as compared to the 1960s and 1970s, African American young people in the former cohort reported significantly higher educational attainment levels than the latter cohort (X = 3.48 vs. X = 2.23). Consistently, just 20 percent of African American young people in the 1960s and 1970s reported having "some college," whereas 36 percent indicated having gone to college in the 1980s and 1990s. Likewise, members of the hip-hop generation showed higher mean levels of occupational prestige and labor force participation than their counterparts in the protest generation, with skilled and service workers experiencing the largest increase. (During the 1960s and 1970s, the percentage of African American young people in the paid labor force as skilled and/or service workers was about 41 percent, by the 1980s and 1990s this number had jumped to 55 percent.) The t-test of differences in means for education, occupational status, and employment status are all significant at p < .01.

Alongside these positive trends depicting a growing educated, gainfully employed African American young adult population, we also see in Table 1 several variables with movement patterns that are negative indicating a more complicated picture. The racial affinity composite measure offers a case in point. Data show that, on average, members of the protest generation were significantly more likely feel an attachment to other black people, believe that government should help improve the conditions of black people, and the conditions for black people have not improved than their counterparts in the hip-hop generation. This is evidenced by the means for racial affinity, which are 4.74 for African American young people who came of age during the 1960s and 1970s, as compared to 3.82 for those who reached political maturity in the 1980s and 1990s.

Family income and interest in politics also experienced declines over time. The mean income for member of the protest generation was noticeably higher (X = 3.55) than it was for members of the hip-hop generation (X = 3.17). In a similar pattern, Table 1 show that African American young people were much more inclined to report an interest in politics in the 1960s and 1970s (X = 1.37) than they were in the 1980s and 1990s (X = 1.26). Further, the t-tests of

Table 1
Means for Key Variables by Generational Cohort: National Elections Study
Cumulative Date File, 1960-1998

Variables	Protest Group (1960 – 1978)	Hip-Hop Group (1980 – 1998)	t-test
Racial Affinity	4.74 (1.05)	3.82 (1.12)	9.48**
Educational Attainment	2.23 (.733)	3.48 (.699)	10.20**
Family Income	3.55 (1.09)	3.17 (1.09)	6.23**
Occupational Status	3.83 (1.56)	4.33 (1.32)	4.24**
Employment Status	1.12 (.333)	1.40 (.402)	12.50**
Interest in Politics	1.37 (.484)	1.26 (.459)	9.09**
Political Campaign Activity	1.65 (1.05)	1.32 (.810)	6.24**

Notes: Numbers in parentheses are standard deviations. Ns for particular items vary due to non-response in particular years.   * p < .05   ** p < .01

differences in means for these items revealed significant differences at the .01 level. Hence, the low feelings of attachment to other black people, the drop in income, and the decrease in interest in politics among African American young adults from 1960 to 1998 connotes actual change and cannot be attributed to measurement error.

In summary, there is little difference in mean levels of political campaign activity among members of the protest and hip-hop generations. By contrast, mean levels of educational attainment and occupational status among African American young people are markedly higher in the hip-hop era than in the protest era. There are also noticeable cohort differences across means for racial affinity and income, but in the opposite direction. Essentially, members of the hip-hop generation reported substantially lower mean levels of racial affinity and income than did members of the protest generation. These data lend some support to a general assumption that African American young people who came of age in the 1980s and 1990s are socially, economically, and politically different than their 1960s and 1970s counterparts. To explore this assumption more directly, as well as the relative impact of socioeconomic status, racial affinity and civic attitudes on levels of political participation for African American young adults over time I turn to a set of logistic regression models in Tables 2 through 5.

Effect of Social Class on Political Campaign Activity

Looking first at the influence of socioeconomic status, Table 2 shows logistic regression coefficients for the effects of education, income, and occupational status on political campaign

Table 2
Logistic Regression Coefficients: Effect of Class on Campaign Activity among

Independent Variables	Protest Group B (S.E.)	Hip-Hop Group B (S.E.)
Socioeconomic Status & Socio-demographic		
Education	.280*** (.077)	.247*** (.064)
Income	.231** (.102)	-.017 (.085)
White-collar	.037 (.283)	.142 (.212)
Employed	-.446 (.355)	.528** (.221)
Not in labor force	-.527* (.305)	-.031 (.263)
Gender (Female=1)	-.061 (.231)	-.500*** (.169)
Urbanism (Urban=1)	.538** (.221)	.366** (.157)
Region (South=1)	.176 (.224)	.006 (.161)
Constants	-2.275*** (.466)	-1.875*** (.347)
Pseudo R2	.130	.068
Model X2	48.708	43.350
DF	8	8
N	487	888

Note: Logistic regression coefficients (B) with standard errors (S.E.) in parentheses are shown for all models.
*p < .10   **p < .05   *** p < .001

activity for two cohorts of African American young people. Overall, the effect of socioeconomic status on the likelihood of participating in politics was significantly stronger in the 1960s and 1970s than in the 1980s and 1990s. This finding is contrary to hypothesis 2, which predicted that the effects of education, income, and occupational status would be much greater in the hip-hop generation, as compared to the protest generation.

The lack of support for hypothesis 2 is also evidenced among the individual level coefficients. As shown in Table 2, education had a noticeably stronger effect on political campaign activity in the protest era than in the hip-hop era. Likewise, the effect of income also declined from 1960 to 1998, but at a much faster rate (than education), going from having a positive and significant influence on political campaign activity in the protest era to having a negative and non-significant effect in the hip-hop era. Replicating this trend of downward movement, I also found the coefficients for labor force participation to be substantially larger in the protest model than in the hip-hop model. Interestingly, the only variable to lend support for hypothesis 2 was employment status. Employed African American young people in the 1980s and 1990s were significantly more likely to get involved in politics (L_i = .528**) than were employed African American young people in the 1960s and 1970s (L_i = -.446).

Effect of Racial Affinity on Political Campaign Activity

Similar to Table 2, the logistic regression models in Table 3 assess the effects of racial affinity on political campaign activities, controlling for the other variables in the equation. The results show that racial affinity was not a significant determinant of whether or not African American young people would get involved in politics in either the protest (L_i = -.138) or hip-hop (L_i = .091) generation. This finding lets me reject hypothesis 1, which asserts that although racial affinity will have a positive effect on political participation among members of the protest and hip-hop generations, its influence will be stronger in the former group than in the latter group.

The relative impact of racial affinity on campaign activity can also be assessed using the summary measures. More specifically, the Pseudo R-square measures the amount of total variance explained. In this regard, a simple comparison of the Pseudo R-square values in Table 2 with those in Table 3 should give us a crude estimate of the overall explanatory power of racial affinity relative to socioeconomic status. If our understanding of African American young adult campaign activity is enhanced by a consideration of racial affinity, then I should observe a noticeable positive difference in the Pseudo R-square values given for socioeconomic status in Table 2 with those given for racial affinity in Table 3. As can be seen, the data does not bear this out.

Consistent with the findings for the individual coefficients, the summary measures highlight an inability of the racial affinity measure to explain participation in politics among African American young adults in either the protest or hip-hop generation. The Pseudo R-square values for the protest models in the respective Tables are identical suggesting no change in the amount of variance explained by adding racial affinity to the equation. Clearly, racial affinity is of much less importance as a predictor to political campaign activity than is socioeconomic status.

Effect of Psychological Political Engagement on Political Campaign Activity

Table 4 presents the results of logistic regressions conducted to test hypothesis 4. Participation in political campaign activity was regressed on indicators of socioeconomic status and socio-demographics, racial affinity, and psychological political engagement—that is, interest in politics and external political efficacy. Together these measures allow me to assess potential dif-

Table 3
Logistic Regression Coefficients: Effect of Race on Campaign Activity among
African-American Young Adults

Independent Variables	Protest Group B (S.E.)	Hip-Hop Group B (S.E.)
Socioeconomic Status & Socio-demographic		
Education	.290*** (.081)	.244*** (.064)
Income	.249** (.107)	-.014 (.086)
White-collar	.068 (.297)	.148 (.213)
Employed	-.511 (.370)	.555** (.222)
Not in labor force	-.627 (.323)	-.023 (.263)
Gender (Female=1)	-.078 (.243)	-.501*** (.170)
Urbanism (Urban=1)	.696*** (.235)	.370** (.157)
Region (South=1)	.349* (.237)	.006 (.161)
Racial Affinity		
Composite Measure	-.138 (.144)	.091 (.114)
Constants	-2.275*** (.466)	-1.875*** (.348)
Pseudo R2	.130	.070
Model X2	48.708	44.246
DF	9	9
N	487	887

Note: Logistic regression coefficients (B) with standard errors (S.E.) in parentheses are shown for all models.
*p < .10   **p < .05   *** p < .001

ferences in the effects of interest in politics and external political efficacy on levels of campaign activity by generational cohort, controlling for other variables in the model. Turning to the results, we see they offer increased support for hypothesis 4. The data reveal a noticeable effect of psychological political engagement on involvement in campaign activity in both the

Table 4
Logistic Regression Coefficients: Effect of Political Attitudes on Campaign
Activity among African-American Young Adults

Independent Variables	Protest Group B (S.E.)	Hip-Hop Group B (S.E.)
Socioeconomic Status & Socio-demographic		
Education	200**	.138**
	(.084)	(.073)
Income	.206*	.039
	(.110)	(.095)
White-collar	.110	-.050
	(.304)	(.240)
Employed	-.413	.573**
	(.379)	(.248)
Not in labor force	-.139	-.599*
	(.333)	(.296)
Gender (Female=1)	.008	-.343*
	(.250)	(.189)
Urbanism (Urban=1)	.630***	.348**
	(.240)	(.177)
Region (South=1)	.289	.028
	(.243)	(.181)
Racial Affinity		
Composite Measure	-.171	.038
	(.150)	(.127)
Political Engagement		
Interest in Politics	.484***	1.018***
	(.138)	(.114)
External Efficacy	.241*	.123
	(.138)	(.107)
Constants	-2.141***	-1.834***
	(.510)	(.386)
Pseudo R2	.197	.226
Model X2	69.171	138.508
DF	11	11
N	441	811

Note: Logistic regression coefficients (B) with standard errors (S.E.) in parentheses are shown for all models.

*p < .10   **p < .05   *** p < .001

protest and hip-hop eras, with the effect being substantially larger among African American young people in the 1980s and 1990s than those in the 1960s and 1970s.

Support of hypothesis 4 is further evidenced by the individual level coefficients. As can be seen, interest in politics and external political efficacy were each found to have statistically significant effects on the odds that African American young adults in the 1960s and 1970s would participate in campaign activity. By contrast, just one (interest in politics) of the psychological political engagement measures was deemed statistically important among African American young adults in the 1980s and 1990s. On its face, the larger number of statistically significant coefficients in the protest model than in the hip-hop model would call for a rejection of hypothesis 4. However, upon closer observation we see that although there are more statistically significant indices of psychological political engagement in the protest model, the size of the coefficient for interest in politics in the hip-hop model is significantly greater, which lend some support to hypothesis 4.

Even more to the point, a comparison of the Pseudo R-squares in Tables 3 and 4 show that consistent with hypothesis 4, the effect of psychological political engagement on the odds of African American young adults participating in campaign activity was less in the protest generation (.197 - .130 = .067) than in the hip-hop generation (.226 - .070 = .156). In other words, interest in politics and external political efficacy accounted for just one percent of the variance in political campaign activity in the protest era, but roughly 16 percent in the hip-hop era.

Effect of Racial Affinity and Social Class on Political Campaign Activity

Up to this point, I have examined the separate effects of racial affinity and social class on political campaign activity. In this section, I extend the previous analyses to consider the interactive effect of these two variables. Table 5 present parallel equations detailing the extent to which the relationship between racial affinity and political campaign activity changes as a result of social class. The results show that contrary to hypothesis 4, interaction effects were found in both cohorts, indicating that the effect of racial affinity on political campaign activity was just as likely to change at different levels of socioeconomic status among members of the hip-hop generation as it was for members of the protest generation.

Among members of the protest generation there was a significant tendency for race-conscious African American young adults with high incomes (top percentile) to get involved in political campaigns to a far greater extent than race conscious African- American young people at the low end of the income scale. Likewise, the effect of racial affinity on political campaign activity is substantially weaker for college-educated members of the hip-hop generation ([-.142 * 5 = -.085] - .625 = -.085) than it is for members of the hip-hop generation with just an elementary school education ([-.142 * 1 = -.142] - .625 = .483). These results are counter to the argument I make in hypothesis 4.

In summary, these data confirm hypothesis 3, but yield very little support for hypotheses 1, 2, and 4. These findings raise the question of why actual changes in African American young people's levels of socioeconomic status, racial attitudes, and civic proclivities, as outlined in Table 1, did not translate into more potent determinants of campaign activity in the hip-hop era and in turn, greater levels of participation. While a plethora of explanations could be advanced to answer this question, I assert that if positive changes in the areas of educational attainment, occupational prestige, and employment status had not been offset by a set of negative changes in the areas of racial affinity, income, and interest in politics and external political efficacy then involvement in campaign activity may have changed more dramatically from 1960 to 1998. In the next section, I confirm and extend this assertion.

Table 5
Logistic Regression Coefficients: Effect of Class and Race on Campaign
Activity among African-American Young Adults

Independent Variables	Protest Group B (S.E.)	Hip-Hop Group B (S.E.)
Socioeconomic Status & Socio-demographic		
Education	.195**	.140**
	(.084)	(.073)
Income	.196*	.038
	(.112)	(.095)
White-collar	.127	-.050
	(.306)	(.241)
Employed	-.449	.596**
	(.381)	(.249)
Not in labor force	-.644**	-.138
	(.336)	(.297)
Gender (Female=1)	.010	-.338*
	(.251)	(.189)
Urbanism (Urban=1)	.608**	.352**
	(.241)	(.177)
Region (South=1)	.292	.044
	(.245)	(.181)
Racial Affinity		
Composite Measure	-.512	.625*
	(.458)	(.401)
Political Attitudes		
Interest in Politics	.461***	1.032***
	(.138)	(.115)
External Efficacy	.248*	.135
	(.139)	(.108)
Interactions		
Race Affinity x Education	-.128	-.142*
	(.116)	(.101)
Race Affinity x Income	.313**	-.064
	(.157)	(.100)
Constants	-2.098***	-1.869***
	(.515)	(.388)
Pseudo R2	.208	.231
Model X2	73.428	141.781
DF	13	13
N	441	811

Note: Logistic regression coefficients (B) with standard errors (S.E.) in parentheses are shown for all models.
*p < .10   **p < .05 *** p < .001

Generational Cohort and Political Campaign Activity

Tables 6 and 7 give a set of logistic regressions for a model of the determinants of political campaign activity that includes the indices of socioeconomic status, socio-demographic characteristics, racial affinity, and psychological political engagement. Looking first at the simple relationship between generational cohort and political campaign activity in model 1 of Table 6, I find that there is a statistically significant difference in the frequency with which African American young adults participated in political campaign activity across the generations. Consistent with results in Table 1, members of the hip-hop generation were found to be significantly less likely to participate in political campaign activity than were members of the protest generation. The negative and statistically significant coefficient given for the effect of cohort in model 1 evidences this finding.

Model 2 of Table 6 show that the generation probability of African American young adult political campaign involvement in the hip-hop is even less likely when the effects of socioeconomic status and socio-demographic characteristics are held constant. To put this differently, model 2 reveals that if the effects of these variables had remained the same across generations, then members of the hip-hop generation would have engaged in political campaign activity at a substantially lower rate than members of the protest generation. However, as revealed in Table 2, we see that the effects of socioeconomic status and socio-demographic characteristics did not remain the same.

Hence, I consider the results in model 3 where the effects of socioeconomic status and socio-demographic characteristics on campaign activity were allowed to vary across the generations. When the effects of these items are allowed to vary, we find that the generational effects move from -.539 to .304. The reason for this change is that the negative effect of the decline in income has disappeared at the same time that the positive effect of the increases in employment status has gotten stronger. Taken together, we see that in the absence of a negative income effect and the presence of a major positive unemployment effect, participation in campaign activity among members of the hip-hop generation increased.

In model 4 of Table 7, I consider the relationship between changes in racial affinity and political participation. The small difference in the value given for the cohort variable in model 4 versus the value given for the cohort variable in model 2 shows that racial affinity played almost no role in promoting general change in political campaign activity among African American young adults from 1960 to 1998. As was evidenced in Table 3, the results in model 4 of Table 7 indicate that socioeconomic status and socio-demographic characteristics were of much greater importance as determinants of change than was racial affinity.

Contrary to the findings for racial affinity, results given for psychological political engagement in model 5 of Table 7 show that interest in politics and external political efficacy are instructive for understanding cohort differences in campaign activity among African American young adults. More specifically, these data illustrate that increased campaign activity among members of the protest generation as compared to members of the hip-hop generation can be explained, in part, by the noticeable decline in the effects of interest in politics and external political efficacy (as observed in Table 4). This is evidenced by the positive and statistically significant relationship between the political engagement variables and political campaign activity in model 5.

The increased role of psychological political engagement in promoting change in campaign activity among African American young adults is further confirmed in model 6. Looking first at interest in politics, we see that the relationship between this variable and political campaign activity among African American young adults was significantly stronger in the hip-hop era ($L_i = 1.018$) than in the protest era ($L_i = .531$). Despite these findings, members of the hip-hop

Table 6
Logistic Regression Coefficients: Effect of Class on Changes in Campaign Activity among African-American Young Adults

Independent Variables	Model 1 B (S.E.)	Model 2 B (S.E.)	Model 3 B (S.E.)
Cohort (Hip-Hop=1)	-.284 (.111)	-.539*** (.128)	.304 (.483)
Socioeconomic Status & Socio-demographic			
Education	---	.246*** (.048)	.274*** (.071)
Income	---	.078 (.064)	.217** (.098)
White-collar	---	.111 (.168)	.105 (.169)
Employed	---	.283* (.168)	-.349 (.338)
Not in labor force	---	-.201 (.197)	-.248 (.200)
Gender (Female=1)	---	-.336** (.135)	-.143 (.218)
Urbanism (Urban=1)	---	.368*** (.126)	.486** (.212)
Region (South=1)	---	.029 (.129)	.059 (.130)
Interactions			
Cohort x Education	---	---	-.025 (.091)
Cohort x Income	---	---	-.240** (.127)
Cohort x Employed	---	---	.818** (.380)
Cohort x Gender	---	---	-.329 (.265)
Cohort x Urbanism	---	---	-.117 (.260)
Constants	-.659*** (.086)	-1.590*** (.275)	-2.167*** (.411)
Pseudo R2	.006	.088	.099
Model X2	6.484	88.630	101.022
DF	1	9	14
N	1592	1375	1375

Note: Logistic regression coefficients (B) with standard errors (S.E.) in parentheses are shown for all models.
 *p < .10 **p < .05 *** p < .001

Table 7
Logistic Regression Coefficients: Effects of Class, Race, and Political Attitudes on Changes in Campaign Activity among African-American Young Adults

Independent Variables	Model 4 B (S.E.)	Model 5 B (S.E.)	Model 6 B (S.E.)
Cohort (Hip-Hop=1)	-.576*** (.131)	-.451*** (.142)	.590*** (.149)
Socioeconomic Status & Socio-demographic			
Education	.248*** (.049)	.148*** (.054)	.154*** (.054)
Income	.073 (.065)	090 (.070)	.092 (.070)
White-collar	.117 (.170)	.038 (.185)	.016 (.186)
Employed	.291* (.187)	.320* (.202)	.309* (.203)
Not in labor force	-.223 (.202)	-.257 (.218)	-.299 (.219)
Gender (Female=1)	-.356** (.137)	-.224* (.149)	-.218* (.149)
Urbanism (Urban=1)	.405*** (.128)	.360*** (.138)	.372*** (.139)
Region (South=1)	.068 (.132)	.054 (.142)	.073 (.143)
Racial Affinity			
Composite Measure	.042 (.089)	(.096)	-.010 -.026 (.097)
Political Attitudes			
Interest in Politics	---	.822*** (.086)	.531*** (.128)
Political Efficacy	---	.133* (.082)	.291* (.159)
Interactions			
Cohort x Interest in Politics	---	--- (.170)	.487***
Cohort x Political Efficacy	---	---	-.194 (.185)
Constants	-1.577*** (.282)	-1.508*** (.303)	-1.449*** (.302)
Pseudo R2	.093	.206	.214
Model X2	91.653	199.425	208.091
DF	10	12	14
N	1330	1252	1252

Note: Logistic regression coefficients (B) with standard errors (S.E.) in parentheses are shown for all models.
*p < .10   **p < .05   *** p < .001

generation reported a lower frequency of participation than members of the protest generation. Interestingly, I did not find the drop in levels of political efficacy over the past thirty to
forty years to have nearly the same effect. In fact, the data show that despite the dip in levels
of political efficacy among African American young adults from 1960 to 1998, the effect of
this item on political campaign activity remained the same during this time period. In this
context, we see that the decline in interest in politics was much more damaging to participation
in campaign activity among members of the hip-hop generation than was the drop in external
political efficacy.

These data not only confirm findings in Tables 1 through 5, but also make clear that if positive changes in the areas of educational attainment, occupational prestige, and employment
status had not been offset by a set of negative changes in the areas of racial affinity, income,
and interest in politics then involvement in campaign activity may have changed more dramatically from 1960 to 1998.

Conclusion

A common observation is that African American young people today do not participate
in politics as much as their 1960s and 1970s counterparts. Drawing on images of African
American young people defiantly sitting at lunch counters, boldly marching in the streets, and
diligently attending protest rallies pundits argue that by comparison African American young
people today, "while eager to live in a world where racism does not exist, do not want to do
the political work of changing themselves or society" (Hooks, 2000: 81). This characterization
of contemporary African American young people as politically apathetic has been even more
troublesome in light of recent changes in their social and economic status, feelings of racial
affinity, and civic attitudes. My results show that members of the hip-hop generation are not
only more educated and likely to be employed in prestigious occupations, but also to possess
feelings of affinity with other African Americans comparable to that of their 1960s and 1970s
counterparts. Despite these widespread changes, which should have lead to increased levels
of participation (Verba et al., 1993; Gurin and Epps, 1975), I observed less political campaign
activity in the hip-hop generation than in the protest generation. While the reasons for the drop
in participation among African American young adults from 1960 to 1998 are complicated, I
highlight noticeable declines in income, labor force participation, and psychological political
engagement.

In summary, my results point to two influential countervailing trends. Looking first at
changes in the social class status of African American young adults, we see that although it has
been primarily in the direction of promoting greater involvement in politics from the protest
to the hip-hop era, the change has not taken the form of a simple uniform increase. Results
show, for example, that while the proportion of African American young people with increased
levels of educational attainment and occupational status was higher in the 1980s and 1990s
than in the 1960s and 1970s, the former group earned less income and was more likely to be
unemployed than the latter group. It is also the case that the effects of education and income
on political participation were noticeably lower in the hip-hop era than in the protest era, while
the influence of holding a white-collar job and being unemployed increased from the protest
to the hip-hop era.

Off setting changes in the social class status of African American young adults that would
promote involvement in politics were changes in psychological political engagement, which
have been primarily negative for participation. Essentially, the proportion of African American
young adults who reported having an interest in politics and felt politically efficacious was lower
in the hip-hop generation than in the protest generation. Yet, the effects of these variables on

involvement in politics grew stronger. We see then, that while changes in psychological political engagement did play a role in promoting general change in political involvement from the protest to the hip-hop era, the change was primarily negative for participation. Basically, if changes in socioeconomic status and socio-demographic characteristics (which were primarily positive for participation) had not been undermined by changes in psychological political engagement (which were primarily negative for participation), then greater differences in levels of participation between African American young adults in the protest and hip-hop generations would have been found.

These results modify current theories at several levels. These results strongly caution against Verba and Nie (1972) and Miller, et al. (1981) claims that group consciousness promote participation among African Americans. My data found no support for the influence of racial affinity on campaign activity among African American young people in either the protest or hip-hop generation. My results also raise questions about the central importance claimed for socioeconomic status as a determinant of political participation (Jackson, 1971; Verba et al., 1995). As can be seen, while education, income, occupational status, and labor force participation were each found to account for some of the variance in campaign activity among African American young adults, the effects of these factors were substantially lower in the hip-hop generation than in the protest generation.

Finally, my results extend and confirm the important role of psychological political engagement in encouraging African American young peoples' involvement in politics (Gurin, Gurin, and Beattle, 1969; Lansford, 1968; Morris, Hatchett, and Brown, 1989). The effects of interest in politics and external political efficacy on campaign activity were strong and positive in protest generation. However, when psychological political engagement declined among members of the hip-hop generation so did its effect on the likelihood of their involvement in politics. This suggest that any effort to increase African American young adults' levels of political participation today must inevitably start with a campaign to raise interest in politics and trust in the efficacy of the political process.

References

Abramson, R. R. 1983. *Political Attitudes in America.* San Francisco, CA: W. H. Freeman.

Abramson, P. R., and J. H. Aldrich. 1982. "The Decline of Electoral Participation in America." *American Political Science Review,* 76: 502-521.

Almond, G., and A. Verba. 1963. *The Civic Culture.* Boston, MA: Little Brown.

Axelrod, M. 1956. "Urban Structure and Social Participation." *American Sociological Review,* 21(1):13-18.

Brady, H. E., S. Verba, and K. L. Schlozman. 1995. "Beyond SES: A Resource Model of Political Participation." *American Political Science Review,* 89(2): 271-294.

Carmines, E. G. 1978. "Psychological Origins of Adolescent Political Attitudes: Self-Esteem, Political Salience, and Political Involvement." *American Politics Quarterly,* 6(2): 167-186.

Carson, C. 1981. *In Struggle: SNCC and the Black Awakening of the 1960s.* Cambridge, MA: Harvard University Press.

Chafe, W. H. 1981. *Civilities and Civil Rights: Greensboro, North Carolina, and the Black Struggle for Freedom.* New York, NY: Oxford University Press.

Chen, M. 2005. Felon Voting Rights Conflict Hits Federal Court. *The New Standard.* (http://www.newstandardnews.net/content/?items=1978&printmode=true).

Dawson, M. C. 1994. *Behind the Mule: Race and Class in African American Politics.* Princeton, NJ: Princeton University Press.

DuBois, W.E.B. 1899. *The Philadelphia Negro: A Social Study.* Philadelphia, PA: University of Pennsylvania Press.

Ferree, M. M. 1992. "The Political Context of Rationality: Rational Choice Theory and Resource Mobilization." In Morris, Aldon, D. & Mueller, Carol McClurg. *Frontiers in Social Movement Theory.* New Haven, CT: Yale University Press.

Glasgow, D. G. 1980. The Black Underclass: Poverty, Unemployment and Entrapment of Ghetto Youth. New York, NY: Vintage Books.

Gurin, P. and E. Epps. 1975. *Black Consciousness, Identity and Achievement.* New York, NY: John Wiley.

Gurin, P., G. Gurin, and L. M. Beattle. 1969. "Internal-External Control in the Motivational Dynamics of Negroes." *Journal of Social Issues,* 25: 29-53.

Guterbock, T. M. and B. London. 1983. "Race, Political Orientation, and Participation: An Empirical Test of Four Competing Theories." *American Sociological Review,* 48: 439- 453.

Hacker, A. 1992. *Two Nations: Black and White, Separate, Hostile, Unequal.* New York, NY: Ballantine Books.

Jackson, J. S. 1971. "The Political Behavior and Socio-Economic Backgrounds of Black Students: The Antecedents of Protest." *Midwest Journal of Political Science,* 15: 661-686.

Jaynes, D. G., and M. R. Williams Jr. (eds.) 1989. *A Common Destiny: Blacks and American Society.* Washington, DC: National Academy Press.

Kluegel, J. R. and E. R. Smith. 1983. "Affirmative Action Attitudes: Effects of Self-Interest, Racial Affect, and Stratification Beliefs on Whites' Views." *Social Forces,* 61(3): 797-824.

Lansford, H. E. 1968. "Isolation, Powerlessness and Violence: A Study of Attitudes and Participation in the Watts Riot." *American Journal of Sociology,* 73: 581-591.

Lasswell, H. D. 1948. *Power and Personality.* New York, NY: Norton.

Lipset, S. M. 1963. *Political Man: The Social Bases of Politics.* Baltimore, MA: Johns Hopkins University Press.

McAllister, I., & Makkai, T. 1992. Resource and Social Learning Theories of Political Participation: Ethnic Patterns in Australia. *Canadian Journal of Political Science,* 25(2), 269-293.

Miller, W. E. and the National Election Studies. 1999. American National Election Studies Cumulative Data File, 1948-1998.

Miller, A. H., P. Gurin, G. Gurin, and O. Malanchuk. 1981. "Group Consciousness and Political Participation." *American Journal of Political Science,* 25(3): 494-511.

Morris, A. D. 1984. *The Origins of the Civil Rights Movement: Black Communities Organizing for Change.* New York, NY: The Free Press.

Morris, A. D., S. J. Hatchett, and R. E. Brown. 1989. "The Civil Rights Movement and Black Political Socialization." In *Political Learning in Adulthood.* Chicago, IL: University of Chicago Press.

Park, B. 1993. "An Aspect of Political Socialization of Student Movement Participation in Korea." *Youth & Society,* 25(2): 171-201.

Payne, C. M. 1995. *I've Got The Light of Freedom: The Organizing Tradition and the Mississippi Freedom Struggle.* Berkeley, CA: University of California Press.

Schuman, H., C. Steeh, L. Bobo, and M. Krysan. 1997. *Racial Attitudes in America: Trends and Interpretations (Revised Edition).* Cambridge, MA: Harvard University Press.

Seeman, M. 1966. "Alienation, Membership and Political Knowledge: A Comparative Study." *Public Opinion Quarterly,* 30: 353-367.

Sengupta, S. 2005. Felony Costs Voting Rights for a Lifetime in 9 States. *New York Times.* (http://www.newyorktimes.org).

Scheff, L. 2003. Winning the Election—The Republican Way: Racism, Theft and Fraud in Florida. *The Weekly Digest,* Boston, MA. (http://www.weeklydig.com/dig/content/2846.aspx).

Shingles, R. D. 1981. "Black Consciousness and Political Participation: The Missing Link." *American Political Science Review,* 75: 76-91.

Sigelman, L., P. Roeder, M. Jewell and M. Baer. 1985. "Voting and Non-Voting: A Multi-Election Perspective," *American Journal of Political Science,* 29: 749-765.

Simpson, A. Y. 1998. *The Tie That Binds: Identity and Political Attitudes in the Post-Civil Rights Generation.* New York, NY: New York University Press.

Verba, S., and L. Nie. 1972. *Participation in America: Political Democracy and Social Equality.* New York, NY: Harper & Row.

Verba, S., K. L. Schlozman, H. Brady, and N. H. Nie. 1993. "Citizen Activity: Who Participates? What Do They Say?" *American Political Science Review,* 87(2): 303-318.

Verba, S., K. L. Schlozman, and H. E. Brady. 1995. *Voice and Equality: Civic Voluntarism in American Politics.* Cambridge, MA: Harvard University Press.

Williams, W. 1982. *The State Against Blacks.* New York, NY: New Press.

Wilson, W. J. 1980. *The Declining Significance of Race: Blacks and Changing American Institutions.* 2nd ed. Chicago, IL: University of Chicago Press.

Wilson, W. J. 1987. *The Truly Disadvantaged.* Chicago, IL: University of Chicago Press.

Let Men be Men: A Gendered Analysis of Black Ideological Response to Familial Policies

Julia S. Jordan-Zachery
Howard University

Introduction

In 1965, Daniel Patrick Moynihan argued, "… ours is a society which presumes male leadership in public and private affairs. The arrangements of society facilitate such leadership and reward it. A subculture such as that of the Negro American, in which this is not the pattern, is placed at a distinct disadvantage" (1965: 75). Thus began our modern engagement with racialized patriarchy. Thirty-five years later, in the revised cultural problem approach, Representative Jessie Jackson Jr. (a black male) argued, "Violent criminals are overwhelmingly males who grew up without fathers and the best predictor of crime in a community is the percentage of absent father households." He concludes, "… states should be encouraged, not restricted, from implementing programs that provide support for responsible fatherhood, promote marriage, and increase the incidence of marriage" (U.S. House 2000). In 2001, President George W. Bush continued the racialized patriarchy movement of promoting marriage and fatherhood. President Bush's approach to institutionalizing patriarchy among the black poor involves spending $1.5 billion over five years to strengthen and promote marriage. The money would be spent on activities such as the development of interpersonal skills, designed to promote healthy marriages, especially among the poor. These marriage initiatives have been embraced at the state level. Indeed many states are utilizing welfare funds to support these programs.[1] Senator Moynihan, Representative Jackson, and President George W. Bush employ a "cultural deficiency" model in their analyses of female solo parenting. Employing this model allows for the argument that government should play the role of ensuring that black women follow a pre-determined patriarchal norm—what Dorothy Smith (1993) refers to as the Standard North American family.

After the publication of the "Moynihan Report", there was much outcry from black academics, etc., concerning the findings of this report (Rainwater and Yancey 1967). However, in current times, there seems to be very little criticism leveled against the similar arguments made by Representative Jackson. In this study, I examine the ideological factors that prevent the black community from addressing the racialized patriarchal nature of current welfare reauthorization proposals. The identification of these factors expands our understanding of interlocking systems of oppression both within and outside the black community. "… The notion of interlocking oppressions refers to the macro level connections linking systems of oppression such as race, class, and gender. This is the model describing the social structures that create social positions" (Cuadraz and Uttal 1999).

As such, I ask why the black community remains relatively silent on a series of state racialized patriarchal initiatives and policies designed to regulate the lives of poor black women. This is not a critique of any antiracist movement tactics, per se, nor is the goal of this article to elevate one gender over another. Instead, the purpose is to encourage the exploration of how the black community can respond to public policies that will limit our ability to achieve social and economic justice since they divert much needed resources from our communities. I suspect that the failure of the traditional black political responses to address gender as an integral element in oppressive structures limits their ability to resist and challenge racialized patriarchal policies. I argue that because of the masculinized approach to black freedom and conservative gender attitudes black liberation ideologies (that opposed racial oppression) can indeed support or be used to justify policies that further subjugate black women.

Historically, Anna Julia Cooper (1892 [1988]), among other black women, called for a simultaneous challenge to patriarchy and racism. This call recognizes that black women are subordinated at multiple levels (see Beal 1970; Crenshaw 1989, 1995; Sizemore 1973). Cooper, among others, recognized that black women function within at least two subordinated groups. Black women are subordinated both along racial and gender lines. One area in which these two oppressive structures converge is in the area of familial ideology. Familial ideology operates from the premise that the family is the basic unit of society. Since this familial edit is both raced and gendered, it has different consequences for women depending on their social location. As a consequence, "women, in general, and minority women in particular are often the victims of the power dynamics between the male leaders of the state and the male leaders" of their group (Stopler 2003).

Black liberation ideologies appear to support the (re)construction of the black man as a patriarch and the protector of the black community. Thus, these ideologies are limited in their challenge to racialized patriarchy policies because any challenge would thwart the efforts aimed at reconstructing black men. Patricia Hill Collins (1996, 14) states, "within African American communities", there is an "unwritten family rule" that "black women will support black men, no matter what" (see also Walker 1983, 316-19; White 1984, 19). This unwritten rule makes it difficult for leaders of the black freedom movement to challenge racialized patriarchy.

Racialized patriarchy has informed both fatherhood and marriage proposals. I make this claim because these policies are about power relations both between and within groups. Patriarchy is first and foremost about power. It is the power of men over women. Patriarchy operates simultaneously in the cultural, economic, political, and social realms to dominate and oppress women.

Higginbotham (1992) challenges the concept of universal patriarchy by asking how does race relate to gender? She argues that gender has always had a racial meaning. Indeed gender is both constructed and fragmented by race. Consequently, in a racialized society, patriarchy serves to oppress not only women of color differently from Euro-American women. It also differentiates men of color from Euro-American men. Zillah Eisenstein (1994, 2-3) in her book, *The Color of Gender: Reimaging Democracy*, employs the term "racialized patriarchy" to "bring attention to the continual interplay of race and gender in the structure of power." As a consequence of racialized patriarchy, black female solo parenting is often viewed as a source of the ills of black communities. Employing the term racialized patriarchy allows us to capture the dynamic and complex interaction of racism and patriarchy. Below I explore how traditional black political ideologies confront racialized patriarchy.

Black Political Thought and Gender

Black political ideologies operate so that some issues are highlighted while others are buried. In this regard, these ideologies have been susceptible to the influence of the American gendered order. Outside of black feminist ideology, traditional black political ideologies have failed to substantively incorporate gender as a mode of analysis (Cade 1970; Giddings 1984; Guy-Sheftall 1995; Springer 1999; White 1999). Indeed, patriarchy is ingrained in many institutions within black civil society (Marable 2001), the result of which is the positioning of women relative to men. In the U.S. society, race is sexualized and sex is racialized. That is, one's experience with race is not gender neutral and vice versa. For example, all women share the same gender categorization, but are made distinct along racial lines. Thus, White women are socially constructed as different from and superior to black women. Based on how the social categories of race and sex intersect black and white women experience different and often inequitable degrees of citizenship, which in turn determine their relationships to societal institutions and practices. Patriarchy also determines inter-group and intra-group relationships. To borrow from the work of Cathy Cohen (1999), black women, are marginalized within an already marginalized group. Black men and women encounter patriarchy differently, thus mediating their experiences with multiple systems of oppression.

The African American struggle for racial liberation and social justice has involved a myriad of ideological responses each with a different vision as shaped by the particular historical context. Dawson (2001, 14) identifies the following six political ideologies: (1) Radical Egalitarian, (2) Disillusioned Liberal, (3) Black Marxists, (4) Black Nationalist, (5) Black feminists, (6) Black Conservative. This article focuses on only two of these political ideologies—Black Nationalism and Integrationism—because they are often identified as two of the oldest schools of thought. While the conclusions of these two ideologies diverge, they share some basic tenets. Central to their paradigms is the notion of autonomy—individual and community based. One other ideological commonality between the above two black political ideologies is their conclusions about the nature and structure of society and the role of men and women in the African American quest for liberation.

Much of the work that has examined black political thought's responses to patriarchy have most closely linked patriarchy with Black Nationalism (Dawson 2001; White 1990). While Black Nationalists have loudly espoused their beliefs on gender and sex, patriarchal beliefs are also evident among cultural pluralists and even integrationists. A common theme connecting many of the approaches of black liberation has been its identification with black manhood. The symbolic equalization of black liberation with black manhood transcends various periods of racial assertion and ideological thought. Below, I focus on these two ideologies and their relationship to gender.

Black Nationalism

Harold Cruse (1967) traces the historical roots of Black Nationalism to the mid-nineteenth century and identifies some of its seminal leaders as Martin Delaney, Edward Blyden, Henry M. Turner, Alexander Crummell, and George Washington Williams. The central organizing principle for Black Nationalism is race and racial oppression. Proponents of Black Nationalism concentrate and focus on group consciousness and solidarity to combat racism and inequality. At the core of Black Nationalism are the concepts of African American autonomy and self-determination. There are variants of Black Nationalism based on the degree to which an adherent believes blacks should seek cultural, social, economic, and/or political separation from America (Bracey 1970).

Black Nationalism (in one form) includes calls for an entirely separate territorial base. Martin Delany (in the nineteenth century) and Marcus Garvey's (in the early twentieth century) are often cited as historical examples in the call for black territorial autonomy. This approach also includes calls for separate black-run institutions within the United States. Additionally, there is a divergence on how African Americans relate to and with Africa and African culture. Some nationalists have also used secular terms to define the parameters of nationalism, while others have couched the ideology in terms of religious beliefs. Common among the variants of Black Nationalism is the concept of group identity (Dawson 2001).

Integrationism

Integrationists such as Ida B Wells, Frederick Douglass, W. E. B DuBois (in his earlier stages of activism), and the Reverend Dr. Martin Luther King, Jr., believed the American socio-political system (or at least its liberal creed) was basically sound, although they recognized the existence and fundamentally harmful affects of racism. However, by subscribing to the approach of moral suasion, the aforementioned individuals believe that the American system can be changed to include African Americans. Proponents of Integrationism hold as their foundation the notion that African Americans are Americans who happen to be of African descent. As such they seek to have African Americans included into Euro-American society via the expansion of civil rights. Specifically, integrationists view the expansion of equal opportunities for African Americans as the venue through which this group will achieve equality. Proponents of integration tend to support policy designed to promote a strong central state with the goal of promoting equality. They subscribe to the American ethos of individual liberty and self-reliance (Dawson 2001).

Black Political Ideology and Womanhood Discourses

Within both Black Nationalism and Integrationism one can find different approaches to the challenge of racial oppression. My linear discussion of these ideologies is not to suggest that they do not overlap. Like other ideologies of resistance, Black Nationalism and Integrationism can range from reactionary to transformative. Generally, a reactionary response to black liberation will not challenge the fundamental societal and cultural institutions, practices, and structures of privilege and power. Following such a path does not allow for a challenge to the ideological assumptions, implications, and outcomes of a patriarchal system. Alternatively, a more revolutionary or transformative paradigm promotes policy and practices that are designed to eradicate systems of inequality. A common thread connecting Black Nationalist and Integrationists ideologies has been their reactionary responses to gender and patriarchy and their failure to fully address these problems. Historically, black liberation movements have not followed a revolutionary or transformative approach on the issue of gender (Brown, Elsa 1990; Brown, Elaine 1992; Higginbotham 1992; Mullings 1997). Gender is a socially constructed phenomenon that envelops power relationships between men and women. Akin to the trope of race, the trope of gender involves a power relationship between men and women and between women and the state. Any progressive black liberation movement has to recognize and challenge this power relationship.

The power relationship between black men and women, that subjugates black women, has been evident regardless of who is championing the cause for freedom and the various tactics employed. The result of this power struggle between African American men and women, has at times, led to the denial of black women's rights during the various quests for civil rights. The rationale for following such an approach was expressed by Nathan Hare (1989, 169) who suggested that "the most basic solution to the black or oppressed female's condition ... will be unavoidably in the reproductive/sexual realm, while the solution to the male's condition will be ably in the sphere of productive/social instrumentality."

The meaning of freedom may differ and has differed based on the ideological lens of its definer. However, black male leaders seem to overwhelmingly define and metaphorically equate freedom with manhood. For many Nationalists, the role of women in the movement is to serve as guardians of the black culture and the nurturer of the children. In essence the role of women is relegated to the domestic sphere. For example, Marcus Garvey often identified the black liberation struggle with the attainment of manhood. Indeed, he would caution his followers and supporters "there is always a turning point of the Negro, where we have changed from the old cringing, weakling, and transformed into full-grown men, demanding our portion as men." (Quoted in Marable 2001, 130). Amy Jacque Garvey—a feminist in her own right—complained about the patriarchal thinking of men in the Garvey Pan-Africanist movement. And forty years later her lament was echoed when African-American women leaders complained about sexism in the Black Panther Party (Dawson 2001).

The Million Man March of 1995, one of the more recent expressions of Black (cultural) Nationalism, shows the tension between race and gender. The March was designed as a Day of Atonement and racial unity. Minister Louis Farrakhan, the national leader of the Nation of Islam, served as the principal organizer of the March. One of his organization's requests was that women stay home, watch the children, and pray. According to Farrakhan:

> We are asking the Black woman, particularly our mothers, to be with our children, teaching them the value of home, self-esteem, family and unity; and to work with us to ensure the success of the March and our mission to improve the quality of life for our people. We take this historical moment to recognize the major contributions that the Black woman has made and continues to make, toward the advancement of our people.
>
> The march is not against females; it's not to say we don't love our women. But we must do something to atone for what we have done to our women and atone for the abuse we have heaped on our women (Quoted in Mullings 1997, 146).

Farrakhan framed the exclusion of women from the March in the language of protection. One goal of the March was to protect women by encouraging and fostering a mindset among black women that would allow them to relinquish leadership roles to black men.

While integrationists have not been as explicit as Black Nationalist, the former have had less than a perfect relationship with gender questions. As Mullings (1997, 137) argues, those who see refers to as inclusionists: "... seek gender privileges within the dominant paradigm: to claim for African American men the privileges of manhood and to seek for African American women the protections of patriarchy denied to them by the dominant culture." Dr. Martin Luther King, Jr., often described freedom as an entitlement to be bestowed on black men. For example, he would assert: "We know, from experiences in past, that the nation does not move on questions involving genuine equality for the black man unless something is done to bring pressure to bear on Congress, and to appeal to the conscience and the self-interest of the nation" (King 1986, 672). Additionally, Martin Luther King Jr., argued, "the primary obligation of the woman is motherhood" suggesting that while black women were important to the movement, their issues are secondary in the race war. Such was evident from the concerns of Ella Baker and Septima Clark that King and other black ministers were dismissive of women's leadership in the Civil Rights Movement. And it was also evident when the courageous, 1972 presidential bid of U.S. Representative Shirley Chisholm, the first black person and black woman to make a contemporary national bid, was strongly criticized by many of the same black male civil rights leaders who were followers of King (Giddings 1984).

Historically is has been all too common in black Liberation Movements for proponents to push for the reinstatement of the black man as the head of the household, according to the patriarchal model. Like so many of his counterparts, Ralph Bunche highlighted the level and types of inequalities endemic in the American society, but excluded gender as a basis of inequality. Bunche in his call for not only a black response but also a state centered-response made the following argument:

> In my view, the United States can pull through this crisis and avert domestic disaster only by a huge amount of heavy thinking by a vast number of people, by good sense and goodwill in tremendous volume, by determination and resources on a war-scale. Indeed, this is a war, a domestic war, that must be waged—against racism, against rejection, against poverty, against slums, against the betrayal of the rich promised of America, inexcusably unfulfilled for *black men* (1995, 301, emphasis added).

Overwhelmingly, gender is relegated to a secondary role in the black liberation struggle. Although not always universally the case (as evident from the many black women who have lead struggles), freedom often appears to be equated with manhood (Hine 1993). The woman's role in the struggle is constructed around motherhood and the domestic sphere. However, such a position does not provide supporters of either Black Nationalism or Integrationism with much hope of challenging policies aimed at eradicating the myth of the "bad" Black Matriarch. Both ideologies implicitly and/or explicitly employ the Black Matriarch as a cultural image and signifier for "dysfunctional" women and families. These schools of thought often couch solutions to the Black Matriarch problem in either a language of "protection" or "rightful place", which overwhelmingly position women in the domestic sphere. With their emphasis on marriage and fatherhood, the current welfare reauthorization proposals, also seek to confine black women to the domestic sphere. The goal of doing such is not necessarily to liberate these women; but instead seems designed to "normalize" their behavior.

Family Intervention by the State

Both marriage and fatherhood initiatives are designed to strengthen "fragile families." Fragile families are those defined as low-income, unmarried couples that have a child (or children). The family is deemed "fragile" because it has a higher risk of poverty, economic insecurity, vulnerable relationships and family dissolution. Recent research focused on these couples and the well being of their children has found that, although the majority of children born to un-wed parents in large U.S. cities are born to parents in committed relationships, theses parents have many barriers to marriage and these relationships often falter.[2] These barriers include low educational attainment, an income below the poverty line, and health limitations (McLanahan, Garfinkel, Reichman and Teitler 2001). Some researchers and policy makers argue that female-headed households perpetuate and foster fragile families. The assumption of this argument is that the causation of poverty is rooted in family formation—particularly the failure to follow the prescribed family norm of two married, heterosexual, parents with children (Thomas 1998). Dorothy Roberts (1997) argues,

> ... It is believed that Black mothers transfer a deviant lifestyle to their children that dooms each succeeding generation to a life of poverty, delinquency, and despair. A persistent objective of American social policy has been to monitor and restrain this corrupting tendency of Black motherhood (8).

The cultural deficiency model is often applied to the familial decisions of black women. The current marriage and fatherhood initiatives capture this approach. Employing a cultural problem approach, the various fatherhood and marriage initiatives are designed to change individual behavior. Allen (1978) identifies the "cultural deviant" theoretical perspective used to study the black family. The cultural deviant model assumes that family formation among African Americans (specifically female headed families) is pathological. Furthermore, this perspective argues that it is the individual's failure to internalize the marital norms of U.S. society accounts for the growth of female solo parenting in the black community (Bernard 1966; Gilder 1981; Mead 1992; Murray 1984, 1996a, 1996b). Following this line of reasoning, welfare reauthorization efforts seek to increase the incidence of marriage in the black community; policy is directed at changing attitudes, lifestyles, and interpersonal skills. Generally speaking, the various marriage initiatives concentrate on an individual, therapeutic approach with the goal of lessening the decline of marriage.

To understand this policy approach, we have to briefly revisit Moynihan's "Black Matriarch" thesis because it is his conclusions that have helped shaped public welfare policies over the past forty years. To be sure, black scholars such as W E. B. DuBois (1969) and E. Franklin Frazier (1948) earlier identified the Black Matriarch as a problem (Giddings 1984). Yet, one central difference between their research and that conducted by Moynihan is that DuBois and Frazier interpreted matriarchal families as a *product* of racial oppression and poverty—not as a central *cause* in the inequitable social and economic position of black families relative to white families.

The Moynihan Report lays out much of what we know of the Black Matriarch and the consequences of this type of family formation. As argued in this work, the Black "Matriarchal" family structure is deviant and causes many of the problems associated with the black community. Moynihan argues that the African American female-headed family is "the principal source of most of the aberrant, inadequate, or antisocial behavior they did not establish, but now serves to perpetuate the cycle of poverty and deprivation" (1965, 76). Employed is the image of a masculinized, domineering "woman." Following this line of argument, Black Matriarchs are depicted as unable to care for and nurture their children (Mullings 1997, 117). According to Collins (1991: 73) "prior to the 1960s, female-headed households were certainly higher in African American communities, but an ideology racializing female-headedness as a causal feature of black poverty had not emerged." As a consequence, of the racialization of female-headedness, the Matriarch is constructed as a bad mother who is responsible for low educational attainment, crime, delinquency of her charges, and for ostracizing black men. Furthermore, "aggressive, assertive women are penalized—they are abandoned by their men, end up impoverished, and are stigmatized as being unfeminine" (Collins 1991, 75). The end result, is that the Matriarch is the purveyor of all that is threatening to white society for she creates a flawed family and then sends her emasculated man and her immoral and inherently flawed children out into the world. Interestingly, "the image of the Black Matriarch emerged at the time as a powerful symbol for both black and white women of what can go wrong if white patriarchal power is challenged (Gilkes 1983, 296). Gilkes suggest that if women fail to follow socially sanctioned patriarchal norms, they will be considered deviant and ostracized.

Fatherhood and marriage initiatives are designed to eliminate the Black Matriarch and "liberate" the emasculated black man by reinstating him in his rightful place. If policy can ensure the reinstatement of these men as leaders of the family, supporters argue everything will be all right in these communities (Horn 2001). These racialized patriarchal policies are all part of the family values platform, which is an attempt by the state to sanction a so-called "normal" family. This concept of normal family represents a particular mode of functioning as well as economic, gender, and social behaviors. Additionally, it speaks to issues of identity and citizenship, for it determines who is valued and protected by the state.

Marriage Related Provisions in Recent Welfare Reauthorization Proposals

In the immediate post welfare reform period, advocates celebrated the "success" of these reforms at reducing welfare caseloads and increasing the numbers of welfare recipients entering and re-entering the workforce. As we move further away from this time and into the reauthorization phase, policy makers are beginning to pay increasing attention to the four family-formation initiatives of the Personal Responsibility and Work Opportunity Reconciliation Act of 1996 (PRWORA). The 1996 welfare reform act, set the stage for the current welfare reauthorization initiatives. The PRWORA has four family-formation objectives:

1. Provide assistance to needy families so that children may be cared for in their own homes or in the homes of relatives;
2. End the dependence of needy parents on government benefits by promoting job preparation, work and marriage;
3. Prevent and reduce the incidence of out-of-wedlock pregnancies and establish annual numerical goals for preventing and reducing the incidence of these pregnancies; and
4. Encouraging the formation and maintenance of two-parent families. (U.S. P.L 104-193, Section 401(a).

These objectives were akin to wallflowers at the dance since they received minimal attention. Most of the initial attention was focused on the requirements of PRWORA related to work, time-limited assistance, and sanctions. There is now a push at both the federal and state level to undertake a series of marriage and fatherhood initiatives designed to accomplish the above stated four family-formation objectives of the PRWORA. As of 2005, four years after the PRWORA should have been reauthorized, there have been a number of federal level initiatives designed to promote marriage and fatherhood among the poor. I now turn my attention to these policy proposals and initiatives.

In November 1999, The Fathers Count Act, introduced by Congresswoman Nancy Johnson (R-Connecticut) was passed in the House of Representatives. In her announcement on the hearing of the fatherhood legislation, Representative Johnson (1999) stated:

> We must support programs that focus on improving relationships between poor young men and women to increase the prospects that they can marry and form two-parent families, or at a minimum, work together to rear their children. Promoting marriage and two-parent families, and aggressively helping these men become responsible parents, is the next step in welfare reform.

This piece of legislation was sent to the Senate on November 16, 1999, but no action was taken. Since then there have been various pieces of legislation designed to promote fathers' involvement in the child's life either by promoting marriage, joint custody, visitation rights, or child support enforcement. Building on the Fathers Count Act, three bills proposed in Congress would fund fatherhood programs with the goal of helping fathers and their families to avoid or leave cash welfare by providing employment services. The bills are the Responsible Fatherhood Act of 2001 (S. 653/ H.R. 1300), the Strengthening Working Families of 2001 (S. 685), and the Child Support Distribution Act of 2001 (H.R. 1471).

In 2002, the House passed H.R. 4737. During that same year, the Senate Finance Committee proposed and passed legislation that included a number of marriage provisions. H.R. 4737 captures the familial ideology of the post 1996 welfare reform efforts. First, this initiative used language more reflective of a particular familial ideology. The revised introductory language reads [the new language is italicized]: "The purpose of this part is *to improve child wellbeing* by increasing the flexibility of states in operating a program designed to "meet the four purposes." References to "parents" in H.R. 4737 were changed to "families." Second, the bill also added a focus on reducing poverty in purpose (2), so that it reads: "end the dependence of needy *families*, on government benefits *and reduce poverty* by promoting job preparation, work, and marriage." H. R. 4737 also altered purpose four to encourage healthy marriage and responsible fatherhood so that it read "encourage the formation and maintenance of healthy two-parent *married* families, and *encourage responsible fatherhood*." (U.S. House 2002; Levin-Epstein, et al. 2002). This piece of legislation also established annual, numerical, and measurable performance goals with respect to each of the TANF purposes, including promoting "healthy marriages."

The 2002 bi-partisan reauthorization bill of the Senate Finance Committee was similar to the goals of H.R. 4737. However, there were some substantial differences between the two bills. First, the Senate bill eliminated the rule that allowed states to impose more restrictive TANF eligibility rules for two-parent families in comparison to solo parenting families. Second, the Senate's bill allocated less money to fund marriage-related activities while allowing for a broader range of allowable activities: such as teen pregnancy prevention, domestic violence prevention, and income stability. One billion dollars in federal dollars, subject to a sate match of an additional $250 million (which could be in-kind), was allocated over a five-year period to fund grants for demonstration programs. These programs sought to strengthen families, encourage marriage as well as evaluate outcomes. Additionally, the Senate Finance Committee bill eliminated the separate two-parent work participation rate. Included in this bill were a series of safeguards designed to ensure that participation in marriage programs was strictly voluntary and required that domestic violence experts be consulted in the development of programs. Finally, the Senate bill did not modify state maintenance of effort requirements, include fatherhood funds, or require "healthy marriage" performance goals in state plans.

Along the lines of the cultural problems approach, the Fatherhood and Marriage Bill (H.R. 2893) attempts to fix the perceived familial dysfunctional formation among low-income individuals. Included in the purposes of this bill are:

(B) Enhancing the abilities and commitment of unemployed or low-income fathers to provide material support for their families and to avoid or leave welfare programs by assisting them to take full advantage of education, job training, and job search programs, to improve work habits and work skills, to secure career advancement by activities such as outreach and information dissemination, coordination, as appropriate, with employment services and job training programs, including the One-Stop delivery system established under Title I of the Workforce Investment Act of 1988, encouragement and support of regular and timely payment of child support in appropriate cases, and other methods.

(C) Improving fathers' ability to effectively manage family business affairs by means such as education, counseling, and mentoring in matters including household management, budgeting, banking, and handling of financial transactions, time management, and home maintenance.

This bill seems designed not only to improve the black man's work situations (with the intention of increasing their paychecks so that they can contribute more money to their children), additionally it prepares them for a particular role as head of the household. Clearly, these men are encouraged to marry and assume responsibility for the family budget and the family home. The suggestion is that "real men" are bankers, handy men, and organizers of their family's schedules.

Although the legislation never reached the Senate floor for a vote, the proposals in augmented forms reappeared over time. In February 2003, the House of Representatives passed H.R. 4, the Personal Responsibility Work, and Family Promotion Act of 2003. The House bill, H. R. 240 and a Senate Finance Committee bill (both introduced in 2005) include a number of marriage initiatives. Most of the marriage initiatives mirror H.R. 4737 in terms of policy proposals and in the general assumptions made about the policy recipients. Common to all of the various bills is the assumption that family formation among poor welfare recipients is deviant and in need of "normalizing." They take the approach that to fix these individuals requires the enforcement of a patriarchal model.

The Bush administration, following the Congress, also sought to promote programs with the goal of normalizing poor black families. The Fatherhood Initiative should be viewed as an extension of child-support enforcement and paternity establishment in that it seeks to "reconnect" the bond between father and child. According to President George W. Bush, he is determined:

> To make committed, responsible fatherhood a national priority. . . . [The] presence of two committed, involved parents contributes directly to better school performance, reduced substance abuse, less crime and delinquency, fewer emotional and other behavioral problems, less risk of abuse or neglect, and lower risk of teen suicide. The research is clear: fathers factor significantly in the lives of their children. There is simply no substitute for the love, involvement, and commitment of a responsible father (2001a).

This Fatherhood Initiative appears to be targeting inner-city males (the accepted euphemism for black and brown men). It is designed, in part, to "improve the job skills of low income fathers; promote marriage among parents; help low-income fathers establish positive relationships with their children" (Bush, Jr. 2001a). In addition, the Office of Faith-Based and Community Initiatives would direct the programs of the Fatherhood Initiative. This organization was directed to develop:

> Resource materials to guide *urban* congregations and other community groups in finding role models for young men who have been raised without fathers. And we will be working with the Office of National Drug Control Policy to enlist dads in our national campaign against drug use (Bush 2001a, emphasis added).

To achieve this goal of reinstating the father into the lives of children, President Bush sold the budget to the public through the use of language that was race- and gender- neutral. The proposals were couched in terms of how much money it would "save" the public. However, a deeper analysis highlights who is being targeted and the projected cause of the problem used to justify the proposals. Various euphemisms were used such as "urban" and "low-income" to give the impression that this was a race-neutral policy initiative. However, it was not. Instead, it was a policy designed to target African Americans who are often projected as deviant and in need of fixing.

The Fatherhood Initiative also claimed that women raising children outside of the institution of marriage are inherently flawed. In addition to targeting low-income fathers, President Bush was clear in specifying the type of woman, who helped to create this situation of "fatherlessness"—black women, the Matriarch in particular. According to Bush his effort to reinstate the male in his rightful place is born out of Daniel Patrick Moynihan's suggestions. Bush informs us:

> The intellectual roots of the fatherhood movement reach back to one exceptional public servant who spoke about the importance of fathers earlier, more often and more eloquently than any other public figure—former United States Senator Daniel Patrick Moynihan, of New York (2001b).

Reminiscent of Moynihan, Bush targets black women as the source of many of the problems faced by solo mothers. Employing the image of the Black Matriarch, (and her counterpart the Emasculated Black Man) allowed President Bush to suggest a causal relationship between the poverty experienced by blacks and the value system of black women. Not only is this woman responsible for the failure of the black man (his ability to follow patriarchal norms), but also she is also responsible for the failure of black children. It is only when this woman is supervised is there any hope of saving the black community. Fatherhood Initiatives appear to be an effort to reverse the effects of the Matriarch—in essence the "bad" black woman—who has emasculated the black man.

Policy makers were concerned with urging poor (black) women to marry and, in the event that this is not possible, to compel fathers to be responsible for their children. In essence policy makers appear to be concerned about children in families that do not conform to the hegemonic nuclear family model. Thus policy is directed at eliminating the Matriarch by reestablishing a male head of the household. However, is it enough to simply enforce marriage among poor African Americans? Because of the Matriarch's behavior, the "nuclear family" will look dangerously close to a solo-mothering household with one additional child, the father. Consequently, the Matriarch must be eliminated and the only way to do such is to un-emasculate the black man/husband—figuratively giving him back his penis/power through various "tools." Thus fatherhood and marriage initiatives appear to be but another form of controlling the "damaged" and "parasitic" black woman. Through a series of familial policies, the state, seeks to control poor black women by allowing black "men to be men."

The Black Politics of Fatherhood Initiatives

Black elected officials and other black leaders appear to be supportive of the various fatherhood and marriage promotion policies, albeit for other reasons than President Bush and his supporters. Black leaders tend to support the promotion of fatherhood and marriage because of the belief that such policies would uplift the black community. The manner in which the African American community frames the issue of gender can lend support to such policies. Black elected officials overwhelmingly supported The Responsible Fatherhood Act of 2001 (H. R. 1300). This Act was introduced by Representative Julia Carson (a member of the Congressional Black Caucus) and supported by twenty-nine members of the Congressional Black Caucus. The Responsible Fatherhood Act of 2001 calls for the promotion of two- parent families and responsible fatherhood. Congressperson Carson uses the following argument to support her introduction of H.R. 1300, "Children who are apart from their biological fathers are, in comparison to other children, five times more likely to live in poverty, more likely to bring weapons and drugs into the classroom, to commit other crimes, to drop out of school, to commit suicide, to abuse alcohol or drugs. Girls are inclined sometimes to become pregnant as teenagers" (2002, H3488). There is an inference to a casual relationship between female headed households and many of the problems confronted by Black America. This casual relationship is often used to suggest that there is a "crisis of black men" and that black men are "endangered". Furthermore, the argument often suggests that African American women are, relative to their male counterparts, in a better social position (see Legette 1999).

The most recent "State of Black America" issued by the Urban League (2006) continues this line of argument. According to the Urban League,

> The gender-specific variables help to account for the increase in the Social Justice index as the data reveals that black females are treated more favorably than their male counterparts. ...Black females found the justice system to be slightly more lenient than for black males. ... when looking at Probation Granted for Felons, the male designation produced an index number of 0.79. The female designation produced an index number of 1.04, which again speaks to black females faring better than black males in the justice system (Thompson and Parker 2006, 4).

This suggests that African American women are better treated by the criminal justice system. Bush-Baskette warns us that black women now "constitute a higher percentage of the incarcerated female population than black males do for the incarcerated male population"

(1998, 113). Using the language of the "endangered black man" also limits us from addressing the relationship between the war on drugs and welfare, housing and education policies (see Jordan-Zachery, 2003). For example, Section 115 of the Personal Responsibility and Work Opportunity Reconciliation Act (PRWORA) denies welfare benefits, cash assistance and food stamps to persons convicted of a state or federal felony offense for using or selling drugs. According to Patricia Allard (2002), of the Sentencing Project, approximately 92,000 women are currently affected by the ban. These include more than 44,000 white women, nearly 35,000 African American women, and almost 10,000 Latinas. "In seven states which implement the ban in part or in full, African American and Latinas represent the majority of women subject to the ban" (Allard 2002, 7).

Additionally, scholars such as Ronald Mincy in *Black Men Left Behind* (2006) lend credence to the debate on the plight of black men being played out in the media. The frame of the "endangered black man" or "black men in crisis" is often used to suggest that we must engage in radical changes to improve the life circumstances of black men. According to Joseph T. Jones, director of the fatherhood and work skills center, the plight of black men stems from the breakdown of the traditional family unit. He argues, "Many of these men grew up fatherless, and they never had good role models. ... No one around them knows how to navigate the mainstream society" (quoted in Eckholm 2006 Section A(1)). As a result of such a frame there has been a policy shift. Erik Eckholm in the *New York Times article* "Plight Deepens for Black Men Studies Warn" states "in response to the worsening situation for young black men, a growing number of programs are placing as much importance on teaching life skills—like parenting, conflict resolution and character building—as they are on teaching job skills" (2006). Legette (1999) warns us of the dangers of not considering how are gendered approach to addressing the ills of the black community can indeed prove harmful to many of the women and girls of the community. He does not suggest that we totally ignore the black "male" crisis; but that we should be equally concerned with the "dangers" confronted by black women. To do such would ensure that all in the black community are uplifted.

Conclusion

The failure of Nationalism and Integrationism to address gender as an integral element in oppressive structures limits their ability to challenge racialized patriarchal policies. Two assumptions under gird these black liberation ideologies. First, both ideologies assume the existence of the family unit. Particularly, they both assume the existence of a heterosexual male dominated family with particular roles for women. As reflected in Black Nationalist and Integrationist theories, the role of women in the freedom struggle is confined to motherhood in terms of nurturers and caregivers. As such, women are confined to the domestic sphere. Second, there is the assumption that the subject of their theories is the male head of a traditional household.

Both Black Nationalists and Integrationists control black women under the guise of protecting them but instead subsume the interests of women. They do so not necessarily to dominate these women, but instead to protect/insulate the community. "Control over women has always been associated with the need to preserve the boundaries of the community and to prevent inter-racial, inter-ethnic, and inter-religious mixing" (Stopler 2003). Embedded in both ideologies is the view of women as: (a) the symbolic representation of nation (blackness); (b) reproducers of the nation; and (c) transmitters of the cultural norms and values of the nation (see Collins 1999). The result of such a construction of the value and role of black women often result in essentializing sameness and difference of gender in the black community. The impact of essentializing sameness and difference is that black women are assumed to have the same interest as black men. Such behavior also has implication for power relations within the black community.

Power is influenced by both race and gender and it also influences how these social categorizations influence the distribution of resources. In the current racialized patriarchy movement, we have an opportunity to critically critique the functioning of gender at both the state level and within group organizing. As argued in this paper, racialized—patriarchy, which allows us to analyze how patriarchy functions along racial lines, should be challenged by African Americans in their quest for freedom. On the surface these policies appear to benefit men, because they allow them to play the socially sanctioned norm of the breadwinner. In promoting a familial ideology, these policies appear to be beneficial to men since they afford them the opportunity to be "normalized"; thereby allowing them to "protect" their women. Black men are "normalized" in the sense that they function in the sanctioned role as the head of the household. Interestingly, however, these policies are not being supported by substantive economic revitalization and educational policies, but are operating within the context of a shrinking social welfare state. In addition, the policies do not necessarily increase the amount of funds available for welfare programs. In fact, some states are diverting welfare funds from programs such as job training, and child care to support marriage and fatherhood programs. However, because they are couched in the language of "reinstating" the black man, which in turn would allow them to "protect" their women and offer them the "benefits" of patriarchy, it is particularly difficult for them to be challenged by traditional black political ideologies. The ability of black political ideologies to mount a challenge is difficult because they operate from similar gender role premises.

There are a number of problems in the failure to simultaneously challenge race and gender oppressions as encouraged by Anna Julia Cooper. Failure to analyze how gender interacts with state policies limits our ability to raise questions such as: can the problem of poverty be addressed solely at the individual level? In their focus on individual behavior, fatherhood and marriage initiatives, do very little to address structural impediments that perpetuate fragile families among the African American poor. For example, these initiatives simultaneously operate with mandatory minimum sentencing policies including: the denial of welfare to those convicted of a drug felony (it should be noted that other criminals are not similarly treated); the denial of public housing as a result of the "one-strike and you're out policy"; and the denial of federally subsidized higher education to those convicted of a drug felony (Brown, et al. 2003). Furthermore, it does little to help challenge sexism, which results in inequitable wages. It appears that Daniel Patrick Moynihan, Jesse Jackson, Jr., and George W. Bush view marriage as an economic panacea for the complex problem of poverty in the black community. This assumes that individual failures to follow the state sanctioned family norm are the source of many of the ills of poor black communities. What this approach ignores is the existence of other oppressive structures and policies that help to promote and perpetuate poverty in these communities.

Any black liberation ideology must recognize the oppressive structures of gender and race. It must not only recognize that these oppressive structures emanating outside of the community, but must also consider how the black community can perpetuate oppression and subordination. Black women have long recognized the intersection of race, class, and gender and have been critical of liberation movements that treat gender as a secondary factor. In fact, black women have sought to move gender from the margin of the freedom struggle. Audre Lorde in *Sister/ Outsider* challenges the rationale for marginalizing black women's concerns and provides a fitting conclusion:

> The threat of difference has been no less binding to people of Color. Those of us who are Black must see that the reality of our lives and our struggle does not make us immune to the errors of ignoring and misnaming differences. Within Black communities where racism is a living reality, difference among us often seem dangerous and suspect. The need for unity is often misnamed as a need for homogeneity, and a Black Feminists vision mistaken for betrayal of our common interests as a people (1984, 119).

Notes

1. A number of states such as **Arizona** (allocated $1.15 million in TANF funds for community-based marriage and communication skills workshops, the development of a "healthy marriage" handbook for marriage license applicants, and vouchers for low-income couples to attend marriage skills courses) **West Virginia** (offers a $100 "marriage bonus" to welfare grant for each month the couple remains married); **Utah** (holds annual marriage conferences since 1994, and earmarked $600,000 in TANF funding to develop an informational video, provide vouchers for counseling and mediation, and promote marriage education); **Michigan** (set aside $400,000 for the development of a pilot Encouraging Family Formation program); **Florida** (was the first state to require that high school seniors take a marriage and relationships skills class, through the Florida Marriage Preparation and Preservation Act); **Wisconsin** (has a "Community Marriage Policy," using TANF funds to develop community-wide standards for marriages presided over by members of the clergy) see the National Council of State Legislatures for additional information (http://www.ncsl.org/statefed/welfare/strength.htm).
2. The Fragile Families and Child Wellbeing Study is designed to provide new information on the capabilities and relationships of unwed parents. In addition, this longitudinal study also analyzes the impact of policies on family formation and child wellbeing. This study follows a birth cohort of (mostly) unwed parents and their children over a five-year period (see http://crcw.princeton.edu).

References

Allard, Patricia. 2002. *Life Sentences: Denying Welfare Benefits to Women Convicted of Drug Offenses.* Washington, DC: The Sentencing Project.

Allen, W. 1978. The Search for Applicable Theories of Black Family Life. *Journal of Marriage and the Family.* 40(1): 111-29.

Beal, Frances. 1970. Double Jeopardy: To Be Black and Female. In *The Black Woman: An Anthology,* (ed.) Toni Cade. New York: Penguin.

Bernard, Jessie. 1966. *Marriage and Family Among Negroes.* Englewood Cliffs, NJ: Prentice Hall.

Bracey, John H Jr., August Meier, and Elliot Rudwick. 1970. *Black Nationalism in America.* Indianapolis, IN: The Bobbs-Merril Company.

Brown, Elaine. 1992. *A Taste of Power: A Black Woman's Story.* New York: Pantheon Books.

Brown, Elsa Barkley. 1990. African American Women's Quilting: A Framework for Conceptualizing and Teaching African-American Women's History. In *Black Women in America: Social Science Perspectives,* (ed.) Micheline R. Malson, Elisabeth Mudimbe-Boyi, Jean F. O'Barr, and Mary Wyer. Chicago, IL: University of Chicago Press, 9-18.

Brown, Michael K., Martin Carnoy, Elliott Currie, et al. (eds.) 2003. *Whitewashing Race: The Myth of a Color-Blind Society.* Berkeley, CA: University of California Press.

Bunche, Ralph J. 1995 [1969]. The Black Revolution. In *Ralph J. Bunch: Selected Speeches and Writings,* (ed.) Charles P. Henry. Ann Arbor, MI: University of Michigan Press. 297-304.

Bush, George W., Jr. 2001a. A Blueprint for New Beginnings: A Responsible Budget for America's Priorities. http://www.whitehouse.gov/news/usbudget/blueprint/budtoc.html. [July 18, 2001].

Bush, George, W., Jr. 2001b. Remarks by the President to the Fourth National Summit on Fatherhood. http://www.whitehouse.gov/omb/budget/fy2002/bud11.html. [June 7 2001].

Bush-Baskette, Stephanie R. 1998. The War on Drugs as a War Against Black Women. In Susan L. Miller (ed.) *Crime control and women* (pp. 113—129). Thousand Oaks, CA: Sage Publications.

Cade, Toni (ed). 1970. *The Black Woman: An Anthology.* New York: Penguin.

Carson, Julia. 2002 (June 12). Supporting Responsible Fatherhood. Congressional Record 107th Cong., 2nd Sess. Congressional Record, 12 June, Vol. 148, No. 77.

Cohen, Cathy. 1999. *Boundaries of Blackness: Aids and the Breakdown of Black Politics.* Chicago, IL: Chicago University Press.

Collins, Patricia Hill. 1991. *Black Feminist Thought: Knowledge, Consciousness, and the Politics of Empowerment.* New York: Routledge, Chapman and Hall.

Collins, Patricia Hill. 1996. What's in a Name? Womanism, Black Feminism, and Beyond. *Black Scholar* 26 (1): 9-17.

Collins Patricia Hill. 1999. Producing the Mothers of the Nation: Race, Class and Contemporary U.S. Population Policies. In *Women, Citizenship, and Difference,* (ed.) Nira Yoval-Davis and Pnina Werbner. London: Zed.

Cooper, Anna Julia. 1988. A Voice from the South. In *The Schomburg Library of Nineteenth Century Black Women Writers*, (ed.) Henry Louis Gates, Jr. New York: Oxford University Press. Originally published in 1892 by Aldine Publishers, Xenia, OH.

Crenshaw, Kimberle. 1989. Demarginalizing the Intersection of Race and Sex: A Black Feminist Critique of Antidiscrimination Doctrine, Feminist Theory, and Antiracist Politics. *The University of Chicago Legal Forum* (139): 141-150.

Crenshaw, Kimberle. 1995. Mapping the Margins; Intersectionality, Identity Politics and Violence Against Women of Color. In *Critical Race Theory: The Key Writing that Formed the Movement*, (ed.) Kimberle Crenshaw, Neil Gotanda, Gary Peller, and Kendall Thomas. 1ˢᵗ ed. New York: The New Press.

Cruse, Harold. 1967. *The Crisis of the Negro Intellectual: From its Origins to the Present*. New York: William Morrow.

Cuadraz, Gloria and Uttal, Lynet. 1999. Intersectionality and In-depth Interviews: Methodological Strategies for Analyzing Race, Class, and Gender. *Race, Gender & Class*, 6 (3). Retrieved June 26, 2004, from http://www.proquest.umi.com.

Dawson, Michael C. 2001. *Black Visions: The Root of Contemporary African-American Political Ideologies*. Chicago and London: The University of Chicago Press.

Eckholm, Erik. 2006. "Plight Deepens for Black Men Study Warns," *New York Times*, Monday, 20 March

Eisenstein, Zillah 1994. *The Color of Gender: Reimaging Democracy*. Berkeley, CA: University of California Press.

Giddings, Paula. 1984. *When and Where I Enter: The Impact of Black Women on Race and Sex in America*. New York: William Morrow.

Gilder, George. 1981 [1993]. *Wealth and Poverty: A New Edition of the Classic*. San Francisco, CA: Institute for Contemporary Studies Press.

Gilkes, Cheryl Townsend. 1983. From Slavery to Social Welfare: Racism and the Control of Black Women. In *Class, Race, and Sex: The Dynamics of Control*, (ed.) Amy Swerdlow and Hanna Lessinger. Boston, MA: G.K. Hall and Co.

Guy-Sheftall, Beverly (ed). 1995. *Words of fire: An Anthology of African American Feminist Thought*. New York: New Press.

Hare, Nathan. 1989. Solutions: A Complete Theory of the Black Family. In *Crisis in Black Sexual Politics*, (ed.) Nathan Hare and Julia Hare. San Francisco, CA: Black Think Tank.

Higginbotham, Evelynn Brooks. 1992. African American Women's History and the Metalanguage of Race. Signs 17: 251-274.

Hine, Darlene Clark. 1993. 'In the Kingdom of Culture': Black Women and the Intersection of Race, Gender, and Class. In *Lure and Loathing: Essays on Race, Identity, and the Ambivalence of Assimilation*, (ed.) Gerald Early. New York: Penguin Books.

Horn, Wade. 2001. Wedding Bell Blues: Marriage and Welfare Reform. *Brookings Review* 19(3): 39-42.

Johnson, Nancy. 1999 (September 29). Johnson Announces Hearing on Fatherhood Legislation. Committee on Ways and Means, Subcommittee on Human Resources. http://www.house.gov/ways_means/humres/106cong/hr-11.htm. [November 11 2001].

Jordan-Zachery, Julia. 2003. The War on Drugs and Welfare Policy: The Impact of Their Intersection on Black Women in Urban America. Midwest Political Science Association Meeting, Chicago, IL.

King, Martin Luther, Jr. 1986 [1968]. Conversation with Martin Luther King. In *A Testament of Hope: The Essential Writings and Speeches of Martin Luther king, Jr.*, (ed.) James M. Washington. San Francisco, CA: Harper and Row.

Legette, Willie. 1999. The Crisis of the Black Male: A New Ideology in Black Politics. In *Without Justice for All: The New Liberalism and Our Retreat from Racial Equality*, (ed.) Adolph Reed, Jr. Bolder, CO: Westview Press. pp. 291-324

Levin-Epstein J, T. Ooms, M. Parke, P. Roberts, V. Turestsky. 2002. *Spending Too Much, Accomplishing Too Little: An Analysis of the Family Formation Provisions of H. R. 4737 and Recommendations for Change*. Washington, DC: Center for Law and Social Policy. Available at http://www.clasp.org.

Lorde, Audre. 1984. *Sister/Outsider: Essays and Speeches*. Freedom, CA: The Crossing Press.

Marable, Manning. 2001. Groundings with My Sisters: Patriarchy and the Exploitation of Black Women in. In *TRAPS: African American Men on Gender and Sexuality*, (ed.) Rudolph R. Byrd and Beverly Guy-Sheftall, (eds.) IN: Indiana University Press.

McLanhan, Sara, Irwin Garfinkel, Nancy Reichman, and Julien Teitler. 2001. Unwed Parents or Fragile Families? In *Out of Wedlock: Trends, Causes, and, Consequences of Nonmarital Fertility*, (ed.) Wu and Wolfe. New York: Russell Sage Foundation.

Mead, Lawrence M. 1992. *The New Politics of Poverty: The Nonworking Poor in America.* New York: Basic Books.

Mincy, Ronald. 2006. *Black Males Left Behind.* Washington, DC: Urban Institute.

Moynihan, Daniel P. 1965. *The Negro Family: The Case for National Action.* Washington, DC: United States Department of Labor, Office of Policy, Research and Planning.

Mullings, Leith. 1997. *On Our Own Terms: Race, Class, and Gender in the Lives of African American Women.* New York: Routledge.

Murray, Charles. 1984. *Losing Ground: American Social Policy, 1950-1980.* New York: Basic Books.

Murray, Charles. 1996a. Keeping Priorities Straight on Welfare Reform. *Society* 33 95): 10-12.

Murray, Charles. 1996b. Reducing Poverty and Reducing the Underclass. In *Reducing Poverty in America: Views and Approaches*, (ed.) Michael Darby. Thousand Oaks, CA: Sage. 82-110.

Rainwater, Lee, and Yancey, William. 1967. *The Moynihan Report and the Politics of Controversy.* Cambridge, MA: MIT Press.

Roberts, Dorothy. 1997. *Killing the Black Body.* New York: Vintage Books.

Sizemore,Barbara A. 1973. (March-April). Sexism and the Black Male. *The Black Scholar*, vol. 4

Smith, Dorothy. 1993. The Standard North American Family: SNAF as an Ideological Core. *Journal of Family Issues* 14:50-65.

Springer, Kimberly (Ed). 1999. *Still Lifting, Still Climbing: African American Women's Contemporary Activism.* New York: New York University press.

Stopler, Gila. 2003. Countenancing the Oppression of Women: How Liberals Tolerate Religious and Cultural Practices that Discriminate Against Women. *Columbia Journal of Gender and the Law*, vol. 12 (1). Retrieved June 26, 2004, from http://proquest.umi.com.

Thomas, Susan. 1998. Race, Gender, and Welfare Reform: The Antinatalist Response. *Journal of Black Studies* 28: 419-46.

Thompson, Rondel and Parker, Sophia. 2006. The National Urban League 2006 Equality Index. Abstracts: The State of Black America 2006. *The State of Black America.* Washington, DC: The National Urban League. Retrieved April 6, 2006, from http://www.nul.org/thestateofblackamerica.html

U.S. House. 2000. The Responsible Fatherhood Act of 2000. 106th Cong., 2nd sess., H.R. 4671, Jesse Jackson Jr., sponsor. 2nd sess. Washington, DC: Government Printing Office.

U.S. House. 2001 (14 September). Promotion and Support of Responsible Fatherhood and Healthy Marriage Act of 2001, H. R. 2893. 106th Cong., 1st Sess. Washington, DC: Government Printing Office.

U.S. House. 2002. Personal Responsibility Work, and Family Promotion Act of 2002, H. R. 4737. 107th Cong., 2nd Sess. Washington, DC: Government Printing Office.

U.S. Public Law 104-193. 1996 (22 August). Personal Responsibility and Work Opportunity Reconciliation Act. 104th Cong. 2nd sess., Washington, DC: Government Printing Office.

Walker, Alice. 1983. *In Search of Our Mothers' Gardens: Womanist Prose.* New York: Harcourt Brace Jovanovich.

White, Deborah Gray. 1999. *Too Heavy a Load: Black Women in Defense of Themselves 1894-1994.* New York: W.W. Norton & Company.

White, E. Frances. 1984. Listening to the Voices of Black Feminism. *Radical America* 18 (2-3): 7-25.

White, E. Frances. 1990. Africa on My Mind: Gender, Counter Discourse, and African-American Nationalism. *Journal of Women's History* 2 (1):73-97.

Part II

Maximizing the Black Vote:
Recognizing the Limits of Electoral Politics

The Impoverished "Culture vs. Structure" Debate on the Woes of Young Black Males and Its Remedy

Ronald B. Mincy
Columbia University

Hillard Pouncy
Princeton University

In an article entitled "Plight Deepens for Black Men, Studies Warn,"[1] Erik Eckholm noted the following from several recent studies on young black men.

(1) The share of young black men without jobs "climbed relentlessly, with only a slight pause during the economic peak of the 1990s. In 2000, 65 percent of black male high school dropouts in their 20s were jobless.... By 2004 that share had grown to 72 percent, compared with 34 percent of white and 19 percent of Hispanic dropouts." Among black males who had graduated high school, half were jobless in 2004.

(2) "In 1995, 16 percent of black men in their twenties who did not attend college were in jail or prison; by 2004, 21 percent were incarcerated. By their mid-thirties, six in ten black men who had dropped out of school had spent time in prison."

(3) "In the inner cities, more than half of all black men do not finish high school."

A dire picture of black unemployment was not news. It was news that black male unemployment and disconnection from mainstream society had grown uniquely in the big economic boom of 1990s and still continues as that boom combined with welfare reform brought gains to poor black women and other groups.

It was also newsworthy that the several studies Eckholm discussed agreed on these matters and reinforced each other. Those works included new books by Holzer, et al (2006); Mincy (2006); Orfield (2004) and Western (2006).

Perhaps the article's most newsworthy aspect came after its publication. It energized long-standing debates on the relevance of cultural versus structural accounts of young black men's. Eli Anderson (Sociology, University of Pennsylvania), Cornel West (Theology, Princeton University) and several other academics gathered at a conference at the University of Pennsylvania. They endorsed the article and then called for national action.[2]

Orlando Patterson (Sociology, Harvard University) and John McWhorter (Linguistics, Berkeley) charged Eckholm and his cited authors with taking a one-sided structural view of the problem and failing to provide solutions.

This chapter examines this latest skirmish in the culture versus structure debate and assesses whether it was either a necessary or helpful encounter. We show that when most structural thinkers critiqued by Patterson and McWhorter turn their attention to policy, their ideas usually anticipate and incorporate the cultural perspectives Patterson and McWhorter claim are missing. In addition Patterson and McWhorter either fail to provide their own policy perspectives, or structural analysts first proposed the policy ideas they present.

We illustrate these two points with material that further exploits the media attention given to Eckholm's article. We take a transcript from an interview last spring between Robin Young, host of the National Public Radio show *Here and Now* and Ronald Mincy about his book *Black Males Left Behind* (2006) and show how these two points can be made in plain language (the italicized text from the broadcast) and how they are referenced in recent academic work (the plain text). We elaborate on these ideas and add several that were left out of the interview. To conclude, we suggest how this latest debate can be made into a fruitful guide to new policies helpful to less well-educated young black males.

The Cultural Complaint

In a *New York Times* op-ed piece entitled "A Poverty of the Mind,"[3] Orlando Patterson complained that Eckholm's article symptomized the mainstream press's reluctance to blame 'hip hop' culture specifically and inner-city culture generally for the woes of young black men. "Hip-hop, professional basketball, and homeboy fashions are as American as cherry pie. Young white Americans are very much into these things, but selectively; they know when it is time to turn off Fifty Cent and get out the SAT prep book," Patterson wrote.

In an address to the American Enterprise Institute John McWhorter, author of *Winning the Race: Beyond the Crisis in Black America* (2006), backed up Patterson's critique. He also accused Eckholm's article of a structural bias and claimed that such a bias was commonplace in mainstream academia.

He pulled a single sentence from Eckholm's article and constructed an entire hidden structural discourse. Here is the sentence:

> Especially in the country's inner cities, finishing high school is the exception, legal work is scarcer than ever, and prison is almost routine.

Here is the hidden structural discourse:

- "Finishing high school is the exception" = inner-city schools are underfunded and fail to inspire students;

- "Legal work is scarcer than ever" = low-skill factory jobs left inner-city areas, so that young black men must turn to selling drugs to make a living; and

- "Prison is almost routine" = the criminal justice system is rigged against blacks.

More expansively McWhorter comments:

> In the summer of 2005, I was struck by accounts of the shooting murder of a twenty-nine-year-old black man at a Saturday night street barbecue. The man was an aspiring rapper, and was shot by rival rappers. This man, as it happened, was a father of four—but more precisely, he had four children by three women and lived with none of them. And yet, he only worked part-time. Nevertheless, interviews

with family and friends showed that this was not thought of as especially abnormal and certainly not wrong. He was even a great father in terms of how he interacted with his children. But he felt no responsibility for paying for their upkeep. Really, one might expect that at the very least, a father of four might work forty hours a week. Yet in his community, this guy was, of all things, normal. Even newspaper headlines fostered this, regularly announcing the shooting of a "Brooklyn father" as if he were a pipe-smoking insurance agent married to a woman who had given birth to all of the kids.

That man, and what he and his nearest and dearest have come to think of as normal, is the problem we are faced with. To describe him is not to evoke a "stereotype," as the Structural types often claim when faced with uncomfortable yet quotidian cases like this man. He is not a "stereotype"—he is a sadly common reality. There is now an entire literature by leftist academics covering his type as a national problem. He is in the work of William Julius Wilson, Ronald Mincy, Harry Holzer, John Foster-Bey, and others who would be surprised to be called "stereotypers." Let's get real and start facing the real problems.

McWhorter is mainly worried that the media and academics are too wedded to William J. Wilson's use of a spatial mismatch hypothesis that blames much of young black men's troubles on the factories that long ago disappeared from their neighborhoods. However, as McWhorter accurately notes, even in cities where blue-collar work has not disappeared the same dismal unemployment pictures emerge for young black males. In addition, there are many new, well-paying blue-collar jobs available for less well-educated males that go begging. And, he correctly notes, in the "old days" before work had "disappeared," the factories were not as close to inner-city neighborhoods and minority workers as the spatial mismatch hypothesis suggests. Back in the day (the 1950s), many black men commuted long distances to their factory jobs.

In reviewing an extensive literature on these challenges to the structural story of how the factories moved out, McWhorter neglects to remind himself that the structural "stereotypers" he castigates are the sources to whom he has turned for this extensive critical of the structural, spatial mismatch hypothesis. Specifically, he relies on Demetra Smith Nightingale and Elaine Sorensen, Holzer, Foster-Bey, Alford Young, and Gary Orfield.[4] With the exception of Gary Orfield's, these are studies drawn from the edited volume *Black Males Left Behind*.

McWhorter is impressed with the 1998 Workforce Investment Act and its Youth Opportunity Centers, which were funded to teach disadvantaged youth how to make their way into serious employment. As we detail below, these types of programs emerged from policy initiatives hosted by structural analysts who had observed the same cultural problems to which McWhorter and Patterson both allude. As we will see below, the structural complaint about these programs is that they are underfunded and not widely available to the young males who desperately need them.

Patterson's complaints are even more divorced from reality. He critiques structural analysts for their failure to provide thoughtful solutions, as he himself remains largely silent on what is to be done. In the section below we review in detail the policies that structural analysts and their associates have recently put forth, and we note how and why these proposals come with many of the same cultural perspectives Patterson and McWhorter have presented.

The Structural Reply

Interviewer: Many of these young men say that the jobs their fathers worked in factories are no longer available. Is that what your research is finding?

Ron Mincy: Absolutely. We have a qualitative chapter in the book based upon interviews with young black men in Detroit, and they talk about the same issues. They want to work; in fact, their vision of a good job is one in which they get dirty, a manufacturing job that offers high wages and good health-care benefits. They think that such evidence of hard work helps them to sustain a certain sense of honor in the community. However, they understand that those kinds of jobs have disappeared from the American landscape. They feel that they can't obtain jobs paying family sustaining wages today, because they lack education, transportation, and those with criminal records, create additional barriers, which they may never be able to overcome. For these reasons, many of these young men feel that they are left out of the information/service economy in which they now live.

McWhorter picked up on similar points from Alford Young's book, *The Minds of Marginalized Black Men: Making Sense of Mobility, Opportunity, and Future Life Chances* (2004): "They often say they will take whatever they can get, but a sentence or two later say that certain wages are wholly unacceptable. This seemingly contradictory talk is consistent with their statements about problems with certain past work experiences, such as the fast food industry, where some men eventually find jobs but abandon them (if not be dismissed) as soon as problems or tensions arise."
See Young, 2004 and Young (2006).

From insights gathered from Young's ethnographic work Demetra Nightingale and Elaine Sorensen (2006) determined that well-paying, non-service sector jobs would be attractive to these men. They then determined that a surprisingly high number of these jobs would be available well into the coming decade.

Interviewer: You also say that there are still jobs where we don't see black men. Why is that?

Ron Mincy: Many of those jobs require lots of customer contact. They require the ability to work in teams. And many of these men have criminal records [which raises employer concerns about: liability; sales; repeat customers; customers at risk and their own safety at risk]. *And those who don't have criminal records are barred from employment because they live in the same neighborhoods as many men who have gone to prison and returned to their communities. Employers don't do background checks, particularly smaller firms, where less-educated workers often apply for jobs. If you're a young black male who has no more than a high school diploma, [and live in a certain community where many men have criminal records] employers simply throw your resume in the trash.*

This is part of a larger conversation on statistical discrimination. McWhorter accurately and anecdotally characterizes statistical discrimination this way:

A rich array of studies all make it … clear that black men of this demographic often have an edgy demeanor and response to conflict as a "code of the streets." The researchers often mark this as necessary in an often threatening environment—okay. But it is still a liability in a job, especially one that involves interacting with the public.... In work by Joleen Kirschenmann and Kathryn Neckerman, J. Henry Braddock and James M. McPartland, Harry Holzer, Philip Moss, and Chris Tilly, and Katherine Neckerman, we meet employers who say that they made a serious effort to hire such black men in the past, only to find that their attitudes made them difficult employees. Importantly, the employers often note that the problem starts with the men's environments—they are not ignorant bigots. The problem is, then, once again, a cultural one.

In testimony before the U.S. Civil Rights Commission (1999) on young black males, Harry Holzer echoed these points when he told commissioners of his experience interviewing a small businessman who confided that he didn't hire black males because "I don't want to be killed." (See reference list[5])

Interviewer: I want to go back to the point that you raised about some of those low-skilled jobs requiring customer contact. Why would that matter?

Ron Mincy: I think we have a curious phenomenon going on in America and in the world. Black male youth culture is one of the biggest selling phenomena that we've experienced in recent decades, not only in the United States but all over the world. The hip-hop music, the dress, the swagger, we celebrate those things every evening when we watch the NBA, when we listen to music, or when our children listen to music, and all of our children, by the way, listen to this music: black children, white children, Chinese children, it's really amazing. However, that behavior, that deportment, may be off-putting when the customer or the employer is an adult who is unfamiliar and, perhaps, uncomfortable with that same subculture. See Majors and Billson (1992) and Patterson (1998).

Interviewer: You watch them on TV, but you don't want to be served by them at the counter at your store.

Ron Mincy: Exactly. We applaud the aggression, bravado, and displays of masculinity on the basketball court, but when we're served at the counter, we may be intimidated by those behaviors.

Interviewer: That must be very confusing and offensive to young black men.

Ron Mincy: That's precisely my point. But do we understand what this means to a sixteen- to eighteen-year-old whose lifelong dream may be to become a player in the NBA, or a rap star. Not unlike the young girl who dreams of becoming a model, or an actress, or the young boy who dreams of becoming a hockey player, these young men have grown up mimicking their heroes, adopting the dress, the cornrows, the bald heads, the style, all of the attributes associated with their dreams. But then they go to apply for a job, and the effects of their dream deny them access to the labor market. How can you help an eighteen-year-old understand what's happening to him? How can you help him avoid becoming embittered at the hypocrisy of American society toward him and people like him?

Sixty Minutes, CBS's national newsmagazine, has twice (May, 1997 and December, 1999) aired reports on a well-regarded job-training program targeting the young, poor, less well-educated minority men and women in New York City, STRIVE, Inc. More recently, *New York Times* discussed the program.[6]

In addition to traditional job skills and job placement content, the program excels at imparting soft skills training to clients who have not learned to "code switch" (Anderson, 1999) in the manner Patterson discusses above. In the early 1990s, the program attracted Ron Mincy's attention when he was at the Ford Foundation developing responsible fatherhood programs targeted to young, less well-educated minority fathers. He encouraged Ford grantees to include the program among a menu of services meant to bring these young men into the mainstream. The Youth Opportunity Centers applauded by McWhorter and funded by the 1998 Workforce Investment Act are an offshoot of the STRIVE model.

In research and evaluations analysts determined three key results. (1) Soft skills and soft-skills training were critical in the current job market generally and especially in connecting the disadvantaged to long-term employment (Cappelli (1995); Moss and Tilly (1995) and Holzer (1999). (2) A key barrier was figuring out how to replicate successful prototypes like STRIVE (Pouncy (2000). Despite this barrier, even generic workforce training programs funded under the old Job Training Partnership Act (JTPA) helped women trainees significantly (Friedlander 1997). The programs were less helpful for men because they provided entry-level skills useful for most women clients, whereas few provided the wage growth skills useful for most men (Friedlander 1997)). (3) The nation's job-training apparatus is severely underfunded (Pouncy 2000), and the relatively few funds available are targeted to women and often linked to work-based welfare reform efforts. In the perverse world of disadvantaged minorities, gender inequity takes on a whole new meaning. Among the less well-educated, men are the unequally treated gender.

Interviewer: And how you can change that. You write that black women are making gains, even though black men are left behind.

Ron Mincy: True, we had a deliberate policy in the 1990s to increase work among young, less-educated single mothers and decrease their dependence on welfare. We also had an economy that fully cooperated with this policy. To achieve the objectives of this policy, we provided training in workplace skills and cultural competence, to help welfare recipients fit in, because many of them have never worked and are unfamiliar with what is expected of them in the workplace. But you were entitled to that training primarily because you were a single mother. See Blank and Gelback (2006). Mincy and Pouncy (2006) elaborate upon this idea.

Interviewer: And the U.S. spent thirty billion dollars a year on the Earned Income Tax Credit, which subsidizes work by about $3,000 per year. It was an anti-poverty program?

Ron Mincy: But if you were a less-skilled man and you didn't have custody of your children, and by the way, a quarter to 50 percent of these men are fathers of children on welfare, you were entitled to none of this assistance. In fact, the opposite was true, because few of these men have custody of their children. So, they were obligated to pay child support, and many of these young men would pay 17 to 25 percent of their income in child support payments. Now they should support their children, <<but?>> doing so reduced their incentives to go to work. In other words, we required and enabled young single mothers to go to work, and since so many young black women are single mothers, their employment experiences benefited from an economy that needed low-educated workers in the 1990s and a set of policies that required and enabled young women to go to work. I think we need a similar set of policies for young men.

Interviewer: Such as?

Ron Mincy: Such as something operating like an Earned Income Tax Credit for young men who have child support obligations. For example, in New York, Governor Pataki's office is working on a variant of the Earned Income Tax Credit for young men who have child support obligations. It says to them: first of all, we will help you get a job, if you have child support obligations that you cannot pay; and if you remain current in your child support payments, we will top off your earnings, supplement your earnings, so that work is better than not working. See Primus (2006 and Holzer, et al. (2005). For a more detailed commentary of the mechanics of this policy idea see Primus and Daugirdas. (2000).

Interviewer: As you said, if some of these young men do get legitimate jobs, they pay 17 to 25 percent of their income in child support payments, so then there's no incentive to work. So they end up working in a cash economy, under the table.

Ron Mincy: Exactly, and I notice, as do most people who travel around the country, that young black men are just missing from the public space. You don't see them in retail stores, or hotels, or grocery stores, or restaurants, or in mail rooms, or even providing janitorial services, or in many of the places that less-educated people work. As a consequence, they end up being net drains on their families and communities. Although they often help mothers in a variety of ways, so I don't want to go too far with this idea that they are not contributing to their families in any way,

But the question I asked myself is: What are the minimum qualifications of citizenship that we actually have for young black men? I begin to answer that question in the same way that we answered it for young women. In the 1990s, we used the phrase that began to program: we want them to be in the mainstream, we want them to be self-sufficient. But I think that's not the goal that we maintained for women. We have seen welfare rolls decline, but many of the young women who were on welfare are now receiving the Earned Income Tax Credit, the Child Care Tax Credit, food stamps, Medicaid; they are simply not self-sufficient. So the minimum standards citizenship for them was that they work, and try to support their children, and we said as a society that we would help them do that.

So I asked myself: What are the minimum standards of citizenship that we have for men? Do we want them to be self-sufficient? Do we want them to be mainstreamed? Or, do we mean that we want them to work, to support their children—maybe it would be good if they didn't have somebody's children, especially if they weren't married to the mothers of those children or if they were unable to support them. We also don't want them to be criminals. Then I ask what we are prepared to do to help them achieve these objectives for minimum requirements of citizenship.

Again, I think we need to revisit how we achieved the recent successes for young women during the 1990s and ask ourselves how can we achieve similar successes for young men. See Katz (2001).

Some studies examining the political implications of welfare reform focused on the "deals" that were required to achieve the 1996 Personal Responsibility and Work Opportunity Reconciliation Act. (For a summary of much of this literature, see Weaver. (2000). As Mincy recounts above, many studies detail the impact of reform on poverty and the welfare rolls (For summaries and guides to this literature visit the MDRC website (http://www.mdrc.org/) and the National Bureau for Economic Research's website (http://www.nber.org/).

Coupled with the boom of the 1990s, the reforms also seem to have reduced employer reluctance to hire ex-welfare recipients see Mead (2005). It will be useful for researchers to determine whether Mead is right in concluding that requiring work as a condition for welfare receipt yields the same "citizenship" (or something like it) that Katz claims for the gainfully employed.

The new research question arising from this discussion is this: Will various policies outlined in *Black Males Left Behind* that impose work or other types of responsible behavior confer "citizenship" on young, less well-educated black males?

Interviewer: Mincy advocates for programs like the now defunct Baraka schools that took black boys from Baltimore to Kenya where they can focus on their studies. Professor Mincy, some would call that segregation, but you say it works?

Ron Mincy: In the late 1980s, in a number of cities around the country, including Baltimore, Maryland and elsewhere, communities created specialized schools for African-American boys. They were intended to give these black boys a positive sense of identity, a sense of pride in their culture, an alternative to subcultural arrangements in their neighborhoods that celebrated different and negative kinds of behaviors. These schools often featured black men as teachers, volunteers or paraprofessionals who gave them outlets for their energy, showed them respect, and demanded respect from them. Those schools were not sustained because of civil liberties challenges. Questions were raised, for example: Why were these schools not open to girls, or to other disadvantaged groups? Do we want to re-create segregation? Our answer in the 1980s was: no, I think that answer was wrong. We're seeing that the educational deficits of black boys are occurring very early, as early as third grade. Dr. Jawanza Kunjufu, an educator, was talking about this in the 1970s, but only a few people listened. Black boys begin to fall behind early; as a consequence they are left back; by the time they reach their late teens, far fewer of them are prepared to a get into college; fewer graduate from college, and so forth. See Lee (1994) and Jeff (1994).

Interviewer: Why do they fall behind from third grade onward?

Ron Mincy: They fall behind because they are in an educational setting that demands respect, but gives them none, that demands that they sit down, pay attention to their teachers, and that rewards academic achievement, but which provides few rewards for young people who have any number of other gifts. I have two black sons, and I recall having to do battle for my sons in schools. They were active, as are many boys, and as they grew older they challenged authority. I had to try to negotiate with teachers to find a middle ground between their demands that my sons respect their teachers and respond to their authority, on the one hand, and my sons' developmental tendencies to test the boundaries of authority. Their teachers were often inflexible, But they endured without losing their interest in learning. It was difficult. Many black male students become totally disillusioned with schools after these skirmishes.

When all other variables are held equal, Margaret Beale Spencer finds that young black males are uniquely disadvantaged in inner-city elementary schools. See Spencer, et al. (1997) and Spencer, et al. (2001).

Interviewer: So you are saying, Professor Mincy, that they need to have specialized, some would say, segregated schooling?

Ron Mincy: Well, I think if we were talking about some other social problem. A medical problem, public health issue, we would be willing to take some risks. And I think that we've reached the point here, where we had better take some risks as well.

Interviewer: Professor Mincy, another issue that you touched on is that because many young black men don't have jobs, they don't have health care. How do you see that manifested where you live, in Harlem?

Ron Mincy: I see a lot of men who are in their thirties or younger who may have been injured. They use canes, they limp, some are in mobile scooters that one commonly sees among the elderly. Their teeth are in disrepair; they have vision problems that are unattended; those who have not gone to prison have mental or physical illness that have been unattended, or if they were attended to in prison they no longer have medical care upon release. If they experienced an injury, they may have obtained emergency medical care, but in the absence of health insurance they did not get the kind of therapeutic treatment required to make a full recovery. This situation really amounts to a human tragedy. Moreover, we could be seeing the beginning of a different kind of crisis, among those who survive into their fifties. What will be the state of their health? Who is going to pay for the health care they need? Because they have been disconnected from their families, who is going to care for them? I been working this area for almost twenty-five years, about half of my life. My view is that we have just gone too long and too far in ignoring this problem.

Conclusion

This latest structure versus culture skirmish was unnecessary, but it has been useful. At one point, structural/cultural debates were necessary correctives to racist traditions, historical studies, and policies that blamed the victims of discrimination for their own discrimination ((Foner 2005). That initial impulse to pit structural versus cultural perspectives against each other morphed into a rigid, stylized blame game in which findings that found fault with structural policies supported the War on Poverty and other government remedies (Clark 1967). Findings that blamed subcultures and minorities for their own troubles reduced support for those remedies (Banfield 1970).

Although demonized as a "victim blamer," Daniel Moynihan (1966) made an early effort at exiting this blame game by mixing together structural and cultural perspectives. Later his 1980 welfare proposals sought to mix personal and governmental responsibility by matching government funding to work efforts expended by welfare recipients.

In his two volumes on the poor, *When Work Disappears* and *The Truly Disadvantaged*, William Julius Wilson saw himself as continuing in the tradition Moynihan began of combining cultural and structural perspectives. A fairer reading than McWhorter gives him would have put Wilson's "the factories moved" argument in its proper context: the cultural problems in the black community.

Researchers who followed up on Wilson's work also continued this impulse to combine structural and cultural perspectives. This happened in part because the main structural policy engine was a booming economy and because evidence from the 1980s and the 1990s indicates that an economic high tide by itself was not enough to bring black men or women into the economic mainstream. In the 1980s, disadvantaged women were not helped by economic progress, whereas the 1990s' economic boom occurred together with welfare reform, the Earned Income Tax Credit, Child Care credits and other work-based policy instruments. Disadvantaged women then took advantage of their employment opportunity.

In addition to noting how and why structural analysts incorporate both cultural structural perspectives in their policy work, we highlighted a number of policies that address the plight of young, less well-educated young black men.

Specifically, we noted that programs like STRIVE, Inc., address the cultural problems on which Patterson and McWhorter focus by providing soft-skills training. We further note that these programs and others like the Youth Opportunity Centers are underfunded and generally unavailable to the men discussed in *The New York Times* last March.

This culture versus structure skirmish was unnecessary because often Patterson and McWhorter were simply inaccurate. Nonetheless the episode has been helpful in that it reveals that we all—those McWhorter calls structural analysts and those he calls cultural analysts—share concern for what has become a national crisis. We share many of the same ideas about what is needed to address this crisis. We differ about what it means to now "get real." It is unreal to still want to play a kind of political correctness game in reverse in which we ask who is "brave" enough to note in public the cultural woes that beset the inner-city poor. "Get real" means funding and supporting the programs and initiatives for young, black males that we already know can work.

Notes

1. The New York Times, March 20, 2006, Page A1.
2. Campbell, Dwayne, "Addressing The Plight Of Young Black Men: A Penn Event Comes As Studies Show Their Situation Worsening." The Philadelphia Inquirer, April 21, 2006, Page B01).
3. The New York Times, March 26, 2006. Section 4, P.13).
4. Nightingale, Demetra and Sorensen, Elaine. 2006. "The Availability and Use of Workforce Development Programs among Less-Educated Youth," in Black Males Left Behind, (ed.) Ronald B. Mincy (Washington, DC: Urban Institute Press). Holzer, Harry and Offner, Paul. 2006. "Trends in the Employment Outcomes of Young Black Me, 1979-2000," in Black Males Left Behind, (ed.) Ronald B. Mincy (Washington, DC: Urban Institute Press). Holzer, Harry, Raphael, Steven and Stoll, Michael. 2006. "How Do Employer Perceptions of Crime and Incarceration Affect the Employment Prospects of Less-Educated Young Black Men?" in Black Males Left Behind, (ed.) Ronald B. Mincy (Washington, DC: Urban Institute Press). Foster-Bey, Jr., John. 2006. "Did Spatial Mismatch Affect Male

Labor Force Participation during the 1990s Expansion?" in Black Males Left Behind, (ed.) Ronald B. Mincy (Washington, DC: Urban Institute Press). Young, Alford. 2006. "Low-Income Black Men on Work Opportunity, Work Resources, and Job Training Programs," in Black Males Left Behind, (ed.) Ronald B. Mincy (Washington, DC: Urban Institute Press).

5.   ListHolzer, Harry J.; Raphael, Steven; and Stoll, Michael, A. 2006, "How Do Employer Perceptions of Crime and Incarceration Affect the Employment Prospects of Less-Educated Young Black Men?" in Black Males Left Behind; Holzer, Harry; Raphael, Steven; and Stoll, Michael. 2001. "Will Employers Hire Ex-Offenders?: Employer Checks, Background Checks, and Their Determinants," Berkeley Program on Housing and Urban Policy, Working Paper Series W01-005, Berkeley Program on Housing and Urban Policy; Pager, Devah, and Western, Bruce. 2005. "Barriers to Employment Facing Young Black and White Men with Criminal Records," Princeton University, manuscript; Moss, Philip, and Tilly, Chris. 1995. "Soft Skills and Race: An Investigation of Black Men's Employment Problems." New York: Russell Sage Foundation Working Paper; Kirschenmann, Joleen, and Neckerman, Kathryn M.. "'We'd Love to Hire Them, But...,' The Meaning of Race for Employers," in The Urban Underclass, ed. Christopher Jencks and Paul E. Peterson. Washington, DC: The Brookings Institution, 1991, 203–232; Braddock II, and J.H., McPartland, J.M., 1987. "How Minorities Continue to Be Excluded from Equal Employment Opportunities: Research on Labor Market and Organizational Barriers," Journal of Social Issues 43: 5–39; and Anderson, Elijah. 1999. Code of the Street: Decency, Violence, and the Moral Life of the Inner City. New York: W.W Norton, c1999.

6.   Mohn, Tanya. 2006. "Sometimes the Right Approach Is Putting the Best Face Forward." The New York Times, May 7. Section 10, Page 1.

References

Banfield, Edward. 1970. *The Unheavenly City: The Nature And Future Of Our Urban Crisis.* Boston, MA: Little, Brown

Blank, Rebecca, and Gelback, Jonah. 2006. "Are Less-Educated Women Crowding Less- EducatedMen out of the Labor Market?" in *Black Males Left Behind* (Washington, DC: Urban Institute Press).

Campbell, Dwayne. 2006. "Addressing The Plight Of Young Black Men: A Penn Event Comes As Studies Show Their Situation Worsening." *The Philadelphia Inquirer*, April 21, Page B01.

Cappelli, Peter. 1995. "Rethinking the 'Skills Gap,'" *California Management Review* Summer Vol. 37 No. 4: 108-124.

Clarke, Kenneth. 1967. *Dark Ghetto; Dilemmas of Social Power.* New York: Harper and Row [1965]

Eckholm, Erik. 2006. "Plight Deepens for Black Men, Studies Warn," *The New York Times*, March 20, Page A1.

Edelman, Peter, Holzer, Harry and Offner, Paul. 2006. *Reconnecting Disadvantaged Young Men.* Washington, DC: Urban Institute Press.

Friedlander, Daniel, Greenberg, David H., Robins, Philip K. 1997. "Evaluating Government Training Programs for the Economically Disadvantaged." *Journal of Economic Literature* 35(4): 1809-55.

Foner, Eric. 2005. Forever Free: The Story of Emancipation and Reconstruction New York: Knopf.

Haskins, Ron. 2006. "Poor Fathers and Public Policy: What Is to Be Done?" in *Black Males Left Behind* (Washington, DC: Urban Institute Press).

Holzer, Harry. 1999. What Employers Want: Job Prospects for Less Educated Workers. New York: Russell Sage.

Holzer, Harry J., Offner, Paul and Sorensen, Elaine. 2005. "Declining Employment among Young Black Less-Educated Men: The Role of Incarceration and Child Support." *Journal of Policy Analysis and Management* 24, no. 2: 329–350.

Jeff, Jr., Morris F.X. 1994. "Afrocentrism and African-American Male Youths." in *Nurturing Young Black Males*, (ed.) Ronald B. Mincy. Washington, DC: Urban Institute Press.

Katz, Michael. 2001. *The Price of Citizenship: Redefining the American Welfare State.* New York: Metropolitan Books.

Lee, Courtland. 1994. "Adolescent Development." in *Nurturing Young Black Males*, (ed.) Ronald B. Mincy. Washington, DC: Urban Institute Press.

Majors, Richard, and Billson, Janet Mancini. 1992. *Cool Pose: The Dilemmas of Black Manhood in America.* New York: Lexington Books.

Mead, Lawrence M. 2005. Government Matters: Welfare Reform in Wisconsin. Princeton, NJ: Princeton University Press.

Mincy, Ronald B., (ed.) 2006. *Black Males Left Behind.* Washington, DC: Urban Institute Press.

Mincy, Ronald B., and Pouncy, Hillard. 2006. "Promoting Marriage Is a Wise Investment," *The Baltimore Sun*, April 11, 17A.

Orfield, Gary. 2004. *Dropouts in America*. Boston, MA: Harvard University Press.

Patterson, Orlando. 1998. *Rituals of Blood: Consequences of Slavery in Two American Centuries*. Washington, DC: Civitas/CounterPoint.

Pouncy, Hillard. 2000. "New Directions in Job Training Strategies for the Disadvantaged," in *Securing the Future*, (eds.) Sheldon Danziger and Jane Walfogel. New York: Russell Sage.

Primus and Daugirdas, Kristina. 2000. "Improving Child Well-Being by Focusing on Low-Income Noncustodial Parents in Maryland." Baltimore, MD: The Abell Foundation.

Primus, Wendell. 2006. "Improving Public Policies to Increase the Income and Employment of Low-Income Nonresident Fathers in *Black Males Left Behind* (Washington, DC: Urban Institute Press).

Spencer, M.B., Dupree, D., and Hartmann, T. 1997. "A Phenomenological Variant of Ecological Systems Theory (PVEST): A Self-Organization Perspective in Context." *Development and Psychopathology* 9: 817–833.

Spencer, Margaret Beale, Noll, Elizabeth, Stoltzfus, Jill; and Harpalani, Vinay. 2001. "Identity and School Adjustment: Revisiting the 'Acting White' Assumption." *Educational Psychologist* 36, no. 1: 21–30.

Weaver, R. Kent, 2000. *Ending Welfare as We Know It*. Washington, DC: Brookings Institution Press.

Western, Bruce. 2006. *Punishment and Inequality in America*. New York: Russell Sage.

Young, Alford, Jr. 2004. *The Minds of Marginalized Black Men: Making Sense of Mobility, Opportunity, and Future Life Chances*. Princeton, NJ: Princeton University Press.

Young, Alford, A., Jr. 2006. "Low-Income Black Men on Work Opportunity, Work Resources and Job Training Programs," in *Black Males Left Behind* (Washington, DC: Urban Institute Press).

Power and Race
in Cross-Group Coalitions

Marion Orr
Dept. of Political Science
Brown University

Darrell M. West
Taubman Center for Public Policy
Brown University

Groups form political coalitions in order to gain benefits for their members. In a heterogeneous society, cross-group alliances create an economy of scale that gives each entity more clout. As Rufus Browning, Dale Rogers Marshall, and David Tabb (1984, p. 3) observed in their award-winning book *Protest Is Not Enough*, this logic is especially applicable to minority groups. According to these authors, African-Americans and Latinos "overcame their exclusion from the political and governmental systems" only when they became major political partners in broader coalitions.

Despite the seeming affinity of African-Americans and Latinos, though, developing cross-group coalitions has not been easy. Minority groups feel competitive with one another and see politics as a zero-sum game. Rather than believing in coalition strategies, disenfranchised groups sometimes fight over scarce resources. Indeed, coalitions between African-Americans and Latinos have emerged when minority leaders have turned politics into a non-zero sum game.

In this chapter, we examine the possibilities for cross-group coalitions in two separate venues: electoral and policy arenas. Although past work has emphasized factors such as racial alienation and prejudice, we argue that cross-group alliances inherently are a political process. Alliances are more likely to form when minorities feel that they have too little political power, especially in arenas involving policymaking. Our results have ramifications for urban areas where demographic changes have created "majority-minority" cities.

The Changing Face of Urban Coalitions

Coalition formation is common in diverse metropolitan areas featuring large populations of different kinds of people. Starting in the late 1960s and early 1970s, cities with significant African-American populations began electing the country's first big-city black mayors (Nelson and Meranto, 1977). A combination of African-American unity and support from liberal whites, elected black mayors in Cleveland, Gary, Detroit, and Los Angeles.

During the 1980s, African-American candidates formed successful electoral coalitions by knitting together support from blacks, liberal whites, and the growing Latino communities. Throughout the 1980s, Los Angeles' incumbent black mayor, Tom Bradley, incorporated Latinos into his electoral coalition (Sonenshein, 1993). In 1983, Chicago's Harold Washington became that city's first African-American mayor, winning nearly 85 percent of the black vote and a majority of the Latino vote. In 1989, David Dinkins defeated Ed Koch, the conservative incumbent mayor of New York City, in part because a majority of Latino voters deserted Koch for Dinkins (Mollenkopf, 1992, p. 178).

Coalitions between African-Americans and Latinos, however, proved more problematic in the 1990s due to changing demographics and increasingly divergent policy preferences (see Meier and Stewart, 1991; Browning, Marshall, and Tabb, 2003). African-American and Latinos argued over policies such as establishing English as an official language, immigration reform, and employer sanctions for hiring undocumented workers. In Chicago and Los Angeles, Wilson (1996) documents the complaints of African-Americans that white employers discriminated against them in favor of Latinos. When African-American alderman Eugene Sawyer attempted to succeed Washington in Chicago, he retained the vast bulk of the black vote, but lost around 70 percent of the Hispanic bloc to Richard Daley (Tedin and Murray, 1994).

Nicolas Vaca (2004) recently argued that many observers incorrectly "presume" that blacks and Latinos will form coalitions. According to Vaca, the tremendous growth in the Latino population (what he called the "Latino tsunami") now challenges African Americans as the dominant minority group. "And as their numbers have grown in urban areas where Latinos … exist shoulder to shoulder with African Americans, conflicts have developed" (Vaca 2004, p. xi). Writing about local politics in Los Angeles, Miami, Houston, and New York, Vaca argues that "unlike the white liberals, Latinos were now in direct competition with Blacks over jobs, housing, and educational opportunity. The interests of the Black voters conflicted directly with the interests of Latinos" (Vaca 2004, p. 105).

In the 2001 Los Angeles mayoral election, city attorney James K. Hahn, a white candidate with African-American support, defeated Antonio Villaraigosa, a Latino. Population gains by Latinos over the last decade and perceptions that African-Americans and Latinos were competing for the same jobs broke up the coalition that had developed in many communities. This allowed white candidates (such as Rudolph Giuliani and Michael Bloomberg in New York City, Richard Riordan and James Hahn in Los Angeles, and Richard M. Daley in Chicago) to win office.

However, in 2005, Villaraigosa became Los Angeles' first Hispanic mayor to be elected since 1872. In a reversal of the 2001 result, the Latino candidate captured 84 percent of the Hispanic vote and regained a large portion of the black vote. With Hahn weakened by ethics scandals within his administration, Villaraigosa was able to earn a seventeen-percentage point victory over Hahn. His election was helped by a twenty-two-percentage point increase in Hispanic voter turnout between 2001 and 2005 (Blood, 2005).

In looking at the factors that affect coalitions involving different racial or ethnic groups (either between whites and minorities, or minorities with other minorities), much of the past work has focused on factors such as racial prejudice and group alienation. Writers such as Lawrence Bobo and Vincent Hutchings (1996) state that group members who feel alienated or encounter prejudice are most likely to feel competitive with other groups. Indeed, the more groups feel oppressed and the object of unfair treatment, the more likely they are to see people in other societal groups as a threat to their own well being. High levels of group competition make it difficult to develop cross-group coalitions because people see politics as a zero-sum game (Blumer, 1958; Jackman, 1994; and Johnson and Oliver, 1989).

In a similar vein, James Dyer, Arnold Vedlitz, and Stephen Worchel (1989) found that "social distance" among various groups limits the formation of cross-group coalitions. Using two surveys in the state of Texas, these authors examine citizen attitudes between Anglos, blacks, and Mexican-Americans in terms of interracial marriage, having children of different races and ethnicities together in school, groups swimming together, being roommates, and working together on a job. To the extent that groups see other group members as more socially distant from themselves, there is less of a chance these groups will work together as political allies.

Using a public opinion survey in Harris County, Texas, Kent Tedin and Richard Murray (1994) demonstrate that the local political culture, beliefs about discrimination and minority opportunities, and political knowledge are important determinants of coalitions. In addition, the social status of the individual matters, with high-status people (measured by education and income) being the least positive about coalitions between African-Americans and Latinos.

McClain, et al. (2002) study the impact of changing demographics and the growing numbers of Latinos on coalitions between whites, blacks, and Latinos. Relying on the case of Durham, North Carolina, an area that long has had a history of biracial coalitions, this research team undertook elite interviews with community leaders on racial and ethnic relations. They found that Latinos are more favorable in their attitudes toward whites than blacks are. However, both Latinos and blacks hold beliefs that are generally negative toward one another. Part of this negativity was due to prejudice each group feels toward one another, but these beliefs also are affected by the feeling that minority politics is a zero-sum game for jobs.

While perspectives emphasizing racial prejudice and group alienation are important, they ignore political factors that affect the incentives groups have to come together. As discussed by Kaufmann (2003), cross-group coalition formation is inherently a political process affected by perceptions about relative power. Those who feel minorities have too little power are more likely to join forces with other groups. These individuals recognize that less powerful sectors need to join forces with more powerful interests to accomplish important objectives. If the feeling of powerlessness is strong enough, it will help overcome negative stereotypes or perceptions of alienation or discrimination groups have toward one another.

The degree of zero-sum or non-zero sum political thinking alters coalitional prospects. If blacks and Latinos feel that one side is gaining power, it threatens the less powerful coalitional member and makes it more difficult to form alliances. Tedin and Murray (1994, p. 786) provide a hint of this in their analysis of Houston. Using a factor such as whether blacks and Hispanics have too little political power, the authors conclude that "the benefits of biracial coalitions are likely undermined by ... the possibility that the other minority group might gain the upper political hand." This suggests that the extent to which groups enter alliances depends on their views about political power and race.

The degree of shared political values is important for coalition formation. Groups come together if they see the political world from a similar perspective. This symmetry can arise through shared partisanship or a similar ideology. It is easier to form alliances within a party and at one end of the political spectrum than across party groupings or ideological camps. Cross-group coalition formation is affected not just by attitudes about race, prejudice, and discrimination, but by political dynamics. The extent to which groups enter alliances depends on their views about minority political power. Groups come together if they think they need one another or if there are perceptions of shared interests based on ideology and partisanship (Sonenshein, 1993).

The Impact of Electoral versus Policymaking Arenas

In making our argument that politics matters, it is important to outline under what conditions political factors affect coalitions. Following the lead of other scholars, we suggest that "arena" affects coalition formation. Arenas are spheres of activity "distinguished by particular institutional frameworks and underlying political cultures that lend a structure" to these activities (Ferman, 1994, p. 4). According to Ferman, arenas "operate according to certain norms, rules, and principles derived from the institutional and cultural frameworks they embody. These norms, rules, and principles shape the types of relationships that develop, the form that political mobilization and organization takes, the types of conflicts that can be aired, the opportunities for leadership, and the policy options that can be considered."

Numerous scholars have documented that segmentation tends to occur within substantive arenas. Frank Baumgartner and Bryan Jones (1993) use the term "policy monopolies" to denote the "existence of numerous independent dependent decision-making subsystems in American politics." They argue that policy monopolies structure group interactions. The particular constellation of institutional arrangements, legal rules, group dynamics, and resource availability affects coalitional possibilities. Since some arenas are more amenable to coalitions than others, it is important to study the dynamics of electioneering and policymaking involving coalitions between African Americans and Latinos.

If cross-group coalitions depend on political calculations, we should see different coalition formation dynamics in various arenas. In particular, one would expect differences in how group members see the prospects for African-Americans and Latinos depending on perceptions about political power and whether the arena is electoral or policy-oriented. Electoral arenas feature several characteristics that make them very public settings. Among other qualities, they exhibit extensive media coverage, political spending, competitive campaigns, and direct citizen involvement owing to the right to vote. Electoral arenas typically are highly visible venues that engage at least some public attention and some media coverage. Candidates must appeal to the general public and seek to mobilize constituencies that are real or potential supporters.

In contrast, policy arenas generally are less visible. With the exception of a handful of issues that galvanize the public, policymaking features less media attention, little spending, few appeals to the general citizenry, and only sporadic public engagement. Citizens do not pay close attention to policymaking and this lack of visibility creates more opportunities for group leaders to engage in bargaining and negotiation.

We hypothesize that there will be greater incentives for cross-group coalitions when minorities are seen having too little political power. This should especially be the case in policy than electoral settings because of the lower visibility of policy arenas. By definition, policy cooperation involves working with other groups, bargaining over differences, and settling for less than what your adherents really want. If the setting in which bargaining takes place is high profile and high visibility, as often is the case in electoral arenas, it will be more difficult for people who see minorities having little political power to engage in cooperation, bargaining, and negotiation. But as the setting becomes less visible, as is true with many policy arenas, there will be more of an opportunity to compromise and cooperate with those different from oneself.

Data and Methods

We examine citizen views about cross-group coalitions using Providence, Rhode Island. Providence is Rhode Island's capital city and New England's second largest municipality. Once a declining industrial city, Providence has recently experienced a comeback, drawing positive reviews for its redeveloped waterfront, splendid restaurants, and its new full-scale downtown shopping mall (Rich, 2000). In 2000, touting its "remarkable rebirth," "quality of life," and low housing prices, *Money Magazine* named Providence "the best place to live in the northeast."

Not surprisingly, the city underwent a significant demographic and political transformation during this period. The Irish, French Canadians, and Italians came in large numbers during the late nineteenth and early twentieth centuries (McLoughlin, 1986). A smaller group of Russians (mostly Jews), Scandinavians, Portuguese, Cape Verdeans, and African Americans joined them. And by the 1970s, the city experienced a remarkable influx of Latinos, many from Puerto Rico and increasingly from Columbia, the Dominican Republic, and Guatemala (Silver, 2001).

The rapid growth of Latino residents, combined with the suburbanization of many of the city's Irish and Italian residents, has made Providence an ethnically diverse city that, according to 2000 U.S. Census, is now "majority-minority." At 30 percent of the total population, Latinos are the largest minority group in Providence, followed by African Americans (17 percent), Asian Americans (7 percent) and Native Americans (2 percent). Combined, Latinos, African Americans, and Asian Americans now outnumber whites 56 percent to 44 percent.

These demographic shifts have had profound political consequences. Since the latter years of the nineteenth century, Providence has been a machine-politics city with a system of personal rewards permeating the electoral arena. For several decades, beginning around the mid-1930s, the Irish and Italians dominated the city's politics. The Irish built a strong Democratic political machine, dispensing patronage and gaining the allegiance of Italians, French Canadians, and Jews (Cornwell, 1960 and Daoust, 1985).

However, in recent decades, the city's African-American and Latino communities have started to gain political strength. As Wilbur Rich (2000) observed, for a long time blacks were "better organized politically" than the city's growing Hispanic community, having arrived in Providence "during an era of strong parties and highly developed patronage systems". Blacks first gained representation on the city council in 1969, and they have held a number of top and middle level positions in city government. Former Mayor Vincent "Buddy" Cianci courted and won the black vote, and appointed African-Americans to several of the city's boards.

Beginning in the late 1990s, though, Hispanics began to flex their muscles. In 1998, to consolidate their growing numbers, Latinos formed Rhode Island Latino Political Action Committee (RILPAC). RILPAC launched voter registration initiatives and endorsed candidates for offices. In 1998, Luis Aponte became the first Latino to win a seat on the Providence city council. In October 2001, former Mayor Cianci created an "Office of Hispanic Affairs." Even though he had once disregarded the Latino community because "Hispanics don't vote," he later asserted "the Hispanic community is playing a more prominent role in every aspect of our lives" (Smith, 2001). Cianci appointed three Latinos to the nine-member school board, and in 1999, the school board named Diana Lam, the city's first Hispanic school superintendent.

The city's 2002 election featured a mayoral campaign where the winning Democrat, David Cicilline made a major pitch for Latino votes. With Latinos representing 30 percent of the population and becoming more politically active, Cicilline established his headquarters in South Providence, the heart of the Latino community. He talked openly about issues of concern to Latinos and African-Americans, such as police brutality, inadequate housing, and a city workforce that remained more than 90 percent white. Cicilline stressed that if elected he would work to bring the Providence "renaissance" to the neighborhoods.

His major opponent, former Providence Mayor Joseph Paolino, ran a campaign that attempted to assemble the traditional white, working class, ethnic coalition that long had dominated Providence city politics. Not only was this the coalition that had helped Paolino serve as mayor from 1984 to 1990, it was the alliance that sustained Cianci from 1991 until 2002.

In the primary, Cicilline beat Paolino and two other white contenders, with 53 percent of the vote. Cicilline ran strongly both in white and minority wards, but local observers emphasized his strong support in the Latino neighborhoods (Milkovits, 2002; Silver, 2001; Bakst, 2003). In an environment where the incumbent mayor had been convicted and minorities felt they were being ignored politically, Cicilline overthrew the old white, ethnic, working class coalition and created a new coalition based on white liberals, Latinos, African-Americans, and Asian-Americans. The 67 percent job approval he has earned at the end of his first year in office demonstrates this new coalition has endured beyond the 2002 election. The way in which he pulled off this major political change reveals interesting factors about the dynamics of cross-group coalitions in mid-sized American cities.

To look at citizen views about cross-group coalitions, we undertook a telephone survey of Providence residents during the 2002 mayoral campaign. We focus on public opinion more than elite opinion because at election time, how citizens feel about group alignments and group power is especially crucial. With the exception of Kaufman (2003), most other studies of urban coalition formation have focused on elite rather than mass opinion.

For example, using Los Angeles as a case study, Sonenshein (1993) developed a theory of interracial coalition in which he argued that ideology, interests, and leadership are central pillars. Ideology, he argued, is the "main basis" for coalition formation. Groups that share political ideology on the liberal to conservative continuum were more likely to form a coalition (Sonenshein, 1993:20). Secondly, "interest alliance, or at least the absence of interest conflict" (ibid.) is another condition for coalition formation. For example, in Los Angeles, African Americans and Jews formed a coalition because both groups were largely excluded from the city's civic arenas. In other words, African Americans and Jews believed they had too little political power. Still, Sonenshein argues that leadership plays an important role in on how groups perceive their interests. "Interests are. . . neither completely objective nor inflexible" (Sonenshein 1993:10). "People come to understand their interests, at least in part, by the actions of leaders either to protect or to jeopardize them" (Sonnenshein, 2003:348). Like Sonenshein, we acknowledge the role of elites in coalition formation. However, we focus on public opinion more than elite opinion because at election time, how citizens feel about group alignments and group power is especially crucial.

Our phone survey was conducted September 14 to 22, 2002 with 688 adults eighteen years or older living in the city of Providence. This was after the primary, but before the general election. Survey interviewing was completed at the John Hazen White Public Opinion Laboratory at Brown University. Interviewers were hired, trained, and supervised in accordance with professional norms. Sampling was undertaken through random digit dialing of the Providence area. Interviewing was conducted either in English or Spanish in order to reach both English and non-English-speaking populations.

The sample for this survey generally was representative of the Providence community, although there was some under-representation of minorities and overrepresentation of whites. In the survey, our sample was 57 percent white, 17 percent Latino, 9 percent African-American, 3 percent Asian-American, 2 percent Native Americans, and 12 percent unknown due to refusal to answer the race question. In the actual population, according to the 2000 U.S. Census, whites comprise 44 percent of the city, followed by Latinos (30 percent), African-Americans (17 percent), and Asian-Americans (7 percent), and Native American (2 percent).

For an analysis of attitudes about coalitional arenas, we employed several questions to measure electoral and policy cooperation. The electoral cooperation item was based on the question "At election time, how much cooperation do you think there should be between African-Americans and Latinos to elect particular candidates? 1) a little 2) some or 3) a lot?" The policy cooperation question was "How much cooperation do you think there should be between African-Americans and Latinos to achieve public policy objectives? 1) a little 2) some 3) a lot?" We inquired about views of job cooperation using the question, "How much cooperation do you think there should be between African-Americans and Latinos to get government jobs for their members? 1) a little 2) some 3) a lot?"

We asked about three public policy questions that sometimes have divided African-Americans and Latinos: affirmative action, bilingual education, and bilingual ballots. The affirmative action question was "Do you think the city of Providence should use affirmative action efforts to hire minority employees? 0) yes 1) no." The bilingual education was "Do you think Providence public schools should offer bilingual education for those who do not speak English? 0) yes 1) no." The bilingual ballots item was "Do you think the government should offer Spanish-language election ballots for Latinos who do not speak English? 0) yes 1) no."

To look at voting behavior in the 2002 election, we employed primary and general election candidate preference questions. The primary election question was a dummy variable item of 0) favor Cicilline or 1) oppose Cicilline. The general election question was a dummy variable item of 0) favor Cicilline or 1) oppose Cicilline.

To explain different models of coalition formation, we used several sets of independent variables derived from past research on race and coalition formation. For the model of racial prejudice, we relied on: "In thinking about your local community, do you believe that minorities are: 0) easy or 1) hard to get along with?" and "How would you feel about having a close relative or family member marry a minority? 1) not favorable 2) somewhat favorable 3) very favorable?" Racial alienation was measured through: "Are the opportunities for minorities in Providence: 1) getting worse 2) staying the same or 3) getting better?" and "How much discrimination do minority populations face in Providence: 1) only a little 2) some or 3) a lot?" Group anger was measured by: "Have whites in Providence ever made you feel angry? 1) rarely 2) sometimes or 3) often?" and "Have whites in Providence ever made you feel afraid? 1) rarely 2) sometimes or 3) often?" Views about relative political power were measured through three different items: "Do you think that African-Americans/Latinos/whites in Providence have: 1) too little, 2) the right amount, or 3) too much political power?"

Recognizing that demographic and ideological factors impinge on beliefs about cross-group coalitions, we employed several of these factors in our analyses. These items included gender (0 male and 1 female), ideology (1 liberal, 2 moderate, or 3 conservative), party identification (1 Democrat, 2 Independent, 3 Republican), age (a six point scale from young to old), race (0 white and 1 minority), education (a five point scale from low to high education), and family income (a six point scale from low to high income).

Citizen Views about Cross-Group Coalitions

We found that there was substantial support for coalitions between African-Americans and Latinos. Forty-two percent believed there should be a lot of cooperation at election time between the two groups to elect particular candidates, 47 percent felt there should be a lot of cooperation between the two groups to achieve policy objectives, and 44 percent wanted a lot of cooperation to get government jobs for group members.

There were differences based on race and ethnicity. On the question about electoral cooperation, 62 percent of African-Americans wanted to see cooperation, while 59 percent of Latinos and 39 percent of whites felt that way. On the subject of policy cooperation, 67 percent of African-Americans and 60 percent of Latinos wanted to see cooperation, compared to 45 percent of whites. And on job cooperation, 68 percent of African-Americans and 63 percent of Latinos wanted to see cooperation, compared to 42 percent of whites.

To determine what factors were important in shaping beliefs, we undertook an analysis of beliefs about electoral, policy, and job cooperation. As shown in Table 1, different factors were important in various venues. For beliefs about electoral cooperation, the significant factors included racial prejudice (views about interracial marriage), racial alienation (opinions about minority discrimination), and age. Those who were favorable to interracial marriage, felt that there was a lot of discrimination against minorities, and were younger were more likely to think there should be cooperation between African-Americans and Latinos to elect candidates for public office. There was no evidence of multi-collinearity in the model.

Table 1
Determinants of Views about Cross-Group Cooperation

	Electoral Cooperation	Policy Cooperation	Job Cooperation
Racial Prejudice			
-Minorities Hard Get Along With	.12(.11)	.03(.10)	-.004(.12)
-Interracial Marriage	.19(.07)**	.20(.06)***	.12(.07)
Racial Alienation			
-Minority Opportunities Worse	.05(.06)	.01(.06)	.01(.07)
-Amount of Min. Discrimination	.24(.07)***	.11(.06)	.16(.07)*
Group Anger			
-Whites Make Angry	.04(.07)	.08(.06)	.04(.07)
-Whites Make Fearful	.09(.09)	.04(.08)	.08(.09)
Political Power			
-Whites Too Little Power	-.04(.07)	.03(.07)	-.03(.08)
-African-Am. Too Little Power	-.15(.08)	-.26(.08)***	-.26(.09)**
-Latinos Too Little Power	.03(.08)	-.09(.07)	-.07(.08)
Control Factors			
-Party Identification	-.09(.07)	-.06(.06)	-.09(.07)
-Ideology	-.06(.06)	-.09(.06)	-.05(.06)
-Gender	.03(.09)	.08(.08)	.05(.09)
-Age	-.08(.03)**	-.09(.03)**	-.04(.03)
-Education	-.02(.04)	-.03(.04)	-.004(.05)
-Family Income	.06(.04)	.03(.03)	.0002(.04)
-Race	.04(.11)	.04(.10)	.19(.12)
Constant	1.54(.54)**	2.23(.48)***	2.24(.57)***
R Square	.25	.35	.24
N	214	217	213

Significance Levels: *p < .05; ** p < .01; *** p < .001

Note: The ordinary least squares regression numbers reported here are unstandardized regression coefficients with standard errors in parentheses.

This result is generally consistent with past research on group competition and coalition formation. As suggested by Bobo and Hutchings (1996), racial prejudice and racial alienation were key factors in the propensity for cross-group cooperation. People who were tolerant and likely to see discrimination were the most likely to want to see electoral cooperation between African-Americans and Latinos. Interestingly, the degree of group anger as measured by the item that whites make you angry and they make you fearful were not significant. There was no association between those reactions and how someone felt about cross-group coalition formation.

However, there were some differences in the results when one looks at policy and job cooperation. As noted by Baumgartner and Jones (1993), policymaking is different from contesting elections. The former generally is less visible and features less media coverage than the latter. Since there are different opportunities for and costs to cooperation across these areas, one would expect there to be differing factors important in each area.

For beliefs about policy cooperation, the most important factors in explaining interest in African-Americans and Latinos cooperating were views about interracial marriage, the opinion that African-Americans have too little political power, and age. Those who were favorable to interracial marriage, felt that African-Americans had little power, and were younger were most likely to think the two groups should cooperate to achieve policy goals. Neither group anger nor racial alienation was associated with views about policy cooperation.

For beliefs about job cooperation, the most important factors were feelings about minority discrimination and the opinion that African-Americans had too little political power. Those who saw considerable discrimination against minorities and felt African-Americans had little power were the most likely to think African-Americans and Latinos should cooperate to get government jobs for their group members. It did not matter how much anger or prejudice there was on this dimension.

Unlike electoral cooperation, views about minority group political power matter to propensity to cooperate in the areas of jobs and public policy. Group members who believe African-Americans have too little power showed significant links to willingness to see cooperation between African-Americans and Latinos. Relative deprivation on the dimension of political power was an enabling quality associated with wanting to see more cooperation between the minority groups.

Coalitions in the Policy Arena

Minority groups come into conflict on various public policy issues. This is particularly the case in policy areas that split the interests of African-Americans and Latinos. Bilingual education and bilingual ballots, for example, are issues that appeal to non-English-speaking Hispanics more so than African-Americans. Affirmative action sometimes has divided people along the lines of race and ethnicity. In reviewing the prospects for cross-group coalitions, then, it is important to look at the factors that affect attitudes on these kinds of divisive policy topics.

There are interesting differences in policy attitudes based on race and ethnicity. Whereas only 46 percent of whites support affirmative action, 80 percent of Latinos and 68 percent of African-Americans do. On bilingual education, 89 percent of Latinos favor it, compared to 76 percent of African-Americans and 57 percent of whites. And on bilingual ballots for people who do not speak English, 60 percent of whites favor that, while 84 percent of Latinos and 76 percent of African-Americans support it.

In looking at possible explanations for differing attitudes in these policy areas, we found interesting differences across our models. As shown in Table 2, race was the only significant factor in attitudes about affirmative action. Even beyond views about racial prejudice, racial discrimination, group anger, or relative political power, minorities were much more likely than whites to favor the city making special efforts to hire minority employees.

The factors that were linked to views about bilingual education were ideology and age. Liberals were more likely than conservatives to offer bilingual education to those who do not speak English. Younger people were more likely than senior citizens to favor bilingual education. There were no significant links based on racial prejudice, racial alienation, group anger, or perceptions about political power.

Table 2
Determinants of Views about Policy Formulation Affecting Minorities

	Affirmative Action	Bilingual Ballots	Bilingual Education
Racial Prejudice			
-Minorities Hard to Get Along With	.34(.41)	.45(.42)	.97(.41)*
-Interracial Marriage	-.24(.25)	.18(.27)	-.38(.26)
Racial Alienation			
-Minority Opportunity Getting Worse	.40(.25)	.06(.25)	.02(.26)
-Amount of Min. Discrimination	.20(.26)	-.36(.28)	-.18(.28)
Group Anger			
-Whites Make Angry	.003(.26)	-.39(.28)	-.45(.28)
-Whites Make Fearful	-.04(.31)	.004(.34)	.45(.34)
Political Power			
-Whites Too Little Power	-.29(.27)	-.02(.29)	-.10(.29)
-African-Am. Too Little Power	.29(.31)	.23(.32)	-.06(.32)
-Latinos Too Little Power	.09(.31)	.20(.31)	.20(.30)
Control Factors			
-Party Identification	.25(.24)	.26(.25)	.09(.27)
-Ideology	.37(.24)	.53(.24)*	.03(.25)
-Gender	-.22(.32)	-.25(.34)	-.51(.34)
-Age	-.05(.12)	.38(.12)**	.51(.13)***
-Education	.20(.17)	.01(.17)	-.22(.18)
-Family Income	-.03(.13)	.21(.13)	.18(.14)
-Race	-1.36(.47)**	-.49(.47)	.004(.47)
Constant	-1.06(1.96)	-3.30(2.13)	-1.52(2.09)
R Square	.21	.28	.28
N	214	218	221

Significance Levels: *p < .05; ** p < .01; *** p < .001

Note: The logistic regression numbers reported here are unstandardized regression coefficients with standard errors in parentheses.

In regard to bilingual ballots, there were significant associations based on racial prejudice (minorities being difficult to get along with) and age. Those who thought minorities were easy to get along with were more likely to support non-English ballots for people who did not speak English. Younger people also were more likely than older individuals to favor bilingual ballots. However, neither anger nor alienation mattered to how someone felt about bilingual ballots or education.

In short, when looking at divisive policy matters, factors such as racial prejudice and political ideology vary in their importance. A factor such as prejudice mattered on a question like bilingual balloting, which is crucial to freedom of expression during elections. However, ideology was more important on bilingual education, which tapped equality of access to educational opportunity.

Coalitions in Electoral Arena

In 2002, the city of Providence faced its first, actively contested election in over a decade. With former Mayor Cianci removed from office due to a felony conviction for racketeering, four Democrats competed in the primary for their party's nomination: David Cicilline, former Providence Mayor Joseph Paolino, David Igliozzi, and Kevin McKenna. In our survey, 56 percent of whites said they voted for Cicilline in the primary, compared to 61 percent of African-Americans and 67 percent of Latinos.

In the general election, there was a four-way race between Democratic primary nominee Cicilline, Republican Dave Talan, Green party candidate Greg Gerritt, and independent candidate Christopher Young. In our survey, Cicilline ran very well among both whites and the minority community. While 71 percent of whites indicated they planned to vote for him in the fall election, 83 percent of African-Americans and 81 percent of Latinos said they favored him.

Our model for the primary vote found that the political factor of ideology was the major factor in people's vote (see Table 3). More liberal voters were the ones most likely to support Cicilline. In contrast, in the general election model, the significant factors were racial prejudice (views about interracial marriage), party identification, age, and race. The individuals most likely to favor Cicilline were those who were favorable about interracial marriage, Democrats, younger people, and minorities.

As shown in the earlier models, the power of sociological and political explanations varies with the campaign setting. Ideology mattered in the Democratic primary, while party identification and racial prejudice mattered in the general election. Each venue brings different forces to the forefront in determining the extent to which African-Americans and Latinos should cooperate politically. In general, group anger and racial alienation were not major factors in how people cast their ballots.

Conclusion

These results demonstrate how characteristics of particular arenas matter in terms of the degree to which coalitions form between African-Americans and Latinos. Policy arenas typically are less public, attract less media attention, and feature less public engagement than electoral ones. As such, they are more likely to be influenced by perceptions about political power. Electoral arenas tend to be more public, get more media attention, and have more citizen involvement. The visibility of these qualities limits the ability of political determinants to outweigh social and cultural forces such as racial prejudice, racial alienation, and group anger.

Speaking more generally, perceptions about relative political power are crucial to propensity to form alliances. Groups that feel they have too little power are the ones most likely to

Table 3
Determinants of Electoral Behavior

	Primary Vote	General Election Vote
Racial Prejudice		
-Minorities Hard Get Along With	-.54(.46)	-.10(.87)
-Interracial Marriage	-.27(.29)	-1.50(.54)**
Racial Alienation		
-Minority Opportunities Worse	.09(.26)	.20(.56)
-Amount of Min.Discrimination	-.02(.29)	-.005(.55)
Group Anger		
-Whites Make Angry	.22(.29)	-.21(.48)
-Whites Make Fearful	.04(.36)	.49(.65)
Political Power		
-Whites Too Little Power	-.20(.30)	.09(.55)
-African-Am. Too Little Power	-.47(.34)	-.85(.65)
-Latinos Too Little Power	.20(.32)	-.46(.70)
Control Factors		
-Party Identification	.38(.31)	1.54(.47)***
-Ideology	.57(.27)*	-.37(.47)
-Gender	-.06(.37)	-.52(.65)
-Age	.02(.13)	-.62(.28)*
-Education	-.24(.20)	-.51(.37)
-Family Income	-.29(.16)	-.33(.31)
-Race	-.61(.45)	-2.40(1.11)*

Constant 1.86(2.14)   8.15(4.32)*

R Square .18   .38

N   169   184

Significance Levels: $*p < .05$; $** p < .01$; $*** p < .001$

Note: The logistic regression numbers reported here are unstandardized regression coefficients with standard errors in parentheses.

be interested in developing coalitions with other groups. Ironically, as Latinos generate additional political resources through larger numbers in a city's population, this may limit their interest in coalition formation with African-Americans. Hispanic residents may conclude they do not need African-Americans to achieve their own group objectives or African-Americans may feel threatened by the political success of Latinos. Even though a number of mid-sized cities are reaching "majority-minority" status, cross-group coalitions are likely to become more difficult and more fraught with risks. This certainly has been the case in Providence as Latinos and African-Americans jockey for political gain in legislative elections. As suggested by Sonenshein (1993), leadership is particularly important to cross-group coalition formation. Political skill matters in terms of how leaders frame issues for voters and encourage them to think in cross-group terms.

As a medium-size city, Providence has a unique constellation of public opinion, political dynamics, and race relations. In large metropolitan areas, cross-group coalition-making is more complex. In larger cities, there is a greater likelihood of having a minority mayoral candidate and media outlets who pay attention to them. Cicilline's ability to oust the old, ethnic coalition in favor of a coalition of white liberals, Latinos, African-Americans, and Asian-Americans was aided by the fact there was no minority candidate to drain votes away from him. As the most clear-cut reformer in the race and the candidate who talked about diversity, police brutality, and minority outreach, he was in a strong position to build a new coalition.

While some of the results may be idiosyncratic to the Providence political environment, we believe the findings reported in this research are of more general interest. Providence has several features that are commonplace elsewhere, i.e., rising numbers of Latino voters, strains between Latinos and African-Americans, varying patterns of cooperation and conflict between racial and ethnic groups, a history of patronage politics, and limited financial resources. These are exactly the conditions that exist in many medium and large cities. As more cities become majority-minority places, it will become even more crucial to understand how these factors affect the political dynamics between Latinos and African-Americans.

References

Bakst, M. Charles. 2003. "Martinez to Keep Carcieri in Touch." *Providence Journal.* January 26., p.H1.

Baumgartner, Frank and Bryan Jones, 1993, *Agendas and Instability in American Politics*, Chicago, IL: University of Chicago Press.

Blood, Michael, "Record Hispanic Turnout Helped Elect Villaraigosa in LA Mayor's Race," *Associated Press*, May 19, 2005.

Blumer, Herbert, 1958, "Race Prejudice as a Sense of Group Position," Pacific Sociological Review, Vol. 1, pp. 3-7.

Bobo, Lawrence and Vincent Hutchings, 1996. "Perceptions of Racial Group Competition: Extending. Blumer's Theory of Group Position to a Multiracial Social Context," *American Sociological Review*, Vol. 61, issue 6 (December, pp. 951-972.

Browning, Rufus, Dale Marshall, and David Tabb, 1984, *Protest is Not Enough*, Berkeley, CA: University of California Press.

_____. 2003. "Mobilization, Incorporation, and Policy in 10 California Cities," in *Racial Politics in American Cities*, (ed.) Rufus P. Browning, Dale Rogers Marshall, and David H. Tabb (New York, Longman Press.), pp.17-48.

Cornwell, Elmer E. 1960. "Party Absorption of Ethnic Groups: The Case of Providence, Rhode Island." *Social Forces*, Vol. 38, pp.205-210.

Daoust, Norma L. 1985. "Building the Democratic Party: Black Voting in Providence in the 1930s." *Rhode Island History*, Vol. 44, No. 3 (August), pp.81-88.

Dyer, James, Arnold Vedlitz, and Stephen Worchel, 1989, "Social Distance Among Racial and Ethnic Groups in Texas," *Social Science Quarterly*, Vol. 70, no. 3 (September), pp. 607-615.

Ferman, Barbara. 1996. *Challenging the Growth Machine: Neighborhood Politics in Chicago and Pittsburgh.* Lawrence, KS: University Press of Kansas.

Jackman, Mary, 1994, The Velvet Glove: *Paternalism and Conflict in Gender, Class, and Race Relations,* Los Angeles, CA: University of California Press.

Johnson, James and Melvin Oliver, 1989, "Inter-Ethnic Minority Conflict in Urban America." *Urban Geography,* Vol. 10, pp. 449-463.

Kaufmann, Karen M. 2003. "Black and Latino Voters in Denver: Responses to Each Other's Political Leadership," Political Science Quarterly, Vol. 118, No.1, (Spring), pp.107-125.

McClain, Paula, Niambi Carter, Victoria DeFrancesca, Alan Kendrick, Monique Lyle, Shayla Nunnally, Thomas Scotto, Jeffrey Grynaviski, and Jason Johnson, 2002. "St. Benedict the Black Meets the Virgin of Guadalupe: Intergroup Relations in a Southern City," paper presented at the annual meeting of the American Political Science Association, Boston, MA, August 28 to September 1.

McLoughlin, William. 1986. *Rhode Island Politics.* New York: Norton.

Meier, Kenneth and Joseph Stewart, 1991, "Cooperation and Conflict in Multiracial School Districts," *Journal of Politics,* Vol. 53, pp. 1123-33.

Milkovits, Amanda. 2002. Latinos give Cicilline Victory. *Providence Journal.* September 11., p.C1.

Mollenkopf, John Hull. 1992. *A Phoenix in the Ashes: The Rise and fall of the Koch Coalition in New York City Politics.* Princeton, NJ: Princeton University Press.

Nelson, William and Phillip Meranto. 1977. *Electing Black Mayors.* Columbus, OH: Ohio State University Press.

Oliver, Melvin L. and James H. Johnson, Jr. 1984. "Inter-Ethnic Conflict in an Urban Ghetto: The Case of Blacks and Latinos in Los Angeles." *Social Movement, Conflicts, and Change,* Vol. 6, pp.57-94.

Pinderhughes, Dianne M. 1994. "Racial and Ethnic Politics in Chicago Mayoral Elections." In George E. Peterson, (ed.), *Big City Politics: Governance and Fiscal Constraints,* 37-62. Washington, DC: Urban Institute Press.

Rich, Wilbur C. 2000. "Vincent Cianci and Boosterism in Providence, Rhode Island. In *Governing Middle-Size Cities,* (ed.) J. R. Bowers and W. C. Rich, 197-214. Boulder CO: Lynne Rienner.

Silver, Hilary. 2001. "Dominicans in Providence: Transnational Intermediaries and Community Institution Building." *Focaal: European Journal of Anthropology,* No. 38, pp.103-123.

Smith, Gregory. 2001. "Fast-growing Latinos Population Given Better Voice in City Hall." *Providence Journal,* October 25, p.C1.

Sniderman, Paul, Philip Tetlock, and Edward Carmines, 1993, *Prejudice, Politics and the American Dilemma,* Stanford, CA: Stanford University Press.

Sonenshein, Raphael J. 1993. *Politics in Black and White: Race and Power in Los Angeles.* Princeton, NJ: Princeton University Press.

Sonehshein, Raphael J. 2003. "The Prospects for Multiracial Coalitions: Lessons from America's Three Largest Cities," in Rufus Browning, Dale Rogers Marshall, and David Tabb (eds.), *Racial Politics in American Cities* (3rd edition) New York: Longman Press, pp. 333-356

Tedin, Kent and Richard Murray. 1994. "Support for Biracial Political Coalitions among Blacks and Hispanics," *Social Science Quarterly,* Vol. 75, no. 4 (December), pp. 772-789.

Vaca, Nick. 2004. Presumed Alliance: *The Unspoken Conflict Between Latinos and Blacks and What It Means for America.* New York: Rayo.

Wilson, William J. 1996. *When Work Disappears.* New York: Knopf.

Testing the Effects of the Otherworldly and Thisworldly Orientations on Black Political Attitudes

Maruice Mangum

Assistant Professor, Department of Political Science
Southern Illinois University at Edwardsville

Religion is an important cognitive source of moral and ethical guidance in the lives of individuals. Religion helps individuals determine their identity, structure worldviews, and establish guidelines for appropriate social thought and behavior. Churches are important institutional entities, for they contribute to the formation of values and help people make sense of the world in which they live. In total, religion and church, by affecting religious life, may plausibly affect and influence one's outlook on politics. More specifically, religion and church may structure and determine political attitudes. Since many public policies and political figures work to advance or hinder the interests of social groups and the ways of life they prefer, religion, as a binding and guiding force, may take on political relevance. Through church, members gain an awareness of political issues from a spiritual or moral perspective, they are encouraged to join civic- and community-enhancing activities, and they develop a value system by which social obligations transcend self-interest (Wald 1992).

A large body of research has examined the influences of religion and church on white political attitudes. Yet, while widely recognized as strong influences on Black Americans, religion and church are not typically investigated as influencing agents in the development of black political attitudes. It is widely accepted that the church has had a profound impact on virtually every facet of black life, socially, economically, and politically, both historically and contemporaneously (Taylor, Thornton, and Chatters 1987). The church is a very prominent and important institution in the black community, exerting many types of influences. The purpose of this investigation is to figure out the extent to which religion and church influence the political attitudes of Black Americans.

We know that the church is highly regarded in the black community, and blacks demonstrate a higher degree of religiosity than whites (Taylor et al. 1987). Controlling for socioeconomic factors, blacks report higher levels of personal religiosity and commitment than whites (Roof and McKinney 1987). Further, there are stark differences in the organization and religious aspects between black and white churches (Ferraro et al. 1994), so one needs to examine the effects of religion and church on political attitudes by separating the races. Because much is already known about these influences on white political attitudes and behavior, I focus solely on the effects of religion and church on black partisanship.

Theoretical Considerations

Unlike the paucity of research conducted that examines the effects of religion and church on black political attitudes, there are a number of works that analyze their effects on black political participation (Marx 1967; Morris 1984; Reed, Jr. 1986; Dawson, Brown, and Allen 1990; Tate 1991, 1993; Brown and Wolford 1994; Harris 1994; Calhoun-Brown 1996; Assensoh and Assensoh 2001). A popular view adopted by the above scholars and for this research is the Adialectical model@ of black churches (Lincoln and Mamiya 1990). That is, two polar-opposite orientations on a continuum, "otherworldly" and "thisworldly," have been used to describe whether religion and church have an impact on black political participation. The dialectic between otherworldly and thisworldly is one of six major pairs of polar opposites discussed in the literature. Lincoln and Mamiya suggest that black churches shift along this continuum between these polar opposites over time. The otherworldly theological orientation posits that religion and church have no effects on black political participation, while the thisworldly theological orientation predicts a positive relationship. This literature paints an "all or none" effect, however, for this investigation there may be a middle ground. That is, I seek to figure out whether religion and church matter more in different types of circumstances and for different types of issues. I test the otherworldly and thisworldly orientations to ascertain the potential effects of religion and church on black political attitudes. Insomuch as the theological orientations help determine behavior, it is plausible that they may aid in the establishment of black partisan attitudes.

Otherworldly

Ellison (1991) states that black churches foster resignation and accommodation than collective action and many have argued that they hinder collective political participation for two reasons. First, black churches advance an otherworldly orientation. An otherworldly orientation places an emphasis on the afterlife where the individual can take comfort in knowing that trials and tribulations of the day are temporary and will be eliminated in the hereafter. Promises of a better life after death, that is, this world, makes the other world more attractive. Also, an otherworldly orientation advocates the elimination of suffering not through social collective action, but through personal piety and worship. Otherworldly theorists contend that religion operates as a mechanism of social control and an avenue to cope with life's difficulties, undermining the willingness to challenge inequalities (Harris 1999). Through religion, oppressed groups accept their subordinate status, which minimizes the impact of temporal concerns and places the focus not on worldly pursuits but the after world.

Second, the beliefs and activities of black parishioners often depend on charismatic pastors and personal loyalty to their pastors. Some argue that this form of personalism does not encourage an intellectual orientation and undermines political participation. Further, the political dominance of black clergymen stunts the growth of black political leadership elsewhere. As a result, religious teachings encourage blacks to be humble, meek, and forgive those who do them wrong (Gordon 1972). Frazier (1974) claims black churches and their instructions have sapped blacks of their intellectual lives and is responsible for the "backwardness" in the community.

The otherworldly orientation of traditional black religions focuses attention on the afterlife for justice and comfort and places an emphasis not on structural explanations for suffering and deprivation, but on individual failings and shortcomings (Ellison and Sherkat 1990). As a result, emotional worship and personal piety are accentuated while solidarity and social and economic improvements are devalued. An otherworldly orientation fosters political acquiescence (Marx 1967; Reed 1986). This is due in part to a greater adherence to or reliance on the sermons given by the pastor at the expense of religious doctrines. Finally, the anti-intellectual and authoritarian nature of black religions is antithetical to democratic participation (Reed 1986). Therefore, if religion and church do not inform black political attitudes, it is because an otherworldly orientation predominates.

Thisworldly

Ellison (1991) states that more recent scholars have discovered a shift from the otherworldly orientation toward the thisworldly orientation that focuses on black social advancement and improvement and the quest for collective justice. That is, there is an emphasis on applying religious doctrine in a universal manner to improve life on earth. Black churches have attempted to improve not only the spiritual well-being of blacks, but their social, economic, and political standing in society. In addition, the work of black churches in legitimizing the civil rights struggle in the 1960s is becoming more widely accepted. Black churches were an important purveyor of information on the civil rights movement and an important communication tool. Calhoun-Brown (2000) says that black churches provided resources to the movement and a context where it can be supported and become effective in achieving its goals.

One of the more effective ways a church achieves its social agenda is through the operation of its community outreach programs (Billingsley 1999). These would include educational, social service, cultural awareness, diaspora, individual, and gender development, employment and economic/community development, and family programs. According to Billingsley, black churches have extensive involvement in community outreach and congregations are actively pursuing social salvation in addition to personal salvation. He finds that in addition to their religious programs, a majority of the black churches he surveyed conduct at least one, sometimes more, community outreach programs. These community outreach programs are of the social service and community development varieties. They seek to address problems within the black community. The most common are family-support programs, designed to support and strengthen families. The next most common programs are children and youth programs, particularly black adolescents. Following behind children and youth programs as the most frequent type of community outreach program are programs to serve the elderly. Billingsley (1990) shows that black churches are very active regarding improving the lives of all its congregants in many aspects of their lives while in this world.

History and recent scholarly trends indicate that a thisworldly orientation is afoot. The church has been and continues to play an integral role in the black community and black political participation is due in part to the influences of religion and church (Tate 1993; Dawson 1994; Calhoun-Brown 1996; Harris 1999). The church and religion encourage political liberation and activism. According to the black theology literature (Cone 1992), black religion engenders feelings supportive of freedom and liberation. It seeks to lessen the effects of the harsh realities of contemporary life (racism and discrimination) to improve the quality of life for blacks. This gives rise to the suspicion that religion and church determine in part black political attitudes. If religion and church do inform the attitudes of blacks, then they have a thisworldly effect.

Data and Methods

Ordinary least squares regression and logistic regression are the methods used to analyze the data. The data set used in this study is the 1996 National Black Election Study (NBES). It has a sample size of 1,216 voting-eligible black respondents in the pre-election wave, 854 respondents in the post-election wave. This data set is beneficial because it has a large number of black respondents, asks opinions on a number of issues, individuals, and groups. More importantly, it asks the essential religion and church variables that serve as a good starting point for an under-tilled line of research. Therefore, I can capture the effects of religion's salience, church attendance, and exposure to politics in church or place of worship.

The 1996 NBES does have shortcomings. The data is ten years old. This might be a problem, but it is still the premier data set on black opinions and the one most appropriate for testing the concepts above. On the other hand, black opinions and attitudes regarding politics, religion, and church may not have changed drastically in such a short time period. Substantively, omitted from the data set are items capturing the effects of church size, demographic composition, and denomination. One could argue that a small religious church or place of worship that is predominantly black would yield different effects than one that is large or a church or place of worship that is much more diverse. Furthermore, attitudinal differences among congregants might be shaped by their denominational affiliation. That is, some denominations are otherworldly while others are thisworldly. However, some scholars have found that black religious denominations are quite similar (Lincoln and Mamiya 1990; Calhoun-Brown 1996). The effects of denomination and orthodoxy are captured to some extent. Members of churches or places of worship whose denominations adhere to the thisworldly orientation would have stated they attended political churches, and those attending churches or places of worship that espouse the otherworldly orientation would state they do not attend political churches.

Dependent Variables

This analysis examines a number of political objects, broadly defined, to learn whether and when religion and church affect black political attitudes. According to Lincoln and Mamiya (1990), the nature of the beliefs espoused by black Christianity is the same as those of white Christians, but there are differences in emphases and valences given to certain theological orientations. For instance, black churches have a much greater emphasis on anti-racial discrimination and freedom. Freedom has come to mean justice in the social, economic, and political arenas. Religion and church in the black community emphasize social justice and liberation from oppression and oppressors. Therefore, religion and church should affect policies to end oppression and perhaps foster feelings of empathy for groups who have been denied equal opportunity and fair treatment in society. Particularly, religion and church should be associated with positive support for affirmative action, and warm feelings toward blacks, Asian Americans, and Hispanic Americans, but cooler feelings toward whites.

In addition, religion and church should lead to support or favorable thermometer ratings toward political parties and individuals who are beneficial for improving the status of black Americans in society. Dawson (1994) finds that blacks support the political party perceived to benefit the race most. More specifically, given the allegiance Black Americans have shown the Democratic Party, it is hypothesized that religion and church will vary positively with Democratic Party identification (seven-point scale and thermometer rating) and Democrats (thermometer ratings of Bill Clinton thermometer and Jesse Jackson). Conversely, religion and church should vary negatively with the Republican Party (seven-point scale and thermometer rating) and Republicans (thermometer ratings of Bob Dole and Colin Powell).

Most assuredly, religion and church are expected to influence positions on moral and social issues. The literature suggests that religion will be most influential on attitudes pertaining to values and institutions, especially moral, sexual, and "family values" issues, and the role of the church in society (Guth and Green 1993). Wilcox (1992) finds that black evangelicals are conservative on social issues. This should translate into low support for gay rights and lower ratings of gays on a thermometer scale.

Key Independent Variables

Table 1
Descriptive Statistics of the Religious Variables, N (%)

1. "Do you consider religion to be an important part of your life or not? Would you say that religion provides some guidance in your day-to-day living, quite a bit of guidance, or a great deal of guidance in your day-to-day life?"

Some	107 (8.8)
Quite A Bit	188 (15.5)
A Great Deal	816 (67.1)
Missing	105 (8.6)

2. "Would you say you go to church or place of worship every week, almost every week, once or twice a month, a few times a year, or never?"

Never	62 (5.1)
A few Times A Year	238 (19.6)
Once or Twice a Month	283 (23.3)
Almost Every Week	216 (17.8)
Every Week	385 (31.7)
Two or More Times a Week	27 (2.2)
Missing	5 (0.4)

3. "Have you heard any announcements or talks about the presidential campaign at your church or place of worship so far this year?"

Yes	463 (38.1)
No	677 (55.7)
Missing	76 (6.3)

4. "Has your church or place of worship encouraged members to vote in this election?"

Yes	789 (64.9)
No	307 (25.2)
Missing	120 (9.9)

Three key independent variables are incorporated in each model. These are the religious and church queries that are Questions 1-4 in Table 1, *Religious Guidance* (Question 1), *Church Attendance* (Question 2), and *Political Church* (Questions 3 and 4), respectively. These survey items capture the essence of religion and church, for they address religion's importance and presence in everyday life, reflect a level of commitment by the individual, and tap contextual effects that can be exerted on the respondent. Specifically, they account for the salience religion and church have in the individual's life, perhaps even the strength of these convictions and commitments. A political church is a church or place of worship where political announcements are made or talk about the presidential campaign takes place. Encouraging others to vote is a political discussion, therefore, Question 3, whether respondents overheard political announcements or discussions about the presidential campaign, and Question 4, whether respondents are encouraged to vote at their church or place of worship, are combined (Pearson $r = .422$, $p < .05$).

Religious Guidance measures general salience and the importance of religion to the individual as a guiding force (Guth and Green 1993). Hoge and de Zulueta (1985) argue that it is the only variable necessary to determine religion's influence on attitudes though Lea and Hunsbeger (1990) contend more variables should be incorporated into models of political attitudes. Given the importance of religion and church to many blacks, Religious Guidance and Church Attendance variables are sufficient, for many have used the items to measure the effects of religion and church on attitudes (Guth et al. 1993) and they should be enough to know whether religion and church have an otherworldly or thisworldly influence. An otherworldly effect would not produce a significant relationship between Religious Guidance and the survey item in question. The otherworldly orientation advances a separation or disconnect between religion and political attitudes. A negative relationship does not mean an otherworldly effect is occurring, but that the variable is inversely related. If the Religious Guidance variable is related, then religion has a thisworldly effect. A positive or negative direction of the coefficient would indicate that religion influences political attitudes in a positive or negative direction, respectively. Church Attendance and Political Church are placed in each model, in addition to the Religious Guidance variable, to determine when church matters.

Control Variables

Undoubtedly, the political attitudes of blacks are shaped by much more than religion and church. Therefore, the possibility that other effects may influence their opinions is taken into account. I control for demographic characteristics, socioeconomic status, political ideology, party identification when not used as a dependent variable, and black solidarity to prevent spurious relationships. These controls are placed in each model. The following model is used to estimate all dependent variables:

$$Y = a + b_1(Age) + b_2(Education) + b_3(Family\ Income) + b_4(Employment\ Status) + b_5(Gender) + b_6(Marriage) + b_7(Political\ Ideology) + b_8\ (Party\ Identification) + b_9(Black\ Common\ Fate) + b_{10}(Religious\ Guidance) + b_{11}(Church\ Attendance) + b_{12}(Political\ Church)$$

Two questions guide this investigation. The first question deals with whether religion and church impact black political attitudes given their high levels of religiosity. I argue that religion and church may have one of two effects on black political attitudes, namely otherworldly or thisworldly. According to the otherworldly orientation, religion and church will not affect black political attitudes. According to the thisworldly orientation, religion and church will affect black political attitudes. If the religion and church variables have null effects on black political attitudes, then we must conclude that an otherworldly orientation prevails. However, if there are a number of relationships detected by the religion and church variables that when taken together form a general pattern, then one must conclude that the thisworldly orientation exists. The second question is, if religion or church matter or both do matter, under what conditions and which political attitudes depend on religion and church? The expectations are that the effects of religion and church will vary according to: (1) the helpfulness of political objects to black interests, (2) social groups who are also disadvantaged, therefore, having a kinship of sorts with blacks that will lead to favorable thermometer ratings, and (3) whether a social group (gays) is reviled by the church and by religious doctrine. The Appendix offers a description of all the variables used in this scholarship as well as their coding schemes.

Empirical Analysis

The purpose of this research is to illuminate the effects of both religion and church on black political attitudes. Therefore, discussion will focus only on the performance of the variables used to capture their effects. Table 2 reports the results of the ordinary least squares regression and logistic regressions (affirmative action and gay rights). Because the primary goal is not to develop models of great explanatory power per se, but to learn of the relationships between religion and church and particular political opinions while controlling for other factors, I report only the unstandardized regression coefficients and standard errors in parentheses for the religious and church independent variables: Religious Guidance, Church Attendance, and Political Church.

Religious Guidance is the variable to examine when determining whether religion has an otherworldly effect or thisworldly effect. The idea here is that stronger adherence to religion as a guiding influence, the more the individual will use them in absolute terms. That is, those who allow religion to shape their views of life and society will likely use religion to structure their political attitudes. Moreover, the religious may project certain responsibilities on the government. The data suggest that religion's salience is modest and it has an otherworldly effect because it fails to detect relationships more than it establishes. Religious Guidance is significant with regard to Party Identification (b = .272, p < .10), where it is associated with identification with the Democratic Party. It is also related positively and significant with the *Clinton Thermometer* variable (b = 1.877, p < .10). Surprisingly, given religion's importance in the black community, Religious Guidance has only a few relationships otherwise, and when it does, it appears to have unsympathetic and intolerant effects. This variable is negative in all models where it is significant: *Asian Americans Thermometer* (b = -2.971, p < .05), *Hispanic Americans Thermometer* (b = -2.859, p < .10), *Support for Gay Rights* (b = -.409, p < .05), and *Gays Thermometer* (b = -6.917, p < .01).

The Church Attendance variable also does a good job at detecting relationships, for it is significant in several models. The direction Church Attendance takes in the Party Identification Model (b = -.149, p < .10) is negative, showing that with increased church attendance, blacks are likely to identify themselves with the Republican Party. In keeping with its conservative influence on black political attitudes, Church Attendance is positive in the *Republican Thermometer* model (b = 1.182, p < .10). It is significant and positive in both the *Dole Thermometer* (b = 1.506, p < .05), and *Powell Thermometer* (b = 1.637, p < .10) models. It is negative in the Support for Gay Rights (b = -.329, p < .01) and Gays Thermometer (b = -5.364, p < .01) models.

The Political Church variable is related to only one dependent variable. It is positive in the Party Identification Model (b = .361, p < .01). These results indicate, as expected, that attending a political church enhances identification with the Democratic Party. A political church is a church that is engaged in politics by definition and when it encourages others to vote, presumably those receiving instructions are also told for which party or candidate to vote. It is

Table 2
Results of Ordinary Least Squares and Logistic Regressions

	Religious Guidance b	Church Attendance b	Political Church b
Dependent Variables			
Support for Affirmative Action	.133 (.135)	-.067 (.077)	-.021 (.114)
Blacks Thermometer	-.938 (1.320)	.176 (.666)	.719 (1.068)
Whites Thermometer	-1.906 (1.413)	1.157 (.713)	-.366 (1.143)
Asian Americans Thermometer	-2.971** (1.461)	.546 (.737)	-.558 (1.182)
Hispanic Americans Thermometer	-2.859* (1.463)	.555 (.738)	-.017 (1.184)
Women's Movement Thermometer	-.323 (1.431)	-.634 (.722)	-1.788 (1.158)
Party Identification	.272* (.151)	-.149* (.076)	.361*** (.121)
Democrats Thermometer	.879 (1.041)	.606 (.525)	1.211 (.842)
Republicans Thermometer	.262 (1.323)	1.182* (.667)	.177 (1.070)
Clinton Thermometer	1.877* (1.100)	.119 (.555)	.565 (.891)
Dole Thermometer	.096 (.009)	1.506** (.673)	-.114 (1.080)
Jackson Thermometer	3.290 (1.265)	-.013 (.638)	1.422 (1.024)
Powell Thermometer	-1.290 (1.305)	1.637** (.658)	.190 (1.056)
Support for Gay Rights	-.409** (.176)	-.329*** (.091)	.127 (.130)
Gays Thermometer	-6.917*** (1.792)	-5.364*** (.904)	-.905 (1.450)

*** = $p < .01$.
** = $p < .05$.
* = $p < .10$.

surprising that the Political Church variable does not do well to find relationships with more political opinions, for the political church is a venue where politics is discussed openly, and the expectation is that those blacks attending such places of worship will use discussions they overhear to form their opinions. Also, if congregants are told to vote, it also likely that they are told what and how to think concerning other social and political figures, groups, and issues.

Summary and Conclusions

The goal of this analysis was to determine whether and when religion and church influence black political attitudes. Two theoretical, theological orientations were tested. Extending its logic, I argued that the otherworldly orientation contends that religion and church do not shape black political attitudes, for the focus is on achieving salvation and focusing on contemporary concerns only serves as interference. Also extending its logic, I stated that the thisworldly orientation suggests that religion and the church are influential forces that play active roles in political thought and the desire to improve life in this world. These opposing schools of thought were tested against several political objects, policies, and positions to determine the occasion(s) when religion and church would have an effect. It appears that religion and church, not necessarily attendance at a political church, however, have a thisworldly effect.

This analysis yielded a number of important findings. First, religion and church have otherworldly effects on black political attitudes. The religion and church variables are not often related to black political attitudes. However, some relationships were established. Religion and church influence thermometer ratings toward other racial groups, political groups, political elites, and political party identification. They had their most consistent impact on gay issues. Both religion and church are related negatively to support for gay rights and thermometer ratings of gays, indicating both have conservative influences on moral, social issues. The Political Church variable was positive regarding gay rights and negative concerning feelings toward gays, but it was not significant in these models. Second, even though black churches and black Christianity focus on ridding society of racial discrimination, stresses freedom, social justice, and liberation from oppression and oppressors, they are not able to get congregants to support a policy intended to achieve those goals. It was expected that religion and church would lead to support for affirmative action, but none of the variables are related to support for the policy. Further, only the Religious Guidance variable is in the positive direction.

Third, religion and church do not work to make blacks more sympathetic, but more intolerant of other people in society. It was hypothesized that religion and church would be associated with feelings of support or empathy for other social groups who have also suffered from discrimination. This did not pan out either, for Religious Guidance was the only variable related in the models constructed to explain thermometer ratings of other social groups and it was in the negative direction. Blacks who stated religion was important and a guiding factor in their lives were cool toward Asian Americans and Hispanic Americans. It should be noted as well that they were also cool toward all other social groups including blacks even though these coefficients were not significant. Religion does not engender empathy or favorable ratings for one's race nor others. These results may be due to black theology's emphasis on freedom and liberation for blacks. The focus is on helping fellow congregants, perhaps thinking others will take care of themselves or they are seen as competitors threatening the way of life of many Black Americans.

Fourth, religion and church have mixed associations with party identification and thermometer ratings for political elites who are considered beneficial to advancing black interests. Black Americans have long shown an affinity toward the Democratic Party because it and its members have been perceived to be most willing to champion the black agenda. It was hypothesized that religion and church would relate positively with identification with the Democratic Party and Democrats, but negatively with the Republican Party and Republicans. However, I find that the Religious Guidance variable performs according to expectations, but Church Attendance does not. That is, religion leads blacks to be supportive of the Democratic Party and Bill Clinton, but attending church with increased frequency leads blacks to be supportive of Republicans, Bob Dole, and Colin Powell. Religion and church have opposite effects, the former Democratic and liberal and the latter Republican and conservative.

Religion and church have some similar and different effects. Both help explain why blacks are conservative on moral and social issues, for the direction of the key independent variables indicate that they foster conservatism and intolerance morally and socially. Black Christianity and black churches speak out against gays and extending rights for gays. However, religion and church are also opposing forces in shaping attitudes. Religion predisposes blacks to be pro-Democratic as for party identification and rating Democratic objects favorably and church facilitates pro-Republican opinions. This may be the case because the liberation and freedom (Cone 1992) messages of black Christianity makes the Democratic Party and Democrats attractive, for they focus on civil rights and equality more than the Republican Party. Furthermore, the emphases on freedom, equality, and liberation for blacks do not extend to other groups in society. Because the focus is so much on improving the status of blacks, Black Americans do not seek to improve the conditions of others, namely Asian Americans, Hispanic Americans, and gays. In fact, even though the coefficients are not significant, they are in the negative direction for blacks, whites, and the women's movement.

The church has the opposite effects on black political attitudes. It makes blacks more inclined to be Republican and conservative. As a religious institution, church emphasizes personal accountability. The church leads blacks to look inwardly to solve problems, not to look to society or government for assistance. The status quo is accepted. It calls for them to accept the world as it is while knowing the after world will be better. Given its focus on individual responsibility and limited government, the Republican Party is more attractive than the Democratic Party. In total, these results support the conclusion drawn by Cook and Wilcox (1990). That is, the messages by pastors in the black community are mixed, for some messages are associated with liberalism, leading to support for the Democratic Party and Democrats and others with conservatism, leading to support for the Republican Party and Republicans.

Political attitudes may vary with religion (Greenawalt 1988). The stronger the adherence to religion and the teachings of the church, the more likely the individual will prescribe to them in absolute terms. Those who allow their religious convictions to shape their view of society will likely allow religion to impact their political attitudes and behavior. Religion and church may influence attitudes toward individuals, groups, ideas, and policies. For instance, one may be instructed to love one's enemies plus themselves, their family, friends, and neighbors. Or one may be very generous to those who are less fortunate than themselves. Also, one may project this responsibility on the government, both working in a tandem to improve the lot of the disadvantaged. Alternatively, those who do not adhere strictly to their religious convictions will think or behave in conditional or variable ways. Some may think it is the individual's sole responsibility to do better, that the government should not play a role in ensuring equality. The middle ground is that a strongly religious person may feel individuals should help the less fortunate, but the government does not necessarily, or vice versa.

Even the religious may believe that some matters are out of the purview of government and politics. Some may believe that people should be allowed to conduct their lives as they wish so long as they do not injure others or infringe on the rights of others. On the other hand, they may believe that certain behaviors and situations are harmful to the natural or social order. Or, the religious may not know their religious convictions are influencing their political attitudes and behaviors or underestimate their impact. In addition, it may be the case that the religious do not perceive a connection or be aware of a connection between their convictions and politics, which is necessary in order for religion to affect their political attitudes and behavior.

References

Alex-Assensoh, Yvette, and A. B. Assensoh. 2001. "Inner-City Contexts, Church Attendance, and African-American Political Participation." *Journal of Politics* 63: 886-901.

Billingsley, Andrew. 1999. *Mighty Like A River: The Black Church and Social Reform.* New York: Oxford University Press.

Brown, Ronald E., and Monica L. Wolford. 1994. "Religious Resources and African-American Political Action." *National Political Science Review* 4: 30-48.

Calhoun-Brown, Allison. 1996. "African American Churches and Political Mobilization: The Psychological Impact of Organizational Resources." *Journal of Politics* 58: 935-953.

Cone, James H. 1992. "Black Theology as Liberation Theology." In *African American Religious Studies*, (ed.), Gayraud Wilmore. Durham, NC: Duke University Press.

Cook, Elizabeth Adell, and Clyde Wilcox. 1990. "Religious Orientations and Political Attitudes Among Blacks in Washington, DC." *Polity* 22: 527-543.

Dawson, Michael. 1994. *Behind the Mule: Race and Class in African-American Politics.* Princeton, NJ: Princeton University Press.

Dawson, Michael, Ronald Brown, and Richard Allen. 1990. "Racial Belief Systems, Religious Guidance, and African-American Political Participation." *National Political Science Review* 2: 22-44.

Ellison, Christopher G. 1991. "Identification and Separatism: Religious Involvement and Racial Orientations Among Black Americans." *Sociological Quarterly* 32: 477-494.

Ellison, Christopher G., and Darren E. Sherkat. 1990. "Patterns of Religious Mobility Among Black Americans." *Sociological Quarterly* 31: 551-568.

Ferraro, Kenneth F., and Jerome R. Koch. 1994. "Religion and Health Among Black and White Adults." *Journal for the Scientific Study of Religion* 33: 362-375.

Frazier, E. Franklin. 1974. *The Negro Church in America.* New York: Knopf.

Gordon, Eugene. 1972. "A New Religion for the Negro." In *A Documentary History of the Negro People in the United States*, Volume 3, (ed.), Herbert Aptheker. New York: Citadel Press.

Greenawalt, Kent. 1988. *Religious Convictions and Political Choice.* New York: Oxford University Press.

Guth, James, and John Green. 1993. "Salience: The Core Concept?" In *Rediscovering the Religious Factor in American Politics*, (ed.), David C. Leege and Lyman A. Kellstedt. New York: M. E. Sharpe.

Harris, Frederick C. 1994. "Something Within: Religion as a Mobilizer of African-American Political Activism." *Journal of Politics* 56: 42-68.

Harris, Frederick C. 1999. *Something Within.* NY: Oxford University Press.

Hoge, Dean R., and Ernesto de Zulueta. 1985. "Salience as a Condition for Various Social Consequences of Religious Commitment." *Journal for the Scientific Study of Religion* 24: 21-37.

Lea, James A., and Bruce E. Hunsberger. 1990. "Christian Orthodoxy and Victim Derogation." *Journal for the Scientific Study of Religion* 29: 512-518.

Lincoln, C. Eric. 1990. *The Black Church in the African-American Experience.* Durham, NC: Duke University Press.

Marx, Gary. 1967. "Religion: Opiate or Inspiration of Civil Rights Militancy Among Negroes." *American Journal of Sociology* 81: 139-146.

Morris, Aldon. 1984. *The Origins of the Civil Rights Movement.* New York: Free Press.

Reed, Adolph, Jr. 1986. *The Jesse Jackson Phenomenon: The Crisis of Purpose in Afro-American Politics.* New Haven, CT: Yale University Press.

Roof, Wade C., and William McKinney. 1987. *American Mainline Religion.* New Brunswick, NJ: Rutgers University Press.

Reese, Laura A., and Ronald E. Brown. 1995. "The Effects of Religious Messages on Racial Identity and System Blame among African Americans." *Journal of Politics* 57: 24-43.

Tate, Katherine. 1991. "Black Political Participation in the 1984 and 1988 Presidential Election." *American Political Science Review* 85: 1159-1176.

Tate, Katherine. 1993. *From Protest to Politics: The New Black Voters in American Elections.* Cambridge, MA: Harvard University Press.

Tate, Katherine. 1998. National Black Election Study, 1996 [Computer file]. ICPSR version. Columbus, OH: Ohio State University [producer], 1997. Ann Arbor, MI: Inter-university Consortium for Political and Social Research [distributor].

Taylor, Robert J., Michael C. Thornton, and Linda M. Chatters. 1987. "Black Americans' Perceptions of the Sociohistorical Role of the Church." *Journal of Black Studies* 18: 123-138.

Wald, Kenneth. 1992. *Religion and Politics in the United States*, 2nd Edition. Washington, DC: Congressional Quarterly Press.

Wald, Kenneth, Dennis Owen, and Samuel Hill, Jr. 1988. "Churches as Political Communities." *American Political Science Review* 82: 531-548.

Walton, Hanes. 1985. *Invisible Politics: Black Political Behavior*. Albany, NY: State University of New York Press.

Wilcox, Clyde. 1992. *God's Warriors: The Christian Right in Twentieth Century America*. Baltimore, MD: Johns Hopkins University Press.

Williams, Rhys H. 1996. "Religion as Political Resource: Culture or Ideology?" *Journal for the Scientific of Study of Religion* 35: 368-378.

Witter, Robert A., William A. Stock, Morris A. Okun, and Marilyn J. Haring. 1985. "Religion and Subjective Well-Being in Adulthood: A Quantitative Synthesis." *Review of Religious Research* 26: 332-342.

Appendix. Description of Variables

Dependent Variables

Support for Affirmative Action	"Because of past discrimination, minorities should be given special consideration when decisions are made about hiring applicants for jobs." 1 = agree, 0 = disagree.
Blacks Thermometer	"Now I'd like to get your feelings toward some of your political leaders and other people, events, and organizations that have been in the news ... I'd like you to rate it using something called the feeling thermometer. You can choose any number between 0 and 100. The higher the number, the warmer or more favorable you feel toward that person, event, or organization; the lower the number, the colder toward them." Coded 0 to 100.
Whites Thermometer	Coded 0 to 100.
Asian Americans Thermometer	Coded 0 to 100.
Hispanic Americans Thermometer	Coded 0 to 100.
Women's Movement Thermometer	Coded 0 to 100.
Party Identification	"Generally speaking, do you usually think of yourself as a Republican, a Democrat, an Independent, or what? Would you call yourself a strong Republican or a not very strong Republican? Would you call yourself a strong Democrat or a not very strong Democrat? Do you think of yourself as a closer to the Republican Party or the Democratic Party?" 1 = Strong Republican, 2 = Weak Republican, 3 = Independent-Republican, 4 = Independent, 5 = Independent-Democrat, 6 = Weak Democrat, and 7 = Strong Democrat.
Democrats Thermometer	Coded 0 to 100.
Republicans Thermometer	Coded 0 to 100.
Clinton Thermometer	Coded 0 to 100.
Dole Thermometer	Coded 0 to 100.
Jackson Thermometer	Coded 0 to 100.
Powell Thermometer	Coded 0 to 100.
Support for Gay Rights	"Do you favor or oppose laws to protect homosexuals against job discrimination?" 1 = favor, 0 = oppose.
Gays Thermometer	Coded 0 to 100.

Independent Variables

Age	Age in years, ranging from 17-90.
Education	1 = grade school (grades 1-8), 2 = some high school, no degree (grades 9-12), 3 = high school degree, 4 = some college, no degree, 5 = Associate's/ 2-year degree, Bachelor's/4-year degree, 6 = some graduate school, Master's degree, doctorate/law degree.

Family Income

Combined income of all members of your family living with respondent, for 1995 before taxes. Range: 1 (up to $10,000) to 11 ($105,000 and more).

Gender

1 = female, 0 = male.

Political Ideology

"Do you think of yourself as more like a liberal or more like a conservative?" 1 = conservative, 2 = neither, refuses to choose, 3 = liberal.

Black Common Fate

"What happens to Black people in this country has a lot to do with what happens to me." 1 = strongly disagree, 2 = somewhat disagree, 3 = somewhat agree, 4 = strongly agree.

Religious Guidance

"Do you consider religion to be an important part of your life or not? Would you say that religion provides some guidance in your day-to-day living, quite a bit of guidance, or a great deal of guidance in your day-to-day life?" 1= some, 2 = quite a bit, 3 = a great deal.

Church Attendance

"Would you say you go to church or place of worship every week, almost every week, once or twice a month, a few times a year, or never?" 1 = never, 2 = a few times a year, 3 = once or twice a month, 4 = almost every week, 5 = every week, 6 = two or more times a week.

Political Church (+)

"Have you heard any announcements or talks about the presidential campaign at your church or place of worship so far this year? Has your church or place of worship encouraged members to vote in this election?" 0 = no discussion, 1 = heard discussion, but not encouraged to vote, 2 = discussion and encouraged to vote.

Federal Enforcement of Voting Rights: Party Competition, Disenfranchisement, and Remedial Measures

Ronald Walters
Professor of Government and Politics
University of Maryland

Introduction

L̲ike so many aspects of African American citizenship rights, the right to vote experienced a tortuous course that led to the enactment of the Voting Rights Act which was signed into law on August 6, 1965. Yet, proof that such rights are still insecure forty years later resides in the substantial degree to which blacks experienced disfranchisement in the elections of 2000 and 2004. This view was echoed by Julian Bond, Chair of the Board of the National Association for the Advancement of Colored People at its 2005 annual conference in Milwaukee, Wisconsin:

> Anyone who claims that voting rights for minority Americans are now secure need only look to Florida in 2000 and Ohio in 2004. A recent report said that 28 percent of all Ohio voters and 52 percent of black voters said they experienced problems voting. And a dismal 19 percent of black voters expressed confidencethat their votes were properly counted.[1]

These problems have existed in perhaps other national presidential elections as well, however, the strength of the competition in more recent elections has been sufficient to allow the flaws in the election process to be exposed to the public.

Nevertheless, some analysts have concluded that the impact of the Voting Rights Act, in legitimizing the creation of single-member districts that resulted in the creation of black majority districts, has also facilitated the emergence of an increased number of republican districts and thereby contributed to party competition. But while agreeing that redistricting has contributed somewhat to the partisan nature of political competition, I argue here that the greater factor has been the conservative shift in the ideology of the political culture over the past forty years and that the strength of such competition has been a major source of the renewed strategies of disenfranchisement of blacks.

Indeed, Professor Larry Sabato and others have pointed to the increasingly polarized state of the political map of the United States according to which states favor one political party or another with an increasing consistency over time, such that 60,000 votes and three states separated Bush from Kerry in 2004.[2] However, the strength of the electoral competition is reflected in the modern notion that the "battleground states" are the terrain over which presidential elections especially are fought and in those states the attention of the media and the campaign organizations have the effect of pouring substantial political resources into these areas and positively stimulating voter turnout. In these states, voter disenfranchisement seems to be a product of the alteration of voting processes by the dominant party in political control in order to advantage their presidential candidate by limiting the impact of votes committed to their opponent party's candidate. Moreover, scholarly studies, such as that by Professor Mark Franklin, indicate that voters react to the character of campaigns by their relative turnout and competitive elections in particular results in higher overall turnout.[3]

The focus on the presidential elections of 2000 in Florida and Ohio in 2004 appear to validate the thesis of the linkage between their status as "battleground states" in the party competition and the resulting massive complaints of voter disfranchisement that in 2000, set off a wave of legislation at both the state and federal levels with respect to election reform. The data below clearly indicates that 62 percent of the sixteen states in the 2004 election regarded by most analysts as "battleground states" also were states with either high black or Hispanic population, historically soft targets for disenfranchisement.

Table 1
Comparison of Battleground States with Election Protection States
by percent vote difference for president in 2000 elections with
the number of Voter Complaints in 2004

Battleground 2000 Percent Election Protection Population

States	Difference	Complaints	% Black	Hisp.
Florida	.01	5,089	14.6*	
New Mexico	.06	1,001	1.9	42.1*
Wisconsin	.22	907	5.7	
Iowa	.32	76	2.1	
Oregon	.44	124	1.6	
Minnesota	2.40	144	3.5	
Missouri	3.34	798	11.2*	
Ohio	3.51	4,166	11.5*	
Nevada	3.54	570	6.8	19.7*
Tennessee	3.87	343	16.4*	
Pennsylvania	4.17	4,835	10.0*	
Maine	5.12	46	0.5	
Michigan	5.13	1,871	14.2*	
Arkansas	5.45	161	15.7*	
Washington	5.58	516	3.2	
Arizona	6.29	1,862	3.1	25.3*

Source: Battleground States: Less than 7.0 percent difference in vote for democratic and republican presidential candidates in the 2000 election. "2004 Election: Battleground States," *Time* magazine, October 24, 2004. Election Protection Complaints: "Nationwide Election Incidents," Election Incident Reporting System, 2004 Election, Verified Voting Foundation and Computer Professionals for Social Responsibility. Population: "Race and Hispanic or Latino: 2000, United States and Puerto Rico, American FactFinder, U.S. Census Bureau, Department of Commerce. (*) high black or Hispanic population—above 10 percent.

Moreover, seven additional states not regarded as "battleground states" in the Election Incident Reporting System database, with black or Hispanic populations over 10 percent also had more than 500 complaints (Louisiana - 811; Georgia - 987; New Jersey - 1,509; North Carolina - 761; New York - 3,210; Texas - 2,473; and South Carolina - 509). This suggests that independent of the competition in Battleground states, minorities in other states also experienced difficulties attempting to vote.

Yet, Thomas Mann, an expert on Congress at the Brookings Institution said that the risk in dealing with election reform was that:

> If it is true that there is a disproportionate representation of lower-income,   minority citizens among those who spoil their ballots, then an effort to reduce the number of spoiled ballots might help Democrats, and therefore, that becomes a disincentive to Republicans getting on board.[4]

While I agree with this formulation, put another way, republicans also have an incentive not to affect a version of election reform that empowers an inordinate number of poor and minority voters that are usually committed to Democratic Party candidates and, indeed, have mounted significant efforts to suppress their vote on the ostensible grounds of preventing "voter fraud." Thus, because blacks and other minority voters exhibit a greater pattern of loyalty to the Democratic Party, they are more prominently the subject of efforts to reduce the size of their vote. This is a critical feature of the electoral landscape both now and in the future, inasmuch as a report by FairVote indicates that competitive states have decreased in number over the past forty years, from twenty-four in 1960 to thirteen in 2004.[5] As such, the prospect is that it will affect blacks and other minority voters disproportionately since, although 30 percent of whites reside in such states and 21 percent of African Americans do.

Thus, effective election reform must take into consideration not only the re-authorization of the Voting Rights Act and the amendment of the VRA, the Help American Vote Act and the National Voter Registration Act. It should also consider how to regulate party competition through more vigorous enforcement of these laws to provide for fair competition and thus, to reduce the outcome of voter disfranchisement.

Therefore, in this work, I will seek to shift the issue of protecting the right to vote by the mere re-authorization of the Voting Rights Act and other measures of election reform, to the responsibility of political leaders to enforce the law. Such enforcement was intended to initiate citizenship rights originally granted to blacks through passage of the Fifteenth Amendment to the Constitution which says that "the Congress shall have the power to enforce this article by appropriate legislation." In arguing for increased federal regulation, I want to examine then, how faithfully administrations have implemented this power. In so doing, I will challenge the view that redistricting under the VRA has been the dominant motivating force of party competition, by asserting that ideology has been the major factor in the persistence of modern disenfranchisement.

The Seeds of Party Competition

The Role of Ideology and the Transition in Party ID

Before examining the enforcement problem in election reform, it is important to reject the proposition that the Voting Rights Act was responsible for the republican transition, especially in the South, rather than the ideological changes based on new attitudes toward social policy. In making this statement, I will partially repeat an argument contained in my most recent book, *Freedom Is Not Enough*,[6] adding support to the consensus that the primary factor in such a transition was ideology and not the creation of single-member districts to enforce Section 2 of the Voting Rights Act.

The point that the Voting Rights Act was not the culpable factor in the political transition of whites to the Republican Party is supported by at least four factors. The first is that the changes in the party identification of Southerners began in 1964 when the republican campaign of Barry Goldwater attracted white Southerners similarly alienated over the expansion of the role of the federal government in civil rights during that era. This shift of party identification, says Professor Charles Hadley, was one that resulted in a dislocation of a significant block of Southern voters from their traditional base inside the Democratic Party and resulted in an independent stance in the 1968 election.[7] This led, he asserts to a period when Southerners adopted a functional "dual political identity."

As Appendix 1 shows, there is a strong correlation between the high point of the Civil Rights movement and the beginning of the downward trend in the public loss of trust in government and the feeling that it was wasting money (on ill-conceived programs that favored blacks). There is also a striking convergence in the downward trend in the public's trust in government and their negative attitude toward the Democratic Party as the precipitator of government actions that appeared to favor blacks. These powerful facts, as I have argued in *White Nationalism*, were the sources of alienation that led to the development of the counter ideology of conservatism and indeed to a movement with that ideology as its dominant characteristic.

Southern political identity begins to clarify even more through a significant alliance that finds 10 million Southern voters joining in coalition with the Republican Party by 1972, motivated partially by President Richard Nixon's use of the "Southern Strategy" in that election. These shifts were far in advance of the impact of the Voting Rights Act on congressional districts, especially in the South, since court decisions allowing such districts occurred in the early 1970s and the districts were created mainly in the 1980s and 1990s.

Second, changes in the party identification of members in the House of representatives elected to single-member districts is more a result of party switching than redistricting. The data below illustrates several factors, one of which is that changes in partisan seats in the House of Representatives were not especially responsive to the redistricting calendar, since in the 1980 and 1990 census and subsequent state redistricting cycles, the greatest changes occurred later than two year after redistricting. One possible exception is the 1990 election, a substantial change in sixteen seats from democrat to republican occurred in 1992. However, such change more than doubled to thirty-four in the mid-term elections of 1994, giving evidence of strong partisan support in the electorate that removed thirty-four incumbents, taking advantage of twenty-two open seats, regardless of the change in the district lines.

The comparison between the significant years where the black members in the House increased as a result of redrawing their congressional boundaries and the subsequent increase in republican members of Congress simply does not present a contiguous picture. In fact, where a large increase in black membership occurs, as in 1987, a subsequent significant change republican members does not increase until five years later in 1992, reflecting perhaps an additional modest increase in black members that year. Otherwise, there is no discernable pattern.

The third explanation is that changes in the partisan identification of these representatives were affected by the greater turnout of voters highly motivated by conservative attitudes. This suggests that changes in the partisan composition of the House of Representatives in this period were more responsive to national political dynamics than the drawing of local congressional district boundaries. Evidence that national politics played a role is found in the fact that the first of the largest partisan changes occurred in 1974, the year Richard Nixon left the White House as a result of the Watergate Scandal. The second most substantial increase in party switching from Democrat to Republican occurred in 1980; that was the year of the first Ronald Reagan

Table 2
Change in Black Members in the House of Representatives
(Greater than 5 %) and Total changes in House Seats, 1978-1996

Total Change in House Seats

	Percent Change	Democrat to Republican
1971	40.0	
1973	14.3	
1974	6.3	
1975	5.9	
1977	5.6	
1978		14
1980		27
1981	- 5.9	
1983	16.7	
1984		13
1987	15.0	
1992	8.3	16
1994		34
1995	5.1	

Source: "Black Elected Officials in the U.S. by Category of Office, 1970-2000: Number and Percent Change From Preceding Year," Table 1, Joint Center for Political and Economic Studies, Washington, DC, 2001, p. 13. Also, Norman J. Ornstein, Thomas E. Mann and Michael J. Malbin, "Vital Statistics on Congress, 1997-1998, Washington, DC: Congressional Quarterly, 2000, p. 57.

election. And the third and fourth largest changes occurred in 1992 and 1994 with the so-called "Republican Revolution."

Fourth, and most important, changes in party ideology have been rooted in the alienation of whites toward social policy issues, with strong race-valued content, as the most dynamic force. For example, Professor Alan Abromowitz has asserted in his 1994 rejection of the Carmines and Stimson view of the "issue evolution" of white voters, that insofar as ideology was involved in changes in party identification, the transition of whites from the Democratic to the Republican Party was more a function of their disapproval of social policy issues such as the expansion of the welfare state and their views on national security rather than their views on racial issues such as opposition to civil rights.[8]

However, Professors Kulinsky, Cobb, and Gilens feel that this provides an inadequate explanation, since their own analysis finds that many in Southerners are still substantially opposed to such issues as the government assisting blacks, than that a black family would move into a white neighborhood. Although this view appears somewhat similar to that of Abramowitz, it hides an important fact which they attribute to Edsall and Edsall, who believe that racial issues are no longer the straight-forward issues they were which corresponded with the attitudes of respondents. The Edsalls are presented as saying:

race is no longer a straightforward, morally unambiguous force in American politics; instead, considerations of race are now deeply embedded in the strategy and tactics of politics, in competing concepts of the function and responsibility of government, and in each voter's conceptual structure of moral and partisan identity.[9]

Kulinski, Cobb, and Gilens perform a list experiment in order to test the salience of Southern racial attitude toward strictly racial policy issues. They conclude that Southerners exhibit the strongest anti-government attitudes, precisely because they are perceived as assisting blacks, a fact which accounts for Abramowitz's interpretation of his finding about Affirmative Action.[10] The work of Kulinski, Cobb, and Gilens supports that of Sears, Van Laar, Carrillo, and Kosterman, in their conclusion that "race-targeted issues" have become more important as old-styled racial responses by survey respondents. In the place of old-styled negative responses to questions about blacks, they assert that there is the new "symbolic racism" that is related to negative attitudes toward policy preferences conceived to advantage blacks.[11]

At local levels of politics, Neimi and Abramowitz conclude that although redistricting after 1970 and 1980 provided a short term partisan advantage to the party that controlled most branches of the national government, partisan control of state governments did little to increase partisan results from redistricting.[12] Their data show that whether the state was under republican control, divided control, or democratic control, the average republican vote in the congressional elections between 1990 and 1992 only increased slightly (2.49 percent, 1.62 percent, and 1.95 percent respectively) and the increase in republican seats also increased modestly (0.00 percent, 1.55 percent and 3.63 percent respectively).[13]

This is all the more striking inasmuch as, again, the gains in black representation in the U.S. House of Representative were much larger a result that appears to strongly discredit the view that Republican advances in redistricting are strongly tied to redistricting for racial affect in accordance with the requirements of the Voting Rights Act.

The Neimi and Abramowitz data also show that in states covered by the pre-clearance requirement, republican gains followed a similar pattern of slight improvement, given the differences in party control of the state.[14] In fact, Professor Gary Jacobson shows rather conclusively that the growth of the conservative trend in American political ideology was more conducive to party displacement in both the House and Senate, between 1972 to 2004.[15]

Disfranchisement in the 2004 Battleground

The surest piece of evidence that the VRA has not had the major role in promoting party transition as a result of redistricting is the more profound political phenomenon of partisan division in the country that has occurred in American elections. The increasing number of uncompetitive districts and states in national elections and the promulgation of a "battleground strategy" of campaigning in closely contested states in presidential elections, are driven by the ideological divide. The battleground strategy intensifies the partisan division by pouring substantial resources into such areas, the effect of which is to politicize the process of elections by influencing the processes involved.

States In The Battleground

In the 2004 elections, Professor Sabato, as others, suggests that the "early research has already indicated that turnout was usually higher in the key battleground states where money and media attention were lavished; in states that featured the controversial gay marriage amendments (to state constitutions); in states where high-profile U.S. Senate elections were being held."[16] So, while campaign resources were important in the creation of contested elections,

Sabato's more expansive profile reveals that emotionally charged issues were also important. The result, Professor Susan MacManus says, is by March of 2004, the battleground consisted of sixteen states, divided into nine "blue" states standing for Democrats and seven "red" states representing Republicans, on the basis of Al Gore's performance in the 2000 elections.[17] These states were as follows:

Table 3
Blue and Red Battleground states
by Pre-Election Spread and Eventual Winner

Blue	PES	W	Red	PES	W
Michigan	K 3.5	K 3.4	Nevada	B 6.3	B 2.6
Washington	*****	K 7.2	New Hamp.	K 1.0	K 1.3
Maine	K 9.5	K 9.0	W. Virginia	B 8.5	B 12.9
Minnesota	K 3.2	K 3.5	Missouri	B 4.2	B 7.2
Penn.	K 0.9	K 2.5	Arizona	*****	B 10.5
Iowa	B 0.3	B 0.7	Ohio	B 2.1	B 2.1
Oregon	K 4.8	K 4.1	Florida	B 0.6	B 4.0
Wisconsin	B 0.9	K 0.4			
New Mexico	B 1.4	B 0.8			

Pre-Election Spread (PES), Bush (B), Kerry (K), Winner (W). "Real Clear Politics Poll Average" (twenty-nine major polls), July and August, 2004. ***** no data available.

It is striking in the above results that, except for Nevada and Virginia, the distance between the predicted outcome and the actual outcome are exceedingly close. And while it may signify that the hyper-contribution of resources, public attention and issues may have made it possible for the outcomes to have this result, it may also mean that even in the "battleground states," the essential competitive framework remained unchanged.

Disenfranchisement: 2000

Modern problems with the enforcement of the Voting Rights Act goes back to at least the 2000 election cycle and beyond, when blacks also experienced serious voter disenfranchisement. In November of 2001, the *New York Times* released a study of 6,000 precincts in Florida which found that, without regard to the voting method, black voters had a rate of spoiled ballots five times that of those in white majority precincts.[18] Then, a study by Caltech/MIT found that although they comprised only 11 percent of voters in the state, 54 percent of the rejected ballots in Florida were from black voters.[19]

Both on and before Election Day, November 2, 2000, voter disenfranchisement experiences of blacks were transmitted to the NAACP which promptly notified the Justice Department of the nature of these complaints. The initial complaints that attracted attention included such things as: numerous problems with the mechanics of voting, disproportionate invalidation of the eligibility of blacks on voter rolls, and failure to pick up a ballot box in a heavily black precinct. After there was no immediate response, Rev. Jesse Jackson met with Attorney General Janet Reno to demand enforcement of the Voting Rights Act in early December of 2000. Reno's reply was that the Department was studying the problem and that in determining whether the VRA had been violated,

... the important ting is to try to make sure that we recognize that it is a matter of state law in most cases, that each state conducts its elections according to state law, and that we do not interfere unless there is a basis for federal jurisdiction.[20]

Somewhat later in this press conference, while noting the complaints of the NAACP, re-emphasized her view on the importance of states rights.

It is important that we adhere to the principles of federalism, recognize that it is primarily a state issue, and again do everything we can to play an important role that doesn't politicize the matter.[21]

Ultimately, Attorney General Reno did not intervene in the Florida case, despite the fact that the Voting Rights Act and the National Voter Registration Act would appear to have provided a clear basis for federal jurisdiction to invoke the injunctive powers they contained.

Disenfranchisement: 2004

Such a conclusion, however, may be considered hasty when one examines other sources. For example, the liberal organization, People for the American Way, was a prime sponsor of a new initiative with over fifty participating organizations, known as the "Election Protection Program" that fielded over 5,000 volunteer attorneys at various polling sites around the country to handle various voter complaints of disenfranchisement. It received complaints from voters in seventeen states, 70 percent of which were in "battleground" states, such as: Florida, Ohio, Pennsylvania, Arizona, Illinois, Michigan, New Mexico, Wisconsin, Colorado, Missouri, Nevada, North Carolina, Arkansas, Minnesota, Texas, Georgia, and Louisiana.[22] This legal initiative resulted in actions where volunteer lawyers brought various suits on behalf of voters, interpreted election law to voters and poll workers, and served in many places as an important liaison with the state and local election officials and the U.S. Justice Department's Voting Rights Division. A "hotline" was established on Election Day and a database was established known as the Election Incident Reporting System that received over 200,000 calls. A large number of these were considered "particularly alarming complaints in all categories" that concerned voter registration and absentee ballot problems, which documented that "incredible barriers ... continue to confront voters through misinformation campaigns and coordinated suppression tactics."[23]

Finally, the state of Ohio came into particular focus even before Election Day, due to various attempts by the Secretary of State, Republican Kenneth Blackwell, who simultaneously, the highest official responsible for election management in the state and a chairman of the Bush/Chaney campaign as well. Without delineating the litany of allegations against him, many citizens of the state, as well as others, believed that his actions were material in the massive complaints of voter disenfranchisement received in that state.

The volume and seriousness of the post-election complaints led Rep. John Conyers, ranking member on the House Judiciary Committee, to hold hearings in Ohio that provided the basis of a subsequent report which concluded:

We have found numerous, serious election irregularities in the Ohio Presidential election, which resulted in a significant disenfranchisement of voters. Cumulatively, these irregularities, which affected hundreds of thousands of votes and voters in Ohio, raise grave doubts regarding whether it can be said the Ohio electors selected on December 13, 2004 were chosen in a manner that conforms to Ohio law, let alone federal requirements and constitutional standards.[24]

In fact, the report pointed to the several actions of the Secretary of State, such as the mis-allocation of voting machines that created unprecedented long lines and waiting times in

minority neighborhoods, restricting provisional ballots, rejecting voter registration applications unless they were submitted on paper of a specified weight, permitting "caging" tactics
that monitored thousands of minority voters, etc. The report concluded that these actions
disenfranchised "hundreds of thousands of Ohio citizens."[25]

Disenfranchisement: Post-2004 Elections

Since the 2004 elections, the Bush administration has shown signs of accepting the new
disfranchisement. First, on March 31, 2005, Governor Sonny Perdue signed House Bill 244
passed by the Georgia legislature, that will have the effect of reducing the number of valid
identifications that render a person eligible to vote in that state from seventeen to six state-
authorized forms of identification with mandatory photo identification. Many groups, such
as the American Civil Liberties Union, considered that such reduction is likely to result in the
exclusion of voters who do not have birth certificates and other documentation to support their
applications for state-issued identification and may not have may not have had previously issued forms of such identification. Their concern that this measure would thereby discriminate
against minority voters, also prompted the Georgia Secretary of State, Cathy Cox to appeal to
Governor Sonny Perdue to request that he veto HB 244 on the grounds that, it is:

1. Unnecessary;
2. creates a very significant obstacle to voting on the part of hundreds of thousands of Geor-
   gians;
3. very unlikely to receive pre-clearance under the Voting Rights Act by the Department of
   Justice;
4. violates Article II, Section I paragraph I of the Georgia Constitution by adding a condition
   on the right to vote that is not contained in the constitution;
5. imposes an undue burden on a fundamental right of all citizens, the right to vote, in violation of both the state and the federal constitutions.[26]

Nevertheless, on August 25, 2005, the Justice Department pre-cleared HB 244, an act that
the ACLU described as a highly partisan action of a republican-controlled Justice Department
acceding to the wishes of a republican-controlled state[27] act. Nineteen states had such ID requirements in 2005.

In addition, the Florida legislature passed HB 1567 in 2005, a measure that ends the practice of allowing voters without sufficient ID to sign an affidavit, shifts all challenged ballots
to provisional status, regardless of whether such challenges are dis-proven, and moves the
counting of such ballots to the end of the period of tallying votes. It also expands the buffer to
100 feet around a polling station as the area within which soliciting to assist voters would be
prohibited. The ACLU indicates that this measure would be retrogressive of the voting rights
previously enjoyed by minority voters which would appear to place it within the prohibitions
of the Voting Rights Act.[28]

Nevertheless, the Department of Justice pre-cleared this law on Tuesday, September 6, 2005.
Florida law professor, Martha Mahoney, says that as a result of this action:

Our data, drawn from counties covered under Section 5, showed that affidavits, provisional
ballots, and declarations of voters using assistance at the polls are used disproportionately by
black and Hispanic voters (with declarations for assistance, the proportion of Hispanic voters
is particularly large).[29]

That these changes would appear to weigh more heavily on black and Hispanic voters is
consistent with the direction of changes or attempted changes in election law by republicans.

The Imperative of Federal Enforcement

In a democratic society, the moderating influence in the free flow of competition among the states and between the states and the federal government is the supremacy of the federal power. Yet the resonance a conservative politics has promoted the devolution of power to states as a mechanism to thwart the ability of government to improve opportunities for blacks and other groups that it has considered unworthy. Thus, fairness in the administration of elections resides in correcting the balance of federalism and challenging the federal government to engage in additional regulation in this area. This conclusion is supported by Professor Alex Kayssar, who notes that since it is the business of the two major parties to win elections, not to restrain their behavior in doing so greater federal oversight and regulation of federal elections is needed. He observed:

> there is nothing inappropriate in the national government enforcing the fulfillment [of democracy]. Throughout our history, the claim that voting was a state matter, rather than a federal one, has invariably been deployed by those who wanted to restrict any expansion of the franchise. "States' rights" was the cry of opponents of the Fifteenth Amendment, the Twentieth Amendment and the Voting Rights Act of 1965. Indeed, the revolution ion voting rights of the 1960s ... came from Congress and the federal courts precisely because both believed that the national government ought to be the guarantor of democracy and that the states with undemocratic political institutions could not be trusted to democratize themselves.[30]

These observations were made in response to the preliminary report of the Carter-Baker Commission on Election Reform.

It should be understood, however, from the experiences of 2000 and 2004 that even if the Voting Rights Act were to be re-authorized or amended that would not automatically insure that the law would be enforced. If we return to the insight of Thomas Mann and the perspective of this paper that so much of modern voter disenfranchisement is driven by party competition that is, in turn, driven by an ideology that contains a strong subtext of animus toward blacks and the Democratic Party, then the project of enforcing voting rights laws is not only complicated, but effectively evaded in many places by the power of the white conservative republican majority. What the massive switching of voters from the Democrat to the Republican Party also indicates is an ideological defection from issues associated with minorities, which includes the Voting Rights Act.

Thus, the enforcement of the VRA has been endangered by the increasing politicization of the electorate, a fact that has been enhanced by the adoption of the concept of the "battle ground state" where it is expected that in states where the political parties are more evenly divided, the competition among candidates for statewide office, such as the senate and president will be more intense. It would appear that in the 2000 and 2004 elections, from the experience of Federal election monitors and the Election Protection program of private organizations that many complaints of voter disenfranchisement emanated from states where political competition was substantially high.

Asserting Federal Accountability: Specific Issues

In calling attention to the responsibility of the federal government to engage in more forceful regulation of elections in order to bring greater integrity into the election procedures and thereby assure American citizens of a fair right to vote, one confronts a major issue of the constitutionality of this responsibility.

Although the federal government has some constitutional responsibility to regulate elections, the primary authority for determining the nature of how local citizens vote is left up to the states, and as we have seen, that was the concern of Attorney General Janet Reno in the 2000 election. This issue was addressed by Associate Attorney General For Civil Rights, Alex Costa in his March 2005 testimony to Congress. After noting that the Constitution in Article 1, Section 4, gave responsibility to the state legislatures for prescribing, "the times, places and manner of holding elections for Senator and representatives," said:

> However, recognizing the national importance of such elections, it continues, "But the Congress may at any time by law make or alter such regulations ..." Thus, except for where Congress has expressly decided otherwise, primary responsibility for the method and manner of elections, and for defining and protecting the elective franchise lies with the several states.[31]

The phrase in Costa's presentation—"except for where Congress has expressly decided otherwise ..." would appear to suggest that ultimate constitutional authority for the process of elections lay with the federal government and that insofar as they have not sought to address certain aspects of these processes, it is not for lack of authority, but respect for the political salience of federalism. Insofar as the balance of power between the states and the federal government is one that fluctuates throughout American history according to the ideological temper of the times, at this time, it swings toward the states.

If it is the case that the passions of party competition, fueled by an ideology which has the effect of closing access of the political system to millions who want to participate is successful, as a country, the quality of citizenship rights would appear to be set nearly back forty years to the beginning of the passage of the Voting Rights Act. The importance of that act was that it was the first federal intervention into this area of protecting voting rights by eliminating the barriers that are faced disproportionally by one particular social group. Now that it has been established that this group has not had its access to the ballot fully protected, and other groups are also vulnerable to disfranchisement, especially by the new electronic voting methods, it is urgent that the federal responsibility be enhanced.

Yet, as indicated above, in an era where the balance of ideological power has swung back strongly toward legitimizing state power, it is an open question whether the attempt to strengthen federal responsibility for election management is politically unfeasible. Nevertheless, I would call attention to a few strategic problems require such enhanced federal attention among the many that have surfaced, if the fair opportunity to vote is to be realized.

Re-authorizing the VRA

Section 2. Moreover, Section 2, should be reauthorized which mandates that certain states and subdivisions provide assistance in a language other than English where such a group consist of at least five percent of the population, should also be retained, in view of its success at empowering Hispanic individuals to vote. In an analysis of Hispanic and Asian voting, Michael Jones-Correa concludes, in an analysis of voter registration data, that:

..language provisions under the Voting Rights Act have a significant effect on voting across all covered groups. The second is that language provisions have a positive impact for first-generation citizens but not necessarily for the native born. Finally, regardless of generation, coverage under the language provisions of the Voting Rights Act has significant positive effects on voting turnout for Latinos but not for Asian Americans.[32]

In fact, his data show that Asians voter turnout has performed in a negative relationship to the language coverage under the VRA. In any case, the fact that such a tool is still useful is indicated in a lawsuit filed by the Justice Department and a simultaneous consent decree resolving the issue on August 25, 2005 against Ector County, Texas that alleged a violation of the rights of Spanish speaking voters by not providing them language assistance at the polls.[33]

Section 5. Some critical sections of the Voting Rights Act of 1965 should be re-authorized to prevent attempts by states to enact new barriers to voting. This law and especially the pre-clearance provision of Section 5 remain as process hurdles that states such as Georgia, Florida, and others must consider when they enact measures which have the force of weakening the black vote by continuing to limit their participation. As seen above, such states have enacted measures limiting the use of forms of personal identification to qualify individuals to vote.

Section 6. Then, Section 6 permits the U.S. Attorney General to assign federal election examiners and Section 8 allows the stationing of federal poll watchers in jurisdictions covered under the Act, both of which should be reauthorized. In 2004, the Justice Department received 1,088 calls and 134 emails that it tracked into an automated database and 600 of these contacts were referred to attorneys. Exemplary of such complaints included:

- a Louisiana 18-year-old who was told that she could not vote for president;
- a poll worker in Illinois who used racially derogatory language to a voter of
  Middle Eastern descent;
- difficulties obtaining provisional ballots;
- illegal closing of a polling station with voter in line.

In his 2005 Oversight Testimony to the House Judiciary Committee, Associate Attorney General for Civil Rights R. Alexander Costa elaborated on the fact that the Justice Department sought to enforce the Voting Rights Act and other laws relating to voting. For example, it dispatched 1,996 federal personnel to observe 163 elections in twenty-nine states, an effort which was greater than that in 2000 when 743 monitors monitored forty-six elections in thirteen states.[34] The activity of monitoring elections began in the Spring and ended on election day in all jurisdictions covered by the Voting Rights Act, and in some non-covered jurisdictions where monitored were requested by state officials. The 148 counties and parishes in nine states include: Alabama, Arizona, Georgia, Louisiana, Mississippi, New York, North Carolina, South Carolina, Texas, California, Illinois, Indiana, Michigan, New Jersey, New Mexico, Pennsylvania, South Dakota, and Washington. Because most of these states were those originally covered at the promulgation of the VRA in 1965, the group has a southern flavor.

In any case, this listing by the Department contains only six states (30 percent) of those included on the "battleground" listing above. A wider perspective is gained, however, when the National Election Reform Commission indicates their contacts with various group produced an awareness of at least 255,000 complaints on Election Day many more of which would have been in such states.[35] This result appears comparable to the Justice Department experience in 2000. Some sense of the scope of this problem is important, because while, in general, the use of federal election examiners to ensure fair elections and prevent disfranchisement waned between 1972 and 2004 in both democratic and republican administrations, the data in Appendix 2 illustrates that there was a dramatic increase in the deployment of federal voting monitors between 2000 and 2004.

There is some evidence in Attorney General Acosta's testimony that there was more attention to enforcement in 2004, but apparently, it was not substantial enough to prevent widespread complaints of disenfranchisement by black voters in Ohio and in other states.

Voting Rights Amendments

Bossier Parish. Next, the VRA should be amended to repeal the decision of the Supreme Court in the Bossier Parish case to conform to the 1982 amendments of the effects test. As a result of the 1990 census, as redistricting plan by the Bossier Parish School board developed a plan that excluded any black majority district. The NAACP found that sufficient black population existed to create at least two black majority districts. The Attorney General of Louisiana objected to pre-clearance and filed suit in federal court. A finding at this level supported the view that the change was subject to pre-clearance, which was appealed to the Supreme Court. The case, argued on December 9, 1996 and decided May 12, 1997, found that the plan of the Board (even though it was racially discriminatory) could not be rejected under pre-clearance solely on the basis that it violated Section 2 of the VRA.[36] The court based its decision on the fact that the plan was not "retrogressive" which is to say that it did not worsen the status of blacks as voters, but merely maintained the status quo. Moreover, the Court resurrected the intent test, by vacating the decision of the district court because it did not prove that the plan was dilutive of the impact of the black vote under Section 2, suggesting that the change may mean that there was an intent to retrogress, but since the evidence was not established, that could not be the basis of their decision. The restoration of the intent test, materially changes the rendering of the attempt by the Congress to institute the effect test as the basis for evaluating whether or not racial discrimination had occurred and thus, its probably effect on the right to vote. As such, the VRA should be amended to restore the effect test.

Felony Voting Rights. The extent to which convicted felons have been denied their voting rights came to light in the examination of the 2000 election in Florida where, since 1868, the State Constitution bars the right of any person convicted of a felony to vote until such right has been restored by way of the executive clemency power of the governor. The 1998 report of the Sentencing Project revealed that while in Florida, 647,100 felons were affected, 31 percent of whom were black men (204,600), nationally 35 percent of the total of felons (1,367 million) were black.[37] Thus, the number of voters who carried the status of felons in the 2000 election, if they had been allowed to vote, may have altered the outcome. In any case, in the period 2000-2002, just over 200,000 people were removed from voter rolls in all states because of their felony status.[38] Here, the author agrees with the recommendation of The Sentencing Project for federal action to eliminate this barrier to the exercise of the vote:

> We believe the best course of action would be to remove conviction-based registration on voting rights. At the federal level, congress should enact legislation to restore voting rights in federal elections to citizens convicted of a felony, so that the ability to cote in federal elections is not subject to varying state laws.[39]

This course would not only guarantee that individual who have paid their debt so society for the commission of a crime could regain their citizenship rights for federal elections, it may also have a positive impact on actions by state legislatures to normalize their eligibility to vote other elections as well.

Provisional Ballots. HAVA could be amended to provide for a uniform procedure for administering Provisional Ballots, to prohibit conflict of interests in election management and to provide for vigorous enforcement of uniform and fair standards in voting technology.

In the 2004 elections, many states attempted to implement the new HAVA provision allowing for voters to have access to vote by provisional ballots in cases where their identity or voting location could not be established. What occurred was the development of differing methods of implementation, based on differing criteria. While some states permitted voters to have provisional ballots who did not reside in a specific voting precinct, others did not; some states permitted access to provisional ballots for voters with identification and others did not; and there were other permutations. In any case, the question remains that in an election for federal office why such different standards should exist.

The County Democratic Party in Sandusky Ohio filed suit against the Secretary of State, J. Kenneth Blackwell for what they considered to be his unfair administration of the Provisional

Ballots, when he denied such ballots to those who were not properly registered in a given voting precinct in which he or she resided. The Justice Department's Voting Rights Section submitted an Amicus Brief in that case arguing that HAVA was not intended to create a private right of action—a position that would prohibit the Sandusky Democratic Party from having standing to suit— suggesting that such complaints should be channeled into the state administrative process that was controlled by republicans. Associate Attorney General R. Alexander Acosta further argued that Congress did not intend through HAVA to preclude States from electing precinct-based voting systems—or for the key election official to administer the law on that basis.[40]

Nonpartisan Election Administration. Then, one of the striking aspects of state adminis-tration of elections is that there is no lawful criteria that it should be a thoroughly non-partisan activity, staffed and directed by non-partisan officials in order to ensure both the presence and the appearance of fair election administration. In 2000 and 2004, Secretaries of State Kath-erine Harris and Kenneth Blackwell respectively were responsible for administering election processes in the states of Florida and Ohio. Simultaneously, they also served as chair of the Bush election committee in each of those years.

This situation has led the Social Science Research Council's Commission on Election Reform to conclude that:

> The partisan control of election administration is problematic in at least two respects. The first .... is that it creates the possibility that administrative decisions will be made to serve partisan purposes. The second is that it creates an unavoidable appearance of a conflict between an election official's administra-tive role and his or her partisan loyalty. These issues loomed large in Florida in 2000; they reappeared vividly in Ohio in 2004 ... with regard to decisions made with regard to provisional ballots.[41]

A most pressing reason for this issue to be taken up at the federal level is the sheer impotence of local action, an example of which is that legislation introduced in the California legislation in March of 2005 to provide for the election of a non-partisan Secretary of State was defeated in committee.[42] In any case, the consideration of this legislation took place in the context of a release issued by the National Association of Secretaries of State which reported that thirty-nine of its members who serve as chief election officials, had pledged to impartially discharge their duties that they conducted their duties in a system bound by checks and balances and were subject to electoral sanction if they did not perform.[43] They further indicated that they were bound by state law and by Congress, by state and federal courts and work with thousands of local officials to administer elections. Nevertheless, these safeguards have not resulted in the perception by the public that elections are being administered fairly.

Voting Rights Equipment Standards. One final area is also ripe for federal intervention. Insofar as the type of voting technology in existence is also material in forms of voter disenfran-chisement, as suggested by the Caltech-MIT studies, the corrective would also be the vigorous enforcement of standards by which such equipment is utilized in federal elections.

However, HAVA does not require that states submit their voting technology for monitoring by it technical committee to conform to uniform high standards, both in ease and effectiveness of accepting and tallying votes, and in the protecting the integrity of votes casts by adequate verification methods, even for federal elections. Instead, such cooperation by states with HAVA in this respect is totally voluntary, but in light of the problems that have emerged in the past two elections, it would appear that such monitoring should be made mandatory.

Conclusion

These recent actions give evidence that protections of the right to vote are still needed and that federal action in that regard is failing. Indeed, perhaps the highpoint of political partisanship in the nineteenth century was the struggle between the major parties over the Michigan Miner's Law, a measure making possible the minority party to obtain votes for presidents by localizing the tally of the vote to congressional districts. Considering the 2000 election to a continuation of the "partisan battleground," Professor Peter Argersinger posited that the example of the Miner's Law fight showed that electoral reform would not move in the direction of non-partisanship, but that since the 1893 Republican legislature in Michigan voted to repeal the Miner's Law, the direction, instead, "was to restrict, not expand, [voting rights] democracy."[44] He explained this by the view that:

> Then as now, those with effective political power over the electoral system used it ruthlessly to promote their own interests without regard to the rights of their opponents, their own expressed ideology, or the claims of democracy.[45]

Thus, at the minimum, existing federal laws should be re-authorized and strengthened, but as stated at the outset, a more sober assessment prevents one from reaching the conclusion that the mere existing of law means that it will be enforced, since many of the disenfranchisement tactics that have been deployed are illegal under current law. It will take aware citizens and governmental officials who are committed to the proposition that the content of democracy is valued by the extent to which its processes of participation have integrity. They, then become the bulwark of the demand for accountability in the electoral process by drawing attention to the necessity to enforce the law and in fact doing so.

In this, they are aided by the final report of the Carter-Baker National Commission on Electoral Reform, issued in September of 2005, contained eighty-seven recommendations, some of which supported greater federal intervention in the election process and the reduction of party competition.[46] For example, the Commission supports a nonpartisan approach to election administration that includes the appointment to national election related institutions, such as the U.S. Election Assistance Commission, as well as the chief election officers in each state (6.1.4). It also feels that Congress should legislate a rule that all electronic voting systems should provide a voter verified paper trail, especially for direct recording electronic (DRE) machines (3.1.1). The federal enforcement role is strengthened by recommendations urging the Justice Department to investigate and prosecute election related fraud, and a federal felony should be established for any person or group that engages in violence or other methods to intimidate or prohibit the right of individuals to vote (5.1.2, 5.1.3, 5.1.4).

The Commission, however, directs most of their recommendations toward the states, affirming their central role in election administration. For example, it supported the right of states, now counties or lower levels of government to provide uniform guidance for the administration of Provisional Ballots (2.3.2). Moreover, they believe that states should allow for the restoration of voting rights for otherwise eligible citizens who have been convicted of a felony, once they have fully served their sentences, probation and/or parole (4.6.1). One of the most controversial recommendations addressed to states was that they should allow voters without proper identification to cast provisional ballots until January 1, 2010, thereafter, the installation of a statewide ID system would be established that would legitimize such ballots (2.5.3). This recommendation drew several published dissents by some Commission members.

However, another conclusion conforms to the politicized environment within which the necessity for enhanced federal accountability rest. It is that the exceedingly partisan nature of the environment has placed a strong incentive for partisan change upon the electoral system as the surest method of achieving the protection of minority voting rights. For if Thomas Mann's views is correct that republicans have an incentive to limit such participation, then democrats have an incentive to expand it and therefore, such measures as suggested above may be delayed until the political atmosphere is conducive to such change as is often the case. And while such a conclusion may not conform to the preferred requisites of a bipartisan approach to democratic theory it may be the most logical conclusion available at this time.

Notes

1. Julian Bond, Speech to the Annual Convention of the National Association for the Advancement of Colored People, Milwaukee, Wisconsin, NAACP, July 11, 2005.
2. Larry J. Sabato, ed., *Divided States of America: The Slash And Burn Politics of The 2004 Presidential Election*, New York: Pearson/Longman, 2005. But see also, ...
3. Mark N. Franklin, "Electoral Competitiveness and Turnout: How Voters React to the Changing Character of Elections," Paper prepared for presentation at the annual Meeting of the Midwest Political Science Association, Chicago, Il., April 2004.
4. Katherine Q. Seelye, "Ideas & Trends: From Selma to Florida; Election Reform, Meet Politics," *New York Times*, March 4, 2001, p. 1.
5. "The Shrinking Battleground: The 2008 Presidential Elections and Beyond, FairVote, The Center for Voting and Democracy, Silver Spring, MD, 2005.
6. Ronald Walters, *Freedom is Not Enough: Black Voters, Black Candidates and American Presidential Politics*, (Rowman and Littlefield, 2005), pp. 88-89.
7. Charles Hadley, "Dual Partisan Identification in the South," *Journal of Politics*, Vol. 47, No. 1, p. 254.
8. Alan I. Abramowitz, "Issue Evolution Reconsidered: Racial Attitudes and Partisanship in the U.S. Electorate," *American Journal of Political Science*, Vol. 38 No. 1 (Feb., 1994), p. 1. This article followed a similar analysis with Kyle L. Saunders, "Ideological Realignment in the U.S. Electorate," *Journal of Politics*, Vol. 60, No. 3 (Aug., 1998), pp. 634-652.
9. James H. Kuklinski, Michael D. Cobb, and Martin Gilens, "Racial Attitudes and the "New South," *Journal of Politics*, Vol. 59, No. 2 (May, 1997), p. 346. This thought is identical to one that I contributed to Tom Edsall in an interview in 1990 on his book, Thomas B. Edsall and Mary D. Edsall, *Chain Reaction: The Impact of Race, Rights and Taxes on American Politics*, (New York: Norton, 1991).
10. Ibid.
11. David O. Sears, Colette Van Laar; Mary Carrillo; Rick Kosterman, *Public Opinion Quarterly*, Vol. 61, No. 1, Special Issue on Race (Spring, 1997), p. 46.
12. Richard G. Niemi ands Alan I. Abramowitz, "Partisan Redistricting and the 1992 Congressional Elections," *The Journal of Politics*, Vol. 56, No. 3 (Aug., 1994), p. 811.
13. Ibid, p. 813.
14. Ibid, p. 815.
15. Gary Jacobson, "Polarized Politics and the 2004 Congressional and Presidential Election," *Political Science Quarterly*, Vol. 120, No. 2, 2005, p. 215. See especially Figures 10 and 11, pp. 215 and 216.
16. Larry J. Sabato, "The Election that Broke the Rules," in Larry J. Sabato, op. cit., p. 55.
17. Susan MacManus, "Kerry in the Red States: Fighting an Uphill Battle from the Start," in Larry J. Sabato, ed., *Divided States of America: The Slash and Burn Politics of the 2004 Presidential Election*, New York: Pearson/Longman, 2005, p. 138.
18. Ford Fessenden, "Ballots Cast by Blacks and Older Voters Were Tossed in Far Greater Numbers," *New York Times*, November 12, 2001, p. A17.
19. "Residual Votes Attributable to Technology: An Assessment of the Reliability of Existing Voting Equipment," Report of the Caltech-MIT Voting Technology Project, March 30, 2001.
20. "Reno Says Justice Department Keeping An Eye On Florida Election," November 8, 2000, http://archives.cnn.com/2000/LAW/11/09/reno.weekly.pol/
21. Ibid.
22. "Shattering The Myth: An Initial Snapshot of Voter Disenfranchisement in the 2004 Elections, People for the American Way, NAACP, Lawyers Committee for Civil Rights Under Law, Washington, DC, December 2004. See also, "Polling Place Problem Stories," Election Protection Program, People for the American Way, Washington DC, November 5, 2004.
23. Ibid, p. 6. The "categories" referred to consisted of: Registration processing, absentee ballots, Machine errors, Voter suppression or intimidation and Provisional Ballots.

24. "Preserving Democracy: What Went Wrong in Ohio," Status Report of the House Judiciary Committee, Democratic Staff, January 5, 2005, p. 1.
25. Ibid.
26. Letter, From Cathy Cox, Secretary of State of Georgia to Honorable Sonny Perdue, Governor, State of Georgia, Atlanta, GA, April 18, 2005.
27. Jeffrey McMurray, "Justice Department Approves Georgia's Law Requiring Photo Identification to Vote," *Associate Press*, August 26, 2005.
28. "Florida Voting Rights Advocates Urge DOJ to Block Florida Voter ID Measure," Daniel Levitas, Ira Glasser, ACLU Voting Rights Project.
29. Ibid.
30. Alex Keyssar, "Reform and an Evolving Electorate," *New York Times*, August 5, 2001, p. 13
31. Ibid, p. 9.
32. Michael Jones-Correa, "Language Provisions Under the Voting Rights Act: How Effective Are They," *Social Science Quarterly*, Vol. 86, No. 3, September 2005, p. 561.
33. "Justice Department Settles Voting Rights Lawsuit Against Texas County," Press Release, U.S. Department of Justice, August 23, 2005.
34. R. Alexander Costa, Prepared Testimony, Annual 2005 Oversight Hearings, Judiciary Committee, U.S. House of Representatives, March 10, 2005, p. 10.
35. "Building Confidence in U.S. Elections: Report of the Commission on Federal Election Reform, American University, September 2005, p. 17.
36. "Reno, Attorney General v. Bossier Parish School Board et al.," Appeal From the United States District Court For the District of Columbia, Supreme Court of the United States, No. 95-1455, May 12, 1997.
37. "Losing The Vote: The Impact of Felony Disenfranchisement Law in the United States," The Sentencing Project, Washington, DC. 1998.
38. "The Impact of the National Voter Registration Act, 2003-2004," A Report to Congress, U.S. Election Assistance Commission, June 30, 2005.
39. Ibid.
40. The Sandusky County Democratic Party, et al, v. J. Kenneth Blackwell, U.S. Court of Appeals, Sixth Circuit, December 2004.
41. "Challenges Facing The American Electoral System: Research Priorities For The Social Sciences," The National Research Commission On Elections and Voting, The Social Science Research Council, New York, N. Y., March 1, 2005, p. 9.
42. "Non-Partisan Secretary of State Efforts Killed in Legislature," Press Release, Assembly member Joseph Canciamilla, 11th Assembly District, March 16, 2005.
43. "Administering Elections in a Nonpartisan Manner, "Statement by 39 Secretaries of State who serve as Chief State Election Officials, National Association of Secretaries of State, February 6, 2005.
44. Peter H. Argersinger, "Electoral Reform and Partisan Jugglery," *Political Science Quarterly*, Vol. 119, No. 3, 2004, p. 519.
45. Ibid.
46. "Building Confidence in U.S. Elections," op. cit.

The Deck and the Sea: The African American Vote in the Presidential Elections of 2000 and 2004

Robert C. Smith
San Francisco State University

Richard Seltzer
Howard University

" The Republican Party is the deck, all else the sea," Frederick Douglass told an audience of African American voters during the Reconstruction era. By this he meant that the Democratic Party was so overwhelmingly hostile to African American interests that it left black voters with little choice except to vote for the Republican Party. Although we do not have precise figures, it is probably the case that from the 1868 election (when African Americans were first allowed to vote in significant numbers) until 1936 the Republican Party averaged more than 90 percent of the black vote in presidential elections.

While the Democratic Party was the sea because of its hostility to black interests, the Republican Party was the deck because it had earned the loyalty of black voters with a series of far reaching, indeed radical, reforms that addressed their concerns for freedom and equality. Beginning with Lincoln's Emancipation Proclamation, these reforms included three constitutional amendments (the Thirteenth abolishing slavery, the Fourteenth requiring the states to treat all persons fairly and equally and the Fifteenth prohibiting the states from denying the vote to black men), three civil rights acts between 1866 and 1875 (the last prohibiting racial discrimination in public conveyances and accommodations) and three civil rights enforcement acts between 1870 and 1875. Partly in pursuance of these acts, the U.S. Army was stationed in the southern states to secure at the "points of bayonets" these newly secured rights.

In addition to these executive and legislative initiatives addressing the civil rights concerns of blacks, the Republican Party created the Freedmen's Bureau, the federal government's first social welfare agency. The Bureau was set up to provide land and work to the newly freed persons, as well as social, educational and medical benefits. Although most of these reforms were subsequently repudiated or fatally compromised,[1] when Douglass spoke in the 1880s the Republican Party had earned the support of blacks with an agenda that addressed their interests.

Since 1964 for African Americans the Democratic Party has been the deck, all else the sea. Since 1968 (the first election since Reconstruction in which most blacks could vote) the Democratic Party has received an average 89 percent of the black vote in presidential elections. And, like the Republican Party during Reconstruction, the Democratic Party during the civil rights era earned the loyalty of blacks. During this period two constitutional amendments were passed (granting the citizens of the majority black District of Columbia the right to cast ballots in presidential elections, and prohibiting the states from requiring a tax as a qualification for voting), and three civil rights acts. These acts included the omnibus 1964 Act which prohibited racial discrimination in employment, federally funded programs and in access to public accommodations. The 1965 Voting Rights Act secured the rights of southern blacks to vote, and to cast an effective, undiluted vote. Finally, the 1968 Act prohibited discrimination in the sale and rental of housing. And, also as in the Reconstruction era, the Democratic Party went beyond the civil rights concerns of blacks for freedom and equality and inaugurated a series of reforms designed to enhance the access of blacks to employment and educational opportunities, and to various social welfare benefits.

The Realignment of the African American Electorate, 1936 – 1964

The Republican Party remained the deck until the election of 1936, albeit a leaky or unstable one. The leaks in the deck began with the so called Compromise of 1877 in which the Republican Party, in exchange for disputed electoral votes from Florida and Louisiana, in effect agreed to abandon blacks in their quest for freedom and equality.[2] From 1877 until the 1960s the Republican Party continued to pay lip service to black interests but essentially the Party took the black vote for granted, since the Democratic Party remained overwhelmingly hostile to black interests. The farewell to the Party of Lincoln started with FDR and the New Deal.[3] Most African Americans remained loyal to the Republican Party in the Depression era 1932 presidential election, in which Franklin D. Roosevelt defeated Herbert Hoover in a landslide. In 1936, however, a majority of blacks abandoned ship and voted for the Democratic Party in a national election for the first time.

African Americans did not vote for FDR because he was a Democrat or because he embraced their civil rights concerns. Roosevelt in his long tenure in office never took a stand in favor of civil rights refusing, despite the urgings of his wife Eleanor, even to speak out against lynching. Like President Kennedy, a generation later, Roosevelt's response was always "I can't take the risk."[4] Can't take the risk of antagonizing the southern white supremacists who controlled powerful committees in Congress and influential states in the Democratic nominating process and the Electoral College. Thus, FDR and the Democratic Party were at best ambivalent about the African American vote, fearing it would destabilize the Party coalition. FDR was able to win black support in 1936 and in subsequent elections in 1940 and 1945 on the basis of his social and economic programs, a few symbolic but highly visible appointments to the bureaucracy and the unwavering support of Mrs. Roosevelt for the cause of equality.[5]

In 1948, the Democratic Party and its presidential candidate, Harry Truman did take the risk, with the Party adopting for the first time a civil rights plank in its platform and President Truman proposing a package of civil rights reforms to the Congress. (Truman also issued an executive order prohibiting discrimination in the armed forces). This was the first time a Democratic President had proposed civil rights legislation, and the first such legislation proposed by any President since Benjamin Harrison in 1889.[6] The risks, however, were plain as South Carolina Governor Strom Thurmond bolted the Party and ran as an independent, segregationist "Dixiecrat" candidate for President. Thurmond carried several southern states and won thirty-nine electoral dates, nearly costing Truman the presidency.

Truman got the message and backed away from his civil rights initiatives, and in 1952 and 1956 Adlai Stevenson, the Democratic nominee, downplayed civil rights while openly courting southern white supremacists. Nevertheless, Truman's embrace of civil rights and his continued support for FDR's social welfare programs reinforced black support for the Democratic Party in presidential elections. However, President Eisenhower in his two campaigns against Stevenson and Vice President Nixon in his campaign against Kennedy in 1960 received from 25 to 40 percent of the black vote.[7]

Although Kennedy won one of the closest presidential elections in history partly on the basis of overwhelming black support, his stance on civil rights during the campaign and early in his administration was hesitant and ambivalent.[8] Kennedy appointed a number of blacks to important positions in his administration and made other racially inclusive gestures, but he refused to propose comprehensive civil rights reforms. Like FDR, he feared such legislation would antagonize southern white supremacists and jeopardize his legislative agenda and his prospects for reelection. Anticipating that he might be reelected by a large margin, Kennedy had decided to postpone action on civil rights until his second term.

The demonstrations led by Dr. Martin Luther King, Jr. in Birmingham in the Spring of 1963 changed this calculus and forced the reluctant President to embrace the cause of civil rights. Fearing that the increasingly militant civil rights movement and the violent reaction of southern racists to it threatened to jeopardize internal security and the nation's international interests, Kennedy in June of 1963 proposed a comprehensive civil rights bill.[9]

Lyndon Johnson, assuming office after President Kennedy's assassination, made enactment of Kennedy's civil rights bill his top priority. Courageously willing to take the risks (he reportedly told his aides as he prepared to sign the 1964 Civil Rights Act that the Democratic Party would lose the South for a generation), Johnson pushed through three major civil rights bills in four years. With his Great Society and War on Poverty Johnson also boldly set in motion policies and programs to achieve racial equality, declaring in a 1965 Howard University address "we seek not just freedom ... but equality as a fact and a result."[10]

The 1964 election was the watershed in the completion of the partisan realignment of the black vote, as well as the racially based realignment of the entire party system.[11]

In 1955 Clinton Rossiter, a leading conservative political theorist, wrote that the "problem of the Negro" presented conservatism and the Republican Party with a choice between expediency—"the cold blooded counting of votes and seats" and principle—"the conscience stricken recognition that Negro should not have to beg and fight for the ordinary rights of Americans."[12]

When confronted with this choice the Republican Party choose expediency, by nominating as its 1964 presidential candidate Barry Goldwater. Goldwater was one of the few non-southern senators to oppose the 1964 Civil Rights Act.[13] Although Goldwater's opposition to the Civil Rights Act was based on conservative not racist principles (he argued that the legislation exceeded congressional authority and was an unconstitutional intrusion by the federal government into the affairs of the states), he and his strategists were fully aware that his vote against the bill would have electoral payoffs in the southern states and elsewhere.[14]

Goldwater lost to Johnson in a landslide, but he did carry five southern states laying the foundations for the Republican Party's southern strategy. As Tali Mendelberg writes "The stage was set for the first racial appeal in American history to win a presidency: Richard Nixon's southern strategy."[15] Emphasizing themes and issues such as "law and order" and busing for purposes of school desegregation, Nixon skillfully appealed to the adversaries of African American freedom and equality.[16] Nixon's 1968 margin over Hubert Humphrey, however, was razor-thin, largely because of the more explicit racial appeal of George Wallace, the segregationist Governor of Alabama who ran as a third party candidate.

In 1969 Kevin Phillips, a special assistant to Nixon's campaign manager, in *The Emerging Republican Majority* wrote in a chapter titled *"The Future of the Republican Party"* that Wallace had done well among Catholics as well as white southerners. Concluding that "Three quarters or more of the Wallace electorate represented Nixon votes," Phillips wrote that the "availability of the Wallace vote was the key to the emerging Republican majority.[17]

Nixon went aggressively after that vote after 1968, with speeches, policies, appointments and symbolic gestures.[18] With Wallace out of the 1972 race because of a failed assassination attempt, Nixon defeated George McGovern, the Democratic nominee, in a landslide carrying forty-nine states. In subsequent elections Republican nominees Ronald Reagan, George H.W. Bush and Bob Dole used implicit racial messages in their campaigns, focusing on issues such paper, we seek to explain the bases or sources of this increased support, and explore its implications for the 20 percent solution and the prospects for the partisan realignment of the black vote.[30] In other words, we consider whether the Democratic Party is still the deck and all else the sea, or whether some blacks—and if so which and for what reasons—may be abandoning ship and risking the hazards of the sea.

Previous studies of blacks and the Republican Party have found little evidence of any shifts toward the Republican Party in presidential elections by any significant segment of the black electorate. Bolce, De Maio and Muzzio in their study of the 1988 election concluded "there is nothing in the data that points to any segment of the black community that can be successfully mined for Republican votes."[31] In their study of the 1992 election Bolce and his colleagues reached similar conclusions, but they also concluded that the 20 percent solution did not work "in part because it was never tried."[32] Unlike his father's administration, strategists in the George W. Bush administration did try, not only by avoiding the race card but by spending money during the campaign and reaching out with appointments and policies calculated to appeal to at least segments of the black electorate.

Republican strategists have identified several segments that might be open to Republican Party appeals. The first is young African Americans who, coming of age after the liberal Democratic administrations of the civil rights era, may be less loyal to the party and more open to certain Republican ideas.[33] Second, Middle to upper income blacks and those who generally feel financially secure it is assumed might be receptive to the Republican message on taxes and spending.[34] Third, those blacks with traditional views on marriage, family and sexuality might be attracted to Republican rhetoric about family values and the Party's position on school prayer, abortion and same-sex marriage. Fourth, born again Christians or religious traditionalists in general might be attracted by the moral values rhetoric, and programs such as Bush's Faith Based Initiative. Finally, some blacks might be attracted to the Party for what Pinderhughes calls "instrumental" or "pragmatic" reasons. This is because some blacks might resent the Democratic Party's taking the black vote for granted, while appealing to the interests and concerns of white moderates and conservatives. Thus, she writes "The combination of high dissatisfaction and high competition within the Democratic Party for what seem to be declining benefits may encourage blacks to make use of the exit option, despite ideological incompatibilities with the Republicans."[35]

We examine the empirical bases for each of these strategic hypotheses, focusing on the 2000 and 2004 presidential elections. Where the data permit, we will make direct comparisons between the two elections. In addition, we present a more detailed analysis of the roles played by candidate qualities and issues in the 2004 election, focusing especially on terrorism, the economy, the Iraq war and moral values.

Data

We rely on the exit polls conducted during the 2000 and 2004 elections. The exit polls are useful for the purposes of this paper because the large sample sizes for the black population permit extensive subgroup analysis in terms of such characteristics as age, gender, class, ideology and partisanship. The 2000 poll was conducted by the Voter News Service (VNS), a consortium of the major national television news organizations and the Associated Press. The 2004 poll was conducted by the National Election Poll (NEP), also sponsored by the same news outlets. VNS and NEP used similar methodologies, questioning voters in sample precincts as they exited the polls. (In some areas, these data are supplemented by telephone surveys because of mail or absentee ballots). Both also conducted separate surveys in each of the states and the District of Columbia. These state surveys have some common questions, but many questions are not asked in all the states. (For example, the questions on the economy discussed below were asked in only twenty three states). The 2000 poll included 13,255 respondents in the national survey and 43,068 in the state surveys. The corresponding figures for 2004 were 13,747 and 63,259. In the 2000 poll 7,317 blacks were sampled; 7,588 in 2004.

Turnout

Although there is disagreement among scholars as to how to appropriately measure turnout,[36] by any standard turnout increased between 2000 and 2004. Both political parties devoted considerable resources to turning out their core constituencies. African American political organizations and other groups associated with the Democratic Party and the Kerry campaign made major efforts to register and mobilize black voters. (This effort included the "Vote or Die" campaign by hip hop artists to register and turnout young blacks). It is estimated that in 2000 African Americans cast 10.5 million votes, making them roughly 10 percent of the electorate, while in 2004 it is estimated that they cast 14.6 million votes constituting 12 percent of the electorate.[37] Among young African Americans (18-29) turnout increased substantially, from 2.1 million in 2000 to 3.7 million in 2004. Overall, young blacks increased their proportion in the electorate from 2 percent in 2000 to 3 percent in 2004.[38]

Age, Class, Gender and Marital Status

Although young African Americans were a larger segment of the electorate in 2004 then in 2000, their support for the Republican nominee was relatively low in both elections. As shown in Table 1 his support did not differ significantly by age. Young blacks may be increasingly disenchanted with the Democratic Party; this has not yet translated into increased support for Republicans. It is likely, as Bositis suggest, young blacks are disenchanted with both parties but like their elders still see the Democratic Party as the deck.[39]

Male and married blacks, like their white counterparts, are more likely to vote Republican. Among married blacks Bush's support in 20004 increased slightly, from 12 to 15 percent. Bush's support also increased slightly among unmarried blacks (from 6 to 11 percent), but if there is anything in the data here to encourage Republican strategists it is that married blacks are somewhat more attracted to the Party than the unmarried.

Class differences also structured the black vote in these two elections in ways that are at odds to some extent with what the literature suggests (see Note 31). Although Bush more than doubled his support among the lowest income blacks (from 7 to 16 percent), in both elections the data in Table 1 show that Bush did better among those with higher incomes. In 2004 he did especially well among those segments of the electorate who earned more then $100,000 a year

Table 1
The African American Republican Vote in the 2000 and 2004 Presidential Elections by Age, Gender, Marital Status, Education, Income And Perception of Financial Situation

% Republican Vote

	2000	2004
OVERALL	10 percent	12 percent
AGE		
18-24	8 (12)	11 (13)
25-29	11 (11)	14 (12)
30-39	9 (23)	10 (22)
40-44	9 (14)	14 (10)
45-49	14 (13)	13 (13)
50-59	9 (14)	14 (16)
60-64	14 (5)	9 (6)
65+	12 (9)	14 (9)
GENDER		
Female	7 (55)	11 (41)
Male	15 (45)	14 (59)
MARITAL STATU.S.		
Married	12 (53)	15 (47)
Not married	6 (47)	11 (53)

The African American Republican Vote in the 2000 and 2004 Presidential Elections by Age, Gender, Marital Status, Education, Income And Perception of Financial Situation

% Republican Vote

	2000	2004
Education		
Less Than High School	5 (6)	14 (6)
High School Graduate	10 (22)	12 (28)
Some College	11 (37)	11 (34)
College Graduate	9 (22)	15 (21)
Post Graduate	19 (13)	8 (12)
INCOME		
<$15,000	7 (10)	16 (14)
15,000 - 30,000	6 (23)	8 (21)
30,000 - 50,000	8 (25)	8 (26)
50,000 - 75,000	10 (25)	14 (17)
75,000 - 100,000	14 (9)	10 (10)
100,000+	21 (8)	23 (12)
Financial Situation		
Better	8 (65)	28 (14)
Worse	33 (8)	6 (49)
Same	14 (28)	12 (37)

• Numbers in parentheses represent proportion of the electorate.

and who thought their financial situation was better in 2004 than 2000, receiving 23 percent and 28 percent of their votes respectively. These, however, were relatively small segments of the electorate. Yet, the data does suggest that to the extent that this upper class segment of the black community continues to grow—as it almost certainty will—then there is a basis to think that 20 percent or more of it will abandon ship.

The Religious Factor

Again, like their white counterparts, African Americans who are religious (as opposed to those with no religious affiliation), attend church weekly and in 2004 those who described themselves as Born Again are more likely to vote Republican. Indeed, as shown in Table 2 those who attend church weekly are almost twice as likely to vote Republican. And unlike the upper income and the financially better off, these groups constitute large segments of the black electorate (half of black voters, for example, attend church weekly and say they are born again). Although the religious variable operates in the black electorate in the same partisan direction as it does among whites, its magnitude is of course much smaller. White evangelicals or Born Again Christians view the Republican Party as the deck, all else the sea.[40]

Ideology, Party, Candidate Qualities and Vote Choice in 2004

For Republican strategists, perhaps the most disappointing news in the data on the 2000 and 2004 elections is the partisan and ideological contours of the African American vote. As Table 3 shows, among Republicans (6 percent of the electorate in 2004) the Party received

Table 2
The Religious Variable and the African American Republican Vote in the 2000 and 2004 Presidential Elections

	2000	2004
RELIGIOU.S. AFFLIATION	%	%
Protestant	13 (25)	19 (21)
Catholic	18 (11)	9 (7)
Other Christian	7 (50)	13 (50)
None	9 (10)	4 (8)
BORN AGAIN		
Yes	NA**	17 (56)
No		8 (44)
CHURCH ATTENDANCE		
Weekly	11 (50)	17 (52)
<Weekly	9 (50)	9(48)

*Numbers in parentheses represent proportion of the electorate.
**Not Available, because questions was not asked in 2000.

more than two thirds of the vote. However, among conservatives (20 percent of the electorate in 2004) Bush received only 29 percent of the vote. Thus, the data show that black conservatives overwhelming view the Party as the sea, as do almost a third of the Republicans. Although this has been the pattern in other post civil rights era elections,[41] it is nevertheless striking that in 2004 the Party did so poorly among its partisan and ideological bases. (Among whites, these groups usually vote near 90 percent Republican.

Table 3 also includes information about how black voters in 2004 evaluated the candidates in determining how to cast their votes. For most blacks the qualities that mattered most in determining their vote was whether the candidate would "bring about needed change" (43 percent) and "whether he cares about people like me" (19 percent). Among these huge segments of the electorate, Bush received infinitesimal 2 and 3 percent of the vote respectively. However, he exceeded 20 percent among the much smaller segments of the electorate who selected such qualities as strong leader (35 percent), honesty (19 percent) and takes a clear stand (21 percent). And, again showing the significance of the religious factor, among the 5 percent of the electorate that selected "strong religious faith" as the most important candidate quality Bush received an extraordinary 59 percent of the vote.

Table 3
Ideology, Party Identification, Candidate Perceptions and the African American Republican Vote in 2000 and 2004

Party	2000	2004
Republican	57 (7)	68 (6)
Democrat	2 (77)	5 (75)
Independent	27 (12)	23 (15)
Other	23 (4)	31 (4)
Ideology		
Liberal	3 (27)	6 (30)
Moderate	10 (56)	9 (49)
Conservative	21 (17)	29 (20)
Candidate Quality That Matters Most***	NA**	
Need Change		2 (43)
Cares About People Like Me		3 (19)
Clear Stand		21 (12)
Strong Leader		35 (8)
Religious Faith		59 (5)
Honest		19 (7)
Intelligent		6 (6)

*Numbers in parentheses represent proportion of the electorate.

**Not Available; question not asked in 2000.

***The question asked: Which candidate quality mattered most in deciding how you voted for President. Respondents were then given the list of seven items.

Issues and Candidate Choice In the 2004 Election

Table 4 reports the choice of the most important issue for African American voters in the 2004 election, and how they voted on the initiatives in the thirteen states banning same-sex marriage. For African Americans, the economy/jobs were by far the most important of the seven issues respondents were allowed to choose from. Thirty-seven percent of blacks selected this issue as the most important in determining their vote and among this group Bush received only 3 percent of the vote. The second most important issues (selected by 13 percent of respondents) were the Iraq War and moral values. Bush received only 1 percent of the vote of those selecting the war. He did best among the 13 percent of the electorate that selected moral values as their most important issue and the 8 percent who selected terrorism, receiving 53 percent and 30 percent respectively.

Thus, the economy and the Iraq war were clearly the key issues in determining the black vote in 2004, issues we explore in greater detail below. But, first the moral values issue should be examined in a bit more detail because it is an issue where Republican strategists believe there is an opportunity to make gains among blacks. The data in Table 4 show this is clearly the case; the problem for the Party is that relatively few blacks view this as a priority issue in determining their vote.[42]

In 2004 same-sex marriage was a specific issue that was thought to be a moral values issue, or at least surrogate for them (along with abortion). Same-sex marriage became an issue in 2004 because of the U.S. Supreme Court decision in 2003 declaring that the Constitution protected the rights of persons to engage in private, consensual homosexual conduct; the 2004 decision of the Massachusetts Supreme Judicial Court legalizing same-sex marriages; and the decision by the mayor of the City and County of San Francisco to order the County Clerk to issue licenses to same-sex couples. As a result of these developments, thirteen states placed initiatives on

Table 4
Most Important Issues, Same-Sex Marriage and the African American Republican Vote In 2004 Presidential Election

Economy/Jobs*	3 (37)
Iraq	1 (13)
Moral Values	53 (13)
Terrorism	30 (8)
Health Care	5 (14)
Education	4 (10)
Taxes	6 (5)
SAME SEX-MARRIAGE***	
Against	15 (70)
For	6 (30)

*Respondents were given a list of these issues and asked to select the one that mattered most in deciding how to vote for President.

**Numbers in parentheses represent proportion of the electorate.

***Represents the vote in thirteen state ballot initiatives on same-sex marriage.

the 2004 ballot defining marriage as exclusively a relationship between a man and woman. Both President Bush and Senator Kerry opposed same-sex marriages, while supporting civil unions. However, President Bush also supported a federal constitutional amendment defining marriage as a union between a woman and man. Kerry opposed the amendment, establishing a partisan divide on the issue.

Same-sex marriage was thus viewed by Republican strategists as an issue that might mobilize their core constituency of white evangelicals and appeal to segments of the black electorate. African Americans—the most liberal and Democratic segment of the electorate—and white evangelicals—the most conservative and Republican segment—are two of the groups most opposed to same-sex marriage. A 2003 Pew Poll found 83 percent of white evangelicals opposed to same-sex marriage, followed by 64 percent of blacks.[43] Among all ethnic groups, support for same sex marriage increased dramatically between 1996 and 2003 except among blacks and white evangelicals where it increased only 1 percent.[44]

The data in Table 4 show that 70 percent of blacks in 2004 were against same-sex marriage (voting yes on the state initiatives banning such relationships) and they were almost three times as likely to vote for Bush.[45] However, this support for Bush was only 15 percent. This points to the fact that black voters tend to give greater priority to the economy and war and peace than to so-called moral issues, such as same-sex marriage or (in earlier elections) abortion.

The Economy and the War

Table 5 shows that perceptions of the economy and which candidate could be trusted to manage it effectively was a critical determinant of the black vote.[46] Among those who thought the economy was in excellent or good condition (4 and 27 percent respectively), Bush crossed the 20 percent threshold receiving 27 percent of the vote of those who rated the economy good. Similarly, he exceeded 20 percent among those who trusted both candidates to handle the economy, and, as one would expect, among those who trusted only Bush (8 percent) virtually all (93 percent) abandoned the Democratic ship.

Table 5
The Economy and the African American Vote in the 2004 Presidential Election

	PERCENTAGE OF THE REPUBLICAN VOTE
WHO TRUST TO HANDLE ECONOMY	
Kerry Only	1 (75)
Bush Only	93 (8)
Both	32 (5)
Neither	27 (11)
Condition of State's Economy	
Excellent	23 (4)
Good	27 (27)
Not Good	11 (46)
Poor	5 (23)

*Numbers in parentheses represent proportion of the electorate.

Table 6
Terrorism, The Iraq War and The African American Vote In the
2004 Presidential Election

2004 Presidential Election

WHO TRUST TO HANDLE TERRORISM	Percentage of the Republican Vote
Bush Only	83 (63)
Kerry Only	1 (13)
Both	0 (9)
Neither	14 (15)
SAFER OR LESS SAFE THAN FOR YEARS AGO	
Safer	31 (26)
Less Safe	5 (74)
APPROVAL OF IRAQ WAR DECISION	
Strongly Approve	54 (6)
Somewhat Approve	32 (12)
Somewhat Disapprove	3 (23)
Strongly Disapprove	10 (58)
HOW THINGS GOING IN IRAQ	
Very Well	40 (3)
Somewhat Well	54 (10)
Somewhat Badly	10 (31)
Very Badly	2 (56)

*Numbers in parentheses represent proportion of the electorate.

Most blacks, however, rated the economy as not good or poor and trusted Kerry to make it better and they voted overwhelmingly Democratic. Those who, for example, viewed the economy as poor and who trusted Kerry gave Bush only 5 and 1 percent respectively of their votes.

The results are similar with respect to terrorism and the Iraq war, as shown in Table 6. Of the 13 percent of the electorate who trusted Bush to handle terrorism, he received 83 percent of the vote and those who thought the country was safer then four years ago (26 percent) Bush was supported by 31 percent. But the 63 percent who trusted only Kerry to deal with terrorism and thought the country was less safe (74 percent) gave the President only 1 percent and 5 percent respectively. Similarly, the tiny minorities of blacks who approved the decision to go to war and thought the war was going well gave Bush strong support. The problem, however, is that from the outset black leaders and the black public were strongly opposed to the war.[47] Indeed, it may be that the Iraq war more then any other issue alienated potential black Republican supporters in 2004. That is, without the war it is reasonable to speculate that Bush might have done better than his overall 12 percent support from blacks.

State Level Analysis

In Table 7 data on the percent of the black vote received by the Republican Party in the 2000 and 2004 presidential elections are presented for the twenty-five states with fifty or more blacks in the sample. Of these states, the Republicans made gains in eighteen, the Democrats in six (the results in Kentucky were unchanged from 2000 to 2004). President Bush's gains in 2004 ranged from 12 in Texas to 1 in Tennessee with an average of 6.5 points. Kerry's gains over Gore ranged from 7 in Arkansas to 2 in Virginia and Alabama, averaging 3 points.

In Texas, Delaware, California and New Jersey Bush nearly reached the 20 percent threshold, receiving 17 percent, or more of the black vote. There is no apparent relationship between the states where Bush gained in 2004 and such variables as region or the size of the state's black population. He made gains in all parts of the country and in states where blacks are a relatively small proportion of the population such as Nevada and California and in states with relatively large black population proportions like South Carolina and Louisiana.[48] Nor is there an apparent relationship between the 2004 vote and the presence of a same-sex marriage initiative on the state's ballot. This finding is contrary to the initial post-election commentaries, which suggested that Bush might have improved his showing in Ohio—the decisive battleground state in 2004 —because of his stance on that issue.

Conclusion

For more than four decades for black voters the Democratic Party has been the deck, all else the sea. For most blacks the Democratic Party remains the deck, however, there is evidence from these two elections that suggests some blacks are abandoning ship. Whether enough are prepared to do so to make the 20 percent solution a viable strategy for the Party is unclear. In 2004 President Bush received only 12 percent of the black vote, which is only a little better than the post civil rights era 9 percent average for Republican presidential candidates. This should be particularly discouraging to Republican strategists, since the Bush campaigns and administrations are the first in the post civil rights era to aggressively reach out to blacks with campaign spending and appeals, and appointments and policies. However, there are some encouraging signs for the Party when one looks more closely at the 2004 results.

Those encouraging signs are not in the voting behavior of young blacks who, while perhaps disenchanted with the Democratic Party, showed only slight movement toward the Republican Party. Although Bush did not reach the 20 percent threshold in any age group, he did somewhat better among middle aged blacks. Generally, the Republican Party does better among married voters and in 2004 it did better among married African Americans.

There are also encouraging signs for Republican strategists in the class data. In 2004 Bush improved his performance among the college graduates and those with the highest incomes. Among the relatively small stratum of blacks earning more then $100,000 and those who thought their financial situation was better in 2004 Bush received 20 percent of the vote or more. Similarly, he met the threshold among those who thought the economy was in good shape and almost 90 percent among those trusted him to manage the economy.

The Party did relatively well in 2004 among blacks who describe themselves as born again, who attend church weekly and who are opposed to same-sex marriage. Among the 5 percent of the electorate who selected religious faith as the quality that mattered most in determining their vote in 2004, the President received almost two thirds of the vote. He also received more than half the vote of the 13 percent of the electorate who selected moral values as the issue that mattered most in the election.

Table 7
The African American Vote for the Republican Presidential Candidate,
Selected States, 2000 and 2004

	2000	2004	REPUBLICAN GAIN LOSS
Texas	5	17	+12
Pennsylvania	7	16	+9
Delaware	9	17	+8
S. Carolina	7	15	+8
Ohio	9	16	+7
Mississippi	3	10	+7
California	12	18	+6
New Jersey	11	17	+6
Florida	7	13	+6
N. Carolina	9	14	+5
Nevada	8	13	+5
Georgia	8	12	+4
Maryland	7	11	+4
Illinois	7	10	+3
Louisiana	6	9	+3
Michigan	8	10	+2
New York	8	9	+2
Tennessee	8	7	+1
Kentucky	12	12	0
Virginia	14	12	-2
Alabama	8	6	-2
District Columbia	6	3	-3
Missouri	15	10	-5
Indiana	13	8	-5
Arkansas	13	6	-7

However, it must be particularly disappointing to Party strategists that among self-identified conservatives the Party continues to barely exceed the 20 percent threshold. And among black Republicans the Party generally receives little more than two thirds of the vote, although Republican support increased from 57 percent in 2000 to 68 percent in 2004.

In 2004 the most important issues for African Americans were the economy and the Iraq war. Most blacks thought the economy was not in good shape and did not trust Bush to make it better, and they voted overwhelmingly Democratic. Similarly, most blacks disapproved of the Iraq war and thought it was going badly, and they too voted overwhelmingly Democratic. The perceived state of the economy and the Iraq war in all likelihood depressed the appeal of the Bush campaign to those who otherwise might have been inclined to respond to the Bush record and his appeals to them on issues of class, faith and values. Given the overwhelming and likely intense opposition of many blacks to the war, it is likely that it in particular made it difficult for Bush's other messages to get through. In other words, the fog of war.

Yet, the question remains can the Republican Party burdened by the legacy of three decades of the southern strategy successfully appeal to a fifth of the black electorate, without fundamental ideological or policy changes. Most scholars think not. Paul Frymer, for example, concludes "Black leaders and their followers, like any rational voter, will not simply run from one party or another if the second party gives them no added value. Offered a choice between political parties making similar vague appeals, a group is likely to maintain its traditional allegiance simply for institutional and historical reasons ... if for no better then historical attachment and habit. For the opposition party, in turn, to shake the negative connotation that the group's voters associate with it require more than vague and halfhearted appeals."[49]

Vague and halfhearted appeals are all the Republican Party appears to be prepared to offer African Americans. Speaking to a nearly all white meeting of the Party's 2005 summer conference Party Chair Mehlman said "we don't have to choose between motivating our base and bringing new faces and new voices into the party ... we're not asking Republicans to become more liberal to lure new voters into the party.... We talk about a compassionate conservative philosophy that not only unites Republicans, but attracts support among discerning Democrats and among independents."[50]

However, some scholars see an inevitable growth in black support for Republicans, even without ideological or policy changes. Mayer, for example, writes of "the inevitability of black bipartisanship "as a result of the lessening of racial prejudice, the continued economic and political progress of blacks, and Republican appeals to upper class blacks and the more religious members of the community.[51]

The results of this study results provides evidence to support both sides of this debate. The Republican Party did have some success in appealing to the wealthy and religious, however, in the case of the former their percent of the electorate is small and among the religious it has not yet reached 20 percent. Nevertheless, in an evenly divided electorate even relatively small shifts in a couple of battleground state can alter the outcome of an election.[52]

Notes

1. W.E.B. DuBois, *Black Reconstruction: An Essay Toward A History of the Part Which Black Folk Played in the Attempt to Reconstruct Democracy in America, 1860-1880.* (1935; reprint, New York: Athenaeum, 1969) and Eric Foner, *Reconstruction: America's Unfinished Revolution, 1863-1877* (New York: Harper & Row, 1988).
2. Rayford Logan, *The Betrayal of the Negro: From Rutherford B. Hayes to Woodrow Wilson* (London: Collier Books, 1965).
3. Nancy Weiss, *Farewell to the Party of Lincoln: Black Politics in the Age of FDR* (Princeton, NJ: Princeton University Press, 1983).

4. Kenneth O'Reilly, *Nixon's Piano: Presidents and Racial Politics from Washington to Clinton* (New York: Free Press, 1995): 111.

5. In response to A. Phillip Randolph's threat of a massive black protest march in Washington, Roosevelt also issued an executive order prohibiting discrimination in employment in industries with defense contracts

6. In 1889 Harrison proposed legislation to enforce African American voting rights; strongly supported the Blair education bill to provide federal aid to education whose primary beneficiaries would have been southern blacks; proposed anti-lynching legislation; and considered using the commerce clause to pass civil rights legislation. See Homer E. Socolofsky and Allan Spatter, *The Presidency of Benjamin Harrison* (Lawrence, KS: University of Kansas Press, 1987).

7. The support of Eisenhower and Nixon in 1960 by blacks was a result of the continued loyalty of many blacks to the party of Lincoln, Stevenson's indifference on civil rights, Kennedy's ambivalent record, the *Brown* school desegregation decision, the support for civil rights among congressional Republicans, and Eisenhower's use of the army (for the first time since Reconstruction) to enforce black rights in the south.

8. Jeremy Mayer, *Running on Race: Racial Politics in Presidential Campaigns, 1960-2000* (New York: Random House, 2002): Chap. 2.

9. Mark Stern, *Calculating Visions: Kennedy, Johnson and Civil Rights* (New Brunswick, NJ: Rutgers University Press, 1992).

10. This speech set forth the philosophical rationale for and gave bureaucratic impetus to the development of affirmative action. See Hugh Davis Graham, *The Civil Rights Era: Origins and Development of National Policy, 1960-1972*, (New York: Oxford University Press, 1990).

11. Edward Carmines and James Stimson, *Issue Evolution: Race and the Transformation of American Politics* (Princeton, NJ: Princeton University Press, 1989).

12. Clinton Rossiter, *Conservatism in America*, (New York: Vintage Books, 1955): 247.

13. Twenty-three of sixty-seven Democrats opposed the bill compared to only six of thirty-three Republicans. Thus, although the Democratic Party was to become the deck after 1964 the Civil Rights Act of that year passed with proportionally more Republican then Democratic support. Each of the civil rights acts of the 1950s, as well as the constitutional amendments referred to earlier, were passed with significant Republican support. Because of the voting behavior of southern Democrats, the Republican congressional delegation continued to be the more liberal party on civil rights throughout the 1960s.

14. Mayer, *Running on Race*, pp. 45-68.

15. Tali Mendelberg, *The Race Card: Campaign Strategy, Implicit Messages and the Norm of Equality*, (Princeton University Press, 2001): 95. Mendelberg's work is an innovative study of the use of race in American elections. Tracing the first use of racial campaign appeals to a New York state election in 1800, she finds that such appeals were openly racist from Reconstruction until the beginning of the 20th Century when race effectively disappeared from national campaigns. When race reappeared as a partisan issue in the 1960s the "norm of racial equality" made explicit racist appeals unacceptable. Thus, Republican candidates beginning with Nixon in 1968 engaged in implicit racial appeals because "If Republicans failed to conform to this norm, they risk losing supporters from their base" (p. 17). Mendelberg shows that historically such appeals, whether explicit or implicit, have revolved around African American sexuality, criminality, economic dependency and laziness and their desire to subjugate whites. On the historical use of these tropes see also Forrest Wood, *Black Scare: The Racist Response to Emancipation and Reconstruction* (Berkeley: University of California Press, 1968).

16. Ibid. pp. 93-98. See also Mayer, *Running on Race*, pp. 69-122.

17. Kevin Phillips, *The Emerging Republican Majority*, (Garden City, N.Y.: Anchor Books, 1970): 462.

18. According to Nixon aide John Ehrlichman, Charles Colson in a 1972 memo to Nixon wrote "The key voters to go after are Catholics, organized labor and the racists" and Ehrlichman notes "That the subliminal appeal to the anti-black voter was always in Nixon's statements and speeches on schools and housing...." See John Ehrlichman, *Witness to Power*, (New York: Auburn House, 1982): 222-23.

19. The most famous or infamous example of playing the race card was the Willie Horton ads during the 1988 Bush-Dukakis campaign. Slickly produced, the ads linked black sexuality and criminality. Lee Atwater, Bush's campaign manager in 1988, two years after the campaign terminally ill with Cancer apologized for the racist implications of the ad. See *"Lee Atwater's Last Campaign," Life Magazine*, (February 1991): 61. On the Horton ad see Mendelberg, *The Race Card*, chapter 5 and

Kathleen Hall Jamieson, *Dirty Politics: Deception, Distraction and Democracy*, (New York: Oxford University Press, 1992): 131-35.

20. Dan T. Carter, *From George Wallace to Newt Gingrich: Race and The Conservative Counterrevolution, 1963-1994*, (Baton Rouge: Louisiana State University Press, 1996).

21. Matthew Holden, Jr., *The Politics of the Black "Nation,"* (New York: Chandler Publishers, 1973): 139-40.

22. Dianne Pinderhughes, *"Political Choices: A Realignment in Partisanship Among Black Voters?"* in *The State of Black America 1986*, (New York: National Urban League, 1986): 96.

23. On Clinton's shifting of the Party toward conservatism or centrism on race see O'Reilly, *Nixon's Piano*, Chap. 10, Mayers *Running on Race*, Chaps 10-11 and Robert C. Smith, *We Have No Leaders: African Americans in the Post Civil Rights Era*, (Albany, NY: State University of New York Press, 1996): Chap. 10.

24. Although the Bush campaign did not play the race card, it was played by African Americans. An NAACP organized group sponsored television and radio ads about the lynching of a black man in Texas that appeared to suggest that Bush condoned lynching.

25. The Faith Based Initiative has awarded millions of dollars to black churches, and in his second administration Bush selected James Towey, an African American, to head the White House office on the Initiative.

26. To some extent homosexuality replaced race as the wedge issue in 2004, with Republican strategists using opposition to same sex marriage to chip away traditionally Democratic voters (including African Americans) and to mobilize the Party's core constituency of white evangelical voters.

27. Lee Atwater, *"Toward A GOP Rainbow,"* *New York Times*, March 26, 1989.

28. RNC Chairman Ken Mehlman's "Remarks at the NAACP National Convention," July 14, 2005. www.gop.com/news/read.aspx?ID=5631. Between January and June Mehlman carried this message to more than a dozen black groups, as did the President in a major address to the Indiana Black Expo on the same day as Mehlman's NAACP address. See Michael Fletcher *"GOP Plans More Outreach to Blacks, Mehlman Says,"* *Washington Post*, July 7, 2005. Anne Kornblut, *"Bush, GOP Leader Woo Black Voters,"* *New York Times*, July 15, 2005.

29. Ibid.

30. All the results or differences reported in the tables are significant at the.05 level.

31. Louis Bolce, Gerald De Maio and Douglas Muzzio, *"Blacks and the Republican Party: The 20 Percent Solution,"* *Political Science Quarterly* 107(Spring 1992):77.

32. Louis Bolce, Gerald De Maio and Douglas Muzzio, *"The 1992 Republican`Tent': No Blacks Walked In,"* *Political Science Quarterly* 108(Spring 1993): 269. They write "The only serious attempt to woo black votes was the nomination to the Supreme Court of Clarence Thomas."

33. Young African Americans are significantly less attached to the Democratic Party and a proportion (between a third and a half) is sympathetic to some Republican positions, such as school vouchers and partial privatization of social security. See David Bositis, *"The Political Orientations of Young African Americans,"* *Souls* 7(Spring 2005): 43-50. In pursuit of the youth vote, Mehlman met and solicited the advice and support of Russell Simmons, the hip-hop impresario and political activist.

34. There is nothing in the scholarly literature to support this strategic calculation. If anything, the literature suggests no class differences in partisan choice among blacks or that middle class blacks are more liberal and Democratic in their partisan leanings. See the studies cited by Bolce and his colleagues above and more generally see Robert C. Smith and Richard Seltzer, *Race Class and Culture: A Study in Afro-American Mass Opinion*, (Albany: State University of New York Press, 1992) and Michael Dawson, *Behind the Mule: Class and African American Politics*, (Princeton, NJ: Princeton University Press, 1994).

35. Pinderhughes, *"Political Choices,"* p. 19. Pinderhughes' instrumental hypothesis is likely to be most attractive to the relatively small stratum of politically active. In any event, the data available to us do not allow for an empirical assessment of this option.

36. Walter Dean Burnham, *"The Turnout Problem,"* in James Reichley (ed.), *Elections, American Style*, (Washington: Brookings Institution, 1987).

37. David Bositis, *The Black Vote in 2004*, (Washington: Joint Center for Political and Economic Studies, 2005): 1. Bositis, using estimates from the committee for the study of the Electorate, estimates overall turnout in 2004 at 60.7 percent compared to 54.3 percent in 2000.

38. Ibid.

39. Young blacks vote less and generally express relatively high degrees of dissatisfaction with both parties. In 2000, for example, 42 percent said neither candidate was worth supporting, 56 percent that politicians don't keep promises, 31 percent that this voting won't make a difference and 34 per-

cent said that not voting was a way to show dissatisfaction with the system. Less then 10 percent of blacks fifty or older agreed with any of these reasons. Bositis, *"The Political Orientations of Young African Americans,"* p.46.

40. Scott Keeter, *"Evangelical Voters: Bedrock of the Republican Party."* Paper presented at the annual conference of the American Association of Public Opinion Research, Miami Beach, Florida, May 12-15, 2005. White evangelicals constituted 35 percent of Bush's total vote in 2004. By comparison, blacks constituted 21 percent of Kerry's vote.
41. See the studies by Bolce and his colleagues cited above.
42. Most scholars view the moral values issue as problematic. As Gary Langer and Jon Cohen write "Against the other items on the list, it's not commensurate, comparable or a discrete political issue. Instead, it served as an ill defined grab-bag for other concerns not listed, especially for Bush voters, who had fewer options offered." *Voters, Values and the 2004 Election."* Paper presented at the annual conference of the American Association of Public Opinion Research, Miami Beach, Florida, May 12-15, 2005. And contrary to the conventional post election commentary, Langer and Cohen conclude that among white voters terrorism rather than moral values was the determining issue in Bush's defeat of Kerry. See also James Campbell, *"Why Bush Won the Presidential Election of 2004: Incumbency, Ideology, Terrorism and Turnout,"* *Political Science Quarterly* 120(Fall 2005): 219.
43. The Pew Forum on Religion and Public Life *"Longitudinal U.S. Public Opinion Polls on Same-Sex Marriage and Civil Unions,"* www.religioustolerance.org/hom_p0115.htm, February, 2004.
44. Ibid.
45. Initiatives banning same-sex marriage were on the ballot in the following states: Arkansas, Georgia, Kentucky, Michigan, Mississippi, Montana, North Dakota, Nebraska, Nevada, Ohio, Oklahoma, Oregon and Utah.
46. The data here are based on questions asked in twenty three state surveys.
47. Chaka Ferguson, *"Blacks Least Likely to Support War,"* *West County Times*, February 25, 2003. Only thirteen percent of the black members of the House voted for the Iraq war resolution, compared to 70 percent of the non-black members.
48. In previous elections there has been what some scholars refer to as "concentration and diffusion effects" where Republican candidates do much better in states where the black population is small. See Bolce, De Maio and Muzzio, *"Blacks and the Republican Party,"* p. 76.
49. Paul Frymeer, *Uneasy Alliances: Race and Party Competition in America*, (Princeton, NJ: Princeton University Press, 1999): 47
50. Marc Sandalow, *"GOP Uncompromising on Far Right Platform, No Moderate Outreach,"* *San Francisco Chronicle*, August 7, 2005.
51. Mayer, *Running on Race*, pp. 295-97.
52. Hurricane Katrina in the short term at least, and perhaps long term depending on the administration's sensitivity to race in its recovery program, may hurt whatever progress the Republican Party may have been making in reaching out to blacks. This is because 66 percent of blacks but only 17 percent of whites thought the government's response to the hurricane would have been faster if most of the victims had been white. See the *Pew Poll for the People and the Press*, September 13, 2005. See also John Whitesides *"Republican Push For Black Votes Hit by Storm,"* *Washington Post,* September 8, 2005. One post-Katrina poll (*NBC News/Wall Street Journal*) found that Bush's job approval rating among blacks had fell to 2 percent (compared to 45 percent among whites and 39 percent among Latinos), the lowest ever seen in presidential approval ratings. Although the small number of blacks in the sample (89) casts doubt on the validity of the 2 percent results, it nevertheless is indicative of the damage the hurricane did to the President among African Americans. See Dan Froomkin *"A Polling Free-Fall Among Blacks,"* *Washington Post*, October 13, 2005.

The Voice of the Congressional Black Caucus in American Foreign Policy

Paige Whaley Eager

Assistant Professor, Department of History and Political Science
Hood College

In the midst of the war on terrorism and the continuous media coverage of Afghanistan and Iraq, the low-level crisis situations which arose in 2003-2004 in Liberia, Sudan, and Haiti may appear to be of minimal importance and salience to the general American public. However, the resignation of Charles Taylor in Liberia, the coup/ouster of embattled former Haitian President Jean-Bertrand Aristide in February 2004, and the continuing attacks in the Darfur region by the pro-government janjaweed militias in Sudan were of significant concern to the Congressional Black Caucus (CBC). The CBC's motto of "acting as the conscience of the U.S. Congress" since its inception in the early 1970s has made the CBC the focus of scholarly analyses on domestic policy issues (Bositis 1993; Singh 1998), voting patterns (Gile and Jones 1995; Pinney and Serra 1999), and how minority U.S. Congresspersons represent their respective districts (Swain 1993; Tate 2003); however, scant attention has been focused upon the CBC's influence on foreign policy issues (Singh 1998; and Copson 2003). Historians have examined the role of African-Americans in influencing foreign policy before the CBC's formation (Skinner 1992; Plummer 1996; Krenn 1998; Henry 2000), and political scientists have examined the role of ethnic lobbies or interest groups, such as the American-Israeli Public Affairs Committee, in influencing the foreign policy making process and outcomes (Said 1981; Ambrosio 2002; Uslaner 2002). However, the few analyses of the CBC's foreign policy preferences go beyond a largely descriptive analysis. Thus, having identified a lacuna in the extant literature, this article is a first cut at articulating how the CBC sought to affect the foreign policy debate in three case studies during the 108th Congress.

In this chapter, I argue that the CBC, as an institutionalized racial caucus is not an interest group in the traditional sense; however, "the CBC could be considered an interest group when it attempts to influence decisions in the executive and judicial branches" (Wright 1996: 23). In the three case studies examined, the CBC acted as a quasi-interest group because it tried to influence executive branch policy, especially toward Haiti and Liberia, but it also tried to shape and influence the debate within Congress as well. The CBC, moreover, does act as a national constituency which promotes and attempts to preserve legislation salient to the African-American population, as well as legislation salient to Africa and the Caribbean. In attempting to promote its interests in foreign policy, one could argue that institutional factors would have the greatest impact on the CBC's relative success[1] in impacting the policy process. Institutional factors would include: (1) whether the Democratic Party controls the White House since all

CBC members of the 108th Congress were Democrats; (2) how many CBC members are chairs of powerful committees and subcommittees; and (3) whether the CBC constitutes a critical mass[2] within Congress to be of importance on crucial votes. In this article, however, I argue that the more salient factors to examine are contextual factors including: (1) the nature of the issue itself—is it an issue which affects U.S. national security interests or is it a "low politics" issue? (2) the breadth and depth of the constituency within and outside of Congress that cares about the issue—is there bipartisan support within Congress on the issue and a wider racial and political constituency outside of Congress?, and (3) the history of African-American influence in lobbying on behalf of the issue.

This article will accomplish four objectives. First, it will provide a brief overview of African-American advocacy in foreign policy as well as the formation and significant foreign policy concerns of the Congressional Black Caucus over the past three decades. Second, the article will examine the policy preferences of the Congressional Black Caucus on the three case studies of Haiti, Liberia, and Sudan.[3] In order to assess the policy preferences of the CBC during the 108th Congress (2003-2004), I will examine: (1) U.S. Congressional hearings; (2) legislation sponsored and co-sponsored by CBC members; (3) CBC press releases and Special Order speeches; and (4) public opinion polling data to gauge whether the American public was in support of the CBC's policy preferences. Third, the analysis will discuss whether the Bush administration's policies and actions in the case studies complemented or diverged from the CBC's stated policy objectives. Finally, the conclusion will assess how the CBC as an institutionalized racial/ethnic lobby continues to advocate on behalf of its policy preferences and suggest future avenues for research.

Racial and Ethnic Politics

A rich area of scholarship has emerged regarding how diasporas try to influence politics in their host and home country. Diasporas, as opposed to ethnicity, accentuates a bond between Americans and their countries of origin. "U.S. diasporas are Americans who maintain some affinity—be it cultural, religious, racial, or national—with their ancestral lands or their dispersed kinfolk elsewhere" (Shain 1995: 70). As Shain notes, the "homeland" may be a person's actual native country, or it may be a place that serves as a symbolic home, as Africa and the Caribbean are for many blacks in America and as Israel is for many American Jews. "Ethnic lobbies are political organizations established along cultural, ethnic, religious, or racial lines that seek to directly and indirectly influence U.S. foreign policy in support of their homeland and/or ethnic kin abroad" (Ambrosio 2002: 2). Some of the best-known ethnic lobbies are the Polish-American Congress, TransAfrica, the Armenian Assembly of America, and the American Israel Public Affairs Committee. Moreover, ethnic lobbies seek to influence policy in at least three ways: (1) framing issues, (2) providing information and policy analysis for the executive and legislative branches through interest groups and other advocacy-related organizations, and (3) engaging in policy oversight.

The Congressional Black Caucus is only one of many actors involved in influencing U.S. foreign policy toward Africa and the Caribbean. However, the CBC is somewhat unique in that it can act, depending on the degree of unity within the CBC and the quality of leadership, as an institutionalized ethnic/racial lobby. The CBC then in turn tries to influence the Executive Branch through meetings with the President and his staff, interfaces with the U.S. State Department's Bureau of African Affairs, and also works with groups such as TransAfrica to bring attention to its issues of concern. Moreover, CBC members constituted one-third of the membership on the Africa Subcommittee within the 108th Congress International Relations Committee in the U.S. House of Representatives;[4] however, Representative Donald Payne

(D-NJ)[5] was the only CBC member also to serve on the Western Hemisphere subcommittee, where the Haitian crisis was discussed.

To argue that all African-Americans, elected or otherwise, are particularly focused on issues affecting the African continent or the Caribbean, is of course an unwarranted claim; however, historians have demonstrated that African-Americans including, but certainly not limited to: Booker T. Washington, W.E.B. DuBois, Marcus Garvey, Josephine Baker, Ralph Bunche and Reverend Jesse Jackson (Skinner 1992; Plummer 1996, Krenn 1998, Henry 2000) have sought to influence American foreign policy towards Africa as well as on numerous other issues, through formal and informal channels.

One cannot discount the historical linkages between African-Americans' problems here at home in the United States with their advocacy against racial oppression of blacks abroad. "The advocacy of black diaspora kinship by Du Bois, Garvey's 'Back-to-Africa' movement, and the civil rights and black power movements all attempted to connect the plight of all those of African descent, whether they be in North America, Africa, the Caribbean or elsewhere" (Scott and Osman 2002: 76). Historically, African-American scholars and diplomats sought often to influence U.S. policy toward Africa before embarking on their own civil rights struggle. They advocated better treatment for the indigenous people by the repressive Americo-Liberian oligarchy, opposed Mussolini's occupation of Ethiopia between 1936 and 1941, and condemned the inhumane treatment of blacks in South Africa (Adebajo 2004: 94). Moreover, African-American identification with Africa is fluid and can change based on political conditions, salience, and the ability of black leaders to rally black public opinion on the issue.

Despite the lack of an institutionalized lobbying apparatus within the Congress before the 1970s, it is readily apparent that African-Americans have through formal and informal outlets sought to influence U.S. foreign policy in many areas, but especially in regards to Africa. With the shift in the black electorate decisively to the Democratic Party by the 1960s, almost all subsequent elected African-Americans to Congress have been Democrats. With its motto "no permanent friends, no permanent enemies, only permanent interests," the Congressional Black Caucus was formally institutionalized in 1971, and the "dean" of the CBC was Representative Charles Diggs (D- MI), who became the first African-American to serve on the House Foreign Affairs Committee. Representative Diggs became Chairman of the House Subcommittee on Africa just as he and others were beginning to organize the CBC (Copson 2003).

> The caucus's emergence as a nationally known organization occurred at a time when the civil rights movement was in a period of decline. Leaders like Malcolm X and Martin Luther King, Jr. were dead, leaving a perceived leadership vacuum. Furthermore, the new emphasis was on electoral politics, and the caucus was seen as the epitome of black political accomplishment (Ross 1975: 36).

The CBC, with its initial thirteen members, gained national attention when it boycotted President Nixon's State of the Union address in January 1971 because the President refused Diggs's request to meet with the black members of Congress separately. Throughout its three decades of existence, the CBC has been vocal on both domestic and foreign policy matters. During the Cold War, the CBC was critical of American support of anti-communist African dictators, drew attention, along with numerous other organizations, to the repressive white minority governments in Rhodesia and South Africa, and lobbied for increased foreign aid to Africa. During the 1990s, the CBC voiced it concern over the Persian Gulf War, lobbied President Clinton to intervene in Haiti, and was instrumental in bringing the issues of debt relief to the attention of Congress.

Liberia

Of the three case studies discussed in this article, the United States has the most direct and special relationship with the small West African country of Liberia. Liberia was founded by freed slaves from the United States in 1820. These freed slaves, called Americo-Liberians, were encouraged to immigrate to Liberia by the American Colonization Society (ACS), an organization which did not necessarily have the best interests of the freed slaves at heart. Despite the intentions of the ACS, out of an estimated 3.3 million people in Liberia today, only 2.5 percent are descended from settlers dispatched by the ACS. Other countries did not recognize Liberia, and the U.S. failed to commit itself in any way to the country despite British consternation. Liberia's statement of independence in 1847 used language reminiscent of the American Declaration of Independence, and Liberia's flag even closely resembled America's. In 1862, a bill finally passed the Congress and was signed into law by President Lincoln recognizing Haiti and Liberia as sovereign countries (Skinner 1992: 52). Over the next century, Liberia was ruled by the Americo-Liberian oligarchy. Indigenous Liberians, approximating at least thirteen distinct ethno-linguistic groups, were largely kept from power which built hostility and resentment toward the seat of Americo-Liberian power in the capital of Monrovia. Thus, for 133 years of independence, the Republic of Liberia was a one-party state ruled by the Americo-Liberian True Whig Party. Liberia supported the U.S. in both WWI and WWII, served as a base of operation for Radio Free Europe, and supplied the U.S. with rubber supplies through the Firestone Company. During most of the Cold War, Liberia was an ally of the United States and received economic assistance from the U.S. for its loyalty.

Americo-Liberian domination ended in 1980 with a coup launched by Liberian Master Sergeant Samuel Doe, from the Krahn ethnic group. Doe's forces brutally executed President William Tolbert and several officials from his government. Some civilians broke into celebrations of what they perceived to be liberation from a century of the settler oligarchy, but ties with the U.S. were strained due to the coup. With Doe's banning of political parties in 1984 and the increasing militarization of life in Liberia, Doe's hold on power was tenuous at best. Then in 1989, a small band of rebels led by Charles Taylor, a former Doe loyalist, invaded Liberia from Côte d'Ivoire and sent the country into one of Africa's bloodiest civil wars from 1989-1996. Taylor's National Patriotic Front of Liberia (NPFL) captured and killed Doe in December 1990. By 1992, several warring factions had broken off from the NPFL, often according to ethnic affiliations. In the midst of the Liberian civil war, the civil war in Sierra Leone was also raging. The issue of "conflict or blood diamonds" became more important as Taylor helped expedite the transit of illegal diamonds. President Taylor has been indicted by the Special Court for Sierra Leone (SCSL) for war crimes and crimes against humanity, especially his financing of the Revolutionary United Front (RUF) which engaged in ghastly executions and amputations throughout Sierra Leone's civil war in the 1990s. The decade of the 1990s saw the destabilization of many West African countries including Sierra Leone, Côte d'Ivoire, Liberia, and Guinea. Moreover, the displacement of nationals from all countries and the porosity of borders contributed to the tremendous humanitarian toll.

In July 1997, Charles Taylor won the presidential elections in Liberia. Many observers could not understand why Liberians would vote overwhelmingly for the man who had caused so much misery in their lives. With an estimated 200,000 Liberians dead as a result of the civil war, the International Crisis Group (ICG) argued that Liberians feared Taylor would continue the civil war if he was not elected. Despite various U.N. Security Council resolutions and the creation of an International Contact Group of Liberia, the misery continued.

In 2003, however, the situation reached the breaking point. Elections were scheduled, but in the meantime two new rebel groups were attempting to take control of Monrovia. Liberians

United for Reconciliation and Democracy (LURD) was created in Freetown, Sierra Leone and operated out of the four countries all mired in conflict in West Africa. Movement for Democracy in Liberia (MODEL), whose formation was announced in March 2003 in Côte d'Ivoire, was composed of anti-Taylor fighters, refugees, and political asylum seekers. MODEL, according to the International Crisis Group, maintained much of its financing from the ethnic Krahn diaspora in the U.S. and was allied with Ivorian President Laurent Gbagbo.

The CBC, the Bush White House, and Liberia

As the LURD and MODEL moved closer to Monrovia, the CBC began to publicly comment on the deteriorating situation. Congressman Donald Payne (D-NJ) wrote a letter on July 2, 2003 to Secretary of State Powell stating the CBC's support for American intervention in Liberia. According to Payne, Liberians were in the streets waving American flags and asking President Bush and Secretary of State Powell to come to the country's aid. As the situation worsened in Liberia and Liberians took refuge at the U.S. embassy in Monrovia, President Bush was preparing for his first trip to Africa. In a press conference on July 3, 2003, National Security Advisor Dr. Rice was asked many questions relating specifically to Liberia. When pressed by a reporter on why the U.S. would not send a few thousand troops to Liberia when there were 140,000 troops in Iraq, Dr. Rice argued that the regional actors (in West Africa) had a stake in this process; however, post 9.11, the Bush Administration also recognized that "failed states" create conditions for terrorism to thrive. Dr. Rice called President Taylor "a menace to his own people," but she made no promise to commit even a few hundred U.S. troops.

A CNN/USA Today/Gallup poll conducted from 25-27 July 2003 assessed public sentiment regarding what Americans thought about potential U.S. involvement in Liberia through a peacekeeping force.[6] Approximately 60 percent of Americans favored the presence of U.S. ground troops (along with troops from other countries) in an international peacekeeping force and 30 percent opposed such involvement. Men were more likely than women to favor U.S. ground troop involvement and Republicans (68 percent) favored intervention over Democrats (60 percent).

Despite this moderate level of support, sentiment among the African-American community for U.S. military intervention in Liberia was not strong. African-Americans have historically been skeptical of military intervention by their country in the affairs of others, at least when compared to non-Black Americans. For example, a *New York Times* survey released on August 3, 2003, which asked whether the U.S. should try to change a dictatorship to democracy or stay out, found that 82 percent of African-American respondents wanted America to mind its own business as opposed to 58 percent of all others (Marquis 2003). In 2003, there was disagreement within the black community over what the U.S. should do, despite the fact that the CBC called on the Bush administration to act. For example, Bill Fletcher, President of the TransAfrica Forum said, "Our view is that the Liberian situation is part of a West African crisis and ultimately needs to be settled by West Africans."[7]

In various speeches, Congressman Payne outlined the long historical ties between the United States and Liberia and argued the U.S. had a moral duty to assist Liberia in the same manner Britain had intervened in Sierra Leone and France in Côte d'Ivoire. In the end, the CBC stated four main policy objectives in House Concurrent Resolution 240: (1) the U.S. should lead a multinational force to help stabilize Liberia; (2) Charles Taylor must step down immediately and unconditionally; (3) the capital of Monrovia must be stabilized and free and fair elections should be organized; and (4) there must be immediate delivery of humanitarian assistance.

By late July 2003, President Bush was calling for President Taylor to immediately step down, and on August 11, 2003, President Taylor left Liberia and was granted political asylum in Nigeria. Initially, the Economic Community of West African States (ECOWAS) again filled the power vacuum and deployed a new peacekeeping operation called the Economic Community in Liberia (ECOMIL). Out of the negotiations in Accra, Ghana, a National Transitional Government was inaugurated in October 2003, led by businessman Gyude Bryant. Also, the United Nations Mission in Liberia (UNMIL) was deployed in late 2003 and embarked upon the arduous mission of Disarmament, Demobilization, Rehabilitation, and Reintegration of the various warring factions. With unemployment around 75 percent, UNMIL faces a difficult mandate. However, presidential elections were successfully held in October 2005, and Liberia has elected Africa's first female head of state, Ellen Johnson-Sirleaf.

The CBC did not sponsor many resolutions pertaining to Liberia during the 108th Congress except for general resolutions condemning the situation in Liberia. While Africa Action, Trans-Africa, the NAACP, Rainbow PUSH, Union of Liberians Association in the Americas, and the Urban League all called for greater engagement in Liberia, the most public and vocal criticism of the Bush administration's policy came in the "U.S. Policy Toward Liberia" congressional hearing held on October 2, 2003.

Congressman Payne chastised the Bush administration for sending an assessment team that traveled like the "Love Boat as they slowly went around to Africa to get to Liberia and then as an old song said, they didn't sit on the dock of the bay, but they sat in their boats watching the tide roll away as this country was wreaked with so much havoc" (p. 8). Later in addressing his comments to Deputy Assistant Secretary for African Affairs at the Department of Defense (DOD) Theresa Whelan, Congressman Payne applauded the Department of State and Secretary Powell for his advocacy for intervention and then lambasted the DOD. Payne said, "I think it is absolutely disgraceful that Defense Secretary Rumsfeld continually argues against deploying a single person in Liberia, and it makes me feel that if it is a black person dying in Africa, Rumsfeld doesn't think they are worth our men on the ground" (p. 24). According to Payne's remarks, "In June 2003, 1,000 people alone died. I would have staked my career that not one shot would have been fired at a U.S. Marine. They (the Liberians) didn't even shoot at the Nigerians, and they don't even like them. They like us. And we stood around and let 1,000 people die while this great execution went on" (p. 25).

Later in the hearing, CBC member Congressman Gregory Meeks (D-NY) supported Payne's accusation that U.S. policy toward Liberia was blatantly racist. Congressman Meeks argued that it was beyond him why the U.S. could afford $87 billion to "rebuild a nation (referring to Iraq) that actually throughout history has not even made a fraction of the same contribution to America as those individuals from Liberia" (p. 27). Meeks asked rhetorically, "what is the true commitment of saving the lives of individuals who happen to be of color?" (p. 27).

In the end, the CBC's stated policy objectives were not met by the Bush administration. No substantial U.S. military presence was deployed, although the U.S. did provide logistical support to ECOMIL and funding for UNMIL. President Bush supported the transfer of Charles Taylor to stand trial before the Special Court in Sierra Leone, which did occur in early 2006. In the final analysis, however, the CBC was the most vocal constituency within the Congress pushing for U.S. military intervention in Liberia. The CBC also supported the transfer of President Taylor to the SCSL and argued that the failure to intervene even on a minimal basis was based on a racist foreign policy. Whether Liberia can stabilize after twenty-five years of chaos through the Doe and Taylor regimes remains to be seen, but in the post 9/11 environment, Liberia definitely fell way below the radar screen on the foreign policy agenda.

In regards to the aforementioned contextual factors, Liberia was viewed as a low U.S. national security threat despite occasional references to the fear that Liberia was becoming a failed state. Second, the breadth and depth of the constituency concerned about the deteriorating situation in Liberia was meager. Within Congress, very few members outside of the CBC articulated much of a concern about Liberia. In fact, House Concurrent Resolution 255, introduced by Representative Ron Paul (R-TX) expressed the view that the United States military should not become involved in the Liberian civil war, either alone or as part of a United Nations peacekeeping force. Moreover, although the CBC supported U.S. military intervention, public opinion was moderately in support if it was done through a U.N. operation; however, at least according to one survey, support among African-Americans for military intervention was very low. Third, the contextual factor of examining the history of African-American lobbying on behalf of Liberia was significant. African-Americans had lobbied on behalf of U.S. diplomatic recognition of Liberia, which did not happen until the Lincoln administration. While African-Americans had been critical of the operations of Firestone Company in Liberia as well as tepid support of Samuel Doe during the Reagan administration, the first two contextual factors seemed to outweigh the third.

Haiti

Haiti, a country of 8.1 million which shares the island of Hispaniola with its neighbor the Dominican Republic, is the poorest country in the Western Hemisphere. Haiti's independence from French control occurred in 1804 when the famous slave revolt, led by Toussaint L'Ouverture, defeated the army sent by Emperor Napoleon Bonaparate. Haiti, therefore, is the world's oldest black republic and the second oldest in the Western Hemisphere. Although Haiti actively assisted the independence movements in many Latin American countries, the independent country did not receive U.S. diplomatic recognition until 1862 for fear that slaves in the U.S. would be inspired by the Haitian revolt against a continental power.

With twenty-two changes of government from 1843 to 1915, Haiti experienced numerous periods of intense political and economic disorder, prompting the U.S. military intervention in 1915 and nineteen-year occupation until 1934. Haiti's instability continued with the brutal dictatorship of the Duvalier dynasty until 1986. After the Duvalier's departure, Haiti embarked on a constitution writing process which called for a French-style hybrid executive. In 1990, Jean-Bertrand Aristide, a charismatic Roman Catholic priest who had been outspoken against the Duvaliers, won 67 percent of the vote in a presidential election that international observers deemed largely absent of major irregularities. Aristide, however, was overthrown in a violent coup in September 1991. Following the coup, Aristide began a three year exile in the United States.

In the interim period, thousands of Haitians took to boats fleeing the political instability and violence in Haiti. During the 1992 presidential campaign, then candidate Bill Clinton called for a humane policy and castigated President George H.W. Bush for cordoning Haiti and using the Coast Guard to forcibly repatriate Haitian economic migrants/refugees. Members of the CBC and TransAfrica were openly critical of President Bush's policy, and were disheartened when President Clinton basically continued his predecessor's policies, albeit with some important modifications. Working through the United Nations and the Organization of American States (OAS), the Clinton administration secured approval of UNSC Resolution 940, which authorized member states to use all necessary means to facilitate the departure of the military government, led by Raoul Cedrás, and to restore Haiti's constitutionally elected government in power. The CBC was supportive of this initiative, as many members of the CBC were personally close to President Aristide.

In September 1994, a multinational force came ashore in Haiti hours after the Carter-Nunn-Powell negotiating team had secured the removal of Cedrás. Aristide returned in October 1994 and in 1995 a pro-Aristide, multi-party coalition called the Lavalas Political Organization swept into power at all levels. In 1995, the first full year after Aristide's return, Haiti received

$730 million from all international donors combined, a sum that represented more than ten percent of the country's GDP. Despite the initial interest from the international donor community, Aristide's term ended in 1996 and René Préval, a pro-Aristide political ally, became President. Parliamentary elections in May 2000 were mired in controversy, but the November 2000 presidential elections[8] brought Aristide back to power as President. Due to the irregularities in the 2000 parliamentary elections, Washington cut off direct aid to the Aristide government but continued to fund Haitian NGOs through USAID. Also, the European Union and other multilateral institutions, including the Inter-American Development Bank, froze funds in 2000.

Between 2000 and the 2004 departure of Aristide, the situation in Haiti continued to worsen. Aristide's political party, Famni Lavalas (LF) consolidated its power at all levels of government, and an organization of anti-Aristide factions coalesced into the Democratic Convergence. CBC members contend, however, that the American government, through the International Republican Institute, has funded and organized anti-Aristide opposition groups since his election win in 2000. As violence continued to worsen in Haiti, again the OAS tried to negotiate a solution to the political crisis. OAS Resolution 822, adopted in September 2002, called for a series of reforms and free and fair elections to be held in 2003. The opposition refused the entreaties of the OAS and Caribbean Community (CARICOM) and called for Aristide's complete removal from power. Political instability and violence continued throughout the summer and fall of 2003. Chiméres, unemployed urban youth who were hired thugs with little ideological commitment and few political objectives, continued to terrorize the Haitian population. Moreover, government-paid armed groups used violence to disperse a public meeting of the Group of 184, a loose alliance of anti-Aristide business and civic organizations, in Cité Soleil.

In January 2004, multilateral efforts continued to broker a solution to the increasing violence. CARICOM took the lead, but in the end the Democratic Platform, an alliance of the Democratic Convergence and Group of 184, rebuffed CARICOM's proposal which called for more power sharing and a new prime minister closer to the opposition. In February 2004, anti-Aristide forces continued their assault on the Haitian capital and Guy Philippe, a former police superintendent who fled to the Dominican Republic in 2000 after being accused of coup plotting, traveled to Goniaves and announced they were joining the armed uprising against Aristide.

The CBC, the Bush White House and Haiti

The relationship between the Bush White House and the CBC was rocky at best. The CBC was vocal in protesting the 2000 Florida recount debacle, rallied behind the president after 9.11, but then reverted to criticism of the war in Iraq and concomitant increases in defense spending. Africa and the Caribbean certainly took a back seat to the war on terrorism. In July 2003, CBC Chairman Elijah Cummings (D-MD) declined a meeting with President Bush to discuss his upcoming trip to Africa because Rep. Cummings wanted President Bush to meet with the CBC in its entirety.[9] Instead, a CBC Special Order speech was held on July 10, 2003 entitled "The Congressional Black Caucus on the State of Africa." While the main concern of the Special Order was the deteriorating situation in Liberia, the CBC clearly articulated its general concerns. CBC member Congresswoman Maxine Waters (D-CA) stated, "It seems to me that if the President is going to five African countries to talk to Africans about what is going on in Africa, he ought to talk to the descendants who are here in the U.S., who are just a few blocks away. I do not believe the President would travel to Israel and take actions on Israel without speaking to the Jewish members of Congress" (p. 36). Congresswoman Barbara Lee (D-CA) reiterated the sentiment by stating, "If it had not been for members of the CBC, there would be no foreign policy as it relates to Africa" (p. 40).

Moreover, during the 108th Congress, a CBC member sponsored eight resolutions on Haiti, and CBC members comprised 50 percent or more of the total co-sponsors on eight out of the eleven U.S. House resolutions pertaining directly to Haiti. The legislation and resolutions mainly addressed the bleak economic and social conditions in Haiti. For example, H.R. 1108 (Access to Capital for Haiti's Development Act) called for the immediate resumption of lending to Haiti through the Inter-American Development Bank, which had been suspended since the 2000 elections. Other legislation called for the establishment of a comprehensive health infrastructure, especially to fight HIV/AIDS, (H.R. 3386) or simply congratulated Haiti on its bicentennial of independence (H.R. 471). Representative Kendrick Meek (D-FL), who represents the largest Haitian constituency in the United States, met with forty Haitian and community leaders in early 2004 and petitioned the Bush administration to grant all Haitians fleeing the violence in the country Temporary Protected Status (H.R. 3867).

In the last two weeks of February 2004, the CBC's involvement increased. On February 19, 2004, the CBC sent a letter to President Bush urging U.S. intervention in Haiti. Then, in a CBC Special Order speech called "Haiti: A Nation in Crisis," CBC Chairman Cummings reported on the CBC's meeting with President Bush, NSA Rice, and Secretary of State Powell on February 25, 2004. Initially, only Rice and Powell received the CBC at the White House; however, the CBC refused to leave until they were granted an audience with President Bush. Within twenty minutes, President Bush appeared. According to Congressman Meek (D-FL), he said the following to President Bush: "If we are in Iraq justifying our presence of being there, of saying that we stand for democracy and we stand for the lives of the Iraqi people, then definitely 650 miles off the coast of the continental U.S., we should stand up for a democracy."[10] The CBC's stated policy preferences, four days before Aristide's departure, were: (1) the establishment of a humanitarian corridor, (2) sending 300-400 U.S. marines to maintain the peace, and (3) assurance of President Aristide's safety.

The events of February 28-29, 2004 are still hotly disputed. On the night of February 29, President Aristide and his family boarded a U.S. chartered plane after Aristide submitted a concise resignation letter. The plane carrying Aristide eventually landed in the Central African Republic, and finally South Africa granted Aristide asylum in June 2004. The CBC's mild criticism of the Bush administration's policy toward Haiti turned to strong rebuke during "The Situation in Haiti" hearings held on March 3, 2004. To characterize this hearing as contentious is a serious understatement. All most all members of the CBC attended the hearing and spoke on record. Opening the hearing, Chairman Cass Ballenger (R-NC) stated the consensus view among House Republicans,

> There have been accusations that officials of the U.S. government have committed a felony punishable by death and that is kidnapping. The head of the Steele Foundation, which was responsible for President Aristide's security, told me personally that if U.S. forces or other forces had tried to kidnap or harm President Aristide, his men had orders to resist and were authorized to use lethal force, if necessary. The accusation that President Aristide was kidnapped is clearly false (p. 2)

On the other side of the aisle, Representative Robert Menedez (D-NJ), a non-CBC member and ranking member of the House Subcommittee on the Western Hemisphere, responded with the consensus view among liberal Democrats and all CBC members,

> The people of this hemisphere watched this Administration turn its back and walk out on a democratically elected President. President Aristide was confronting a violent, step-by-step takeover of his country by rebel leaders and not simply protests in the street. They watched and they got clear messages that this Administration sent. This Administration will not stand up for a democratically elected Head of State they do not like and this Administration will stand idly by as rebels, thugs, and prisoners topple a democratically elected government (p. 3)

The most embattled witness before the hearing was Roger Noriega, former Assistant Secretary of State, Bureau of Western Hemisphere. The exchanges between CBC members and Mr. Noriega were hostile. For example, CBC member Congresswoman Barbara Lee (D-CA) asked Noriega, "When did you decide that Mr. Aristide had to go and what did you do to make sure that happened?" (p. 44). Congressman Charles Rangel (D-NY), a long-time CBC member, then asked Mr. Noriega if the U.S. forced Aristide's departure by implying indirectly or even directly that the U.S. would not protect Aristide and his family, who were holed up in the presidential palace in Port-au-Prince, unless he submitted his resignation. Noriega denied this accusation by Representative Rangel and argued that Aristide voluntarily resigned to save the country from more violence. CBC member Congresswoman Maxine Waters (D-CA) stated that she had spoken with President Aristide on the morning of March 3, 2004, and Aristide directly communicated to her that he was kidnapped (p. 51). CBC member Congresswoman Sheila Jackson-Lee (D-TX) raised the question of CIA involvement, and Congresswoman Corrine Brown (D-FL) proceeded to argue that the Administration's policy in Haiti is racist because Iraq has oil and Haiti does not (p. 57). Finally, a non-CBC member, Congresswoman Jan Schakowsky (D-IL) said,

> Let me just say it is obvious, Mr. Noriega, that you think that the very distinguished CBC, members of Congress, who, in my view, have the most expertise and the most interest in Haiti, not only for President Aristide, but for the people of Haiti, are all wrong. And it seems to me that would justify a full and objective investigation of what exactly happened (p. 62).

Other hearing witnesses concurred, to a degree, with the CBC's accusations against the Bush administration. Observers of U.S. policy towards Haiti have stated that it is extremely partisan in nature (Erikson 2005), and the Congressional testimony confirms that judgment. It is also important to note Congresswoman Lee introduced H.R. 3919[11] on March 9, 2004, which called for the establishment of the "Independent Commission of the 2004 Coup d'Etat in the Republic of Haiti." The commission would have subpoena power, a $5 million budget, staffers, and the purview to examine the role the CIA, the International Republican Institute, the National Democratic Institute for International Affairs, and other organizations funded by USAID played in undermining and/or overthrowing President Aristide.

After Aristide

In the evening of February 29, 2004 as President Aristide and his family left on a plane chartered by the U.S., the United Nations Security Council in an emergency session, passed Resolution 1529 which authorized the deployment of a U.S.-led Multinational Interim force to be replaced in ninety days by a U.N. stabilization force (Erikson 2005: 88). The Interim Force was supported by U.S., Canadian, and French troops but in the end the Brazilians have led the MINUSTAH (UN Stabilization Mission in Haiti). A transitional government, largely comprised of technocrats, was sworn in on March 17, 2004. The transitional Prime Minister Gerard Latortue, who lived abroad for more than thirty years, appeared to have the support of the international community. The CBC met with Prime Minister Latortue, and the Bush administration organized a donor conference in July 2004 for Haiti. However, hurricanes in 2004 created a massive humanitarian crisis for an already traumatized country. Legislative elections were held in October and November 2005 with a high degree of international scrutiny. In early 2006, former President René Préval has been elected once again to serve as President, and there is speculation that Aristide may return from exile.

As of this writing, the CBC, most African-American newspapers, and TransAfrica maintain that President Aristide was forced out by the Bush administration. Even the OAS remains extremely critical and passed a resolution in June 2004 calling for an investigation into the circumstances surrounding Aristide's exile. Some CBC members have a close personal friendship with Aristide and his family, while other CBC members are more concerned about the plight of the Western Hemisphere's poorest country. The stated objectives of the CBC regarding its preferences for White House policy during the February-March 2004 crisis were largely unmet. President Bush did meet with the CBC, though, on the February 25, 2004, which appears to indicate the CBC did have some legitimacy on the Haiti crisis. The U.S. has not played a significant role in MINUSTAH; however, Secretary of State Powell did travel to Haiti in December 2004 and FY 2005 financial assistance for Haiti was $200 million.

In relation to the contextual factors, Haiti was again an issue of low national security concern. Second, the breadth and depth of the constituency within and outside of Congress in relation to Haiti was more robust than the case of Liberia; however, the ability of CBC members to encourage more support within Congress was lacking. Outside of Congress, lobbying organizations such as the NAACP and TransAfrica did support U.S. military intervention, but the ability to appeal to more conservative-minded organizations to pressure the Bush administration to respond with military intervention was limited. Third, although the historical record of lobbying on behalf of Haiti is extensive, again it appears that the first two contextual factors, as in the case of Liberia, outweighed the third.

Sudan

Even though the United States does not have the same historical connection with Sudan as is the case with Liberia and Sudan, the misery of Sudan since its independence in the 1950s, has been of concern to the United States. In September 2001, former Senator John Danforth was designated Presidential Envoy for Peace in Sudan. Danforth's role was to explore the role the U.S. could play in searching for an end to Sudan's civil war, which has now claimed approximately 2 million lives and finally end the humanitarian catastrophe. It is important to note that well before Secretary of State Colin Powell's September 2004 declaration that genocide was taking place in Darfur, members of the House of Representatives, including CBC members, were already calling the Khartoum government a genocidal regime.

In a 2001 Congressional hearing called "America's Sudan Policy: A New Direction?" CBC member Congressman Payne talked about his trips to Sudan in the 1990s with various elected officials, including non-CBC members, and stated unequivocally that the Khartoum regime could not be trusted. Moreover, the U.S. Commission on International Religious Freedom found in May 2000 the government of Sudan to be the world's most violent abuser of the right to freedom of religion and belief and stated that the Government of Sudan (GOS) was committing genocidal atrocities against civilian populations in the southern part of the country. The 2001 hearing focused on how the GOS was obstructing the ability to deliver humanitarian supplies through Operational Lifeline Sudan, which was launched in 1989, and what types of policies could be employed to discourage foreign countries from doing business in Sudan for lucrative oil contracts. Similar to the campaign against the apartheid government in South Africa, African-American leaders have been arrested before the Sudanese Embassy in Washington, DC.

In July 2002, the GOS and the Sudanese People's Liberation Movement/Army (SPLM/A) reached an historic agreement (the Machakos Protocol) regarding the role of state and the right of southern Sudan to vote on possible secession after a six-year interim period. In October 2002, President Bush signed into law H.R. 5531, (the Sudan Peace Act).[12] The act, according to the U.S. State Department, calls for continued U.S. engagement in the peace talks between the GOS and SPLM through Senator Danforth's efforts and appropriated $100 million in FY 2003-2005 for assistance to areas outside governmental control. The Sudan Peace Act required that the President certify every six months from the date of enactment that the GOS and the SPLM were negotiating in good faith and that the negotiations should continue. If the President determined that the GOS was not negotiating in good faith, then the U.S. may seek to: pass a UNSC Resolution for an arms embargo against the Sudanese government, instruct all U.S. executive directors to vote against and actively oppose loans and credits by international financial institutions, and deny the GOS access to oil revenues to ensure the funds are not used for military purposes. Finally, the legislation also required the Secretary of State to collect information about incidents which may constitute war crimes, crimes against humanity, and genocide.

The CBC, the Bush White House and Sudan

Out of the three case studies examined for this article, the CBC and the Bush White House were most in agreement regarding policy towards Sudan. The main reason for this agreement was due to the widespread condemnation on both sides of the aisle regarding the actions of the Sudanese government as the situation in Darfur worsened during the 108th Congress.

Despite the progress of the Machakos Protocol, violence in the western part of Sudan began to intensify in early 2003. The first attacks were initiated by a newly formed insurgent organization, the Sudan Liberation Movement/Army (SLM/A), followed a few weeks later by a second new group called the Justice and Equality Movement (JEM) (Kasfir 2005). After executing attacks on military planes and government soldiers, the GOS in return unleashed the notorious Janjaweed. The Janjaweed came from mostly previously existing nomadic tribal militias of Arab background. In the mainstream press, the situation in Darfur has often been presented as Muslim vs. Christians or animists, but this is not factually accurate. While some groups of the American "religious right" did become engaged in the Sudanese issue due to the North/South civil war and the modern-day slavery issues where Arabs kidnap and enslave black Sudanese, the civilians who have been killed, raped, and pillaged in Darfur are mainly black Muslims while the Janjaweed are Arab Muslims. As Kasir (2005) and the International Crisis Group note, it is difficult to isolate the GOS's motives with the Darfur crisis. For the SLM/A and JEM, the fact that the GOS is negotiating with the SPLM/A is proof enough that they must form a serious rebel movement to make the GOS listen to their demands. With the world focused on the war in Iraq in 2003, Darfur received little coverage; however, the coverage intensified in 2004 as the refugees from Darfur spilled over into neighboring Chad, and organizations such as Doctors Without Borders, Oxfam, and various U.N. agencies issued alarming reports about the world's worst humanitarian catastrophe.

Congress also reacted to the Darfur crisis. Even though the Bush administration has been somewhat mollified by the Sudanese government's agreement to assist the U.S. in the war on terror, several congressional hearings were held on the topic of Sudan during the 108th Congress. In April 2003, President Bush sent his determination to Congress that in accordance with the terms set forth in the 2002 Sudan Peace Act, both parties (the GOS and SPLM/A) were negotiating in good faith and the U.S. must remain engaged with its troika partners (Britain and Norway) under the leadership of Kenyan General Sumbeiywo. Also in April 2003, H.R. 194[13] was introduced which called for the end to slavery and other human rights abuses in Sudan. In March 2004, the Subcommittee on Africa held a hearing entitled "Sudan: Peace Agreement Around the Corner?" and in June 2004 Secretary Powell traveled to Sudan and visited Darfur.

The Africa subcommittee Chairman Ed Royce (R-CA) began the hearing by commending Rep. Donald Payne for his tireless work on trying to bring peace to Sudan. The hearings on Sudan were characterized by extensive bipartisanship unlike the congressional hearings held on Haiti and to an extent even Liberia during the 108th Congress. Congressman Payne did not ask whether "black lives" were worth less than "white lives" as he and other CBC members did during the hearings on Haiti and Liberia. During the hearings, there was unanimous condemnation among Republicans and Democrats on the genocidal nature of the Sudanese government. Even the legislation introduced on Sudan has had non-CBC members as the main sponsors, unlike the Haiti legislation introduced in the 108th Congress. For example, House Concurrent Resolution 402 was co-sponsored by Representatives Tancredo (R-CO) and Donald Payne (D-NJ) and called for war crimes and crimes against humanity investigations against particular Sudanese officials, including the First Vice President, Ali Osman Mohammed Taha.

In April 2004, House Concurrent Resolution 403 was sponsored by non-CBC member Frank Wolf (R-VA). This resolution unequivocally condemned the GOS for its attacks against the civilians of Darfur. Probably most important to the spotlight placed on Darfur during the spring of 2004 was the tenth anniversary of the Rwandan genocide. In fact, a hearing was held entitled "Rwanda's Genocide: Looking Back." Congressman Payne began the hearing by expressing his outrage that the U.N. Human Rights Commission would not pass a resolution condemning the GOS and that African countries will not take a stronger stand on the issue in Sudan. Payne asked rhetorically, "One of the supposedly outstanding leaders in Africa is Thabo Mbeki. How can they sit by and actually watch this happen in Darfur when the whole world community fought to end apartheid in South Africa?" (p. 8).

The momentum on Darfur continued with a CBC Special Order speech on May 13, 2004. CBC members Payne, Cummings, Jackson-Lee and others unequivocally condemned the situation in Sudan, but again Congressman Payne alluded to the bipartisan nature of the issue and particularly thanked conservative politicians, including Representatives Tom Tancredo (R-CO) and Chris Smith (R-NJ) and Senators Brownback (R-KS) and Bill Frist (R-TN) for their leadership on the issue. The bipartisan support displayed in Congress on Darfur is even partially reflected in a July 2004 poll, conducted by the Program on International Policy Attitudes. A majority of Republicans and Democrats supported a U.N. military force to stop the killing in Darfur, although Republicans were less supportive of contributing U.S. troops (54 percent) than Democrats (64 percent).[14] In June 2004, leading members of the CBC joined the advocacy group Africa Action for a press conference on Capitol Hill where they called attention to the genocide taking place in Darfur and urged the U.S. to lead an immediate intervention to stop the killing. In late July 2004, House Concurrent Resolution 467, sponsored by Congressman Payne, declared that genocide is occurring in Sudan and urged the Bush Administration to "seriously consider multilateral or even unilateral intervention to stop genocide in Darfur, should the UN Security Council fail to act."

During the fall of 2004 and amidst the presidential election cycle, protestors continued to flood the steps of the Sudanese embassy in Washington, DC, a one-day vigil was held as part of a national day of conscience by the Save Darfur Coalition, the Holocaust Museum in Washington, DC stepped up its efforts to draw attention to the genocide in Darfur, city councils throughout the country began passing resolutions condemning the Darfur crisis and calling for divestment from public pension funds, and other groups such as the NAACP called for massive intervention in Sudan. Even Presidential candidate Senator John Kerry remarked at the CBC Foundation's Legislative Conference held in September 2004 that he would act now in Darfur if elected.

In October 2004, non-CBC member Rep. Tancredo introduced H.R. 5061 (Comprehensive Peace in Sudan Act of 2004). This resolution, with a companion Senate resolution, became law in December 2004 and called for the extension of the terms of the Sudan Peace Act of 2002 to the Darfur crisis. Throughout the ongoing negotiations to end the North/South civil war, the GOS declined to include discussions about the situation in Darfur. According to H.R. 5061, the GOS must demonstrate it is making real efforts to stop the Janjaweed militias, permit humanitarian assistance to Darfur, and permit the return of internally displaced persons and refugees.

Peace at Last?

In January 2005, the Comprehensive Peace Agreement was signed by the GOS and the SPLM. The Africa Union Mission in Sudan (AMIS) deployed a few thousand troops on the ground in early 2005, but the International Crisis Group has argued it is not enough. Rapes, looting, destruction of livestock, and aerial bombardment continued throughout 2005-2006 in Darfur.[15] In March 2005, UNSC Resolution 1590 was passed which established the United Nations Mission in Sudan (UNMIS) to include 10,000 military personnel and 715 police personnel. However, UNMIS's main goal is to support the implementation of the 2005 Comprehensive Peace agreement in southern Sudan; its current mandate does not extend to Darfur.

In March 2005, Representative Payne sponsored H.R. 1424 (Darfur Genocide Account-ability Act of 2005), which permits the U.S. government to: (1) prohibit visas for civil and military officials of the GOS and militia members implicated in the Darfur atrocities; (2) enforces strict sanctions on Sudan; (3) prohibits any entity engaged in commercial activ-ity in Sudan from raising capital in the U.S.; and (4) authorizes the President to stop the genocide in Darfur through the establishment of a no-fly zone and use of unmanned armed planes. In July 2005, NATO began ferrying troops from African countries to Darfur to increase the effectiveness of UNMIS.[16] Moreover, the SLA and the JEM signed a declara-tion of political principles with the GOS outlining a long-term solution to the Darfur crisis in July 2005. With almost 200,000 dead and two million displaced as a result of the Darfur crisis, the ICG argues that at least 15,000 troops are needed immediately compared to the approximately 7,700 which hope to be deployed by the end of September 2005. On July 9, 2005, in an elaborate ceremony in Khartoum, Sudanese President Bashir appointed Dr. Garang his top deputy; however, in late July 2005 Dr. Garang died in a plane crash on a return trip from Uganda. With the death of Garang, the fate of the peace process hangs precariously in the balance.

As far as analyzing the efficacy of the CBC in this issue area, a few generalizations are warranted about the contextual factors. First, the national security interest factor of Sudan was important to the United States. Even before September 11, 2001, the U.S. had been highly concerned about the Sudanese government's support for global terrorism. This concern became even more heightened after 9/11. The ongoing civil war between northern and southern Sudan, while not immediately linked to terrorism, was increasingly making Sudan a failed state. Sec-ond, the constituency within and outside of Congress was diverse in breadth and depth. Out of the three case studies examined for this article, bipartisan support condemning the Khartoum government was overwhelming. The most conservative of Republicans and most liberal of Democrats coalesced in a "strange bedfellows" coalition to introduce legislation on Sudan in the 108th Congress. Moreover, the CBC was able to find support across the aisle. In a number of speeches, the CBC's main voice on affairs in Africa, Donald Payne, spoke about how grateful he was to his Republican colleagues for their support. The third contextual factor, the history of African-American lobbying on behalf of Sudan was not a significant factor in this case. In comparison to Haiti and Liberia, historically there has not been a significant African-American lobbying initiative within Congress or outside of Congress on Sudan; however, African-American newspapers and elected officials have become increasingly more vocal about the slavery issue in Sudan. It is important to note, that many white Christian conservative groups throughout the 1990s had been portraying the Sudan civil war as a conflict between Arab Muslims and black Christians and animists in the South. Finally legislation, congressional hearings, press releases, and secondary sources consulted demonstrated robust bipartisan and cross-racial support on Sudan as compared to Liberia or Haiti.

Analysis

Over the course of the 108th Congress, the Congressional Black Caucus was active in attempting to influence the Bush Administration's policy towards Liberia, Haiti, and Sudan. Measuring the efficacy of the CBC's efforts is a difficult endeavor; however, in this article, I have examined the CBC's policy preferences in the three case studies and then examined how the Bush administration ultimately responded.

In the case of Liberia, the CBC lobbied for U.S. military intervention in the summer of 2003; however, the Bush administration never sent more than a few hundred U.S. marines to Liberia. The CBC and the Bush administration both called for President Taylor to step down from power. Public opinion moderately supported U.S. military intervention in Liberia, albeit through a U.N. mission with U.N. Security Council authorization. However, African-Americans, at least according to one public opinion poll, were less supportive of U.S. military intervention than white Americans.

In the case of Haiti, the distance between the CBC's stated policy preferences and the Bush administration's response was the most pronounced. First, the CBC argued that the Bush administration had covertly or overtly participated in a coup to overthrow President Aristide. Second, the CBC has routinely argued that U.S. policy toward Haiti and Haitian refugees/migrants is racist. Third, the CBC was in favor of U.S. military intervention in Haiti, which did not happen on a large-scale. Finally, CBC members were the main sponsors of legislation directly pertaining to Haiti during the 108th Congress.

In the case of Sudan, there appears to be the most agreement between the CBC and the Bush administration's actions on the Darfur crisis which worsened during the 108th Congress. The CBC argued for robust sanctions against the Khartoum regime and perhaps even military intervention to stop the genocide. At the time of this writing, the U.S. has not deployed any ground troops to Sudan, nor is a no-fly zone being enforced in Darfur; however, the U.S. is helping to transport African troops, under NATO auspices, to Darfur in order to increase the AMIS force capacity. Furthermore, the voices lobbying the Bush administration on Sudan have been more diverse than was the case for Haiti and even Liberia. In fact, while CBC member Congressman Donald Payne has been instrumental in the Sudan issue over the past decade, white members of Congress including Tom Tancredo (R-CO) and Chris Smith (R-NJ) have been very vocal as well. The Sudanese issue has engendered a great deal of bipartisan support in the Congress, unlike the Haiti situation in 2004. The tone of congressional hearings held on Haiti was extremely partisan, whereas the hearings held on Sudan were much more bipartisan.

Some would argue that the CBC's access and ability to influence foreign policy might increase when the Democratic Party controls the White House, since all the members of the 108th CBC were Democrats. However, the more immediate factors which may influence the CBC's access and influence are: the nature of the issue itself, the breadth and depth of the constituency that cares about the issue, and the history of African-American influence in lobbying on behalf of the issue. First, in the cases of Haiti and Liberia, direct U.S. national security interests were not at stake despite the attention now paid to "failed states" becoming havens for terrorists. Sudan, on the other hand, has been prominent on the Bush administration's agenda for its role as a state sponsor of terrorism, which facilitated more interest in the issue within and outside of Congress. Second, the breadth and depth of the constituency was much more bipartisan inside and outside of Congress on the issue of Sudan as opposed to Haiti and Liberia. Without a doubt, the most partisanship was displayed in the Haiti case; moreover, military intervention did not attract any support across the aisle from Republicans in Congress. For that matter, white liberal Democrats were not particularly vocal on the Liberia situation either. In contrast, the Sudan issue elicited a great deal of bipartisan support within both chambers of Congress, including from the leadership. Moreover, Christian conservatives outside of Congress already had established a significant lobbying force on Sudan prior to the situation becoming worse in Darfur in 2003-2004. Third, the history of African-American lobbying on these issues would have seemed to work in favor of Haiti and Liberia as opposed to Sudan. Even well before the CBC's formation, African-Americans have focused a great deal of effort on shaping American foreign policy towards these two countries with special links to the United States. In CBC Special Order speeches, CBC members often alluded to the historical linkages shared with these two countries. On the other hand, there has not been as significant of a record of African-American lobbying outside or inside Congress on Sudan. Of course, TransAfrica and Congressman Donald Payne (D-NJ) have been criticizing the government in Khartoum since the early 1990s, but Sudan has not carried the same symbolic significance for African-Americans as compared to Haiti and Liberia. However, in this analysis, Sudan did have the other two contextual factors in its favor—the country was of concern for U.S. national security interests and there was a broad and deep bipartisan constituency committed to Sudan inside and outside of Congress.

Conclusion

Over the course of the 108th Congress, the Congressional Black Caucus was active in attempting to influence the Bush Administration's policy towards Liberia, Haiti, and Sudan. Measuring the "success" of the CBC's efforts is a difficult endeavor; however, I have delineated the CBC's stated policy preferences in the three case studies and then examined how the Bush administration ultimately responded. History has demonstrated that African-Americans have played a vital role in articulating policy preferences on various foreign policy issues. Over the past three decades, the CBC has been one actor participating in this process with varying degrees of success. However, in order to gain a more accurate representation of the foreign policy making process, I fully recognize other players in the policy process need to be addressed in future research including, the African Affairs Bureau at the U.S. State Department, other African-American lobbying organizations, and even the Department of Defense. Moreover, I look forward to conducting personal interviews with members of the Congressional Black Caucus who have a long institutional memory of working on issues affecting Africa and the Caribbean.

Notes

1. It is difficult to operationalize the dependent variable "success." One could examine the ability of the CBC to get its preferences incorporated in mark-ups of legislation, for example. However, all the bills introduced the CBC regarding Haiti and Liberia died in committee. Therefore, one cannot examine mark-up sessions of these bills or voting behavior of CBC members. It is important to keep in mind, however, that almost 90 percent of all legislation introduced in Congress dies in committee.
2. Most scholars who examine critical mass arguments for minorities (racial and gender) use a 30 percent threshold for critical mass. African-American members of Congress comprise almost 11 percent of the total members of Congress (combining the U.S. Senate and House of Representatives).
3. These three case studies were selected for their importance to the CBC during the 108th Congress as well media coverage. Eventually, the White House would have to articulate its policy on all three of these case studies as well.
4. The Africa Subcommittee had nine members. They were: Edward Royce (Chairman), Amo Houghton, Thomas Tancredo, Jeff Flake, Mark Green, Donald Payne, Gregory Meeks, Barbara Lee, and Betty McCollum. In the 109th Congress, the Africa Subcommittee has been renamed the Subcommittee on Africa, Global Human Rights, and International Operations.
5. Congressman Payne was first elected in 1988 as New Jersey's first African American Congressman. Representative Payne is a CBC member who has been particularly active in foreign policy toward Africa and has visited numerous countries on fact-finding missions.

6. "Should the US Keep the Peace in Liberia?" Released by the Gallup Organization on August 5, 2003.
7. Black intellectuals and activists cite several reasons for their reluctance to commit troops. African-Americans, they note, are a disproportionately large group within the armed forces. Nearly 20 percent of active service members are black, while blacks make up about 13 percent of the overall population. Suspicion about the true intentions of the American government is another motivator.
8. All major opposition parties boycotted the elections for president and nine Senate seats. Aristide ran for the presidency against three virtual unknowns, winning 92 percent of the vote. Turnout for the election was estimated at 5-10 percent (ICG, "A New Chance for Haiti").
9. President Bush met with the CBC in January 2001, February 2004 to discuss Haiti, and January 2005. The CBC in the 108th Congress was thirty-nine members. The CBC in the 109th Congress is forty-three members (all Democrats, and now including Senator Barack Obama (D-IL).
10. Special Order on Haiti, "A Nation in Crisis," February 25, 2004.
11. Also H.R. 946 in the 109th Congress has been introduced by Congresswoman Lee with the verbatim language as H.R. 3919.
12. The main sponsor of this legislation was Tom Tancredo (R-CO). Other CBC members which co-sponsored the legislation were Barbara Lee (D-CA), Donald Payne (D-NJ), and Chaka Fattah (D-PA). The Act was passed in the US House of Representatives on October 7, 2002 by a vote of 359-8. The Senate passed the same language by unanimous consent on October 8, 2002.
13. H.R. 194 was sponsored by Rep. Michael Capuano (D-MA), a non-CBC member but CBC co-sponsors included Representatives Payne and Rangel.
14. See "Americans on the Crisis in Sudan." The Program on International Policy Attitudes. July 20, 2004.
15. See ICG Report, "Darfur: The Failure to Protect," March 8, 2005.
16. A new bill H.R. 3127 was sponsored by Rep. Tancredo in June 2005 and is similar to Payne's H.R. 1424, except for more robust language authorizing the president with broad flexibility to reinforce the AMIS mission in Darfur and leaves open the option of a NATO bridging force and a no-fly zone should the AMIS fail to stop the genocide in Darfur.

References

Adebajo, Adekeye. 2004. "Africa, African Americans and the Avuncular Sam." *Africa Today*, 50, 3: 92-110.

Ambrosio. Thomas. 2002. "Legitimate Influence or Parochial Capture? Conclusions on Ethnic Identity Groups and the Formulation of U.S. Foreign Policy." In T. Ambrosio (Ed). *Ethnic Identity Groups and US Foreign Policy*, p. 199-216. Westport: Praeger.

America's Sudan Policy: A New Direction? Joint Hearing before the Subcommittee on Africa and Subcommittee on International Operations and Human Rights of the Committee on International Relations. U.S. House of Representatives, 107th Congress, First Session, March 28, 2001. Retrieved online at http://commdocs.house.gov on February 28, 2005.

Barnett, Marguerite Ross. 1975. "The Congressional Black Caucus." *Proceedings of the American Academy of Political Science*, 32, 1: 34-50.

Bositis, David A. 1993. *The Congressional Black Caucus in the 103rd Congress*. Washington, DC: Joint Center for Political and Economic Studies.

CBC Chairman Comments on Meetings Today with Interim Haitian Prime Minister Latortue and US Secretary of State Powell. May 5, 2004. Press Release from CBC Chairman Elijah Cumming. Retrieved online at www.house.gov/cummings.

CBC Special Order on Helping the People of Haiti. U.S House of Representatives, April 30, 2003. Floor speech retrieved online at http://www.house.gov/cummings on February 28, 2005.

CBC Special Order on the Future of Africa. U.S. House of Representatives, July 8, Floor speech retrieved online at http://www.house.gov/cummings on February 28, 2005.

CBC Special Order on Haiti: A Nation in Crisis. U.S. House of Representatives, February 25, 2004. Floor speech retrieved online at http://www.house.gov/cummings on February 28, 2005.

CBC Special Order on Sudan. U.S. House of Representatives, May 13, 2004. Floor speech retrieved online at http://www.house.gov/cummings on February 28, 2005.

Copson, Raymond W. 2003. *The Congressional Black Caucus and Foreign Policy (1971- 2002)*. New York: Novinka Books.

Darfur: The Failure to Protect. International Crisis Group, Africa Report. No. 89 Released March 8, 2005. Retrieved online at www.crisisweb.org.

Do Americans Care About Darfur? International Crisis Group/Zogby International Opinion Survey., Africa Briefing, No. 26. Released on June 1, 2005. Retrieved online at   www.crisisweb.org.

Dr. Condoleezza Rice Discusses the President's Trip to Africa. July 3, 2003. Press Briefing on July 3, 2003. Retrieved online at www.state.gov on May 30, 2005.

Erikson, Daniel P. February 2005. "Haiti After Aristide: Still on the Brink." *Current History*, p. 83-90.

Giles, Roxanne and Charles E. Jones. 1995. "Congressional Racial Solidarity: Exploring Congressional Black Caucus Voting Cohesion, 1971-1990." *Journal of Black Studies*, 25, 5: 622-641.

Haiti's Transition: Hanging in the Balance. International Crisis Group, Latin American/Caribbean Briefing, No. 7. Released on February 8, 2005. Retrieved online at www.crisisweb.org.

Henry, Charles P., (ed.) 2000. *Foreign Policy and the Black International Interest.* New York: State University of New York Press.

Kasfir, Nelson. May 2005. "Sudan's Darfur: Is it Genocide?" *Current History*, p. 195-202.

Krenn, Michael. 1998. *The African American Voice in U.S. Foreign Policy since WWII.* New York: Garland Publishing, Inc.

Liberia Unravelling. International Crisis Group, Africa Briefing. Released on August 19, 2002. Retrieved online at www.crisisweb.org.

Marquis, Christopher. August 3, 2003. "Blacks Counsel Caution on Liberia." *New York Times*. Retrieved online at www.nytimes.com on May 15, 2004.

A New Chance for Haiti. International Crisis Group, Latin American/Caribbean Report, No. 10. Released on November 18, 2004. Retrieved online at www.crisisweb.org.

A New Sudan Action Plan. International Crisis Group. Policy Briefing, Africa, No. 24. Released on April 26, 2005. Retrieved online at www.crisisweb.org.

Payne, Richard J. and Eddie Ganaway. 1980. "The Influence of Black Americans on U.S. Policy toward Southern Africa." *African Affairs*, 79, 317: 585-598.

Pinney, Neil and George Serra. 1999. "The Congressional Black Caucus and Vote Cohesion: Placing the Caucus within House Voting Patterns." *Political Research Quarterly*, 52, 3: 583-608.

Plummer, Brenda. 1996. *Rising Wind: Black Americans and U.S. Foreign Affairs, 1935-1960.* Chapel Hill, NC: University of North Carolina Press.

President Bush Meets with Congressional Black Caucus to Discuss the Political Situation in Haiti. February 26, 2004. Transcript retrieved online from www.lexis-nexis.com on August 31, 2004.

Rebuilding Liberia. International Crisis Group. Africa Report, No. 75. Released on January 30, 2004. Retrieved online at www.crisisweb.org.

Reviewing the Sudan Peace Act Report. Hearing before the Subcommittee on Africa of the Committee on International Relations. U.S. House of Representatives, 108th Congress, First Session, May 13, 2003. Retrieved online at http://commdocs.house.gov on February 28, 2005.

Rwanda's Genocide: Looking Back. Hearing before the Subcommittee on Africa of the   Committee on International Relations. U.S. House of Representatives, 108th Congress, Second Session, April 22, 2004. Retrieved online at http://commdocs.house.gov on February 28, 2005.

Said, Abdul Aziz, 1981. "A Redefinition of National Interest, Ethnic Consciousness, and U.S. Foreign Policy." In A.A. Said, (ed.) *Ethnicity and U.S. Foreign Policy*, p. 1-18. New York: Praeger Publishers.

Scott, Fran and Abdulah Osman. 2002. "Identity, African-Americans, and U.S. Foreign Policy: Differing Reactions to South African Apartheid and the Rwandan Genocide." In T.   Ambrosio (ed). *Ethnic Identity Groups and U.S. Foreign Policy*, p. 71-92. Westport: Praeger.

Shain, Yossi. 1995. "Multicultural Foreign Policy." *Foreign Policy*, 100: 69-87.

Singh, Robert. 1998. *The Congressional Black Caucus: Racial Politics in the U.S. Congress.* Thousand Oaks, CA: Sage Publications.

The Situation in Haiti. Hearing before the Subcommittee on the Western Hemisphere of the Committee on International Relations. U.S. House of Representatives, 108th Congress, Second Session, March 3, 2004. Retrieved online at http://commdocs.house.gov on February 28, 2005.

Skinner, Elliot. 1992. *African Americans and U.S. Policy Toward Africa 1850-1924: In Defense of Black Nationality.* Washington, DC: Howard University Press.

Spoiling Security in Haiti. International Crisis Group, Latin American/Caribbean Report, No. 13. Released May 31, 2005. Retrieved online at www.crisisweb.org.

Sudan: Peace Agreement Around the Corner? Hearing before the Subcommittee on Africa of the Committee on International Relations. U.S. House of Representatives, 108th Congress, Second Session, March 11, 2004. Retrieved online at http://commdocs.house.gov on February 28, 2005.

Swain, Carol M. 1993. *Black Faces, Black Interests: The Representation of African Americans in Congress.* Cambridge, MA: Harvard University Press.

Tackling Liberia: The Eye of the Regional Storm. International Crisis Group, Africa Report, No. 62. Released April 30, 2003. Retrieved online at www.crisisweb.org.

Tate, Katherine. 2003. *Black Faces in the Mirror: African Americans and Their Representation in Congress.* Princeton, NJ: Princeton University Press.

Uslaner, Eric M. 2002. "Cracks in the Armor? Interest Groups and Foreign Policy." In A. Cigler and B. Loomis (eds.) *Interest Group Politics*, p. 355-377. Washington, DC: CQ Press.

U.S. Policy Toward Liberia. Hearing before the Subcommittee on Africa of the Committee on International Relations. U.S. House of Representatives, 108th Congress, First Session, October 2, 2003. Retrieved online at http://www.commdocs.house.gov on February 28, 2005.

Wright, John R. 1996. Interest Groups & Congress: Lobbying, Contributions, and Influence. Boston, MA: Allyn and Bacon.

Just Another Interest Group?
The Organized Representation of Ethnic
Groups in American National Politics

Matt Grossmann
Department of Political Science
University of California, Berkeley

Research on ethnic political mobilization and representation is due for a broad review. Current subfield divisions promote studying ethnic political mobilization as a distinct category of mass behavior, with a primary focus on voter turnout. Similarly, ethnic political representation is investigated as a distinct problem, primarily associated with the composition of legislatures. There is no research program to analyze how ethnic political mobilization and representation differs from that of other political constituencies. There is also little attempt to connect studies of ethnic representation in national political institutions with studies of the mass behavior of ethnic groups. Though ethnic voter turnout and support for minority legislators are the focus of the current literature, studies of the history of national policymaking about minority rights and concerns demonstrate that ethnic representative interest organizations working in several political institutions were often responsible for policy change (e.g., Skrentny 2002; Haney and Vanderbush 1999). It is time to ask whether the behavior of ethnic groups and their organized representatives constitute a unique class of political activity or a series of dissimilar case studies of the general patterns of mobilization and representation in American national politics.

I hope to provoke that discussion by analyzing American ethnic groups as a category of political factions with organized representation in national policymaking. I examine more than one hundred organizations that claim to speak on behalf of American ethnic groups in national politics and I compare their structure and involvement to that of more than one thousand other constituency interest organizations. Rather than study the behavior of advocates in institutions in isolation from the groups they claim to represent, however, I provide an account of the differences among the public groups that serve as the constituencies for 140 sectors of these national advocacy organizations. The goal is to give a description of ethnic mobilization and representation and to highlight similar and distinct features of ethnic politics and other forms of political activity.

The payoff is fourfold. First, we can assess whether the organized representatives of ethnic groups pursue distinct strategies and are subject to unique political opportunities and constraints or whether their behavior is contingent on the same factors that affect all interest organizations. If ethnic representation is merely an arbitrary category of interest representation, organizational resources may offer a better explanation for political influence than specific circumstances of ethnic mobilization. Second, we can build connections between the literature on ethnic political mobilization and the generic literature on interest group mobilization. The former emphasizes identity, perceptions of common fate, and civic institutions and the latter emphasizes individual incentives and entrepreneurship by national elites. Both theoretical foundations are likely to be important for building theory about political participation. Third, we can better understand the empirical differences among the political activities of ethnic groups by widening the scope of analysis. Ethnic politics researchers rely primarily on comparisons among ethnic groups rather than comparisons to other constituencies such as religious, occupational, or ideological groups. The appropriate basis for comparison in evaluating the political activities of groups such as Latinos and Asian-Americans, however, may turn out to be groups other than African-Americans. We can better understand the differences by broadening the basis of comparison. Fourth, we can provide an empirical foundation for current debates about the normative implications of identity politics. If the differential political involvement of ethnic groups is a product of the same factors that generally distort political participation and influence, normative critiques should be directed toward the general biases of political institutions, rather than toward the particular difficulties of ethnic representation or the specific patterns of ethnic mobilization.

Research on Ethnic Mobilization and Representation

The intellectual background of studies of American ethnic group mobilization and representation is in-depth historical case studies, especially of African-Americans during the civil rights movement (see McAdam 1985; Lee 2002). Yet most contemporary ethnic politics research is focused on the individual-level dynamics of political behavior. In this literature, researchers draw on a wealth of public opinion survey data. For African-Americans, scholars find that ethnic identity, perceptions of common fate, and belief in government responsiveness all influence political perspectives and mobilization (see Shingles 1981). Bobo and Gilliam (1990) further emphasize the importance of attentiveness, efficacy, and trust in African-American political participation. This behavioral analysis uses ideas from social psychology and empirical findings from the literature on voter turnout. Researchers of ethnic political behavior also examine the effects of context on ethnic mobilization. Bledsoe et al. (1995) and Oliver and Wong (2003), for example, demonstrate that aggregate features of a neighborhood, such as the presence of local ethnic institutions, the opinions of neighbors, and the threats generated by living in close proximity with other groups, affect the precursors to ethnic mobilization. These context studies have few equivalents in research on non-ethnic political constituencies, despite their potential applicability.

Recent research has attempted to extend the behavioral model of African-American participation to other ethnic groups. In their review of the literature on the political participation of Latinos and Asian-Americans, Segura and Rodrigues (2006) find that most of the existing scholarship focuses on voter turnout and support for minority candidates. They argue that Latino and Asian-American politics has unjustifiably been studied primarily through the lens of scholarship on African-American politics. Yet Verba et al. (1993) argue that most differences in political participation between ethnic groups are accounted for by differences in their levels of resources, civic skills, and organizational memberships. Leighley and Vedlitz (1999) also find that resources, attitudes, and social connectedness help predict individual participation across four ethnic groups. Much of the literature on ethnic mobilization has focused on potential partnerships among these ethnic groups, rather than partnerships with other types of constituencies.

Some scholars combine correlates of political participation at the individual-level with group-level characteristics to predict the relative mobilization of ethnic groups. Leighley (2001), for example, argues that elite mobilization is central to the electoral participation of different minority groups. Research on African-Americans, Latinos, and Asian-Americans demonstrates that membership in organizations helps determine other types of political participation (see Wong et al. 2005). Elite behavior and organizational development thus both affect individual mobilization. Because of these connections, Kaufmann (2003) argues that the future direction of mass Latino participation will depend on the activities of the leaders of Latino organizations. Given consistent findings of the importance of elite mobilization and organizational context, the paucity of broad-based studies on the national political representation of American ethnic groups is surprising.

Ethnic politics scholars do study ethnic involvement in national political institutions but the literature is quite focused. The most common area of investigation is the effect of electoral institutions and ethnic candidates on representation (see Swain 1993; Lublin 1997). In their review of research on race in American politics, Hutchings and Valentino (2004) indicate that race-based redistricting has been the focus of studies of ethnic representation. They criticize the division in the literature between the institutional implications of race in American politics and the mass behavior literature on ethnic participation. This problem is enhanced when it comes to analyzing the determinants of changes in public policy. Studies of policies designed to enhance minority rights often point to the influence of political elites, rather than mass mobilization. Skrentny (2002), for example, argues that federal administrators and Washington organizations advance many policies in support of minority rights without broad-based constituency support. Haney and Vanderbush (1999) argue that organized ethnic representatives are also influential in foreign policy debates.

Yet researchers that jointly study elite politics and mass ethnic behavior find their linkage important. In their different explanations of the success of the civil rights movement, for example, McAdam (1985) and Lee (2002) both find the connections between elite and mass support for African-American rights critical. Lee (2002) and Frymer (1999) also argue that the strategic choices of minority leaders were important to the electoral and legislative results of mass ethnic mobilization. Frymer (1999) further argues that the success and failure of African-Americans in the Democratic Party is associated with their organized representation and grassroots mobilization. Based on these case studies, however, we cannot conclude that the relevant causal factors are specific to ethnic political mobilization; we also do not know whether the findings are generalizable to other categories of political activity. In their review of comparative research on ethnic politics, Hechter and Okamoto (2001) emphasize the need for studies of the mechanisms of national minority group mobilization. They argue that we cannot yet assess current models of ethnic collective action due to their lack of specificity or empirical confirmation.

Research on ethnic interest organizations provides an opportunity to link studies of public mobilization with organized policy influence. Yet current studies generally adopt a case study approach (e.g., Haney and Vanderbush 1999). Some of these case studies provide little evidence of the effects of organizational activity on national policymaking or mass mobilization (e.g., Kurien 2001). In contrast to the literature on religious organizations (see Hertzke 1988; Hofrenning 1995), there has been no broad comparison of ethnic organizations in Washington with other interest organizations. Instead, scholars often implicitly assume that the individual-level findings of ethnic mobilization research and the history of the civil rights movement demonstrate that ethnic organization takes a distinct form.

This assumed distinctness has given rise to an extensive debate about the normative implications of identity politics. Warren (1992), for example, argues that identity politics involves competition over new categories of public goods and thus should feature new patterns of political conflict and cooperation. Stokes (2002) contends that identity politics poses both practical and ideological challenges to democratic theory because claims of group rights are contrary to liberal notions of citizenship and individual identity. In most cases, this literature analyzes the implications of identity politics without offering specific hypotheses or desiderata. Gutmann (2003), for example, argues that identity politics raises new types of risks and opportunities for democracy; she claims that identity groups must be differentiated theoretically from interest groups but does not systematically analyze their similarities and differences. Kane (2002) notes that the new concerns about identity politics in political theory have replaced many of the traditional critiques about the relative influence of social classes.

Ethnic Groups as Political Factions with Organized Representation

We should not assume a priori that the categories we use to analyze the mobilization and representation of public groups necessarily correspond with the objectives, structures, or environments of interest organizations or their constituencies. There are several reasons to believe that the category of ethnic representation used by researchers will not match up with similarities in the behavior of ethnic organizations. First, all national interest organizations respond to a universally similar lobbying environment that includes many of the same governing and mediating institutions. Second, the organizations that claim to speak on behalf of a particular ethnic group share a unique constituency with distinct challenges for mobilization. Third, each organization has a different capacity for influencing policymaking based on its own structure and resources. Each interest organization therefore has some unique features and shares some relevant characteristics with all other interest organizations and with the other organizations that represent the same ethnic group. Yet each organization shares few characteristics with only organizations that represent different constituencies in the same category (i.e. other ethnic representatives). Each organization competes for constituency support with other organizations representing the same ethnic group and competes for policymaker attention with other organizations that participate in the same policy issue debates. Our conventional category for dividing the study of organizations, ethnic representation, should therefore not necessarily predict the behavior or success of ethnic representatives.

The category of ethnic representation that we use in current scholarship is based on assumed differences in the kinds of constituencies that ethnic organizations attempt to mobilize and represent. Yet each ethnic group offers different strengths and weaknesses because they have different capacities for mobilization and different cleavages of internal differentiation. The mobilization of any political faction could be affected by their basic demographic features, their political engagement and participation levels, or their political views. These features of political constituencies are unlikely to be consistent across different ethnic groups.

Instead of building a unique theoretical framework for analyzing ethnic mobilization and representation, using traditional interest group theory offers an appealing alternative. In this intellectual tradition, Truman (1951) originally argued that social groups differ in their potential to mobilize an organized leadership. Gray and Lowery (2004) and McFarland (2004) combine this original framework with recent research on organizational behavior; they argue that theories of social competition and organizational development offer a compelling account of interest mobilization and influence. According to Wilson (1995), interest group research has identified many purposive, solidary, and instrumental incentives that promote individual mobilization. Walker (1991) and Salisbury (1992) add that national leadership entrepreneurs and institutional patrons affect the development of interest organizations. This research suggests that the organizational resources of interest groups and the features of their issue agendas are likely to influence their level of involvement in national policymaking, rather than the category of interests they advance.

If these generic factors account for the mobilization and representation of ethnic groups in national policymaking, identity politics may not raise distinct challenges for democratic theory. The unequal distribution of political influence certainly has important normative implications. The complicated process by which ethnic groups get represented by organized advocates may also fail to live up to some expectations for democratic governance. Yet the generic problem of factions was recognized by the American founders; its modern incarnation has been often discussed by proponents and critics of American democracy (see Dahl 1963; Skokpol 2003). In analyzing the normative implications of ethnic mobilization and representation, we should be attentive to these generic problems of democratic governance and ask whether identity groups raise new types of concerns or new incarnations of the same concerns. To advance our critiques of American governance, we should first understand how groups get represented in American national politics. If ethnic groups follow a different pattern of mobilization and representation, we can adapt our empirical studies and our normative critiques to account for the differences.

Data and Method

This analysis of ethnic mobilization and representation in national politics includes four components. First, I present descriptive statistics from data that I collected on the prominence and involvement of organizations representing American ethnic groups in Washington. Second, I compare the structure, prominence, and involvement of the ethnic sectors of organizations to other constituency representatives. Using a wider data set that I collected, I assess how and why ethnic representative organizations differ from others. Third, I use General Social Survey (GSS) data to present descriptive statistics on the characteristics of American ethnic groups that might be relevant to ethnic mobilization. Fourth, I compare ethnic groups to the public constituencies for other sectors of interest representatives in order to assess the characteristics that make ethnic groups unique as political constituencies.

The information on the organized representation of American ethnic groups uses compiled data on 141 organizations with a political presence in the Washington area. The names, reference text descriptions, and Web sites of these organizations indicate that they seek to represent an ethnic group in national politics.[1] To identify organizations, I use the *Washington Representatives* directory.[2] Below, I aggregate the organizational data into nineteen sectors of organizations that represent nineteen different American ethnic groups. Because some scholars consider Jews to be an ethnic group, I also provide information on the Jewish sector.[3] Each sector has at least two organizations.[4] Some organizations are included in multiple sectors, even if they only represent a subconstituency of the sector. For example, the Organization of Chinese Americans is included in both the Chinese sector and the Asian-American sector.

For each sector, I provide information on their organizational characteristics, their prominence, and their involvement in policymaking. For organizational characteristics, I report the number of organizations in the sector and the total number of representative political staff.[5] For the prominence of each sector, I report the number of times that the organizations were mentioned in two kinds of media from 1995-2004: the Washington print media, which is directed at policymakers, and the television news media, which is directed at the public.[6] For the policymaking involvement of each sector, I report the number of times that organizations in the sector gave testimony before congressional committees and the number of times they participated in public political events in Washington from 1995-2004.[7] To check reliability, I content analyzed a subset of the mentions of each organization.[8]

To compare ethnic political organizations to other interest organizations, I contrast this information with data that I collected on the structure, prominence, and involvement of more than 1,600 other organizations in the Washington area that speak on behalf of public constituencies.[9] In addition to ethnic political organizations, the population includes representatives of religious groups, occupational groups, single-issue perspectives, ideological perspectives, and other social groups. To test for differences between ethnic representatives and other constituency organizations, I report the mean or proportion among ethnic groups and among all other organizations and I look for statistically significant differences between the categories. I also add several indicators of organizational structure: the mean organizational age and the proportion of organizations with public members, state or local chapters, and Political Action Committees (PACs).[10] I also report the mean number of external lobbyists hired by each category of organizations and the size of their issue agendas.[11] To assess organizational involvement in the venues of policymaking, I report the number of times organizations in each category were mentioned in congressional floor proceedings, in the finals rules and decisions of administrative agencies, in federal court documents, and in the *Papers of the President* from 1995-2004.[12] To assess whether the differences I find are due to organizational characteristics or features of ethnic representatives as a category, I regress several indicators of organizational prominence and involvement on whether organizations represent an ethnic group and several organizational characteristics.

My analysis of the constituencies for these interest organizations uses pooled public opinion survey data from the GSS from 1972-2004. I use the cumulative GSS to identify constituencies among the 45,803 total respondents.[13] I present aggregate demographic data along with information on each ethnic group's political views and their levels of political engagement. For demographics, I report each group's size, the difference between their mean socioeconomic status (SES) and the overall means among Americans, and their level of geographic concentration.[14] For political views, I report each group's ideological cohesion and level of confidence in government along with a scale of the extremity of their opinions on five issue areas.[15] For political engagement, I report the difference between the overall means and the group mean on level of attention to news, level of interest in politics, level of political efficacy, level of personal trust, number of civic organizational memberships, and voting rate.[16]

To assess how ethnic political constituencies differ from other political factions, I compare information on the characteristics of ethnic groups with data that I collected on the constituencies for other sectors of representative organizations in Washington. As a basis of comparison, I use the aggregate features of eight religious groups, forty-three occupational groups, eleven ideological groups, forty-eight groups of supporters for single-issue perspectives, and sixteen other social categories.[17] For these constituencies, I collect the same information on their demographics, political views, and political engagement. For each characteristic, I report the mean among ethnic groups and the mean among other political constituencies and I test for statistically significant differences between the categories. I can thus assess how ethnic groups in the American public differ from other political factions, in addition to investigating how and why their organized representation differs from that of other constituencies.

The Organized Representation of American Ethnic Groups

Table 1 reports the characteristics of nineteen sectors of organizations representing American ethnic groups in national policymaking. The African-American sector, including organizations such as the *National Association for the Advancement of Colored People*, has the most organizations and political staff. It is also the most prominent and involved of the ethnic sectors; African-American organizations are the most commonly mentioned sector in the media and

Table 1
The Prominence of Organized Ethnic Representation in Washington

Organizational Sector	# of Orgs	Political Staff	DC Media Mentions	TV News Mentions	Testimony in Congress	DC Events
African-American	38	52	4498	43148	69	1511
Hispanic	26	39	787	2893	28	712
Native American	15	26	286	1191	159	342
General Minority	7	12	44	131	5	33
Arab-American	5	13	722	2430	10	449
Greek	5	7	39	9	3	6
Asian-American	4	4	61	88	8	71
Korean	4	7	11	58	0	6
Italian	4	2	125	251	2	42
Puerto Rican	4	1	45	229	1	23
Cuban	3	8	203	3323	7	46
Indian	3	2	13	20	1	4
Chinese	3	1	52	296	1	16
Turkish	3	3	40	6	5	7
Irish	2	1	16	17	0	24
Kurdish	2	2	18	12	2	5
Armenian	2	6	22	22	0	35
Japanese	2	2	71	339	0	9
Afghan	2	2	8	8	0	10
Jewish	22	61	2098	14160	61	668

Data for the number of organizations and representative political staff are compiled from Washington Representatives. Data for the other columns are from searches for organizational names in databases of articles, transcripts, and event announcements from 1995-2004.

the most active in Washington political events. The Hispanic sector, with organizations such as the *National Council of La Raza*, is the second largest in terms of organizations and political staff. The sector also ranks second in media mentions and Washington event participation. The Native American sector, with organizations such as the *Alaska Federation of Natives*, places first in congressional testimony. The general minority sector, which includes organizations such as the *National Association of Minority Contractors*, is moderately large and well-staffed. The Arab sector, with organizations such as the *American Arab Anti-Discrimination Committee*, is moderately well-staffed; it is also well represented in all types of media.[18] Most of the other sectors of ethnic representatives are quite small and feature organizations with few political employees. To allow for comparison, I also include representatives of Jews, such as the *American Jewish Committee*. The Jewish sector is the largest and most well-staffed sector of religious organizations and is substantially more prominent than most ethnic sectors.

Is Ethnic Representation Different?

Despite the heterogeneity among the sectors of ethnic representative organizations, ethnic organizations as a category do have unique features in comparison to other constituency interest organizations. Table 2 reports means and proportions among ethnic organizations and all other organizations. Despite the emphasis on local mobilization in the ethnic politics literature, ethnic

Table 2
Differences between Ethnic Representatives and Other Advocacy Organizations

	Ethnic Organizations	Other Constituency Representatives
% of Organizations with Members	44.4%	48.0%
% of Organizations with Chapters	19.3%	19.2%
% of Organizations with PACs	5.6%*	11.9%
Organizational Age	33.7***	42.7
Staff Political Representatives	1.5***	2.7
External Lobbyists	0.5***	1.0
Issue Areas	1.1***	2.2
DC Print Media Mentions	51.5**	98.8
TV News Mentions	384.5	609.0
DC Event Calendar Mentions	25.8**	46.2
Floor of Congress Mentions	22.0***	37.5
Mentions in Admin. Agency Rules	28.4***	41.1
Mentions in Federal Court Docs.	12.0***	34.0
Mentions in Presidential Papers	1.2	1.1
Testimony in Congress	2.4***	4.9

Table entries are proportions or means among ethnic organizations and among all other organizations. The significance indicators for proportions are based on a chi-square test. For differences in means, I use a two-sample t-test that does not assume equal variances. ***$p<.001$; **$p<.01$; *$p<.05$ (two-tailed).

organizations are not more likely than other advocacy organizations to have public members or sub-national chapters. Yet they are significantly less likely to have associated PACs. They are also significantly younger, on average, than other advocacy organizations and they have significantly smaller issue agendas. In terms of organizational structure, the primary important difference is that ethnic organizations have fewer staff political representatives and external lobbyists working on their behalf. Among the smallest ethnic organizations are those representing intersectional identities, such as members of an ethnic group in a particular occupation.

Ethnic organizations are also less prominent and involved, on average, than representatives of other constituencies. They appear in the Washington print media significantly less often and do not participate in as many Washington events. They are mentioned less frequently in congressional floor debates and they testify less often before congressional committees. They are also mentioned significantly less often in administrative agency rules and in federal court documents, though they are mentioned a similar number of times in presidential papers. Many organizations representing the smallest ethnic groups are rarely involved in policymaking in any branch.

In each indicator where ethnic organizations differ significantly from other advocacy groups, they are less prominent and less involved in Washington policymaking. Does this indicate a bias against representatives of ethnic groups? A more likely explanation is that the basic organizational features of ethnic representatives reduce their prominence and involvement. In support of this hypothesis, Table 3 presents the results of regressions to predict organizational prominence and involvement.[19] The models explain mentions in the Washington print media, on the floor of Congress, in administrative agency rules, and in federal court documents using organizational age, size of political staff, and size of issue agenda in addition to an indicator of whether the organization represents an ethnic group. The models are intended as descriptive and do not include the full causal process that produces organizational prominence and involvement. Yet the results confirm that, after controlling for basic organizational characteristics, representing an ethnic group does not reduce an organization's prominence or involvement in any branch of government. Representing an ethnic group is not a significant predictor of any indicator of involvement. Even though the average ethnic group has significantly fewer mentions in bivariate analyses, the coefficient for representing an ethnic group in these regressions is always positive and insignificant. Yet the age, size, and agenda breadth of an interest organization has a uniformly significant effect on their prominence and involvement. This indicates that ethnic organizations are less prominent and involved, but only because they lack the longevity, staff, and broader issue agendas of other advocacy organizations.

The Character of Ethnic Groups as Political Constituencies

In the ethnic politics subfield, scholars most often look for explanations of differences in ethnic political mobilization and representation at the individual level-of-analysis. Many scholars seek to explain why some people within an ethnic group are more likely to mobilize for

Table 3
Regressions to Predict Organizational Prominence and Involvement

	Mentions in Washington Print Media	Mentions on Floor of Congress	Mentions in Admin. Agency Rules	Mentions in Federal Court Documents
Organizational Age	.82***	.51***	1.71***	.81***
	(.20)	(.07)	(.24)	(.14)
# of Staff Political Representatives	48.2***	13.4***	9.2***	8.5***
	(2.2)	(0.7)	(2.7)	(1.6)
# of Issue Areas	9.3***	4.1***	6.1**	7.1***
	(1.7)	(0.6)	(2.1)	(1.2)
Org. Represents Ethnic Group	29.3	10.0	19.9	2.1
	(22.3)	(7.4)	(25.7)	(15.0)
Constant	- 84.4	- 28.2	- 67.5	- 37.2
R2	.354	.341	.069	.108
N	1604	1604	1558	1558

Table entries are OLS regression coefficients, with standard errors in parentheses. The dependent variables cover the period 1995-2004. ***$p<.001$; **$p<.01$; *$p<.05$ (two-tailed).

Table 4

Demographic Characteristics and Political Views of Ethnic Groups in the American Public

Constituency Group	Population Size	SES	Opinion Extremity	Ideological Cohesion	Confidence in Gov.
African-American	12.4	-6.513	0.979	-0.074	-0.037
Hispanic	5.8	-4.758	0.362	-0.026	0.180
Native American	4.3	-5.743	0.378	-0.032	-0.196
Mexican	3.0	-6.521	0.316	0.001	0.232
Puerto Rican	1.0	-4.262	0.720	-0.036	0.126
Asian-American	1.2	5.315	0.427	0.010	0.388
Chinese	0.4	12.229	0.669	-0.010	0.383
Japanese	0.3	8.374	0.517	0.113	0.239
Indian	0.4	13.265	0.662	0.216	0.226
Arab-American	0.2	5.221	0.850	-0.236	-0.061
Italian	5.6	2.110	0.291	0.087	0.044
Greek	0.4	1.578	0.308	-0.076	0.148
Irish	12.0	1.262	0.088	0.019	-0.026
Jewish	2.1	13.368	0.794	-0.030	-0.025

Table entries are based on pooled GSS data. Population size is the percent of the U.S. population in the ethnic group. SES compares the group mean with the overall mean in the U.S. population. Opinion extremity and confidence in government are based on comparisons of scaled indicators. Ideological cohesion is a comparison of the relative dispersion of ideological perspectives within a group.

political activity. Comparison between ethnic groups is more often conducted in a qualitative manner, usually with African-Americans as the implicit basis of comparison for other groups. To search for explanations of both the common patterns of mobilized representation among American ethnic groups and the differences among their mobilization processes, we can start by analyzing the aggregate characteristics of ethnic constituencies. The profiles of ethnic groups as political factions show vast differences and some common patterns.

In terms of traditional demographic characteristics, ethnic groups vary widely in population size and SES. Table 4 indicates that Indians and Jews have higher SES, with African-Americans, Mexicans, and Native Americans averaging far lower SES. Table 4 also shows that there is substantial variation in relevant features of the political perspectives of American ethnic groups. African-Americans and Arab-Americans, for example, are substantially more extreme in their opinions than many other ethnic groups. The ideological cohesion data indicates that some ethnic groups are less cohesive than the general population but others are more cohesive. The data for confidence in government comports with other research demonstrating that ethnic groups with more recent immigrants have more positive views (see Uhlaner and Garcia 2002). The political perspectives of different ethnic groups seem quite varied, both in terms of their attitudes toward government and their opinions on policy issues.

In terms of political engagement, there is also substantial variation among ethnic groups. Table 5 illustrates their differences in attention to news, political interest, political efficacy, interpersonal trust, civic membership, and voting rate. Ethnic groups with more recent immigrants are somewhat less attentive and involved. Many ethnic minority groups have less political interest, personal trust, and involvement in civic organizations than the general population. Most ethnic minority groups also vote at a substantially lower rate than the general population.

Table 5
Political Engagement of Ethnic Groups in the American Public

Constituency Group	Attention to News	Political Interest	Political Efficacy	Personal Trust	Civic Membership	Voting Rate
African-American	-0.256	-0.037	-0.112	-23.57	-0.248	-5.85
Hispanic	-0.430	-0.264	-0.098	-14.95	-0.541	-23.90
Native American	-0.410	-0.263	-0.219	-13.97	-0.360	-13.29
Mexican	-0.509	-0.229	-0.141	-12.67	-0.565	-24.95
Puerto Rican	-0.420	-0.555	-0.368	-23.73	-0.724	-27.05
Asian-American	-0.322	-0.048	0.238	-9.59	-0.322	-32.36
Chinese	-0.099	-0.055	0.011	0.85	-0.449	-32.41
Japanese	0.046			6.27	-0.387	-20.19
Indian	-0.287			-14.01	-0.023	-30.09
Arab-American	-0.133			-3.23	0.117	-29.20
Italians	0.057	-0.061	-0.005	-2.51	-0.213	-0.74
Greek	0.021			0.76	-0.116	-3.98
Irish	0.050	0.101	-0.028	4.96	-0.033	3.87
Jewish	0.361	0.185	-0.137	6.61	0.593	17.34

Table entries are based on pooled GSS data. Each column compares the group mean or percent with the overall mean or percent in the U.S. population. For some ethnic groups, sufficient data was unavailable for the years that the GSS asked questions about political interest and efficacy.

In the indicators of political engagement, Jews differ substantially from the ethnic groups with their higher levels of organizational involvement, attentiveness, and voting. To draw conclusions about which group attributes help generate organized representation, one would need a larger group of constituencies. Yet the low levels of political engagement and participation among some ethnic groups offer one potential explanation for differential levels of organized representation.

Are Ethnic Constituencies Different?

Though American ethnic groups differ substantially in their demographic attributes, levels of political engagement, and political views, as a category ethnic groups share some traits that make them unique in comparison to other political constituencies. The thirteen ethnic groups differ significantly from other public groups that have representative organizations in Washington, especially in terms of their social and political engagement. Table 6 presents differences between the mean among ethnic organizations and among other political constituencies. Ethnic groups have lower average socio-economic status, but the results are not statistically significant. The primary demographic difference is that ethnic groups are more concentrated geographically. McAdam (1985) argues that this geographic concentration may stimulate mobilization; yet it may also inhibit the development of national organizations.

Table 6
Differences between Ethnic Groups and Other Political Constituencies

	Ethnic Groups in the American Public	Other Public Constituencies
Socio-Economic Status	1.7	4.4
Geographic Concentration	56.7***	18.1
Extremity of Opinion	.53	.48
Ideological Cohesion	-.01	.03
Confidence in Government	.11***	- .03
Attention to News	- .18***	.03
Interest in Politics	- .13**	.04
Political Efficacy	- .09	- .03
Interpersonal Trust	- 8.1***	1.4
Civic Membership	- .26***	.17
Voting Rate	- 16.2***	2.4

Table entries are the means among ethnic groups and among all other constituencies. The significance indicators are based on a two-sample t-test with Levene's test used to assess equality of variances. ***$p<.001$; **$p<.01$; *$p<.05$ (two-tailed).

The characteristics of the political views of ethnic groups are not very different from the views of other constituencies. Ethnic groups and other constituencies have similar levels of opinion extremity and ideological cohesion. On average, they are significantly more confident in government than other constituencies. Government confidence is sometimes thought to influence the degree to which constituencies choose mobilization strategies outside of traditional institutional mobilization. Despite the difference in government confidence, ethnic groups do not differ significantly from other constituencies in their levels of internal political efficacy.

Yet there are several important differences in the political engagement levels of American ethnic groups in comparison to other social constituencies. First, their interest in politics is, on average, lower than other groups. Interest in politics is traditionally linked to individual political participation and may potentially affect organizational mobilization at the group level. Second, ethnic groups have lower levels of interpersonal trust than other political constituencies. Whereas most mobilized constituencies have higher levels of trust than the general population, many ethnic groups have lower levels of trust. Third, ethnic groups have a lower level of civic involvement; ethnic group members are, on average, likely to join fewer civic organizations. Some authors hypothesize that interpersonal trust and civic organizational involvement are key steps in the generation of social capital for political influence (see Skokpol 2003); many ethnic groups appear to lack this social capital. Fourth, ethnic groups also have significantly lower voting rates than other political constituencies. Whereas most mobilized groups have higher voting rates than the general population, ethnic groups have lower voting rates, on average, by more than sixteen percentage points. This is likely to negatively affect their ability to influence elected policymakers. The lower levels of civic and political engagement among ethnic groups are thus apparent in their attention, interest, organizational membership, and voting. Combined, these differences offer a potential explanation for the minimal national organized representation that speaks on behalf of many ethnic groups.

Implications

By evaluating ethnic mobilization and representation in a comparative framework, we can not only illustrate similarities and differences between ethnic groups and other types of political constituencies, but also advance our understanding of how organized ethnic representatives become involved in national policymaking and why all ethnic groups do not achieve the same level of influence. The results of this initial analysis have important implications for our view of the distinctness of ethnic representation, our explanations of the process of ethnic mobilization, and our concerns about the normative repercussions of identity politics.

As a category, ethnic organizations do differ descriptively from other sectors of interest organizations. Yet ethnic political representatives are far from a homogenous sector of similar organizations. In fact, the differences in the prominence and involvement levels of ethnic organizations as a category only reflect the different attributes of ethnic organizations, especially their recent formation, their small size, and their limited issue agenda. Ethnic organizations appear to be subject to a similar set of opportunities and constraints as religious, occupational, ideological, and single-issue organizations. The elite-level organized participation in policymaking found in Skrentny's (2002) analysis of minority rights interventions may be the normal course of policy influence in the U.S., rather than the mass-based mobilization that he envisions based on the model of the African-American civil rights movement. Ethnic organizations appear to use the same multiple tactics as other organizations to influence policymakers and mobilize constituents. The most important difference in their organized representation may be structural, rather than strategic. Because the representative organizations generated by many ethnic groups are new, small, and focused, their involvement is limited. Organizations that do not share these features, such as many African-American and Jewish groups, are not typically subject to these same constraints. Rather than rely on specific features of ethnic representation to explain the relative success of ethnic organizations, researchers should build on the framework offered by interest group research (e.g., McFarland 2004; Walker 1991).

Scholars should also expand their notions of ethnic representation to include ethnic interest organizations. The current literature's focus on representation by minority legislators may be justified by the importance of legislators in advancing the concerns of ethnic groups in American politics. Yet the limited definition of representation implied by legislative research may miss important routes to ethnic group influence and may not offer a full explanation for the differential influence of some ethnic groups in national policymaking. The different levels of organized representation among ethnic groups and in comparison to other political constituencies is likely an understudied part of the explanation for why some ethnic groups gain advantage in the political process, and other groups lack influence.

At the mass level, ethnic groups also differ from other American political constituencies in important ways. They are more geographically concentrated and more confident in government but they report less interest in politics, less attention to news, less interpersonal trust, less involvement in civic organizations, and lower voting rates. There are still major differences within the category of ethnic groups on these measures, but the average differences are substantively and statistically significant. The relevance of these constituency characteristics to national political mobilization at the group level remains unclear but the lower overall levels of political engagement among ethnic groups may be related to the limited nature of their organized representation in Washington. The current emphasis on the multi-causal explanation for individual minority political mobilization may be useful beyond the current literature's predictions about political attitudes and voter turnout. Researchers have found important and influential individual-level differences in resources, attentiveness, trust, social connectedness, and political participation. The individual characteristics that promote mobilization, when aggregated to the group-level, may have important implications for the involvement of ethnic representatives in national policymaking. The national political organization of ethnic groups may also be an important contextual factor in shaping mobilization, beyond the local context for mobilization addressed in current research.

The results presented here suggest some explanations for important differences among ethnic groups in terms of their political mobilization and representation. There is little reason to believe that the organized representatives of Mexicans, Asian-Americans, or other ethnic groups should behave similarly to representatives of African-Americans, Jews, and Cubans or achieve a similar level of success. There are not only important and consequential differences in the structural characteristics of the representative organizations, but also potentially relevant differences in the demographic features, political views, and levels of political engagement of their constituencies. Scholars interested in political differences between ethnic groups may want to expand their basis of comparison to other categories of political factions such as religious, occupational, or ideological groups. The current focus on inter-ethnic comparison identified by Segura and Rodrigues (2006) may be stifling for theoretical development. In addition, the focus on context effects, collective identity, and common fate perceptions within the ethnic politics literature may be relevant for other constituencies, such as religious and ideological groups. By integrating ethnic mobilization and representation research into the broader analysis of factional competition, we can improve studies of ethnic politics and studies of political participation by other public groups.

The analysis presented here can also help to provide a more informed background for normative debates over identity politics. No empirical investigation can provide answers to questions about how groups should pursue mobilization around collective identities or about how democratic government should respond to identity-based representation. Yet the current tendency to separate theoretical concerns over identity politics from other problems related to the competition among political factions (e.g., Warren 1992; Gutmann 2003) may do a disservice to analyzing the implications of ethnic politics. Before reconstructing democratic theory in response to ethnic mobilization and representation, scholars should ensure that the concerns raised by identity politics are actually distinct from the long-running problems of public mobilization, representation, and differential group influence that arise in all democratic governance. We are unlikely to advance our normative critiques or our empirical knowledge by arbitrarily separating ethnic politics from other examples of the mobilization and representation of political factions.

Notes

1. If an organization claimed to represent ethnic groups in national policymaking, it was included in the population. We used reference text summaries and organizational Web sites; in a reliability analysis of a sample of organizations, my research assistant and I reached the same coding decisions for more than 95 percent of organizations.
2. I also checked with other directories such as the Encyclopedia of Associations, The Capital Source, the Government Affairs Yellow Book, Public Interest Profiles, and the Washington Information Directory.
3. I do not include Jewish organizations in the ethnic group category when analyzing the differences between ethnic groups and other interest representatives.

4. I do not provide information on sectors with only one organization representing an ethnic group. There are seven other ethnic groups represented by only one political organization in the Washington area, including Polish, Mexican, Latvian, Albanian, Croatian, Filipino, and Southeast Asian Americans. All organizations that speak on behalf of these groups are included in the overall population of ethnic organizations.

5. I use the number of political staff reported in Washington Representatives.

6. For Washington media mentions, I search for organizational names in Roll Call, The Hill, National Journal, Congress Daily, The Hotline, Congressional Quarterly, and the Washington Post. For television news mentions, I search for organizational names in the LexisNexis database of broadcast transcripts recorded by the Video Monitoring Services of America. The database includes television transcripts of national cable and network news programs and local news broadcasts in major metropolitan areas. All searches include material from January 1, 1995 through December 31, 2004. The collection and measurement of these indicators are described in Grossmann (forthcoming).

7. For congressional testimony, I search for organizational names in the LexisNexis database of the Federal Document Clearing House Congressional Hearing Transcripts. The database includes a record of committee and subcommittee hearings along with written material submitted by those who provide testimony. For participation in Washington political events, I search for organizational names in the Federal News Service Daybook, The Washington Daybook, and the LexisNexis database of Federal Document Clearing House Political Transcripts. The listings and transcripts provide information on organizations that participated in conferences, panel discussions, and public hearings that took place in Washington. These measures are also described in Grossmann (forthcoming).

8. I used multiple forms of the organizational name when appropriate. I assessed thirty mentions of each organizational name to ensure that the references were to the correct organization.

9. The population includes organizations that speak on behalf of social groups or political perspectives and have a presence in the Washington area. To be included in the population, organizations must have an identifiable constituency that is larger than their official membership. Corporate policy offices, trade associations, and governmental units are not included in the population.

10. I use Washington Representatives for information on associated PACs. I use reference directories and organizational Web sites to determine whether organizations have public membership and whether they have affiliated sub-national chapters.

11. I use Washington Representatives for information on the number of lobbyists hired and the number of issue areas on an organization's policy agenda.

12. For congressional floor mentions, I search for the organizational names in the Congressional Record. For involvement in administrative agency decisions, I search for organizational names in the LexisNexis database of the final rules and decisions of administrative agencies. For involvement in federal court litigation, I search for organizational names in the LexisNexis database of all federal court case documents. For presidential involvement, I search for organizational names in the Papers of the Presidents. These measures are also described in Grossmann (forthcoming).

13. GSS data is weighted to exclude oversamples of African-Americans and non-respondents. I was only able to collect data for thirteen ethnic groups. I provide data for Jews as a basis of comparison, but Jews are not included in my analysis of differences between ethnic groups and other constituencies.

14. For size, I report the percent of survey respondents who self-identify as a member of the ethnic group or report an associated country of origin. For SES, the group mean is compared to the overall mean among respondents to the same set of surveys. For geographic concentration, I report the total difference between the mean population percent and the group population percent in the nine geographic regions identified by the GSS.

15. I measure ideological cohesion by estimating the difference between the overall and group standard deviation in reported ideological positions on a five-category left-right scale. For government confidence, I report the difference between the overall and group mean on a five-point scale. For opinions, I use the average of the absolute values of the distances between the overall mean and the group mean on responses to questions about the appropriate level of spending on the environment, health, education, welfare, and the military.

16. For attention to news, I use a five point scale measuring newspaper reading. For interest in politics, I use a four point scale of self-reported level of interest. For internal efficacy, I use a five point scale of belief that average people can influence the political process. For personal trust, I use the percent of respondents who say that you can trust other people most of the time. For civic involvement, I use the organizational memberships reported by respondents. For the voting rate, I use the percent who

reported voted in the last presidential election. For all categories, I report the difference between the group mean and the overall mean among respondents to the same surveys.

17. To identify ethnic, religious, ideological, and demographic constituencies in the survey data, I use respondent self-reports. To identify occupational constituencies, I use my coding of the International Standard Occupational Codes used by the GSS. To identify single-issue constituencies, I use strong supporters of the sector's issue position where the GSS contained relevant questions. For some organizational sectors, I had to construct scales of multiple questions to identify the relevant constituency.

18. This is likely to be an artifact of requests for comment from journalists regarding the events surrounding September 11 and the two U.S. wars covered in the period.

19. I use ordinary least squares regression, even though the dependent variables are counts of mentions, with many organizations producing zero mentions. Using zero-inflated count models makes the results more difficult to interpret and does not change the substantive results.

References

Bledsoe, Timothy, Susan Welch, Lee Sigelman and Michael Combs. 1995. "Residential Context and Racial Solidarity Among African Americans." *American Journal of Political Science* 39(2): 434-458.

Bobo, Lawrence and Franklin D. Gilliam, Jr. 1990. "Race, Sociopolitical Participation, and Black Empowerment." *American Political Science Review* 84(2): 377-393.

Dahl, Robert A. 1963. *A Preface to Democratic Theory*. Chicago, IL: University of Chicago Press.

Frymer, Paul. 1999. *Uneasy Alliances: Race and Party Competition in America*. Princeton, NJ: Princeton University Press.

Gray, Virginia and David Lowery. 2004. "A Neopluralist Perspective on Research on Organized Interests." *Political Research Quarterly* 57(1): 163-175.

Grossmann, Matt. "Environmental Advocacy in Washington." Forthcoming in *Environmental Politics*.

Gutmann, Amy. 2003. *Identity in Democracy*. Princeton, NJ: Princeton University Press.

Haney, Patrick J. and Walt Vanderbush. 1999. "The Role of Ethnic Interest Groups in U.S. Foreign Policy: The Case of the Cuban American National Foundation." *International Studies Quarterly* 43(2): 341-361.

Hechter, Michael and Dina Okamoto. 2001. "Political Consequences of Minority Group Formation." *Annual Review of Political Science* 4: 189-215.

Hertzke, Allen D. 1988. *Representing God in Washington: The Role of Religious Lobbies in the American Polity*. Knoxville, TN: University of Tennessee Press.

Hofrenning, Daniel. 1995. *In Washington But Not Of It: The Prophetic Politics of Religious Lobbyists*. Philadelphia, PA: Temple University Press.

Hutchings, Vincent L. and Nicholas A. Valentino. 2004. "The Centrality of Race in American Politics." *Annual Review of Political Science* 7: 383-408.

Kane, John. 2002. "Democracy and Group Rights." *In Democratic Theory Today*, (eds.) April Carter and Geoffrey Stokes. Cambridge, UK: Polity Press.

Kaufmann, Karen M. 2003. "Cracks in the Rainbow: Group Commonality as a Basis for Latino and African-American Political Coalitions." *Political Research Quarterly* 56(2): 199-210.

Kurien, Prema. 2001. "Religion, Ethnicity, and Politics: Hindu and Muslim Indian Immigrants in the United States." *Ethnic and Racial Studies* 24(2): 263-93.

Lee, Taeku. 2002. *Mobilizing Public Opinion: Black Insurgency and Racial Attitudes in the Civil Rights Era*. Chicago, IL: University of Chicago Press.

Leighley, Jan E. 2001. *Strength in Numbers? The Political Mobilization of Racial and Ethnic Minorities*. Princeton, NJ: Princeton University Press.

Leighley, Jan E. and Arnold Vedlitz. 1999. "Race, Ethnicity, and Political Participation: Competing Models and Contrasting Explanations." *Journal of Politics* 61(4): 1092-1114.

Lublin, David. 1997. *The Paradox of Representation: Racial Gerrymandering and Minority Interests in Congress*. Princeton, NJ: Princeton University Press.

McAdam, Doug. 1985. *Political Process and the Development of Black Insurgency, 1930-1970*. Chicago, IL: University of Chicago Press.

McFarland, Andrew S. 2004. *Neopluralism: The Evolution of Political Process Theory*. Lawrence, KN: University of Kansas Press.

Oliver, J. Eric and Janelle Wong. 2003. "Inter-Group Prejudice in Multi-Ethnic Settings." *American Journal of Political Science* 47(4): 567-582.

Salisbury, Robert H. 1992. *Interests and Institutions: Substance and Structure in American Politics.* Pittsburgh, PA: University of Pittsburgh Press.

Segura, Gary M. and Helena Alves Rodrigues. 2006. "Comparative Ethnic Politics in the United States: Beyond Black and White." *Annual Review of Political Science* 9: 375-395.

Shingles, Richard D. 1981. "Black Consciousness and Political Participation: The Missing Link." *American Political Science Review* 75(1): 76-91.

Skocpol, Theda. 2003. *Diminished Democracy: From Membership to Management in American Civic Life.* Norman, OK: University of Oklahoma Press.

Skrentny, Johnathan D. 2002. *The Minority Rights Revolution.* Cambridge: Harvard University Press.

Stokes, Goeffrey. 2002. "Democracy and Citizenship." *In Democratic Theory Today,* (eds.) April Carter and Geoffrey Stokes. Cambridge, UK: Polity Press.

Swain, Carol M. 1993. *Black Faces, Black Interests: The Representation of African Americans in Congress.* Cambridge, MA: Harvard University Press.

Truman, David B. 1951. *The Governmental Process: Political Interests and Public Opinion,* 2d ed. New York: Knopf.

Uhlaner, Carole Jean, and F. Chris Garcia. 2002. "Latino Public Opinion." In *Understanding Public Opinion,* (eds.) Barbara Norrander and Clyde Wilcox. Washington, DC: C.Q. Press.

Verba, Sidney, Kay Lehman Schlozman, Henry Brady, and Norman H. Nie. "Race, Ethnicity and Political Resources: Participation in the United States." *British Journal of Political Science* 23(4): 453-497.

Walker, Jack L. 1991. *Mobilizing Interest Groups in America: Patrons, Professions, and Social Movements.* Ann Arbor, MI: University of Michigan Press.

Warren, Mark. 1992. "Democratic Theory and Self-Transformation." *American Political Science Review* 86(1): 8-23.

Washington Representatives. 2002. New York: Columbia Books.

Wilson, James Q. 1995. *Political Organizations.* Princeton, NJ: Princeton University Press.

Wong, Janelle S., Pei-te Lien, and M. Margaret Conway. 2005. "Group-Based Resources and Political Participation among Asian Americans." *American Politics Research* 33(4): 545-576.

Deracialization and White Crossover Voting in State Legislative Elections

Atiya Kai Stokes-Brown
Department of Political Science
Florida State University

Race has an enduring influence in American campaigns and elections. With issues of race often heightened in elections, it has been argued that voter discrimination toward African American candidates is certain (Terkildsen 1993; Perry 1996; Reeves 1997). Students of campaigns and elections point to the vast underrepresentation of African Americans among elected officials and the paucity of African American candidates who have been able to win outside of African American majority settings as evidence that white voters continue to vote along racial lines and are not yet willing to embrace African American candidates (e.g., Davidson and Grofman 1994; Lublin 1997).

There are those, however, who argue that the significance of race has declined in elections and point to the small but growing trend of African Americans that have been elected from majority-white constituencies since the 1990 (e.g., Thernstrom 1987; Swain 1993). The success of these candidates is often credited to candidates' willingness to pursue a strategy of deracialization in which candidates adopt a non-threatening image, emphasize substantive issues that have mass appeal, and avoid direct appeals to African American voters (McCormick and Jones, 1990; Jones and Clemons 1993). By using this strategy, it is it is argued that African Americans can send a message to white voters "that there are no meaningful differences between constituents or policies on the basis of race" (Canon 1999; 48).

While many scholars have examined the concept of deracialization and/or white crossover voting in urban and congressional elections (e.g., Bullock 1984; Carsey 1995; Liu 2001; Liu and Vanderleeuw 2001; Perry 1996; Reeves 1997), few studies have investigated the efficacy of this electoral strategy in state legislative elections. Research suggests that cross-racial voting exerts different dynamics in elections given the level and symbolic importance of office (Longoria 1999). Since the 1990s, state legislative elections have become increasingly visible and competitive, due in large part to the devolution of federal responsibilities to the states and to the ascendancy of the Republican Party in the South. As states have become the nation's key service providers, state legislators play a central role in public policymaking. Moreover, many state legislatures have become more professional and serve as a training ground for ambitious politicians seeking higher offices. Two hundred thirty five of the 435 House members in the 109th Congress were former state legislators, as were thirty-nine of the 100 senators (NCSL 2004). As of January 2005, twenty-four governors served as members of state legislatures (NGA 2005).

Given the importance of state legislative office and elections for public policy at the state and national level, the impact of candidate race in these elections warrants greater attention.

In this study, I examine the effectiveness of deracialization on white crossover voting in biracial state legislative elections.[1] Focusing specifically on the issue component of deracialization, I discuss the development of political deracialization within the literature. Next, I discuss how particular campaign issues may provide a strategic benefit to African American candidates, given voters' perceptions about the ideological leanings of minority candidates and the performance of political parties. Finally, I analyze the impact of African American candidates' issues on white crossover voting, and examine under what conditions issues increase white crossover voting in state legislative elections.

Deracialization, White Crossover Voting, and Issues

Modern campaigns and elections are characterized by intense focus on the candidate, rather than political parties. As agents of information, campaigns are replacing parties as the primary source of information about the candidate. When evaluating candidates, voters tend to rely on cognitive shortcuts that provide information about the candidate in a readily available form. While partisanship and incumbency are the most well known informational cues (Campbell et al. 1960; also see Popkin 1991), candidate demographic cues are also important because attitudes about groups often serve as central organizing principles in the minds of voters when it comes to politics (Berelson et al. 1954; Converse 1964; Conover 1984). Cues such as race and gender can activate stereotypes that simplify the decision making process (Conover and Feldman 1989).

Much of the research focusing on candidate race in campaigns and elections shows that voters cast their ballots for candidates of their same race (e.g., Kinder and Sanders 1996; Dawson 1994). In biracial elections, studies show that white voters are significantly less likely to vote for African American candidates (Reeves 1997; Terkildsen 1993; Citrin et al. 1990; Voss and Lublin 2001; but see Highton 2004), in part because the continuance of existing racial stereotypes (e.g., Bianco 1998). While white Americans' negative stereotypes of African Americans have softened to some degree as part of a broader liberalization of racial attitudes (Schuman et al. 1988), by many accounts, white Americans continue to ascribe negative attitudes, opinions, and characterizations to African Americans (e.g., Bobo and Kluegel 1993; Kinder and Mendelberg 1995). As a result, African American candidates are often perceived as being more liberal than average, solely concerned with racial issues, less experienced and capable of handling the task of office holder, and less likely to have personal attributes desired in elected officials, such as honesty and trustworthiness (Williams 1990). For example, when Rep. Sanford D. Bishop, Jr. ran for re-election in his conservative, rural majority white district in 1998, many white supporters noted that they had to reject deep prejudices to vote for him because they "just wouldn't have thought a black man would know enough to do the job" (see Sack 1998).

In the face of these existing prejudices, a growing body of research suggests that white voters are willing to vote for African American candidates under the right circumstances. Voters' perceptions of candidates are influenced by the messages candidates communicate during the campaign. Consequently, the manner in which African American state legislative candidates construct their campaigns and frame issues can shape voters' assessments of political candidates. The implications of this research may well be reflected in the changing styles employed by African American candidates since the late 1960s, when the Civil Rights Movement was at its peak. The predominant campaign strategy at that time was that one of insurgency—"direct challenges to prevailing political order; explicit attacks and criticisms on elected officials, institutional processes ... resulting in mobilization of interests and bias in local political context"

(Persons 1993; 45). Because insurgent campaigns are characterized by mobilization based on racial appeals, African American candidates garnered most, if not all, of African American vote with little white crossover vote (Bullock 1984; see Persons 1993; 45). Running in districts with large African American populations, candidates using this strategy gained entry to state and local positions.

Insurgent voting strategies have declined and deracialized campaigns have become more common (McCormick and Jones 1993). Deracialized electoral strategies encourage African American candidates to promote non-threatening images, emphasize substantive issues that have mass appeal, and avoid direct appeals to minority voters (Perry 1996; Persons 1993). Issues are important in political campaigns and elections because candidates use issues not only to convey their positions on salient issues of the day, but also to present themselves to potential voters and convey impressions of competence and trustworthiness (Fenno 1978). For African American candidates, focusing on the issue component of deracialization is essential given that many issues like crime, welfare, and affirmative action have strong racial overtones, and are implicitly associated with racial minorities in the minds of many Americans (Peffley et al. 1997; Gilens 1996). The deracialization framework encourages African American candidates to purposefully avoid race-specific issues, and to emphasize mainstream, diffuse issues that allow a candidate to build a larger set of supporters. Thus, the true purpose of a deracialized issue strategy is to make it more difficult for white voters to rely on negative racial stereotypes.[2]

However, some issues may prove to be more beneficial than others. I propose that African American candidates, like female candidates, gain a strategic advantage when they stress race neutral issues that voters associate favorably with African Americans candidates. Research suggests that female U.S. House and state legislative candidates are significantly more likely to win the general election when they run "as women," stressing issues that are perceived to be "women's" issues (Herrnson et al. 2003). By focusing on social welfare issues, African American candidates may benefit from voters' stereotypes as well as the advantages of party affiliation. With the exception of welfare, there has been a great deal of support for social spending in the United States. Many social welfare issues, including health care, education, social security, and child care, enjoy widespread support among the electorate (e.g., Gilens 1999), and are commonly cited among the most important problems facing the nation (see Table 1). Social welfare issues are "bridge issues" that can connect African American candidates with a larger electorate. Voters, relying on racial stereotypes, may be more likely to infer African American candidates to be more supportive of governmental spending for these favored programs because African American candidates are viewed as more liberal than their white counterparts (Williams 1990).

African American candidates may also benefit from these issues because of the Democratic Party's ownership of these issues. According to Petrocik (1996), certain issues are positively associated with either major political party. When voters are most concerned about those issues, that party's candidates tend to do better at the polls. An overwhelming percentage of African Americans run for office as members of the Democratic Party – the party that is perceived by voters to better handle social welfare issues.[3]

Yet, it is also likely that African American candidates gain a strategic advantage when they stress economic issues that convey a moderate or fiscally conservative message (e.g., Sigelman et al. 1995). Voter's electoral decisions are often influenced by personal and national perceptions of the economy and economic conditions (e.g., Campbell et al. 1960; Kinder and Kiewiet 1981). If white voters perceive African American candidates to be more liberal than other candidates, running on moderate to fiscally conservative economic issues may make white voters more inclined to respond favorably to the campaign simply because the candidate's stance on the issue diverges from voters' expectations (e.g., Peffley et al. 1997). Voters' opinions about

Table 1
Most Important Issues for Voters 1996-2000

Rank	1996	1998	2000
1	Economy/Jobs	Education	Moral/Ethical Values
2	Medicare/ Social Security	Economy/Jobs	Economy/Jobs
3	Federal Deficit	Social Security	Education
4	Education	Health care	Social Security
5	Taxes	Taxes	Health care/Medicare/Taxes

Note: Polls were collected from the following sources: Voter News Service National Exit Poll (1996), AFL-CIO Post Election Survey (1998), and the Los Angles Times National Exit Poll (2000).

which party best handles economic issues tend to favor Republicans (Petrocik 1996: 831). However, African American candidates who focus on these issues are likely to be perceived as a "serious" candidate, who can focus on issues "that transcend the racial question" (Jones and Clemons 1993). Using these issues, they are able to project a conservative image that helps them mitigate the effects of racial stereotyping, thereby increasing their chances of winning crossover votes.

Hypotheses, Data, and Methods

In this study, I test two hypotheses about the effect of deracialization on white crossover voting. The first hypothesis addresses the influence of campaign issues.

Hypothesis 1: Economic and social welfare issues, as part of a deracialized campaign, significantly increase white crossover voting.

While the concept of deracialization has been well developed in the literature, empirical assessments of this strategy have been limited. To characterize a campaign as deracialized requires deep knowledge of the campaign. Where deracialization strategies have been studied, it has typically been with a proxy or underdeveloped techniques. For example, Liu (2003) uses endorsements by white owned newspapers as a proxy for a deracialized campaign. Longoria (1999) uses articles summarizing candidate's stance on key issues. The research presented here expands our understanding of deracialization by measuring the actual issue components of candidates' campaigns. This is an important shift from using approximate measures to assess what has been hailed as critical political strategy.

I examine candidates' issue platforms using a two step process to determine whether the candidate ran a deracialized campaign. The first step required the use of Nexis-Lexis, a full text news database, to learn about the candidates, the tone of the campaign, and key issues in their campaigns. Having identified these issues, each candidate was then contacted and asked to define the most important issue in their campaign. In each case, this issue was the issue candidates spoke about most often in public appearances and used consistently in campaign literature. Candidates were then asked to describe the manner in which they framed the issue. For example, after a candidate mentioned improving health care as the most important issue, the candidate was prompted to talk about the specifics of the message. Did the candidate's message about healthcare stress racial disparities in healthcare, or did the candidate more generally stress the importance of better healthcare for working Americans? This form of questioning was asked of all the candidates to discern whether the candidates presented issues to the electorate in an explicitly race neutral manner. The list of issues and distribution among candidates will be discussed later in the next section of the chapter.

The second hypothesis addresses the impact of campaign issues and the racial context of the precinct to assess under what conditions issues increase white crossover voting.

Hypothesis 2: The impact of issues on white crossover voting will be greater in districts where the percentage of African American registered voters is greater than or equal to 55 percent.

The influence of racial context on white crossover voting has been examined in great detail. Several studies conclude that as the size of the African American population increases, whites are more likely to perceive a racial threat, which leads whites to vote against African American candidates (Key 1949; Huckfeldt and Kohfeld 1989). Yet a growing literature suggests that the racial context positively influences white political behavior (e.g., Carsey 1995; Voss 1996; Liu 2001). It is possible that greater contact and interpersonal interactions with African Americans will result in higher levels of crossover voting. Building on social interaction theory, I posit that deracialized issue strategies will increase white crossover voting in majority African American precincts because in addition to responding positively to the message, these voters are less likely to believe that race hinders the candidate's ability to handle the job. Living in close proximity with African Americans increases the development of casual and personal friendships, which then influences political attitudes and behaviors (e.g., Huckfeldt 1986; Carsey 1995). The social interaction process and the universality of the campaign issue should make these voters more likely to support these candidates.

To test these hypotheses, I examine white crossover voting in twelve biracial state legislative elections between 1996 and 2002 in four states: South Carolina, North Carolina, Florida, and Georgia. Each election district is majority white. The unit of analysis is the electoral precinct and the data includes a total of 422 precincts (see Table 2). These particular elections were chosen for evaluation because: 1) in each district whites are a majority; 2) the African American candidate ran as Democrat and the white candidate ran as a Republican; and 3) in each state voter registration statistics are collected by race. This last criterion is most important because voter registration by race is superior to other aggregate measures, such as voting age population data, and allows for more direct estimate of racial voting (Mc-Clerking 2001). I relied on Lexis-Nexis and state party executive directors and office staff in each state to verify the racial identity of the candidates. I used the *Almanac of American Politics* to verify the racial composition of the district drawn from 1990 Census data. The 2002 election districts were verified using *Maptitude*. This software package provides geographic and demographic data for the United States. Clearly there are some disadvantages to this data that limit generalizability. Because all of the states in the sample are in the South, there is no control for regional effects. While a larger dataset is ideal to decisively conclude that the observed results are generalizable to the national as a whole, it can be argued that southern states permit a more rigorous examination of white voter discrimination given the legacy of racism and prejudice in this region of the country. In other words, southern districts provide a "tough case" test of the white crossover voting hypothesis because white voters in the South are less likely to crossover than those in the North. Thus, if evidence of white crossover voting is found in this study, it is likely that a national sample would have even stronger effects.

Table 2
Election Statistics – African American State Legislative Candidates (1996-2002)

Composition of the District

State	Year	District*	# of Precincts	% African American voters	% white crossover voting	%white	% African American	% Latino
FL	2000	26	67	10.3	40.5	79	11	9
		3*	152	23.3	55.3	65	30	3
GA	1996	64	13	34.1	40.7	69	23	3
	1998	64	13	48.6	53.6	69	23	3
NC	2000	97	23	44.8	64.6	50	47	1
	1998	92	21	6.3	23.1	86	9	1
SC	1998	16	19	28.1	33.9	87	32	1
	2002	11	20	20.5	27.7	72	28	0
		15	22	24.9	27.1	70	29	0
		43	19	24.6	24.0	72	26	0
		58	31	19.4	28.1	69	30	1
		86	22	26.2	27.8	68	31	1
(N)			(422)					

Note: * denotes Senate districts. % African American is the percentage of registered voters within each precinct who are African American.

Source: Voter information collected by author from county boards of elections.

Dependent variable

In an effort to measure racial crossover voting, I use King's (1997) solution to the ecological inference (EI) problem to estimate race-specific individual level information from aggregate data. Drawing individual-level inferences from aggregate data can lead to ecological fallacy. To minimize the potential for errors and biases, I use precinct level data as opposed to district level data. State legislative districts are fairly large, heterogeneous units whereas precincts are smaller and more homogeneous. While some scholars have had success finding individual level data from national exit polls to examine voting behavior (Highton 2004; Wright-Austin and Middleton 2004), major survey efforts rarely address voting behavior at the state legislative level.[4] In the absence of data that evaluates individual level responses from state legislative elections, this technique is the best method to approach this specific research problem.

Estimating the dependent variable, white crossover voting, is a two step process. The first stage of EI applies a model of ecological inference to estimate African American and white turnout in each precinct using the following observed data provided by state board of elections: the proportion of the voting age population who turned out to vote, the proportion of registered African Americans voters, and the total number of voting age people in the precinct. These data were used to estimate race-specific turnout. The second stage of EI, uses an additional variable, the proportion of votes received by the African American candidate to estimate the proportions of white and African American voters that voted for the African American candidate. While this procedure has drawn fire from scholars (e.g., Freedman et al. 1998; Herron and Shotts 2003), it is widely used to study racial voting (e.g., Liu 2001; Liu and Vanderleeuw 2001; Gay 2001). As shown in Figure A-1, King's procedure is less successful at predicting estimates in precincts with large percentages of African American registered voters. As a result, the precincts included in the analysis are those in which at least 25 percent of the registered voters are white, lowering the total number of precincts included in the analysis to 405 (see Table A-1; also for similar analysis, see Liu 2003).[5]

The results presented in Tables 3 and 4 are robust regression models. The models were also tested using weighted least squares (WLS) analyses, which yielded similar results. I use robust regression because like WLS, it takes into account the uncertainty in the estimates, and is best when dealing with data sets with a small number of observations (Draper and Smith 1998; Wooldridge 2000).

Independent variables

The candidates focused their campaign on five major issues: economic development, balancing the state budget, affordable health care, improving public education, and protecting the environment. The data show that five candidates (36 percent) ran on education, three candidates (27 percent) ran on health care, and two candidates (18 percent) ran on economic development. Of the remaining two candidates, one focused on the budget and the other focused on the environment (19 percent). In the analysis, each issue is coded as a binary variable, and then recoded into three issue groups: social issues (environment), social welfare issues (affordable health care, improving public education), and economic issues (economic development, balancing the state budget). Each variation of the issue variables will be tested in separate models to examine the individual and additive effects of the issues.[6]

To measure the impact of social context, I use two variables. The first variable (*Percent African American*) measures the percentage of African American registered voters in each precinct. This continuous variable ranges from 0 percent to 75 percent. The second variable also measures the percentage of African American registered voters but is a dichotomous variable where 1=55 percent or more African American registered voters, and 0 otherwise (*Racial context*). This measure of the African American density level will be used to test Hypothesis 2.

The models also include several control variables thought to influence white crossover voting. *Financial advantage* measures African American candidates' total receipts minus white opponents' total receipts. This information was collected from the National Institute on Money in State Politics. *Political experience* is scaled from low to high, where 0 = no political experience, 1 = some political experience but never held elective office, and 2 = previously held elected office. Previous studies suggest that incumbency and newspaper endorsements (from white newspapers) are positively related to white crossover voting (Reeves 1997; Bullock 1984). *African American Incumbent* is coded 1 if the African American candidate is an incumbent and 0 otherwise. Newspaper endorsement is coded 1 if the candidate was endorsed, 0 otherwise. *Democratic strength*, measures the Democratic Party's share of the general election vote in each precinct in the previous state legislative election. The final variable, *time*, controls for the year of the election. The variable ranges from 0 (1996) to 3 (2002).

Findings

Table 3 tests the impact of a deracialized issue strategy on white crossover voting. The findings for both models demonstrate that candidates' issues significantly influence white crossover voting. In Model 1, white crossover voting increases by 18 percent when African American

Table 3
Issues and White Crossover Voting

	Model 1	Model 2
Social welfare issues	18.23***	-
	(4.25)	
Economic issues	8.06*	-
	(4.31)	
Health care	-	7.26
		(4.68)
Education	-	12.09**
		(4.64)
Economic development	-	21.70***
		(4.49)
Balancing the budget	-	15.02***
		(4.03)
percent African American	.71***	.76***
registered voters	(.04)	(.03)
Endorsement	32.16***	.03
	(4.72)	(5.01)
Financial advantage	.01***	.01***
	(.00)	(.00)
Political experience	8.16***	3.08*
	(2.13)	(1.59)
Incumbency	10.54**	12.54***
	(3.66)	(3.50)
Democratic strength	.10***	.09***
	(.03)	(.02)
Time	2.64	.23
	(1.60)	(1.21)
Intercept	-35.41	18.09
R^2	.68	.72
(N)	(405)	(405)

$*p<.05, **p<.01, ***p<.001$ (one tailed)

candidates run on those issues broadly categorized as social welfare issues (affordable health care, improving public education), and increases 8 percent when they run on economic issues. Model 2, however, provides a richer understanding of how individual issues influence white voting. Here, we find that several issues—education, economic development, and balancing the state budget—are significant predictors of white crossover voting, whereas health care provides little strategic advantage.

Contrary to the group threat theory, both models show that the presence of African Americans in the precinct has a positive and significant impact on white crossover voting. For every one percentage point increase in the percentage of African American registered voters, there is a .71 percentage point increase (Model 1) or .76 percentage point increase (Model 2) in white

Figure 1
Predicted Effect on African American Density on White Crossover Voting

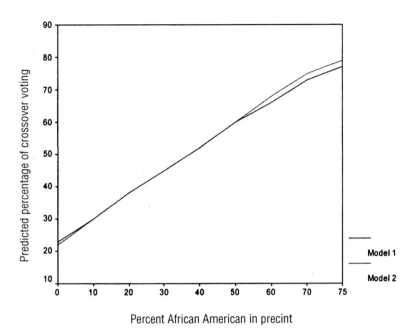

Percent African American in precint

crossover voting. While the effect of the variable on white crossover voting is much smaller than that of issues, Figure 1 demonstrates the substantive influence of African American density on white voting. Holding all other variables constant at their mean, the predicted probability of white crossover voting increases steadily as the percentage of African American registered voters increases.

Most of the control variables are in their expected direction and are statistically significant. Endorsements are highly influential in Model 1 where candidates' issues are coded in broad issue categories, but are less influential when each issue is coded separately in the model. Campaign spending has a positive and significant impact on white crossover voting, and candidates with more political experience garner more white votes. We also find that incumbents draw more support from white voters, suggesting that African American political representation improves white attitudes toward African Americans (e.g., Hajnal 2001). The results also show that white crossover voting for African American state legislative candidates is more likely to occur in precincts with higher levels of Democratic partisanship. Overall, these models are statistically significant, and correctly predict 68 percent and 72 percent of the cases, respectively. The results provide strong evidence for the conclusion that economic and social welfare issues, as part of a deracialized campaign, significantly increase white crossover voting.

The models presented in Table 4 test the second hypothesis about the influence of deracialized issue strategies and racial context. Recall we expect deracialized issue strategies to have a greater impact on white crossover voting in precincts where African Americans are the racial majority. In this table, the measure of African American density is a dichotomous variable where 1=55 percent or more African American registered voters, and 0 otherwise.[7] The findings in Model 1 show that the impact of social welfare issues on white crossover voting is greater in precincts with 55 percent or more African American registered voters. The variable for social welfare issues is negative and statistically insignificant, whereas the racial context variable is

Table 4
Issues, Racial Context, and White Crossover Voting

	Model 1	Model 2
Social welfare issues	-4.12	-
	(5.49)	
Economic issues	-2.43	-
	(5.35)	
Social welfare issues * Context	25.22***	-
	(5.99)	
Economic issues*Context	7.97	-
	(6.07)	
Health care	-	21.51***
		(6.31)
Education	-	5.13***
		(6.25)
Economic development	-	22.97***
		(6.04)
Balancing the budget	-	.82
		(5.44)
Health care* Context	-	25.91***
		(5.66)
Education* Context	-	23.85***
		(7.66)
Economic development* Context	-	18.21**
		(6.98)
Balancing the budget* Context	-	5.84
		(6.44)
Racial Context	24.24***	24.23***
	(5.36)	(5.38)
Endorsement	18.47***	-2.17
	(4.99)	(6.24)
Financial advantage	.01*	.01***
	(.00)	(.00)
Political experience	3.77*	.70
	(1.97)	(1.83)
Incumbency	-2.44	11.99*
	(6.89)	(6.69)
Democratic strength	.13***	.02
	(.03)	(.03)
Time	1.25	.04
	(1.44)	(1.40)
Intercept	4.78	39.01
R2	.57	.59
(N)	(405)	(405)

*p<.05, **p<.01, ***p<.001 (one tailed)

Note: Entries are robust regression coefficients. Robust standard errors are in parentheses.

positive and highly significant. However, the interaction term is both positive and significant. Running on social welfare issues in precincts where African American registered voters are a numerical majority increases white crossover voting by 25 percent. Running on economic issues, however, does not have the same effect.

Model 2 also tests the impact of deracialized issue strategies and racial context on white crossover voting. Here we see that the results largely support Hypothesis 2. The conditional effects of each social welfare issue (health care and education), economic development, and racial context significantly influence white crossover voting. For each variable, the coefficient is positive and statistically significant. It is interesting to note, however, that the positive effect of both social welfare issues in majority African American precincts is larger than the positive effect of economic issues in the same social context. These finding suggest that the social interaction process and the universality of campaign issues, particularly social welfare issues, increases white crossover voting.

Conclusion

This study demonstrates that campaign issues, as part of a deracialized campaign, provide a strategic benefit to African American state legislative candidates. Social welfare and economic issues positively influence white crossover voting in biracial elections. In other words, when African American state legislative candidates stress these issues in a race-neutral manner throughout the campaign, they are able to win the support of a significant percentage of white voters. However, the results also show that African American density, or the percentage of African American registered voters in the precinct, significantly influences the impact of these issue strategies. They are most influential in precincts where African Americans are the majority.

The results are somewhat encouraging for those who are concerned about African American representation in this post-*Shaw* era. Beginning with *Shaw v Reno* (1993), several Supreme Court rulings have steadily impeded the creation of majority African American districts. While there remain conditions under which the Court will uphold the creation of majority-minority districts, the future of these districts remains uncertain. It is likely that the limits have been reached in terms of the number of African American elected officials who have been elected in predominately African American districts. One could argue that "the greatest growth potential for increases in the number of BEO (black elected officials) will likely be in districts without black voting majorities" (Bositis 2002). If attitudes about race continue to place strategic imperatives on African American candidates as many scholars suggest, then it is indeed necessary to further investigate under what conditions African Americans can win crossover votes in majority white districts. This study suggests that candidates' issue strategies may be one way to ensure that the number of African Americans in state legislatures continues to increase. Focusing on social welfare and economic issues as part of a broader deracialization strategy, African American candidates can increase white crossover voting, ultimately increasing their chances of winning elections outside of predominately African American districts. Thus, deracialization can be an effective strategy for integrating more African Americans into political institutions.

Currently, African Americans remain underrepresented in elected offices. Two percent of all elected officials in the U.S. are African American, while African Americans make up over 12 percent of the population (Bositis 2002). Increasing limits placed on the creation of majority- minority districts has exacerbated this inequality in representation. This study suggests that under certain conditions, majority white districts can provide a fertile ground for future African American representation. By running in these districts, African American candidates can continue to increase the presence of African Americans in state legislatures. Therefore,

Carol Swain's (1993) argument that African Americans need not limit their political campaigns to majority African American districts is an important one.

However, the results clearly show that while social welfare and economic issues, as part of a deracialized campaign, are significant predictors of white crossover voting, they are most effective in precincts where African Americans are the racial majority. As Liu (2003; 587) suggests, this reveals an important dilemma for African American candidates running for election in majority-white districts. With the limitation of this campaign strategy revealed, it is necessary to build upon this strategy that "challenges white voters to look to be less race-bound in their voting preferences" (Perry 1996: 3).

Finally, this study also has significant implications for the nature of the electoral process. If, despite its limitations, deracialization can change how voters view African American candidates, then African Americans, who in the past have been constrained by race, face real possibilities of winning elections outside of minority-majority districts. The salience of campaign strategies in elections ultimately strengthens the argument that campaigns play important role in the electoral process—in effect, campaigns do matter (Holbrook 1996).

Appendix

Figure A1
King's Estimated of Precinct White Turnout

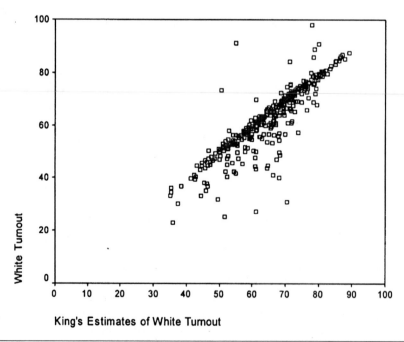

Note: The numbers in the figure represent the percentage of white registered voters in each precinct. Sixty-six precincts did not have voter turnout statistics by race and are excluded from the figure.

TABLE A.1
Estimates of White Turnout in Precincts with up to 75 % African American Registered Voters

Absolute Error |true precinct turnout-King's estimate of precinct turnout|	Number of Precincts	(percent)
<1	142	41.9
1 to <5	127	37.5
5 to <10	36	10.6
10 to <15	23	6.8
15 to <20	8	2.2
> 20	3	1.0
Total	339	100

Note: Sixty-six precincts did not have voter turnout statistics by race and are excluded from the table.

Notes

1. Biracial elections in this study are defined as contests featuring white and African American candidates.
2. It should be noted that African American candidates can also choose an alternative to deracialization—the "balancing commonality" approach outlined by Canon (1999). In this approach to racial representation, African American candidates address and openly recognize racial differences and distinctive black interests, while balancing those concerns with nonracial issues. This is distinct from the approach I describe in this paper, in which no differences between the races are openly addressed by the candidate.
3. A poll conducted by the Washington Post/Kaiser/Harvard in July 2000 shows that 51 percent of Americans surveyed thought that Democrats are better for health care whereas only 38 percent of those polled believed Republicans best handle this issue.
4. The Voter News Service (VNS) provides individual level data from national exit polls for gubernatorial, senatorial, and congressional elections. Had the data included state legislative candidates, this would be an appropriate dataset. However, there is some doubt about the extent to which respondents would answer truthfully to racially sensitive survey questions (Traugott and Price, 1992). When asked whether any polls were conducted during an African American candidate's campaign, one consultant commented "in the midst of a campaign however, with a limited number of questions to ask, these particular questions [questions about race and attitudes toward candidates of a different race] wouldn't be used because I wouldn't know how much faith to put into the numbers."
5. Voter statistics by race were not found for 6 counties in three states: Duplin, NC, Sampson NC, Wake NC, Jefferson, FL, Wakulla, FL, and Dekalb, GA. For these 66 precincts, the absolute value of the difference between actual white voter precinct turnout and King's estimate of white voter turnout was not calculated (see Table A-1). Registration statistics, however, were available. Frequencies of the data show that in these precincts, the percentage of African American registered voters ranged from 1 percent to 73 percent. These precincts are therefore included in the analysis, bringing the total number of observations to 405.
6. In Model 1, social issues (the environment) is the base.
7. The models were also tested with a continuous measure of the racial context. In both Model 1 and 2, the continuous racial context variable was positive and statistically significant. In addition, the variables measuring the interaction between racial context (continuous measure) and the social welfare issues were also positive and statistically significant.

References

Berelson, Bernard R., Paul F. Lazarsfield, and William N. McPhee. 1954. *Voting.* Chicago, IL: University of Chicago Press.

Bianco, William T. 1998. "Different Paths to the Same Result: Rational Choice, Political Psychology, and Impression Formation in Campaigns." *American Journal of Political Science* 42: 1061-1081.

Bobo, Lawrence and James R. Krugel. 1993. "Opposition to Race Targeting: Self Interest, Stratification Ideology, or Racial Attitudes?" *American Sociological Review* 58: 443-464.

Bositis, David A. 2002. "Latest Report of Black Elected Officials: A Statistical Summary." Washington, DC: Joint Center for Political and Economic Studies.

Bullock III, Charles S. 1984. "Racial Crossover Voting and the Election of Black Officials." *Journal of Politics* 46: 239-251.

Campbell, Angus, Philip Converse, Warren E. Miller, and Donald E. Stokes. 1960. *The American Voter.* New York: Wiley.

Canon, David T. 1999. *Race, Redistricting, and Representation: The Unintended Consequences of Black Majority Districts.* Chicago, IL: University of Chicago Press.

Carsey, Thomas. 1995 "The Contextual Effects of Race on White Voter Behavior: The 1989 New York Mayoral Election." *Journal of Politics* 57: 221-228.

Citrin, Jack, Donald Philip Green and David O. Sears. 1990. "White Reactions to Black Candidates: When Does Race Matter?" *Public Opinion Quarterly* 54: 74-96.

Conover, Pamela Johnston and Stanley Feldman. 1989. "Candidate Perception in an Ambiguous World: Campaigns, Cues, and Inference Processes." *American Journal of Political Science* 33: 912-940.

Conover, Pamela. 1984. "The Influence of Group Identifications on Political Perception and Evaluation." *Journal of Politics* 46: 760-785.

Converse, Philip E. 1964. "The Nature of Belief Systems in Mass Publics." In *Ideology and Discontent,* (ed.) David E. Apter. New York: Free Press.

Davidson, Chandler and Bernard Grofman, (eds.) 1994. *Quiet Revolution in the South: The Impact of the Voting Rights Act, 1965-1990.* Princeton: Princeton University Press.

Dawson, Michael C. 1994. *Behind the Mule: Race and Class in African-American Politics.* Princeton, NJ: Princeton University Press.

Draper, N.R. and H. Smith. 1998. *Applied Regression Analysis,* 3rd ed. New York: Wiley.

Fenno, Richard F., Jr. 1978. *Homestyle: House Members in Their Districts.* Boston, MA; Little, Brown and Co.

Freedman, D.A., S.P. Klein, M. Ostland, and M.R. Roberts. 1998. "Review of 'A Solution to the Ecological Inference Problem.'" *Journal of the American Statistical Association 93: 1518–22.*

Gay, Claudine. 2001. "The Effect of Black Congressional Representation on Political Participation." *American Political Science Review* 95: 589-603.

Gilens, Martin. 1999. *Why Americans Hate Welfare: Race, Media, and the Politics of Antipoverty Policy.* Chicago, IL: University of Chicago Press.

Gilens, Martin. 1996. "'Race Coding' and White Opposition to Welfare." *American Political Science Review* 90: 593-604.

Hajnal, Zoltan. 2001. "White Residents, Black Incumbents, and a Declining Racial Divide." *American Political Science Review* 95: 603-617.

Herrnson, Paul S., J. Celeste Lay, and Atiya Kai Stokes. 2003. "Women Running 'as Women': Candidate Gender, Campaign Issues, and Voter-Targeting Strategies." *Journal of Politics* 65: 244-255.

Herron Michael C. and Kenneth W. Shotts. 2003. "Using Ecological Inference Point Estimates as Dependent Variables in Second-Stage Linear Regressions." *Political Analysis* 11: 44-64.

Highton, Benjamin. 2004. "White Voters and African American Candidates for Congress." *Political Behavior* 26: 1-25.

Holbrook, Thomas M. 1996. *Do Campaigns Matter?* CA: Sage Publications.

Huckfeldt, Robert. 1986. *Politics in Context: Assimilation and Conflict in Urban Neighborhoods.* New York: Agathon Press.

Huckfeldt, Robert and Carol Weitzel Kohfeld. 1989. *Race and the Decline of Class in Americans Politics* Urbana, IL: University of Illinois Press.

Jones, Charles E and Michael L. Clemons. 1993. "A Model of Racial Crossover Voting." in Georgia A. Persons, (ed.) *Dilemmas of Black Politics: Issues of Leadership and Strategy.* New York, NY: HarperCollins College Publishers.

Key, V.O., Jr.1949. *Southern Politics in State and Nation.* New York: Knopf.

Kinder, Donald R. and Tali Mendleberg. 1995. "Cracks in American Apartheid: The Political Impact of Prejudice among Desegregated Whites." *Journal of Politics* 57: 402-424

Kinder, Donald R. and D. Roderick Kiewiet. 1981. "Sociotropic Politics." *British Journal of Political Science* 11: 129-161.

King, Gary. 1997. *A Solution to the Ecological Inference Problem" Reconstructing Individual Behavior from Aggregate Data*. Princeton: University of Princeton Press.

Liu, Baodong. 2003. "Deracialization and Urban Racial Contexts." *Urban Affairs Review* 38: 572-591.

Liu, Baodong. 2001. "Racial Contexts and White Interests: Beyond Black Threat and Racial Tolerance." *Political Behavior* 23: 157-180.

Liu, Baodong and James M. Vanderleeuw. 2001. "Racial Transition and White Voter Support for Black Candidates in Urban Elections." *Journal of Urban Affairs* 23: 309-322.

Longoria, Jr., Thomas. 1999. "The Impact of Office on Cross-Racial Voting: Evidence form the 1996 Milwaukee Mayoral Election." *Urban Affairs Review* 34: 596-603.

Lublin, David I. 1997. "The Election of American Americans and Latinos to the U.S. House of Representatives, 1972-1994." *American Politics Quarterly* 25: 269-286.

McClerking, Harwood. 2001. "Looking for 'Threats' in all the Wrong Places: A Critique of the Current Use of Race as a Contextual Effect in Political Science." *Politics & Policy*   29:637-49.

McCormick, Joseph and Charles E. Jones. 1990. "The Conceptualization of Deracialization: Thinking Through the Dilemma." In Georgia A. Persons, (ed.) *Dilemmas of Black Politics: Issues of Leadership and Strategy*. New York, NY: HarperCollins College Publishers.

McDermott, Monika L. 1998. "Race and Gender Cues in Low-Information Elections." *Political Research Quarterly* 51: 895-918.

National Conference of State Legislatures. 2004. "Former State Legislators in the 109th Congress." Available on-line at < http://www.ncsl.org/statefed/fsl.htm>

National Governors Association. 2005. "Fast Facts on Governors." Available on-line at <http://www.nga.org/governors/1,1169,C_TRIVIA^D_2163,00.html>

Perry, Huey L., (ed.) 1996. *Race, Politics, and Governance in the United States*. Gainesville, FL: University Press of Florida.

Persons, Georgia A. 1993. "Black Mayoralities and the New Black Politics: From Insurgency to Racial Conciliation." in *Dilemmas of Black Politics: Issues of Leadership and Strategy,* Georgia A. Persons, (ed.) New York: HarperCollins

Petrocik, John R. 1996. "Issue Ownership in Presidential Elections, with a 1980 Case Study." *American Journal of Political Science* 40: 825-850.

Peffley, Mark, Jon Hurwitz, and Paul M. Sniderman. 1997. "Racial Stereotypes and Whites' Political Views of Blacks in the Context of Welfare and Crime." *American Journal of Political Science* 41: 30-60.

Popkin, Samuel L. 1994. *The Reasoning Voter: Communication and Persuasion in Presidential Campaigns* 2nd edition. Chicago, IL: University of Chicago Press 1994.

Reeves, Keith. 1997. *Voting Hopes or Fears? White Voters, Black Candidates, and Racial Politics in America*. New York, NY: Oxford University Press.

Sack, Kevin. "In the Rural White South, Seeds of a Biracial Politics." *New York Times* Dec. 30, 1998. Late ed. A1.

Schuman, Howard, Charlotte Steeh, and Lawrence Bobo. 1988. *Racial Attitudes in America: Trends and Interpretations*. Cambridge, MA: Harvard University Press.

Sigelman, Carol K., Lee Sigelman, Barbara J. Walkosz and Michael Nitz. 1995. "Black Candidates, White Voters: Understanding Racial Bias in Political Perceptions." *American Journal of Political Science* 39:243-65.

Swain, Carol M. 1993. *Black Faces, Black Interests: The Representation of African Americans in Congress*. Cambridge, MA: Harvard University Press.

Thernstrom, Abigail M. 1987. *Whose Votes Count? Affirmative Action and African American Voting Rights*. Cambridge, MA: Harvard University Press.

Traugott, Michael W. and Vincent Price. 1992. "Exit Polls in the 1989 Virginia Gubernatorial Race: Where Did They Go Wrong?" *Public Opinion Quarterly* 56: 245-253.

Terkildsen, Nayda. 1993. "When White Voters Evaluate Black Candidates: The Processing Implications of Candidate Skin Color, Prejudice and Self-Monitoring." *American Journal of Politics* 37: 1032-1053.

Voss, D. Stephen, and David Lublin. 2001. "Black Incumbents, White Districts: An Appraisal of the 1996 Congressional Elections." *American Politics Research* 29: 141-82.

Voss, D. Stephen. 1996. "Beyond Racial Threat: Failure of an Old Hypothesis in the New South." *Journal of Politics* 58: 1156-1170.

Williams, Linda F. 1990. "White/Black Perceptions of the Electability of Black Political   Candidates." *National Political Science Review* 2: 45-64.

Wooldridge, Jeffrey M. 2000. Introductory Econometrics: A Modern Approach. OH: South Western College Publishing.

Wright-Austin, Sharon and Richard Middleton, IV. 2004. "The Limits of the Deracialization Concept in the 2001 Los Angeles Mayoral Election." *Political Research Quarterly* 57: 283-293.

A Systematic Analysis of the Deracialization Concept*

Byron D'Andra Orey
Department of Political Science
University of Nebraska, Lincoln

Boris E. Ricks
Department of Political Science
University of Missouri, Kansas City
& Mellon Postdoctoral Fellow (2004-2006),
Pomona College

*Acknowledgements: An earlier version of this paper was presented at the Western Political Science Association's annual meeting in Denver, Colorado. We are especially thankful to Michael Preston, Richard Engstrom, William Nelson, Janelle Wong and Renford Reese for their prior comments. Of course, only the authors can be responsible for the analyses and interpretations presented here. We would like to especially thank Dan Orey, Jr. (1941-2006) who encouraged both of us to make the best of our education while matriculating as student/athletes at his/our alma mater, Mississippi Valley State University.

Introduction

The concept of deracialization gained notoriety following elections held in November of 1989. During these elections, a number of African-American candidates captured victories in majority-white electoral jurisdictions, leading McCormick (1989: 1) to coin this Election Day as "Black Tuesday." Among those elected on "Black Tuesday" include: L. Douglas Wilder as governor of Virginia, David Dinkins as mayor of New York City, Norman Rice as mayor of Seattle and Chester Jenkins, mayor of Durham, North Carolina. In this article we systematically examine the deracialization construct/strategy and the potentially damaging impact that such a strategy might pose on the black community.

The evolution of the deracialization concept

McCormick and Jones (1993) formally define deracialization as, "conducting a campaign in a stylistic fashion that defuses the polarizing effects of race by avoiding explicit reference to race-specific issues, while at the same time emphasizing those issues that are perceived as racially transcendent, thus mobilizing a broad segment of the electorate for purposes of capturing or maintaining public office" (76). The concept was first introduced in 1973 by political scientist, Charles Hamilton, at a National Urban League meeting. The purpose of the meeting was to assemble a group of scholars, activists, and public officials to discuss strategies for organizing in the "post-protest" phase of the civil rights movement. During this meeting, Hamilton presented a brief essay that offered some possible strategies for achieving his goal. He encouraged blacks to develop coalitions with other races, especially whites (Hamilton 1973). As a means of gaining white support, Hamilton suggested that blacks should address social issues that made broad appeals to society as a whole. For Hamilton, one such issue was "full employment," which he considered the most important issue facing the black community and also an issue equally appealing to whites.

In 1976, Hamilton revisited the concept of deracialization in a position paper commissioned by the Democratic Party. During this presentation, he advised presidential candidates to emphasize issues that would attract voters across racial lines (Hamilton 1977). Hamilton argued that programs targeted directly at minorities failed to capture white votes. Thus, he urged civil rights groups and the Democratic Party to work for "deracialized solutions" such as national health insurance and an income maintenance program (McCormick and Jones 1993: 70). William Julius Wilson (1990) expanded upon Hamilton's message by suggesting that the Democratic Party embrace a progressive "race neutral program." Wilson stated that blacks and liberals who have pushed "a race specific agenda" (e.g., affirmative action, minority set-asides, busing) create a major barrier to those advocating broader programs that would be more attractive to white voters.

Hamilton's advocacy for the deracialized strategy sparked an interest among students of black politics (see e.g., Persons 1993; Perry 1991 and 1996). The preponderance of studies employing the concept of deracialization, however, has not been based on the systematic analysis of evidence. A typical study in this area simply presents conclusions drawn by the researcher with no indication of the methods or standards employed to arrive at such conclusions. In this article our goal is to improve upon the extant literature by creating a quantifiable measure of the deracialization construct. In doing so, we conduct an empirical analysis for the purpose of systematically testing the construct's validity.

Deracialization and its Application

According to McCormick and Jones (1993: 76), a deracialized political strategy affects the issues candidates stress, their mobilization tactics and the style of their campaigns. Their model cautions black candidates who run in racially competitive districts/jurisdictions to avoid race-specific campaigns. According to this model, black candidates in such positions should avoid using explicit references to issues such as welfare, affirmative action and set-asides. Rather, they should place emphasis on issues that appear to be race-neutral. In addition to the avoidance of race-specific issues, the deracialized strategy also involves the campaign tactics employed by black candidates to mobilize voters. The authors contend that black office seekers who run deracialized campaigns should avoid public appeals to the black community. Black candidates risk the potential of alienating the white electorate with the use of race-specific campaign tactics. In short, black candidates should be careful of not giving white voters the impression that they are only interested in representing blacks. The final component of McCormick and Jones's model is political style. The success of black candidates in attracting white support depends, in part, on their ability to project a nonthreatening image. It therefore is necessary for black candidates to project a reassuring image to the white electorate. Black candidates, for example, should avoid associating themselves with people that white voters will view as racial partisans.

The scholarly debate on the issue of deracialization has evolved both normatively and empirically. Borrowing from the normative front, political scientist Ron Walters notes that "the available political jurisdictions that are majority black are drying up. So to increase the number of Black elected officials, they will have to come from majority white districts. You cannot run there in the same way as in a majority Black district and be successful." (quoted by Gurwitt 1990: 30). Confronted with this reality, both scholars and political pundits have argued that new strategies such as deracialization are necessary in order for more black candidates to be successful in the future. Others, on the other hand, view the use of this strategy with a jaundiced eye. Starks (1991), for example, has argued that the concept:

> ... cannot be permitted to divert attention from the essence of American politics—that is, the acquisition and maintenance of group power. Nor can it be permitted to divert from the substance of what constitutes African-American politics—using electoral politics as a lever to maximize group power in the fight against racism, exclusion, and marginalization while promoting African-American-specific policy preferences within the political system (Starks 1991: 216).

In a case study of L. Douglas Wilder's election as governor of Virginia in 1989, Jones and Clemmons (1993), note that Wilder presented himself as a "social moderate and fiscal conservative who represented the 'New Virginia Mainstream'—a major theme of the campaign" (140). In determining whether Wilder conducted a deracialized campaign, these authors systematically examine Wilder's appointment book. The results reveal that between June 19 and September 4, 1989, Wilder appeared before the public eighty-four times. Jones and Clemons (1993) dichotomize the groups Wilder addressed, as being predominantly-white or predominantly-black, finding that only ten of these appearances were before black audiences. This research serves as one of the few systematic analyses conducted on the deracialization concept to date.

Schexnider (1990) extends his analysis to move beyond Wilder's gubernatorial race. He argues that Wilder's deracialization strategy can be traced back as far as his 1985 campaign to become lieutenant governor of Virginia. According to the author, Wilder did not present himself to the Virginia electorate as a black candidate in 1985, rather Wilder focused on his legislative record and issues that appealed to all voters (e.g., economic, educational, and environmental). Schexnider cites the work of Yancey (1988) as support for his claims. Yancey states:

> Wilder never mentioned race. He hammered away at why he was more qualified until the media and white voters finally had to pay attention. But his campaign never took on the aura of a black crusade. But Wilder knew he had to have the redneck and suburban vote to win and he went after it (Yancey quoted in Schexnider 1990: 155).

However, Yancey himself does not provide a systematic analysis for his conclusions (see, Yancey 1988: 17).

Wilson Goode was elected as the first black mayor of Philadelphia, Pennsylvania in 1983. In examining Goode's campaign strategy, Ransom (1987) writes, "Goode did not portray himself as a 'black' candidate for mayor; instead, he campaigned as the former city managing director—he was familiar with city services; he knew the budget; he had demonstrated his managerial skills; and he had a vision of Philadelphia on the move" (276). Ransom continues by stating that Goode placed emphasis on his experience and background, and voiced the necessity of a partnership between the public and private sectors. Despite such claims, the author fails to reference any support for his claims.

The above examples are typical of studies in this area. They simply present conclusions drawn by the researchers with very little mention of the methods or inferential standards employed to arrive at such conclusions. Such presentations are difficult, if not impossible, to replicate and evaluate.[1] For example, no systematic content analysis of the media coverage of a campaign is provided. In only a few cases, as well, are there references to elite interviews with people in a position to know about the election campaigns (e.g., Summers and Klinkner 1996).

Even in the few cases in which a systematic analysis was attempted, it is often flawed. Katherine Underwood (1997) utilizes the deracialization concept in her investigation of the campaigns of Latino candidates for the city council elections in Los Angeles, California. She reports that Latino candidates were able to build cross-racial support by running deracialized campaigns. Underwood employs multiple regression to examine the causation of the vote for Latino candidates as a function of the voting age population by ethnic group. However, Underwood's findings are marred by mistakes. Criticism of the analysis is best stated in her own words: "The independent variables constructed result in near perfect multicollinearity. To the extent that the four ethnic categories (white, African American, Latino, and Asian) exhaustively include the precinct population, the value of the fourth category is almost perfectly determined by the other three" (Underwood 1997: 13). In the worst case, multicollinearity inflates the standard errors of the correlated variables and attenuates the statistical significance of the unstandardized coefficients.

Sharon Wright's (1996: 157) racially polarized voting analysis of the 1991 mayoral election in Memphis, Tennessee serves as one of the few analyses to systematically examine the impact of a candidate's campaign strategy. According to her analysis, Willie W. Herenton, the black candidate, is reported to have received roughly 98.5 percent of the black vote and only 1.5 percent of the white vote. On the other hand, Richard Hacket, a white candidate, received 98.5 percent of the white vote and only 1.5 percent of the black vote.

Elsewhere, Orey has attempted to strengthen the literature examining the deracialization construct, by conducting systematic analyses. In one analysis, Orey (n.d.) argues that the media should be employed as a contextual variable/effect, when examining the deracialization construct. Using content analysis, he finds that the print media helped to create a racialized environment, even when the black candidate attempted to run a deracialized campaign. Specifically, in using Jackson, Mississippi as a case study, Orey finds that the leading mainstream newspaper (i.e., paper with the highest circulation in the state), *The Clarion Ledger*, made more references to race in 1993 when the leading black candidate loss, than in 1997 when he won. Further, in a separate analysis, Orey (1999), in following the lead of Wright (1996), employs ecological inference to examine racial bloc voting in the 1993 and 1997 Jackson, mayoral election. He finds that the black candidate received more votes from both blacks and whites when he ran a race-specific campaign, than when he ran a deracialized campaign. In running a deracialized campaign, the candidate failed to win the primary, however, when he ran a race-specific campaign he was elected as the city's first black mayor.

Where do we go from here?

Albritton, et al. (1996) provide us with a template as to how to proceed in our efforts to measure deracialization. These authors create a typology for racial campaigns. They identify four categories of racial campaigns: (1) race-specific, (2) modified race-specific, (3) race-neutral and (4) extremely race-neutral. Conceptually, the authors make a much-needed contribution to the deracialization literature. However, these authors fail to provide a systematic method for distinguishing among their categories. In failing to create replicable measurements for their categories, the authors are unable to systematically analyze their data, which makes it very difficult to evaluate their work.

Data and Methods

The data employed in this analysis are derived from the 2001 *California Black Elected Officials Survey* (Ricks, 2003*).* We first retrieved addresses for the 238 black elected officials in the state of California from the Joint Center for Political and Economic Studies. A survey was then mailed to all of the black elected officials in the state of California on August 15, 2001. The responses included seventy-four completed surveys. An additional twelve surveys were returned as undeliverable (because of incorrect addresses). As a result, our response rate, excluding the twelve undeliverable questionnaires, dips to 33 percent. Admittedly, this rate is somewhat lower than the 40 percent reported within the extant literature.

Dependent Variables

Using the above typology offered by Albritton et al., we operationalize deracialization based on the following item: "which of the following strategies best describe your campaign?" The responses included "race neutral (e.g., absence of racial cues; colorblind)", "race moderate (e.g., low use of racial cues, coalition building)" and "race specific (e.g., high use of racial cues; Afro-centric)." Given the fact that our analysis focuses on deracialization, we code the variable as a dichotomy, taking on a value of one, if the response is race neutral and zero otherwise. Given the dichotomous nature of the variable, logistic regression is employed.

In addition, we have created a measure for Black Interests to determine whether a black candidate who runs a deracialized campaign is more or less likely to support a black interest bill. To operationalize the Black Interest variable, we have created an additive-index scale based on three Likert response-format items: The leadership style of black elected officials differs from that of white elected officials; black voting districts should be exclusively represented by black elected officials; for black office seekers, identification with black issues is more important than coalition building. The scale's reliability is moderate, achieving an alpha score of .61. The additive-scale ranges from strongly agree to strongly disagree. Given the continuous nature of this variable, ordinary least squares regression is used.

Independent Variables

Deracialization also is measured on the right hand side of the equation. In addition, other independent variables include racial identification, which takes on a value of one if the respondent indicated that African-American best described his/her race and zero otherwise (i.e., Negro, Black, Colored, African, or some other label). Additionally, a number of control variables are included for the purpose of correctly specifying the model. Gender is a dichotomous variable that takes on a value of one if the respondent is male and zero for females. Education is a continuous variable ranging from lowest level of education (high school diploma or less) to highest level (postgraduate). Similarly, income ranges from lowest level of income (under 40K) to highest level of income (over 100K). Age is the actual age of the respondent. Ideology is based on a four point scale ranging from conservative to radical, with both moderate and liberal occupying the middle categories, in the order presented here. Democratic identification is represented as a dummy variable taking on a value of one if the respondent is Democrat and a zero otherwise.[2]

For ease of interpretation, all variables have been mapped onto a [0, 1] interval, with the exception of age.

Thus, our proposed models suggest the following relationships:

(1) **Deracialization** = f(Age, Income, Education, Income, Racial Identification, Ideology, Democrat, Gender).

(2) **Black Interests** = f(Deracialization, Age, Income, Education, Income, Racial Identification, Ideology, Democrat, Gender).

Findings

Based on the descriptive statistics, black elected officials are more likely to identify their political campaign as being a race-neutral or a race-moderate campaign, as opposed to a race-specific campaign. According to Table 1, approximately 41 percent of the respondents indicated that their campaign style can best be described as race-neutral. A majority of the respondents (51 percent), however, identified their campaign as race-moderate. Only about eight percent of the respondents identified as running race-specific campaigns.

In addition to the campaign strategy, Table 2 provides a frequency distribution of the agree/disagree responses of the Likert-items used to measure Black Interests. Based on these findings, roughly 52.2 percent of the respondents disagreed that "the leadership style of black elected officials differs from that of white elected officials, compared to 34.3 percent that agreed. Approximately 60 percent disagreed that "black voting districts should be exclusively represented by black elected officials, compared to 31.4 percent who agreed. Lastly, approximately 70 percent disagreed that "for black office seekers, identification with black issues is more important than coalition building," compared to 17.2 percent who agreed.

Using logistic regression, Table 3 provides the results for the explanations of deracialization. Based on the Odds-Ratios reported in Table 3, the findings reveal that older African-American leaders are roughly 5 percent more likely to adopt a deracialized strategy when compared to younger blacks. Additionally, those blacks who self-identify with the label African-American are found to be approximately 73 percent less likely to adopt a deracialized strategy when compared to those blacks identifying with some other label describing blacks. Lastly, blacks who self-identify as Democrats are 88 percent less likely to describe their leadership as race neutral. The models pseudo r-square is respectable at .28.

Table 4 affords us the opportunity to determine if deracialization serves as an explanation for opposition to Black Interests. Based on the results, the deracialization variable achieves statistical discernability at the .05 level. No other variable in the analysis achieves statistical significance. The results presented here support the normative literature suggesting that those black leaders who identify with the deracialized leadership style are more likely to oppose/disagree with interests that are deemed to be progressive for the black community.

Conclusion

The preponderance of scholars conducting research on deracialization has failed to provide systematic analyses in drawing their conclusion. The typical study in this area has drawn conclusions without providing any indication of the methods or standards employed to make such inferences. The research here has created a quantifiable variable measuring deracialization. The construct is based upon previous definitions of the deracialization strategy. Here, we have focused on the issues and the campaign style. The validity of the measure was tested, by examining the impact of the deracialization variable on opposition to black interests. Based on the findings, those black elected officials who have identified their campaign strategies as race-neutral/deracialized, were less likely to support interests that have traditionally been found to be pertinent to the black community. Admittedly, we rely on extreme categories, due to data limitations. However, these issues are consistent with traditional issues addressed by black elected officials. Despite this shortcoming, this research note has provided us with a useful means for operationalizing the deracialization construct.

The implications of this study suggest that African Americans who run race-neutral campaigns have moved away from the protest approach used in the 1960s and 1970s to more accommodating campaign strategies. The overwhelming percentage of race-neutral and race-moderate campaigns endorsed by the respondents in this analysis suggest that African Americans have become more responsive to other groups, and place less emphasis entirely on Black Interests. Indeed, our multiple regression analysis finds that respondents who ran deracialized campaigns were less likely to endorse black interest policies. Interestingly, our findings also reveal that older legislators are more likely to identify their campaigns as race-neutral, when compared to their younger counterparts.

The findings discussed here have broader implications for students of black politics. black elected officials who run deracialized campaigns will also support race-neutral bills. Or, more important, these officials may fail to support black-interest bills. Future research examining the sponsorship of bills is needed if we are to gain a full understanding of the impact of the deracialization strategy on candidate's performance in office. Clearly, the current research is limited by our data and as a result, one should be careful in making generalizations based on our findings. Similarly, as always, when conducting case studies, caution should be used in making generalizations. Despite these shortcomings, we have attempted to generate research questions that may be answered in future research.

Table 1
Which of the following best describes your campaign strategy?

	Percent	**Respondents**
race-neutral (colorblind)	41%	30
race-moderate (coalition-building)	51%	38
race-specific (pro-Black)	4%	3

Source: California Black Elected Officials (Ricks, 2003).

Table 2 [3]
Questions used to construct the Black Interests Index
N=70

		Percentage who indicated:	
		agree	disagree
1.	The leadership style of black elected officials differ from that of white elected officials.	52.2%	34.3%
2.	Black voting districts should be exclusively represented by black elected officials.	60%	31.4%
3.	For black office seekers, identification with black issues is more important than coalition building.	70%	17.2%

Source: California Black Elected Officials

Table 3
Logistic regression predicting Deracialization.

Variable	b	s.e.	Odds ratio
Age	0.052	(0.024)**	1.05
Racial Identification			
(African-American)	-1.324	(0.613)**	0.27
Income	0.592	(1.205)	1.81
Education	0.525	(1.035)	1.70
Ideology	-2.375	(1.124)	0.09
Gender (male)	-0.059	(0.629)	0.94
Democratic Identification	-2.114	(1.06)*	0.12
Constant	-2.142	(1.543)	

Pseudo R2	
(Nagelkerke)	0.28
χ^2	16.61
Prob. $> \chi^2$	0.02**
N	70

Note: **p < .05; *p< .10

Table 4
Opposition to Black Interests

Variable	b	s.e.
Deracialization	0.15	(0.07)*
Ideology	-0.10	(0.13)
Education	0.02	(0.12)
Income	0.07	(0.13)
Racial Identification		
(African-American)	0.003	(0.07)
Age	-0.002	(0.002)
Gender (Male)	0.02	(0.07)
Constant	0.60	(0.16)**

R2	0.12
Adj. R2	0.02
N	70

Note *p < .05 **p < .01

Notes

1. Krippendorf (1980: 145) suggests that the researcher "must describe the conditions under which data are obtained, justify the analytic steps taken, and see to it that the process is not biased in the sense that if favors one kind of finding rather than another. Explicitness about the process is required so that others may evaluate his work, replicate the process, or qualify the findings."
2. This decision was made because there is limited variation beyond identification with the Republican Party (e.g., Democrats represent roughly 84 percent and Republicans represent 13 percent of the sample).
3. All strongly agree/agree categories are collapsed into one category of agree, and all strongly disagree/disagree categories were collapsed. Also, the percentages do not add up to 100 because a separate middle category capturing undecided respondents is not presented here.

References

Albritton, Robert B., George Amedee, Keenan Grenell and Don-Terry Veal. 1996. "Deracialization and the New Black Politics" in *Race, Politics and Governance in the United States*, (ed.) Huey L. Perry. Gainesville, FL. University Press of Florida: 96-106.
Gurwitt, Robert. 1990. "A Younger Generation of Black Politicians Challenges Its Elders." *Governing the States and Localities* (February).
Hamilton, Charles. 1973. "Full Employment as a Viable Issue." In *When the Marching Stopped: An Analysis of Black Issues in the '70s*. New York: The National Urban League: 87-91.
———. 1977. "Deracialization: Examination of a Political Strategy." *First World*. March/April: 3-5.
Jones, Charles E. and Michael L. Clemons. 1993. "A Model of Racial Crossover" in *Dilemmas of Black Politics*, (ed.) Georgia Persons. New York. Harper Collins College Publishers, 66-84.
Krippendorff, Klaus. 1980. *Content Analysis: An Introduction to its Methodology*. Beverly Hills, CA: Sage Publications.
McCormick, J.P., II and Charles E. Jones. 1993. "The Conceptualization of Deracialization" in *Dilemmas of Black Politics*, (ed.) Georgia Persons. New York. Harper Collins College Publishers, 66-84.
McCormick, J.P., II. 1989. "Black Tuesday and the Politics of Deracialization." Paper delivered at a symposium, Blacks in the November '89 Elections: What is Changing." Sponsored by the Joint Center for Political Studies, Washington, DC. December 5, 1989.
Orey, Byron D'Andra. Forthcoming. "Framing the Issue, When the Issue is Race." *International Journal of Africana Studies*.
———. 1999. *Deracialization, Racialization or Something in Between: The Making of a Black Mayor in Jackson, Mississippi*. Ph.D. Dissertation, University of New Orleans.
Perry, Huey. 1991. "Deracialization as an Analytical Construct in American Urban Politics." *Urban Affairs Quarterly* 27, 2 (December): 181-91.
———, (ed.) 1996. *Race, Politics and Governance in the United States*. Gainesville, FL: University Press of Florida.
Persons, Georgia A. 1993. *Dilemmas of Black Politics: Issues of Leadership and Strategy*. New York: Harper-Collins College Publishers.
Ransom, Bruce. 1987. "Black Independent Electoral Politics in Philadelphia and the Election of Mayor W. Wilson Goode." In *The New Black Politics*. (ed.) Michael Preston, Lenneal J. Henderson, Jr. and Paul L. Pureyar. White Plains: Longman: 256-293.
Ricks, Boris E. 2003. *California Black Elected Officials Survey Data/Codebook*. In Black Elected Officials, Leadership Style and The Politics of Race: Los Angeles, 1963-2000. Ph.D. Dissertation, University of Southern California.
Schexnider, Alvin J. 1990. "The Politics of Pragmatism: An Analysis of the 1989 Gubernatorial Election in Virginia." *Urban Affairs Quarterly*, 27 December (2): 216-222.
Starks, Robert. 1991. "Commentary and Response to Exploring the Meaning and Implications on Deracialization in African-American Urban Politics." *Urban Affairs Quarterly*, 27 December (2): 216-222.
Summers, Mary E. and Phillip Klinkners. 1996. "The Election and Governance of John Daniels as Mayor of New Haven." *In Race, Politics, and Governance in the United States*, (ed.) Huey L. Perry. Gainesville, FL. University Press of Florida: 127-150.
Underwood, Katherine. 1997. "Ethnicity is Not Enough." *Urban Affairs Review* September 33 (1): 3-27.

Wilson, William Julius. 1990. "Race neutral policies and the Democratic coalition." The American Prospect 1: 74-81.

Wright, Sharon. 1996. "The Deracialization Strategy and African American Candidates in Memphis Mayoral Elections." *In Race, Politics and Governance in the United States*, (ed.) Huey L. Perry. Gainesville, FL. University Press of Florida: 151-164.

Yancey, Dwayne. 1988. *When Hell Froze Over*. Roanoke, VA: Taylor Publishing Co.

Conservatives, Federalism, and the Defense of Inequality

Donald J. Matthewson
Shelly Arsneault
Department of Political Science
California State University, Fullerton

Introduction

Modern American conservatives, following a tradition that dates back to Plato, have consistently demonstrated an aversion to the egalitarian aspects of democracy. Conservative thinkers as diverse as Michael Novak (1996), Leo Strauss (1968), and Richard Weaver (1948) have all argued that modern democracy, which inexorably reduces distinctions among citizens, is the most "pernicious result" of liberal political thought. In applying their philosophy to public policy issues, conservatives have argued that remedial policies designed to correct structural inequalities threaten the "traditional order" of society. While we accept the view that modern conservatism plays a critical role in contemporary politics by raising questions that must be answered by liberals, we contend that conservatism's constructive role in fashioning public policy is limited. We agree with the observation of Christopher Jencks that conservative principles applied to public policy increase income inequality and, in turn, increase social and political inequality.[1] We extend the argument of Jencks and show that in its critical mode conservatism raises important questions that must be considered when fashioning public policy, however, in its constructive mode, conservative policies often undermine equality thereby undermining democratic values.

Specifically, we demonstrate that "new" conservatives argue for a type of federalism that promotes decentralization of government functions, urges close government cooperation with segments of the private sector, and creates social and economic inequality without corresponding economic and social mobility. Modern conservatives are not unlike their older counterparts in that the goal of each is to support and maintain a social and political order that is hierarchical or, as Wilmoore Kendall (1985) has phrased it, "to maintain aristocracy without aristocrats." As we will show, both the old and the new conservatives hold in common a deep distrust for democracy. The fear of democracy that is characteristic of conservative thinking operates to undermine the very goals that conservatives wish to promote. The liberal model of democracy that is most disparaged by conservative thinkers embodies the tradition which emphasizes that equal rights for all citizens pre-exist the formation of the state. Contemporary liberal theories of democracy argue for a relatively strong state to secure the promise of equal civil, political, and social rights. At the same time, liberals hold that the state not be intrusive with respect to individual freedoms and liberties.

By contrast, American conservatism derives from three intellectual traditions: "neoconservatism," traditional conservatism, and religious conservatism. While the model of democracy envisioned by the "new" or neoconservatives differs from that of the "old" traditional conservatives, the ends of the polity, for each, remain the same. For conservatives, whether "new," traditional, or religious, the primary purpose of philosophy is to stop the "liberal revolution," which they believe is destined to turn the U.S. into a "collectivist," egalitarian state.

The first of the three traditions, neoconservatism is discussed in detail by Peter Steinfels (1979). He notes that, "one of the most perplexing aspects of neoconservatism is its apparent belief that America is in the grip of implacable egalitarianism" (1979: 274). According to Steinfels, neoconservatives fear most the shift from equality of opportunity to equality of results, and the shift from equality between individuals to equality between groups. The concern about equality expressed by neoconservatives in the 1970s and 1980s converged during this time period with similar views that had been expressed by classical conservatives much earlier. Robert Devigne observes, "The neoconservatives, believing that postindustrialism had eroded public belief in the veracity of the political and social mores required for a stable liberal democracy, advanced a political prescription similar to one offered by the Straussians: the development of public policies and institutions that conform to public standards of a political and moral good and bad" (1994: 64).

Traditional conservatives, taking their inspiration from Plato, argue against democracy and particularly the liberal view of democracy that emphasizes equality. The antipathy to democracy has prompted conservatives such as Richard Weaver (1948) to note that "pure democracy" fails because of its inability "to stand for anything intelligible." Traditional conservatives argue for a model of American democracy that turns Madisonian democracy into a modified aristocracy. Such a model must move control of politics as far as possible from control by the *demos*. This conservative model emphasizes the regeneration of aristocratic leadership that preserves "reverence, discipline, order, and class" (Kirk 1985).

Further, the third main intellectual source of conservatism, religious conservatism, also expresses hostility toward equality. For example, Richard John Neuhaus and Peter Berger argued in 1976 that the real threat to modern society is the encroachment of the secular state in the name of egalitarianism on the free market and "constructive" role of religion in public life. By the late 1970s, all three intellectual strands of conservatism converged in their opposition to egalitarian trends in American life in general and, specifically, to the concept of social welfare embodied in the reforms of the Great Society. Rather than focus on a broad treatment of the fusion between classical conservatism, neoconservatism, and religious conservatism, we are most concerned in this paper with their joint defense of inequality and their institutional recommendations for the promotion of a specific vision of democracy that many liberals consider anti-democratic.

We divide this paper into three parts, first outlining the conservative defense of social and economic inequality. We find that the conservative commitment to inequality is not simply based on support for a market system, nor can the defense of inequality be viewed merely as a reaction to the expansion of the welfare state in the 1960s and 1970s. On a more fundamental level, the defense of inequality derives from a particular view of human nature, which finds its origin in a specific interpretation of the Judeo-Christian concept of original sin.

Second, we identify the political structures that conservatives wish to establish in order to promote the goal of inequality. Specifically, we examine the conservative conception of federalism, relying primarily on the literature of public choice theory, and we attempt to show how conservatives have used this literature to argue for a specific version of American federalism.

In general, their view of federalism holds that the worst features of American democracy can be eliminated by reducing the size of decision- making units. Smaller decision-making units, in the language of public choice theory, can create conditions that can, overtime, lead to results that approximate unanimity in decision making. Furthermore, smaller units are more receptive to civic groups, reducing the possibilities for opportunistic behavior that often lead to "rent seeking."[2] We show that the institutions essential to this form of federalism actually undermine, rather than promote, democratic decision making.

Finally, we use the 1996 Personal Responsibility and Work Opportunity Reconciliation Act (PRWORA) to demonstrate that the devolutionary federalism advanced by conservatives subverts equality, thereby subverting democracy. Roeder (1994) argues that competition between local communities improves democracy as politicians respond to the demands for services by constituents who can, in Tiebout's (1956) words, "vote with their feet." However, many scholars have noted that, in fact, American politicians at the state and local level are more responsive to development and business interests than the interests of average citizens (Bowman and Kearney, 1986; Peterson, 1981; Peterson, Rabe and Wong, 1986; Rom, 1989; Shannon, 1989; Feiock, 2002); and they are far less interested in serving the needs of low income citizens (Piven and Cloward, 1985; Piven, 2002). The poor vote and participate in the political system less often than their wealthy neighbors, thus insuring that economic inequality and political inequality co-exist. Economic and social inequality have also been linked to political instability, which often leads to government restrictions on political activity that further erode political rights and thereby eroding democracy. Put simply, economic and social inequality foster political inequality and political inequality precludes a truly democratic system.

The Conservative Defense of Inequality

The first part of our paper attempts to reconstruct the conservative defense of inequality. We explore the central paradox of conservative philosophy, which is its claim to be a democratic ideology while at the same time supporting political, social, and economic inequality. The conservative justification for inequality is curious because it involves the reassertion of a moral order and at the same time a redefinition of human freedom based upon economic foundations. How this conjunction is worked out gives us insight into the modern conservative philosophy. The following are the main steps in the conservative argument and represent views held in common by all three variations of conservatism:

1. The decay in modern society, for conservatives, represents a decline from an absolute fixed moral order.
2. The trend toward increasing equality is a reflection of the decline from an absolute moral order and an attempt to replace the natural order of society with man made utopianism.
3. The increasing democratization that accompanies egalitarianism threatens the traditional order. The *demos* cannot be relied upon to exhibit either virtue or restraint. Elites, whether produced through education or a competitive economic system, are important to the maintenance of an ordered society.
4. To re-establish morality human freedom must be restrained.
5. Human freedom can be restrained either through coercion or the reconceptualization of freedom in economic terms or a combination of both.
6. Freedom in the private realm is relatively more important than political freedom.
7. Inequality is thus a natural consequence of the re-introduction of a well-ordered society and reaffirmation of "traditional American values."

Before turning to the question of how the conservative vision is institutionalized, it is necessary to examine the supporting evidence for their main argument.

First, whether secular or religious, conservatives begin their analysis of modernity by arguing that contemporary society is in a state of decline. The decay that is being experienced in modern society is illustrated both by nihilism and a disregard for the "traditional rules" of moral conduct by society as a whole. Daniel Patrick Moynihan (1993) referred to this trend as "defining deviancy down," while Charles Krauthhammer (1993) called it "defining deviancy up." In both cases conservatives maintain that moral decline and relativism are proximate results of the "moral deregulation" of the 1960s.

The decline of modern society is rooted in the conservative view of the nature of man. Whether religious or secular, conservatives believe that the natural characteristic of man is his tendency to engage in evil. Peter Viereck once defined conservatism as "the political secularization of the doctrine of original sin" (1949: 6). Modern conservatives derive their view of human nature from sources such as Plato and St. Augustine. While Plato writes in the classical Greek tradition and St. Augustine in the Christian tradition, both share the view that evil is a part of the human condition. In the classical view, the context of evil was man himself; he could choose virtue, or alternatively evil, which is viewed as a departure from natural harmony or from happiness. In any case, according to Strauss, good or evil derives from human action which has the potential of diverging from the "natural order" of the soul (1968: 13).

On the other hand, the Christian view of sin is somewhat more complex. On one level, Christianity is egalitarian, radical, and progressive. There are no strings attached to salvation. In fact, Paul opened the early Church even to Gentiles, arguing that every man, through the grace of God, had the ability to progress to eternal salvation. But even with its radical vision of time, which emphasized progress and infinite development of man's moral capacities, early Christian writers such as Augustine insisted on a version of original sin. There was a state in time in the past where man lived in harmony, as Augustine writes, "the peace of the body and the soul is the ordered life and well-being of a living thing. The peace between a mortal man and God is an ordered obedience, in faith, under the eternal law" (XIX, Chapter 13). It is the act of sin that violates this harmony. Presumably, Christ died in order to forgive man of this sin, as Augustine puts it, through grace. But, grace alone cannot take sin out of the world. Since sin is always present, all human associations depend on an ordered structure to control man's instinct to evil. "The peace of the household is an ordered concord concerning commanding and obeying among those who dwell together. The peace of the city is an ordered concord concerning commanding and obeying among the citizens" (XIX, Chapter 13).

For Strauss, evil and virtue can be understood in secular terms. Philosophy is the methodology by which an understanding of ultimate truths can be attained. In contrast, politics is merely a quest for human ends, and since humans are flawed and possess varied levels of comprehension and perception, many are not capable of the philosophical understanding of good and evil. Since politics is fallible, Strauss, as well as early Christian writers, agreed that an ordered state is necessary to control the evil that is a natural presence in the world.

Second, since sin is natural, and hierarchy is a natural way to control the effects of sin, conservatives are opposed to any attempt to replace the natural order of things with man-made utopianism. Voegelin (1952) called this desire for perfectibility modern "Gnosticism" and locates its egalitarian impulse in "progressivism, positivism, Hegelianism, and Marxism" (p. 247). For many conservatives, such as Frank Meyer (1964) and Russell Kirk (1953 [2001]), the replacement of the authority of traditional norms by "reason" has been one of the major mistakes of the twentieth century. Others such as Aaron Wildavsky have commented that "a few pundits aside, there is not now, if there ever was, a social stratum able to support a conservative ethic against the forces in favor of pushing public policy over the egalitarian precipice" (1973: 32).

Most conservative writers reject institutions that foster equality as a threat to the traditional order. In modern versions of conservatism, the argument against egalitarian institutions focuses either on the moral chaos that occurs as a result of the abandonment of traditional hierarchies or on some idea of natural meritocracy that is facilitated by a free market economy. There is an implicit assumption in conservative philosophy that "merit," of the sort that is recognized by a market economy, results in a preferred set of conservative values. By substituting merit for equality, conservatives have successfully equated capitalism to preferred middle-class values. In this way conservatives are able to support market distributions with a moral argument. As John Roemer (2000) has pointed out, conservatives believe that a market economy based exclusively on merit will create a "larger economic pie." Conservatives have thus politicized private values in a way in which public policy can be used to reinforce inequalities. It is an easy transition to the argument that poverty is a personal problem, a view that helped launch the conservative attack on the welfare state in the late 1970s.[3]

Fourth, conservatives argue that while freedom is certainly an important value, it also has the potential of being harnessed by an activist state as ideological support for equality. It is interesting that liberalism, in its justification for social welfare, has never been particularly interested in the equality of outcomes, and like conservatism generally seeks to ensure that public institutions increase equality of opportunity. However, conservatives believe that any increase in freedom, employed in an effort to provide equality of opportunity, would quickly be misused. For the conservative, there is always a distinction between freedom and authority. Freedom is a means to an end, not an end in itself, and thus must be tempered by authority. Freedom is the means by which man achieves virtue, and results of free acts by humans that do not aspire to virtue are, for the conservative, suspect. For example, Fareed Zakaria (2003) has argued that the democratization of religion in modern society produces something that is "popular" rather than something that is spiritual. Freedom, in and of itself, is not a primary virtue but is to be valued to the extent that it produces preferred values.

Freedom can be restrained either by virtuous authority or by reconceptualizing freedom in economic terms. For the conservative, whether religious or traditional, "the chief purpose of politics is to aid the quest for virtue." [4] In general terms, virtue means actions that are in accord with the transcendental order, whether this is expressed either in traditional or religious terms. Conservatives have also attempted to define markets as mechanisms that will enforce virtues that promote order. For example, Lee and McKenzie (1988) have argued that distributions of goods produced by markets are much more efficient than distributions attempted by government precisely because of the threat of poverty. In capitalist societies, poverty is not only inevitable, but serves a social purpose in that it forces participants into desirable modes of behavior.[5]

Conservatives thus end up with an argument which states that private freedom is relatively more important than public freedom. The values that conservatives wish to emphasize are those values most associated with the private realm, family and middle-class industriousness. The rhetoric of the Bush Administration's claim that tax cuts are simply a refund of our "own money" is another example of the valorization of private over public freedom. It is less important to participate in politics than it is to participate in the market.

Inequality is simply a natural by-product of the elevation of the private realm over the public. According to Dunn and Woodward (2003), there are three reasons why conservatives believe that the toleration of some inequality is beneficial. First, government can be kept relatively small because there is no need for a large apparatus to enforce equality. Second, inequality gives people an incentive to excel. Finally, as Edmund Burke observed in this *Reflections on the Revolution in France,* equality can undermine the fundamental order of society. The degree of wealth or poverty is not the real measure of virtue in society. Civil life, based on the virtue of tradition, can work for the rich as well as the poor. According to Burke, it is the societal commitment to the transcendent value of order that works best for all. For Burke, as with contemporary conservatives, equality is considered a threat rather than an ideal.

Conservative Models of Democracy

Now that we understand why conservatives distrust equality, we can proceed to an analysis of the institutional arrangements preferred by modern conservatives. In his recent book, *A Political History of the American Welfare System,* Brendon O'Connor argues that the conservative attack on welfare comes from two intellectual sources. First, the work by authors such as Charles Murray (1984) and George Gilder (1981) emphasize the perverse incentive systems that characterized Great Society programs. Certainly, their work emphasizes the conservative values of hard work, discipline, and industriousness. In this paper, we wish to focus on the second source of the conservative argument, the emphasis on structural reform. With regard to institutions, conservatives launched two simultaneous attacks. First, public choice economists, using the metaphor of markets, argue that institutions at the federal level cannot adequately amalgamate the preferences of a diverse population. Second, they argue that bureaucratic structures designed to deliver services to the poor are inefficient at best and pathological at worst. As Walter Williams (2003) has pointed out, ideologues in the Reagan Administration employed the logic of public choice to launch an all out attack on the institutions of the federal government. Williams argues that this attack ultimately was successful in that "it led the nation into plutocracy and a much diminished brand of democracy" (p. 17). We will consider this charge in some detail.

Public choice theorists, in general, support what Ian Shapiro (2003) has referred to as an aggregative theory of democracy. Public choice economists are intrigued by the "market metaphor" by which private preferences are articulated and amalgamated. Applying this theory to politics, public choice theorists thus privilege "the unanimity principle" (Buchanan and Tullock, 1962; Buchanan, 1974). But, according to Buchanan, the cost of unanimous decision making far outweighs perceived benefits. However, without the protection of unanimity, there is always a risk that government will act either opportunistically or in an arbitrary manner, which means that coercion is often used, which inevitably leads to inefficiency.

Buchanan (1985) argues that there is no likelihood that any welfare function could be developed independent of what participants prefer. This means that any conception of social justice is, by definition, arbitrary. Therefore, aside from the decision making rule employed there can be no standard of evaluation. This means, that we must direct our attention to the development of decision rules. Such rules, to be efficient, must be related to desired outcomes. Since unanimity is impossible to achieve, the next best option is majority rule in smaller decision-making units.

According to Buchanan, smaller decision making units, operating under majority procedures, can approximate the unanimity principle over time. Decisions approach unanimity for three reasons: First, individuals understand that while they may not prevail in the short term, over the longer term their preferences will be incorporated into policy as they participate in numerous decisions. Second, local decision-making institutions promote closer ties between and among the people who are most concerned and impacted by the decisions. It is probable that preferences are more clearly articulated to decision makers in localized decision making units. Finally, even if preferences are not clearly articulated, or realized, individuals have the ability to leave and find a community whose policies are more closely attuned to their own. The threat of exit is also important because it restrains government from "confiscatory" taxation (1985).

In addition, smaller decision making units make it easier for civic groups to connect with government. The literature addressing this issue presumes that policy preferences are formed as part of participation in civic groups. The extent to which these civic groups can interact with government is the extent to which more relevant preferences can be included in the decision-making process. This process will obviate the need for coordination by a central government bureaucracy.

This literature by economists lent itself easily to conservatives interested in dismantling the welfare state altogether and supplanting it with more localized approaches to charity. Thus the "faith based" initiative in the Bush Administration was motivated by writers such as Marvin Olasky (1992). As Charles Murray stated in the Introduction to Olasky's Book: "The error of contemporary policy is not that it spends too much or too little to help the poor, but that it is fundamentally out of touch with the meaning of those needs" (xviii).

Related to the public choice preference for smaller government units is the critique of bureaucracy itself. Bureaucracies create distributions that are (a) inefficient, and (b) reflective of groups that are able to capture "rents." In both cases, distributions of societal resources for which bureaus are responsible are not optimal.

Tullock (1965) is usually credited with initiating the public choice attack on classical models of bureaucracy. Tullock begins his analysis by taking *homo economicus* from the market and placing him in the bureau. This character, when placed in a hierarchical, rather than a market setting, will tend to pursue his own interests rather than the public interest and will inevitably hide information from his superiors.

Building on Tullock's argument, Niskanen's (1971) contribution is to focus on the relationship between bureau and sponsor. Using, as does Tullock, the assumption of rationality, Niskanen argues that the bureaucrat will attempt to maximize his budget. The consequence is more output than one would expect in a private market. Niskanen observes that bureaucrats have informational advantages that allow them to exploit legislative sponsors. Finally, since there is no market, bureaus have no way of evaluating output in relation to the costs of input. Therefore, democracy can never achieve any socially optimum distribution of goods and services as long as it relies on bureaucracy.

Traditional conservatives were drawn to the arguments of public choice economists and neoconservatives because the argument provided justification for the elimination of government structures that conservatives believed were responsible for the egalitarian trends in modern society.

Conservative Federalism Meets Welfare Reform

Conservative arguments about social order, the value of inequality in advancing the market, and a decentralized political system converged in 1996 in the Personal Responsibility and Work Opportunity Reconciliation Act (PRWORA), better known as the Welfare Reform Act.[6] Widely hailed as the greatest success of the 1995 "devolution revolution," PRWORA transformed a sixty-year entitlement for the poor into a temporary, block-granted program intended to retract the long-standing obligations of society for its neediest members. Among the key changes occurring in 1996 is the replacement of Aid to Families with Dependent Children (AFDC) with the Temporary Assistance to Needy Families (TANF) program. TANF granted greater flexibility to states to design their welfare programs to meet their own specialized needs. In addition to ending benefits after sixty months with a goal of recipient self-sufficiency, the TANF block grant allows states to determine their own rules, benefit levels, and time limits because, according to conservative arguments, each state knows best its own resources and needs. In their analysis of TANF implementation, Nathan and Gais (1999) note what they call "second-order" devolution of welfare: efforts by most states to devolve major responsibilities for welfare and other social service programs to the local level. As they explain, second-order devolution is a natural consequence of the structure of welfare reform because "so much of what needs to be done to get and keep a person off of welfare has to be decided, arranged, and carried out locally" (36). The devolution of authority for rule making and policy implementation of welfare was advanced by conservatives and became federal law in 1996 regardless of the fact that economists and political scientists for years have argued that redistributive policies, such as public assistance, are most efficiently administered and equitably financed at the federal level.

The distinction between developmental policies, which "attempt to enhance the economic competitiveness of a political jurisdiction," (Rom, 1989: 61), and redistributive policies, which offer assistance from the well-off in society to the needy, is well established (Peterson et al., 1986; Rom, 1989; Peterson, 1995; McGuire, 1991; Nathan, 1993, 1996). In this tradition, McGuire (1991) makes a distinction between the efficient competition and the destructive competition models, arguing that states are more prone to engage in destructive competition due to their taxing mechanisms, their service priorities, and the diversity and mobility of their residents. McGuire concludes that destructive competition leads to inefficient levels of public goods and services, therefore, federal grants are the most appropriate means to assist states in providing more efficient levels of service.

Similarly, it has been argued that because states compete with one another over limited tax dollars, they tend to focus their attentions on developmental policies like worker training, tax exemptions, deregulation, and other economic development projects that broaden both their residential and commercial tax bases (Tiebout, 1956; Bowman and Kearney, 1986; Peterson, Rabe and Wong, 1986; Shannon, 1989; Rivlin, 1992; Feiock, 2002). Thus, many scholars advocate centralized administration of redistributive policy based on concerns about equity and state reluctance to offer redistributive programs (Ladd and Doolittle, 1982; McKay, 1985; Rom, 1989; Peterson and Rom, 1990; McGuire, 1991; Oates and Schwab, 1991; Nathan, 1993, 1996; Williams, 1994; Quigley and Rubinfeld, 1996; Piven, 2002; Whitaker and Time, 2001).

Because economic competitiveness leaves states reluctant to offer high benefit levels to the needy, liberals have worried about a "race to the bottom" in welfare provision: Rather than risk attracting welfare recipients through the "welfare magnet" effect, states have incentives to offer lower benefit levels to discourage immigration from less generous states and, possibly, to encourage out-migration. Volden (2002) finds that a "cautious slide" may better describe the condition of state competition over welfare benefits than a "race to the bottom." While the research is mixed on either the existence of a welfare magnet effect or a race to the bottom, there is evidence that politicians in the states base decisions on these theories nonetheless (Peterson and Rom, 1990; Schram and Krueger, 1994; Schram and Beer, 1998; Rom, Peterson and Scheve, 1999; Weaver, 2000).

In addition to ignoring the fact that state and local politicians are more likely to cater to business interests than the interests of the poor, conservative arguments in favor of devolution ignore resource disadvantages faced by many poor states and local governments (Nathan and Gais, 1999; Weaver, 2000; Whitaker and Time, 2001; Parisi, et al., 2003). In its multi-state evaluations of welfare reform implementation, the Rockefeller Institute found significant differences in administrative resources between urban, rural, small and large communities (Nathan and Gais, 1999). In 2003, Parisi, et al. note that devolving TANF implementation to the lowest level can fail because, "In many cases, poor economic conditions, low human capital, minority concentration, high inequality, and low civic engagement occur together, magnifying the disadvantages the poor experience in these communities" (2003: 508). Finally, Ingrid Philips Whitaker and Victoria Time (2001) note that because state wealth has always varied dramatically, the history of welfare in the United States is characterized by vastly unequal levels of cash benefit. They fear that preexisting inequality will be exacerbated under the welfare reform. In other words, states and local governments may not need to race or slide to the bottom in welfare provision—benefit levels will simply fall on their own in resource-poor jurisdictions.

Another problem with the theory of welfare devolution is that reform has not been as empowering for local governments or community organizations as conservatives projected. In 1969, O'Donnell and Chilman noted that unless the poor are able to participate as full-fledged members of community organizations, they will be alienated by the political and bureaucratic process. James Jennings (2002) and Ann Whithorn (2002) illustrate these problems under PRWORA. For example, Jennings found that contrary to the hopes of devolution advocates, welfare reform in Massachusetts has had a chilling effect on neighborhood organizations and their ability to serve clients, as community-based organizations "chase low-paying jobs for their clients rather than strengthening the economic infrastructure of the area," (2002: 129). He explains that "TANF policy (specifically, time limits to benefits, regulation forcing individuals to find any available job, regulations against schooling as a way to earn benefits, and work-first rules), coupled with erroneous perceptions of and civic biases against our poorer black and Latino neighborhoods, is weakening the social and institutional fabric of neighborhoods with relatively high levels of poverty" (2002: 130). Devolution of the welfare program has done little to facilitate economic growth in poor communities and strict work and participation requirements leave the poor little time to organize their own lives, let alone become empowered at the local level.[7]

In assessing welfare reform, James Q. Wilson's summary epitomizes the conservative argument about social order and the poor. He writes that "successful welfare work programs make women feel that they *must* work. Paternalism without compulsion is simply advice" (1997: 339). Further, he argues that the poor will benefit from "being told what to do and how to do it" and thus will be encouraged to continue to follow the direction of the government as they realize the benefits obtained by doing so. He notes that many people are suspicious of paternalism directed toward adults because, "Our desire for autonomy leads us to insist on the same freedom for others, even people who have great difficulty in making use of it" (1997: 339-40). Such reservations, Wilson explains, are unfounded. In fact, Wilson argues that paternalism should be "enlarged and extended for people—the homeless, criminals, drug addicts, deadbeat dads, unmarried teenage mothers, and single mothers claiming welfare benefits—who have by their behavior indicated that they do not display the minimal level of self-control expected of decent citizens" (p. 340-341).

The paternalism argument is fascinating from the standpoint of consistency in conservative thinking. While the 1996 Welfare Reform has been touted as devolving federal responsibility back to the states and local governments, the neo-conservative arguments of Wilson and Lawrence Mead in *The New Paternalism* (1997), clearly indicate that the central government should control many important life decisions for certain segments of the population, including decisions about whether or not to marry or when and with whom to have a child. The freedom to make one's own decisions on such matters should be extended only to "decent citizens." While somewhat shocking to those with liberal sensibilities, these arguments are reminiscent of early twentieth century reformers who, along with advocating that welfare offer poor mothers the ability to remain in the home, were also "eager to supervise and improve the home conditions of recipients... they advocated rules and intervention to regulate the lives of poor single mothers, such as home visits by social workers" (Mink and Solinger, 2003: 42).

Until the welfare reforms of the 1960s, for example, welfare mothers were under strict "man in the house rules" which often involved late-night raids on the homes of recipients; if welfare caseworkers found a man in the home of a single mother, benefits were rescinded. Other tactics of the welfare bureaucracy further restricted the size of the AFDC rolls, both discouraging and eliminating unwed mothers and black women from welfare recipiency throughout the 1930s, 1940s and 1950s (Cammisa, 1998; Piven and Cloward, 1993; Hancock, 2004).

In the 1960s, welfare reform and the civil rights movement came together to take some of this power out of the hands of government and put it in the hands of welfare mothers. As Linda Gordon writes, for many women "going to the welfare office was a step toward citizenship, not only for the first entrance into a relationship with the government but also as a statement of self-esteem." She adds that claiming their entitlement to welfare benefits "was a strategy for upward mobility, especially for one's children" (2002: 19). Thus, the return to paternalism and government direction over the poor, which began in the 1980s, is a return to earlier, conservative traditions of social and moral control. In such a relationship, the poor are not active participants but are, as Wilson suggests, "told what to do and how to do it." Rather than foster the self-sufficiency purported by welfare reform advocates, TANF offers a system in which welfare recipients are under strict regulations and constant monitoring to ensure that they are in compliance with program rules. Under such a system the poor are not even superficially treated as full members of society. As Albelda (2002) points out, "The rights imperiled by TANF policies range from basic expectations of autonomy and privacy among civilized and respectful people to liberty guarantees that have been deemed fundamental to constitutional citizenship" (2002: 99). Furthermore, Whitaker and Time (2001) argue that the Fourteenth Amendment rights to equal protection for welfare recipients are infringed upon when resource availability varies dramatically by state. This is a particular problem under a devolved welfare system in which only the federal government has the ability to equalize economic disparities. Welfare reform is an example of the conservative agenda fostering political inequality and infringing upon the civil rights of the nation's most needy, an untenable position if one is concerned with advancing democratic norms of participatory citizenship.

Finally, welfare reform can be considered a success only when counting the numbers of recipients that have left the welfare rolls; empirical evidence indicates that families that have left welfare are living in worse conditions in a number of ways. For example, extreme childhood poverty for families off of welfare has grown since 1996 (Rice, 2001; Wycoff, et al., 2002). Several studies indicate that work is still elusive for welfare leavers as 35 to 50 percent remain unemployed (Anderson and Gryzlak, 2002; Wycoff, et al., 2002). In addition, thousands of female welfare recipients who had been in college in 1996 were forced to drop out after welfare reform (Rice, 2001). Most importantly, the typical family remains near or below the poverty line when it leaves TANF (Rice, 2001; Schram and Soss, 2002; Danziger, 2002; Weber, et al., 2002; Anderson and Gryzlak, 2002; Wycoff, et al., 2002).

Continued high levels of poverty can hardly be surprising when research on income inequality and social mobility are considered. For example, Holly Sklar and her colleagues (2001) found that the real value of the $5.15 minimum wage was 35 percent less in 2000 than the value of the minimum wage in 1968. During this same time, they note, national productivity grew by 74.2 percent; if the minimum wage had kept pace with productivity, it would have been $13.80 in 2000. Even in rural Kentucky, where the cost of living is typically low, Julie Zimmerman found that the wage earner in a family of three would need to earn over $10 an hour to make ends meet (Zimmerman, 2000).

These findings are particularly troubling for adult women with low levels of education and skills who make up two-thirds of the minimum wage work force and compose the bulk of welfare recipients. As Joy K. Rice (2001) notes, the problem is not the glass ceiling but "the sticky floor;" forty percent of women formerly on assistance "are concentrated in low-paying service industries such as restaurants, bars, nursing homes, home child care, and temporary help service firms" (2001: 360). In addition, many former welfare recipients face a revolving door of employment and unemployment; those with spotty work histories are far more likely to return to TANF (Anderson and Gryzlak, 2002).

The growth of income inequality is further highlighted by the fact that in 1980, business CEOs earned ninety-seven times the income level of a minimum wage employee, and by 2000 CEOs earned 1,233 times the minimum wage earner (DeNavas-Walt and Cleveland, 2002). Between 1980 and 2003, the share of all income earned by households in the top twenty percent increased from 43.7 to 49.8 percent. For the bottom twenty percent, share of income declined from 4.3 to 3.4 percent (DeNavas-Walt, Proctor and Mills, 2004; see Table 1). Incredibly, between 1980 and 2001, the top five percent of households had increased their share of income from 15.8 to 22.5 percent (DeNavas-Walt and Cleveland, 2002). These high levels of inequality are tolerated in America, explains Charles T. Stewart, Jr. (2002), because of our belief in progress and upward mobility. Unfortunately, these beliefs have no basis in fact. In summarizing research on social and economic mobility, Charles E. Hurst notes that while America tends to have more upward mobility than downward mobility, "the upward mobility is of short distance," and more prevalent in the early twentieth century than in the decades at century's end. In fact, he writes, "the last couple of decades have witnessed at least a stabilization, if not a decline, in overall occupational mobility in the United States" (2004: 296). Thus, the realities of America's economic system, coupled with conservative public policy leave the welfare poor in a precarious state. They are no longer able to receive public assistance for longer than sixty months (and in many states the time limit is shorter), and they are unable to seek education and training opportunities for more than a year in most states. Thus welfare recipients are unlikely to find quality employment that will lead to the self-sufficiency imagined by reform advocates. For conservative economist Stewart (2002), Americans will not find the solution to the problem of inequality by allocating "a larger share of resources for redistribution." Instead, Stewart concludes that "an alternative is to preserve the conditions under which inequality is widely accepted" (2002: 510). The general acceptance of vast economic inequality is facilitated by our preservation of political inequality, the root of the conservative enterprise.

Defending Political Inequality

To be considered a democracy, a system of government requires the participation and involvement of its citizens, yet the economic inequality fostered by conservative policy precludes large segments of the citizenry from participation. Ultimately this political inequality is the most dangerous aspect of the conservative defense of socio-economic inequality. Rosenkranz and Hasen (1999) note that since 1976, when the Supreme Court legitimized campaign spending as a form of free speech in *Buckley v. Valeo*, proponents of campaign finance reform have had a difficult time arguing that wealth illegitimately advantages some parties, candidates, and issues. *Buckley v. Valeo* is, of course, a conservative application of the market model to voting: the presumption is that the free competition of the "political market" will bear out the best candidates and the winning platforms. Electoral winners experience a sort of mandate by fiat:

Table 1
Household Share of National Income, 1980 and 2003

	1980	2003
Top 20% Households	43.7%	49.8%
Bottom 20% Households	4.3	3.4

they won so they must have offered what the voters want. While the veracity of this claim (or this system) is not within the scope of our inquiry, the implications of this system are within our scope.

It is well known that those at the highest levels of the socio-economic ladder tend to run for and win office, contribute to political campaigns, initiate ballot proposals via direct democracy, and vote more often than their neighbors at the lower end of the socio-economic spectrum.[8] Linda Fowler (1996) notes that while most western democracies responded to universal suffrage with the creation of labor parties to represent working class interests, the U.S. did not. In fact, most members of Congress continue to hail from the ranks of the banking, law, and business industries. In the 107th Congress, for example, 39 percent of members held law degrees, while 18 percent were millionaires. Burt Neuborne (1999) addresses the question of why the American system tolerates such a large amount of "wealth-driven political inequality." "Could it be that, deep down, we want to tilt the political playing field towards the rich (or away from the poor) because, despite formal and rhetorical protests to the contrary, our political culture still regards wealth as a proxy for talent, and poverty as a mark of inferiority?" (1999: 1610).

Our argument is that Neuborne is absolutely correct. The conservative proclivity toward social order, the neoconservative prioritization of market mechanisms, and the religious conservative belief that those who ascribe to the Protestant work ethic will be justly compensated, leads to the idea that wealth signifies merit, and merit should be rewarded. Poverty, which signifies personal, professional, and moral failure, should be sanctioned. Political rewards come in the form of positions of authority inside the government, access to those with positions of authority, and the ability to shape the political and policy process. Those subject to political sanctions rarely hold positions of political authority or, enjoy access to those with such authority, and they are more likely to be made *subject to* public policy than to be policy makers. Ange-Marie Hancock (2004) makes this case well in her account of the "politics of disgust" in welfare reform: using the heuristic of the "welfare queen" allowed elites to deny political legitimacy to welfare recipients, thus ignore their voices during the reform debates of 1996.

Neuborne calls those at the lowest levels of the socio-economic and political spectrums "spectator-citizens." They "are formally entitled to participate in the political process, and may occasionally be drawn into the voting population. Ordinarily, however, spectators do not perceive themselves as players in the game of politics" (1999: 1611). As he notes, our system further burdens the spectator-citizen in our most basic democratic norm: Voting, which is laden with institutionalized transaction costs that advantage the wealthy and well educated. He notes that while we compel citizens to do everything from serve on juries, to obtain vaccinations, and cooperate with census takers, we compel neither voting nor voter registration in the United States; in fact, as he notes, we continue to hold elections on workdays. Perhaps it is not too conspiratorial to suggest that the explanation lies in conservative efforts to create the *appearance* of democracy while actually creating a neo-Platonic plutocracy.

Concluding Thoughts

Conservative thinkers since Plato and St. Augustine have embraced inequality, and modern American conservatives, rhetoric aside, continue to do the same. More than simply espousing the values of inequality, however, conservative politicians have created structures which further institutionalize inequality; an excellent example of this is the 1996 welfare reform act. Because conservatives believe that social, moral, and economic order is jeopardized by a generous welfare state, their solution has been to create a system that fosters inequality and keeps the poor under state control. While espousing the values of "devolution" and "decentralization," conservative policy makers have sought greater regulation of the lives of the poor and those who may upset the "moral order."[9] State and local levels of government have long been recognized as least likely to assist the poor in a consistent manner for precisely the reasons that public choice theorists have argued: smaller units of government are more responsive to constituent preferences than is the central government. As discussed here, the problem with the conservative policy of decentralized welfare provision is that destructive competition leads state and local governments to ignore the preferences of less affluent constituents in favor of the interests of the wealthy and business owners.

According to public choice theorists, devolution of welfare would purportedly allow for local solutions to poverty and create a more efficient system of welfare provision. While this is supposed to provide for a more democratic system through the amalgamation of local preferences, leaving decisions about the most vulnerable in society to the lowest levels of government actually undermines democracy by chiseling away at social, economic and political equality. Rather than creating a more democratic process, devolution fosters economic, social and political inequality. When neoconservative economic theory, classical conservative political ideology and religious moral conservatism converged on welfare policy in the 1980s and 1990s, welfare reform became an amalgam of preferences with a singular goal: enforce the economic, social, and moral order through the defense of inequality.

Notes

1. For example Jencks has observed: "Conservatives have argued for centuries that trying to limit economic inequality inevitably reduces both the incentive to work and the efficiency with which work is organized. As a result, they think egalitarian societies have fewer goods and services to distribute than societies that allow the market to determine household incomes" (2002, 53). This view is certainly at odds with political economists such as J.S. Mill who have argued that redistribution, to a point, is beneficial to a political economy in that it increases total demand, and hence results in the production of more goods and services.
2. "Rent seeking" is a term used to refer to the process by which certain groups obtain subsidies from the government at below market prices.
3. Arrow, Bowles and Durlauf (2000) argue that the conservative argument has won over large segments of the public for three reasons: First, the idea that ability should determine rewards has shifted the public perception of the poor from people who have been left out of the capitalist system to the idea that the poor should simply "smarten up." Second, massive media coverage of crime, drug use and other social pathologies in low income communities convince the public that the poor need "moral uplifting," particularly a sense of personal responsibility. Third, the massive conservative propaganda campaign that asserts that government policies are failures have convinced the public that government redistribution should be diminished.
4. L. Brent Bozell. Quoted by George H. Nash (1998, 163).
5. George Lakoff (2002) points out, "In the conservative moral worldview, the model citizens are those who best fit all the conservative categories for moral action. They are those: (1) who have conservative values and act to support them; (2) who are self-disciplined and self-reliant;(3) who uphold the morality of reward and punishment; (4) who work to protect moral citizens; and (5) who act in support of the moral order. Those who best fit all these categories are successful, wealthy, law-abiding conservative businessmen who support a strong military and a strict criminal justice system, who are against government regulation, and who are against affirmative action. They are the model citizens" (169-170).
6. It is important to note that while welfare reform has been discussed in terms of a bi-partisan consensus, the bulk of the policy was first offered in the 1994 Republican "Contract with America." It has been argued that Clinton signed PRWORA for two key political reasons: first, in his 1992 presidential campaign, he had promised to "end welfare as we know it," yet by 1996 he had not yet done so. Second, was the upcoming presidential election; approving welfare reform in the midst of his re-election campaign struck many as simply a wise political move, albeit one that had many detractors. Notably, groups such as the Children's Defense Fund, the National Organization for Women, and the Roman Catholic Bishops loudly opposed the legislation. In addition, top Democrats in Congress, including Senators Christopher Dodd (CT) and Paul Simon (IL) were vocal opponents

of PRWORA. Finally, several of President Clinton's top welfare advisors, including Mary Jo Bane and David Ellwood, resigned as a result of PRWORA's passage. For a clear discussion of PRWORA as a Republican rather than a bi-partisan policy, see O'Connor's *A Political History of The American Welfare System* (2004).

7.   For detailed examples of life under TANF, see LynNell Hancock's *Hands to Work: The Stories of Three Families Racing the Welfare Clock.*

8.   There are many examples of these phenomena including: Piven and Cloward, 2000; Alexander, 1992; Fowler, 1996; Garrett, 1999; and Neuborne, 1999).

9.   An excellent example is the millions of state and federal dollars spent to reduce the levels of "illegitimate child bearing" even among well educated and wealthy women. Under PRWORA, states have been awarded $20 million bonuses for reducing their levels of out-of-wedlock births while not increasing their abortion rates.

References

Albelda, Randy. 2002. "Fallacies of Welfare-to-Work Policies," in *Lost Ground: Welfare Reform, Poverty, and Beyond*, Randy Albelda and Ann Withorn, (eds.) Cambridge, MA:South End Press.

Alexander, Herbert E. 1992. *Financing Politics: Money, Elections, and Political Reform.* Washington DC: CQ Press.

Anderson, Steven G. and Brian M. Grylak. 2002. "Social Work Advocacy in the Post-TANF Environment: Lessons from Early TANF Research Studies." *Social Work* 47:3:301-314.

Arrow, Kenneth. Samuel Bowles and Steven Durlauf. (eds.) 2000. *Meritocracy and Economic Inequality.* Princeton, NJ: Princeton University Press.

Bowman, Ann O'M., and Richard C. Kearney. 1986. *The Resurgence of the States.* Prentice-Hall: Englewood Cliffs, NJ.

Buchanan, James N. and Gordon Tullock. 1969. *The Calculus of Consent.* Ann Arbor, MI: University of Michigan Press.

Buchanan, James N. 1975. *The Limits of Liberty.* Chicago, IL: University of Chicago Press.

——. 1991. *Constitutional Economics.* Oxford: Basil Blackwell.

Cammisa, Anne Marie. 1998. *From Rhetoric to Reform? Welfare Policy in American Politics.* Boulder, CO: Westview Press.

Daedalus. 2002. *Inequality.* (Spring)

Danziger, Sheldon H. 2002. "Approaching the Limit: Early National Lessons from Welfare Reform," in Rural Dimensions of Welfare Reform, Bruce A. Weber, Greg J. Duncan, and Leslie A. Whitener, (eds.) Kalamazoo, MI: W.E. Upjohn Institute for Employment Research.

DeNavas-Walt, Carmen and Robert W. Cleveland. 2002. *Money Income in the United States: 2001.* Washington, D.C.: US Census Bureau, United States Department of Commerce.

DeNavas-Walt, Carmen, Bernadette D. Proctor, Robert J. Mills. 2004. *Income, Poverty and Health Insurance Coverage in the United States: 2003.* Washington, DC: US Census Bureau, United States Department of Commerce.

Devigne, Robert. 1994. *Recasting Conservatism: Oakeshott, Strauss, and the Response To Postmodernism.* New Haven, CT: Yale University Press.

Dunn, Charles W. and J. David Woodard. 2003. *The Conservative Tradition in America.* New York: Rowman and Littlefield.

Feiock, Richard C. 2002. "A Quasi-Market Framework for Development Competition," *Journal of Urban Affairs* 24:2:123-142.

Fowler, Linda. 1996. "Who Runs for Congress?" *PS: Political Science and Politics* 29:2:430-434.

Garrett, Elizabeth. 1999. "Money, Agenda Setting, and Direct Democracy." *Texas Law Review* 77:7:1845-1890.

Gilder, George. 1993. *Wealth and Poverty.* ICS.

Hancock, Ange-Marie. 2004. *The Politics of Disgust: The Public Identity of the Welfare Queen.* New York: New York University Press.

Hancock, LynNell. 2002. *Hands to Work: The Stories of Three Families Racing the Welfare Clock.* New York: William Morrow, and Imprint of HarperCollins Publishers.

Hurst, Charles E. 2004. Social Inequality, 5th edition. Boston, MA: Allyn and Bacon.

Jennings, James. 2002. "Welfare Reform and Neighborhoods: Race and Civic Participation," in *Lost Ground: Welfare Reform, Poverty, and Beyond*, Randy Albelda and Ann Withorn, (eds.) Cambridge, MA: South End Press.

Gordon, Linda. 2002. "Who Deserves Help? Who Must Provide?" in *Lost Ground: Welfare Reform, Poverty, and Beyond*, Randy Albelda and Ann Withorn, (eds.) Cambridge, MA: South End Press.

Kirk, Russell. 1985. *The Conservative Mind from Burke to Eliot.* 7th Revised Edition. Washington, DC: Regnery Publishing.

Krauthammer, Charles. November 22, 1993. "Defining Deviancy Up." *The New Republic.* P. 20.

Ladd, Helen F. and Fred C. Doolittle. 1982. "Which Level of Government Should Assist the Poor?" *National Tax Journal* 35:3:323-336.

Lee, Dwight R. and Richard McKenzie. 1988. "Helping the Poor Richard E. Wagner, (eds.) *Public Choice and Constitutional Economic. Greenwich: JAI Press.*

McGuire, Therese J. 1991. "Federal Aid to States and Localities and the Appropriate Competitive Framework," in *Competition Among States and Local Governments, Efficiency and Equity in American Federalism*, Daphne A. Kenyon and John Kincaid, (eds.) Washington DC: The Urban Institute Press.

McKay, David. 1985. "Theory and Practice in Public Policy: the Case of the new Federalism." *Political Studies* XXXIII:203-217.

Mead, Lawrence M., (ed.) 1997. *The New Paternalism: Supervisory Approaches to Poverty*, Washington, DC: The Brookings Institution Press.

Meyer, Frank. (ed.) 1964. *What is Conservatism.* New York: Holt, Rinehart and Winston.

Mink, Gwendolyn and Rickie Solinger, (eds.) 2003. *Welfare: A Documentary History of U.S. Policy and Politics.* New York:NY: New York University Press.

Morgen, Sandra and Jeff Maskovsky. 2003. "The Anthropology of Welfare 'Reform': New Perspectives on U.S. Urban Poverty in the Post-Welfare Era." *Annual Review of Anthropology* 32:315-338.

Murray, Charles. 1984. *Losing Ground.* New York: Basic Books

Nash, George H. 1998. *The Conservative Intellectual Movement in America since 1945.* Delaware: ISI.

Nathan, Richard P. 1993. *Turning Promises into Performance: The Management Challenge of Implementing Workfare.* New York: Columbia University Press.

Nathan, Richard P. and Thomas L. Gais. 1999. *Implementing the Personal Responsibility Act of 1996: A First Look.* Albany, NY:The Nelson A. Rockefeller Institute of Government.

Neuborne, Burt. "Is Money Different?" *Texas Law Review* 77:7:1609-1625.

Neuhaus, John, Richard. 1996. "A New Order of Religious Freedom." in,Gerson, (ed.).

Nice, David C. 1987. *Federalism: The Politics of Intergovernmental Relations.* New York: St. Martin's Press.

Niskanen, William A. 1975. "The Pathology of Politics" in, Selden, (ed.).

Novak, Michael. 1999. *On Cultivating Liberty: Reflections on Moral Ecology.* New York: Rowman and Littlefield.

Oates, Wallace E. and Robert M. Schwab. 1991. "The Allocative and Distributive Implications of Local Fiscal Competition." in *Competition Among States and Local Governments, Efficiency and Equity in American Federalism*, Daphne A. Kenyon and John Kincaid, (eds.) Washington DC: The Urban Institute Press.

O'Connor, Brendon. 2004. *A Political History of the American Welfare System.* Boulder: Rowman and Littlefield.

O'Donnell, Edward J. and Catherine S. Chilman. (1969 [2003]). "Poor People on Public Welfare Boards and Committees: Participation in Policy-Making?" in, *Welfare: A Documentary History of U.S. Policy and Politics.* Gwendolyn Mink and Rickie Solinger, (eds.) 2003 New York: NY: New York University Press.

Neuborne, Burt. 1999. "Is Money Different?" *Texas Law Review* 77:7:1609-1625.

Patterson, James T. 2000. *America's Struggle Against Poverty in the Twentieth Century.* Cambridge, MA: Harvard University Press.

Parisi, Domenico, Diane K. McLaughlin, Steven Michael Grice, Michael Taquino, Duane A. Gill. 2003. "TANF Participation Rates: Do Community Conditions Matter?" *Rural Sociology* 68:4:491-512.

Peterson, Paul E., Barry G. Rabe and Kenneth K. Wong. 1986. *When Federalism Works.* Washington, DC: The Brookings Institution.

Peterson, Paul E., and Mark Rom. 1990. *Welfare Magnets.* Washington, DC: The Brookings Institution.

Peterson, Paul E. 1981. *City Limits.* Chicago, IL: University of Chicago Press.

Peterson, Paul E. 1995. *The Price of Federalism.* Washington, DC: The Brookings Institution.

Piven, Frances Fox. 2002. "Globalization, American Politics, and Welfare Policy," in *Lost Ground: Welfare Reform, Poverty, and Beyond*, Randy Albelda and Ann Withorn, (eds.) Cambridge, MA: South End Press.

Piven, Frances Fox, and Richard A. Cloward. 2000. *Why Americans Still Don't Vote: and Why Politicians Want it that Way*. Boston, MA: Beacon Press.

———. 1985. *The New Class War*. New York: Pantheon.

Quigley, John M. and Daniel L. Rubinfeld. 1996. "Federalism and Reductions in the Federal Budget." *National Tax Journal* 64:2:289-302.

Rice, Joy K. 2001. "Poverty, Welfare, and Patriarchy: How Macro-Level Changes in Social Policy Can Help Low-Income Women." *The Society for the Psychological Study of Social Issues* 57:2:355-374.

Rivlin, Alice. 1992. "A Vision of American Federalism," *Public Administration Review* 52:4:315-320.

Roeder, Phillip W. 1994. *Public Opinion and Policy Leadership in the American States*. Tuscaloosa, AL: University of Alabama Press.

Rom, Mark. 1989. "The Family Support Act of 1988: Federalism, Developmental Policy, and Welfare Reform." *Publius: The Journal of Federalism* 19:57-73.

Rom, Mark, Paul E. Peterson, and Kenneth F. Scheve, Jr. 1999. "Interstate Competition and Welfare Policy," in *Welfare Reform: A Race to the Bottom?* Sanford F. Schram and Samuel H. Beer, (eds.) Washington, DC: Woodrow Wilson Center Press.

Rosenkranz, E. Joshua and Richard L. Hasen. "Symposium Introduction: Money, Politics, and Equality." *Texas Law Review* 77:7:1603-1608.

Schram, Sanford and Joe Soss. 2002. "Success Stories: Welfare Reform, Policy Discourse, and the Politics of Research," in *Lost Ground: Welfare Reform, Poverty, and Beyond*, Randy Albelda and Ann Withorn, (eds.) Cambridge, MA: South End Press.

Schram, Sanford F. and Samuel H. Beer, (eds.) 1999. *Welfare Reform: A Race to the Bottom?* Washington, DC: Woodrow Wilson Center Press.

Schram, Sanford F. and Gary Krueger. 1994. "Welfare Magnets" and Benefit Decline: Symbolic Problems and Substantive Consequences." *Publius: The Journal of Federalism* 24:61-82 (Fall).

Selden, Richard T. (ed.) 1975. *Capitalism and Freedom: Proceedings of a conference in Honor of Milton Friedman*. Charlottesville, VA: University Press of Virginia.

Shannon, John. Winter, 1989. "Competition: Federalism's 'Invisible Regulator.'" *Intergovernmental Perspective* 15:1:28-30, 39.

Shapiro, Ian. 2003. *The State of Democratic Theory*. Princeton, NJ: Princeton University Press.

Sklar, Holly, Laryssa Mykyta and Susan Wefald. 2001. Raise the Floor: Wages and Policies that Work for all of Us. Cambridge, MA: South End Press.

Steinfels, Peter. 1979. *The Neoconservatives*. New York: Simon and Shuster.

Stewart, Charles T. 2002. "Inequality of Wealth and Income in a Technologically Advanced Society." *The Journal of Social, Political and Economic Studies* 27:4:495-512.

Strauss, Leo. 1953. *Natural Right and History*. Chicago, IL: University of Chicago Press.

———. 1968. *Liberalism Ancient and Modern*. Chicago, IL: University of Chicago Press.

Tiebout, Charles M. 1956. "A Pure Theory of Local Expenditures," *Journal of Political Economy* (October):416-2.

Tullock, Gordon. 1975. "The Pathology of Politics." in, Selden, (ed.).

Viereck, Peter. 1949. *Conservatism Revistited: The Revolt against Revolt*. New York: The Free Press.

Voegelin, Eric. 1952. *The New Science of Politics*. Chicago, IL: University of Chicago Press.

1997. *The Collected Works. Vol. 19. Hellenism, Rome, and Early Christianity*. Columbia: University of Missouri Press.

Volden, Craig. 2002. "The Politics of Competitive Federalism: A Race to the Bottom in Welfare Benefits?" *American Journal of Political Science* 46:2:352-363.

Weaver, R. Kent. 2000. *Ending Welfare As We Know It*. Washington DC: Brookings Institution Press.

———. 1996. "Deficits and Devolution in the 104th Congress." *Publius: The Journal of Federalism* 26:3:45-85.

Weaver, Richard. 1948. *Ideas Have Consequences*. Chicago, IL: University of Chicago Press.

Whitaker, Ingrid Phillips and Victoria Time. 2001. "Devolution and Welfare: The Social and Legal Implications of State Inequalities for Welfare Reform in the United States. Social Justice 28:1:76-90.

Whithorn, Ann. 2002. "Friends or Foes? Non-profits and the Puzzle of Welfare Reform," in *Lost Ground: Welfare Reform, Poverty, and Beyond*, Randy Albelda and Ann Withorn, (eds.) Cambridge, MA: South End Press.

———. 1997. "Paternalism, Bureaucracy and Democracy," in, *The New Paternalism: Supervisory Approaches to Poverty*, Lawerence M. Mead, (ed.) Washington, DC: The Brookings Institution Press.

Williams, Walter. 2003. *Reaganism and the Death of Representative Democracy*. Washington, DC. Georgetown University Press.

Wilson, James Q. 1997. "Paternalism, Democracy and Bureaucracy," *The New Paternalism Supervisory Approaches to Poverty*. Lawrence C. Mead, ed, Washington DC: Brookings Institution Press.

Wolff, Kurt, (ed.), Emile Durkheim. 1960 [1895]. *Writings on Sociology and Philosophy*, New York: Harper & Row.

Wycoff, Susan, Maristella Bacod-Gebhardt, Susan Cameron, Marielle Brandt and Bruce Armes. 2002. "Have Families Fared Well from Welfare Reform? Educating Clinicians about Policy, Paradox, and Change." *The Family Journal: Counseling and Therapy for Couples and Families* 10:3:269-280.

Zakaria, Fareed. 2003. *The Future of Freedom*. New York: W.W. Norton.

Zimmerman, Julie N. 2000. Thinking about Poverty Policy and Economic Development. *Social and Economic Education for Development*, Lexington, KY: University of Kentucky, College of Agriculture.

Rhetoric, Responsiveness, and Policy Moods: Testing the Issue of Social Welfare

Virginia H. Jordan
James Madison University

Phillip B. Bridgmon
University of North Alabama

Introduction

Congress and the Presidency were designed, normatively speaking, to represent the interests of the public. Whether these institutions accomplish this is the subject of several scholarly treatments (Arnold 1990; Asher and Weisberg 1978; Fenno 1978; Fiorina 1996; Herrnson 1998; Mayhew 1974; Mouw and MacKuen 1992; Light 1991; Shull 1997). Shifts in policy responsiveness is a measure of representation (Arnold 1990; Peterson 1990; Kingdon 1984; Light 1991; McCool 1995; Meier 1993; Page and Shapiro 1983; Ripley 1985; Ripley and Franklin 1991; Shull and Gleiber 1991; Shull 1997; Stimson et al. 1995). This study also examines the relationships between the public, policy responsiveness and representation by means of the dynamic representation model developed by Stimson, Makuen and Erikson (1995).

Dynamic representation posits that public preferences guide elected officials in their response to policy. Moreover, shifts in public opinion cause shifts in public policy. Such shifts may be measured on a directional, liberal-conservative continuum (e.g., Stevens 2000). The model provides support for majoritarian arguments that public interests are represented. The model also challenges arguments that political institutions are insulated or non-responsive to the public's preferences. By linking policy shifts as dependent upon public opinion shifts, an empirical measure of the theoretical concept of representation is provided.

We follow the assumptions used in the original model. In addition, the role of issue saliency is examined. The authors specifically state that dynamic representation does not necessarily address responsiveness to specific policies. Because public opinion is often measured issue by issue, different trends in responsiveness for different issues surface. In particular, the importance of saliency has long been debated as a potential factor in responsiveness. Dynamic representation's use of a liberal-conservative continuum may capture shifts in policy actions for a salient issue.

We explore whether the liberal-conservative continuum and the dynamic representation model manifests a change when we examine the salient issue area of social welfare policy.

Dynamic Representation

Stimson et al. propose that, "public opinion moves meaningfully over time, that government officials sense this movement, and that those officials alter their behavior in response to the sensed movement. This is dynamic representation" (543). In the analysis, Stimson et al. aggregate the global policy preferences, also described as the general domestic policy preferences of the public for policy activity in each institution—Congress, Presidency, and Courts. Results of the dynamic representation model demonstrate that regarding government as a whole, current policy is responsive to the public's mood (544). This responsiveness is measured by a liberal-conservative continuum. The dynamic representation model finds that the more *liberal* the public's mood (meaning the more supportive of spending and programs), the more *liberal* the policy actions of elected officials.

Election outcomes are essential to the measurement of responsiveness. It is argued that election outcomes are considered the ultimate indicator of public opinion (Shull, Gleiber and Garland, 1991). Stimson, et al. states, "public attitudes are real, knowable and likely to be relevant to the electoral future" (545). Specifically, the dynamic representation model posits two ways in which policy is influenced by public opinion through elections. Policy is influenced by: 1) the *rational anticipation* by officials of the electoral consequences of policy responsiveness to public opinion, and 2) *election turnover* when officials fail to respond to public sentiment. Stimson et al. assert that, through time and electoral outcomes, shifts in public opinion produce shifts in policy:

In layman's terms, elected officials may sense a shift in public opinion and anticipate what this may mean election-wise. They will support or adopt policy preferences supporting such a shift and responsiveness is actualized. Alternatively, however, elected officials may not sense a shift in public opinion or may not anticipate what this may mean election-wise. Elected officials are then booted out of office; new faces are elected which support or adopt policy preferences and responsiveness is actualized. Representation through policy responsiveness, therefore, determines a candidate's election, re-election or defeat.

The presidency and Congress represent and respond to public opinion. These institutions are led by elected officials designed to represent and reflect public sentiment. The devices necessary for responsiveness vary by institution (Kingdon 1984; Light 1991; McCool 1995; Meier 1993; Mayhew 1974; Peterson 1991). For example, Congress directly responds by Congressional voting, while the president responds by position-taking, public statements, bureaucratic management and bargaining. It is through these devices that the presidential and Congressional institutions transform preferences into policy (Monroe 1979; Page and Shapiro 1983; Wright, et al. 1987).

The dynamic representation model's assumptions are supported by a number of scholars. Mayhew (1974) holds that one of the major concerns of members of Congress is re-election. Fenno (1978) also states that Congressmen will attempt to support legislation that has an impact on their constituents and gives the impression that he is responsive of their individual interests. Wright and Berkman (1986) find that candidates believe issues are important to voters, and voters, in turn, are influenced by a candidate's positions. Herrick et al. (1994) conclude that representatives seeking re-election keep in constant touch with their districts more often, employ staff assistance for constituency work and legislation, research and attend more roll call votes and are more legislatively active. Elected officials, therefore, partake in representing and responding to the preferences of the public because of electoral consequences. Dynamic representation can be illustrated in this manner:

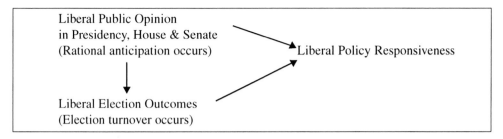

By developing a liberal-conservative continuum and aggregating across issues over time, the dynamic representation model finds that policy responds dynamically to public opinion through rational anticipation and electoral outcomes.

However, scholars debate the extent to which the public's global policy preferences, or even specific policy preferences, affect overall legislative voting behavior. Some find evidence that preferences on highly salient issues, such as abortion, taxation or entitlements, can indeed be a primary determinant in voter choice. Yet others argue that vote choice is dependent upon a multitude of measurable and immeasurable factors such as emotions, general gut instincts and a candidate's appeal (Goren 1999; Marcus 1998; Ragsdale 1991; Rahn 1993). These views challenge the assumption of electoral consequences and policy preferences of the public, implicit in the dynamic representation model.

This study contributes to this debate by adapting the dynamic representation model to a salient policy issue. Guided by the work of Stimson et al., dynamic representation is tested for the House, Senate and Presidency using multiple indicators of changes in social welfare policy. It examines dynamic representation and explains changes elected officials' support for social welfare policy.

Social Welfare Policy

Social welfare policy administers social services to the elderly, the poor, and the temporarily and permanently disabled. Largely because such a "redistributive" policy relies upon the sacrifices of one group to contribute to another group, this issue ranks as a salient public issue (Meier 1993; Gallup, 2005). For this research, welfare is concerned with programs designed to address poverty and income maintenance. This study, therefore, focuses on policy issues implemented under public assistance (PA) programs that offer cash benefits to those below the poverty threshold. Programs administering this are Supplemental Security Income (SSI) and Temporary Assistance to Needy Families (TANF).

TANF, the program formerly known as Aid to Families with Dependent Children (AFDC), emerged under the 1935 Social Security Act. President Franklin D. Roosevelt signed the Act into law, and in more than sixty years of its of existence there has been observable shifts in policy and public opinion. Given the background of the Great Depression, the original intent of SSA was to provide relief and a safety net for the poor (Dobelstein 1996). Public sentiment at the time preferred governmental intervention to such dire economic conditions, and officials responded by adopting SSA (Katz 1994; Dobelstein 1996). In 1938, over 81 percent of those polled approved Social Security Laws providing public assistance to the poor (Roper Center 1995). Between 1935-1959, many Americans received PA. However the vast *majority* of the poor did not fully utilize such programs. Regional and cultural factors often influenced the decision to apply for governmental funding. Further barriers to applying for PA, such as lack of or refusal to be given public information, caused certain population segments to be underrepresented. For example, minorities often did not know the existence of such programs (Katz 1994). Until the 1960s, the conditions and plight of the poor in America were largely underreported and undocumented.

In the 1960s, a strong civic responsibility emerged. The public obtained greater awareness of people living in poverty through investigative reporting by Edwin R. Murrow and Michael Harrington's pivotal work, *The Other America*. The issue influenced the agendas set by Presidents Kennedy and Johnson, and the War on Poverty movement emerged (Dobelstein 1996). Although ambitious, the intent of introducing new, innovative welfare programs and expanding social services was to ultimately end poverty. However, despite expanding social programs, poverty was far from eliminated. By the 1970s, the expansion of social programs saw a tremendous increase in the growth of bureaucratic agencies and social spending. Many liberals who had expected a more positive outcome were largely disappointed; consequently conservatives saw the opportunity for initiating their preferred reforms (Rexroat 1998). Ten years have passed since significant welfare reform occurred with the passage of Personal Responsibility and Work Opportunity Reconciliation Act (1996). Since the 1996 reform, welfare has been a salient issue that has shown shifts in policy as well as shifts in public opinion. Given the background of social welfare, the question now is whether the changing policies over the past forty years adapt to the notion of dynamic representation. As the public's sentiment for welfare policy has shifted over time, has policy responded? Further, does a liberal-conservative continuum explain such shifts?

Hypotheses

In adapting the model for a salient policy-specific issue such as welfare, Stimson et al.'s assumptions are followed, but data and measurements are tailored for welfare. Policy responsiveness by elected officials is a form of representation. Public opinion is perceived as the public's mood on government. A political representative is one who is voted on to act on behalf of others. The choice of such a representative is primarily based on shared views between the representative and voter. Thus public opinion on issues influences not only a representative's electoral chances, but also his/her policies. The dynamic representation model asserts, then, that if the public's sentiment changes, officials respond to this; or the public has the opportunity to elect another leader who will respond to preferences.

As in the original model, the hypotheses address three specific inquiries: 1) does opinion move policy? 2) does opinion influence election outcomes?, and 3) through what mechanisms does opinion work on policy? The hypotheses describe the expected direction of the relationships based on a liberal-conservative continuum. Liberal means more government assistance and more government spending, while conservative means the opposite.

Given this, the following hypotheses are posited:

H1: *Liberal shifts in public opinion's preferences for welfare policy influence liberal shifts in welfare policy.*

Rational anticipation of the public's preferences by elected officials is expected. Elected officials sense the mood of the moment, assess its trends and anticipate its consequence for future elections. Shifts in public opinion will lead politicians to change policy accordingly. If the public prefers a more liberal welfare policy, the president and Congress will respond with more liberal policy.

H2: *Liberal shifts in the public's preferences for welfare policy influence liberal shifts in election outcomes.*

Public opinion in support or opposition of welfare will directly influence who is elected. The more liberal the public's preferences are on welfare policy, the more liberal politicians will be elected.

H3: *Liberal shifts in election outcomes influence liberal shifts in welfare policy.*

Public opinion will be seen through elections. By changing the personnel in these institutions, causing election turnover, the aggregated preferences of elected officials will shift. The more liberal politicians elected, the more liberal changes in welfare policy.

Methodology and Data

The authors of the dynamic representation model predict that indirectly through election turnover and directly through the anticipation of elections, public opinion will influence policy. The authors model this relationship for each governmental institution, providing more than one dependent variable. Using causal modeling and path analysis, therefore, the dynamic representation model shall be replicated to test if public opinion influences policy in social welfare between 1956-1996. This is the selected period because we are interested in determining policy responsiveness that led up to the passage of welfare reform. Path analysis measures the magnitude of the linkages between the variables to provide information on the total effects of the causal process that makes up dynamic representation.[1]

The policies of the presidential and Congressional institutions are examined by identifying year as the unit of analysis. Implicit in the model, as discussed earlier, is the element of time. The latent preferences of the public influence current policy responsiveness. An estimate of previous public opinion on current policy responsiveness is necessary. The cycles of presidential and Congressional elections must also be considered. Given this, data has been gathered for every other year between 1956-1996. Therefore our unit is measured bi-annually for Congress and every four years for the presidential election.

As mentioned, the indicators for Congress and the presidency will be tailored to fit welfare policy, instead of the global policy preferences tested in the original model. The data for these indicators have been compiled through public records in the *Congressional Quarterly Almanac*, *Weekly Compilations of Presidential Statements*, the United States Bureau of the Census, the Americans for Democratic Action (ADA), *Vital Statistics on the President* (Ragsdale, 1996), and survey data from the National Election Studies, 1956-1996.

Dependent Variable: Liberal Welfare Policy. For the dependent variable in the dynamic representation model, Stimson et al. net out the sum of many indicators of policy to capture its overall liberalism or conservatism. The reasoning given for this is that there is not a "defensible measure" that explains how Congresses or presidents can be more or less liberal than other Congresses or presidents. "We will exploit several indicators of annual policy output," they argue, "each by itself dubious. But when they run in tandem with one another, the set will seem much more secure than its members" (549).

The dependent variable tested in this model is liberal welfare policy responsiveness. Such policy is measured by the extent to which governmental actors support a more liberal approach to welfare over time. It shall be measured under the Congressional and presidential institutions in the following manner:

1.*Congressional policy responsiveness.* It is presumed that a more liberal Congress reflects a more liberal public, which in turn produces more liberal policy options for welfare. The indicators of Congressional welfare policy are the net sum of these indicators:

a) The ADA rating scale of Congress (one for the House, one for the Senate) will measure the liberalness of Congress.

b) The number of key liberal roll call outcomes on welfare votes will act as another, more specific, measure of the extent to which Congress is more liberal on welfare policy.

2. *Presidential policy responsiveness.* It is presumed that a more liberal president reflects a more liberal public, which in turn produces more liberal policy options for welfare. One the most direct and measurable mechanisms that the president has to influence policy is by public position taking and public statements. Thus, the indicators of presidential welfare policy preferences are the net sum of the following measures:

a) The percentage of liberal presidential positions on key welfare votes will measure the president's liberalness on welfare policy.

b) The percentage of liberal presidential statements on poverty issues will also measure the president's liberalness on welfare policy, as poverty is the primary eligibility requirement for welfare recipients of cash benefits.

Independent Variable 1: Public Opinion. The first independent variable measures the preferences of public opinion. The liberalness of the public's mood regarding welfare (meaning more government spending and governmental assistance) will be captured to reflect public preference. The survey question from NES asking whether government should spend more or less on programs to improve citizens' standard of living will be used to calculate the bi-annual percentage of liberal response to welfare policy.

The justification for the use of this question, as opposed to other questions asked by NES, GSS, NORC, etc., is that this question is asked more consistently than other survey questions during the time examined. A similar survey question that asks about public assistance focuses on the specific issues of health and education. The question selected for this study attempts to measure how the public feels about government assisting people's living standards. This question, therefore, offers more face validity than the other questions considered.

Independent Variable 2: Election Outcomes. The second independent variable measures the role of election outcomes in the dynamic representation model. Election turnover, as mentioned, affects changes in welfare policy, as those elected are the authoritative decision-makers of policy. Scholars argue the extent of influence of party identification, but nonetheless agree that party identification is a valid and reliable measurement of voting behavior. Because Democrats and Republicans identify with differing ideologies (liberal and conservative), the breakdown of Democrats elected in governmental institutions reflects the liberalness of government and public preference. This can reflect the liberalness of the public for governing (Quaile Hill and Leighley 1996), which can be further interpreted to reflect the liberalness of the public for welfare policy. Thus, the percentage of Democrats elected as president and as members of the House and Senate will measure to extent to which the primary decision making institutions are more liberal or more conservative. Through election outcomes (the percentage of Democrats in office), public preferences for policy responsiveness is measured and election turnover is explained.

Also, recall that election turnover of public opinion will guide elected officials in shaping welfare policy over time. Because House and Senate members, as well as the president, all follow different election cycles, three time lags (t, t-2, t-4) of public opinion and election outcomes are factored into the model. These time lags follow the original model of dynamic representation, and fit nicely with the bi-annual NES data.

Control Variable: Economic Conditions. Finally, because measuring changes in welfare policy is greatly influenced by economic conditions, a control for the economy is also calculated into the relationship. An extensive literature review exists in discussing the connection between economic and political variables in policymaking (Erikson 1989, 1990; Hofferbert 1966; Lewis-Beck 1977; Browning 1985). Hofferbert and Lewis-Beck contend that a relationship between economic factors and policy exists, and cannot be dismissed. This relationship not only influences the policy process, but also the actors shaping policy. In welfare policy, Browning (1985) noted that both political actors and citizens respond to poor economic conditions that, in turn, affect policy preferences and responsiveness on issues such as welfare expenditures and recipient eligibility. Therefore, the yearly sum of the unemployment rate and the consumer price index (CPI), commonly known as the misery index, is employed as a control measure of economic influence. Given the hypotheses and measures presented, the dynamic representation model for welfare policy now takes this form:

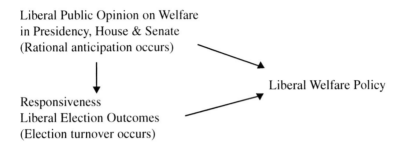

Liberal Public Opinion on Welfare
in Presidency, House & Senate
(Rational anticipation occurs)

Responsiveness
Liberal Election Outcomes
(Election turnover occurs)

Liberal Welfare Policy

The dynamic representation model developed by Stimson et al. captures global policy preferences only and establishes a liberal-conservative continuum for such preferences. If the hypothesized relationships are confirmed, the model will be shown to fit not only global policy preferences, but also within a salient policy-specific issue. If estimated correctly, the hypotheses tailored for welfare policy will support and expand the explanatory and predictive value of dynamic representation. It can be said that such a continuum explains a salient, policy-specific issue. In addition, the relationship between elected officials and the public can be more accurately described. A greater understanding of democratic representation will be established. It is further expected that this will advance theoretical development in public policy studies within political science. Finally, it is expected that this model will contribute to research in welfare and poverty issues, by determining the significant and influential factors involved in decision making.

Findings

Interesting and conflicting results are revealed when the dynamic representation model is estimated for the salient welfare policy issue. Figures 1, 2, and 3 identify the significant path coefficients for the presidency, House and Senate, respectively. Table 1 reports path coefficients for all of the relationships estimated, indicating their direct and indirect influences on liberal welfare policy. In determining the total influences for path analysis, all relationships that are estimated must also be significant. This does not occur in any of the institutions, but this nonetheless is computed to present the accuracy of path specifications. Overall, however, the findings reveal that the dynamic representation model produces no total effects on shifts in welfare policy.

To fully understand the differences in findings between the "global" policy preferences of dynamic representation and shifts in a specific policy area, the findings of this study's analysis of the model are compared with Stimon et al.'s.

Welfare Policy and the President

Global policy preferences: Policy is demonstrated to be a function of public opinion both directly and indirectly through election outcomes. The hypothesized relationships are confirmed. The party of the president is a function of public opinion and election outcomes. The more liberal the public's preferences, the more liberal the president responds. Rational anticipation occurs.

Findings
Dynamic Representation in the President, House and Senate For Welfare Policy

Figure 1
Dynamic Representation Model in Presidency
(Significant relationships only)

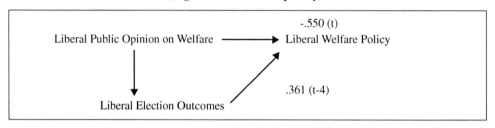

Welfare policy preferences: The results in Figure 1 demonstrate two significant relationships. First, liberal public opinion on welfare is inversely related to liberal welfare policy. The relationship does not fit with the dynamic representation model that calls for a liberal public opinion-policy connection. The inverse relationship reported finds that the more conservative the public's opinion on welfare, the more liberal the president responds. Thus our first hypothesis is not confirmed. Further, this counters the argument for rational anticipation.

No significant relationships are reported to confirm the second hypothesis, positing a liberal public opinion-electoral outcome connection. Public opinion in support or opposition of welfare does not have a direct influence on who is elected. The second significant relationship reported in Figure 1 confirms the third hypothesis, however. Liberal election outcomes influence liberal welfare policy. Election turnover has a partial influence. Significant positive relationships must result in this path analysis to confirm dynamic representation.

Welfare Policy and the House

Global policy preferences: Regarding policy in the House of Representatives, policy is a function of public opinion. Yet their findings reveal no significant relationship for a liberal public opinion-electoral outcome connection; therefore it cannot be said that the public's preferences affect House elections. However, all other relationships, including the direct relationships testing rational anticipation and election outcomes, are highly significant and show a liberal direction. The authors conclude that in testing for global policy, dynamic representation is largely present.

Welfare policy preferences: Figure 2 reports only one significant relationship for the House of Representatives that confirms H3-liberal shifts in election outcomes influence liberal shifts in welfare policy. The first and second hypotheses are not confirmed, as significant path coefficients are not reported. Rational anticipation of the public's preferences on welfare by elected officials, therefore, does not occur. A liberal public opinion-election outcome connection also finds no support. (This finding, however, is consistent with the global policy model of dynamic representation, as they too did not find support for the House with this measure.)

The findings that support H3 partially support the model's election turnover assumption. At t-2, election outcomes resulting in more liberal representatives produces more liberal shifts in welfare policy. Yet, Table 1 indicates weak explanatory power for this relationship (.068). Given this as well as a lack of significant relationships, it cannot be said with any real confidence that a liberal public influences liberal welfare policy, either through rational anticipation and election turnover. Dynamic representation is not confirmed for the House.

Figure 2
Dynamic Representation Model in House
(Significant relationships only)

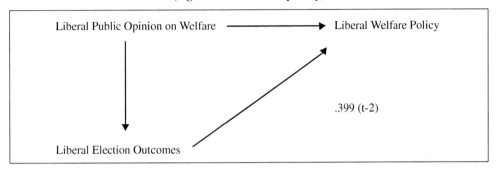

Welfare Policy and the Senate

Global policy preferences: Regarding policy in the Senate, it is a function of public opinion. Senate elections respond to public opinion. The hypotheses (testing both direct and indirect influences) support rational anticipation, election turnover, and the overall dynamic representation model. The findings of this group of policymakers offered the strongest explanatory power for dynamic representation. Thus, the Senate more than any other group significantly responds to public opinion.

Welfare policy preferences: The findings for the first hypothesis do not support shifts in liberal welfare policy as a function of shifts in liberal public mood. Figure 3 reports a significant but inversely related relationship between public opinion and election outcomes that tests H2. The public opinion-elections outcome connection, posited in H2, reports a significant path coefficient at t-2. The inverse relationship, however, implies that as the public opinion on welfare favors governmental assistance, more conservative representatives are elected. This counters the hypothesized relationship in dynamic representation. Election turnover does not occur in the hypothesized manner. No significant coefficients are reported for the third hypothesis.

Table 1 reports that, in testing both institutions, shifts in public opinion do not significantly influence shifts welfare policy. Moreover, the coefficients demonstrate an inverse relationship for the presidency, House and Senate. Initially, this implies that, regarding welfare, policy responsiveness of elected officials is not necessarily influenced by the public's mood. Other influences such as party affiliation, special interest groups, ideology, etc. may play a role.[2] Additionally, this evidence does not expand the notion of a liberal-conservative continuum to explain the shifts of a salient policy-specific issue.

Figure 3
Dynamic Representation Model in Senate
(Significant relationships only)

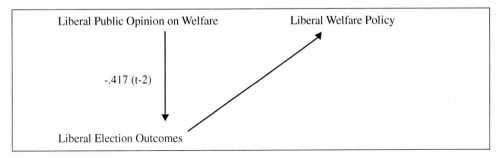

Table 1
Path Analysis of Dynamic Representation in Welfare Policy:
Influences on the President, House and Senate

	Direct Influence: Public Opinion through rational anticipation by elected officials	Indirect Influence: Public opinion through election turnover	Indirect Influence: Election outcomes	Total Influence Public opinion through election outcomes
President	-.550* (R^2 .321)	-.563	.411* (R^2 .283)	-.780
t-2	n/a	n/a	n/a	n/a
t-4	-.113	.361* (R^2 .360)	-.590	-.342
House	.-.599	-.259	.152	-.630
t-2	-.278	.399* (R^2 ..068)	-.709	-.588
t-4	.286	.592	-.429	.449
Senate	-.949	-.272	.133	-.989
t-2	-.417* (R^2 .236)	.152	-1.012	-1.277
t-4	.175	-.294	-1.004	-1.123

Standardized coefficients reported.
*$p < .10$

Implications

Several implications for public opinion, policy responsiveness and representation, are found in the results of this study. First, what can be said about these relationships by institution? Dynamic representation occurs in the presidential institution when testing for global policy. However, the welfare policy model finds that liberal public opinion on welfare does not influence more liberal policy, neither through election turnover nor by rational anticipation. Given the inverse relationship of public opinion on policy, it is implied that other influences, perhaps ideology or party position on welfare, influence the presidential institution over public opinion. This also meets more closely with literature describing presidential policies as influenced by a multitude of factors, not just public opinion (Barber 1992, Light 1991).

The findings of the original model in the House challenge the dissenting views that suggest House members are not directly responsive to public opinion and that the House is insulated beyond the public's ability move it (Fiorina 1989; Jacobsen 1991). When testing for a salient policy-specific issue, however, the findings support such views. House members do not anticipate constituents' messages and produce appropriate responses. Because those elected determine the liberalness of welfare policy more so than liberal public opinion on welfare, other factors appear to influence policy greater than the public's preferences on welfare.

In the Senate, global policy preferences of the dynamic representation model found that rational anticipation and election outcomes matter greatly. This differs from the constitutional design of the Senate, which prescribes limited electoral pressure, as it should not have to react to short-term public opinion. In the welfare policy model, neither election turnover nor rational anticipation dominate. The Senate does not respond to public opinion as dynamic representation posits for global policy. In this respect, the Senate is indeed consistent with the constitutional design for this branch of Congress and counters Stimson et al.'s conclusion.

In addition, what can be said about the adaptability of the dynamic representation model? The model does not fit within a salient policy-specific issue. The liberal-conservative continuum adapts only to shifts in general preferences. The overall implications of the welfare policy model of dynamic representation do not support the original assertions. Other factors besides public opinion determine shifts in welfare policy. Further, the public's preferences on specific policies do not necessarily impact elections, nor policy responsiveness. As discussed, some scholars of voting behavior suggest that a number of influences determine the final vote for a candidate. This is influenced not only by the political sophistication of the voter, but by the voter's emotions and overall candidate appeal. It is often challenged, in fact, that the public does not vote for candidates based on issue preferences alone (Neimi and Weisberg 1993; Sniderman et al. 1994). Thus, policy responsiveness does not necessarily come from public opinion when examining a salient policy issue.

Conclusion

Stimson et al. state that they do not look at a single policy issue for their model, but general representation of general policy preferences (543). The model provides clear evidence that, in the aggregate, a relationship exists. Additionally, it also utilizes an important device in measuring representation (the liberal-conservative continuum). At this level, it can be said we have representation. However, testing for specific policy preferences may not adapt to a model positing global policy preferences. As this study concludes, the dynamic representation model, when testing for a policy-specific issue, does not imply policy shifts as influenced by shifts in the public mood. Although the authors hold that the model is not necessarily meant to describe trends in specific policy issues, the explanatory and predictive value of dynamic representation is limited. Without the potential to expand such a model to explain shifts in at least salient issues with ongoing policy reforms, we have reached a limited understanding of representation. If the model posits only that general "global" preferences guide policy, then the most that can be said is that our representatives respond to the status quo.

Another potential area this examination exposes is the politics of the welfare issue. It may be that in the universe of all public policies, some may adhere closer to the public's mood than others. On an issue such as welfare, those who benefit the most from welfare—corporations—have different interests than those who must pay for the programs. Elite business interests such as agriculture, health care, and real estate may allow slight modifications to the welfare state, but not its entire elimination. Counter to the elite position is the middle class electorate that bears the burden of supporting welfare subsidies. Politicians can easily demagogue the welfare issue for votes since welfare recipients are not their reelection constituents. Thus, what we may have captured, at least on this issue, is the idea that welfare policy is one of those policies that is shaped by elites as policy entrepreneurs. Rather than view elected officials as the receiver of marching order, it may be that we need to view them as opinion leaders. Recently, as an example, President Bush attempted to be a policy entrepreneur on the issue of Social Security reform, but public opinion did not go with him. It seems the public did not buy the argument that elder recipients of Social Security benefits posed a policy problem that could be solved by his proposals.

Future examinations of single policy issues should include some fleshing out of ideological salience. While welfare reform had its flashpoint around ten years ago, the overall debate does not stir the masses as it once did. Policy concerns change places on the public's radar screen. We think perhaps some of the vacillating interest in welfare policy by the public lends additional weight to the argument that it is an easily recognizable policy that shows up as salient in the public opinion measures, but individuals may not hold the issue at their forefront of the ideological spectrum. Simply stated, salient policy issues are not always intently considered by the masses.

Notes

1.   This will slightly differ from the original model in that the authors chose to use a more sophisticated method to estimate the relationships (Kalman filter). However, path analysis and linear regression were cited as alternatives (548, 557), and will therefore be used in this analysis.
2.   Also important to note is that the overall estimations for each relationship tested for the Senate appear misspecified, as the total influence comes to slightly more than $|1.000|$. Path analysis states that the path coefficients, when calculating its total influences, cannot exceed more than 1.000 coefficient.

References

Arnold, R. Douglas. 1990. The Logic of Congressional Action. New Haven, CT: Yale University Press.

Asher, Herbert. 1983. Causal Modeling. Newbury Park, CA.: SAGE Publications.

Asher, Herbert B., and Herbert F. Weisberg. 1978. "Voting Change in Congress: Some Dynamic Perspectives on an Evolutionary Process." American Journal of Political Science 22:391-425.

Barber, James D. 1992. The Presidential Character: Predicting Performance in the White House. Englewood Cliffs, NJ: Prentice-Hall.

Dobelstein, Andrew W. 1996. Social Welfare Policy and Analysis. 2nd ed. Chicago, IL: Nelson-Hall Publishers.

Erikson, Robertson S. 1989. "Economic Conditions and the Presidential Vote." American Political Science Review 83:567-73.

Erikson, Robert S. 1990. "Economic Conditions and the Congressional Vote: A Review of the Macrolevel Evidence." American Political Science Review 83:567-73.

Fenno, Richard. 1978. Home Style: House Members in Their Districts. Boston, MA: Little, Brown.

Fiorina, Morris P. 1989. Congress: Keystone to the Washington Establishment. 2nd ed. New Haven, CT: Yale University Press.

Fiorina, Morris P. 1996. Divided Government. 2nd ed. Boston, MA: Allyn and Bacon.

Goren, Paul. 1997. "Gut-Level emotions and the Presidential Vote," American Politics Quarterly 25:203-229.

Herrick, Rebekah, Michael K. Moore and John R. Hibbing. 1994. "Unfastening the Electoral Connection: The Behavior of U.S. Representatives when Re-election is No Longer a Factor." The Journal of Politics.

Herrnson, Paul S. 1998. Congressional Elections: Campaigning at Home and in Washington. 2nd ed. Washington, DC: Congressional Quarterly.

Katz, Michael B. 1989. The Undeserving Poor: From the War on Poverty to the War on Welfare. New York. Pantheon Books.

Kingdon, John W. 1984. Agendas, Alternatives and Public Policies. Boston, MA: Little, Brown.

Light, Paul C. 1991. The President's Agenda: Domestic Policy Choice from Kennedy to Reagan. Baltimore, MD: Johns Hopkins.

Marcus, George. 1988. "The Structure of Emotional Response: 1984 Presidential Candidates" American Political Science Review. 82: 737-62.

Mayhew, David R. 1974. Congress: The Electoral Connection. New Haven, CT: Yale University Press.

McCool, Daniel C. 1995. Public Policy, Theories, Models and Concepts: An Anthology. Englewood Cliffs, NJ: Prentice-Hall.

Meier, Kenneth J. 1993. Politics and the Bureaucracy: Policymaking in the Fourth Branch of Government. 3rd ed. Belmont, CA: Wadsworth.

Mishler, William and Reginal Sheehan. 1993. "The Supreme Court as a Countermajoritairan Institution? The Impact of Public Opinion on Supreme Court Decisions." American Political Science Review. 87: 87-101.

Mouw, Calvin, and Michael MacKuen. 1992. "The Strategic Agenda in Legislative Politics." American Political Science Review 86:87-105.

Niemi, Richard G. and Herbert F. Weisberg. 1993. Controversies in Voting Behavior. 3rd ed. Washington, DC: Congressional Quarterly Press.

Page, Benjamin I., and Robert Y. Shapiro. 1983. "Effects of Public Opinion on Policy." American Political Science Review 77:175-90.

Peterson, Mark A. 1990. Legislating Together: The White House and Capitol Hill from Eisenhower to Reagan. Cambridge, MA: Yale University Press.

Quaile Hill, Kim and Jan Leighley. 1996. "Political Parties and Class Mobilization in Contemporary United States Elections," American Journal of Political Science 40:683-691.

Ragsdale, Lyn. 1991. "Strong Feelings: emotional Responses to Presidents." Political Behavior. 13:33-65.

Ragsdale Lyn. 1996. Vital Statistics on the President. Washington, DC: Congressional Quarterly.

Rahn, Wendy. 1993. "The Role of Partisan Stereotypes in Information Processing about Political Candidates," American Journal of Political Science 37:472-496.

Rexroat, Jennifer. 1998. "The 1996 Welfare Reform Bill and Its Impact on States and Urban Areas." Presented at the annual meeting of the Southern Political Science Association, Atlanta.

Ripley, Randall B. and Grace A. Franklin. 1991. Congress, the Bureaucracy and Public Policy. 5th ed. Pacific Grove, CA: Brooks/Cole.

Ripley, Randall B. 1985. Policy Analysis in Political Science. Chicago, IL: Nelson-Hall.

Shull, Steven A., Dennis W. Gleiber and David Garland. 1991. "Ideological Congruence Between the General Public and Government Institutions: The Case of Civil Rights." prepared for delivery at the 1991 Annual Meeting of the Western Political Science Association, Seattle, Washington, DC. March 21-23.

Shull, Steven A. Presidential-Congressional Relations: Policy and Time Approaches. Ann Arbor, MI: University of Michigan Press.

Sniderman, Paul M., Richard A. Brody and Philip E. Tetlock. 1994. Reasoning and Choice: Explorations in Political Psychology. Cambridge University Press.

Stevens, Daniel. 2000. "Public Mood and Public Policy: The Case of Kennedy and Civil Rights." Presented at the annual meeting of the Midwest Political Science Association.

Stimson, James A. 1991. Public Opinion in America: Moods, Cycles and Swings. Boulder, CO: Westview.

Stimson, James A., Michael B. Mackuen and Robert S. Erikson. 1995. "Dynamic Representation." American Political Science Review 89:543-564.

Wright, Gerald C. and Michael B. Berkman. 1986. "Candidates and Policy in the United States Senate Elections." American Political Science Review.

"Welfare: American Dilemma." February/March 1995. The Public Perspective. Published by the Roper Center: 40-45.

War and Morality: An Examination of African Americans, the Republican Party, and the 2004 Presidential Election: A Research Note

Kevin A Pirch
Department of Political Science
Lehman College, CUNY

During the presidential election of 2004, the Republican Party made a concerted effort to court African American voters who traditionally have supported the Democratic Party en masse for the past forty years. These appeals were made primarily by questioning whether the Democratic Party takes the African American community for granted and by appealing to more conservative positions some African Americans may have on social issues. While the Republican Party increased support among other traditional Democratic groups such as Catholics and Hispanics during the 2004 campaign, George W. Bush also made progress within the African American community. In this election Bush increased his support among African Americans from 7 percent in 2000 to 10.94 percent of the total vote in 2004. This increase gave Bush nearly 550,000 more votes from African Americans in 2004 than in 2000, to a total of approximately 1.54 million votes from African Americans. In garnering nearly 11 percent of the African American vote, Bush received more of this community's vote than any other Republican candidate for the presidency since Richard Nixon received 13 percent of the vote in 1972 and Ronald Reagan received 11.28 percent in 1984. Moreover, Bush was only the third Republican candidate to receive more than 10 percent of the African American vote since at least 1968.

While there are volumes of literature describing the Republican Party's base of support among the nation as a whole, there are fewer studies on African American support for the modern Republican Party. Because of this, it is not clear if African American support for the Republican Party is correlated to income, education, religion, or some other factor. The purpose of this article, then, is threefold: using data from the 2004 American National Election Survey, it will undertake to explain the factors leading to support for the Republican Party among African Americans, determine if the Republican Party's strategy to court African Americans by talking about moral issues had any effect, and discover if African American Bush voters supported him for the same reasons as other Americans. To do this, we will first explore the relationship between the African American community and the Republican Party, the connection between African Americans and the conservative movement, and the context of the 2004 presidential election.

Graph 1
Republican Percentage of the African American Presidential Vote by Year, 1968-2004

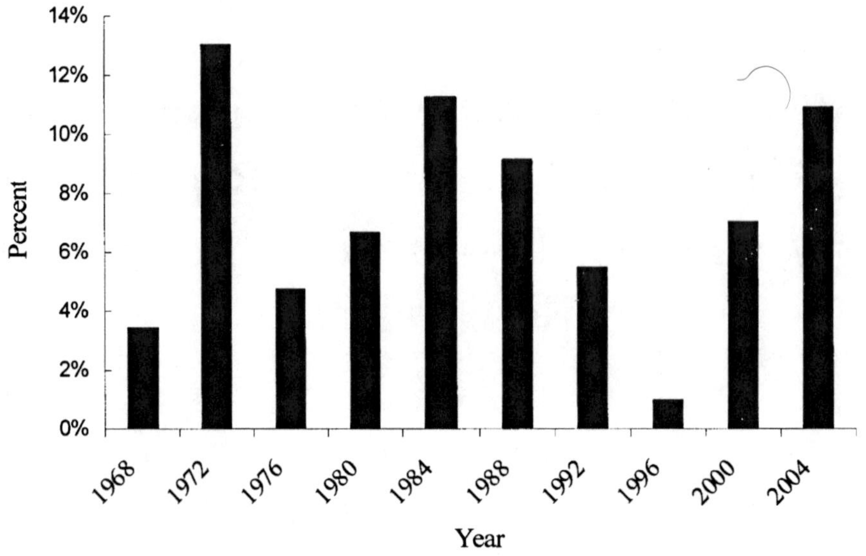

Source: American National Elections Studies Cumulative Data File

African Americans and the GOP

While almost universally committed to the Republican Party during Reconstruction, African Americans became more alienated from the party during the early twentieth century as Republican leadership made an effort to attract white, southern voters (Dawson 1994; Ferguson 1983; Campbell 1960). This transformation in party allegiance continued in earnest in the 1930s as African Americans generally supported Franklin Roosevelt's presidency and his economic priorities. However, the vote of many African Americans was not wholly committed to the Democratic Party until the 1960s (Dawson 1994). Much of this support was related to the Democratic Party's position on Civil Rights, voting rights, Affirmative Action, and other domestic programs which supported their economic and political interests (Black and Black 1987; Sundquist 1983). This allegiance to the Democratic Party continued through the 1980s as more African Americans went to the polls, in part because of the presidential candidacy of Jessie Jackson, and supported the Democratic Party (Tate 1991).

During this time the relationship between the African American community and the Republican Party became a two-way street of neglect. African Americans, deeply committed to the policies of the Democratic Party and distrustful of a party which was less supportive of Civil Rights and other important issues, became almost reflexively supportive of the Democrats. While the Republican Party, eager to court conservative white Southerners and philosophically opposed to major federal programs, did not assertively try to press their message to the African American community. This is readily seen during campaigns where the Republican Party almost totally ignored the African American community. Studies of campaign outreach have found that while the percentage of African Americans who were contacted by the Democratic Party during campaigns from 1952 until 1996 was roughly representative of their percentage of the voting population, the percent of African Americans contacted by the Republican Party was substantially less (Wielhouwer 2000).

The conservative effort to influence public opinion among African Americans during this time was done using commentators and activists rather than by direct appeals during political campaigns. Conservative think tanks and Republican government leaders, in this method, promoted conservative African Americans to express their viewpoints and to act as a counterpoint to more liberal leaders. These appointments allowed conservative African Americans access to more conservative press outlets and appearances on talk radio (Walton 2002). However, in his study, Walton finds that this effort did not substantially change African American public opinion.

The Republican approach to voter outreach began to change during the 2000 presidential election when African Americans were seen in more important roles during the Republican National Convention. Having more African Americans speak in prominent times during the convention increased the perception among many viewers that the Republican Party was reaching out to attract African Americans and other minorities. An analysis of viewers' attitudes found that those who spent more time watching the 2000 Republican National Convention on television had increased positive perceptions of the Republican Party's attitudes towards minorities (Philpot 2004). This attitude was especially significant among conservatives, whites, and those with higher levels of education. However, this feeling was not universal and the attempt to influence one critical audience appeared to have failed. Specifically, African Americans did not experience this increased positive perception of the GOP after the 2000 convention (Philpot 2004).

African Americans and the Modern Conservative Movement

There remains a strong conservative streak among some in the African American community based on individualism, a belief in the importance of personal achievement over race, and a view that believing in the African American community as a collective good is unattainable and promoting a collective good is undesirable (Smith 2002). For many African American conservatives, race is just one of many aspects of their lives, and one that is not a primary concern. Rather than defining themselves as African American, many Black conservatives define themselves primarily by their family, their occupation, their religion, and nationality. Additionally, African American conservatives tend to equate success with an individual ethos. "Individualism is linked with success. Collectivism is linked with being poor. ... In essence, those who advocate a collective consciousness fear their freedom" (Smith 2002, pp 127). This view has created differing opinions in the African American community among liberals and conservatives concerning social issues, economic issues, and civil rights, as well as philosophical differences based in part on geographic and demographic differences. Those who are richer, live in rural areas, or have weak racial identification are more likely to consider themselves conservative. Additionally, unlike many other groups, younger African Americans are more likely to consider themselves conservative while older individuals consider themselves more liberal (Tate 1993). In the South, Earl and Merle Black (1987) found that 21 percent of African Americans considered themselves conservative, and 13 percent believed in "greater stress on individual responsibility," a central hallmark of conservativism.

The idea that African American conservatives can be attracted to the GOP is rooted in many of the community's beliefs. In 2004, half of all African Americans reported being evangelical Christians, compared to 28 percent of whites (Pew 2003). Because the Republican Party has a two-to-one advantage over the Democratic Party among white evangelical Christians, it seems reasonable that the Republican Party could make some in-roads into the African American community based simply on religious affiliation. Moreover, African American Protestants,[1] while not necessarily affiliating with the Republican Party, have been leaving the Democratic

Party and becoming independents over the past decade. Since 1992, the number of African American Protestants claming association with the Democratic Party declined by 6 percent (Green 2005).

Additionally, these African American Protestants tend to have conservative views on salient social issues in the 2004 election such as same-sex marriage and abortion. Opinions of African American Protestants have become increasingly conservative over the past fourteen years. In 2004, 40 percent of African American Protestants believed that homosexuals should have the same rights as other Americans, compared to 59 percent who believed so in 1992, making it the only religious group with declining support in the percentage of people who supported homosexual rights during this time (Green 2005). Similarly, 10 percent of African American Protestants supported same-sex marriage and 18 percent supported civil unions, the least sup- portive group of this policy besides white Evangelicals (Green 2005). Like white Evangelicals, African American Protestants were more likely to believe that AIDS was God's punishment of homosexuals (36 percent) than other religious groups (Pew 2003).

This trend in conservative views on social issues was also found concerning abortion. In surveys, 32 percent of African American Protestants said they believed that there should be more legal restrictions on abortions and 21 percent said abortions should always be illegal (Pew 2003) (Green 2005). Again, these figures are similar only to the views of white Evangelicals. Simply put, if social issues are salient to the election, the Republican Party should hope to get more than the seven percent of the African American vote Bush received in 2000 (Janofsky 2004; Stevenson 2004).

The 2004 Election

The 2004 election was the first presidential campaign since the terror attacks on September 11, 2001 and the subsequent War on Terror. Consequently, foreign policy became a much more salient issue during this campaign than in many elections since the end of the Cold War. In response to the September 11 attacks, more than 100,000 troops were deployed in Iraq and thousands more went to Afghanistan, a new government department, Homeland Security, had been created, airport security was now the responsibility of the federal government rather than the private sector, and a host of other laws and regulations were created.

Despite the conflicts in Iraq and Afghanistan, many exit polls indicated that the most important issue for a plurality of voters during 2004 was the "Moral Issues." More than 20 percent of the electorate polled said social policy questions were the critical questions of the campaign, rather than Iraq, the economy, health care, or other issues (Nelson 2005; CNN 2005). Specifically, the controversy over whether same-sex marriages should be legally permitted, the use of stem cells in medical research, and the debate over abortion were the major social issues which came to the forefront during the 2004 presidential election (CNN 2005).

With the 2004 election appearing to be a close contest in many pre-Election Day polls, many Republicans believed that even a minimal increase in African American support for the GOP could be the difference in the contest with Senator John Kerry (Janofsky 2004). Appealing to minorities on moral issues was part of the Republican Party's broader attempt to break apart the Democratic coalition by bringing to the forefront issues such as abortion, embryonic stem-cell research, same-sex marriage, and euthanasia in an attempt to split conservative Catholics, Jews, and others from the Democrats majority coalition (Lampman 2004). By focusing on those issues which might be more inline with the Republican Party, Republican strategists hoped to trump the traditional economic interests which were so salient to the Democratic Party in past elections (Lampman 2004).

Asserting that the Democratic Party has taken African Americans for granted, President Bush and others campaigned that the African American community would benefit from his faith-based initiatives and tax cuts (Stevenson 2004). Many Republicans believed that Bush's policies such as school vouchers might increase his popularity among some African Americans, as would his appointments of African Americans such as Colin L. Powell and Condoleezza Rice to important government positions. To help with this effort, the President created a steering committee of African American community leaders and increased his advertising and get out the vote operations to encourage African American conservatives to vote for the Republican Party (Janofsky 2004).

The Analysis

Using data from the American National Election Studies 2004 data set this article examines whether certain beliefs were more likely to cause a person to vote for George W. Bush rather than another candidate.[2] The variables tested consist of traditional demographic and socio-economic factors, as well as a measurement of peoples' belief on certain key issues during the 2004 campaign. Specifically, this analysis will examine variables such as age, income, amount of education, gender, and partisanship to determine if there is any relationship between these factors and a decision to vote for the Republican candidate among all Americans, non-African Americans, and African Americans. It also will test three issue positions which were salient during the 2004 presidential election to gauge voters' support for Bush: support for the war in Iraq, opinions on moral issues such as gay marriages and abortion, and views on the economy. Additionally, to assist in determining if there was another, more subtle, connection between the moral issues and voting from George Bush, this analysis will include an index of religiosity, which will determine if those people who consider themselves to be highly religious were more likely to vote for the President, which could be closely tied to beliefs on moral issues.

Because this analysis involves a dichotomous dependent variable, voting for Bush or not, OLS regressing analysis assumptions are violated and probit analysis is used to estimate the effect of each of the independent variables.

The following equation was estimated:

$$Pr(Y_i=1) = Pr(a+B_1X_i+...+B_jX_k)$$

Where Y is 1 if the individual voted for George W. Bush and 0 if he or she did not, and Pr denotes a probability of voting for Bush to be estimated. Probit estimates (MLEs) are presented in Table 1.

In the first model, examining the entire electorate, education is the only significant standard demographic variable for supporting George W. Bush. Surprisingly, while there is a possibility of a Type II error, there is no significant relationship in this model between income and the decision to vote for Bush. All of the variables concerning policy issues also were significant in explaining a decision to vote for Bush. Support for the war in Iraq, belief in the strength of the economy, and a conservative view on moral issues, all were factors in the decision to vote for Bush, as was identification with the Republican Party. Additionally, the variable measuring religiousness was not statistically significant at the 0.05 level, nor did it have the expected sign for a candidate who focused on religion and moral issues.

The findings for non African-American voters, demonstrated in Model 2, are similar to Model 1. Again, education is the only standard demographic variable significant in explaining a choice for Bush. Neither a voter's income, age, nor sex is capable of significantly explaining a voter's choice. However, all three of the policy issues, again, have significant explanatory power for voting for the Republican, as does an individual's party identification. In addition, claiming strong religious convictions also did not have a significant impact and had an unexpected sign. Belief that the nation's economy was doing well had a relatively strong impact on a voter's decisions to select Bush. Similarly, supporting the U.S. mission in Iraq was a significant variable in deciding to vote for Bush among Americans as a whole—people who believed that the war in Iraq was worth the cost and George Bush had done a good job handling the war were more likely to vote for the president. Lastly, a conservative position on moral issues such as abortion and gay marriage was a significant factor in voting for the Republican among non African Americans.

Table 1
Support for George W. Bush in the 2004 Presidential Election

	All Americans (Model 1)	Non African-Americans Only (Model 2)	African-Americans Only (Model 3)
Age	0.004 (0.003)	0.004 (0.003)	-0.008 (0.016)
Male	-0.101 (0.103)	-0.1220 (0.110)	.452 (0.412)
Income	0.000 (0.002)	0.002 (0.003)	-0.008 (0.009)
Education	0.181** (0.034)	0.185** (0.036)	0.237 (0.139)
Religious	-0.034 (0.019)	-0.040 (0.020)	0.108 (0.098)
Republican	0.663** (0.066)	0.644** (0.71)	0.501 (0.268)
Support Iraq	0.422** (0.069)	0.395** (0.074)	0.879** (0.237)
Economy	0.205** (0.051)	0.210** (0.055)	0.086 (0.167)
Moral Issues	0.215** (0.032)	0.241** 0.034)	0.002 (0.110)
Constant	-3.771** (0.291)	-3.798** (0.310)	-3.867** (1.187)
N	1155	954	183
Pearson's Goodness-of-fit-chi-square	1030.125	876.675	130.68
DF	1145	949	173
P	0.993	0.954	0.993

Note: Number in parentheses are standard errors.

*p 0.05; **p 0.01

There is a substantial difference between African American support for Bush and the rest of the electorate, as seen in Model 3. Support for Bush among African Americans does not have the broad philosophical backing as it does among the electorate as a whole. There is no significance between voters' demographic characteristics, including education, and their decision to vote for Bush. Unlike all Americans there also is no significant link between those who believed the economy was doing well or those who shared a similar conservative belief in the moral issues and support for Bush. Nor did claiming affiliation with the Republican Party have an impact on the decision to vote for Bush. Moreover, positions on abortion or gay marriage had no significant influence on African Americans' decision to vote for the Republican. Among African Americans who voted for President Bush, the only significant issue was their support for the war in Iraq—those who supported the war were, like all Americans, significantly more likely to vote for Bush than Kerry. There also was some variation between African American Bush supporters and other Bush voters. Religion and age also are different in this model then in the other two models. Religion, among African Americans, has a positive association with voting for Bush, but not at a statistically significant level, while age had a negative association with voting for Bush—which is consistent with previous research by Tate (1993).

Conclusions

In conclusion, although much was made in the media immediately after the election about the importance of moral issues in deciding the outcome of the 2004 presidential contest, factors such as gay marriage and abortion were not a mobilizing force for African American Bush supporters. Additionally, appeals to religious values did not influence vote choice of African American voters. Despite the findings of other research that wealthier African Americans were more likely to be conservative, there was no relationship between that factor and voting for Bush in 2004. While conservative views on social issues is a strong predictor of voting for Bush among other Americans, it appears that the Republican Party could not capitalize on the socially conservative views of some African Americans on abortion and same sex marriage, nor their inherent conservatism.

Rather, the only significant variable explaining African Americans' vote for president Bush is their feelings about the war in Iraq. This could reflect a belief that the Republican Party is more dominant on defense and national security issues, or it might be because of a desire to support the incumbent president during times of war. It is interesting to note that the only other times a Republican candidate polled more than 10 percent of the African American vote since at least 1964 was in 1972, when, like 2004, the Republican was an incumbent presiding during a war and 1984 during a time of heightened tensions with the Soviet Union.

That being said, changing decades of partisan predispositions in one election cycle would be a monumental task. While focusing on social issues, the Republican Party also must address economic and racial issues which the Democratic Party has dominated for decades among African American voters. It also remains to be seen whether the Republican Party can capitalize on gains that it had made through its stances on national security issues among this community. In the past, African American support for presidents has waned as the number of soldiers killed in action increases (Dawson 1994). Moreover, some of this increased level of support for Bush in 2004 could be due to incumbency advantage, rather than any successes from a shifting campaign strategy.

Secondly, it is important to note that while some demographic variables such as income had been predictors of vote choice in previous elections for all Americans, only education had a significant effect on the vote choice among Bush supporters in 2000. This could indicate that the Republican Party has succeeded in attempts to capture the votes of the middle- and working-class and now voters across all income brackets and ages are identifying with the party.

The final major finding of this paper is that the magnitude of both Iraq and the economy should not be overlooked as factors in determining support for Bush among all Americans—with the war showing a greater impact than moral issues and the economy showing a similar impact as moral issues in support for Bush. Despite the fact that many polls stated that "moral issues" were the paramount concern of many voters, both a belief that the economy was doing well and headed in the right direction, and support for the war in Iraq were strong predictors of support for the president. In addition to benefiting from moral issues, Bush benefited from support for the war in Iraq and the military—a traditional strength of the Republican Party—and belief in his command of a strong economy—a traditional strength for incumbents.

Appendix

Variable Description

Dependent Variable
   0 = Did not vote for Bush and 1 = Did vote for Bush

Independent Variables
Age – Respondent's age in years

Education –
   1. 8 grades or less and no diploma or equivalency
   2. 9-11 grades, no further schooling (incl. 12 year without diploma or equivalency)
   3. High school diploma or equivalency test
   4. More than 12 years of schooling, no higher degree
   5. Junior or community college level degrees (AA degrees)
   6. BA level degrees; 17+ years, no advanced degree
   7. Advanced degree, including LLB

Income – Respondent's Household Income: 23 point scale where 1 = less than $2,999 and 23 = $120,000 and above

Male – Male respondents = 1; Female respondents = 0

Support Iraq – Factor score based on responses to:
   1. Do you approve or disapprove of the way George Bush is
   Handling the War in Iraq? (0 = no; 1 = yes)
   2. Taking everything into account, do you think the war in Iraq
   has been worth the cost or not? (0 = no; 1 = yes)

Moral Issues – Factor Score based on responses to:
   1. Should same-sex couples be allowed to marry, or do you think
   they should not be allowed to marry? (not allowed=1; allowed or civil unions = 0)
   2. View on abortion (4 point scale 4 = never permitted; 3 = only in case of rape, incest, or when the woman's life is in danger; 2 = for other reasons, but only after the need for has been clearly established; 1 = woman should always be able to obtain an abortion as a matter of personal choice)

Economy – Factor based on a four point scale, where 4 = strongly approving
Bush's handling of the economy, and 1 = strongly disapprove of Bush's
handling of the economy.

Party – Republican respondents = 1; Democrat respondents =0.

Religion – Factor Score based on responses to:
1. Importance of religion? (4 point scale: not important = 0; very important = 3)
2. How often do you pray? (5 point scale: never = 0; 4 = many times a day)
3. Do you attend religious services? (no = 0; yes = 1)

Notes

1. In Green et al's study, African American Protestants, both Evangelical and non-Evangelical were grouped together because of the homogeneity of modern American Protestant churches.
2. The National Election Studies, Center for Political Studies, University of Michigan. Electronic resources from the NES World Wide Web site (www.umich.edu/~nes). Ann Arbor, MI: University of Michigan, Center for Political Studies [producer and distributor], 1995-2006.

   These materials are based on work supported by the National Science Foundation under Grant Nos. : SBR-9707741, SBR-9317631, SES-9209410, SES-9009379, SES-8808361, SES-8341310, SES-8207580, and SOC77-08885.

   Any opinions, findings and conclusions or recommendations expressed in these materials are those of the author and do not necessarily reflect those of the National Science Foundation.

References

Aldrich, J.H. & Nelson, F.D. 1984, *Linear Probability, Logit, and Probit Models*, Sage Publications, Newberry Park.

Bartels, L.M. 2000, "Partisanship and Voting Behavior, 1952-1996," *American Journal of Political Science*, vol. 44, pp 35-51.

Black, E. & Black, M. 1987, *Politics and Society in the South*, Harvard University Press, Cambridge, MA.

Bolce, L. & De Maio, G., 2002, "Our Secularist Democratic Party." *The Public Interest*. Fall 2002 139:3-22.

Budge, I. & Farlie, D.J. 1983, *Explaining and Predicting Elections: Issue Effects and Party Strategies in Twenty-Three Democracies*, George Allen and Unwin, London.

Cable News Network, 2005, Presidential Exit Poll, retrieved from http://www.cnn.com/ELECTION/2004/pages/results/states/US/P/00/epolls.0.html

Campbell, Angus, et al. 1960, *The American Voter*, New York, Wiley.

Cassel, C.A. & Hill, D.B., 1981, "Explanations of Decline: A Multivariate Test." *American Politics Quarterly*, vol. 9, pp181-195.

Dawson, M.C., 1994, *Behind the Mule: Race and Class in African American Politics*, Princeton, NJ: University Press Princeton.

Downs, A., 1957, *An Economic Theory of Democracy*, Harper Collins, New York.

Ferguson, T., 1983, "From Normalcy to New Deal: Industrial Structure, Party Competition, and American Public Policy in the Great Depression," *International Organization*, vol. 38, pp41-129.

Green, J.C. et al., 2005, "The American Religious Landscape and the 2004 Presidential Vote: Increased Polarization," Pew Forum on Religion and Public Life, Washington, DC.

Holder, K., 2006, "Voting and Registration in the Election of November 2004," U.S. Census Bureau, Washington, DC.

Janofsky, M., 2004, "GOP Seeks Better Share of Black Vote," *The New York Times*, July 21, pp 14.

Lampman, J., 2004, "A 'Moral Voter' Majority? The Culture Wars are Back," *Christian Science Monitor* (Boston, MA), November 8, pp 04.

Miller, W. & Shanks, J.M., 1996, *The New American Voter*, Harvard University Press, Cambridge, MA.

Nelson, M., *The Election of 2004*, CQ Press, Washington, DC.

Niemi, R.G. & Weisberg, H.F., (eds.), 2001, *Controversies in Voting Behavior*, CQ Press, Washington, DC.

Pew Research Center for the People and the Press, 2003, *The 2004 Political Landscape: Evenly Divided and Increasingly Polarized*, Washington DC.

Philpot, T.S., 2004, "A Party of A Different Color? Race, Campaign Communication, and Party Politics," *Political Behavior*, vol. 26, pp 249-270.

Putnam, R.D., 2000, *Bowling Alone: The Collapse and Revival of American Community*, Simon and Schuster, New York.

Smith, S., 2002, "The Individual Ethos: A Defining Characteristic of Contemporary Black Conservativism," in *Dimensions of Black Conservatism in the United States*. (eds.) Tate, G.T. & Randolph, L.A., Palgrave, New York.

Stevenson, R.W., 2004, "Bush Urges Blacks to Reconsider Allegiance to Democratic Party," *The New York Times*, July 24, p1.

Sundquist, J., 1981, *The Decline and Resurgence of Congress*, Brookings Institution, Washington, DC.

Tate, K., 1991, "Black Political Participation in the 1984 and 1988 Presidential Elections," *American Political Science Review*, vol. 85, pp 1159-1176.

Tate, K. 1993, *From Protest to Politics: The New Black Voters in American Elections*, Russell Sage Foundation, New York.

Teixeria, R., 1987, *Why Americans Don't Vote: Turnout Decline in the United States 1960-1984*, Greenwood Press, New York.

Walton Jr., H., 2002, "Remaking African American Public Opinion: The Role and Function of African American Conservatives" in *Dimensions of Black Conservatism in the United States*. (eds.) Tate, G.T. & Randolph, L.A., Palgrave, New York.

Wielhouwer. P.W., 2000, "Releasing the Fetters: Parties and the Mobilization of the African-American Electorate," *Journal of Politics*, vol. 62, pp 206-222.

Wolfinger, R.E., & Rosenstone, S.J., 1980, *Who Votes?* Yale University, New Haven, CT: New Haven Press.

Race, Preemption, and Autonomy in the District of Columbia

Sekou M. Franklin
Middle Tennessee State University

Richard Seltzer
Howard University
Department of Political Science

As citizens of the nation's capitol, Washingtonians lack some of the political rights and prerogatives shared by many Americans. They do not have voting representation in Congress; although Washingtonians are able to elect a delegate to the House of Representatives, this representative is relegated to a non-voting status. Moreover, the District of Columbia lacks the budget autonomy afforded to most cities and its political and economic decisions are regulated by Congress (Rowat, 1973: 342; Hanson and Ross, 1973: 96). The congressional subcommittees exercising supervision over the District of Columbia are the Committee on Government Reform's Subcommittee on the District of Columbia (formerly the House Committee on the District of Columbia[1]) in the House of Representatives, the House of Representatives Appropriations Subcommittee on the District of Columbia, the Senate District of Columbia Appropriations Subcommittee, and the Senate Governmental Affairs Subcommittee on General Services, Federalism, and the District of Columbia.

Political scientist Charles Harris (1995: 213) uses the concept, "anticipatory colonialism," to describe the relationship between the federal government and the District of Columbia. Anticipatory colonialism, or what we refer to as federal preemption, emerges when cities are consigned to a permanent or long-term state of subordination by federal or state governments, thus ruining the prospects for local self-governance. Cities that operate under these conditions have no substantive input in managing their budgets and public expenditures without the close scrutiny of higher levels of government. In fact, District residents often refer to their city as the "last colony" because they have relatively less sovereignty over their financial and political affairs, when compared to most mainland American cities. Illustrating this sentiment is the slogan, "taxation without representation," which has been adopted by the District and officially placed on all of the automobile vehicle license plates issued by the city.

This article examines the intersection between federal preemption and the politics of race and class in the District. We argue that federal preemption has exacerbated long-standing racial divisions among blacks and whites, particularly when assessing their outlooks about the federal government's role in the city's affairs. It has further shed light on class divisions among black

Washingtonians. To examine these trends we relied upon data from five surveys administered by *The Washington Post* from 1995-2002 and a survey conducted by Howard University's Department of Political Science in 1998.

Although this article focuses on federal-local relations through the prism of black and white attitudes, it is worth noting that Washington, DC has experienced an influx of Latino immigrants over the last two decades. Latinos make up eight percent of the population (U.S. Census, 2001). Most live in poor and working-class neighborhoods—primarily the Mt. Pleasant, Columbia Heights, and Adams Morgan neighborhoods—and are isolated from well-paid, civil service jobs (Sanchez, 1991, B3; Escobar, 1993, A1). Since Latinos only comprise a small percentage of the survey samples, we are cautious about making broader conclusions about them. Thus, our study is limited to the black/white encounter.

It is also significant to point out that there has been a sharp decline in the District's black population over the last fifteen years. In the 1980s, blacks comprised over 70 percent of the population, yet by the end of the century, they declined to just a little over 60 percent of the population. Simultaneously, the number of whites increased during the same period from 25 to 30 percent (State of the Cities Data Systems, 2000). From 1970-1998, the majority black wards in the city depopulated at a rate two and three times more than the affluent, mostly white ward three (De Vita, Manjarrez, and Twombly, 2000: 5). Many blacks moved to neighboring Prince George County, having been forced to move out of the District due to an increase in rental and housing costs (Henig, 1993).

We assess black/white attitudes toward political institutions that influence the District's administrative and political functions and aspirations for home rule and statehood. We hypothesize that blacks tend to link the federal government's anticipatory authority over the District to racial antagonisms among conservative lawmakers. As a result, they at will be less sympathetic to federal supervision, when compared to white residents. The second hypothesis is that intra-racial divisions will emerge among blacks regarding their viewpoints about the federal design. This is important to consider since the District is racially and economically stratified (Frazier 1957; Henig 1993). We also look at the impact that gender and age have on black and white perceptions.

In summary, our two hypotheses suggest that the nature of federal-local relations produced noticeable inter-racial divisions between blacks and whites. Where there are similarly held views across racial lines, we expect class (measured by education) to have the greatest effect. We test these two hypotheses against the backdrop of political battles over the past decade involving the District's budget and finances, home rule, mayoral politics, and Congress-District relations.

The remainder of this study assesses how racial politics intersects with the movement for political sovereignty in the District. We then outline our methodological approach for the study, which is followed by a discussion of the findings.

Racial Politics, Federal Preemption, and Political Autonomy

It is virtually impossible to examine local politics in the District of Columbia and the larger debates over home rule and statehood without situating racial conflicts between blacks and whites at the center of the discussion. As early as 1871, during the Reconstruction era, conservative business leaders lobbied Congress to change the District's government structure because they feared that the black electorate (at this time only black males could vote) had gained too much political influence in the city. In reaction to the growing black presence (at this time blacks comprised 33 percent of the population), this coalition of business and congressional leaders abolished local elections and formed a territorial government (GPPP, 1997: 5). This was followed by a reorganization of the government in 1874 that abolished home rule for 100 years (Haskins, 2001-2002: 47-48).

The chief antagonistic to DC home rule and statehood in the twentieth century was the racially conservative Dixiecrat, John McMillan of South Carolina. As Chair of the House Committee on the District of Columbia from 1945-1972, McMillan belligerently opposed numerous Senate proposals that supported statehood for the District (Harris, 1995; Meyers, 1996: 37-38). (After being defeated in 1972, Charles Diggs (D-Michigan), a supporter of home rule and statehood and a founding member of the Congressional Black Caucus, was selected to lead the House Committee on the District of Columbia.)

Not surprisingly civil rights activists linked their struggles to the home rule/statehood movements that encapsulated the District from the 1960s-1980s. Many of the leading activists in the home rule/statehood movement were members of prominent social justice and civil rights organizations. Julius Hobson, a prominent activist and perhaps the most vocal proponent of political sovereignty, formed the Statehood Party in 1971. After winning a seat to the city council in the 1970s, he used the position to rally support for statehood (Haskins, 2001-2002). Reverend Walter Fauntroy of the Southern Christian Leadership Conference (SCLC) became the city's first congressional (non-voting) delegate of the twentieth century. While in Congress, he developed what came to be known in political circles as the "Fauntroy strategy," which targeted white congressional representatives who came from majority-white districts that had sizable and influential, non-majority black populations (i.e., 25 or 30 percent) (Barnett, 1982: 39-40; Walters and Smith, 1999: 152). Fauntroy claimed that five or six dozen white representatives could be pressured to vote for DC home rule or statehood, especially if the black vote could be leveraged to influence the outcome of close elections in their congressional districts.

The efforts of these activists resulted in a significant legislative victory with the passage of the District of Columbia Self-Government and Governmental Reorganization Act (also called the Home Rule Act of 1973) (House Committee on the District of Columbia 1974; Schrag 1984; Kurland 1992; Bangura 2000). As table 1 indicates, the Home Rule Act eliminated the commissioner-mayoral-city council style of government and granted District residents the power to elect a mayor and city council for the first time since the 1870s. Later, with the assistance of the Congressional Black Caucus and liberal congressmembers, the sovereignty movement pressured Congress to pass a proposed constitutional amendment in the late 1970s that attempted to grant the District senatorial representation and a voting congressional representative. Yet this amendment failed to garner the approval of the thirty-eight states required for ratification.

Congressional hostility to sovereignty claims and the historical baggage of racism in the District have made federal-local relations an acutely sensitive issue for many blacks. According to Meyers, "Many blacks are insulted when they hear comments that DC residents are not ready for self-rule or representation in Congress. They feel as ready as any other Americans and tend to interpret such comments as part of the ageless question of who will control this minority-populated jurisdiction" (1996: 98). Thus, the struggle for self-governance in the District has served as a lens through which many blacks view federal-local relations and racial politics in the city.

A major reason why blacks are suspicious towards federal preemption is because of what has been commonly referred to, half-jokingly and half-seriously, as the *plan*. The plan is a District folklore which asserts that federal preemption of local self-governance is part of a larger conspiracy (Smith and Seltzer, 2000: 118), in which whites want "to regain political power over the [majority black] city and would use whatever means necessary to do so" (Barras, 1998: 181). This concern re-emerged after the 1998 election produced the District's first majority white city council in decades. In the aftermath of the election, a debate ensued in the city's newspapers about whether the majority-white city council signaled the beginning of the end of black political power in the nation's first majority-black large city. This reinvigorated the age-old debate about *the plan* or the take-over of the District by whites. Whether real or

Table 1
Key Dates in the Evolution of the Political-Fiscal-Racial Crisis in the District of Columbia

1961   The 23rd Amendment to the Constitution is ratified to give District residents the right to vote for the President of the United States.

1967   President Lyndon B. Johnson sent his Reorganization Plan No. 3 to Congress in June. This plan abolished the Board of Commissioners that had existed since 1874. In its place the Plan created a single Commissioner and a nine-person city council appointed by the President.

1968   Congress authorizes the direct election of a Board of Education for the DC Public Schools.

1971   Walter Fauntroy is elected as the first non-voting delegate to Congress in the twentieth century. Also, Julius Hobson forms the DC Statehood Party.

1972   Chairman of the House Committee on the District of Columbia, John McMillan (D-South Carolina), was defeated in his reelection bid. He had been a consistent opponent of Home Rule for the District and since he assumed the responsibilities of Chair of this committee, he was an ardent opponent of Home Rule and Statehood for the District. After his defeat, black congressman Charles Diggs was selected to chair the House Committee on the District of Columbia.

1973   Congress authorizes the District of Columbia Self-Government and Governmental Reorganization Act (Public Law 93-198), which changed the structure that had been created by Reorganization Plan No. 3. Under this legislation, the offices of elected mayor and city council were established. General elections were held a year later in 1974 for Mayor and the City Council.

1974   Walter Washington takes office as the first elected black mayor in the City of Washington in the twentieth century.

1978   Congress approves the District of Columbia Voting Rights amendment, which was designed to give District residents voting representation in the House and the Senate. This proposed constitutional amendment was not ratified by the necessary number of states (thirty-eight) within the allotted seven years.

        Marion Barry is elected to his first term as mayor.

1982   Marion Barry is elected to his second term as mayor.

1986   Marion Barry is elected to his third term as mayor.

1989   Marion Barry authorizes the creation of the Commission on Budget and Financial Priorities of the District of Columbia (the first Rivlin Commission).

1990 Marion Barry is arrested for drug abuse. He loses the mayoral election to Sharon Pratt Kelly who becomes the first black women mayor in the District.

1991 The Rivlin Commission issues a report which stated that the District faced a budget deficit of at least $90 million that could potentially balloon to $700 million by fiscal 1996.

1992 Barry successfully wins a council level election and takes office in 1993.

1994 Barry announced his intention to run for a fourth term as mayor. He captures 47 percent of the primary vote and 56 percent of the vote in the general election.

   In November, the Republican Party wins the majority of the contested seats in both the House of Representatives and in the Senate.

   In December, the Rivlin Commission issues another report, entitled Four Years Later—The Rivlin Report Revisited: An Assessment of Progress in the District of Columbia. The report finds that the majority of the Rivlin Commission's recommendations had been fully or partially implemented, and that the District's fiscal situation continued to deteriorate.

1995 Congress passes the District of Columbia Financial Responsibility and Management Assistance Act (Public Law, 104-8) which intended to combat the budget deficits and management inefficiencies of the District. The law established the District of Columbia Financial Responsibility and Management Assistance Authority [also called the Control Board] to manage the District for six years. The Control Board begins taking over much of the political and administrative powers assigned to the Mayor, City Council, and Board of Education.

1999 Anthony Williams takes over the mantle as Mayor of the city after winning the mayor's race in the November 1998 election. Barry's decision not to run for office was a major reason why Williams was able to win the election without strong resistance.

2000 On September 30, the Control Board was formally abolished after a six-year reign in the District of Columbia.

Source: This is a modified table adapted from Joseph P. McCormick, 2nd, "The Evolution of a Political-Fiscal-Racial Crisis in the District of Columbia: A Chronological Overview," A Paper Prepared for a discussion before the Executive Leadership Institute of the National Forum of Black Public Administrators, Howard University, September 11, 1997, 5-8.

perceived, the larger significance of the plan is that it is frequently used to explain why many blacks believe anti-home rule/anti-statehood officials in Congress are ambivalent to the idea of self-governance for District residents.

The Decade of the 1990s and Beyond

Our study is concerned with how federal preemption shapes contemporary attitudes among blacks and whites in the District. Our data covers a crucial period in the District (1995-2002) that experienced several major political events that altered the political landscape of the city. First, in 1994, Marion Barry was elected to his fourth term as mayor after a short jail sentence stemming from a highly publicized crack cocaine possession charge. In his political comeback, he defeated incumbent Sharon Pratt Kelly, who was elected in 1990. Kelly's ties to the city's older black elite, her base of support among the black middle-class, fiscal moderates, and the predominantly white and affluent third ward, were considered out of step with the District's poor and working-class black communities (Gillette, 1995: 204). In contrast to Barry, Kelly's leadership was warmly received by congressional moderates and conservatives and Congress gave her an additional $100 million in federal aid (Harris, 1995: 17). Yet to the disappointment of moderates and activists of all political stripes, who were concerned about the city's deficit, Kelly failed to bring fiscal discipline to the city (Gillette, 1995: 204).

Second, Barry's re-election as mayor in 1994 occurred concurrently with the republican takeover of Congress in the same year. Immediately, Congress eliminated the House Committee on the District of Columbia, and placed freshman congressman Tom Davis (R-Virginia) in charge of the newly formed House Committee on Government Reform's Subcommittee on the District of Columbia. Barry's re-election angered conservative lawmakers on Capitol Hill who charged that he was incapable of resolving the city's budget and fiscal problems. Republican Senator Lauch Faircloth of North Carolina, the Chair of the Senate District of Columbia Appropriations Subcommittee from 1995-1998, vehemently scolded the mayor as an inept leader and pushed to replace the District's mayoral system with a city manager form of government (Ibid., 244-245).

Third, just a few months after Barry's mayoral victory, Congress passed the District of Columbia Financial Responsibility and Management Assistance Act of 1995 (Public Law, 104-8). The Act established the Office of Chief Financial Officer (OCFO) and the D.C. Financial Responsibility and Management Authority (also called the Control Board). Once the Control Board was created it assumed administrative and financial control of the District (Fauntroy, 2003; Boyd, 2003; Fauntroy and Boyd, 2000). It was given a six-year mandate to balance the budget and stabilize the city's service delivery system (Dearborn and Meyers, 1997; Fauntroy, 2003). The Act also required "the District to produce four consecutive years of balanced budgets as a prerequisite for the termination of the Authority [the Control Board] and the return of home rule" (Boyd and Fauntroy, 2002: 2).

Financial control boards work with municipal officials to help economically distressed cities balance their budgets and lay out multi-year expenditure plans (Harvard Law Review Association, 1997; Palmer, 1997). For example, financial control boards were implemented in Philadelphia, Chicago, Cleveland, Boston, Yonkers, and Orange County, California (House Government Reform Committee, 1995). The District's Control Board, however, operated in a politically contentious environment. It was perceived as a partisan political formation and an appendage of the republican power brokers in Congress. Marion Barry, perhaps the Control Board's foremost critic, stated that its creation was an attempt to "re-colonize the citizens of the District" (Chan, 2001: B1). Within two years after its creation, the Control Board seized nearly all of the political authority from the mayor's office and school board.

Proponents of the Control Board believed that it would bring responsible governance and fiscal discipline to city hall. Under both Barry and Kelly's (1991-1995) leadership, but mostly Barry's, the District's economy spiraled downward and it was in a state of fiscal shock; its deficit reached $90 million in 1991, and by 1995 when Barry returned to the mayor's office, the deficit ballooned to $350 million (Cook, 1998).

The implementation of the Control Board was one of several measures, initiated by the federal government, restricting the authority of local government officials in the mid-to-late 1990s. Prior to the Control Board's formation, several city agencies were placed under federal receivership due to neglect, mismanagement, security concerns, and sexual harassment (Cook,

1998). In 1997, two years after the Control Board's formation, Congress passed the National Capital Revitalization and Self-government Improvement Act. The bill transferred the authority to appoint or dismiss the heads of nine city departments from the mayor to the Control Board: Administrative Services, Consumer and Regulatory Affairs, Corrections, Employment Services, Fire and Emergency Services, Housing and Community Development, Human Services, Public Works, and Public Health (Noto, 1998). This temporary restructuring dealt a serious blow to home rule advocates who argued that it was another sign of the federal government's anticipatory authority over the District of Columbia.

Heading into the 1998 mayoral election, it was apparent to most political observers that Mayor Barry and Congress were incompatible together, and that Barry's chance of a re-election victory was uncertain. Hence, he decided not to seek re-election, and instead, his Chief Financial Officer, Anthony Williams, successful won the open seat. Williams was considered a pragmatic bureaucrat, having been initially recruited by Barry to repair the city's financial problems. Yet during his tenure, he distanced himself from Barry's charismatic style, and in a controversial decision that angered many blacks, he fired a number of government workers as part of a balanced budgeting, cost-saving measure.

As mayor, black activists often admonished Williams during his first term for being less racially conscious than Barry, less attentive to the poorest communities, and for his advocacy of pro-growth, economic development policies (Woodlee, 1999; Gillette, 2001). These criticisms were fueled by some controversial decisions that Williams made during his first term in office. In 1999, he was criticized for not responding fast enough to reprimand the head of the District's Office of the Public Advocate who made racially insensitive comments in a staff meeting. A year later, Williams led an effort to shut down the emergency services wing of the Greater Southeast Community Hospital, which was located in the poorest section of the city (Rivlin, 2000). In 2000, he attempted to restructure the school board by reducing its size and replacing half of its elected body with mayoral appointees. Despite the opposition of the city council to this measure, he won the support of a slight majority of voters after a modified version of the plan was put before the electorate through a ballot initiative (Raspberry, 2000; Browne, 2000; DC Board of Elections, 2000).

Since becoming mayor, Williams has been portrayed as Barry's antithesis and as a repudiation of Barry's four mayoral terms. Whereas Barry was criticized for excessive spending, Williams is considered a fiscal disciplinarian. In contrast to Barry, whose popularity was found among poor and working-class black residents, Williams is well-liked among moderates and fiscal conservatives in Congress, and drew much of his support from whites and the black middle-class. Despite the revulsion of his drug use (Jaffe and Sherwood, 1994; Barras, 1998; and Agronsky, 1991), Barry was applauded for opening up the city's workforce to the black community during his first term, for creating a popular summer youth jobs program, and for providing opportunities to minority business owners. His popularity and resiliency earned him the acrimonious title, "the mayorforlife," by local media pundits. Because of his strong advocacy for statehood, as well as his use of race-conscious appeals to mobilize low-income blacks, many of his supporters linked the attacks on Barry by members of Congress and the city's newspapers, as attacks on black self-governance and democracy.

Data and Methodology

We utilize data from five surveys conducted by *The Washington Post* in 1995, 1996, 1997, 2000, 2002, and one survey administered by Howard University's Department of Political Science from February-April 1998. The respondents in the surveys are residents of the District of Columbia and all over eighteen years of age.

We conducted cross-tabulations to measure black/white attitudes toward three political institutions: Congress, the Control Board, and the mayor's office [Mayors Marion Barry (1979-1990, 1994-1998) and Anthony Williams (1998-2006)]. Perceptions about these institutions are used as proxies for assessing how District residents view federal-local relations. The surveys provide further insight into whether District residents believe these institutions are capable of resolving the city's fiscal problems and quality of life. To make the study more readable and for purposes of clarity, we chose to display only black-white differences, rather than the full-set of socio-demographic differences (education, gender, and age) found within the two groups. Yet we used log-linear analyses to determine if inter-racial differences were a function of the aforementioned socio-demographic variables.

As we discussed earlier, we expect that blacks will be more antagonistic than whites toward Congress. We predict that this animosity will extend to the Control Board, given its close ties to moderate and conservative congressional leaders and its take-over of District affairs beginning in 1995. Our hypothesis suggests that because blacks feel passionate about home rule and self-governance, they will express support for the institutions that have been the strongest advocates of these initiatives. Hence, they will probably show more enthusiasm toward the mayor, primarily under the leadership of Barry, given his close ties to the home rule and statehood movements.

In order to measure political opinion regarding the federal-local partnership, we divided our discussion into two sections: federal preemption and local autonomy/self-governance. The first section looks at Congress and the Control Board. These institutions are external to local elected leadership and have been criticized for subordinating the city's autonomy. We use them as proxies for adequately assessing federal-local relations and support for federal supervision. Under the second section, we discuss the mayor's office. We anticipate some variation in black attitudes toward the mayor's office that will swing from huge support for Barry to tepid support for Williams.

Preemption and Local Autonomy

Congress

Next we discuss black and white attitudes toward Congress. In comparison to whites, we expect blacks to be less enthusiastic about Congress playing an overly deterministic role in the city's affairs. The republican congressional takeover, along with the establishment of the Control Board, and the abolition of the House Committee on the District of Columbia, all occurring in 1995, intensified these antagonisms over the last decade.

Table 2 reveals that inter-racial differences appeared on all eight questions that looked at the four major issues related to Congress and self-governance: congressional control over the District and its finances; Congress's ability to make budget cuts for the District in a fair way; the overall trust among District residents in Congress; and whether budget problems were attributed to the way Congress set-up home rule. On all of these issues, blacks expressed less favorable attitudes about Congress. Almost 51 percent of blacks compared to 89 percent of whites, said that they trusted Congress to make fair budget cuts in 1995. Although the black-white divide on this issue closed in 1996 and 1997, the racial gap was at least 20 percent in both years.

We also found some intra-racial cleavages among blacks and whites. Older residents, primarily among whites, along with men and less educated respondents were more supportive of congressional preemption. In fact, they were supportive of Congress having temporary or permanent control over the District and its finances.

Table 2
Congressional Supervision and Preemption

	(1) Permanent Control City's Finances (1995)	(2) Budget Problems Due to Set-up of Home Rule (1995)	(3) Trust Make Fair Budget Cuts (1995)	(4) Permanent Control of City Finances (1996)	(5) Trust to Make Fair Budget Cuts (1996)
	Favor	Big Reason	Lot/Little	Favor	Lot/Little
Whites	34.1 p=.0001	44.4 p=.03	88.5 p=.0001	34.8 p=.001	62.6 p=.001
Blacks	16.7	48.9	50.5	15.2	37.9

	(6) Permanent Control of City Finances (1997)	(7) Trust to Make Fair Fair Budget Cuts (1997)	(8) Congress Have Control Over D.C. (1998)		
	Favor	Lot/Little	Same/Less		
Whites	36.4 p=.001	75.1 p=.0001	48.9 p=.04		
Blacks	22.5	55.1	62.9		

Interestingly, less educated respondents—those who were economically insecure—were less antagonistic to Congress playing a supervisory role than higher educated respondents. Many of these residents, most of whom are black, live in deep-seated poverty. Thus, they probably looked to any institution, even Congress, to resolve the economic deprivation that shaped much of their lives.

This last point is important, considering the substantial number of impoverished Washingtonians. Despite the economic prosperity of the 1990s, the gap between the haves and have-nots actually grew in the District during this period (De Vita, Manjarrez, and Twombly 2000: 3). In fact, the influx of whites into the city, along with the exiting of the black middle-class in the 1990s, created more pockets of concentrated poverty. Furthermore, the poorest areas in the District experienced a withdrawal of non-profit service and community development organizations, despite the fact that they had the greatest need. Many of these groups relocated or opened up offices in more accessible and secure areas of the city (Ibid.). These conditions underscore the seemingly insurmountable challenges confronting the District as it attempts to combat poverty. They suggest that when faced with the predicament of poverty, the District's poorest residents may look to any institution for relief, including a conservative Congress.

The aforementioned results confirm our first hypothesis that blacks and whites have different understandings of the congressional role in the District's affairs. However, contrary to our second hypothesis, middle-class blacks were not as supportive of Congress as we expected. On the other hand, the most economically insecure blacks are more receptive of congressional intervention than we initially predicated.

Control Board

A major debate in DC politics over the last decade involved the functions of the Control Board. The establishment of the Control Board, along with the diminution of the mayor's power, angered the District's grass-roots activists, statehood advocates, and the long-standing black political establishment. Many of these activists viewed the Control Board as the political arm of the moderate and conservative wings of Congress.

Twenty-six questions measured the respondents' concerns about the Control Board. Table 3 points out that inter-racial divisions emerged between blacks and whites on all but two questions. Overall, blacks had less favorable attitudes about the Control Board's handling of the budget, finances, and the implementation of spending cuts, with a racial gap ranging from 18-40 percent on these sets of issues. In addition, there was less optimism among blacks regarding the Control Board's overall authority, accessibility, and job performance. For example, in 1997, over 77 percent of whites compared to about 44 percent of blacks approved of the Control Board's job performance. A similar racial divide appears when rating the job performance of the chair of the Control Board. Additionally, blacks were pessimistic about the board's capacity to improve education, to protect city services, to eliminate government waste and fraud, and to make the District a safer and better place to live. Less than 35 percent of blacks said that the Control Board made the city more livable and even a smaller portion said it improved the education system. In terms of safety, over 50 percent of blacks said that conditions deteriorated under the Control Board. In 1997 and 1998, both blacks and whites offered low support for permanent congressional control over the city's finances, although in 1997, there was slightly more approval for this proposal among whites.

The sharpest contrast in black-white opinion materializes when looking at how District residents view the so-called *plan*. As we talked about earlier in the study, the plan is a city folklore which asserts that Congress, moderate political elites, and the Control Board, will make a concerted attempt to remove black control from the city and turn it over to whites, or that they will

Table 3
The Financial Control Board

#	Item (Year)	Response	Whites	Blacks
(1)	Budget Problems Due To Set-up of Home Rule (1995)	Big Reason	44.4 p=.03	56.1
(2)	Manage City Finances/ Make Spending Cuts (1995)	Favor	73.8 p=.0001	34.1
(3)	Deal w/City's Budget (1996)	Trying Hard	79.4 p=.004	60.6
(4)	Makes Needed Budget Cuts (1996)	Favor	56.8 p=.0001	24.2
(5)	Trust to Make Budget Cuts (1996)	Lot/Little	88.1 p=.0001	62.4
(6)	Should Have More/Less Power Council (1997)	Less	14.3 p=.0001	48.2
(7)	Reject Mayor/ Decisions (1997)	Approve	78.6 p=.0001	44.5
(8)	Improved City Services (1997)	Good	38.4 p=ns	33.6
(9)	Make District More Livable (1997)	Good	74.4 p=.0001	33.6
(10)	Permanently Placed Over City's Finances (1997)	Yes	33.3 p=.05	27.1
(11)	CB's Job Performance (1997)	Approve	77.2 p=.0001	43.5
(12)	CB Chair's Job Performance (1997)	Approve	82.5 p=.0001	49.0
(13)	Education Worse w/CB (1997)	Worse Off	31.4 p=.0002	21.7
(14)	District Safer w/CB (1997)	Less Safe	34.1 p=.0001	52.6
(15)	CB Will Make Things Better for You (1997)	Better	48.4 p=.0001	20.8
(16)	Trust to Make Fair Budget Cuts (1997)	Lot/Little	87.9 p=.0001	61.7
(17)	Eliminate Gov't. Waste (1997)	Good	53.0 p=.0001	38.9
(18)	Protect Needed Services Gov't. (1997)	Good	52.7 p=.0001	31.8
(19)	Reduce City Spending (1997)	Good	62.6 p=.0001	38.4
(20)	Eliminates Fraud in City Gov't. (1997)	Good	50.6 p=.01	40.6
(21)	D.C. Better Before CB's Creation (1997)	Better	62.6 p=.0001	28.9
(22)	Make District Better (1998)	Better (Yes)	74.1 p=.0001	44.4
(23)	Should Be Accessible (1998)	More Accessible	42.2 p=.0001	80.6
(24)	CB Have Control (1998)	Same/Less	15.6 p=.0001	51.2
(25)	Permanently Placed Over City Finances (1998)	Yes	31.8 p=ns	27.3
(26)	Plan to Subvert Black Control (1998)	Plan Exists	12.4 p=.0001	72.3

implement policies that have the effect of pushing blacks out of the District. Over 70 percent of blacks believed that the management structure of the city—the Control Board—was part of a larger plan to remove local government from black control. Slightly more than 12 percent of whites supported this claim. The racial divide on this issue is to be expected, considering that many black leaders and activists routinely talk about the plan during local political campaigns. This belief was intensified by the racial antagonisms of conservative members of Congress such as Senator Fairclough. Black gentrification, the influx of whites into the city, and Williams's pro-growth agenda, also heightened fears among blacks about the plan.

Intra-racial divisions, across age, education, and gender emerged regarding the role of the Control Board. Older respondents, mainly among whites, favored the formation of the Control Board (LR=11.5, DF=3). Overall, older respondents trusted the Control Board to make necessary budget cuts, they believed that the Control Board had done a good job of improving police protection, and they trusted that it would personally improve their circumstances. Men, in contrast to women, claimed that the Control Board did a good job of reducing and eliminating government spending, waste, and fraud, as well as protected needed services.

Similar to our discussion of congressional preemption, we found interesting results when taking into accounting educational status. Across both racial groups, higher educated respondents expressed more approval for the Control Board's job performance and its ability to reduce government spending. Higher educated respondents, especially among whites, further said that the city was better off after the Control Board was established. Yet in 1997 and 1998, when the respondents were asked about whether they believe the Control Board should be permanently placed in charge of the District's finances, the least educated respondents expressed more support for this proposal than we anticipated. This is probably due to the fact that the city's poor communities look to any government entity for relief.

The Mayor's Office: Local Autonomy/Self-Governance

Next we examine black/white attitudes toward the mayor's office. Table 4 looks at fourteen questions measuring Mayor Barry's job performance, his handling of the city's budget and management problems, and the respondents' overall impression of him. On every question blacks had more favorable attitudes of Barry. The black-white divide regarding Barry's job performance was between 40-55 percent, and in terms of their overall impression of Barry, the racial divisions were between 49-66 percent. Similar gaps were found when measuring the respondents' trust in Barry, his management of the city, and control of the budget. This black-white divide points to what Smith and Seltzer (2000, p. 119) call a "canyon" of public opinion regarding Barry's role in the city.

Interestingly, we found an inverse set of findings when measuring racial attitudes toward Williams. Table 4 reveals that whites, in contrast to blacks, had a very favorable impression of Williams and his overall job performance, with the intra-racial differences ranging from 11–31 percent. The widest racial gap emerged in the 2000 survey when the respondents were asked if Williams understood their concerns. About 81 percent of whites agreed with this statement as opposed to about 6 percent of blacks. Another gulf appeared when the respondents were asked if they agreed with the mayor's proposal to eliminate government jobs as a solution to bringing fiscal discipline to the District. Over 90 percent of whites, compared to 33 percent of blacks, agreed with this proposal. Whites further believed that Williams would infuse ethics into the mayor's office, and they rejected arguments by his opponents that he is uninterested in the concerns of low-income residents.

The intra-racial differences offer a complicated picture of the perceptions of DC's mayors among blacks and whites. The economically vulnerable residents, especially among blacks,

Table 4
The Mayor's Office: Marion Barry and Anthony Williams

Marion Barry

Column	Item (Year)	Category	Whites	Blacks
(1)	Job Performance (1995)	Approve	38.9 p=.0001	79.2
(2)	Trust to Make Fair Budget Cuts (1995)	Lot of Trust	9.5 p=.0001	43.7
(3)	Overall Impression of Barry (1995)	Favorable	29.7 p=.0001	86.8
(4)	Overall Impression of Barry (1996)	Favorable	11.2 p=.0001	73.3
(5)	Job Performance (1996)	Approve	13.0 p=.0001	68.6
(6)	Trust to Make Fair Budget Cuts (1996)	A Lot	3.6 p=.0001	34.1
(7)	Handling of D.C.'s Budget Problems (1996)	Trying Hard	38.7 p=.0001	76.2
(8)	Job Performance (1997)	Approve	4.4 p=.0001	46.4
(9)	Overall Impression of Barry (1997)	Favorable	5.2 p=.0001	54.9
(10)	Trust/Distrust Barry (1997)	Distrust	74.3 p=.0001	36.9
(11)	Have Control Over Management of City (1998)	More Control	10.2 p=.0001	59.5
(12)	Job Performance (1998)	Approve	9.9 p=.0001	51.3
(13)	Overall Impression of Barry (2000)	Favorable	5.4 p=.0001	70.9
(14)	Overall Impression of Barry (2002)	Favorable	7.1 p=.0001	64.5

Anthony Williams

Column	Item (Year)	Category	Whites	Blacks
(15)	Job Performance (2000)	Strong Approve	47.0 p=.0000	35.2
(16)	Understands Your Concerns (2000)	Agree	81.4 p=.0000	5.6
(17)	Overall Impression of Williams (2000)	Favorable	95.4 p=.0001	77.4
(18)	Eliminate Hundreds of D.C. Jobs (2000)	Good Idea	90.8 p=.0001	33.0
(19)	Job Performance (2002)	Approve	90.2	58.9
(20)	Understands Your Concerns (2002)	Agree	78.8 p=.0001	40.7
(21)	Has "Ethical" Administration (2002)	Agree	77.7 p=.0001	54.8
(22)	Not Helping Low-Income Residents (2002)	Agree	48.1 p=.001	60.3
(23)	Overall Impression of Williams (2002)	Favorable	92.0 p=.0001	61.1
(24)	Williams High-Income Residents to the City (2002)	Agree	27.3	50.5

had the most confidence in Barry. They trusted him more than higher educated respondents, had a more favorable impression of him, and approved of his job performance. Support for Barry among low-income blacks continued well into his last two years in office and after he left office. Men and younger blacks also showed more approval for Barry's job performance, and young people in particular, had a favorable impression of him.

We found a different trajectory of results for Williams. Whereas Barry shored up support among lower educated and younger residents, Williams was backed by older and higher educated respondents who believed he understood their concerns. He received support from higher educated respondents, including middle-class blacks who had a more favorable impression of him, and expressed a higher level of interest for his proposal to eliminate city jobs to balance the budget.

The "canyon" between Barry and Williams is accentuated by social class. Since his first mayoral campaign, Barry built a base of support in wards seven and eight, the poorest and blackest districts in the city. Yet Williams received lukewarm support in these districts in the 1998 mayoral race.[2] Middle-class blacks expressed declining support for Barry, despite the fact that many were the beneficiaries of his expansionist government programs of the late 1970s and early 1980s. Many of these blacks became disillusioned with the Barry administration as a result of his drug use, his management of the city's finances, the cronyism practiced under his administration, and the city's dysfunctional bureaucracy (Gillette, 2001).

Finally, it is ironic that the least educated residents expressed some hope that Congress and the Control Board could alleviate the city's fiscal problems, yet they are also among the most loyal supporters of Mayor Barry who was a vocal critic of these two institutions. Their attraction to Barry is partly due to his historic role in the civil rights and statehood movements and his distribution of government jobs to blacks during his first mayoral term. In fact, blacks in wards seven and eight were intensely partisan—almost militantly partisan—in terms of their loyal support for Barry. For them Barry symbolized the transcendent, race-conscious leader who fought for the interests of the District, chiefly its black poor and working-class residents. They further viewed the struggle for self-governance through the prism of Barry's battles with Congress and the Control Board.

Conclusion

Our study examined the federal-local partnership as it relates to the District of Columbia, or what we have described as federal preemption. We explored black/white perceptions of federal preemption and self-governance by looking at their attitudes toward Congress, the Control Board, and Mayors Barry and Williams.

Our study found noticeable differences between blacks and whites, particularly toward the Control Board and Marion Barry. This confirms our hypothesis that blacks and whites have come to different conclusions about federal oversight. However, we are somewhat cautious about these conclusions, since white attitudes may reflect a negative reaction to the Barry years, rather than staunch support for the Control Board and congressional preemption. Likewise, many blacks are protective of Barry and believe he received unequal treatment from conservative lawmakers.

The findings partially confirm our second hypothesis that similarities would appear among middle-class blacks and whites. Although the black middle-class was less enthusiastic about congressional oversight of the District, they expressed general approval for the creation of the Control Board. Yet, to our surprise, low-income blacks expressed some support for Congress and the Control Board, but only when it pertained to their management of the city's finances.

Finally, it is important to note that black Washingtonians are probably more supportive of self-governance and local autonomy when compared to other blacks around the country. They may also be less enthusiastic about the federal government playing such an overly deterministic role in the usurpation of their political and economic affairs. However, they do distinguish federal intervention from federal subordination or preemption. An affirmative interventionist strategy by Congress, as exhibited through the lobbying and advocacy of Fauntroy, Hobson, and other home rule/statehood advocates, takes place when Congress provides more economic assistance to the District, and more importantly, when it grants the local officials more decision-making power. Preemption, on the other hand, takes place when the federal government takes control over the District, even at the expense of self-governance.

These findings are important and perhaps more transparent in the District because it has yet to experience the type of democratic self-governance that is seen in most jurisdictions across throughout the nation. Future studies on federalism should consider how political processes that preempt or usurp local autonomy and self-governance shape local political cultures and exacerbate racial tensions in municipalities. This would be useful given the recent preemptive policies by state and federal governments of urban school districts, housing agencies, child welfare departments, and even some local governments.

Notes

1. After the 1994 mid-term elections, the republican majority in the House of Representatives abolished the Committee on the District of Columbia.
2. Since close to 80 percent of the voters are democrats, the candidate who wins the democratic primary election is guaranteed a victory in the general election. In the 1998 primary, which only saw a little over 30 percent voter turnout, Williams obtained 50 percent of the vote. The general election saw only 40.2 percent voter turnout (Powell and Cottman 1998).

Book Reviews

Katznelson, Ira, 2005; *When Affirmative Action Was White: An Untold History of Racial Inequality in Twentieth Century America,* (New York: W.W. Norton) xv+ 238pp. ISBN 0-393-0521-3 (cloth)

My colleague Mack Jones over the years in his discussion of scholarly analyses of race in the United States has frequently invoked a quote from Ralph Ellison. In the 1966 essay "The World and the Jug" Ellison asked "why is it so often true that when critics confront the American as *Negro* they suddenly drop their advanced critical armament and revert with an air of confident superiority to quite primitive modes of analysis."[1] Ellison's observation immediately came to mind when I completed reading Ira Katznelson's *When Affirmative Was White: An Untold History of Racial Inequality in Twentieth Century America.* Interestingly, in an essay of his own on affirmative action Jones alludes to Ellison when he writes "ordinary rules of logic are rarely if ever followed in the discussion of race and public policy in America."[2] With respect to affirmative action, Jones writes:

No intelligent proponent of democracy would argue that special consideration should be given any individual or group merely because of race. But in the context of the struggle for racial justice in America, that is not the appropriate question to raise now nor has it ever been the question. The pertinent question is: Should special consideration be given to individuals who belong to a group that was singled out for unequal treatment by the Constitution of the United States and by statutory law at all levels of government, national, state and lo-cal, whose unequal treatment was sanctioned by social custom and reinforced by the use of terror and economic intimidation, and who, as a result of that government—mandated and culturally sanctioned oppression, lag behind white Americans on practically every indicator of socio-economic well-being? The question is: Should members of that oppressed group receive special consideration until such time that the gap between them and the dominant group on these indicators of well-being is eliminated?[3]

Instead of focusing on the question of oppression, discussions of affirmative action since *Bakke* have focused on issues of "diversity" and the inclusion of "minorities" in various societal institutions. This narrow focus—owing much to Justice Lewis Powell's controlling opinion in *Bakke*—Jones contends is illogical because it makes "affirmative action... an act of majority benevolence rather than one of reparations to atone for past and continuing crimes against humanity."[4]

The point of departure for when *Affirmative Action Was White* is President Lyndon Johnson's 1965 address to Howard University's graduating class. (The text of the speech is reprinted as an appendix). In retrospect, President Johnson's speech has to be considered one of the most important ever given by an American president on the subject of race. It established the philosophical and conceptual rationales for the bureaucracy to design and implement affirmative action public policies. The address established first the idea that merely ending racism and white supremacy and treating all persons the same without regard to race was not enough to overcome the effects of centuries of discrimination. Second, it articulated the principle that fairness required that groups disadvantaged by discrimination receive more than a theoretical opportunity to compete. Instead, disadvantaged groups deserved compensatory or remedial policies to overcome or remedy the consequences of past discrimination, thus making opportunity a reality. Finally, the speech set forth the idea that equality was to be measured by the results or effects of policies, rather than their intent or stated purposes.

While applauding the address, Katznelson contends that its historical account was "vague" and that it substituted "expressive language for hard-edged analysis" (p. 10). The absence of historical grounding in the speech he believes means affirmative action advocacy is weakened legally and politically, and contemporary public policy debate is uninformed. This then is a major purpose of the book; to provide the necessary history of public policy left untold in the president's speech.

The untold history of racism is limited to New Deal era public policies because in addition to anchoring the book in Johnson's speech, Katznelson also wishes, following Justice Powell's opinion in *Bakke*, to use this recent history because it allows for the identification of affirmative action recipients "who have a direct relationship to the harm being remedied" (p. 170). He believes this direct connection of remedies to specific harms will make affirmative action more defensible legally and politically, as well as more appealing to "the broad middle of the political spectrum" (p. 159). This narrow approach allows Katznelson to ignore all except thirty years (1930s-1960s) of the history of when affirmative action was white.

In Katznelson's "untold history" affirmative action was white during the New Deal. Specifically, he tells the story of how in their design and implementation each of the major New Deal programs—Social Security, minimum wage, unemployment compensation, unionization of the workforce, and the GI Bill—were racist. The racism in these programs he traces to the disproportionate power exercised in Congress by southern racists and white supremacists in coalition with conservative Republicans. In this telling of the story these New Deal programs became the basis for the

creation of the post-war, white, middle-class, and the development of the enormous economic gap between blacks and whites referred to by President Johnson in his speech.

As Katznelson acknowledges, this is not an untold story. It has, as he writes "been discussed and analyzed by an array of talented social scientists and historians" (p. xiv), most recently Linda Williams in *The Constraint of Choice: The Legacies of White Skin Privilege in America*.[5] What is new in Katznelson's work is his bringing together the story in a compelling narrative with an arresting title. (He writes that the title was suggested to him by E. J. Dionne, the *Washington Post* columnist, at the 2002 meeting of the American Political Science Association).

While affirmative action was clearly white during the formation of New Deal social policies, it has of course always been white as even the most obtuse American knows. Indeed, in looking back over the history of the country affirmative action was perhaps least white in the New Deal period. The enormous gaps in well being and wealth between blacks and whites in the U.S. today are not a product of the New Deal; rather the New Deal merely reinforced older and more pernicious policies and practices of white affirmative action.

The first and worst affirmative action program for whites was of course slavery. (Economists who try to estimate how much whites benefited from slave labor *begin* their estimates at a trillion dollars). In the midst of the war that would result in the emancipation of the slaves, Congress enacted the 1862 Homestead Act. This policy ultimately resulted in the giving away—mainly to whites—of more than 250 million acres of land (10 percent of the entire land area of the country). The Homestead Act is in some ways as significant as the New Deal in laying the foundations for today's white middle-class; an affirmative action program for whites that is the source of much of the wealth of the virtually all white Great Plains states.

After emancipation as the freed Africans in America struggled to accumulate a little wealth, the long and brutal chapter of Jim Crow era affirmative action for whites was soon inaugurated. Blacks during this period, with the sanctions of the state, faced widespread theft of their land, destruction of businesses, separate and grossly unequal education, and thousands of lynchings in a systematic strategy of terror that assaulted both their minds and bodies.

Slavery and Jim Crow affirmative action programs were centered in the South, where most African Americans lived. However, in the northern states there was also affirmative action for whites. In an innovative historical case study Theodore Hershberg and his colleagues at the Philadelphia Social History Project of the University of Pennsylvania analyzed the experiences of separate waves of immigrants to Philadelphia during three historical periods. First, the Irish and Germans who settled in the "industrializing city" of the mid to late nineteenth century; then the Poles, Italians and Russian Jews who settled in the "industrial city" at the turn of the century; and African Americans who, although present throughout, arrived in their greatest numbers in the "post industrial city" after World War II. In both the industrializing and the industrial city, immigrant whites found employment in the manufacturing sector throughout the occupational hierarchy, laying the foundations for the upwardly mobile status of their grandchildren and children during the New Deal. African Americans, however, were virtually excluded from these jobs, relegated instead to the low paying domestic and laborer jobs at the bottom of the occupational structure.

Of the industrial city Hershberg and his colleagues write "Although 80 percent of the blacks lived in the city within one mile of 5,000 industrial jobs, less then 13 percent of the black work force found gainful employment in manufacturing."[6] Earlier in the industrializing city "blacks were not only excluded from the new and well-paying positions, they were uprooted as well from many of their traditional unskilled jobs, denied apprentice ships for their sons, and prevented from practicing the skills they already possessed."[7] During this period, the authors also note, blacks were denied the right to vote and were the victims of frequent race riots in which their homes, churches and schools were destroyed over and over again, experiences unlike those of any other ethnic group.

Affirmative action for whites in manufacturing employment did not begin to come to an end in Philadelphia until the emergence of the post industrial city after World War II. Although in this period blacks were still disproportionately concentrated in low skill, low wage jobs, they for the first time penetrated the relatively higher paying manufacturing employment. Yet, just as employment began to become somewhat colorblind, manufacturing jobs in the city begin disappearing. (Between 1930 and 1970 Philadelphia lost 75,000 manufacturing jobs, and of every ten manufacturing jobs in the city, the three-mile ring from downtown had nine jobs in 1930 but only four in 1970). Hershberg concludes "Precisely at the moment when the worst of the racist hiring practices in industry appear to have abated, the most recent immigrants find themselves at considerable remove from the industrial jobs that remain and thus are unable to repeat the essential experience of earlier white immigrant groups."[8]

Thus, while Katznelson is correct in calling attention to the role of affirmative action for whites during the New Deal in the expansion and consolidation of the white middle-class, he overlooks the historical origins of this middle-class in affirmative action programs for whites in the private sector throughout American history. At the same time all of these affirmative action programs for whites relegated blacks to unequal employment, housing and schooling, laying the foundations for what is now referred to as the black underclass.

In concluding their work on Philadelphia Hershberg and his colleagues write "Since our sense of history—conscious or not—exercises a real power in the present, it should sensitize us to the dangers of ahistorical social science."[9] *When Affirmative Action Was White* is a work of historical synthesis by an able social scientist. Yet it is by design ahistorical; and untold history of affirmative action for whites that deliberately leaves untold all but a few decades of that history. How can one account for this quite primitive mode of analysis by one of the nation's leading political scientists (he is currently president of the American Political Science Association), and one who is sympathetic to the African American struggle for justice and equality? The explanations lie in the ideological and political purposes of the book.

One of those purposes is to discredit the movement for reparations. A comprehensive history of when affirmative action was white might logically lead to reparations as a comprehensive remedy. On reparations, Katznelson writes:

> In truth, the brutal harms inflicted by slavery and Jim Crow are for too substantial ever to be properly remedied. Epic historical crimes such as slavery, unremitting racial bigotry and segregation are injuries that cannot be requited. There are no adequate rejoinders to losses on this scale. In such situations, the request for large cash transfers places bravado ahead of substance, flirts with demagoguery, and risks political irrelevance. These calls also have practical problems. They suffer from slack precision and all-inclusive, grand dimensions. Who would qualify – only blacks descended from slaves or more recent African immigrants? What scale could cash transfers achieve? How could they ever be more than tokens? Whatever the abstract merits of such claims, this utopian politics seems entirely symbolic, not really serious (pp. 157-58).

This is more than primitive analysis. It is not analysis at all, and it does suggest what Ellison referred to as a confident air of superiority. There is an extensive body of philosophical, historical, econometric, and political science scholarship on reparations that addresses each of the concerns and questions raised by Katznelson. Rather then engage this literature, Katznelson responds with shibboleths.

Katznelson's second reason for ignoring all except thirty years of white affirmative action is to place affirmative action for blacks on what he believes are firmer intellectual and political grounds. He believes that the opponents of affirmative action for blacks have "succeeded in occupying the high ground of color-blind equality" (p. 150). This is a puzzling conclusion that is not developed with any detail or rigor. Puzzling because it is difficult to see how invoking the principle of color blindness should be persuasive to the author of a text that compellingly demonstrates the historical hollowness of this principle. As Justice Ruth Bader Ginsberg wrote in her dissent in *Gratz and Hamacher v. Bollinger* et al. "This insistence on [color blindness] would be fitting were our nation free of the vestiges or rank discrimination long reinforced by law. But we are not far distant from an overtly discriminatory past, and the effects of centuries of law—sanctioned inequality remain painfully evident in our communities and schools."[10]

Katznelson believes that Justice Powell's "deeply historical approach" and "fine-grained assessment" provide the appropriate intellectual and political underpinnings for affirmative action for blacks (pp. 158, 160). Yet Powell's opinion in *Bakke* specifically rejected affirmative action as a means for narrowing the gap between blacks and whites in the medical profession specifically and in the society generally. Powell also rejected the use of affirmative action to remedy the effects of historical racism. Instead, he upheld the University of California's affirmative action program on the basis of the University's First Amendment right to select a diverse student body."[11] While Justice Powell may be correct that an ethnically diverse student body may be "essential to the quality of higher education,"[12] it is not logically or constitutionally compelling as a rationale for remedying the effects of two hundred or thirty years of affirmative action for whites (As an alumni of a historically black institution of higher education, I am a bit skeptical as to whether ethnic diversity is *essential* to quality education). Katznelson himself, white applauding Powell's opinion, concedes that diversity is "too light and limited" as a purpose for affirmative action (p. 170). What is useful about Powell's opinion for his purposes is its requirement that affirmative action for blacks should be limited to "identified," "specific instances of discrimination."[13]

Powell's narrow targeting of affirmative action is what makes Katznelson's narrow history of white affirmative action useful. His untold story of New Deal racism allows him to craft an affirmative action program for blacks that can "search for identifiable individuals who have been harmed—even at a distance of one or two generations—by the pattern of exclusions and local administration this book has documented" (p. 171). Slavery, the Homestead Act, Jim Crow era racism in the South and in Philadelphia and other cities are too distant to identify specific harms and remedies.

In addition, the New Deal programs were public policies enacted by the state and therefore remedial actions by the state are appropriate, whereas actions by slaveholders, lynchers, and employers in Philadelphia were private actions and therefore, arguably, beyond remedial public policies. As he puts it "Injuries dealt by government count for more than private patterns of institutional racism" (p. 172).

Following this line of reasoning Katznelson proposes the following examples of affirmative action for blacks that could remedy the racist policies and practices of the New Deal. First, to remedy the racist exclusion of blacks from the Social Security system the excluded or their heirs could be offered one-time grants to be paid into designated retirement funds. Second, for absence of access to minimum wage, tax credits could be provided. Third, for lack of access to the GI bill, subsidized mortgages, business loans, and educational grants could be provided. (In order to hold down costs and target the policy to those most in need, he proposes that the benefits be taxed back at a certain, unspecified level of income).

These programs of "corrective justice" narrowly tailored to the injustices of the New Deal, Katznelson believes, are more likely to gain popular and political support and judicial legitimacy than the narrow diversity programs, or the broader calls for reparation.

The affirmative action policies proposed by Katznelson are interesting and represent a modest kind of reparations. It is unlikely, however, that they would gain more popular, political or judicial support than current affirmative action programs or comprehensive reparations. Sadly, this is because the majority of white Americans refuse to recognize the wrongs done to blacks in the past or that continue to be done to them today. In her dissent in the Michigan affirmative action case referred to earlier, Justice Ginsberg cited studies documenting continued affirmative action for whites in the form of preferences for whites in employment, the real estate market and consumer transactions.[14] In 1968 in a case involving whether the Thirteenth Amendment could be employed to prohibit housing discrimination Justice William O. Douglas wrote "The true curse of slavery is not what it did to the black man, but what it has done to the white man. For the existence of the institution produced the notion that the white man was superior in character, intelligence, and morality. ... Some badges of slavery remain today. While the institution has been outlawed, it has remained in the minds and hearts of many white men. Cases which come to this Court depict a spectacle of a slavery unwilling to die."[15]

A 2000 survey conducted by Michael Dawson and Bobo found that only 30 percent of whites thought the "federal government [should] apologize to African Americans for the slavery that existed in this country." This survey also found that only 4 percent of whites thought the "federal government [should] pay monetary compensation to African Americans whose ancestors were slaves."[16] In 1996 the General Social Survey of the University of Chicago asked respondents the following question: Some say because of past discrimination, blacks should be given preference in hiring and promotion. Others say that such preference in hiring and promotion is wrong because it discriminates against whites. What about your opinion—are you for or against preferential hiring and promotion of blacks? Only 10 percent of whites responded affirmatively.

It is unlikely that if Katznelson's proposals to remedy the injustices of the New Deal were put to white Americans in the form of survey questions that the responses would differ significantly from those cited above. European Americans are unwilling to compensate African Americans for the injustices done to them whether these injustices are centuries or decades old; whether they were done by the government or private entities or whether there are identifiable victims of a specific harm. In a 2003 Dawson survey whites were asked whether compensation should be paid to the specific survivors of the white destruction of the black communities of Tulsa, Oklahoma in 1921 and Rosewood, Florida in 1923. Only 11 percent of whites said "yes."[17]

In the course of the long campaign to end affirmative action for whites in education, Thurgood Marshall and his colleagues initially sought only judicial enforcement of the equality mandated by *Plessey*. After winning a series of such cases, Marshall, at considerably risk of losing, said "Let's go for the whole hog" and ask the Court to declare that separate but equal itself was inherently unequal. The result was *Brown*, celebrated on its fiftieth anniversary as one of the most important Supreme Court decision of the twentieth century and one of the two or three most important in the history of the court.

Given the "untold" history that Katznelson recounts and the history he does not tell; the effects of these histories in creating the huge gaps in social and economic well being between blacks and whites; and the sentiments of the white public on affirmative action and reparations, those interested in justice for blacks should go for the whole hog. Going for this whole hog, however, will require not a new strategy of litigation or lobbying, but a new strategy of protest. Joe Feagin, perhaps the leading social science scholar of racism in America, has concluded that reparations will require a large scale, multiracial, mass movement of destabilizing protests. As Feagin writes "The destabilizing effects of protest and resistance can alter the cost-benefit calculus so that changes favorable to blacks actually comes to be in the interest of dominant forces."[18] It was, after all, only with such a movement that the whole hog of school desegregation was achieved some fifteen years of *Brown*.

Notes

1. Ralph Ellison, "The World and the Jug" in Ellison, *Shadow and Act*, (New York: New American Library, 1966): 115.
2. Mack H. Jones, "Affirmative Action: What is the question – Race or Oppression," *National Political Science Review* 7(1999): 250.
3. Ibid, p. 249.
4. Ibid, p. 252.
5. Linda F. Williams, *The Constraint of Choice: The Legacies of White Skin Privilege in America*, (University Park, PA: Pennsylvania State University Press, 2003).
6. Theodore Hershberg, et al. "A Tale of Three Cities: Blacks and Immigrants in Philadelphia, 1850-1880, 1930 and 1970." *Annals of the American Academy of Political and Social Science* 441(1979):75.
7. Ibid, p. 66.
8. Ibid, pp. 73-74.
9. Ibid, p. 80.
10. *Gratz and Hamacher v. Bollinger* et al., U.S. Supreme Court (slip opinion) #02-516 (2003).
11. *Regents of University of California v. Bakke*, 438 U.S., 265 (1978).
12. Ibid.
13. In response to Justice Powell, Justice Marshall in *Bakke* wrote "It is unnecessary in the twentieth century America to have individual Negroes demonstrate that they have been victims of racial discrimination; the racism of our society has been so pervasive that none, regardless of wealth or position, has managed to escape its impact." Ibid.
14. *Gratz and Hamacher v. Bollinger*.
15. *Jones v. Alfred H. Mayer*, 392 U.S., 409(1968).
16. Michael Dawson and Rovana Popoff "Reparations: Justice and Greed in Black and White," *DuBois Review* 1(2004): 61-62.
17. "Wealth of White Nation: Blacks Sink Deeper," *The Black Commentator*, October 22, 2004.
18. Joe R. Feagin, *Racist America: Roots, Current Realities and Future Reparations*, (New York: Routledge, 2000).

Robert C. Smith
San Francisco State University

Simien, Evelyn M., 2006; *Black Feminist Voices in Politics,* State University of New York Press, 184 pp. ISBN: 0-7914-6790-2

Evelyn Simien argues that she wrote this book because, "in spite of the progress that has been made in recent years, too few political scientists deem African American women and Black feminist theory worthy of intellectual inquiry."

She claims that only Michael Dawson and herself have used the evidence from the 1993-1994 National Black Politics Study to pursue the question of gender equality and feminist priorities among African American men and women. I disagree with this, because in 1998 Todd C. Shaw, Robert A. Brown, Cathy Cohen, and Marwin Miller presented a paper at the Midwest Political Science Association entitled, "Lessons Learned? Black Gender and Intergenerational Differences on Attitudes toward Black Nationalism and Black Feminism" that used data from the 1993-1994 study.

Where Simien's book differs from their work and Dawson's chapter on Black Feminist Ideology in Black Visions is that she provides a critique of the dominant approaches used by political scientists to measure black feminist consciousness.

Simien breaches the wall between black feminist theorizing and mainstream political science by identifying ways in which public opinion scholars have ignored, conceptualized, measured, and modeled the intersection of race and gender consciousness.

Her book wishes to show that the omission of black feminist voices causes survey researchers to ask the wrong questions. She argues that using survey items designed for white women results in a measurement of support of white feminism among black women—not black feminist consciousness.

Her critique is that political scientists have measured gender identification and race identification and then used the interaction of these two variables to create a measure of the politicized group identification of black women. She claims that this measurement strategy is faulty because it assumes that race and gen-

der identification are separate constructs. She argues that this has several problems, because this measurement approach fails to assess the simultaneity of oppression, and the hierarchy of interests within the black community.

What I think makes Simien's work most interesting is that she observes that another limitation of the empirical research is its tendency to focus on feminist support among women without assessing the level of support for these same principles among men. Simien makes the important point that given the emphasis of black feminists on building coalitions with black men and the rise of the men's movement to end patriarchy, it seems most appropriate to examine the extent to which black men endorse black feminist ideals.

The heart of this text is compelling because she challenges the way public opinion scholars and survey researchers measure race or feminist consciousness and neither the intersection of nor interaction between these two variables.

Simien praises such works as Katherine Tate's, From Protest to Politics: The New Black Voter in American Elections (1994), Michael C. Dawson's, "Behind the Mule: Race and Class in African-American Political Activism (1999), and Frederick C. Harris's, Something Within: Religion in African American Political Activism (1999) for their highly sophisticated and comprehensive explanatory models of black political behavior, which place African American political thought at the center of their empirical analysis. Simien states, however, that despite the valuable information they provide, these studies often fail to recognize the importance of theorizing gender.

She makes the claim that for the most part, African American women's public opinion and political behavior have been measured against those of black men and white women, and other women of color. She argues that Tate's book tends to consider black men's political attitudes as the norm against which black women's political attitudes are measured and found lacking.

In her book, Tate writes that, "Black women have weaker racial identities than Black men" and speculates that Black women might form weaker racial identities because they are less likely than Black men to see themselves as victims of racial discrimination." Simien refutes this. She posits that Tate stops short of empirically investigating the why question: Why don't black women possess stronger racial identities than black men? If black women participated in higher numbers than black men in the Civil Rights Movement and vote at higher rates than black men despite their reported lower levels of trust in government, Simien argues that black women's public opinion and political behavior are long overdue for reinvestigation.

She then goes on to address the work of Dawson and Harris. Simien's critique of Behind the Mule is that Dawson asserts that "whether an African American believes his or her own fate is linked to that of the race as a whole is not predicated on socioeconomic status or gender, but by the extent to which "an African American individual is integrated into the Black community and tied to Black information networks." Dawson also argues that socioeconomic status is significant. Simien states, "It is my view that what is defined as linked fate must be determined, in part, by an appreciation for the lived experiences of both African American men and women. That is to say, survey researchers and public opinion scholars must develop measures of race identification that consider in-group variation. She claims that the use of a single survey item that asks about Blacks in general is insufficient because this approach fails to consider difference between and among individual members of the Black community."

She also argues that the use of a single item to measure race identification should be avoided in survey research. She recommends the use of parallel items that ask, "Do you think what happens to Black women and Black men in the country will have something to do with what happens in your life?' By doing so, Simien believes that political scientists expand the traditional linked fate model to include items that assess in-group attachments. Where she falls short however, is in not updating this disserta-

tion-turned book by engaging Dawson's more recent book, Black Visions, in this section. If she did, she would have to acknowledge that this work has a more refined statement and analysis of in-group variability.

Finally, Simien examines Fred Harris's book. The value that she finds in his text is that he challenges conventional definitions of politics by adopting an approach that puts the perspectives and experiences of Black women at the center of his analysis. But at the same time, he casts male clergy as the model of leadership against which women are found lacking in regard to assumption of authority roles. Simien acknowledges that he devotes some attention to the obstacles to equality and empowerment of African American women, but claims that he falls short of making the case for the feminist implications of his work by not compelling us to consider how current Black politics research might be changed if the lives of these women were taken into consideration.

This is where I think Simien has an important observation: African American men and women must also dispel false universalism, which sets up African American men (in this case, clergy) as the norm against which black women are judged, and who in this context, appear to be deviant cases. Simien's hope is that her book will persuade researchers to refine their conceptualization of group consciousness so that intersecting identities can be taken into account.

So what does Simien's book offer that others don't? She provides evidence that black feminist consciousness is empirically distinct from feminist identification and race identification. After looking at the 1993-1994 National Black Politics Study Survey, she actually finds that black men are more likely to support black feminism than black women! How does she explain this? Well she finds it to be questionable and turned to another data set which operationalizes the distinction between black women and men. She's concerned that the items in the 1993-1994 study failed to raise the bar high enough to truly separate those with genuine commitment to black feminist principles from those with only a fleeting recognition of the discrimination faced by black women. Using data from the 1984-1988 National Black Election Study, she found that black women and men differ in their related beliefs toward sex role socialization and the comparative influence of women in society.

Now this is where I critique Simien. Although I agree with her that the gender of the interviewer is significant, and that male respondents are likely to respond differently to women than men, I don't think Simien takes into account the historical moment in which her data is collected. Methodologically, I'm not sure how it's OK, for results from 1993-1994 which are counterintuitive to her thesis can be disregarded by data that is five to ten years older.

In short, I think the data is a-historicized. She says that she turned to the 1984-1988 data set because she thought the results in 1993-1994 were "politically correct." This leaves out an entire chapter in African American history. The Clinton Administration was important for African American Women. Two black women—Maggie Williams and Alexis Herman—held two of the most powerful jobs in Washington, DC. Williams was the first Black chief of staff to a first lady—a first lady who, many argue, was the second most powerful person in the government. Alexis Herman was chosen to direct the White House Office of Public Liaison, and Hazel O'Leary was appointed Secretary of Energy. Even though Clinton erred with Lani Gunier's nomination, the data for the 1993-1994 Survey would have been done before he asked Dr. Joycelyn Elders to resign as Surgeon General. For Simien to disregard the high placement of four Black women in Clinton's cabinet, erases an important explanation as to why black men might have changed their views after the two Jesse Jackson Presidential runs.

In fact Shaw. Brown, Cohen and Miller argue that according to the 1993 National Black Politics Study, 75 percent of young black men and 83 percent of older black men saw Anita Hill and Lani Gunier as having been persecuted. In her dissertation, but not the book, Simien dismisses this data. She writes, "Another item asked respondents whether there is a tendency for white society to attack and silence strong black women like Anita Hill and Lani Guinier, this item was discarded because a large percentage of respondents refused to answer the question (19%). It is this writer's view that the average respondent, who has not graduated from college, may have felt uncomfortable responding to the item when they knew very little about Lani Guiner and her nomination to the U.S. Justice Department post."

I would argue that this is the limitation of survey data. Some might argue that Simien has stayed within the confines of her discipline and respected its methods and even provided new alternatives. However, I think she could have taken a cue from Melissa Harris-Lacewell. Simien does not engage Harris-Lacewell,'s 2004 book, Barbershops, Bibles, and BET which makes the important point that, "The distribution of Black feminism in the (1994) NBPS sample shows it to be clearly more popular than Conservatism, but not nearly as pervasive as Nationalism. Harris-Lacewell argues that, "Feminism emerges in informal political discussions, Black media exposure, organizational membership, and political discussions in the church, which are all associated with a stronger sense of linked fate with women" (108-109).

I think this is an extremely important point and it would be useful for other scholars to conduct research around this point, utilizing different methods. I believe that multiple methods provide more answers and a richer analysis. Simien clearly respects historical methods because she chooses to provide a historical narrative of a different black woman at the outset of each chapter, which I think engages the readers and also helps to resurrect black feminist voices in politics. I just wish that these black feminist voices weren't so obscured by data analysis.

Duchess Harris
American Studies, Macalester College

Invitation to the Schoarly Community

The National Political Science Review (NPSR), a refereed publication of the National Conference of Black Political Scientists, is seeking to expand its contributor and subscriber base.

The NPSR was conceived with emphasis particularly on theoretical and empirical research on politics and policies that advantage or disadvantage groups by reason of race, ethnicity, or gender, or other such factors. However, as a journal designed to serve a broad audience of social scientists, the NPSR welcomes contributions on any important problem or subject which has significant political and social dimensions.

The NPSR seeks to embrace the socio-political dimensions of all disciplines within the social sciences and humanities, broadly defined. Generally, the NPSR seeks to incorporate analysis of the full range of human activities which undergird and impinge upon political and social life. Thus, in addition to contributions from political scientists, the NPSR seeks relevant contributions from historians, sociologists, anthropologists, theologians, economists, ethicists, and others. The NPSR strives to be at the forefront of lively scholarly discourse on domestic and global political life, particularly as disadvantaged groups are affected. While not meant to be exhaustive, the listing below is illustrative of the different areas of scholarly inquiry which the NPSR wishes to draw upon:

Public policy (general)	Global studies
Health policy	Economics
Social policy (general)	Criminology and Criminal Justice
Educational policy	Race and ethnicity
Science and technology policy	Gender politics and policy
Policy history	Anthropology and ethnography
Communications and media	Public management
History	Ethics
Sociology	Language and communication
Philosophy	Religion and public affairs
African studies	Law and legal studies

The NPSR welcomes conventional manuscripts as well as research notes on important issues. The NPSR is particularly interested in contributions which set forth research agendas in critical scholarly areas within the context of past scholarship and ongoing contemporary developments. The Editor encourages collaborative efforts by two or more contributors as well as contributions by single authors.

For the initial review, manuscripts may be submitted in two formats. (1). Manuscripts may be submitted electronically as an email attachment. This will greatly facilitate timely review. However, *it is the author's responsibility to ensure that the electronic attachment does NOT bear the author's name*. In addition to an electronic format, two hardcopies of manuscripts must also be submitted with one copy bearing the author's name, academic institution, and email address on the cover page. One hardcopy should be a blind copy. (2). Authors may choose to submit only hardcopies for the initial review, in which case 4 hardcopies are required, only one of which should carry the author's name, institutional address, email and telephone number.

Manuscripts should not exceed thirty typewritten pages double-spaced, inclusive of notes and references; and must be prepared according to guidelines which are available from the publisher. Tables, figures, and graphs must be submitted in camera ready condition for publication. For tables, use a uniform typeface. (preferably Times Roman).

Correspondence and manuscripts should be sent to:

Georgia A. Persons, Editor
National Political Science Review
School of Public Policy (0345)
Georgia Institute of Technology
Atlanta, GA 30332-0345

Phone: (404) 894-6510. FAX (404) 894-0535.
Email: georgia.persons@pubpolicy.gatech.edu.

Matters regarding reviews of books should also be sent to the Editor at the above address.